CRITICAL RACE THEORY

A Primer

KHIARA M. BRIDGES
Professor of Law
Professor of Anthropology
Boston University

CONCEPTS AND INSIGHTS SERIES®

444 Cedar Street, Suite 700
St. Paul, MN 55101
1-877-888-1330

Printed in the United States of America

ISBN: 978-1-68328-443-7

To Dr. James Bridges, my beloved Uncle J, who loves me so much that he reads all of my books.

ACKNOWLEDGMENTS

I am grateful to the many people who helped bring this book to life. Thanks to Khaled Beydoun, Osagie Obasogie, and David Rossman for offering incisive comments on several of the book's chapters. I am incredibly indebted to Kristina Fried, Michael Onah, and Chelsea Tejada for their impeccable research assistance. Thanks to Ryan Pfeiffer at Foundation Press for inviting me to write this book and for being such a wonderful editor. (And thanks to Jim Fleming, my brilliant and generous colleague, for sending Ryan my way!) Thanks as well to Staci Herr at Foundation Press for all of the help that she provided.

I am forever grateful to Kendall Thomas, my mentor and friend, for introducing me to Critical Race Theory when I was just a baby. Thank you to the community of critical race theorists and progressive race scholars who insist upon challenging the status quo and dreaming of a just world. Thank you for developing the audacious, powerful, inspired theory that I humbly describe in this book.

A special debt of gratitude is owed to my immediate family—Clive Bridges, Deborah Bridges, Khari Bridges, and Algeria Bridges—for making me into who I am today. Thanks to Mams and Paps Reynaert, *mijn schoonouders*, for welcoming me into the family and being so very good to me. And, of course, thank you to Gert Reynaert, *mijn perfecte echtgenoot*, for making my life so very sweet. On a scale of 1 to 10, I love you a 79.

Portions of chapter 2 were previously published in Jens Meierhenrich and Martin Loughlin, eds., *The Cambridge Companion to the Rule of Law* (Cambridge: Cambridge University Press, 2019), reproduced with permission.

Portions of chapters 5 and 7 were previously published in Khiara M. Bridges, "Excavating Race-Based Disadvantage Among Class-Privileged People of Color," 53 Harv. C.R.-C.L. L. Rev. 65 (2018).

SUMMARY OF CONTENTS

PART IV. CONTEMPORARY ISSUES

TABLE OF CONTENTS

CRITICAL RACE THEORY

A Primer

INTRODUCTION

- During the 2016 campaign for the Republican presidential nomination, hopefuls Jeb Bush and Donald Trump both asserted that it was damaging to the country when noncitizen women give birth to their children within U.S. borders. They referred to the infants of these women as "anchor babies"—children whose birthright citizenship allow them to function as anchors, mooring their undocumented mothers to the country and ensuring that these women could not easily be moved back to their countries of origin. While the term "anchor baby" is race neutral in the sense that it does not explicitly mention race, most would agree that the term is racially loaded. It acquires its racial connotation from the fact that those who employ the term typically use it to refer to undocumented immigrants who hail from Mexico and Central America. Thus, "anchor baby" *implicitly* refers to Latinx[1] infants. As such, "anchor baby" allows people who use the term to talk about race without ever explicitly mentioning race. Perhaps that is why many people understand the term to be, at best, politically incorrect, or, at worst, a slur.

  We might understand the issue of undocumented immigration, as a general matter, to be racially loaded. This is because close to three-quarters of those who have immigrated to the U.S. without authorization are from Mexico and Central America. Thus, when we talk about curbing undocumented immigration, we are talking about restricting the numbers of Latinx people who may enter the country; when we talk about making it easier for undocumented immigrants to naturalize, we are talking about making it simpler for Latinx people to become citizens. This may make us wonder whether ideas about race have informed our immigration laws as well as the views that politicians, pundits, scholars, and we, as citizens, have about those laws.

- In the last weeks of 2015, a married couple, Syed Rizwan Farook and Tashfeen Malik, walked into a holiday party at a conference center in San Bernardino, California and sprayed a crowd of unarmed people with bullets. Fourteen people were killed and 21 others were wounded. Although Farook worked for the San Bernardino County health

[1] This book uses the term *Latinx*, instead of *Latino/a* or *Latin@*, as a gender inclusive, non-binary reference to people of Latin American descent.

department, which was hosting the party, many news outlets almost immediately began reporting that the shooting was a "terror attack" and not, say, a "workplace shooting." However, other mass shootings have not been similarly understood as acts of terrorism: the attack at a Planned Parenthood in Colorado Springs by a "warrior for the babies," in which three persons lost their lives; the homicides of six people in Kalamazoo, Michigan by an Uber driver who picked up and dropped off passengers between shootings; the shooting deaths of nine black churchgoers in Charleston, South Carolina by a self-proclaimed white supremacist whose stated intent was to spark a race war; the attack at a company in Hesston, Kansas that left three people dead. We might wonder whether the names of the shooters in the latter incidents provide some insight as to why the public and the media largely failed to conceptualize them as perpetrators of terrorism: Robert Lewis Dear, Jason Brian Dalton, Dylann Roof, and Cedric Larry Ford. If the Kansas shooting, for example, had been perpetrated by a "Saleem Majid Ibrahim" instead of a "Cedric Larry Ford," would the public have been willing to accept the interpretation that police offered soon after the events transpired—that the incident was nothing more than a "workplace shooting" and not a "terror attack"?

- In April 2014, Flint, Michigan—a city that is predominately black and where 40 percent of the residents live below the poverty line—stopped purchasing treated Lake Huron water from Detroit and started using the Flint River as its water source. The Flint River, however, has a high chloride concentration, making its water more corrosive than Lake Huron water. When Flint officials failed to add anti-corrosive agents to the river water, it leached lead from the lead service pipes that pump water into Flint homes. Thousands of adults and children were unwittingly exposed to dangerous levels of lead until the problem was made known to the public in November 2015.

  That Flint used lead pipes to pump water into and out of homes is not all unique. In fact, many older cities across the nation and around the globe use lead pipes. Thus, everyone living in these places—rich and poor, white and nonwhite—is endangered by an infrastructure that, under certain circumstances, can be harmful. Further, the latent potential for harm increases as these infrastructures age and crumble. However, some communities will be wealthy enough to repair or replace its infrastructure. Some communities will be able to afford to rip out the lead pipes and substitute them with safer alternatives. And some people will be able to move out of toxic neighborhoods and into newer, healthier ones. The communities unable to afford to manage the risks associated with their risky infrastructures, and the people left behind there, inevitably will be poor. In a country where race follows class closely, these people and communities will disproportionately be nonwhite.

- On March 12, 2012, Dante Servin, an off-duty police officer, shot Rekia Boyd in the back of the head, killing her, as she talked to a group of friends in her Chicago neighborhood. The encounter began when Servin, who remained employed by the Chicago Police Department for years after the shooting, told the group to quiet down. He opened fire when the group ignored his command. On July 17, 2014, Eric Garner died after police offer Daniel Pantaleo put him in an illegal chokehold during an arrest. The encounter between Pantaleo and Garner began after Pantaleo, who is white, approached Garner, who was black, because he suspected that the latter was selling "loosies"—single cigarettes from a pack. On August 9, 2014, Michael Brown, an unarmed black teenager, was shot and killed by a white police officer, Darren Wilson, in Ferguson, Missouri. The city erupted in protests twice—initially after Brown's killing, and again after a grand jury declined to indict Wilson on any charges connected to the shooting. On November 27, 2014, Tamir Rice, a 12 year-old black boy who had been playing with a toy gun outside of a recreation center in Cleveland, Ohio, was shot and killed by police officers who reported that they believed that the gun that Rice held was real. Ohio is one of many U.S. states that permit the open carry of handguns. On March 30, 2015, Mya Hall was shot and killed after she took a wrong turn onto National Security Agency property and crashed into a security gate and a police car. There was no evidence that Hall, a black transgender woman, had posed any threat to the facility or to anyone present. On July 10, 2015, police in Waller County, Texas stopped Sandra Bland, a black woman, for failing to signal a lane change. She was arrested for allegedly assaulting the white police officer who had pulled her over. Bland was found dead in her jail cell three days later. On July 6, 2016, a police officer in Falcon Heights, Minnesota pulled over Philando Castile, a black man, as he drove in his car with his girlfriend and her four-year-old daughter. The officer asked Castile for his license and registration. He fatally shot Castile, who had informed the officer that he had a firearm in the car, when he reached for the items that the officer had requested. On March 18, 2018, police officers in Sacramento, California responded to a report that someone was damaging property in a neighborhood. The incident ended with officers firing twenty shots at Stephon Clark, who they said had run away from them, in his own backyard. Clark, who died, was unarmed. He was also black.

Many will explain these events in terms of race. They will believe that, had the victims been white, they would still be alive. However, these explanations compete with other accounts that focus not on race, but rather on the victims' behavior: Boyd had disobeyed an off-duty police officer's commands; Garner had resisted arrest; Brown had gotten into a physical altercation with a police officer; Rice had a toy weapon that could be mistaken for an actual gun; Hall had been driving a stolen car; Bland failed to extinguish her cigarette when directed to do so; Clark ran away from the cops.

- Black Americans have higher rates of diabetes, hypertension, heart disease, and asthma than any other racial group. They also have higher rates of most cancers, and they are much less likely to survive prostate cancer, breast cancer, and lung cancer relative to white people. Latinx people have higher rates of diabetes than white people, and they are much more likely to die from the disease than are their white counterparts. The prevalence of obesity is highest among indigenous persons. They are also 60 percent more likely than their white counterparts to suffer a stroke; indeed, the rate of stroke among indigenous women is twice that of white women.

- Approximately 1.5 million people are presently incarcerated in the U.S. About 500,000 of those people are white, 350,000 are Latinx, and 550,000 are black. While white people make up 63% of the U.S., they make up only 33% of those who are presently incarcerated. While Latinx people make up 16% of the U.S., they comprise 23% of those who are presently incarcerated. And while black people make up 13% of the U.S., they constitute close to 37% of those who are presently incarcerated.

  About 500,000 people are in jail for nonviolent drug offenses. Two-thirds of those persons are racial minorities.

Some will read the preceding vignettes and take them to be definitive proof that race still matters in the contemporary U.S. They will conclude that these stories and statistics show that race powerfully impacts how a person's behavior will be understood, whether he will be under the jurisdiction of this country's criminal justice system or free, whether she will be sick or healthy, and whether he will live or die.

However, some will reach a different conclusion. They will conclude that the preceding vignettes are about race only to the extent that we make them about race. They will say that race might be *descriptive*: it might describe who acted and who was affected by the actor's action. For example, race can be used to describe those who were affected in Flint. We can state, quite accurately, that the people in Flint who were exposed to lead in the city's drinking water were predominately black. But, they will argue that race is not at all *explanatory*: it does not explain *why* the people who were exposed to lead in Flint were black. Indeed, they will argue that race cannot be used to explain any of the vignettes.

The belief that race does not and cannot explain the stories and statistics that open this chapter is consistent with the idea of post-racialism. According to this philosophy, if the racial arc of the nation bends towards a place where racial differences, if they exist, are completely irrelevant to social, cultural, economic, and political life, then we are almost there.[2] It claims that we are closer to that utopic racial destination than we are to our dystopic racial origins, where race brutally determined the content and trajectory of individuals' lives. Post-racialism denies that the nation today is in any important way proximate to its historical past. It argues instead that, at present, racism is an aberration, a rarity. It posits that enduring racial inequality is not the effect of race or racism, but rather is the effect of other forces, like class or individual behavior.

Importantly, the law has come to reflect post-racialism. In 1994, the Supreme Court held in *Adarand Constructors, Inc. v. Peña* that courts will be as skeptical of the constitutionality of laws that seek to benefit historically disadvantaged racial groups as they are of laws

---

[2] The reader should note that there are other definitions of post-racialism. *Post-racialism* might refer to the idea that society has arrived at a historical moment that is racially different from the one that came before it, although that troubled racial past continues to inform the racial present. Kimberlé Crenshaw analogizes this alternative definition of *post-racialism* to the terms *post-colonial* or *post-apartheid*. She writes that "the 'post' in post-colonial or post-apartheid signals that the past does not simply precede the present but partly constitutes it. In this sense, the significance of 'post' is not in the signaling of a before and an after, but in signaling a range of factors—potentially undefined—that make the contemporary social order a variation of the prototype, not its opposite." Kimberlé Williams Crenshaw, *Twenty Years of Critical Race Theory: Looking Back to Move Forward*, 43 CONN. L. REV. 1253, 1313 (2011) [hereinafter Crenshaw, *Twenty Years*].

that seek to benefit white people, who historically have enjoyed significant advantages on account of their race.[3] In essence, the Court said that affirmative action programs (which are intended to bring racial minorities into institutions from which they had been excluded historically) and Jim Crow laws (which reflected their authors' belief that black people are inferior to white people) are indistinguishable under the Equal Protection Clause of the Fourteenth Amendment. *Adarand* manifests a post-racial philosophy. The doctrine that it establishes echoes the sense that actors act culpably, and therefore unconstitutionally, whenever they make race significant in their decision-making processes. Indeed, the idea that the Constitution is *colorblind* and can only improperly distinguish between the races is in keeping with post-racialism.

Post-racialism also motivates the Court's analysis in *Parents Involved in Community Schools v. Seattle*, in which the Court struck down two school districts' plans to integrate schools that, because of residential segregation, had become racially segregated.[4] The Court essentially found that the school districts' efforts to desegregate their schools were constitutionally equivalent to the efforts made under Alabama Governor George Wallace's pledge to fight for "segregation now, segregation tomorrow, [and] segregation forever." Chief Justice Roberts ended his plurality opinion with a truism of post-racialism: "The way to stop discrimination on the basis of race is to stop discriminating on the basis of race."[5]

Post-racialism is the current flowing beneath the Court's decision in *Shelby County, Alabama v. Holder*, in which it struck down section 4(b) of the Voting Rights Act ("VRA").[6] The VRA was passed in 1965 to realize the promises of the Fifteenth Amendment by addressing rampant racial discrimination in voting. Section 4(b) of the VRA contains the formula that determines which jurisdictions ("covered jurisdictions") would have to get preclearance by the Attorney General or a panel of three judges for any changes to their voting laws. Covered jurisdictions are those that had a documented history of racial discrimination in voting. At the time of the initial passage of section 4(b), these covered jurisdictions had deplorable statistics that demonstrated the pervasiveness of racial discrimination in voting. However, things had changed in the five decades that had elapsed since the Act's passage: the statistics that the covered jurisdictions boasted in 2013 told a story in which racial discrimination in voting had declined significantly. This prompted

---

[3] Adarand Constructors, Inc. v. Peña, 515 U.S. 200, 222–27 (1995).

[4] Parents Involved in Cmty. Sch. v. Seattle Sch. Dist. No. 1, 551 U.S. 701, 729–32 (2007).

[5] *Id.* at 748.

[6] Shelby Cty. v. Holder, 570 U.S. 529, 557 (2013).

the *Shelby County* majority to write, "Blatantly discriminatory evasions of federal decrees are rare. And minority candidates hold office at unprecedented levels."[7] The majority found that this was reason enough to strike down section 4(b), as covered jurisdictions endured federal oversight because of a lamentable history that no longer accurately described their present. The Court's decision in *Shelby County* adopts the perspective that racism has been conquered. It proceeds from the post-racial assumption that, in the present-day, race is insignificant.

Critical Race Theory ["CRT"] proceeds from the opposite assumption. It takes the vignettes that open this chapter as incontrovertible evidence that race remains highly significant in the present-day U.S. And, quite radically, it proposes that the law plays a crucial role in maintaining the significance of race.

As Part I of this book explores, CRT emerged in the 1970s and 1980s, at a time when the prevailing sense was that the law was not at all involved in creating and sustaining racial hierarchies. Prior to the advent of CRT, most in the legal academy had embraced the idea that norms of fairness, equality, and justice guided the law. Accordingly, they found it difficult to contemplate that the law could be involved in creating a society that, racially speaking, is unfair, unequal, and unjust. The intellectual forefather of CRT, Derrick Bell, was one of the first to challenge this view. Bell, the first black tenured professor at Harvard Law School, devoted his scholarship to exploring how it came to be that black people remained at the bottom of practically every measure of social wellbeing, even though the Civil Rights Movement had forced the passage of laws that ostensibly were designed to end black people's subordination. Bell concluded that racial inequality endured in a post-civil rights era because, among other things, the vision of racial justice that civil rights lawyers had championed was a weak and impoverished one. The result was that the civil rights laws that had been passed, which reflected this vision, were equally weak and impoverished. Thus, Bell argued that if racial inequality persisted in a post-civil rights era, then the law was central to explaining that persistence.

Bell's scholarship, along with the writings of many others, eventually coalesced into CRT. Today, CRT is an intellectual movement, a body of scholarship, and an analytical toolset for interrogating the relationship between law and racial inequality.

But, is Critical Race Theory a *theory*? Well, it depends on one's definition of "theory." If one defines a "theory" as an idea that one can test with experiments in order to prove its truth or falsity, then CRT is not a theory. There is no test that can prove that CRT is "right" or

---

7 *Id.* at 558.

"wrong" when it argues that the law constructs, naturalizes, and justifies racial inequality.

However, if we embraced a more expansive definition of "theory"—defining it as an analytical framework that can be used to explain or examine facts or events—then CRT would qualify.

Consider the incarceration rates described above. Social theories, like CRT, are sets of ideas that can help us explain or otherwise make sense of those statistics.

- A person employing a Marxist social theory, for example, may conclude that the capitalist class's need to control the laboring class explains those numbers. To a Marxist theorist, the criminal law and the prison are tools that the bourgeoisie uses to manage the proletariat.
- A person employing a Foucauldian social theory may think that the U.S.'s incarceration rates are interesting because, according to French philosopher Michel Foucault, the prison is a model of modern power at its most perfected. Thus, to a Foucauldian theorist, the high rates of incarceration in the U.S. make sense, as the state is most powerful when its subjects are as visible as they are when they are incarcerated.

Like Marxist and Foucauldian social theories, CRT is a social theory that we can use to explain or examine the U.S.'s incarceration rates. CRT would argue that the fact that the U.S. has the largest prison population in the world, together with the fact that people of color are overrepresented among those who are incarcerated, show that the law—the criminal law, in this case—is deeply implicated in sustaining racial subordination.

Kimberlé Crenshaw, one of the founders of CRT and the individual who coined the term *Critical Race Theory*, explains that she chose to use "theory" in CRT's name in order to signify "the desire to develop a coherent account of race and law."[8] Nevertheless, one would be hard pressed to describe CRT as *coherent*, if one uses that term to mean unified or internally consistent. (However, if one means "coherent" in the sense of "capable of being understood," then most—even those who disagree with CRT's assumptions and conclusions—would say that CRT is *coherent*.) Scholars who have reflected on the framework acknowledge that there are host of different approaches, ideas, and trajectories within the body of work that may be called

---

[8] Kimberlé Williams Crenshaw, *The First Decade: Critical Reflections, or "A Foot in the Closing Door,"* 49 UCLA L. REV. 1343, 1361 (2002) [hereinafter Crenshaw, *The First Decade*].

CRT. As Jerome McCristal Culp puts it, there is no Critical Race *Theory*; instead, "there are critical race *theories*. There are many theories that unite and divide everyone who could be accused of being or claim to be members of the critical race theory movement."[9] The one thing—perhaps, the only thing—that all of those folks have in common, according to Culp, is the "belief in an opposition to oppression."[10] Crenshaw herself would agree. She describes CRT as "fundamentally eclectic" and has argued that although it has "achieved some intellectual coherence," it is far from "a fully unified school of thought."[11] Elsewhere, she states that CRT is neither a "stable project" nor "an intellectual unit filled with natural stuff—theories, themes, practices, and the like."[12] She asserts that CRT is not a noun, but rather is a verb—an entity that shifts as it interacts with its environment.[13]

In some sense, then, CRT might simply be a political position. The "theory" in its name might do no more than refer to its status as a location from which a critique of the prevailing racial order might be launched. Indeed, it is because of the eclecticism within CRT that this primer largely refers to persons who produce CRT scholarship not as "critical race theorists," but rather as "critical thinkers about race," "progressive race scholars," or similar. Many authors of scholarship that is fairly described as CRT identify as *critical race theorists*; however, many others do not. Because this primer understands CRT to be a political position from which to criticize the racial status quo, it proceeds from the assumption that one need not be a self-identified *critical race theorist* in order to do CRT. In recognition of this fact, this primer only uses "critical race theorist" to refer to the author of a text who self-identifies as such.

That said, simply expressing a dissatisfaction with the existing racial order is not enough to make a piece of scholarship a part of the CRT oeuvre. It seems fair to say that in order for a something to be appropriately described as CRT, it has to embrace—or, at least, be consistent with—a couple of basic ideas. But, what are these ideas? Scholars have schematized these foundational commitments in different ways, identifying anywhere from two to eight essential tenets of the CRT framework. Four are named here.

---

9 Jerome McCristal Culp, Jr., *To the Bone: Race and White Privilege*, 83 MINN. L. REV. 1637, 1638 (1999).

10 *Id.*

11 Crenshaw, *The First Decade*, *supra* note 8, at 1362.

12 Crenshaw, *Twenty Years*, *supra* note 2, at 1261.

13 *Id.*

1. *CRT believes that race is not a biological entity, but rather is a social construction.*

Scholars working within the CRT paradigm deny that race is a genetic entity; indeed, they deny that race is "natural" in any sense of the word. Nevertheless, race has persevered. Progressive race scholars take it as their charge to examine the role that law plays in that perseverance.

However, to argue that race is a social construction poses a bit of a problem for CRT. This is because some claim that if race is a social construction, then it is not "real." Arguments that "race is not real" and "there is no such thing as race" tend to lead to statements like, "Well, if race is not real, then we should stop talking about it." "Because there's no such thing as race, we should stop taking it into consideration." "Because race is not real, there's no point in thinking about it or studying it. Thinking about it and studying it serve to just perpetuate this false thing."

Critical thinkers respond that although race may not be biologically or genetically real, it is socially real. They feel that because of the social reality of race, they are justified in talking about it, taking it into consideration, thinking about it, and studying it. In fact, CRT is committed to the idea that being conscious of race is not what perpetuates race and racial inequality. Rather, it proposes that being unconscious of race—or pretending that it does not exist—may be that which is most responsible for the perpetuation of race and racial inequality in this post-civil rights era.

Because one of CRT's basic ideas is that race is a social construction, the body of work that can be referred to as CRT scholarship seems to be united by the questions that it asks about the law's role in constructing race. These questions include:

- How exactly does the law fabricate race?
- How has the law protected racism(s)?
- How does the law reproduce racial inequality?
- How can the law be used to dismantle race, racism(s) and racial inequality?

Note that these questions all suggest that law is part and parcel of the racial order. Indeed, CRT assumes that the law is not merely *regulating* race and the relations between the various races, but is actively *constituting* race and the relations between the various races. Thus, if white people enjoy racial dominance and people of color are subordinate to them, CRT argues that, despite protestations to the contrary, the law has produced that state of affairs.

It is important to note that although CRT scholarship might be united by the questions that it asks about the law, it is in no way united by how it goes about answering those questions. That is, there is no CRT "methodology." Collectively, the scholars who produce CRT are an interdisciplinary bunch, and they bring a broad range of investigative tools—including anthropology, history, qualitative and quantitative sociology, political theory, and economics, among many others—to bear in their inquiries.

Finally, while CRT scholarship might be joined by the questions that it asks about the law, it is not joined by the answers that it gives. There is no CRT "solution" to what CRT takes to be the U.S.'s race problem. Some CRT scholarship argues that the solution lies in reparations. Other work argues that legal reform is the answer. Still other work rejects incremental reform and champions revolution—taking it to the streets—as the remedy. While CRT scholarship might disagree about how to solve the problems that it identifies, it is uncompromising in its belief that there is a problem. Which leads to another one of CRT's basic ideas . . . .

2. *CRT believes that there is a race problem, that racism is a* normal *feature of American society (and not a deviation from an otherwise fair and just status quo), and that institutions, like the law, have worked to perpetuate racial inequality.*

   CRT denies that the vignettes that begin this chapter are a series of unfortunate coincidences involving individuals who just happen to be people of color. CRT argues that these stories are linked, and it endeavors to investigate the systems that link them.

   It deserves underscoring that CRT places emphasis on the systems that subordinate people of color. Thus, scholars operating within the CRT paradigm remain largely uninterested in explanations of racial inequality that focus on individual bad actors. These explanations tend to define racism as discrete, identifiable, intentional, irrational acts perpetrated by bad individuals. These accounts diagnose the racist's error as thinking about race, and they go on to conclude that this is what racism is: racism is what happens when we think about race. Accordingly, it posits that racism will stop happening when we stop thinking about race. Here, we arrive again at Chief Justice Roberts's maxim that "[t]he way to stop discrimination on the basis of race is to stop discriminating on the basis of race." We see, then, that implicit in the definition of racism as "thinking about race" is a commitment to colorblindness.

Interestingly, this definition of racism is not something that only political conservatives, like Chief Justice Roberts, have embraced. Importantly, liberals have embraced it as well. Which brings us to another one of CRT's basic ideas. . . .

3. *CRT rejects traditional liberal understandings of the problem of racism and how racism will be defeated.* CRT is convinced that liberal understandings of racism are deficient and that this deficiency partially explains why racial inequality persists well after the Civil Rights Movement achieved such significant triumphs in the 1960s. Chapter 2 explores CRT's dissatisfaction with liberal race discourse in greater depth.

While CRT does not deny that individual bad actors do bad acts that harm racial minorities, it does not conceptualize these acts as bearing the primary responsibility for racial inequality's persistence. Instead, CRT proposes that, in the post-civil rights era, rational structures, institutions, and discourses do the bulk of the work of creating and maintaining racial hierarchies. Which is to say: CRT proposes that racial disenfranchisement is an entirely rational mechanism.

There are two additional reasons for CRT's refusal to define *racism* as "being conscious of race" and *racists* as "people who are race conscious." First, if racism is what happens when you are conscious of race, then efforts to address racial inequality that require consciousness of race become the stuff of racism. Such efforts include affirmative action programs that allow admissions offices to be aware of the race of the applicant, initiatives to desegregate schools that consider the race of a student when assigning him to any number of schools, efforts that attempt to ensure the effective political representation of racial minorities that consider the racial composition of neighborhoods when crafting voting districts, and many more. Because all of these practices involve being conscious of race, they are "racist," according to the definition of racism that CRT rejects. Moreover, if they are racist, then their supporters have to apologize for them—citing them as temporary departures from the norm of colorblindness. They have to be conceptualized as necessary evils. CRT contends that there is no need to apologize for these programs because, according to CRT, race-conscious efforts to address racial inequality are not racist. According to CRT, racism is not simply being conscious of race. It is something much more, and much more pernicious, that that.

Second, CRT believes that defining racism as race consciousness is problematic because it narrows our field of vision. If racism is defined as irrational bad acts perpetrated by bad actors, then it disallows us from seeing all the other social practices that may also function to maintain racial inequality—like residential segregation, the financing of public schools through property taxes, the way that we have instituted the social safety net, etc.

4. Finally, *CRT believes that scholarship is not, cannot, and should not be disconnected from people's lives on the ground. Thinkers using a CRT framework produce their scholarship with the hope of dismantling systems that subordinate people of color.* CRT believes that all knowledge is political. It believes that scholarship that ignores race is not demonstrating "objectivity" or "neutrality," but rather is demonstrating its own political commitments to the existing racial order. As Francisco Valdes explains this idea, "[B]y looking the other way—by seeking to ignore the foreseeable effects of our disengagement with the everyday lives of those whom the law slights—legal scholars effectively take sides with the privileged and powerful who prefer to sustain a status quo that favors them at the expense of others."[14]

[14] Francisco Valdes, *Beyond Sexual Orientation in Queer Legal Theory: Majoritarianism, Multidimensionality and Responsibility in Social Justice*

Thus, CRT is dedicated to the production of politically engaged scholarship. It allows race to figure centrally in its analyses, and it rejects the criticism that this is an analytical error. CRT argues that when race figures centrally in legal scholarship, it allows us to see how racial hierarchies are reflected in and reproduced by areas of law that seemingly have nothing to do with race—like the tax code, securities laws, land use laws, and intellectual property laws.

But, it is it possible that CRT misrecognizes the complexity of social life by conceptualizing race as an essential element in understanding why our present looks the way that it does? Is it not possible that other factors are operating—like class, gender, or religion? For example, the debate over immigration might not be about race, but rather about protecting scare resources within the U.S. nation state. Identifying as "terrorism" acts of violence committed by people with "Muslim sounding" names might not be about race, but rather about the likelihood of political radicalization. The lead poisoning of Flint water might not be about race, but rather about a city that was on the verge of bankruptcy that tried to save money by switching the city's water source to a cheaper, albeit more corrosive, supply. The death of Mya Hall and Stephon Clark might not be about race, but rather about individuals who were fleeing from the cops. Racial disparities in health might not be about race, but rather about class and poverty.

CRT responds that class, gender, religion, and even an individual's behavior are important in explaining social life. But, they insist that *race is also important.* CRT proposes that race intersects with class, with gender, with religion, with sexuality, and with other factors (including individual behavior) to produce a society that is racially stratified. Indeed, it insists that one cannot understand the inequalities within society if one fails to understand classism, sexism, religious intolerance, homophobia, transphobia, etc. The insight upon which CRT insists is that race, almost invariably, is a factor. Race intersects with other axes of identity and -isms to produce the world in which we exist. It claims that the occasions in which race is irrelevant are

---

Scholarship or Legal Scholars as Cultural Warriors, 75 DENV. U. L. REV. 1409, 1462–63 (1998).

> rare exceptions; they are most certainly not the rule. Thus, CRT believes that we miss something crucial when we fail to analyze the role that race plays in society.

The balance of the book will be a presentation of Critical Race Theory. Its goal is to explain the theory's basic commitments, examine its strengths, and identify its weaknesses. Part I will provide a history of CRT—exploring CRT's emergence out of Professor Bell's scholarship and student agitation at Harvard Law School, its critique of liberal and other leftist discourse about race, and interventions made by scholars who criticized CRT's initial erasure of the racial experiences of nonblack racial minorities. Part II will introduce and explore several core concepts in the theory—including institutional/structural racism, implicit bias, microaggressions, racial privilege, the relationship between race and class, and intersectionality. Part III will build on Part II's discussion of intersectionality by exploring the intersection of race with a variety of other characteristics—including, sexuality and gender identity, religion, and ability. Part IV will then explore several contemporary issues to which CRT speaks—including health disparities, affirmative action, the criminal justice system, the welfare state, and education.

* * *

Before continuing, it might be useful for me to identify myself—the author of this text. I am a legal scholar who identifies as a critical race theorist. (I am also a feminist, an anthropologist, a dancer, a living constitutionalist, a reality TV enthusiast, a person who believes that her own jokes are *hilarious*, and a host of other identities and subjectivities.) I was drawn to CRT when I was introduced to it in my second-year of law school because the theory struck me as exciting and generative. I had been underwhelmed with the liberal legal scholarship about race that I had encountered at that early stage of my legal career. I found the ways that this scholarship talked and thought about race and racial inequality to be inadequate. There *had* to be something wrong with it, I thought. If it was right, then why hadn't the U.S solved its race problem? Why did racial inequality persist? And why were so many people comfortable with this state of affairs?

I loved CRT because it offered what I believed to be a convincing explanation of why the subordination of people of color persisted despite our predecessors' belief that we had "overcome" in the 1960s. I also respected CRT's rejection of legal conventions. I admired its questioning of the legitimacy of social institutions, like law schools and the Supreme Court. Further, I found Patricia Williams's prose to be poetic. I thought that Ian Haney López's *White By Law* was simply breathtaking.[15] I believed that Cheryl Harris's "Whiteness as Property" article offered one of the most mind-blowing conceptions of racial privilege that I had ever encountered.[16] Thoroughly moved, I have allowed CRT to inspire my scholarship and to inform my views of the world.

Now, my identity as a critical race theorist certainly influences my presentation of CRT. (Indeed, a person's *refusal* to identify as a critical race theorist would also influence her presentation of the theory. That is, there is no *unbiased* way to describe CRT. We are all simply differently biased.) However, this identity does not prevent me from seeing CRT's shortcomings, from taking seriously the criticisms that have been launched against it, or from recognizing that it represents one of many ways of thinking about race, racism, and racial inequality. In the pages that follow, I endeavor to provide an accurate description of CRT while pointing out the many alternative ways of thinking through the thorny problems with which CRT concerns itself.

I. Questions and Discussion

1. When was the last time that you had a conversation about race with someone who did not share your views? How would you describe that conversation? Did you learn something from that person? Do you think that person learned something from you? Do you think that it is possible for people to change their deeply held beliefs about race?

2. Scholars who produce CRT scholarship are all committed to racial justice, but they disagree on just what racial justice looks like. Some imagine that a racially just world is one where race exists (i.e., people have racial identities and there are differences between racial group); but, there is no inequality between racial groups. Others imagine that a racially just world is one where race has been eliminated; it is no longer a category that usefully describes groups or people. What does racial justice look like to you? Why?

3. CRT does not hesitate to describe the institutional and structural forces that produce and reproduce racial inequality as "racist." For example, as Chapter 20 explores, public schools tend to be funded by property taxes. This means that schools in wealthier neighborhoods, where property is more valuable, are better funded than schools in poorer neighborhoods, where property values are lower. Because race follows class closely in the U.S., this ends up

---

[15] IAN HANEY LÓPEZ, WHITE BY LAW: THE LEGAL CONSTRUCTION OF RACE (10th ed. 2006).

[16] Cheryl I. Harris, *Whiteness as Property*, 106 HARV. L. REV. 1707 (1993).

meaning that wealthier schools tend to have largely white student bodies, while poorer schools tend to be predominately nonwhite. As this funding structure operates to reproduce racial inequality, many critical thinkers describe it as "racist." They cite it as an example of "structural racism." What is the value of using the language of "racist" and "racism" when describing this phenomenon? What are the dangers of using this language? What language might we use instead?

4. What do you think is the attraction of colorblindness? Why do you think many people are committed to the idea that the country is a post-racial one?

5. As the chapter explains, CRT believes that race intersects with class, gender, religion, and other factors to produce a society that is racially stratified. If this is true, why center race in analyses of law and society, as CRT does? If other factors, acting in concert with race, explain why society looks the way that it does, then why should we not foreground those other factors? Why allow *race* to figure centrally in these investigations?

6. As noted above, CRT believes that all scholarship is political; for this reason, CRT commits itself to racial justice. In this sense, CRT scholarship is *instrumental*—endeavoring to understand the mechanisms that subordinate people of color so that they can be dismantled. Some observers have critiqued this aspect of CRT. For example, Douglas Litowitz has argued that the instrumentality of CRT weakens it. He suggests that CRT "eschews the realm of abstract, ahistorical, normative debate" and chooses to focus "instead on the relationships between doctrine and concrete change, and the extent to which doctrine can be manipulated to produce more change."[17] Litowitz believes that this singular focus leads CRT to lack "balance, nuance, and a weighing of insider and outsider perspectives."[18]

Do you believe that CRT's commitment to using scholarship to further the cause of racial justice—that is, its instrumentality—poses a problem? If so, what problem does it pose? Do you believe that instrumental scholarship necessarily lacks "balance, nuance, and a weighing of insider and outsider perspectives"? Is there a way for instrumental scholarship to be both political *and* evenhanded?

Is it possible that scholarship that features "abstract, ahistorical, normative debates" is *also* instrumental—also serving a purpose? If so, what purpose might it serve?

---

[17] Douglas E. Litowitz, *Some Thoughts on Critical Race Theory*, 72 NOTRE DAME L. REV. 503, 522 (1997).

[18] *Id.* at 527–28.

7. As noted above, CRT believes that a racial hierarchy exists in the U.S. (and around the globe) and, further, that the mechanisms that reproduce this hierarchy are everywhere. According to CRT, they exist in the Court's interpretation of the Constitution as well as in the tax code; they exist in society's approach to dealing with crime as well as the way that it regulates securities. Further still, CRT is devoted to uncovering the ubiquitous devices that create and sustain racial inequality. According to CRT, many of these devices are obvious; but, many of them are not.

Some observers have found fault with this orientation. For example, Daniel Farber and Suzanna Sherry argue that CRT's belief that the mechanisms that subordinate people of color are ubiquitous but often concealed results in scholars operating within the framework to possess a "paranoid mode of thought"[19]—leading them always "to be on the look-out for hidden threats."[20]

Do you think that Farber's and Sherry's critique of CRT is a fair one? Is it ever appropriate to be *paranoid*?

8. As described in the chapter, if *theories* are supposed to be unified, CRT might not be a theory. Yet, self-identified critical race theorists embrace the somewhat disjointed nature of the enterprise. John Calmore affectionately writes that CRT is "actually improvisationally incoherent, diffuse, and stunningly eclectic in both method and message."[21] But, there may be some problems with this approach. Devon Carbado and Mitu Gulati describe CRT as a "big tent." They go on to acknowledge that its "broad-ranging approach makes CRT appear to be substantively and theoretically diffuse and . . . . unruly. In short, the disparate body of work that occupies space in CRT's tent renders CRT difficult to manage and articulate as a positive theory."[22] Elsewhere, Carbado writes that "a theory without clear boundaries is hard to mobilize and describe as a theory."[23]

What are some problems with CRT being a diffuse and disparate effort? What are some of the strengths of that approach?

---

[19] DANIEL A. FARBER & SUZANNA SHERRY, BEYOND ALL REASON: THE RADICAL ASSAULT ON TRUTH IN AMERICAN LAW 136 (1997).

[20] *Id.*

[21] John O. Calmore, *Random Notes of an Integration Warrior—Part 2: A Critical Response to the Hegemonic "Truth" of Daniel Farber and Suzanna Sherry*, 83 MINN. L. REV. 1589, 1592 (1999).

[22] Devon W. Carbado & Mitu Gulati, *The Law and Economics of Critical Race Theory*, 112 YALE L.J. 1757, 1767 (2003).

[23] Devon W. Carbado, *Critical What What?*, 43 CONN. L. REV. 1593, 1602 (2011).

Part I
CONTEXTUALIZING CRT

Chapter 1

THE ORIGINS OF CRITICAL RACE THEORY

The architects of Critical Race Theory have described the theory as a "left intervention into race discourse and a race intervention into left discourse."[1] By this, they are referring to CRT's emergence in the late 1980s and the early 1990s as a response to the perceived failures of two intellectual formations.

On the one hand, those who would come to found CRT were disappointed with the fact that the consortium of critical thinkers of the day, the Critical Legal Studies movement (or CLS), seemed uninterested in thinking about questions of race, racism, and racial justice. The adherents of CLS—or crits, as they came to be called—were a largely white, predominately male "collection of neo-Marxist intellectuals, former New Left activists, ex-counter-culturalists, and other varieties of oppositionists in law schools."[2] What united them[3] was an interest in exposing the law's role in creating, sustaining, and naturalizing a society that they believed to be woefully oppressive and alienating. The crits brought an impressive catalogue of theoretical tools to the task of critiquing the law, including "Marxian and neo-Marxian social theory, phenomenology, semiotics, structuralism, post-structuralism and the deconstructive techniques of post-modern literary criticism."[4] However, on the whole, they did not use these tools to think about racial hierarchy and subordination. CRT ought to be understood as a reaction to CLS's perceived bankruptcy in this regard.

And on the other hand, the foremothers and forefathers of CRT were disappointed with the way that political liberals had come to conceptualize racism. These incipient critical race theorists felt that a dissatisfying conservatism had crept into liberal discourse around race as a result of its failure to adopt an avowedly critical approach

---

1 KIMBERLÉ CRENSHAW ET AL., CRITICAL RACE THEORY: THE KEY WRITINGS THAT FORMED THE MOVEMENT, at xix (1995) [hereinafter CRENSHAW ET AL., CRITICAL RACE THEORY].

2 *Id.* at xvii.

3 It might be important to offer the same caveat about CLS that the Introduction offers about CRT: CLS ought not to be understood as a homogeneous intellectual formation. As one scholar wrote during CLS's heyday, "Over 150 of us identify ourselves with the movement, and I suspect that there are about that many positions among us on any given concrete issue." Richard Michael Fischl, *Some Realism About Critical Legal Studies*, 41 U. MIAMI L. REV. 505, 507 (1987).

4 Elizabeth Iglesias, *Latcrit Theory: Some Preliminary Notes Towards a Transatlantic Dialogue*, 9 U. MIAMI INT'L & COMP. L. REV. 1, 9 (2001).

to thinking about racial inequality. This arguable conservativism was particularly dangerous in the 1980s, as this was the time of the "Reagan Revolution"—a political moment when "social programs coded 'black,' such as 'welfare' and 'affirmative action[,]' were under attack by a well-organized right-wing committed to rolling back the social welfare state."[5] Thus, if liberal discourse around race was itself conservative, there was nothing that the left could do or say to challenge the more avowed and direct conservatism that was sweeping the nation. CRT ought to be understood as a reaction to liberal discourse's perceived bankruptcy in this regard.

Perhaps it is because of CRT's status as both a confrontation with liberal discourse around race and a confrontation with critical discourse about law that the stories that circulate about CRT's origins—numerous though they may be—tend to invariably recount two historical moments. The first is the student protests that erupted at Harvard Law School (HLS) after Professor Derrick Bell left the school in the early 1980s. The second is the discontent that a swath of legal scholars of color felt with CLS in the mid- to late-1980s. The protests at HLS dramatize CRT's status as a left intervention into race discourse, while the discontent with CLS dramatizes CRT's status as a race intervention into left discourse.

I. Student Protests at Harvard

Professor Derrick Bell was not only the first black tenured professor at HLS, but he was also one of the first legal scholars to be critical of the court victories that civil rights lawyers had secured in the 1950s and 1960s—victories that had brought formal racial equality to the country. While most of his contemporaries wrote with a certain satisfaction about all of the gains that people of color had achieved as a result of the Civil Rights Movement, Bell was less sanguine. In his scholarship and teaching, he sought to disturb many of the racial truisms that had come to be accepted. Bell challenged the assumption that the litigation strategies adopted by civil rights lawyers actually reflected the desires and needs of the marginalized people that the lawyers purported to represent. He disputed the belief that the grant of civil rights to people of color solely (or, even, mostly) benefited people of color. And he contested the proposition that society was well on its way to expunging itself of racial injustice. Importantly, Bell did not worry solely about racial issues that were "out there" in society; he was also quite concerned about racial issues that were much closer to home—at HLS, to be exact. Bell was distressed by the dearth of faculty of color at the school. After the

---

[5] Berta Hernández-Truyol, Angela Harris & Francisco Valdes, *Beyond the First Decade: A Forward-Looking History of LatCrit Theory, Community and Praxis*, 17 BERKELEY LA RAZA L.J. 169, 177 (2006).

school failed to hire or tenure any black female professors after a number of years, Bell left in protest.

Bell's departure from HLS meant that the course on race that he had taught in semesters past—a course that explored how various aspects of American law created and sustained a racial hierarchy in which people of color resided at the bottom—would go unoffered. Several students of color approached the administration and asked that the school hire a black professor to teach the course in Bell's place. The school responded by saying that there was no black professor alive who could meet HLS's standards of excellence in hiring. However, the school did promise to offer a three-week "mini-course" on civil rights that would be taught by Jack Greenberg, the white director of the NAACP Legal Defense Fund, and Julius Chamber, a well-respected black civil rights attorney.

The students insisted that the proposed mini-course on civil rights was not an adequate replacement for the course that Bell had offered. While the former would examine how the law managed and sought to resolve racial antagonisms, the latter examined how the law *created* and *justified* those very antagonisms. Moreover, the students maintained that a black person ought to be hired to teach the desired course. They believed that living a life on the losing side of racial power provided a valuable, unique perspective on the law—a perspective that would invariably enhance the presentation and assessment of the law. HLS's administration was unconvinced, and the dean of the law school is reported to have infamously asked the students, "[W]ouldn't you prefer an excellent white professor over a mediocre Black one?"[6]

The students boycotted the school's mini-course on civil rights. Instead of enrolling in the class that the school offered, they organized an "Alternative Course" that they could take instead. Under the sponsorship of HLS professor Charles Ogletree, the "Alternative Course" featured law professors of color from other institutions who were invited to give lectures that offered critical analyses of the relationship between law and race. Writes Kimberlé Crenshaw, who was one of the student protestors at HLS, "The Alternative Course is a useful point to mark the genesis of Critical Race Theory," as "it was one of the earliest attempts to bring scholars of color together to address the law's treatment of race from a self-consciously critical perspective."[7]

---

[6] Kimberlé Williams Crenshaw, *Twenty Years of Critical Race Theory: Looking Back to Move Forward*, 43 CONN. L. REV. 1253, 1267 (2011) [hereinafter Crenshaw, *Twenty Years*].

[7] CRENSHAW ET AL., CRITICAL RACE THEORY, *supra* note 1, at xxi.

Further, the Alternative Course is a useful point to mark the genesis of CRT as it also demonstrates CRT's resistance to and departure from liberal discourse around race. The school's position vis-à-vis the student protestors embodies this discourse. According to CRT, liberal discourse is blind to, or simply uninterested in, the way that the law might construct the very racial inequality that it purports to be interested in remedying. In CRT's view, liberal discourse does not interrogate how ostensibly race-neutral "standards"—around who is qualified for a job, for example—are not at all race-neutral. Because it is not sensitive to how these "standards" are both a cause and an effect of racial power, it is not disquieted when "standards" are deployed in a manner that justifies excluding people of color from jobs, institutions, and other opportunities. Further, CRT critiques liberal discourse for its commitment to colorblindness as the moral compass of the post-civil rights era. Liberal discourse sees an equivalence between the race consciousness involved with seeking to hire a person of color to teach a course about race and the race consciousness involved with seeking to avoid hiring people of color altogether. It is one that does not recognize a vast dissimilarity between those two uses of race and, therefore, is guided by the conviction that, absent exigent circumstances, any and all awareness of race must be avoided. The following chapter explores CRT's dissatisfaction with liberal discourse around race in greater depth.

II. Critical Legal Studies and Critical Race Theory

What exactly is CLS, and why did CRT come to disapprove of it?

CLS is appropriately understood as a logical extension of legal realism, which first emerged in the 1920s and 1930s. Legal realism was a reaction to classical legal thought, which proposed that law and politics were entirely separate and that the process of deciding cases was "scientific, apolitical, principled, objective, logical, and rational."[8] Classical legal thought contended that legal decisions were nothing more than logical deductions of the relevant legal principles; moreover, it proposed that these principles were identifiable, finite, and led to only one result in any given case. According to this tradition, the judge's job was simply to mechanically ascertain the lone answer that was required by the governing principles.

Legal realism denied that legal principles led invariably to only one answer. Instead, they proposed that a certain *indeterminacy* characterized the law. That is, just as the relevant principles could

[8] Joseph William Singer, *Legal Realism Now*, 76 CALIF. L. REV. 465, 499 (1988).

lead a reasonable judge to decide in favor of the plaintiff, they could just as easily lead another equally reasonable judge to decide in favor of the defendant. In light of the indeterminacy of the law, legal realists proposed that judges ought not to pretend that the law was divorced from social context when deciding cases. Instead, the realists proposed that judges ought to acknowledge that the law ordered society. In this view, judges ought not to think that they were engaged in an effort to find the *right* answer to legal disputes; they ought to think that they were engaged in an effort to find the *best* answer—the answer that would order society in the most desirable way.[9] Further, realists proposed that the social sciences—specifically, economics and sociology—were the tools that judges ought to use when attempting to identify the *best* rules with which to regulate society.

In important ways, CLS picked up where legal realism left off. Like the realists who came before them, the crits believed that the law was indeterminate and that the relevant legal principles in any given case could lead to at least two competing or contradictory results. However, CLS used this observation to launch a critique of law that was much more total than the one that interested the realists. Whereas the realists observed the indeterminacy of law *in specific areas of the law* in order to encourage judges to be more pragmatic and result-oriented in their decision-making, crits observed the indeterminacy of law *in general* in order to destabilize the authority of the law. That is, while the realists argued that the law was indeterminate in order to encourage judges to replace abstract, formal logical reasoning with the concrete identification of the legal result that would make for better social policy, crits argued that the law was indeterminate in order to call into question the possibility of law itself. As one observer summarizes it, "while the Realists used analytic critique selectively, to discredit existing dogmas and suggest specific avenues of law reform, the critical legal

[9] Part of the reason for the realists' belief that judges ought to consider themselves to be engaged in a search for the *best*, as opposed to the *right*, answers is that realists were convinced that the formal logic that classical legal thought claimed ought to guide quests for right answers did nothing more than mask the judge's own political and/or moral choices. As one observer explains, "The Realists embraced the view that legal questions are inevitably 'social policy' questions, even if the judges and lawyers involved are utterly unaware of the fact. Left to their own devices, judges would invariably decide those questions on the basis of their own unstated (and often subconscious) psychological, sociological, and economic assumptions, and then rationalize their decisions by invoking legal rules and principles." Fischl, *supra* note 3, at 519–20. Accordingly, the realists concluded that it was better if judges were more forthcoming about the motivations behind their decisions, arguing that "judges should consciously and frankly engage in sophisticated and fact-sensitive social science analysis so that they could make better policy." *Id.* at 520.

scholar is more concerned with the entire framework of liberal thought."[10]

The crits were invested in destabilizing the authority of the law because they believed that law played an indispensable role in sustaining an unjust social order. This belief went beyond the recognition that the law contained and enforced rules that allowed some to have a lot while others had very little or nothing at all. It included the conviction that the law naturalized the social order, operating so that even the most subordinated individuals believed that the way that society was organized was inevitable and, at a basic level, fair. Thus, the crits were interested in the law as *ideology*; they were interested in the law as a body of thought that served to legitimate an unequal status quo. To the crits, destabilizing the law meant destabilizing a powerful means of legitimating a society that disempowered so many. As such, the crits understood their efforts to expose the incoherence and contradictions of the law to be in the service of liberation and social justice.

One can see, then, why CLS was attractive to the thinkers who would go on to found CRT. As Crenshaw and her coauthors explain, "While many in the legal community were, to put it mildly, deeply disturbed by the CLS assault against such ideological mainstays as the rule of the law, to scholars of color who drew on a history of colored communities' struggle against formal and institutional racism, the crits' contention that law was neither apolitical, neutral, nor determinate hardly seemed controversial."[11] These scholars of color understood these insights as foundational to "any serious attempt to understand the relationship between law and white supremacy."[12]

However, while many aspects of CLS were appealing to the nascent critical race theorists, they were disquieted by some of CLS's claims and rhetorical moves. First, they were disturbed by the crits' wholesale rejection of the possibility that law could be valuable to the subordinated. To the crits, the law was nothing more than a technique of alienation and a tool for sustaining hegemonic dominance. Consistent with this conception of law was the belief that legal rights could serve no real role in the liberation of subordinated people. Indeed, crits suggested that winning rights might thwart liberation goals: being granted rights that had been fought for might make the marginalized self-satisfied, blinding them to—or making

---

10 *'Round and 'Round the Bramble Bush: From Legal Realism to Critical Legal Scholarship*, 95 HARV. L. REV. 1669, 1680 (1982).

11 CRENSHAW ET AL., CRITICAL RACE THEORY, *supra* note 1, at xxii.

12 *Id.*

them patient with—the fact that the rights had not actually relieved them of their marginalization.

Yet, this critique of rights did not ring true to the burgeoning critical race theorists. In fact, it struck many of them as tone-deaf to black people's specific historical experience with rights. As Patricia Williams wrote in response to the crits' critique of rights:

> For the historically disempowered, the conferring of rights is symbolic of all the denied aspects of humanity: rights imply a respect which places one within the referential range of self and others, which elevates one's status from human body to social being. For blacks, then, the attainment of rights signifies the due, the respectful behavior, the collective responsibility properly owed by a society to one of its own.
>
> . . .
>
> "Rights" feels so new in the mouths of most black people. It is still so deliciously empowering to say. It is a sign for and a gift of selfhood that is very hard to contemplate reconstructing (deconstruction is too awful to think about!) at this point in history. It is the magic wand of visibility and invisibility, of inclusion and exclusion, of power and no-power. The concept of rights, both positive and negative, is the marker of our citizenship, our participatoriness, our relation to others.[13]

Mari Matsuda expresses a similar thought. She writes that people of color *know* that the law is not a guarantor of fairness, equality, justice, and all the other idyllic things that we are taught to believe. The experience that people of color have had with the law has given them firsthand knowledge that law can be an instrument of subordination. However, their experience has also taught them that law can be an instrument of emancipation. As a result, Matsuda claims that people of color embrace the law, despite the contradiction involved in simultaneously critiquing and venerating it. She writes:

> There are times to stand outside the courtroom door and say "this procedure is a farce, the legal system is corrupt, justice will never prevail in this land as long as privilege rules in the courtroom." There are times to stand inside the courtroom and say "this is a nation of laws, laws recognizing fundamental values of rights, equality and personhood." Sometimes, as Angela Davis did, there is a need to make both speeches in one day. Is that crazy? Inconsistent? Not

[13] Patricia J. Williams, *Alchemical Notes: Reconstructing Rights from Deconstructed Ideals*, 22 HARV. C.R.-C.L. L. REV. 401, 416, 431 (1987).

to Professor Davis, a Black woman on trial for her life in racist America. It made perfect sense to her, and to the twelve jurors good and true who heard her when she said "your government lies, but *your* law is above such lies."[14]

Thus, while many crits thought that law had no place in the fight for a just society—indeed, many crits were convinced that the law impeded the realization of a just society—the incipient critical race theorists were not entirely convinced. In their view, law had done powerful things for the vulnerable. As such, they were not ready to dismiss law as nothing more than an ideological weapon of hegemonic power.

Second, although the crits proclaimed to be invested in exposing the indeterminacy, incoherence, and contradictory nature of law because of an overarching interest in freeing minds and producing social justice, at times, it appeared as though they were simply interested in critique for critique's sake. The budding critical race theorists thought that critique for critique's sake was a waste of time—a luxury that they simply could not afford. As Richard Delgado puts it, "Racism will not go away simply because Crits show that legalisms are indeterminate, that rights are alienating and legitimizing, and that law is a reflection of the interests of the ruling class. Whatever utility these concepts may have in other settings and in attempting to explain the angst of CLS members, they have limited application in helping to understand, much less cure, racism."[15]

Thus, the emergent critical race theorists were not interested in engaging in critique in order to see who could generate the fanciest theory. Instead, they were interested in engaging in critique in order to end racial subordination. If they were going to expose the indeterminacy, incoherence, and contradictory nature of the law, they were going to do it with the goal of dismantling existing racial hierarchies. They were going to do it with the emancipation of people of color on their minds.

Observing that CLS had not developed a theory of racism or racial domination, those who would become critical race theorists pushed the crits to pay closer attention to the race question—to use the impressive theoretical tools at their disposal in the service of antiracism. In response to these pushes, the organizers of the annual CLS conference in 1987 decided to make race the focus of that year's event, and they invited several nascent critical race theorists to

---

[14] Mari J. Matsuda, *When the First Quail Calls: Multiple Consciousness as Jurisprudential Method*, 11 WOMEN'S RTS. L. REP. 7, 8 (1989).

[15] Richard Delgado, *The Ethereal Scholar: Does Critical Legal Studies Have What Minorities Want?*, 22 HARV. C.R.-C.L. L. REV. 301, 309 (1987).

present papers that addressed issues of race from a decidedly critical perspective. Many of these papers were subsequently published in the *Harvard Civil Rights-Civil Liberties Law Review*, and they would become "key documents in the critical-race-theory corpus."[16] Several architects of CRT identify the 1987 CLS conference and the symposium edition that was published thereafter as "the final step in the preliminary development of CRT as a distinctively progressive critique of legal discourse on race."[17]

Now, while CLS was, at some level, open to hearing the racial critiques launched by the emergent critical race theorists, it was not willing to incorporate those critiques into a CLS-identified theory. This unwillingness resulted from a disbelief that it was actually appropriate to allow race to be the focal point of theory, analysis, and/or political activity. As Crenshaw and her co-authors describe it, many crits had "an abiding skepticism, if not outright disdain, toward any theoretical or political project organized around the concept of race."[18] If these crits were right, and if centering race in legal scholarship was a sign of intellectual laziness or a lack of analytical sophistication, then the incipient critical race theorists' desire to generate a theory of the relationship between law and racial subordination was foolish. The budding critical race theorists' sense that CLS was dead wrong about this assessment of their desires suggested that they would not be able to do their work under the banner of CLS. They would have to create a new banner.

And this is precisely what they did. Two years after the 1987 CLS conference, twenty-four scholars of color[19] met at the University of Wisconsin during the summer to pursue the race-centered project that many crits had suggested was inadvisable, unrefined, or simply uninteresting.[20] The summer workshop was designed to give

---

[16] Richard Delgado, *Liberal McCarthyism and the Origins of Critical Race Theory*, 94 IOWA L. REV. 1505, 1514 (2009).

[17] CRENSHAW ET AL., CRITICAL RACE THEORY, *supra* note 1, at xxvi.

[18] *Id.*

[19] These scholars were Anita Allen, Taunya Lovell Banks, Derrick Bell, Kevin Brown, Paulette Caldwell, John Calmore, Kimberlé Crenshaw, Harlon Dalton, Richard Delgado, Neil Gotanda, Linda Greene, Trina Grillo, Isabelle Gunning, Angela Harris, Mari Matsuda, Teresa Miller, Philip Nash, Elizabeth Patterson, Stephanie Phillips, Benita Ramsey, Robert Suggs, Kendall Thomas, and Patricia Williams. Kimberlé Williams Crenshaw, *The First Decade: Critical Reflections, or "A Foot in the Closing Door,"* 49 UCLA L. REV. 1343, 1361–62 (2002) [hereinafter Crenshaw, *The First Decade*].

[20] We should note, though, that this gathering at the University of Wisconsin was made possible through the support of David Trubek, one of the co-founders of CLS. As the Director of the Institute for Legal Studies at University of Wisconsin's law school, Trubek provided the institutional support to host the workshop. This demonstrates that the relationship between CLS and CRT is not one of bitter antagonism—at least, not all the time. Instead, the relationship between the two frameworks might be better described as one of respectful disagreement.

thinkers interested in examining questions of race, law, and justice from an emphatically critical stance the space to develop their ideas while in conversation with a small number of similarly-minded and equally-motivated colleagues.

We might identify this summer meeting as the moment when the entity known as Critical Race Theory finally emerged—the event when the critical race theorists *to-be* finally became *critical race theorists*. Indeed, their efforts received their appellation shortly after this initial summer workshop. Crenshaw, who coined the name "Critical Race Theory," describes her intention to "signify the specific political and intellectual location of the project through 'critical,' the substantive focus through 'race,' and the desire to develop a coherent account of race and law through the term 'theory.' "[21]

The CRT summer workshops continued for nine years, finally coming to an end in 1997. CRT, however, lives on.

III. Questions and Discussion

1. Professors Sumi Cho and Robert Westley contend that if CRT lives on, it is in part because of student agitation at law schools in the late 1980s and 1990s. In addition to the protests at HLS discussed above, students at the University of California, Berkeley agitated in response to the school's failure to hire faculty of color. When the school did not respond by hiring a significant number of professors of color, the students led a strike, which subsequently spread to other law schools around the country. In the wake of this nationwide strike, the pace of the hiring of racial minorities in the legal academy picked up. Further, some of the newly hired professors were identified with, or would come to identify themselves with, CRT. Thus, scholars operating within a CRT framework found institutional homes in the academy and, therefore, platforms from which to disseminate their work.

Cho and Westley contend that student activism plays a crucial role in CRT's persistence because it "directly impacted critical race scholars' access to top law reviews, their legitimacy and popularity, and subsequently, placement in top law schools."[22] They insist that it is important not to erase this activism and/or dismiss its significance:

> To overlook the role of local and national student organizing in bringing about these changes is dangerous to CRT as a long-term project. Such oversight buttresses the liberal myth of self-correcting societal institutions that respond to

[21] Crenshaw, *The First Decade*, *supra* note 19, at 1361.

[22] Sumi Cho & Robert Westley, *Critical Race Coalitions: Key Movements that Performed the Theory*, 33 U.C. DAVIS L. REV. 1377, 1399 (2000).

"better argument." In this narrative, law schools diversified when exceptional candidates of color miraculously presented and proved themselves worthy. Sustained and heated political activism was merely incidental or detrimental to the process. As critical race scholars, we should be wary of histories of our inclusion that perpetuate the myth of institutional openness to racial justice.[23]

2. CLS's skepticism about pursuing an intellectual project that centers race is similar to the skepticism that many people feel about identity politics. Indeed, when describing crits' uncertainty about the CRT project, Crenshaw and her co-authors speak about it in terms of the crits' disdain of the concept of identity. They write that these crits had adopted a "post-modern critique of identity" that led them to believe that "since racial categories are not 'real' or 'natural' but instead socially constructed, it is theoretically and politically absurd to center race as a category of analysis or a basis for political action."[24]

The distaste for identity politics has not gone anywhere. For example, some pundits have attributed Donald Trump's election to the presidency to identity politics. The argument is that, for many years, politicians had focused on identity and, in the process, had ignored or overlooked those who had not organized around identity or whose concerns were not a product of their identity. Thus, politicians had appealed to, and responded to the needs of, those making claims on the basis of their race (i.e., black people), gender (i.e., women), and sexuality (i.e., lesbian, gay, and bisexual persons)—with race, gender, and sexuality being understood as identity categories. However, politicians were not responsive to the needs of those making claims on the basis of their class (i.e., the poor, the working class)—with class being understood as something other than an identity category. Trump, the argument goes, paid attention to class and appealed to voters who had been disadvantaged on that basis. Consequently, he was able to win the presidential election.

The difficulty with this analysis is that it does not help us discern which categories should be understood as identity-based ones versus those that should not. Why is "class" not an identity-based category? How is making an appeal to the "working class" not making an appeal to a person's or group's identity? It is not enough to say that "class" is non-identitarian because it cuts across identity categories. For example, it is not enough to argue that an appeal to "the working class" is not an appeal to identity because "the working class" includes people of all races, genders, and sexualities. First, this

---

[23] *Id.* at 1404.

[24] CRENSHAW ET AL., CRITICAL RACE THEORY, *supra* note 1, at xxvi.

definition still does not tell us which categories are properly conceptualized as identities and which ones are not; it does not tell us what qualities or characteristics must be present (or absent) before something can be categorized as an identity. Second, if we define categories as non-identitarian by virtue of their ability to cut across identity categories, then many of the categories that we understand as identity-based would qualify as non-identitarian. If, for example, that which makes a category non-identitarian is its ability to cut across identity categories, then "black people" is non-identitarian, as it includes people of all sexualities and genders (and classes).

Others propose that "class" is non-identitarian because it allows for a broader critique than the categories that we understand to be identities. The argument is that addressing the problems or issues affecting marginalized *classes* requires structural transformations, while addressing the problems or issues affecting marginalized *races, genders, or sexualities* does not require similar structural changes. For example, the argument is that in order to respond to the needs of the working class in the U.S., we have to contend with globalization and the transnational movement of labor and capital. But, in order to respond to the needs of black people in the U.S., we do not have to contend with such large-scale processes; we only have to include them in existing structures and institutions. However, it may not be true that addressing the problems or issues affecting marginalized identities does not require structural transformation. That is, if white supremacy, or patriarchy, or heteronormativity is systemic and endemic to society, then resolving the concerns of the identity groups that these institutions subordinate (i.e., nonwhite people, transgender and cisgender women, LGBTQ people) might require structural transformation. If so, then making race-based, or sex-based, or sexuality-based claims might allow for an extremely broad critique.

With this is in mind, how do you feel about "identity politics"? Why do you think they have gotten such a bad rap? Are they divisive, or narrow, in a way that non-identity-based politics are not and, if so, why? Do you think that identity politics ought to be reimagined or redeemed? Why or why not? How might we go about this task?

3. The student protestors at HLS received some pretty harsh criticism—even from those on the left. A lot of the criticism focused on the students' desire that a *black* professor teach the course that Bell once taught. For example, Bayard Rustin, a leader in the Civil Rights Movement, wrote in a letter to the editor published in the New York Times that the students' refusal to be taught by a white

professor was "nothing more than blatant racism."[25] He continued, "Blacks, as victims of racial discrimination, should be the first to reject the view that race can disqualify one from any particular pursuit."[26]

How do you feel about the students' insistence that a black professor teach the course? Do you think they were right in wanting to learn from someone "who had not only acquired legal expertise in fighting racism but who had also experienced its dynamics individually and institutionally"?[27] Or do you think they did nothing more than replicate the discourses that racial justice activists had fought—discourses that avow that you can know a person's qualifications by knowing his race?

4. As the chapter describes, the burgeoning critical race theorists had a complicated way of thinking about the law. On the one hand, they agreed with the crits that law was indeterminate, alienating, and a tool of oppression; on the other hand, they recognized the emancipatory potential that the law possesses.

Angela Harris describes this as CRT's simultaneous postmodernism and modernism. In its postmodern moments, CRT is as pessimistic as is CLS about the work that the law can do to produce a just society. However, in its modern moments, CRT believes in *truth, objectivity,* and *reason*. In these moments, CRT proposes that if we think about things correctly, and if we use the law in the right way, we can produce a nation where racial inequality has been vanquished. Harris explains that "CRT's commitment to the liberation of people of color" and to the belief that scholarship can help bring about that liberation

> suggest a faith in certain concepts and institutions that postmodernists lack. . . . [M]odernist narratives have faith that once enough people see the truth, right action will follow: that enlightenment leads to empowerment, and that empowerment leads to emancipation. Modernist narratives, then, are profoundly hopeful. They assume that people of color and whites live in the same perceptual and moral world, that reason speaks to us all in the same way despite our different experiences, and that reason, rather than habit or power, is what will motivate people. Modernist narratives also can be profoundly romantic. They imagine heroic action by a formerly oppressed people rising up as one, "empowered" to be who they "really" are or

[25] Bayard Rustin, Letter to the Editor, *A Misguided Protest by Blacks at Harvard*, N.Y. TIMES, Aug. 17, 1982, at A26.

[26] *Id.*

[27] Crenshaw, *Twenty Years*, *supra* note 6, at 1266.

choose to be, breathing the thin and bracing air of freedom.[28]

Because of the modernism that is part and parcel of CRT, Harris describes the theory as, at bottom, "redemptive, not deconstructive."[29]

Similarly, Charles Lawrence writes that the simultaneous embrace of and rejection of the law—what Harris describes as CRT's concurrent modernism and postmodernism—can also be observed in the scholarship of CRT's founding father, Derrick Bell, who had both a "critical skepticism about the achievements of civil rights law and [a] commitment to using the law as a vehicle for social change."[30]

What do you think about CRT's love/hate relationship with the law? In what way might this relationship—this inconsistency—weaken the theory? In what ways might it strengthen it?

---

[28] Angela P. Harris, *Foreword: The Jurisprudence of Reconstruction*, 82 CALIF. L. REV. 741, 753 (1994).

[29] *Id.* at 743.

[30] Charles R. Lawrence, III, *The Word and the River: Pedagogy as Scholarship as Struggle*, 65 S. CALIF. L. REV. 2231, 2241 (1992).

Chapter 2

THE CONSERVATISM OF LIBERAL DISCOURSE ON RACE

As Chapter 1 discusses, Critical Race Theory considers itself to be not only an intervention into critical discourse about law, but also an intervention into liberal discourse about race. With respect to the former, CRT sought to center the race question in the Critical Legal Studies movement—an organization of scholars who had taken a decidedly critical stance towards the law and who were developing a theory that they hoped would explain the law's complicity in social injustice. And with respect to the latter, CRT sought to identify the weaknesses—indeed, the conservatism—in the way that liberals had come to conceptualize and talk about race, racism, and racial justice. Further, it endeavored to develop an alternative discourse that would explain the persistence of racial inequality in an era of formal equality, revitalize the way that lawyers and lay persons thought about race and racism, and lead to more racially just outcomes if operationalized in the law.

At the time of CRT's emergence in the 1980s, many liberals perceived the country to be in the midst of a retreat from the commitment to racial justice that the Civil Rights Movement had seemingly forced the nation to make. Then-President Ronald Reagan had filled the federal judiciary with politically conservative judges who handed down exceedingly narrow interpretations of the newly minted civil rights laws, drastically limiting their reach and effect. Moreover, he appointed as heads of the agencies charged with implementing and enforcing civil rights laws individuals who were hostile to racial justice reforms.[1] In this way, the political climate at the time of CRT's advent was one in which the limits of the civil rights laws were becoming crystal clear. CRT endeavored to analyze the origins of these limits. It concluded, quite controversially, that the source of what it thought to be the inefficacy and inadequacy of civil rights laws was not a conservative judiciary and executive branch; instead, it argued, the source was liberal civil rights discourse itself. CRT's willingness to lay blame for the frustration of

[1] Indeed, in 1982, Reagan tapped Clarence Thomas to be the Chairman of the Equal Employment Opportunity Commission, which enforces Title VII of the Civil Rights Acts of 1964. Thomas's subsequent tenure as a Supreme Court Justice, having revealed in great detail his extremely conservative conception of racial justice and the role that law ought to play in achieving it, illuminates the nature of the Reagan era reversal on racial justice reform.

liberals' racial justice goals with *liberals* might be that which has earned CRT its "radical" label.[2]

While CRT certainly critiqued the impediments to substantive racial equality that it believed conservative judges and politicians had erected, it also critiqued the liberal understandings of race, racism, and racial justice that were embodied in civil rights laws—reformist and integration-oriented laws that liberals had fought for, championed, and continued to defend. CRT argued that conservatism was part and parcel of the way that liberals thought and talked about racism and racial equality, and they claimed that this conservatism explained why it was so easy for conservatives to coopt the language of civil rights to limit the scope of the civil rights laws. As Gary Peller describes it, conservatives had used "the very rhetoric of tolerance, color-blindness, and equal opportunity that once characterized progressive discourse to mark the limits of reform. But it would be a mistake to think that today's conservative discourse is simply a bad faith distortion of a progressive worldview. Serious limits to the integrationist vision existed from the beginning."[3] The balance of this chapter examines the limits that CRT saw in the liberal vision of racial justice.

I. Defining Racism

Traditional civil rights discourse tends to define racism as discrete, easily identifiable, invariably intentional, always irrational acts perpetrated by bad actors. Let's unpack this definition a bit.

If acts of racism are *discrete*, it means that they are cut off and isolated from other acts, individuals, and institutions. If acts of racism are easily *identifiable*, it means that recognizing the mechanisms that disadvantage individuals and/or groups on account of race is straightforward, unambiguous, and involves no great effort (or theory). If acts of racism are *intentional*, it means that the actor who engages in the racist behavior purposefully disadvantages an individual because of her race; indeed, disadvantaging the individual because of her race is the actor's sole, or primary, reason for engaging in the racist behavior. If acts of racism are *irrational*, it means that it does not make sense for the racist person to do them. So, for example, the racist storeowner acts irrationally when she refuses to serve Asian patrons, as she is denying herself the money that those patrons would otherwise spend inside of her establishment. Finally, if acts of racism are perpetrated by *bad actors*, it means that when we are trying to figure out how to dismantle racial hierarchies, we need to be on the lookout for culpable individuals. We can safely

[2] *See, e.g.*, Angela P. Harris, *Foreword: The Jurisprudence of Reconstruction*, 82 CALIF. L. REV. 741, 747 (1994) (describing CRT as possessing a "radicalism").

[3] Gary Peller, *Race Consciousness*, 1990 DUKE L.J. 758, 762 (1990).

ignore the structures within which individuals exist, and we can safely ignore the institutions that operate within society.

Essentially, traditional civil rights discourse defines racism as individually-held bias or prejudice. As Peller explains this idea,

> [t]he mental side of racism is . . . represented as either "prejudice"—the prejudging of a person according to mythological stereotypes—or "bias"—the process of being influenced by subjective factors. The key image here is of irrationalism—the problem with prejudice is that it obscures the work of reason by clouding perception with beliefs rooted in superstition. . . . [R]acism achieves social form when the distortion of prejudice in consciousness subsequently translates into practice. Here racism manifests itself in the practice of "discrimination," in the disparate treatment of whites and blacks that the irrational attribution of difference is supposed to justify.[4]

CRT proposes that this definition of racism is woefully inadequate. While defining racism as a "discrete, identifiable, intentional, irrational act perpetrated by a bad actor" describes a type of racism that may have been ubiquitous in the pre-civil rights era (and that may tenaciously persist today), CRT argues that it does not describe the mechanisms that do most of the work of maintaining white people as the dominant racial group in the country at present. CRT contends that far from being discrete, racism and racial dominance are oftentimes the result of the interactions of many institutions across multiple domains.[5] CRT claims that far from being easily identifiable, racism (and the recognition of an act or omission as a species thereof) frequently requires a theoretical framework to help us ascertain which societal choices inflict racial subordination and, consequently, ought to be designated as *racism*. CRT proposes that racism is not invariably intentional; in the post-civil rights era, it is oftentimes the unintended (if foreseeable) consequences of choices that we make. CRT also denies that racism is unvaryingly irrational; it posits that more often than not, racism makes all the sense in the world. Finally, CRT argues that while racism may be perpetrated by bad actors, it more frequently is the result of institutional, structural processes in the post-civil rights era.

---

4 *Id.* at 768–69 (footnote omitted).

5 So, for example, the fact of black children disproportionately finding themselves attempting to acquire educations in underfunded schools is the product of jurisdictions' constitutionally protected choice to fund schools through property taxes interacting with residential housing segregation (which, in turn, is the result of a slew of institutions interacting across multiple domains). Chapter 20 explores this phenomenon in depth.

CRT offers that defining racism in the way that traditional civil rights discourse proposes is dangerously problematic. When racism is only understood as bias or prejudice practiced by a bad actor, it puts outside of the field of vision all of the institutions and structures that function to maintain what critical thinkers perceive to be the nation's current racial hierarchy. For example, consider the questions that the traditional liberal definition of racism leads us to ask when Eric Garner, an unarmed black man, was killed by police after being placed in an illegal chokehold on the streets of Staten Island, New York.[6] The definition directs our focus to the police officer who killed him, Daniel Pantaleo, and it guides us to an interrogation of Pantaleo and his views on race. So, we ask whether Pantaleo, a white man, has ever used the *n-word*. We ask whether he has any black friends. Does he listen to hip-hop? Does he think that Rihanna is attractive? Has he seen the movie *Black Panther*? Did he like it more than *Deadpool*? Essentially, the liberal definition of racism leads us to ask whether Pantaleo is a bigot. If we determine that he is not, then Garner's death cannot be understood as a manifestation of racism.

However, when racism is defined in the way that the CRT proposes, we are encouraged to ask different questions about Garner's death. When we learn that Pantaleo initiated the encounter that ended in Garner's death because Garner was illegally selling individual cigarettes from a pack, we can ask why that act had been proscribed. Indeed, why had the New York State legislature decided to make that particular act *criminal*? Further, why had Garner felt compelled to engage in it? What does it reveal about the economic opportunities available (or not available) to Garner that an able-bodied adult man of sound mind considered selling individual cigarettes from a pack something that was worth his time and energy? Also, what empowered Pantaleo (or any police officer, for that matter) to engage with Garner, an individual who was suspected to be engaging in a nonviolent, victimless crime? Why has our Constitution—specifically, the Fourth Amendment guarantee against unreasonable searches and seizures—been interpreted to give the police the latitude to initiate contact with individuals suspected to be engaging in nonviolent, victimless crimes?

Moreover, when we learn that Garner had a host of health issues, including asthma, that made the illegal chokehold in which Pantaleo put him much more likely to be deadly, we can ask questions about why Garner had come to inhabit such a state of unhealth. Why did Garner, as well as so many other indigent folks in

[6] Joseph Goldstein & Nate Schweber, *Man's Death After Chokehold Raises Old Issue for the Police*, N.Y. TIMES (July 18, 2014), https://www.nytimes.com/2014/07/19/nyregion/staten-island-man-dies-after-he-is-put-in-chokehold-during-arrest.html.

our country, suffer from obesity? Why did Garner, as well as so many other poor people of color, suffer from asthma? Why did Garner, as well as so many other black people, suffer from hypertension and heart disease? The answers to this batch of questions do not involve malicious actors, but rather deadly *systems* and *structures*. Defining racism in the way that the liberal tradition proposes disallows us from asking these broader questions. Instead, it keeps our attention squarely focused on Pantaleo and his beliefs and intentions.

In this way, we see how the liberal definition of racism suggests that in order to fix any race problem the nation continues to have, no great societal reformation is necessary. Few would argue that there are large numbers of bigots roaming the streets in the post-civil rights era. Surely, individuals who hate or dislike others simply because they belong to a racial outgroup certainly exist—and they might even occupy positions of power. However, liberals, conservatives, moderates, and radicals would probably all agree that these types of individuals are few and far between. Now, if racism is only individually-held bias or prejudice, and if biased or prejudiced individuals are few and far between, then racism is an *aberration*. And if racism is an aberration, then racial justice will be achieved when these aberrant individuals are identified and denied the ability to harm others. The work of antiracism, then, is simply to remove these blemishes from an otherwise perfectly good body politic.

But, if racism is more broadly defined, then there is nothing simple, pat, or easy about the work of antiracism. Let's return to Eric Garner's death at the hands of Daniel Pantaleo. The liberal definition of racism suggests that the work of antiracism is to remove Pantaleo from the police force if he is, indeed, a racist; it also suggests that we need to implement procedures that would prevent other racist individuals from becoming police officers. If we do those two things—*Ta da!* Problem solved. But, if racism is defined in the way that CRT proposes, then more wide-reaching changes are necessary. These changes involve:

- addressing society's decision to criminalize nonviolent activities in which the poor, because of their indigence, primarily engage—like selling individual cigarettes from a pack;
- creating legal opportunities for individuals to support themselves and their families financially;
- constructing a durable, generous, and non-punitive social safety net for those who find it difficult or impossible to be financially self-supporting;

- reconsidering the Court's interpretation of the Fourth Amendment;
- addressing the siting of environmental hazards in poor communities of color, which contributes to the high rates of asthma and other health problems among the residents of these communities;
- remedying the dearth of healthy foods that are available in poor neighborhoods;
- tackling the myriad reasons for people of color in this country being sicker and dying earlier than their white counterparts—including our two-tiered healthcare system and the deleterious toll that racism-related stress takes on the bodies of people of color.

This example reveals that CRT's definition of racism requires an extensive, some would say *radical*, reordering of society. But, this makes sense, CRT claims, because society was ordered at a time when people of color were unable to participate in it. Indeed, CRT says, society was ordered at a time when the exclusion of people of color from the body politic was an accepted and valued feature of society. As a result, CRT claims, we should have little faith that the institutions that we created during that time of racial exclusion are legitimate. We might, in fact, expect that white dominance is embedded in these institutions—that it comprises the very essence of our systems and conventions. It is for this reason that CRT encourages us to adopt a definition of racism that allows us to put "the entire range of everyday social practices in America—social practices developed and maintained throughout the period of formal American apartheid—[within] the scope of critical examination or legal remediation."[7]

II. Racism as Race-Consciousness

Traditional civil rights discourse defines racism as the fact of simply thinking about race. This is what white supremacists did during the pre-civil rights era: they thought about race. They thought about race when they concluded that black people were unfit to sit in the same railway coaches as white people. They thought about race when they designated some schools for white children and other schools for black children. They thought about race when they declared that black people and white people ought not to marry and passed anti-miscegenation laws to criminalize these unions. Traditional civil rights discourse identifies this constant race-thinking as the flaw of the pre-civil rights era. Thus, it prescribes

---

[7] KIMBERLÉ CRENSHAW ET AL., CRITICAL RACE THEORY: THE KEY WRITINGS THAT FORMED THE MOVEMENT, at xv (1995).

never thinking about race—race unconsciousness—as the appropriate cognitive mode of the post-civil rights era. It designates colorblindness as the moral, legal, and political compass that ought to guide the nation. Hence, we arrive at Dr. Martin Luther King, Jr.'s dream of a nation where people "would not be judged by the color of their skin, but by the content of their character."[8]

It is worth noting that both liberals and conservatives declare colorblindness to be the approach to racial justice that our increasingly racially enlightened society should adopt. Consider the Court's 2007 decision in *Parents Involved in Community Schools v. Seattle*.[9] In an effort to achieve a small measure of racial integration in their schools, two school boards allowed a student's race to be one factor in determining the school to which she would be assigned. The school boards' plans were eventually challenged, and the Court struck them down, holding that they violated the equal protection clause of the Fourteenth Amendment. In the course of so doing, Chief Justice Roberts declared that "[t]he way to stop discrimination on the basis of race is to stop discriminating on the basis of race."[10] In essence, Roberts, writing for a plurality, declared that colorblindness ought to be our constitutional guide. Because the liberal conception of racism as race consciousness is identical to its conservative counterpart, liberals do not have a convincing retort to Roberts' claim. They best that they can say is, "Yes, colorblindness *ought* to be our constitutional guide. Just not now. Not yet."

It is certainly hard to deny the intuitive appeal of colorblindness. As Barbara Flagg explains, "Race consciousness—the explicit use of racial classifications as a means of disadvantaging nonwhites—has been the primary vehicle of racial subordination until quite recently. . . . [C]olorblindness appeared to be the exact antithesis of the form of race consciousness that had been the root cause of racial subordination. If 'color' had marked an individual as inferior, then the refusal to recognize "color" would be the way to elevate him to equal status with whites."[11]

However, there are a number of consequences to understanding race consciousness to be racism and colorblindness to be the repudiation of racism. First, this understanding problematizes all race consciousness *equally*. Thus, for example, the white person who thinks about race when deciding to burn a cross on her black neighbor's lawn commits the identical cognitive and behavioral error

---

8 Martin Luther King, Jr., I Have a Dream (Aug. 28, 1963) (transcript available at http://www.thekingcenter.org/archive/document/i-have-dream-2#).

9 Parents Involved in Cmty. Sch. v. Seattle Sch. Dist. No. 1, 551 U.S. 701 (2007).

10 *Id.* at 862.

11 Barbara J. Flagg, *"Was Blind But Now I See": White Race Consciousness and the Requirement of Discriminatory Intent*, 91 MICH. L. REV. 953, 1013 (1993).

as the black person who thinks about race when deciding to patronize a black-owned business in her neighborhood. CRT challenges the construction of equivalents between these two modes of thinking about race, disputing the suggestion that they are anything *like* one another. Surely, says CRT, there is a difference between thinking about race in order to continue the exclusion of a group from an institution from which they have been historically excluded and thinking about race in order to finally bring that group into the institution. There has to be a difference, they say, between thinking about race in order to maintain the dominance of a racial group and thinking about race in order to empower a subordinated racial group.

Second, if thinking about race is racist, then attempting to dismantle the nation's racial hierarchy by race conscious means is racist. Accordingly, race consciousness when making school assignments in order or achieve mildly integrated schools; race consciousness in the construction of voting districts; race conscious affirmative action programs in hiring and university admissions, race consciousness when evaluating the impact of changes in voting laws or practices. . . . All of these efforts become conceptualized as racist. Consequently, liberals—unwilling to challenge their conception of racism, but also committed to the existence of such remedial efforts—are forced to apologize for these programs. They are compelled to frame these programs as "necessary evils"—as "a merely 'exceptional' remedy for past injustice, a temporary tool to be used only until equal opportunity is achieved."[12] CRT proposes that there is something deeply problematic about styling such efforts as *evils*, albeit necessary ones. If they are evil, it becomes harder to argue that they are the *right* and *moral* thing to do given our nation's history and present of racial inequality. Further, if such programs are evil, then it becomes easy to equate them with the evils of racial exclusion that they are attempting to address. One can just hear conservative opponents saying, "Well, two wrongs don't make a right. . . ."

CRT unreservedly rejects conceptualizing racism as race consciousness. It concedes that race consciousness was a salient feature of the days of chattel slavery, Jim Crow, the Chinese Exclusion Act,[13] Japanese internment during World War II,[14]

---

[12] CRENSHAW ET AL., *supra* note 7, at xv.

[13] Act of May 6, 1882 (Chinese Exclusion Act), ch. 126, 22 Stat. 58 (repealed 1943) (terminating Chinese immigration for ten years and prohibiting Chinese nationals from becoming naturalized citizens).

[14] Korematsu v. United States, 323 U.S. 214, 216–17 (1944) (holding that the Civilian Exclusion Order directing all persons of Japanese ancestry to be excluded from "Military Areas" in the West Coast was constitutional due to "pressing public necessity").

Operation Wetback,[15] and the requirement that an individual be a "free white person" in order to naturalize as a U.S. citizen.[16] However, they argue that the error practiced in those days was not simply thinking about race. Rather, it was thinking about race *in the service of white supremacy*. According to CRT, the race consciousness of Jim Crow and the race consciousness of affirmative action, for example, ought not to be lumped together in the same boat. They are on different continents, oceans away from each other.

Accordingly, CRT embraces race consciousness *in the service of racial justice*. This acceptance of race-thinking—indeed, the unapologetic championing of race-thinking as necessary, right, and *good*—represents, perhaps, the most significant departure between CRT and traditional civil rights discourse.

CRT observes that both conservatives and liberals offer colorblindness as the best means for achieving racial equality. Conservatives and liberals say that if we simply stop thinking about race in the public sphere, people of color will be able to get decent educations, find competitive jobs, acquire wealth, be healthier, and live longer—things that the race consciousness of the pre-civil rights era denied them. However, claims CRT, if this is what colorblindness is supposed to do, it has not succeeded. Indeed, CRT understands colorblindness to be a "failed social policy."[17]

CRT derides colorblindness for more than its failure to achieve racial justice. It decries it because it is convinced that in an era of formal equality, colorblindness perpetuates racial oppression. So, the "Whites Only" signs have been taken down. The covenants that forbid the sale of a home to a black person have been declared unenforceable. The bylaws that maintain that nonwhite people cannot be admitted into an organization have been removed. The persons who believe that nonwhite people are, as a rule, incompetent and unqualified have had changes of heart, have been run out of public life, or have been advised that they can no longer make decisions in accordance with those beliefs. CRT's distaste for colorblindness results from its refusal to believe that some kind of social osmosis is going to happen and, in the absence of formal barriers, people of color are just going to float over into the neighborhoods, institutions, halls of government, and arenas of

---

[15] Operation Wetback was a large-scale campaign to identify and remove undocumented Mexican aliens from the U.S. who had entered the country in response to an increase in demand for labor. The campaign resulted in the deportation of one-sixth of the Mexican-origin population in the country. *See* Gilberto Cardenas, *United States Immigration Policy Toward Mexico: An Historical Perspective*, 2 CHICANO L. REV. 66, 79–81 (1975)

[16] Uniform Naturalization Act of 1790, ch. 3, 1 Stat. 103 (repealed 1795) (restricting the right to naturalization to "free white persons").

[17] Flagg, *supra* note 11, at 1014.

power from they have been excluded. CRT proposes that we have to think about race and actively move people of color into these spaces. Colorblindness prevents us from doing that.

III. Formal Equality as the Best Means to the Desired End

Since the passage of the Civil Rights Act of 1964, formal equality has been the legal order of the day with respect to racial justice. Formal equality requires that all competent adults be given equal legal status and that the government endow them with the same bundle of rights. The state is thus compelled to treat all individuals in an evenhanded manner, affording everyone the same privileges and imposing upon everyone the same obligations. Thus, for example, formal equality means that the person of color must have the right to attend Suburban School X if other persons have that right. The demands of formal equality are satisfied as long as the government treats everyone equally—allowing all individuals to attend Suburban School X, or prohibiting everyone from doing the same.

Liberals do not deny that racial stratification in the country persists. However, they do not attribute the persistence of racial inequality to the nation's commitment to formal equality as its civil rights policy. On the whole, they believe that there is nothing wrong with the concept of formal equality. The problem that they see is in its implementation. They tend to believe that if conservative judges would not erect so many procedural barriers in front of plaintiffs seeking to vindicate their formal rights, or if the agencies charged with enforcing the civil rights laws would be funded properly or led by commissioners and chairs that are committed to civil rights, then formal equality will achieve what it is designed to achieve, and the nation's existing racial hierarchies will be dismantled.

CRT departs from its liberal counterpart on this issue. Whereas traditional civil rights discourse sees no conceptual shortcomings in formal equality, CRT believes that formal equality has a defective premise. It proposes that similar treatment—the analytical mainstay of formal equality—makes sense when individuals are similarly situated. Indeed, CRT does not deny that understanding equality as treating similar people similarly is perfectly logical. However, it contends that when individuals are dissimilarly situated, treating them similarly is not to treat them equally. Quite the opposite, similar treatment under conditions of inequality is *unequal* treatment; it is to treat unequal individuals in a manner that perpetuates their inequality.[18]

---

[18] This, of course, is what Anatole France was getting at when he penned the oft-quoted phrase, "The majestic quality of the law which prohibits the wealthy as well as

Having laid down that conceptual framework, CRT observes what, to it, is obvious: white and nonwhite people are dissimilarly situated. As such, the symmetrical treatment that is part and parcel of formal equality is inapposite. CRT proposes that we should not be at all surprised that formal equality has not managed to eliminate white racial dominance. It contends that to expect anything from formal equality but the maintenance of the unequal status quo is absurd.

Now, formal equality is usually distinguished from substantive equality. Contrary to formal equality, the demands of substantive equality are not satisfied with a mere affirmative answer to the question of whether the government is treating everyone the same. The obligations of substantive equality are not discharged with the assurance that individuals have the same *abstract* ability to engage in the same behavior because the government has bestowed everyone with the same rights. Instead, substantive equality asks whether an individual can *actually* do what the right allows him to do in theory. Thus, if a person of color cannot actually attend Suburban School X—because she cannot afford it, because she cannot physically get to the school, or because she is prohibited from attending it because it is outside of her assigned school district, for example—then the person of color is not substantively equal to her white counterpart who can attend Suburban School X.

CRT embraces substantive equality—something that our civil rights laws do not reflect and, according to CRT, are incapable of achieving as drafted. CRT recognizes that in order to achieve this substantive equality, there must be some dissimilar treatment of the dissimilarly situated individuals and groups in society.

IV. Commitment to Integration

It would be an exaggeration to say that CRT is not committed to racial integration. Many critical thinkers about race believe that the ideal society is one that features the peaceful, mutually beneficial coexistence of people of all races on terms of equality. However, it is also accurate to say that many critical thinkers are not as committed to racial integration as are liberals. They do not conceptualize integration as a categorical imperative—something that must be

---

the poor from sleeping under bridges, from begging in the streets, and from stealing bread." ANATOLE FRANCE, *Madame Has Her Way, in* THE RED LILY 95 (Maison Mazarin 1905) (1894). To treat the rich and poor the same—as dissimilarly-situated as they are—and to proscribe both groups from sleeping under bridges, begging, and stealing is to perpetuate the poverty and marginalization of the poor, as only the poor will find themselves prohibited from engaging in the activities that allow them to meet their basic needs.

pursued at all costs. As a result, they tend to be much more tolerant of racial separation than their liberal counterparts.

Traditional civil rights discourse has come to understand the evil of the pre-civil rights era as the segregation of the races. The most apparent remedy to this legally-mandated racial apartheid is, of course, integration. For this reason, liberals have tended to be steadfast in their allegiance to efforts that enable the races to share the same physical space as one another. This faithfulness is probably most on display in the war that liberals waged to integrate the schools. They fought for the full-throated integration of all schools even when it became apparent that white opposition to that goal was making it nearly impossible to achieve—even when it became apparent that black children were suffering from both the daily exposure to white hostility in newly-integrated schools as well as the abandonment of the schools in their communities as sites where a proper education could be acquired.[19]

Part of the reason for critical thinkers' greater toleration of some degree of separation of the races is their refusal to understand *segregation* as the evil of the pre-civil rights era. Instead, they submit that *white supremacy* was the evil of the pre-civil rights era. Segregation was simply a physical manifestation of that ideology; indeed, segregation was just an exercise in making physical space display society's commitment to white superiority and black inferiority. If the evil of the pre-civil rights era is understood as white racial dominance—the amassing of racial power in the hands of white people—then the most appropriate remedy appears to be something along the lines of the redistribution of racial power. Critical thinkers about race have proposed that racial separation can be consistent with this redistribution. For example, if the schools that are attended predominately by black children are funded on the same level as the schools that are attended predominately by white children—and if those black children are acquiring the same quality of education as their white counterparts—then segregation, in this particular

---

[19] Derrick Bell made this provocative argument in his formative "Serving Two Masters" article. One of the first to be anything less than celebratory about the efforts made by the civil rights lawyers fighting for school integration, Bell observed that "court orders mandating racial balance may be (depending on the circumstances) educationally advantageous, irrelevant, or even disadvantageous. Nevertheless, civil rights lawyers continue to argue that black children are entitled to integrated schools without regard to the educational effect of such assignments." Derrick A. Bell, Jr., *Serving Two Masters: Integration Ideals and Client Interests in School Desegregation Litigation*, 85 YALE L.J. 470, 480 (1976) [hereinafter Bell, *Serving Two Masters*]. Bell challenged the conventional wisdom, which offered that integration was the *only* thing worth fighting for, by suggesting that "court-ordered remedies that emphasize educational improvement rather than racial balance" may be what civil rights lawyers ought to seek. *Id.* at 487.

context, might actually be a manifestation of the redistribution of racial power.

Another reason for CRT's relatively greater toleration of racial segregation is the reality that integration has usually required people of color to shed the accouterments of their cultural specificity as a prerequisite to their integration into white institutions. Now, one reason for traditional civil rights discourse's devotion to integration, argues CRT, is that it does not recognize institutions—the schools, the universities, the organizations, the neighborhoods—as *white*. Instead, viewing these institutions through an uncritical lens might lead one to believe they are racially neutral. However, CRT denies this, asserting instead that the institutions that were constituted during the regime of formal racial apartheid reflect white culture, norms, practices, and interests. CRT claims that the white domination of the pre-civil rights era has "inform[ed] the broader self-definition of white institutions."[20] Thus, CRT does not share the uncomplicated impulse to integrate people of color into these institutions. Rather, its impulse may be to dismantle the institutions—and then to rebuild them with the equal participation of white and nonwhite people. As such, the institutions would not be integrated; they would be *co-constituted*. And as a direct consequence of this co-constitution, they would reflect society in all of its racially pluralistic glory.

V. Commitment to Neutrality

As discussed above, traditional civil rights discourse has defined racism as bias and/or prejudice held by individuals, and it has measured the nation's racial problem by the number of individuals holding biased or prejudiced beliefs. A corollary to this understanding is that neutrality is what happens when people stop being biased or prejudiced. The goal, then, of civil rights reform is to get rid of bias and prejudice so that society can finally be neutral.

CRT is skeptical about the "neutrality" that is imagined to be what is left when bias and prejudice are cleared away. It is suspicious on two front. First, it is doubtful that the institutions that had been constructed and administered during the days of formal racial inequality, as well as their practices and procedures, are neutral. Second, it is skeptical about the possibility of neutrality itself.

On the first front, liberals that subscribe to traditional civil rights discourse assume the neutrality of existing social institutions. As such, they assume that society will come to be a racially equal and just one when the biased individuals working in these institutions are removed from their posts (or are asked not to be biased during

---

[20] Peller, *supra* note 3, at 802.

business hours).[21] This supposition ignores the likelihood, says CRT, that racial inequality has been baked into the institutions. What if dominance has been formative of institutional practices and procedures? What if the institutions that had been "constructed or maintained during segregation . . . . reflected deeper aspects of a culture within which the explicit exclusion of blacks seemed uncontroversial"?[22] If institutional norms, practices, and procedures do, in fact, reflect a culture that ratified white supremacy in its most ostentatious forms, then *neutrality* would not reign when biased or prejudiced individuals are removed from institutional life. Instead, white racial power—albeit in a subtler, more oblique form—would remain. That racial power would remain as long as the institutions remain.

CRT's critique is most clearly demonstrated in the context of the battle over standards in hiring and university admissions, which Chapter 17 extensively explores. Traditional civil rights discourse does not question the legitimacy of these standards. For example, it does not question the requirement that one needs to score highly on a standardized test in order to be admitted into college. It does not have a problem with the fact that involvement in extracurricular activities, volunteering and other forms of community service, and the ability to speak a language that is neither English or a "mother tongue" is considered the stuff of a competitive application. In the arena of hiring, liberals have no issue with "qualifications" being constructed in such a way that they seem to mirror perfectly the resumes of the white elite. In the liberal (and conservative) worldview, these qualifications are neutral, objective, rational, not racial, apolitical, and entirely outside of social power. Inasmuch as they are not explicitly and obviously connected to white racial dominance, liberals have no problem with them.

CRT denies that these standards are what liberals (and conservatives) imagine them to be. It proposes instead that they are the products of power and politics—echoing the perspectives,

---

[21] In a "funny if it wasn't so not funny" observation, Peller notes that there was not a significant level of personnel turnover in institutions when the pre-civil rights days of *de jure* racial segregation evolved into the post-civil rights era of *de jure* equality. He writes:

> The same whites who once carried out the formal program of American apartheid actually kept their jobs as the decisionmakers charged with evaluating merit in the employment offices of companies and in the admissions offices of schools in the post-segregation world. In institution after institution, progressive reformists have found themselves struggling over the implementation of racial integration with the former administrators of racial segregation, many of whom soon constituted an old guard "concerned" over the deterioration of "standards."

Id. at 778.

[22] *Id.*

worldviews, interests, and ideologies of a particular segment of society. In other words, the standards themselves are not neutral. If this is true, then expelling the obvious bigots from the hiring and admissions committees will not make employment and admissions decisions "neutral." As long as these decisions rely on traditional standards—even if the decisions are made by the most unbiased and unprejudiced of individuals—they will be unmistakably "un-neutral."

On the second front, CRT is simply skeptical that a "neutral" standard,[23] an "objective" rule, or a "rational" regime exists. Neutrality, objectivity, and rationality are supposed to be outside of power. But, CRT proposes that power—white racial power, to be precise—created those concepts. CRT argues that white dominance formed the very condition of possibility for the idea that something could be apolitical. The concepts of neutrality, objectivity, and rationality, argues CRT, are "historical, contingent and rooted in the particularities of culture," and they do not represent "the transcendence of perspective itself."[24]

The result is that CRT tends to understand "neutrality", "objectivity," and "reason," to be traps. They are excuses for maintaining the current maldistribution of racial power, deployed when the persistence of racial hierarchies needs to be defended. Now, CRT certainly understands their appeal. Crenshaw and Peller write that the concepts are seductive because they seem "to be able to do what [they] cannot do—resolve issues of social power, racial power, once and for all"[25] without making the slightest mention of the dirty word of race and the uncomfortable truth that power has been (sometimes purposefully, sometimes unintentionally) distributed unevenly between racial groups. But, they cannot do what their proponents have promised they will do. CRT proposes that instead of placing our faith in these concepts, we ought to come to terms with the fact that racism is not a splotch on the body politic, but rather constitutive of it. It is not a blemish on society's face, but rather embedded in the very DNA of the thing. If racism is conceptualized as such, CRT offers, society might be moved to take very different

---

[23] As Patricia Williams explains in the context of constitutional law, "neutrality is far from neutral." She writes, "Blacks and women are the objects of a constitutional omission which has been incorporated into a theory of neutrality. It is thus that omission is really a form of expression, as oxymoronic as that sounds: racial omission is a literal part of original intent; it is the fixed, reiterated prophecy of the Founding Fathers." Patricia Williams, *The Obliging Shell: An Informal Essay on Formal Legal Equality*, 87 MICH. L. REV. 2128, 2142–43 (1989).

[24] *Id.*

[25] Kimberlé Crenshaw & Gary Peller, *Reel Time/Real Justice*, 70 DENV. U. L. REV. 283, 290–91 (1993).

measures than the ones that it has been taking to rid ourselves of this dignity- and humanity-denying fact of American life.

VI. Questions and Discussion

1. As this chapter explains, CRT has criticized liberals for having an impoverished vision of what racial justice looks like. CRT argues that racial justice, from a liberal standpoint, is society as presently arranged sans racist individuals in positions of power. Once those with biases and prejudices are removed from public life, liberals imagine that people of color will come to occupy the social, cultural, political, and economic roles that they ought to occupy.

However, as discussed above, CRT is skeptical of this vision, arguing that it presupposes the fairness of the way that society is presently arranged. CRT observes that U.S. society was ordered during a time of formal racial exclusion. Consequently, it argues, we should not assume the legitimacy of the institutions that were created during this time. Society might look entirely different if people of color (as well as sexual minorities and all women) were able to participate in it *as equals* during its formative stages. CRT suggests that if we want to know what racial justice looks like, we have to ask what society would look like if people of color were equal members of the body politic at the nation's inception. Would it have public schools and, if so, how would they be funded? Would it have prisons and jails? What systems would it erect to ensure the health of the population? What systems would it erect to ensure the safety of the population? Would it give the state the power to execute its citizens? Would it support its poor and, if so, how? Answer these questions as a thought experiment. How different is your racially just society from our present? How different is your racially just society from the liberal vision of it?

2. As noted above, liberals have tended to define racism in terms of individual bias and prejudice. According to this definition, racism is what happens when a racist individual externalizes his deeply-felt bias and prejudice. On the contrary, CRT tends to understand racism in terms of institutions and structures. According to this definition, racism is what happens when a racist individual externalizes his deeply-felt bias and prejudice, *but it is also what happens when institutional processes function to unfairly disadvantage a racial group*.

However, the dichotomy between individual racism and institutional racism may be a false one. Institutions may play an important role in creating and legitimating individual racism, and individuals may play an important role in producing institutional racism. While the latter point may be easy to grasp—individuals create and administer institutions, after all—the former may be a bit more difficult to fathom. How can an institution create individual bias or prejudice?

Well, consider the example of an employer who does not want to hire an ex-convict and refuses to offer jobs to black males because they are statistically overrepresented in the population of ex-convicts. Most will offer, at least initially, that this is an example of individual racism: an *individual* has taken an act that harms members of a racial group because they are members of that racial group. However, there are significant structural elements to the story. Many theorists have argued that the spectacularly disproportionate incarceration of black males is a product of institutional racism. Michelle Alexander, in her widely-read book *The New Jim Crow*, has described mass incarceration as the result of "a tightly networked system of laws, policies, customs and institutions that operate collectively to ensure the subordinate status of a group defined largely by race."[26] Thus, if our hypothetical employer discriminates against black males, large-scale processes that have made black males an overrepresented population within the employer's disfavored group necessarily inform her individual decision. In other words, her individual act of racism is, in important ways, a product of institutional racism.

What this example illustrates is that individual and institutional racism are not perfectly dichotomous. As such, we might need to challenge formulations of individual racism that are overly individualizing. Conceptions of individual racism at present tend to disconnect the harborers of racist sentiment from the structures that make the sentiment "make sense." A more promising conception might be to understand individual racism to be far from a character flaw, but rather a belief system that undergoes constant reality testing. To the extent that there is obvious and undeniable racial stratification and inequality, then we might *expect* individual racism. Such beliefs should only be unexpected when we have created a world in which there are no external data that could be used to give them validity—when we have dismantled the institutions that produce a society that gives those beliefs some degree of rationality and believability.

Recognizing that institutional racism may help to constitute individual racism might lead to the insight that individual racism is not necessarily a personality trait that a person either has or does not have. Institutions and structures may *produce* individual racism and *create* individual racists. And the converse is likely true: institutions and structures can dismantle individual racism and eliminate individual racists.

---

[26] MICHELLE ALEXANDER, THE NEW JIM CROW 13 (2012).

What do you think about this idea? Do you find it hopeful? Or pessimistic?

3. Many have perceived as radical CRT's claim that school integration might not have been the most advantageous route for civil rights lawyers to pursue. Indeed, many have been angered by Bell's claim that black children may have been better off—educationally, socially, and psychically—in well-funded black schools as opposed to hostile white schools. This anger might be expected inasmuch as the claim poses an acute challenge to the conventional wisdom about what racial justice looks like.

Recently, however, conservatives have argued against the constitutionality and/or advisability of plans designed to achieve school integration, and some of their arguments sound eerily similar to Bell's position. As discussed above, *Parents Involved* concerned a constitutional challenge to two school boards' plans to integrate the schools in their districts. The Court struck down the race-conscious plans as a violation of the Constitution's equal protection guarantee. Justice Thomas concurred in the Court's judgment and, in a separate opinion, disputed the contention that black children had to attend integrated schools in order to receive decent educations. He stated that, "[i]n reality, it is far from apparent that coerced racial mixing has any educational benefits, much less that integration is necessary to black achievement."[27]

Thus, Bell and Thomas both are receptive to racial segregation. Of course, they are receptive to it for different reasons. Bell expresses a willingness to countenance segregation in the course of arguing that in the face of fierce, sometimes violent, opposition to integration on the part of white parents and communities, it might have been best for civil rights lawyers to change course and pursue another avenue—i.e., the improvement of schools in black communities—that was constitutionally available. Thomas, on the other hand, expresses a willingness to countenance segregation in the course of arguing that the pursuit of integration ought not to be constitutionally available when that pursuit is race-conscious. Nevertheless, the skepticism towards integration is the same in both Bell's and Thomas's arguments. What are your reactions to the similarity between an ostensibly radical position and a decidedly conservative one? As the chapter discusses, CRT has accused liberals of being conservative in their approach to thinking about racism and remedying racial inequality. But, does the similarity between Bell and Thomas on the question of school integration suggest that CRT is equally conservative? Or does it raise entirely different questions—

[27] Parents Involved in Cmty. Sch. v. Seattle Sch. Dist. No. 1, 551 U.S. 701, 761 (2007) (Thomas, J., concurring).

questions about the utility (or disutility) of the labels "conservative," "liberal," and "radical"?

4. Critical race theorists have offered a number of different theories to explain why liberal discourse on race has not been quite as progressive as it could be.

- Richard Delgado has proposed that the conservatism of traditional civil rights discourse is a function of the identities of the individuals who have developed it. In a provocative article published in 1984, Delgado observes that the "heavyweights" in civil rights scholarship—the persons who are the most prominent and most cited—are white men working at elite law schools. After doing an extensive review of the existing civil rights literature, he concludes that, at its most influential core, there exists "about a dozen white, male writers who comment on, take polite issue with, extol, criticize, and expand on each other's ideas. It is something like an elaborate minuet."[28] He argues that the identities of these authors—specifically, their whiteness and class privilege—have influenced the content of civil rights discourse. He observes that many of them are "unaware of basic facts about the situation in which minority persons live or ways in which they see the world."[29] He found that the authors appeared to be concerned much more with procedure and less so with the substance of civil rights law—a concern that Delgado attributes to a "failure of empathy, an inability to share the values, desires, and perspectives of the population whose rights are under consideration."[30] He observed that the scholars were more willing than their counterparts of color to make "safe" arguments for racial justice—arguments that sounded more in utilitarian theories of justice and less in retributive theories. The problem with utilitarian arguments, according to Delgado, is that they rob the proposed remedies "of their moral force."[31] Finally, he found that the authors appeared to be most sympathetic to approaches to racial justice reform that would not disturb the property, capital, interests, and

[28] Richard Delgado, *The Imperial Scholar: Reflections on a Review of Civil Rights Literature*, 132 U. PA. L. REV. 561, 563 (1984).

[29] *Id.* at 567–68.

[30] *Id.* at 568.

[31] *Id.* at 570.

sensibilities of the white middle and upper-middle class—classes to which the authors belonged.

- Derrick Bell has made two arguments that might explain the conservatism that CRT sees in traditional civil rights discourse. The first is the proposition that the lawyers who were crafting civil rights litigation strategies and litigating civil rights cases in court were not actually representing the interests of their clients—poor and working class black people and communities. He argues that, in the context of the fight for school desegregation, poor and working class black parents were most concerned with the quality of their children's education—not with integration. They wanted to send their children to schools that would provide them with a stellar education; to them, it was neither here nor there whether those schools enrolled a single white child. Thus, they would have been happy with court-ordered remedies that focused on improving the schools located in black neighborhoods. Civil rights lawyers, on the other hand, were singularly committed to school integration. They did not contemplate reversing course even when their clients asked them to do so, and even when it was becoming patent that attempting to integrate schools would be disadvantageous to black children. Bell identifies the reason for the disconnect between the litigation strategies pursued by civil rights lawyers and the communities they were purporting to represent is that the former were not being financially supported by the latter, but rather "by middle class blacks and whites who believe fervently in integration."[32] He concludes that racial reform would look different had civil rights lawyers actually listened to the communities bearing the heaviest burdens caused by segregation and not to the more privileged communities that believed that they knew what was best for everyone.

  The second theory that Bell offers to explain the perceived conservatism of traditional civil rights discourse is "interest-convergence." This theory proposes that the law will only yield to the demands of civil rights activists when that concession will benefit—or at least not harm—white people with class

[32] Bell, *Serving Two Masters*, *supra* note 19, at 489.

privilege. Thus, civil rights gains to blacks are actually gains to whites. Bell explains,

> The interest of blacks in achieving racial equality will be accommodated only when it converges with the interests of whites. However, the fourteenth amendment, standing alone, will not authorize a judicial remedy providing effective racial equality for blacks where the remedy sought threatens the superior societal status of middle and upper class whites. It follows that the availability of fourteenth amendment protection in racial cases may not actually be determined by the character of harm suffered by blacks or the quantum of liability proved against whites. Racial remedies may instead be the outward manifestations of unspoken and perhaps subconscious judicial conclusions that the remedies, if granted, will secure, advance, or at least not harm societal interests deemed important by middle and upper class whites.[33]

What do you think about Bell's and Delgado's explanations for the arguably non-progressive nature of traditional civil rights discourse? Do you find their explanations compelling? Why or why not?

---

[33] Derrick A. Bell, Jr., Brown v. Board of Education *and the Interest Convergence Dilemma,* 93 HARV. L. REV. 518, 523 (1980).

Chapter 3

CRITIQUES OF CRITICAL RACE THEORY

I. Introduction

Critical Race Theory has received its fair share of criticism over the years. This is to be expected: as discussed in Chapter 1, the architects of CRT quite intentionally situated the theory in opposition to two frameworks that, at the time of CRT's emergence, had many adherents both inside and outside the legal academy: the Critical Legal Studies movement and mainstream liberal approaches to civil rights. Because CRT purposefully challenged influential ways of thinking about the law and society, it ought to come as no surprise that, while devotees of these challenged frameworks were sympathetic to CRT's claim that the country had not achieved anything that approximated racial justice, they criticized CRT in the course of defending their preferred ways of thinking. Thus, CRT sustained critique from not only those with conservative politics (who were more likely to dispute that the United States had a "race problem" that deserved any degree of sustained intellectual attention), but also politically left-leaning, would-be allies.

That we might expect CRT to be on the receiving end of a negative appraisal or two does not explain the bitterness that characterized some attacks on CRT, however. A case in point is the vitriolic review of CRT that then-Seventh Circuit judge, Richard Posner, wrote in the late 1990s. He described critical race theorists as "lunatics" who "have swallowed postmodernism hook, line, and sinker."[1] He continued by asserting that critical race theorists are

> [l]aw professors with little to say about the law itself. . . . .By exaggerating the plight of the groups for which they are the self-appointed spokesmen, the critical race theorists come across as whiners and wolf-criers. By forswearing analysis in favor of storytelling, they come across as labile and intellectually limited. By embracing the politics of identity, they come across as divisive. . . .Their grasp of social reality is weak; their diagnoses are inaccurate; their suggested cures (rigid quotas, 1960s-style demonstrations, transformations of the American spirit, socialism, poverty law practice) are tried and true failures. Their lodgment in the law schools is a disgrace to legal

[1] Richard Posner, *The Skin Trade*, THE NEW REPUBLIC, Oct. 13, 1997, at 40 (book review).

> education, which lacks the moral courage and the intellectual self-confidence to pronounce a minority movement's scholarship bunk. . . . [They] have gotten a free ride for too long because they have wrapped themselves in the mantle of race.[2]

Of course, Posner may have had an honest aversion to the methodological moves and the substantive claims that critical race theorists writing in the 1980s and 1990s made in their scholarship. However, the not-so-thinly-veiled contempt, wholesale dismissiveness, and alarming hostility with which Posner writes suggests that something more fundamental is in operation: Posner might simply have had an issue with CRT's refusal to be satisfied with the racial progress that had been made. That is, Posner's willingness to reject CRT as the stuff of "lunatics," and his hope that everyone else would do the same, may be a product of his anger at its radicalism. This is to say that while we should assume that many of the critiques of CRT that this chapter explores were made in good faith, we should be attuned to the possibility that some critiques "reflect the cold fact that many, in the legal academy and beyond, just don't want to hear what Critical Race scholars have to say."[3]

This chapter describes the more controversial methodological choices that scholars operating within the CRT paradigm have made (namely, the choice to tell stories in legal scholarship) and the substantive claims that they have made that have been subject to the most criticism. Before beginning, it is worth reiterating that those who employ a CRT framework in their scholarship are a motley crew. Thus, while *some* critical race theorists have engaged in storytelling and have made the provocative claims explored below, it would be an error to assert that *all* critical race theorists have done the same. CRT is capacious enough to accommodate those who find storytelling incompatible with their own disciplinary methodologies; and it is roomy enough to include those who disagree with the claims described below. To put it more bluntly, CRT is a theoretical approach; it is not a cult.

II. Storytelling

Perhaps the most contentious intervention that critical race theorists have made into legal scholarship is not substantive, but methodological: they have used narrative in their explorations of law. These narratives have taken many different forms, including "personal histories, parables, chronicles, dreams, stories, poetry, fiction, and revisionist histories."[4]

---

[2] *Id.*

[3] Robin D. Barnes, *Race Consciousness: The Thematic Content of Racial Distinctiveness in Critical Race Scholarship*, 103 HARV. L. REV. 1864, 1871 (1990).

[4] MARI J. MATSUDA ET AL., WORDS THAT WOUND: CRITICAL RACE THEORY, ASSAULTIVE SPEECH, AND THE FIRST AMENDMENT 6 (1993).

Introducing eCRT

In recent years, CRT has taken an empirical turn. Helmed by Osagie Obasogie, a group of critical scholars have endeavored to bring the social sciences to CRT, and vice versa. The excerpt below explains the impulses that led to the emergence of empirical Critical Race Theory, or eCRT.

* * *

SYMPOSIUM ISSUE: CRITICAL RACE THEORY AND EMPIRICAL METHODS: FOREWORD: Critical Race Theory and Empirical Methods, 3 U.C. Irvine L. Rev. 183, 184–186 (2013)

[T]here seems to be an unacknowledged schism between critical race scholarship and the social sciences. To be sure, individual scholars have examined particular areas of race scholarship—most notably, the social psychology of implicit bias—through a lens that uses social science methods to measure these dynamics and critical race perspectives to frame their legal significance. However, there has not been a sustained conversation beyond this literature concerning the importance of building bridges between these two communities to tease out the opportunities and challenges associated with extending a joint critical race and empirical effort to other areas of race scholarship, whether it be health disparities, gaps in educational achievement, or issues pertaining to criminal justice.

Why is this important? Both critical race theory and empirical research on race are at crossroads. On one hand, critical race theory has been around now for a few decades and it has made important contributions. Of particular importance, it has provided a conceptual and theoretical basis from which to understand the extent to which race is not only socially but legally constructed, how racial subordination is not merely aberrational but a structured part of social relations, and how legal rules and doctrines—even those designed for antidiscrimination purposes—often produce outcomes that systemically disfavor racial minorities. While these insights are profound, the methods used to substantiate them have often not been as robust as they could be. Critical race theory has often focused on internal inconsistencies in legal doctrine or historical and theoretical critiques that, while important, often do not offer a measureable basis from which to understand the depth of these on-the-ground trends and social dynamics. On the other hand, social scientists have been developing quantitative and qualitative tools to measure the social world for several decades. They have refined statistical measures and qualitative analyses that are able to tease out the subtle human dynamics that shape everyday life. While theory is an important aspect of all social science research, the theories social scientists draw upon often serve overly descriptive ends in cataloguing the social world as it currently exists rather than embracing a normative orientation towards racial justice that questions inequalities produced by social and legal structures.

Linking social science methods with critical race theory provides a remarkable opportunity to pursue race scholarship that is both theoretically sophisticated and empirically robust. That is to say, it is an opportunity to think about and measure race in new and exciting ways that builds upon the strengths of multiple disciplines to assess, document, and theoretically extrapolate the hidden ways in which not only law and society construct race, but the way that race constructs law and society.

. . . .

The goal . . . is not to simply "improve" critical race theory by incorporating empirical methods, nor is it to simply "improve" social science research through integrating critical race perspectives. Instead, we seek to rethink and change the premise of race scholarship in general by eschewing theoretical and methodological silos in pursuit of deepening our understanding of race and racism to advance racial justice.

There is much disagreement among self-identified critical race theorists about the centrality of storytelling to the framework. Some have argued that one is not doing CRT if one is not using narrative in one's scholarship. Others disagree, arguing that storytelling is just one methodology among many that a critical race theorist might employ. The latter position appears to be the better one, as making the presence of storytelling a prerequisite for a finding that a piece of scholarship "counts" as a contribution to the CRT oeuvre would disqualify a lot of scholarship that *clearly* "counts" as contributions to the CRT oeuvre. As Adrienne Davis writes,

> Critical Race Theory is an expansive genre that . . . includes Gerald Torres's work on pluralism, Kendall Thomas's work on historiographic practices, Lani Guinier's transformation of voting rights scholarship, Regina Austin's revision of outlawry and underground economies, Richard Delgado's and Charles Lawrence's work on hate speech, as well as Derrick Bell's parables about civil rights tensions, Mari Matsuda's recovery of litigant histories, and Patricia Williams's descriptions of personally negotiating structures of law. Clearly, narrative jurisprudence is one methodology and mode of analysis among many employed by critical race theorists. To make this one method the sum total of the

scholarship erases the work of many who utilize different, or combined, methodologies in their scholarship.[5]

That being said, it is true that many critical race theorists—including those who we might identify as the most foundational and influential voices within the framework—have employed storytelling in their work. Consider the opening of one of the most well-cited pieces of CRT scholarship, Charles Lawrence's "The Id, the Ego, and Equal Protection"[6]:

> It is 1948. I am sitting in a kindergarten classroom at the Dalton School, a fashionable and progressive New York City private school. My parents, both products of a segregated Mississippi school system, have come to New York to attend graduate and professional school. They have enrolled me and my sisters here at Dalton to avoid sending us to the public school in our neighborhood where the vast majority of the students are black and poor. They want us to escape the ravages of segregation, New York style.
>
> It is circle time in the five-year old group, and the teacher is reading us a book. As she reads, she passes the book around the circle so that each of us can see the illustrations. The book's title is *Little Black Sambo*. Looking back, I remember only one part of the story, one illustration: Little Black Sambo is running around a stack of pancakes with a tiger chasing him. He is very black and has a minstrel's white mouth. His hair is tied up in many pigtails, each pigtail tied with a different color ribbon. I have seen the picture before the book reaches my place in the circle. I have heard the teacher read the "comical" text describing Sambo's plight and have heard the laughter of my classmates. There is a knot in the pit of my stomach. I feel panic and shame. I do not have the words to articulate my feelings—words like "stereotype" and "stigma" that might help cathart the shame and place it outside of me where it began. But I am slowly realizing that, as the only black child in the circle, I have some kinship with the tragic and ugly hero of this story—that my classmates are laughing at me as well as at him. I wish I could laugh along with my friends. I wish I could disappear.
>
> . . . .

---

5 Robert S. Chang & Adrienne D. Davis, *The Adventure(s) of Blackness in Western Culture: An Epistolary Exchange on Old and New Identity Wars*, 39 U.C. DAVIS L. REV. 1189, 1232–33 (2006).

6 Charles R. Lawrence III, *The Id, the Ego, and Equal Protection: Reckoning with Unconscious Racism*, 39 STAN. L. REV. 317 (1987).

> [Time passes.] I am thirty-three. My daughter, Maia, is three. I greet a pink-faced, four-year old boy on the steps of her nursery school. He proudly presents me with a book he has brought for his teacher to read to the class. "It's my favorite," he says. The book is a new edition of *Little Black Sambo*.[7]

In the balance of the article, Lawrence argues that the Court's decision in *Washington v. Davis*, requiring a finding of discriminatory intent before a law will be found to contain a racial classification and reviewed with strict scrutiny, was in error. He contends that, in the post-civil rights era, individuals frequently are not conscious of the racist stereotypes and racial aversions that they have. Lawrence offers the story of *Little Black Sambo* as an example of unconscious racism exhibited by well-meaning white people—folks whose actions, though harmful and hurtful to people of color, are not cognizable as discrimination under the *Washington v. Davis* test because but they are not the product of a conscious intent to discriminate. The story of *Little Black Sambo* is a prelude to an explanation of why the disparate impact test, which would find constitutionally suspect all laws that have the effect of disproportionately burdening a racial group, would be a more appropriate, effective doctrine.

Most would agree that Lawrence's doctrinal analysis and proposal for revision does not *depend* on the story of *Little Black Sambo*. His inquiry into the requirements of the Equal Protection Clause would be just as rigorous had he chosen not to lead the article with the story. So, we have to ask why. Why does Lawrence—and a good number of other prominent critical race theorists, including Derrick Bell, Patricia Williams, and Richard Delgado—use storytelling within their scholarship? Several reasons explain their choice.[8]

A. Arguments in Favor of Storytelling

1. *The Pedagogical Function of Storytelling*

According to its proponents, storytelling is pedagogical inasmuch as it educates readers about what racial

---

[7] *Id.* at 317–18.

[8] One reason for engaging in storytelling that is not explored in-depth in this section relates to storytelling's status as an important part of many nonwhite cultural traditions. As Adrien Katherine Wing has explained, many people of color "prize our heritages in which the oral tradition has had historical importance—where vital notions of justice and the law are communicated generation to generation through the telling of stories." Adrien Katherine Wing, *Global Critical Race Feminism: Legal Reform for the Twenty-First Century*, 34 DE JURE 446, 451 (2001). Employing narratives in legal scholarship, then, is a way to remain connected to nonwhite cultural traditions while participating in a largely white cultural form.

disenfranchisement in the modern era looks like and, perhaps more importantly, *feels* like when one has to endure it. After reading Lawrence's story about *Little Black Sambo*, readers know that a little black boy can be made to feel ugly even when there is no white supremacist calling him an ape or monkey to his face—something that might have occurred in the bad old days of yore. The story demonstrates that the message that black lives are not to be taken seriously—that they exist for others' use and enjoyment—need not be explicitly stated in order for people to hear and understand it. The story instructs us that this new-fangled racial oppression—just like its old-school predecessor—feels like a "knot" in the stomach, like panic and shame. Finally, the story suggests that being the daughter of a well-respected law professor offers no immunity from the lessons that there are to learn about black ugliness, inferiority, and insubstantiality.

Elsewhere, Lawrence has written that it is important that people of color tell stories like the one with which he opens his "Id" article—and it is important that they tell them inside of law review articles and within law journals—simply because nonwhite people's stories had not appeared in these spaces. "Our stories have, for the most part, not been told or recorded in the literature that is the law. Accordingly, the first reason for embracing narrative is that more of our stories must be told and heard."[9] Hearing stories that previously have been unheard might be valuable beyond the simple sense that it is good, in and of itself, to hear everyone's tale. Instead, it might be valuable because stories are a source of information that, together with other sources of information, help us to gather a full, complex, detailed understanding of an issue. As Kathyrn Abrams states, there are myriad ways by which we can come to *know* phenomena. The more pluralistic our approach to gathering knowledge, the more complete will be the knowledge that we develop. Abrams writes that each source of data "may supply insights that the others fail to tap and when they coincide, they create a stronger impression—the pieces of a puzzle falling together."[10] Stories—whether fictional, factual, or somewhere in between—"may offer a limited, yet salient, claim for experiential ways of knowing that are not systematic, and cannot be comprehensively verified or documented. They represent a valued, though not necessarily a privileged, way" of coming to know facts about the world.[11]

Skeptics may respond that stories are not a particularly *good* way of coming to know facts about the world. These skeptics may find

---

[9] Lawrence, *supra* note 6, at 2279.

[10] Kathyrn Abrams, *Hearing the Call of Stories*, 79 CALIF. L. REV. 971, 995 (1991).

[11] *Id.*

more compelling other forms of knowing that describe the world in a way that is generalizable in a way that stories are not. That is, many of the stories that some critical race theorists tell are valuable for their specificity—because they describe the author's subjective experience of being a person of color who lives in a society in which people of color reside at the bottom of most measures of social wellbeing. Consider Lawrence's story of encountering *Little Black Sambo* as a child and as an adult. We know from the story that being forced to confront the reality that black people have been, and continue to be, viewed as minstrels caused Lawrence to develop a knot in his stomach, to panic, to feel shame, to want to disappear. But, although this subjective account allows us to know what encountering racism felt like *to Lawrence*, we are left not knowing whether encountering racism feels the same way to all people of color. Thus, the skeptic may privilege other forms of knowing, like statistics, that allow us to know *general* truths, and not just specific ones.

However, Devon Carbado and Mitu Gulati remind us that this specificity is precisely why some critical race theorists use stories in their scholarship. Particularity is the very thing that is lost when one generalizes in order to describe universal, or at least wide-ranging, truths. A story "focuses on the specific and provides detail. Statistical analyses do the reverse. When an outsider is trying to describe an experience to someone who cannot readily relate to it, an insider, narrative provides the detail that can help the insider empathize and relate to the experience."[12] So, for example, consider racial disparities in infant mortality. We might wonder whether a statistic that relates that twice as many black infants as white infants die during the first year of life will cause the average, otherwise unconcerned person to come to care about the phenomenon—as compared to a story told by a mother who gave birth to a baby that never drew its first breath. It should be clear how proponents of the use of narrative in legal scholarship would answer that question.

2. *Persuasiveness*

Because stories provide information about a social fact in a way that allows those who are otherwise removed from it to empathize with the storyteller, they arguably are persuasive in a way that other forms of knowing are not. Delgado writes that stories allow the hearer to "overcome otherness" and to see commonality with the storyteller, someone who might be in a social outgroup.[13] Abrams

---

[12] Devon W. Carbado & Mitu Gulati, *The Law and Economics of Critical Race Theory*, 112 YALE L.J. 1757, 1785 (2003) (book review).

[13] Richard Delgado, *Storytelling for Oppositionists and Others: A Plea for Narrative*, 87 MICH. L. REV. 2411, 2438 (1989) [hereinafter Delgado, *Storytelling*].

makes a similar point. She recounts a story that Patricia Williams tells about her failure to rebuke an individual who had made anti-Semitic remarks in her presence, and she states that she believes Williams' story because it "resonate[s] with something I know about myself or those around me. . . . In short, I believe Williams' stories the way I believe a good piece of literature. . . . [I]t is not only their representation of the particular, but their subtle invocation of something common and recurring that triggers my assent."[14] The resonance that a story produces in a hearer may be more compelling—more persuasive—than even the best statistics or doctrinal analysis.

3. *Challenges the Objectivity of Truth*

CRT, like its Critical Legal Studies predecessor, has been heavily influenced by postmodernist and poststructuralist philosophy and literary criticism—which has been identified with thinkers like Michel Foucault, Jacques Derrida, Judith Butler, Julia Kristeva, and Jacques Lacan. One of the many ideas that postmodernism introduced was the possibility that there is no such thing as objective truth. Postmodernism proposes that truth is not a unitary thing that is "out there" and is entirely independent of context. Instead, it proposes that truth is contingent; it depends on the frameworks and the systems of knowledge that society has created to ascertain what "truth" is. According to postmodernism, the truth is that there are many truths, all of which are dependent on the perspective that the truth seeker brings to the quest to know it. Truth, then, is profoundly subjective.

Many critical race theorists embrace the use of stories in legal scholarship because stories challenge the existence of objective truth.[15] Much of legal scholarship—as well as court opinions, legislative findings, and other legal texts—is written as if there is an objective truth that is out there, waiting to be discovered. Further, at the dawn of CRT, most of the legal scholarship around race suggested that things were getting better, objectively speaking. Formal equality had arrived, and the doors of opportunity had swung open. The *truth* of the matter, according to most legal scholarship at the

---

[14] Abrams, *supra* note 10, at 1002–03.

[15] However, Robert Chang has observed that stories need not necessarily challenge the existence of objective truth. They might solely be used to demonstrate that the truth that society believes to be objective actually is not. Narrative may be used to "reveal[ ] bias in supposed objectivity [and then to] reconstruct[ ] it to include previously excluded perspectives." See Robert S. Chang, *Toward an Asian American Legal Scholarship: Critical Race Theory, Post-Structuralism, and Narrative Space*, 81 CALIF. L. REV. 1241, 1278 (1993). If narrative is used in this way, it is offered only "to challenge the current formulation of objectivity, but not the notion of objectivity itself." *Id.*

time, was that there was much to celebrate and little to lament when it came to racial inequality.

The stories that critical race theorists offered showed that while this story about racial progress was "true," it was "true" *from the perspective of those with racial privilege.* CRT narratives demonstrated that even in an era of formal equality—an era in which people of color sat on the faculties of the most elite law schools in the country—there were many opportunities for people of color to be reminded that they lack racial privilege. Sometimes these reminders only stung a little bit; other times, they felt like spirit murder.[16]

Crucially, proponents of storytelling in legal scholarship assert that by inserting their unconventional stories into law review articles and the like, it functions to reveal that more conventional legal scholarship—with its doctrinal analysis, dispassionate language, pretenses of objectivity and neutrality, and incorporation of accepted social sciences, like economics, political science, or history—was itself a story, too. As Gary Peller explains, "[B]y posing personal, subjective, and impassioned voices, narrative critical race scholarship reveals the ways in which identity and emotion have been artificially marginalized in the discursive space, thus revealing how mainstream scholarship is itself a particular kind of narrative of what is important and what is not. The point is not that narrative is a better way to relate 'truth,' but rather that all discourse is a form of narrative, a telling of stories about what the world is and should be."[17]

If what Peller proposes is true, then it forces us to ask why the more conventional narratives that appear in legal scholarship have been privileged and why the more unconventional narratives that some CRT scholarship employs have been marked as deviant, unsophisticated, and properly excluded from law reviews, court opinions, legislative findings, and the like.

4. *Healing to Victims of Racial Injustice*

Some proponents of narrative within legal scholarship have argued that telling stories can help restore both the teller and hearer of the stories to health. As Delgado writes, "[S]tories about oppression, about victimization, about one's own brutalization—far from deepening the despair of the oppressed, lead to healing, liberation, [and] mental health."[18] Delgado suggests that part of the reason for stories' effect of healing those who have endured racial

---

[16] *See* PATRICIA WILLIAMS, THE ALCHEMY OF RACE AND RIGHTS: DIARY OF A LAW PROFESSOR (1992)

[17] Gary Peller, *The Discourse of Constitutional Degradation*, 81 GEO. L.J. 313, 335 (1992).

[18] Delgado, *Storytelling*, *supra* note 13, at 2437.

discrimination is that they create a community. Others who have had similar experiences may hear a story and realize that they are not alone—that others have survived comparable injuries. These shared experiences are the stuff upon which a spirit of kinship can be built and from which strength can be derived.

Lawrence proposes that storytelling may be a healing modality for nonwhite people because stories allow people of color to be in charge. Storytellers are empowered to direct the narrative, to relate events from their perspective, to create characters, and to do things with the characters that they create. In other words, storytelling allows people of color to be *subjects* that act in the world. This may be uniquely profound to nonwhite people, as, for so long, they have been *objects* upon which others have acted.[19]

Because stories allow people of color to relate their vision of the world and themselves, they function as a mechanism for countering images of nonwhite deviance. CRT observes that there are innumerable negative portrayals of nonwhite people circulating in our society. We hear about black welfare queens, the primitive nature of indigenous people, Muslim terrorists, Latinx people who threaten "American" culture and ways of life, and Asian people who aberrantly overachieve. Stories present an opportunity to engage in what Margaret Montoya calls "discursive subversions" by countering problematic representations with those that are "truer" to the reality of the storyteller.[20]

B. Arguments Against Storytelling

While proponents of storytelling in legal scholarship see a lot of upside in its use, it is not an overstatement at all to say that many opponents truly loathe the practice. They have offered multiple reasons for their tremendous distaste of unconventional narratives in legal scholarship and law, more generally.[21]

---

[19] Lawrence, *supra* note 6, at 2265.

[20] Margaret F. Montoya, *Celebrating Radicalized Legal Narratives*, *in* CROSSROADS, DIRECTIONS, AND A NEW CRITICAL RACE THEORY 243, 243 (Francisco Valdes, Jerome McCristal Culp & Angela P. Harris eds., 2002).

[21] One critique of narrative in critical race scholarship that will not be explored here relates to the *quality* of the stories in some CRT scholarship. A number of critics have complained that some critical race theorists are not particularly talented storytellers.

It may be more appropriate for those with a specialty in literary criticism to evaluate whether some critical race theorists' stories are "bad." It may suffice to say that if they are "bad," then we ought not to be surprised. As Carbado and Gulati write, "[M]ost CRT scholars are not trained in the use of narrative—for the most part, they have had the same legal training as their non-CRT colleagues." Carbado & Gulati, *supra* note 12, at 1784.

1. Stories Persuade Through Emotion, Not Reason

Many critics of storytelling in legal scholarship are disturbed by the fact that unconventional stories—the fables, autobiographies, chronicles, and science fiction tales that some CRT scholarship features—do not seek to persuade readers through rational modes of argumentation. These alternative narratives do not attempt to convince readers to accept or reject a legal rule through an analysis at the legislative history of a statute, by arguing that an outcome is inconsistent with established precedent, or by making a philosophical argument about the nature of rights. Instead, many stories seek to convince by engaging the emotion of the reader. This is problematic for two reasons, say critics. First, the failure to make reason-based arguments plays into stereotypes about the intellectual inferiority of people of color. Critical race theorists' *choice* not to employ rational modes of argumentation can easily be interpreted as a race-based *inability* to do so. Second, seeking to persuade through engaging readers' emotions does not persuade in the manner in which people ought to be persuaded. As one commenter writes, "The problem with convincing people in this way is that it is circuitous and skirts the real issues; it is a way of convincing people at any cost, in order to serve a higher cause."[22] This is inadequate, writes this commenter, because it leads "people to adopt a position without giving them a doctrinal basis for it.[23]" According to this point of view, issues "*should* be decided on doctrinal grounds."[24]

Proponents of narrative in legal scholarship would respond: "Says who?" Who says that issues *should* be decided on doctrinal grounds? More importantly, what makes deciding an issue on doctrinal grounds better than deciding an issue on the basis of emotion? If there is an injustice in the world, and if one's emotions lead one to feel that the injustice ought to be rectified, why look to doctrine for permission to right the wrong? One's emotions might lead one to *create* new doctrine that will allow the wrong to be righted.

In the view of storytelling's defenders, the critique that narrative ought not to be used in legal scholarship because it is not based in reason misses the point. Proponents of storytelling are well aware that the arguments for social change that stories make are not grounded in reason. Indeed, that is the point of many stories: to persuade by striking an emotional cord with the reader. In order for this particular critique to have some traction, say storytelling's

---

[22] Douglas E. Litowitz, *Some Critical Thoughts on Critical Race Theory*, 72 NOTRE DAME L. REV. 503, 522 (1997).

[23] *Id.*

[24] *Id.* (emphasis added).

supporters, critics need to explain why reason-based argumentation is superior to emotion-based argumentation. It is not enough simply to declare that stories are inappropriate because they engage in the latter and not the former.

Now, one answer that a critic might give as to why we ought to prefer reason-based to emotion-based argumentation is that emotions do not necessarily lead us down the path of justice. Instead, emotions might lead us to make illiberal, morally indefensible choices. Writes one critic of narrative:

> There is a danger in storytelling precisely because it can lead in any and every direction, politically speaking. . . . If one set of narratives can make us *more* sympathetic to people of color, it stands to reason that a different set of narratives can make us *less* sensitive. We can easily imagine the emergence of narratives and stories in which white authors describe the experience of being denied entry into professional schools when they would have been accepted had they been black or female. In extreme cases it might be imagined that such authors would use storytelling to glorify a white utopian society without minorities. The error by CRT is to think that storytelling is inherently liberating when in fact it is inherently neutral—neither liberal nor conservative, neither constraining nor freeing.[25]

Valid point. However, respond storytelling's defenders, we might say the same thing of the reason-based arguments that are traditionally found in law reviews and other legal texts. These defenders would likely point out that reason does not inexorably lead to just outcomes. They might note that the Framers' *reason* led them to create a document, the Constitution, that not only tolerated slavery, but protected it. They would point out that the Court's decisions in *Dred Scott v. Sandford* (in which the Court declared that black people were not citizens of the country, as they had been "regarded as beings of an inferior order" and "had no rights which the white man was bound to respect")[26], *Plessy v. Ferguson* (in which the Court upheld the doctrine of "separate but equal")[27], *Korematsu v. United States* (in which the Court found that the Japanese internment during World War II did not run afoul of the Constitution)[28], and the *Insular Cases* (in which the Court held that the nonwhite people inhabiting the Philippines, Puerto Rico, and other lands that the U.S. had acquired in the Spanish-American War

---

[25] *Id.* at 521.

[26] Scott v. Sandford, 60 U.S. 393 (1857).

[27] Plessy v. Ferguson, 163 U.S. 537 (1896).

[28] Korematsu v. United States, 323 U.S. 214 (1944).

would not enjoy the constitutional rights that people on the mainland enjoy, as they were "alien races, differing from us in religion, customs, . . . and modes of thought"[29]) were all well-*reasoned* opinions. Indeed, these defenders would observe that, like storytelling, reason is "neither liberal nor conservative, neither constraining or freeing," and thus, not an obviously superior mechanism for achieving justice.

2. Stories Are Not Clearly Normative

Another criticism of the use of storytelling in legal scholarship is that stories are not clearly normative. That is, they do not clearly tell us which rule ought to be adopted or what the law ought to look like. So, when we read Lawrence's tale of his first encounter with *Little Black Sambo*, we learn about the psychic (and physical) injury that the encounter caused him; however, the tale does not tell us what to do with the law. What does Lawrence's experience with *Little Black Sambo* mean for the Equal Protection Clause, or antidiscrimination law more generally?

Of course, the rest of Lawrence's "The Id" article explains what, in Lawrence's opinion, *Little Black Sambo* ought to mean for the Equal Protection Clause. This suggests that stories are not inherently non-normative; they are not inevitably unconnected to rules. They are capable of being deployed to suggest a particular law. Some may choose not to connect the stories that they tell to a normative framework. But, that choice is not demanded by the stories themselves.

The problem that some critics have with storytelling may not be due to stories' inability to lead to rules—they can. Rather, it may be due to critics' beliefs that we ought not to rely on stories as the basis for new rules. Abrams has described this as a skepticism about "whether prescriptions derived from narrative are entitled to be taken as normative by legal actors."[30] This is a skepticism about whether narratives should be regarded as "legitimate sources of legal prescriptions."[31] This is a different problem. Further, it is a harder problem to solve, as it involves asking difficult questions about why more widely-accepted sources of legal prescriptions—like legislative intent, policy-based arguments, moral philosophy, empirical data, and economic analyses—are superior to the stories that some critical race theorists tell. It involves asking hard questions about why these alternative stories ought to be excluded from the expansive universe of things considered "proper" sources of legal prescriptions.

---

[29] Downes v. Bidwell, 182 U.S. 244, 287 (1901).

[30] Abrams, *supra* note 10, at 978.

[31] *Id.*

3. Atypicality

Some critics of narratives would answer the prompt above—asking why stories ought to be excluded from the universe of things considered proper sources of legal prescriptions—by noting that it is difficult to know when an experience that an author relates is a typical one. So, for example, are many black children made to look at pictures of *Little Black Sambo* in elementary school? Do these children feel the shame that Lawrence felt? Do most black children feel that *Little Black Sambo* portrays black people as ugly, unintelligent, and the stuff of white entertainment? Or do some black children simply find *Little Black Sambo* amusing? Is the embarrassment that Lawrence felt due to his being the only black person in his kindergarten class? Would black children in a more mixed-raced setting or in a predominately black environment feel the humiliation that Lawrence felt? And so on and so forth. Critics who ask these types of questions are likely motivated by the sense that Lawrence's story can only be the basis of a legal prescription if it describes an experience that is universal among black people.

Proponents of storytelling in legal scholarship respond to concerns about the typicality of stories by noting that these concerns evince a commitment to modernist beliefs that there is one truth that is out there and that there are certain criteria that can help us know whether we have found it. One of those criteria is universality: if something is true for everyone, then it is likely the *truth*. Accordingly, if all black children come across *Little Black Sambo* at some point in their young lives and feel the shame that Lawrence felt, then it is likely *true* that the representation of blackness contained in the book is degrading and, further, is clearly communicated to youth. However, if some black children never find themselves having to confront *Little Black Sambo* and, if they do, do not have the same reaction that Lawrence had to it, then Lawrence's claims about the meaning of the book are not *true*. And, according to this way of thinking, proper sources of legal prescriptions must be *true*.

Many proponents of narrative reject these modernist conceptions of truth. As explained above, many of these proponents would consider themselves postmodernists and, as such, disbelieve that there is one truth that we can come to know with the proper tools. They believe instead that there are many contingent truths out there. Thus, they reject the idea that an atypical story has no relationship, or only an attenuated relationship, to *truth*. (Indeed, many postmodernist storytellers believe that even a fictional story can be true: fiction, while not factual, can be true when it is felt as such within the hearer and/or when it reveals something insightful about society, the nation, the law, or humankind.) Insisting upon the typicality and universality of stories measures stories by standards that many storytellers have rejected. Indeed, critics who insist upon typicality and universality view stories within an approach to knowledge that the tellers of the stories have challenged quite intentionally, and then criticize stories for failing to meet the rebuffed approach's requirements.

4. Stories Make Dialogue Difficult, if Not Impossible

Finally, some critics of narrative in legal scholarship argue that personal narratives, specifically, are not a proper source of legal prescriptions because their very nature—they are *personal* and their authority derives from the speaker's status (as a woman, as a person of color, as a sexual minority, etc.)—makes it difficult to engage in productive conversations about the substance of the narrative. Write Daniel Farber and Suzanna Sherry, who have probably offered the most comprehensive critique of CRT, "[A]ny criticism of the stories is inevitably seen as a personal attack on the storyteller. . . . [Conversations] can become sidetracked from discussing the merits of the message itself into bitter disputes about the speaker's authenticity and her right to speak on behalf of an oppressed group."[32] Similarly, some have argued that personal narratives about experiences that the storyteller has had make dialogue about the substance of the narrative difficult because it excludes from the conversation anyone who has not had the same or a similar experience or anyone who does not want to respond by offering their own experiences. The assumption underlying these arguments is that robust conversation is a necessary component of good rule-making, and any approach that inhibits discussion ought to be rejected.

Proponents of the use of personal narratives in legal scholarship would likely admit that the intimate nature of these narratives might increase the possibility that storytellers will be offended by critiques of their stories and the rule changes that those stories prompt. However, they would also likely note that enmity is not *inevitable*, and storytellers and their critics can develop and deploy techniques that can help them engage in productive conversations about personal narratives. (Further, proponents might also remind us that hostility and incivility are not at all unique to dialogues about personal narratives. One can find in the pages of law reviews intensely acrimonious debates about whether originalism is a better approach to constitutional interpretation than living constitutionalism, whether the *Chevron* doctrine is defensible, etc.)

---

[32] DANIEL FARBER & SUZANNA SHERRY, BEYOND ALL REASON: THE RADICAL ASSAULT ON TRUTH IN AMERICAN LAW 12 (1997).

On the issue of personal narrative excluding from the discussion those who have not had the same or a similar experience or who do not want to respond by offering their own experiences, Abrams writes, "I have no doubt that some forms of experiential narrative scholarship tend to discourage those unwilling to respond in experiential terms; but it could also be said that forms of scholarship based on assumptions of scientific rationality discourage those discussants unwilling to strive for objectivity in their perspective or universality in their claims."[33] In essence, *someone* is going to be excluded from the conversation. No approach guarantees full participation by all.

III. The Claim That People of Color Speak in a Distinctive Voice

While the debate over whether narrative is an appropriate methodology for producing legal scholarship has occupied many pages of law reviews, observers have also critiqued some of the substantive claims that thinkers writing within the CRT framework have made. One of these is the claim that there exists a unique "voice of color."

Matsuda, one of the founders of CRT, has offered one of the most eloquent articulations of the assertion that nonwhite people possess a perspective—a voice—that is always and in every case different from that possessed by white people. Matsuda has argued that because racism is an unavoidable ubiquity in the United States, all people of color living in the country have endured it. According to Matsuda, this common experience of racial oppression has created in every nonwhite person a distinct way of viewing the world and the law that organizes it. This view is inevitably one that will not countenance the unjust subjugation of any person or group. As such, it is a view that is best able to describe a world in which racial justice reigns. Writes Matsuda, "Those who are oppressed in the present world can speak most eloquently of a better one. Their language will not be abstract, detached or inaccessible; their program will not be undefined. They will advance clear ideas about the next step to a better world. The experience of struggling against racism has taught much about struggle, about how real people can rise up, look power in the eye and turn it around."[34]

Central to Matsuda's argument about the "voice of color" is the proposition that it is shared by all nonwhite people—without regard to socioeconomic status. Matsuda disavows that affluence allows

---

[33] Abrams, *supra* note 10, at 1044.

[34] Mari J. Matsuda, *Looking to the Bottom: Critical Legal Studies and Reparations*, 22 HARV. C.R.-C.L. L. REV. 323, 346–47 (1987).

nonwhite people an escape from racial disadvantage. The conclusion that she draws from this is that the standpoints of poor people of color are indistinguishable from the standpoints of wealthy people of color. She writes:

> A minority perspective cuts across class lines. Reading the editorials and letters in *Black Enterprise*, a slick and conventional magazine directed at an audience of black entrepreneurs, reveals that even economically successful black capitalists are critical of the Reagan Administration's effect on the poor. There is something about color that doesn't wash off as easily as class. The experience of racism, it seems, causes the normative choices of black capitalists to diverge from the choices of others in their class.[35]

It is easy to see why Matsuda's argument raised a few hackles. The problem, in her critics' view, is that it is inconsistent with what we observe on a day-to-day basis. They point out that we can observe the incredible heterogeneity of people of color at any given moment on any given day. We know that political conservative Clarence Thomas replaced political liberal Thurgood Marshall on the Court. We know that anywhere from 18% to 28% of Latinx persons voted for Donald Trump in the 2016 presidential election—despite his describing Mexican immigrants as "rapists," "criminals," and "bad hombres" and promising to build a wall along the U.S.-Mexico border if elected. Thus, even if Matsuda is correct that racism is an omnipresence in the U.S. and no person of color living in the country has managed to remain untouched by it—a proposition with which most, if not all, persons operating within the CRT paradigm would agree—it seems extremely unlikely that all people of color have responded to that omnipresent racism *in the same way*.

Additionally, the suggestion that there is a similarity of perspective among people of color that crosses class lines is one that critics of Matsuda's argument find incredulous. They would argue that while class privilege may not entirely immunize people of color from racial oppression, class privilege certainly does allow for different experiences of that racial oppression. Is not the racial disenfranchisement endured by the indigent person of color trapped in a hypersegregated, heavily policed, disinvested neighborhood different from the racial disenfranchisement endured by his more affluent counterpart in the suburbs? Is not the racial oppression sustained by a transgender woman of color who relies upon public benefits for her financial viability different from the racial oppression sustained by her economically self-sufficient cisgender counterpart? If we answer these questions in the affirmative, then it might be

---

[35] *Id.* at 360–61.

reasonable to expect that the "voices" of these different groups of people of color will be different, as their experiences with racial disadvantage have been quite different. When some critical race theorists appear to deny this, they appear to claim that all nonwhite people—including the relatively privileged few who have managed to acquire law degrees and become professors at law schools—have endured the exact same racial oppression as the most economically dispossessed of their racial group. As Alex Johnson, Jr. has written of this view, "The erroneous assumption is that, although all members of the oppressed and economically disadvantaged class are not people of color, all people of color—including scholars of color—are members of this oppressed class, at least in terms of perspective and viewpoint, and speak from that perspective and in that voice. Nothing could be further from the truth."[36]

To its critics, the "voice of color" argument fails not only because it denies *class* stratification among nonwhite people, but also because it denies all of the tremendous stratification that exists along lines other than class. Johnson writes that "[m]atters of gender, class, sexual orientation, educational opportunity, environment—the list is endless—affect who the scholar of color is and what she says. Conceding the existence of a monolithic voice of color negates the rich and variegated diversity that scholars of color possess, which is our strength as a collective body."[37]

If Johnson is right, the claim that people of color speak with a distinctive voice requires some nuance. Other scholars writing within the CRT framework have supplied that nuance. Prominent critical race theorist Richard Delgado, for one, has rejected the proposition that there is a singular voice of color, instead positing the existence of *many* voices of color. He has noted that Matsuda's original claim is best understood modestly; he reads her as suggesting nothing more and nothing less than the likelihood that "persons who have grown up in the minority community may have information not easily

---

[36] Alex M. Johnson, Jr., *The New Voice of Color*, 100 YALE L.J. 2007, 2038 (1991).

Several other critical race theorists have rejected the monolithic "voice of color" claim, including Robert Chang, the father of Asian Pacific American Critical Race Theory (or APACrit, which is explored in chapter 5). Chang has noted that some feminists once argued that women spoke with a "different voice" that was more relational and interdependent, but that "feminist theory has, for the most part, moved beyond the idea of a different voice arising out of some unitary female experience that binds all women. Instead, feminist theory has recognized for some time now that identities are contradictory, multiple, partial, and strategic, giving rise to a multiplicity of voices. *It is time now for critical race theory to do the same, to move beyond the false issue of voice and its accompanying question of authenticity*. ROBERT S. CHANG, DISORIENTED: ASIAN AMERICANS, LAW, AND THE NATION STATE 63 (1999) (emphasis added).

[37] Johnson, *supra* note 36, at 2034.

accessible to others and a special stake in disseminating it."[38] He notes that in a society that is "deeply structured by racism," that structure will give the stories that people of color tell "a commonality warranting the term 'voice.' "[39] Delgado's reimagining of the "voice of color" claim avoids the essentialism present in the less nuanced version of the claim. That is, Delgado recognizes a shared experience of racial oppression while simultaneously recognizing that differences along lines of class, gender, sexual orientation, citizenship status, etc., will impact the form that racial oppression takes as well as the individual's subjective experience of it.

Johnson has also added nuance to the "voice of color" claim. He agrees with Delgado that the "voice of color" is a varied thing—born from the heterogeneous experiences that nonwhite people have had with racial disenfranchisement as inflected through their other axes of identity. (Johnson refers to the differences in the "voice of color" that are due to the multiplicity of nonwhite people's experiences as "dialects.") Moreover, he adds that one only hears a "voice of color" when a nonwhite person calls upon the insight that she has gained as a person of color. Thus, nonwhite people will not always and in every case speak in a "voice of color." They will only speak in their voice of color when they use their lived experience as a racial minority as a source of insight. So, for example, a black scholar might analyze the tax code. However, that scholar only writes in her "voice of color" if she calls upon her experience as a person of color to yield some verity about that code. Thus, people of color are free to always, never, or sometimes speak in a voice of color. This understanding of the voice of color removes the sense of inevitability that attached to it when it was first described in the CRT literature.

Adding refinement to the position that people of color speak in a distinctive voice might be important, as the unrefined version of the argument is vulnerable to the charge that it is nothing more than a stereotype about nonwhite people—a generalization about the group that denies the particularity of the individuals within the group. In this vein, Randall Kennedy, whose critiques of CRT caused quite a stir in the late 1980s, wrote that the monolithic voice of color claim "replicates deeply traditional ideas about the naturalness, essentiality, and inescapability of race . . . Chief among these baneful notions is the belief that race is destiny—that knowing a person's race can properly lead to certain assumptions or conclusions about

---

[38] Richard Delgado, *When a Story is Just a Story: Does Voice Really Matter?*, 76 VA. L. REV. 95, 99 (1990).

[39] *Id.* at 97.

the worthiness of that person or her knowledge or her capacity to accomplish a certain task."[40]

A productive revision to the monolithic voice of color argument—a revision that would be completely consistent with the CRT paradigm—might propose that, in a society built upon racial inequality and wherein racial stratification remains the order of the day, one can comfortably assume that any individual person of color has encountered racial disadvantage. This does not mean that race is destiny; it simply means that racial oppression, in some mode or manner, is unavoidable. When that individual allows the racial oppression that he has experienced, in whatever form that it has taken, to be a source of insight, he may have a perspective, a voice, that is different from the one possessed by a person who has not endured and survived racial disadvantage. This is the "voice of color" claim, redux.

IV. The Claim That Merit Is Biased

Critical scholars thinking about race during the 1980s and 1990s looked around them and noticed that the number of law professors of color was distressingly small. When the deans of law schools were asked why this was so, they usually responded by saying that they would love to increase the size of their nonwhite faculty; however, there were precious few people of color who were qualified to work as law professors. In those days (and at present), persons interested in teaching in a law school had to boast certain credentials: a JD from an elite law school, high grades on her law school transcript, membership on the school's law review, a published paper, and usually a clerkship with a federal judge. Most deans explained the dearth of faculty of color in terms of the dearth of people of color who had these credentials.

This prompted critical thinkers about race to question why these characteristics counted as "credentials." Essentially, these thinkers interrogated why merit had been defined in the way it had been defined. They wanted to know why it was largely accepted that in order for an individual to be a successful, effective, productive law professor, she needed to have attended an elite law school, earned high grades, worked on the law review, published a substantial paper, and clerked for a judge. Why were other things excluded from the criteria used to identify those who are qualified to teach the law—like employment at a civil rights organization and practical experience with using law to effect social change, or a deep knowledge of the lives that marginalized people live and awareness of how the law has failed them (or helped them), or the ability to

---

[40] Randall L. Kennedy, *Racial Critiques of Legal Academia*, 102 HARV. L. REV. 1745, 1801 (1989).

incite in students the desire to produce social justice? Why had other indicia that might identify talented individuals been rejected as the stuff of merit?

CRT answered that those who had constructed the standards of excellence had created them in their image. Those with the power to define merit had defined it in terms of the characteristics that they themselves possessed: *they* had attended elite law schools, earned high grades, worked on the school's law review, etc. It was not *objectively true* that individuals who had these credentials were more qualified than those without them. The former individuals were only more qualified than the latter individuals when judged by standards that powerful people had erected.

CRT insisted that, contrary to the claims made by those who defended the criteria by which excellence was measured, these criteria were not at all neutral; they were not decontextualized, ahistorical, apolitical things that were wholly disconnected from power. Instead, these criteria were socially embedded, and deeply so. Moreover, they were biased: they favored affluent white males, who had a much easier time achieving the stuff of merit than other groups in society. As such, CRT argued that traditional qualifications functioned to exclude people of color from the legal academy. Further, it asserted that in preventing nonwhite people from becoming law professors, the criteria helped to maintain law schools as spaces that were free from truly progressive, radical thought; the criteria functioned to produce law schools as mechanisms for maintaining the status quo.

Expectedly, not everyone agreed with these arguments. Some insisted that the way that merit had been defined *was* objective—that it was, in fact, *true* that persons who had the qualifications that law schools traditionally looked for in candidates for law teaching jobs were more talented and had more promise than persons without those qualifications. Farber and Sherry, for example, defended the conventional indicia of merit as completely disconnected from race, religion, gender, and socioeconomic status. They argued that because the conventional definition of merit does not *explicitly* judge persons on account of their race or other personal characteristics, it was objective. They argued that in making personal characteristics irrelevant, traditional understandings of merit prevent our society from returning to the days of yore, when people were formally excluded from occupying certain positions and from participating in certain aspects of society because of their race, gender, religion, etc.[41]

Other critics were more circumspect. Kennedy, for example, agreed with CRT that the standards by which excellence was

---

[41] *See* FARBER & SHERRY, *supra* note 32.

measured were subjective and socially constructed; he agreed that powerful actors had selected the criteria that would identify candidates as attractive for jobs in the legal academy.[42] However, he disagreed with CRT when it argued that other criteria were equally capable of identifying individuals who would have stellar careers as legal academics. Kennedy wanted CRT to *prove* that the alternative criteria that they proposed for judging candidates for law teaching jobs were as good as the criteria that had been traditionally accepted. He implored CRT to identify the specific individuals of color who could be brilliant law professors, but who could not get a job in legal academia because they were "unqualified" pursuant to traditional measures.

Essentially, Kennedy and others demanded that CRT substantiate its claims. When critical race theorists denounced the fact that the civil rights scholarship written by scholars of color was not cited as frequently as that written by white scholars, Kennedy wanted them to *prove* that the excluded scholarship was as good as the stuff that was being cited. When critical race theorists argued that many professors of color were unfairly denied promotion and tenure because their scholarship was thought not to be as rigorous, thoughtful, or insightful as white professors' scholarship, Kennedy demanded that critical race theorists *prove* that the scholarship of these nonwhite academics was as good as white professors' scholarship.[43]

There were two responses to Kennedy's critiques. First, many critical scholars observed that the demand that CRT identify individuals of color who could not get jobs in the legal academy although they were qualified to work there, as well as the demand that it prove that the scholarship of progressive academics of color was as good as that of white academics, completely missed the point. Similar to the critique that stories cannot serve as the basis for normative proposals because they were not typical or universal, critics were asking progressive scholars to prove that individuals and their scholarship met the very standards that these scholars were challenging. In essence, critics of CRT insisted upon judging progressive scholars and progressive scholarship by the same old measures—the measures that CRT rejected as complicit in producing

---

[42] Kennedy, *supra* note 40, at 1763.

[43] Perhaps the most controversial part of Kennedy's critique was his suggestion that the scholarship that academics of color produced was, objectively speaking, not as good as that produced by their white counterparts and his conjecturing as to why that might be. He postulated that because professors of color were few and far between in law schools, they "probably find themselves beset by far greater demands from students (particularly black students) and administrators than their white counterparts. This is a burden that cannot help but impede efforts to produce top-grade written legal scholarship." *Id.* at 1769.

a society that accepted racial inequality and racial hierarchy as an inevitable (indeed, valid) feature of modern life.

Second, many critical scholars responded to Kennedy's critiques by asking why *they* had to bear the burden of proving their claims. For example, why did not those who defended traditional indicia of merit bear the burden of proving that those criteria were the best mechanism for identifying talented candidates? Why did not those who claimed that the most cited scholarship was in reality, the most rigorous, thoughtful, and insightful work out there bear the burden of proving that all other scholarship has, in every conceivable respect, less to offer? Essentially, why did not defenders of the status quo have to prove that the status quo was better than any of the alternative worlds that we can imagine?

The question of who bears the burden of proof is an important one, as it is likely true that whoever bears that burden loses. Writes Jerome McCristal Culp, "[I]f the status quo has no burden to defend itself, it will often win whether it is right or not."[44] Critical thinkers seemed willing to admit that they could not prove that the alternative conceptions of merit that they proposed would produce better law schools. But, they insisted that their critics could not prove that the traditional conception of merit had generated the best version of these institutions.

V. Questions and Discussion

1. Why do you think some of the critiques lobbed against CRT have been so acerbic? What about CRT may have incited this acerbity?

2. Did you find the story about *Little Black Sambo* from Lawrence's "The Id, the Ego, and Equal Protection" compelling? Note that the story was offered in support of his claim that most individuals harbor implicit biases and are largely unaware of their negative feelings towards members of racial outgroups. Do you think that the story made that claim more or less plausible?

Did the story make you more sensitive to the possibility that unintended racial slights are not only ubiquitous, but are also profoundly painful to those on the receiving end of the slights? Do you think that sensitivity matters? Why or why not?

3. Some scholars have proposed that part of the anxiety that many critics have over storytelling in legal scholarship is due to their lack of knowledge about how to evaluate narrative works. Legal scholars understand how to assess an argument about the original

---

[44] Jerome McCristal Culp, Jr., *To the Bone: Race and White Privilege*, 83 MINN. L. REV. 1637, 1669 (1999).

intent of the Framers, or a philosophical argument about the right to privacy, or an economic analysis of law. However, they do not know how to evaluate a story. Some scholars have proposed that the use of narrative in legal scholarship will become more accepted if legal scholars become familiar with the conventions of narrative work and learn how to distinguish well-executed and poorly-executed stories. Abrams writes that in the disciplines in which narrative is an essential element—like literary criticism, for example—narratives do not become credible only when they correspond to actual events that have taken place in the real world. They may also become credible "through revealed pain, through the cohering, particularized knowledge of the expert witness, [or] though the ignition in the reader of a flash of recognition."[45]

Do you think this explains the anxiety surrounding narrative in legal scholarship? If not, what do you think explains this anxiety?

4. In his critique of the argument that people of color speak with a distinctive voice, Kennedy writes that the proposition that there is a "black experience" that produces a unique perspective in black people is both overinclusive and underinclusive. It is overinclusive because some black people will not have had the "black experience" and, consequently, will not have the associated perspective; and it is underinclusive because some nonblack people will have had the "black experience" and, consequently, will have the associated perspective. He continues by noting that, if the above is true, "blackness" is "the description for a state of mind or set of beliefs that a person, regardless of race, can choose to adopt, discard, use, or modify. Having gone this far, however, toward separating blackness as a sociological condition from blackness as an intellectual category, it would seem useful to drop the racial identification of the latter. Instead of referring to a 'black' perspective, we should articulate the substantive content of the perspectives to which we refer."[46]

How do you feel about Kennedy's proposal? Do you believe that we lose something by failing to identify something as a *black* (or Asian, or Muslim, or white) experience? If so, does identifying black experiences—plural—regain what you believe was lost? Why?

5. Consider the alternative criteria mentioned above by which candidates for law teaching jobs might be measured: employment at a civil rights organization and practical experience with using law to effect social change; deep knowledge about the lives that marginalized people live and awareness of how the law has failed (or helped) them; and the ability to incite in students the desire to produce social justice? Do you feel that these are desirable

[45] Abrams, *supra* note 10, at 1024.

[46] Kennedy, *supra* note 40, at 1803.

credentials to demand of persons interested in becoming law professors? Why or why not? How might law schools change if law faculty had to possess these credentials? How might society change? Do you view these changes as attractive?

Chapter 4

THE LATCRIT INTERVENTION

LatCrit is a mode of enquiry that centers Latinx people in the analysis and critique of law. It is "a movement to articulate the particularities of Latina/o perspectives and experiences within the regime of white supremacy."[1] There is some disagreement about whether LatCrit is a branch of scholarship that exists within the larger intellectual project of CRT, or whether it is entirely distinct from CRT—existing alongside it, but not within it.[2] What is undisputed, however, is that LatCrit emerged in the mid-1990s as a response to the failure of early iterations of CRT to theorize the unique forms of race-based subordination that Latinx people experience.

I. Shortcomings of Early CRT

A. The Black-White Paradigm

Although many nonblack scholars—including Mari Matsuda, Gerald Torres, and Neil Gotanda—helped to found CRT, the primary focus of early CRT scholarship was on black people's experiences with racism in the U.S.[3] In retrospect, it is clear that early CRT deployed a *black-white paradigm* of race in the U.S. This paradigm understands race relations in the country to consist entirely of white people's efforts to dominate black people and black people's struggles to free themselves from that domination. Wholly obscured by the black-white paradigm are the experiences of Asian, indigenous, and Latinx people with race and racial power.

---

[1] Elizabeth M. Iglesias, *Identity, Democracy, Communicative Power, Inter/National Labor Rights and the Evolution of LatCrit Theory and Community*, 53 U. MIAMI L. REV. 575, 622 (1999).

[2] It is worth noting that although there may be some uncertainty about LatCrit's relationship to CRT, the primary architects of LatCrit understand it to be distinct from CRT. Indeed, they have described it as a " 'close cousin' to CRT" that "welcomes CRT, both in spirit and in the flesh, to its gatherings." *See* Francisco Valdes, *LatCrit: A Conceptual Overview*, LATCRIT, http://www.latcrit.org/content/about/conceptual-overview/ (last visited July 14, 2018).

[3] Professor Stephanie Phillips, who has been involved in the CRT movement since its infancy, has argued that early CRT's failure to consider and theorize forms of racial subordination that affect nonblack-nonwhite groups was not intentional; it did not result from a principle that prioritized the experiences of black Americans over all others. Phillips writes that the exclusion of nonblack-nonwhite groups from early CRT's analytical purview simply "was a function of ignorance." Stephanie L. Phillips, *The Convergence of the Critical Race Theory Workshop with LatCrit Theory: A History*, 53 U. MIAMI L. REV. 1247, 1252 (1999).

While the myopia that the black-white paradigm induces is offensive because it erases the histories and present realities of all nonblack racial minorities in the country, it is also damaging because it results in an incomplete understanding of racism. The black-white paradigm leads to the conclusion that the mechanisms that have subordinated black people in the U.S. constitute the entire universe of techniques of racial exclusion. Thus, the black-white paradigm leads us to suppose that racism is *only* anti-black institutions, laws, and practices: chattel slavery, Jim Crow laws, vagrancy statutes, convict leasing systems, poll taxes, literacy tests, redlined neighborhoods, mass incarceration, etc. This limited paradigm disallows us from seeing the mechanisms that have oppressed Asian, indigenous, and Latinx peoples throughout history. As Leslie Espinosa has written, racism is *also* "immigration laws and internment camps; it is stolen land grants and silenced languages; it is standardized tests based on standardized culture; it is invisibility and lost identity."[4] In critical thinkers' view, seeing these latter techniques of exclusion and marginalization—and identifying them as *racism*—is important because it allows us to recognize the multiplicity of practices that have sustained white people at the top of racial hierarchies in the U.S. and abroad.

LatCrit's critique of the black-white paradigm also leads us to complicate our definition of race. The black-white paradigm encourages us to focus only on black and white people and, consequently, to conceptualize racial difference as the differences between those two groups. Thus, we think of racial difference as the stuff of skin color, hair texture, nose width, lip size, and other physical attributes. This, in turn, leads us to think of *race* as categorizations of humans in terms of differences in skin, hair, noses, lips, and other physical characteristics.

LatCrit proposes that this definition of race is incomplete. It suggests that if we free ourselves from the constraints of the black-white paradigm—and if we think of racial differences as not only those differences between white and black people, but *also* those differences between white and *nonblack minorities*, like Latinx people—we will expand our understanding of racial difference and race. For the most part, skin, hair, noses, lips and other physical attributes have not distinguished white people from Latinx people. Instead, language, accent, immigration status, nationality, and culture have differentiated the two groups. Thus, LatCrit suggests that our definitions of race are incomplete if we allow them to reflect only physical distinctions. It contends that the *nonphysical*

---

[4] Leslie Espinosa & Angela P. Harris, *Embracing the Tar Baby: LatCrit Theory and the Sticky Mess of Race*, 85 CALIF. L. REV. 1585, 1593 (1997).

distinctions that have been used to divide and subordinate groups of people are *also* the stuff of race.

Now, there is an argument against expanding our definition of race in a way that allows us to understand nonphysical characteristics as the stuff of racial difference. The argument is that nonphysical characteristics—like language, accent, national origin, and culture—actually denote *ethnicity*. Thus, the argument is that traditional schemas, which define race in terms of physical attributes, are actually *correct*. Accordingly, revising our understandings of race to recognize nonphysical characteristics as racial is inadvisable because it is inaccurate.

The counterargument to this position, explored in depth in Chapter 6, reminds us that traditional definitions of race, which define race in terms of physical attributes, are products of a largely discredited science that claims that biological or genetic differences distinguish the races: according to this science, biological or genetic variations produce distinct physical types among the racial groups. However, if we reject these schematizations of race as pseudoscience, it leaves us to wonder why we ought to prioritize physical characteristics in our definitions of race. What principle warrants continuing to define race as a categorization of physical variations among humans?

In the absence of a clear principle, LatCrit and CRT propose that we should define race not by asking what race *is*, but instead by asking what race *does*. While race has done many things throughout history, one important role of race is to justify subordinating some groups of people.[5] According to this line of thought, race justified enslaving black people. It justified exterminating indigenous people and removing them from their ancestral lands. It justified preventing Asian people from entering the nation and interning those who were here. And it has justified denying citizenship and concomitant rights to Latinx people. Following this understanding of race, those characteristics that have served as bases for thinking of indigenous, Asian, and Latinx people as nonwhite people—language, national origin, culture, tribal affiliation, etc.—become racial characteristics.

Notably, U.S. antidiscrimination law has embraced the traditional definition of race as physical difference. Accordingly, when persons endure negative treatment because of the language

---

[5] In this vein, sociologist Paul Gilroy has described race as an "impersonal, discursive arrangement, the brutal result of the raciological ordering of the world, not its cause." PAUL GILROY, POSTCOLONIAL MELANCHOLIA 39 (2005). Here, Gilroy argues that race does not produce racism; instead racism produces race. Following this sentiment, CRT and LatCrit would look to see whether some need for subordination has produced a group as a race. The theories would conclude that because there has been a need to subordinate Latinx people, they have been created as a race.

that they speak, because they speak with an accent, because they were born outside of the U.S., or because they embrace or display certain "nonwhite/non-American" cultural traditions, the law does not understand it to be *racial* discrimination. As a result, persons seeking relief from this negative treatment have had to fit their experiences within other legal categories. Specifically, they have looked to the category of "national origin" to offer them the protections that the category of race cannot. However, LatCrit has argued that thinking of the marginalization that Latinx people have experienced as a type of discrimination on the basis of "national origin" is far from ideal.

According to LatCrit, the first flaw lies in courts having constructed the category of "national origin" so as to fail to protect individuals from language and accent discrimination. Courts have interpreted it as only prohibiting discrimination on the basis of immutable characteristics. Because individuals can learn new languages and learn how to speak English without an accent, courts have deemed language and accent to be mutable characteristics and, consequently, have denied relief to individuals alleging language and accent discrimination.[6] LatCrit problematizes this result, arguing that it functions to subordinate nonblack minorities, to exclude these same groups from the polity, and to maintain the U.S. as a white nation. As Matsuda has observed, employers' refusals to hire those who speak accented English, together with "[t]he recent push for English-only laws[ ] and the attack on bilingual education, may represent new outlets for racial anxiety now that many traditional outlets are denied. The angry insistence that 'they' should speak English [or speak English without an accent] serves as a proxy for a whole range of fears displaced by the social opprobrium directed at explicit racism."[7] LatCrit proposes that just as the explicit racism of yesteryear maintained the U.S. as a white nation, the modern techniques—operating in terms of language and accent prohibitions—do the same.

Second, LatCrit contends that forcing plaintiffs to allege national origin discrimination when they experience language or accent discrimination is flawed because *national origin* appears to

---

[6] *See, e.g.*, Garcia v. Gloor, 618 F.2d 264 (5th Cir. 1980) (finding that an employer's English-only policy did not violate Title VII by discriminating against Mexican American plaintiffs on the basis of national origin); Fragante v. City & Cty. of Honolulu, 888 F.2d 591, 595–99 (9th Cir. 1989) (denying a Title VII national origin discrimination claim brought by a plaintiff who was not hired for a civil service job because he spoke with a "[h]eavy Filipino" accent); Garcia v. Spun Steak Co., 998 F.2d 1480, 1483 (9th Cir. 1993) (upholding employer's English-only policy and denying that it was a form of discrimination on the basis of national origin in violation of Title VII).

[7] Mari J. Matsuda, *Voices of America: Accent, Antidiscrimination Law, and a Jurisprudence for the Last Reconstruction*, 100 YALE L.J. 1329, 1397 (1990).

refer to the country of one's birth. However, many plaintiffs who have experienced adverse employment actions because they spoke Spanish at work or spoke with Spanish accents were born in the United States. Juan Perea observes the discursive problem that the doctrine creates: nonwhite persons born in the U.S. have to allege that they were discriminated against on the basis of their national origin—in essence, they have to allege that they were not born in the U.S.—in order to gain the protections of antidiscrimination law. He notes, "Such individuals must deny their actual national origin . . . . [They] must claim a treacherous fiction, that they belong to another country, in order to fit a constitutionally recognized category of claims."[8] LatCrit and CRT query the work that this does to preserve constructions of the U.S. as a white nation where nonwhite persons are always and in every case outsiders—never *truly* belonging to the nation.

One final note on the black-white paradigm: LatCrit theorists have proposed another reason for rejecting it. They claim that it is simply not familiar to many individuals hailing from Latin American countries. For example, Berta Hernández-Truyol has observed that in many nations in the Caribbean and Latin America, the relevant distinctions between people are not racial, but rather are cultural. She has observed that "the Latina/o identity narrative—for those raised outside and within U.S. borders alike—is based upon ethnic/national origin/social/cultural identity"; this is an identity narrative that starkly contrasts with the " 'American' model in which race plays a nuclear, primary, defining, and pivotal role."[9] Theirs is a "culture-based normativity" that has to yield to the racial classification system that the U.S. imposes upon them.[10]

LatCrit challenges us to think about the desirability of importing Latinx conceptions of identity, and race, into the U.S. Hernández-Truyol observes that in Latin America, race is a shifting entity. "[T]he reality of racial admixtures developed the concept of 'race' as a fluid continuum, rather than the absolutist black/white paradigm. This fluid model, where the construction of race is imbued with values based upon class, education, economics, and culture, lacks rigid borders . . . and allows traveling in and out of categories."[11] LatCrit challenges us to wonder how racial disenfranchisement in the U.S. might change if the country conceptualized race in a way that is more fluid than it is now—if class

---

[8] *See* Juan F. Perea, *Ethnicity and the Constitution: Beyond the Black and White Binary Constitution,* 36 WM. & MARY L. REV. 571, 578 (1995).

[9] Berta Esperanza Hernández-Truyol, *Borders (En)Gendered: Normativities, Latinas, and a Latcrit Paradigm,* 72 N.Y.U. L. REV. 882, 895 (1997).

[10] *Id.* at 902.

[11] *Id.* at 901.

privilege, for example, might allow individuals to change racial groups. Would things be better or worse for racial minorities?

B. Black Exceptionalism

LatCrit also emerged as a response to an idea that might be implicit in the black-white paradigm of race relations in the U.S.: *black exceptionalism*. Black exceptionalism argues that the black-white paradigm *rightfully* obscures the experiences of nonblack-nonwhite racial groups in the U.S. It argues that this is because black people's experiences in this country are foundational to understanding every other racial group's experiences in the nation. Thus, black exceptionalism concludes that black people *ought* to be centered in our analyses of race in the U.S., as comprehending anti-black racism is the key to comprehending the racial oppression endured by Latinx, Asian, and indigenous peoples.

As support for this provocative position, black exceptionalism makes two additional claims. The first is that white people have defined themselves in contradistinction to black people—not Latinx, Asian, or indigenous peoples. That is, white people have been able to understand themselves as intelligent, industrious, tidy, moral, and god-fearing because they have constructed black people—and not other racial minority groups—as stupid, lazy, unkempt, immoral, and godless. As Angela Harris describes this idea:

> The people who now call themselves "whites" originally developed that identity, and continue to maintain it most insistently, in contrast to "blacks." Our slavery became their freedom: our degraded labor produced their "free labor," our political nonexistence, their political belonging. Our ugliness, our promiscuity, our simple natures reflected their beauty, continence, and refinement. Our simple joys and pleasures, our songs and dances and folktales (mocked and admired in their minstrelsy) enabled their sophistication and formed a basis for their nostalgia.[12]

In other words, whiteness is the opposite of *blackness*; it is not the opposite of Latinidad, or Asian-ness, or indigeneity. Thus, black exceptionalism proposes that blackness ought to be centered in our analyses because doing so is the only way to discover the content of whiteness.

The second claim in support of black exceptionalism posits that black people are foundational to the country in a way that other racial groups are not. Antidiscrimination law in the U.S. is, in many respects, responses to black people's demands for inclusion. The

---

[12] Espinosa & Harris, *supra* note 4, at 1597.

Thirteenth, Fourteenth, and Fifteenth Amendments—which, among other things, proscribe involuntary servitude and guarantee all persons equal protection of the law—were efforts to bring *black people* into the body politic. Further, the Civil Rights Act of 1964—which provides the statutory framework under which all racial minorities (as well as women) are protected from discrimination in public life—is a response to the demands that *black people* made during the Civil Rights Movement. Further still, the language that black people used during the Civil Rights Movement has been deployed by other groups in their fights for justice. As Harris writes, "The moral claim to inclusion that African Americans made during the 1960s civil rights movement has become the rhetorical template for all subsequent civil rights struggles. Abortion protesters now sing 'We Shall Overcome'; gay and lesbian activists liken marriage restrictions to miscegenation laws."[13] Thus, other groups' struggles for dignity, inclusion, and social transformation have depended on black people's struggles. Black exceptionalism takes this as a justification for centering black people's experiences—even if it renders invisible or diminishes the importance of the experiences of other groups.

Most modern progressive thinkers about race reject black exceptionalism. (And it is unlikely that many critical race theorists at CRT's inception embraced the concept.) This is, in part, due to the fact that the two claims upon which black exceptionalism rests might be false—or, at least, they may not be entirely true.

First, while few would gainsay the proposition that whiteness has been defined in contradistinction to blackness, few ought to gainsay the proposition that whiteness also has been defined in contradistinction to Latinidad, Asian-ness, and indigeneity. That is, just as whiteness is *not* possessing the characteristics that have been attributed to blackness (i.e., ugliness, laziness, inability to delay gratification), whiteness is *not* possessing the characteristics that have been attributed to Latinidad, Asian-ness, and indigeneity. Whiteness is *not* a lack of citizenship. It is *not* being born in another country. It is *not* speaking with an accent (or, at least, not with "those" accents). It is *not* having a language other than English as one's first language. It is *not* having an affiliation with a tribe. It is *not* having a feeling of cultural affinity with people who have been marked as nonwhite.

Second, it is true that the Civil Rights Movement produced much of the country's antidiscrimination laws and developed a language that has been borrowed by subsequent movements for social justice. Yet, it is also true that black people were not the only ones marching,

---

[13] *Id.* at 1600.

protesting, and dying in the struggle against racial power during this time. The movement for social justice in the 1950s and 1960s was one that was peopled by persons of various racial identities and ascriptions.

Moreover, black exceptionalism's critics believe that there are many other reasons for finding the claim unsupportable. Their primary reason derives from a recognition that the racial order of things has been maintained through various mechanism, and not all of these mechanisms have been directed at or against black people. While it is undeniable that the institution of chattel slavery and the discursive and legal construction of black people as unfit for freedom functioned to place white people at the top of the racial hierarchy, it is also undeniable that restrictive immigration laws and the discursive and legal construction of various nonwhite peoples as unfit for citizenship functioned to do the same. While it is undeniable that Jim Crow laws produced and reflected white supremacy, it is also undeniable that the genocide of indigenous peoples did the same. And so on and so forth.

Further, black exceptionalism's critics worry that the claim might lead to an "oppression sweepstakes," wherein nonwhite racial groups attempt to establish that they have suffered "the most."[14] In essence, black exceptionalism identifies black people as "the winner"; they are the racial group that has been the most dispossessed throughout U.S. history. This framing might incentivize nonblack minority groups to argue that *they* are actually "the winners"—that, contrary to black exceptionalism's claims, *they* have been subjected to the most inhumane, degrading, and dignity-denying treatment.

Most CRT and LatCrit scholars would agree that this "race to the bottom" is not at all productive. This competition encourages nonwhite groups to focus on each other as opposed to the racial power that subordinates them all. CRT and LatCrit assert that it may be infinitely more productive to shift attention to the institutions and structures that have caused nonwhite groups to suffer, rather than attempting to calculate the "weight" of those respective sufferings. This shifted focus may allow us to identify threads of commonality that link the different subordinations.

For example, Elizabeth Iglesias notes two different readings of the Court's decision in *Dred Scott v. Sandford*, which infamously held that not only was an enslaved black man not emancipated by his residence in a free territory, but also that black people were not and could not become citizens of the country, as they were "regarded as beings of an inferior order" and, consequently, "had no rights which

---

[14] *Id.* at 1641.

the white man was bound to respect."[15] One might read *Dred Scott* through the lens of black exceptionalism and conclude that the opinion demonstrates that chattel slavery was the most dehumanizing institution ever imposed in U.S. history—a reading that identifies black people as the uniquely-suffering "winners" of the oppression Olympics. But, Iglesias notes an alternative reading. If we are interested in identifying threads of commonality that unite the experiences of all those who have struggled to exist beneath the weight of white racial power, we might read *Dred Scott* as a case about

> the configuration of state power around a citizen/non-citizen dichotomy. . . . [T]he decision not only denied free Blacks citizenship, but in doing so, transfigured a representative government of limited powers into an imperial state. This is because the constitutional framework of government underpinning the *Dred Scott* decision reveals a state that claims the power to govern, without any legal limitations, a class of persons whose interests it does not even pretend to represent. . . .Read through this discourse, the reasoning of *Dred Scott* is still alive and well in the present day configuration of white supremacy. Its present day target is no longer the Black American, as such, but the foreign, the poor, and those who are cast as "national security" threats.[16]

LatCrit proposes that the latter reading is more productive than the traditional reading because, in allowing us to see commonalities in the treatment of black people and "the foreign, the poor, and those who are cast as 'national security' threats," we have a platform upon which we can build intergroup solidarity. Intergroup solidarity may be key because, as Iglesias notes, "[d]ismantling one racial system will not necessarily dismantle the others. On the contrary, it may actually reinscribe the remaining systems and enable their more virulent entrenchment in American society."[17]

II. Key Contributions of LatCrit

A. The Heterogeneity of Latinidad

Latinx people are an incredibly diverse group. They are white, black, Asian, and indigenous; they are U.S.-born and born abroad; they are fervently religious and fiercely agnostic; they speak only Spanish and speak no Spanish at all; they are undocumented immigrants and birthright citizens; they are cisgender men and

[15] Dred Scott v. Sandford, 60 U.S. 393, 407 (1857).

[16] Iglesias, *supra* note 1, at 593–94.

[17] *Id.* at 676.

transgender women; they have extreme amounts of wealth and live in the most destitute of poverties.

Recognizing the heterogeneity of Latinidad is important because it makes the "Latinx subject" difficult to identify. For example, when one speaks about this subject as if she always speaks Spanish, it erases those Latinx people who speak only indigenous languages. When one imagines that the subject is always Catholic, it makes invisible those Latinx people who are Muslim or atheists. The "Latinx subject" cannot be a fixed, unitary, singular thing; instead, in order to accommodate the multiplicity that characterizes those who are Latinx, it must be a multiple, shifting, capacious concept. In this way, speaking about the "Latinx subject" in a way that does not erase any Latinx individual is a feat of antiessentialism; it is coup inasmuch as it avoids reducing a heterogeneous group to one of its many parts. Those who have been accused of essentializing its membership—i.e., when feminists speak about "women," but only mean affluent cisgender white women; when advocates for racial justice speak about "black people," but only mean black men[18]—might learn from LatCrit about how to "do" antiessentialism.

B. Centering Latinx Subjects Reveals Insights About Issues That Are Not Specifically About Latinx Subjects

LatCrit insists that the theory is not "just" about Latinx subjects. Indeed, it proposes that it can make productive contributions to matters that have universal import. Further, LatCrit proposes that it is the practice of centering Latinx subjects that generates these valuable insights about issues of general concern.

For example, consider LatCrit's critique of the failure of antidiscrimination law to protect individuals' ability to speak Spanish in the workplace or to speak English with an accent. While this critique of antidiscrimination law is born of a concern for Latinx people, it can be applied to issues that are not specifically about Latinx people and that exist well outside the genre of language and accent discrimination. As Iglesias explains it:

> [T]he struggle over language rights reflects only one instance in a more general struggle against relations of domination organized by and effectuated through the legal production of differential access to the means of communication. This is because the compelling personal and collective interests at stake in the struggle against the suppression of non-English languages are equally

[18] Kimberlé Crenshaw, *Mapping the Margins: Intersectionality, Identity Politics, and Violence Against Women of Color*, 43 STAN. L. REV. 1241, 1298 (1991).

implicated in such matters as the regulation of political speech and the ownership and control of new technologies of communication. Indeed, in each of these contexts, the matter at stake is the power to communicate—to express oneself—meaningfully and effectively.[19]

Thus, LatCrit may be able to make important contributions to conversations around the First Amendment, the regulation of the telecommunications industry, and campaign finance reform—all matters of universal import.

C. Immigration

LatCrit has made many contributions to the conversation around immigration. LatCrit has argued that the debate around immigration is invariably one about race and that politicians have mobilized fears of the racial other in order to generate support for restrictive immigration laws. Further, LatCrit has offered that debates around immigration are better understood not as contests over who will be kept out or permitted entrance into the country, but rather as contests over who will be allowed to benefit from "the increased migration flows that are all but inevitable given the push-pull factors of an increasingly interconnected and global economy."[20] If the U.S. declines to give visas or other legal protections to the foreign-born workers whom the global economy pushes out of their countries of birth and pulls into the U.S., the biggest beneficiaries of this legal order are employers—who can avail themselves of a vulnerable and, consequently, cheap and exploitable pool of labor. LatCrit offers that the immigration debate is not really about whether we will allow those workers into the U.S., but about whether we will allow them to reap a larger share of the wealth that their labor generates.

D. Globalization

LatCrit has also made incisive contributions to the literature around globalization—a term that refers to the processes by which capital, labor, goods, and services travel across the borders of individual countries, producing a world that is economically (and, invariably, politically) linked. LatCrit has been interested in globalization for many reasons. One of these reasons is that the *immigrant*, an implicitly racialized subject that LatCrit has theorized extensively, frequently becomes an immigrant because of globalization. As noted above, the global economy has created push-and-pull forces—pushing laborers out of countries where their labor cannot be utilized and pulling them into countries where their labor

---

[19] Iglesias, *supra* note 1, at 647.

[20] *Id.* at 669.

can produce profits and wealth. The large numbers of immigrants to the U.S.—and the racialized debates that they have sparked—is an expected consequence of globalization.

Another reason for LatCrit's interest in globalization is the effect that it has had of disempowering and subordinating poorer countries (and the people living in them). LatCrit thinkers contend that while these countries were once disenfranchised by powerful nations' militaries, globalization does the same today. As Margaret Montoya has written, "If the conquest of peoples and nations in the last century was accomplished and maintained through militaristic force, the conquest during this first part of the next millennium is being extended through transnational capitalism and other forms of globalization. The United States now occupies unchallenged domination in every part of the globe through its control of capital, munitions, information and technology."[21] LatCrit suggests that if scholars are critical of the subordination of nonwhite nations by bombs, tanks, and guns, they might also be critical of the subordination of nonwhite nations by free trade agreements, the unobstructed movement of capital, and restrictive immigration laws. Through globalization, LatCrit argues, "the West has been able to successfully reproduce the basic structure of differentiation that underlies earlier racialized forms of imperial domination."[22]

LatCrit has observed that there is an analogy between the domestic context and the international context as it concerns the transformation of the mechanisms by which nonwhite people and nations are dominated. Racial minorities living in the United States were once subordinated by laws and policies that relied on explicitly racist discourses about the inferiority of these groups; analogously, nonwhite people living in colonized nations were once subordinated by systems of colonialism that relied on explicitly racist discourses about their inferiority. Fast forward to the present day. The U.S. now has embraced formal equality with respect to racial minorities living within its borders, but it largely has not problematized the racial disenfranchisement that results from colorblind, race-neutral laws and policies; analogously, champions of globalization have embraced the formal equality of nonwhite nations, but they largely have not problematized the racial disenfranchisement that results from colorblind, race-neutral efforts to produce and maintain a global economy.

Critics of the black-white paradigm of race relations cite this as another limitation of the framework. The "black" in the black-white

---

[21] Margaret E. Montoya, *Class in LatCrit: Theory and Praxis in a World of Economic Inequality*, 78 DENV. U. L. REV. 467, 482 (2001).

[22] Gil Gott, *Critical Race Globalism? Global Political Economy and the Intersections of Race, Nation and Class*, 33 U.C. DAVIS L. REV. 1503, 1506–07 (2000).

paradigm oftentimes has stood for "U.S.-born black." This functions to erase black people living outside of the nation and their experiences with racial power—despite the fact that their experiences mirror those of U.S.-born black people.[23] Thus, according to these critics, the black-white paradigm has disallowed thinkers from seeing the interconnected nature of systems of subordination. Narrowing one's focus to domestic issues—and believing that racial justice is a purely domestic issue—precludes scholars from recognizing that global capitalism invariably produces conflicts between groups, and that these conflicts are frequently played out in racialized terms. Moreover, if globalization has linked racial conflicts in other nations with those in the U.S., then fighting for racial justice abroad might be essential to the realization of racial justice "at home."

Another reason for LatCrit's interest in globalization is that globalization frequently prioritizes above all else the desire to create a world system wherein capital, labor, goods, and services can move freely. According to critics of globalization, it puts any concern that we may have about distributive justice in the backseat. They have argued that the lack of a commitment to ensuring that all receive some portion of the gains that a global economy produces invariably results in some gaining nothing at all. Similarly, they say, globalization has placed any concern that we may have about respecting different cultural forms in the backseat. Concurrent with the circulation of goods, services, labor, and capital is the circulation of values, ethics, and worldviews. A treacherous byproduct of globalization, say its critics, is cultural imperialism, wherein the values of the West (i.e., individualism over community-orientation, wealth accumulation over producing enough to satisfy one's needs, rationality over things deemed irrational) are privileged over values that might be labelled "non-Western." The consequence is the denigration—and possible disappearance—of some cultural forms and ways of life.

In this way, globalization may present many problems—with racial minorities bearing the brunt of these problems. But, LatCrit has warned challengers of globalization to be wary about the tools with which they contest it, as those tools may also be harmful to racial minorities. For example, one might be tempted to answer the

---

[23] Of course, this is not to deny that there were and continue to be important differences in the marginalization of people of color in the U.S. and the marginalization of people of color abroad. Whereas people of color are a minority in the U.S., they were often a majority in the colonized countries abroad. "[C]olonial techniques had to allow for the suppression of a majority population by a minority colonialist group, usually entailing the creation of a comprador, or middle-man economic and bureaucratic class. In the United States, struggling against racial oppression meant taking on the *majority* whose interests thoroughly structured the state itself." *Id.* at 1513.

threats that globalization poses by appealing to the needs of the people within the nation-state. One might claim that the needs of the citizens of one's own country ought to be prioritized over everything else. However, there is just a short hop from this type of argument to xenophobia, which is frequently racialized in the most problematic of ways. In a similar vein, one might oppose globalization because it has worked to produce the unskilled immigrant laborer as an extremely exploitable subject. But, if one recognizes that immigration restrictions are essential to the production of this subject's vulnerability—especially when these restrictions make him "illegal"—one might believe that the answer is to get rid of immigration restrictions altogether. Indeed, one might believe that the answer is to guarantee every individual the right to move freely across borders. However, this resolution of the issue would simply facilitate globalization, dependent as it is on the free movement of people, things, and money. Moreover, the resolution would be "inadequate to the task of reversing the deeper problem of transnational racialized divisions of labor,"[24] whereby white people are typically those who own the capital and nonwhite people are typically those who have only their labor to sell. LatCrit continues to think through the thorny issues that globalization poses, offering nuanced analyses of a complex problem.

III. Questions and Discussion

1. What are some arguments in favor of thinking of "Latinx" as a racial category? What are arguments in favor of thinking of "Latinx" as an ethnicity?

2. It may overstate the case to say that globalization has harmed poor nations. While policies that aim to facilitate free movement of labor and capital around the globe certainly have harmed the poor in these nations, they have also improved the lot of the middle class in these countries. When considered in this light, it might deny the nuances of globalization to think of it as white people in white nations impoverishing nonwhite people in nonwhite nations. How should CRT and LatCrit think about the issue in light of *some* people of color—the elites in nonwhite developing nations—benefitting from globalization?

Relatedly, while many reasons explain Donald Trump's victory in the 2016 presidential election, at least one of these reasons is that he challenged the wisdom of the U.S.'s participation in processes of globalization. During his campaign, Trump claimed that he would significantly reduce the presence of foreign labor within the U.S.—labor that he argued took jobs away from U.S.-born workers. Further,

---

[24] *Id.* at 1508.

he promised to implement policies that would prevent U.S.-based industries from moving to other nations, thus increasing the number of jobs available to U.S-born workers living in the U.S. In essence, he promised to opt the U.S. out of globalization, insulating the country from the forces that would open its borders to free flows of labor and capital. Trump's appeal resonated with a portion of the U.S. electorate that had been negatively impacted by globalization—a portion of the electorate that was largely white. This shows that globalization had not only negatively impacted nonwhite people in developing nations, *but also white people in developed nations*.

Some LatCrit and CRT scholars have suggested that our critiques of globalization are radically incomplete if they ignore the issue of race. For example, Gil Gott has written that the 1999 "protests at the [World Trade Organization] conference in Seattle, led by traditional, mostly white, contingents from the organized labor, environmental, and human and animal rights movements, only serve to confirm that a specifically race-based perspective is missing from our critique of global capitalism."[25] In light of globalization having made winners and losers of white and nonwhite people, do we need a specific racial justice-based critique of globalization? What do we gain by such a critique? What do we lose if we do not have this critique?

3. Some LatCrit scholars have proposed that, in addition to all of the reasons detailed above as to why race scholars should reject the black-white paradigm, the paradigm is limiting because it disallows black people from seeing the subordination of *other black people*. For example, immigrant workers are usually imagined to have an antagonistic relationship to U.S.-born black people, as the two groups purportedly compete for the same jobs. Many U.S.-born black people favor immigration restrictions for that reason. (Indeed, 13% of black men voted for Donald Trump in the 2016 presidential election.[26] It is possible that his anti-immigrant stance informed this group's support of him.) However, Cheryl Little has noted that because the *black* in the black-white paradigm usually means *U.S.-born black people*, it makes invisible the reality that restrictive immigration policies harm many black people.[27] She notes that immigrants from Haiti are subjected to particularly restrictive immigration exclusions. She proposes that if U.S.-born black people see that the harsh treatment that Haitians receive is, in part, because many Haitians seeking to immigrate to the U.S. are black,

---

[25] *Id.* at 1512.

[26] *Exit Polls,* CNN: ELECTION 2016 (Nov. 23, 2016), https://www.cnn.com/election/2016/results/exit-polls.

[27] Cheryl Little, *InterGroup Coalitions and Immigration Politics: The Haitian Experience in Florida*, 53 U. MIAMI L. REV. 717 (1999).

then U.S.-born black people may feel a kinship with Haitian immigrants; U.S.-born black people might recognize that Haitians are "like" them inasmuch as both groups have been subjected to anti-black racism. This recognition might dissolve the antagonism that purportedly describes the relationship that U.S.-born black people have to immigrants.

Do you find this reasoning compelling? Iglesias has criticized Little's proposal, contending that it relies on black exceptionalism and the belief that black people—in this case Haitians—have it worse than everyone else because they are black. She argues that Little's argument forces us to rank subordinations: we have to compare Haitians' experiences with U.S. immigration policies with the experiences of other immigrant groups. She argues that this gets us involved in the unproductive business of comparing oppressions when our energies are better spent on analyzing "the U.S. imperial state, the production of poverty in the international political economy, and the failures of the interstate system of sovereign nations to sustain a world order based on respect for international human rights."[28] Do you agree? Or do you believe that we can engage in the broad critique of the U.S. as an imperial state and the racialized nature of the immigration system while simultaneously recognizing that the U.S. has treated black immigrant groups "the worst"?

4. Interestingly, some LatCrit scholars have offered careful defenses of the black-white paradigm and the black exceptionalism that might be the logical conclusion of the paradigm. Consider the following:

> [While LatCrit] was itself born of the critical need to move beyond the essentialism of the Black/White paradigm toward a more inclusive theoretical framework that focuses, broadly and comprehensively, on the way the institutionalization and cultural performance of white supremacy affect *all* peoples of color, though in different ways, still the political impact of uncritically abandoning the Black/White paradigm would be indefensibly regressive. . . . If LatCrit theory were to abandon uncritically the Black/White paradigm, it would marginalize a substantial portion of the Latina/o community and betray our aspirations to substantive intergroup justice. Thus, the objective must be to move our understanding of white supremacy progressively beyond the Black/White binary of race, even as we acknowledge the particular and virulent forms of anti-Black racism that are

[28] Iglesias, *supra* note 1, at 600.

> institutionalized and expressed in virtually every society across the globe, including Latina/o communities. Doing so requires that we center the particularities of Black subordination long enough to recognize the way anti-Black racism operates in Latina/o communities and the way the struggles of Black peoples, who are not Latina/o, are also implicated in the LatCrit project.[29]

What do you think of this defense of the black-white paradigm? Do we need the black-white paradigm in order to acknowledge "the particular and virulent forms of anti-Black racism that are institutionalized and expressed in virtually every society across the globe"? Is this acknowledgement important? Why or why not?

5. One issue with understanding LatCrit as an analytical approach that is distinct from CRT, as opposed to as a genre of scholarship that falls within the umbrella project of CRT, is that it may lead to the conclusion that the limitations that characterized CRT before the LatCrit intervention have not been rectified within CRT. If so, then CRT remains a theory that continues to embrace the black-white paradigm and an understanding of race as physical difference; LatCrit, on the other hand, would be the theory that thinks outside of the black-white paradigm and that rejects narrow definitions of race that center physical difference. In truth, however, the critical race theorist who embraces the black-white paradigm and a narrow definition of race is a rarity. Which is to say: CRT has taken the LatCrit critique to heart.

Thus, if LatCrit is distinct from CRT, then the distinction is not in the way that the two approaches conceptualize race, racism, and racial subordination. Neither would the distinction be found in the groups that are the subjects of the scholarship: many self-identified critical race theorists analyze the experiences of Latinx, indigenous, and Asian peoples, just as many self-proclaimed LatCrit theorists analyze the experiences of Asian, black, and indigenous peoples. Thus, it may be difficult to discern a distinction—at least, not one that matters—between CRT and LatCrit.

What do you think is at stake in the question of whether CRT and LatCrit are distinct theoretical frameworks? Do you think that it is important to answer the question definitively?

---

[29] *Id.* at 623–24.

Chapter 5

OTHER CRITS

Critical Race Theory has sparked the development of several other critical approaches to thinking about law. Like LatCrit, many of these "other crits" emerged as responses to early CRT's exclusive focus on the subordination of black people in the U.S.

The question that Chapter 4 raises about whether we ought to understand LatCrit to be analytically distinct from CRT is also relevant here. That is, there might be uncertainty about whether the "other crits" that this chapter explores are genres within CRT or, alternately, are distinct intellectual formations and scholarly movements. The former might be the better answer. This is simply because CRT is not a static entity. It can evolve, and it can rectify the oversights and omissions that were part of the theory at its inception. Accordingly, we might understand these "other crits" to be corrections to the myopia that once characterized CRT. If so, then APACrit, QueerCrit, TribalCrit, ClassCrit, DisCrit, and Critical Race Feminism ought to be thought of as specific areas of emphasis within the larger CRT project—as opposed to theories that were merely inspired by, and are now separate from, CRT.

I. APACrit

As LatCrit coalesced in response to the failure of early CRT to include Latinx people within its analyses of race and racism, Asian Pacific American Critical Race Theory, or APACrit, coalesced in response to the failure of early CRT to analyze the experiences of Asian and Asian American people with racial power in the United States. APACrit interrogates the racial marginalization that persons of Asian descent have endured. As explained by Robert Chang, who first outlined the contours of a program for using a critical lens to investigate Asian Americans' lives within the law, the discrimination that has been directed at Asian Americans in the past and in the present is "quantitatively and quantitatively different from that suffered by other disempowered groups."[1] If true, then it might be productive to study the particularities of this discrimination. This is what APACrit sets out to do. APACrit proposes that this endeavor reveals things not only about Asian Americans, but also about race, the nation, the "rule of law," and white domination, more generally.

---

[1] ROBERT S. CHANG, DISORIENTED: ASIAN AMERICANS, LAW, AND THE NATION-STATE 45 (1999).

For example, APACrit scholars have offered incisive analyses of the internment of people of Japanese descent during World War II. Gil Gott has observed that we tend to believe that there is a dichotomy between the domestic and the international.[2] In Gott's analysis, the domestic is imagined to be the site of the rule of law—a place where the Constitution constrains the state. The international, on the other hand, is imagined to be the site of impunity and raw power. While this dichotomy may be bad for those unfortunate enough to reside in the international realm (i.e., "foreigners" might find themselves subjected to unrestrained power), it is comforting for those residing in the domestic realm. But, what happens when the international sphere infiltrates the domestic sphere? What happens when "foreigners" manage to penetrate the nation's border? Gott answers that unrestricted, lawless power reigns down upon them. This was the Japanese internment.

Gott suggests that the idea and practice of "national security," wherein the state is empowered to protect its citizens from "foreign" threats, destabilizes the dichotomy between the international and the domestic. "National security" enables the state to deploy lawless power domestically at any time. This might be especially ominous for nonwhite people. Writes Elizabeth Iglesias, "The vulnerability of domestic minorities is particularly apparent given the fact that race and 'foreignness' are so easily conflated in the master narratives of white supremacy."[3] However, it might also be true that one need not be nonwhite to figure as a "foreign" threat. Continues Iglesias:

> [T]hough race is certainly a central feature of the conjured enemy, national security ideology makes an enemy of anyone who resists the dominant structure of privilege and power. The ensuing violations of basic civil rights and otherwise fundamental legal norms are then justified through a totalitarian logic in which the struggle for social justice and political change is recoded and attributed to 'subversive elements' whose subversiveness constitutes a threat so overwhelming it cannot be stopped unless basic rights are suspended or fundamental legal norms violated.[4]

Thus, organizers of social movements, the poor, and political activists might all feel the brunt of lawless power if the state can be

---

[2] Gil Gott, *A Tale of New Precedents: Japanese-American Internment as Foreign Affairs Law*, 19, B.C. THIRD WORLD L.J. 179 (1998).

[3] Elizabeth M. Iglesias, *Out of the Shadow: Marking Intersections in and Between Asian Pacific American Critical Legal Scholarship and Latina/o Critical Legal Theory*, 19, B.C. THIRD WORLD L.J. 349, 361 (1998).

[4] *Id.* at 367.

build a plausible case that it is acting in the interests of "national security."

APACrit has also offered trenchant analyses of the U.S.'s immigration policies with respect to persons of Asian descent. For most of the country's history, the law explicitly provided that only "white persons" could naturalize as citizens of the United States.[5] In *Ozawa v. United States*[6] and *United States v. Thind*,[7] the Supreme Court determined that people of Asian descent were not "white persons" within the meaning of the law. As such, Asian people were precluded from becoming citizens of the United States. Then, in 1924, Congress passed a law that prohibited "persons ineligible for citizenship" from immigrating to the United States.[8] Thus, Asian people were not only *politically* excluded from the nation (inasmuch as they could not become citizens), they were also *physically* excluded from the nation (inasmuch as they could not even immigrate to the country).

APACrit has taken Asian people's political and physical exclusion from the U.S. to be more than an interesting, albeit unfortunate, historical fact. Instead, they propose that it reveals a fundamental characteristic about the country: race is inextricably interwoven into the nation-state. To be more precise, APACrit argues that the U.S. nation-state is white. The political and physical exclusion of Asians as a racialized Other functioned to produce and sustain the whiteness of the nation-state. Precluding Asians—a "foreign," nonwhite Other—from being a part of the U.S. constructed the U.S. as *not* Asian," *not* "foreign," and, most importantly, *not* "nonwhite." APACrit proposes that ignoring the particularity of Asian Americans' encounter with racial power in the United States may prevent us from seeing the racialized character of the nation-state.

Indeed, APACrit insists upon the consideration of the "unique forms of exclusion and oppression" to which Asian Americans have been subjected.[9] One unique form of marginalization that Asian Americans have experienced is the "model minority" myth, which proclaims that people of Asian descent are ideal immigrants. The myth declaims that Asian immigrants work hard, possess unimpeachable values, persevere in the face of adversity, and refuse

---

[5] Naturalization Act of 1790, ch. 3, 1 Stat. 103 (repealed 1795). It was only in 1952 that all racial restrictions in naturalization were lifted.

[6] Ozawa v. United States, 260 U.S. 178 (1922).

[7] United States v. Thind, 261 U.S. 204 (1923).

[8] Immigration Act of 1924, Pub. L. No. 68-139, 43 Stat. 153 (current version at 8 U.S.C. ch. 12 (1952)).

[9] Robert S. Chang, *Toward an Asian American Legal Scholarship: Critical Race Theory, Post-Structuralism, and Narrative Space*, 81 CALIF. L. REV. 1241, 1251 (1993).

to accept assistance from the government. Their work ethic and value system lead them, as a group, to be highly successful—enjoying high income levels, high levels of education, and high rates of family stability.

At first blush, the model minority myth does not appear to be oppressive; indeed, it seems to be a compliment of the highest order. But, APACrit argues that it is insidious because it both "den[ies] the existence of present-day discrimination against Asian Americans and the present-day effects of past discrimination" and "legitimiz[es] the oppression of other racial minorities and poor whites."[10]

APACrit asserts that through the emphasis that it places on Asian Americans' success, the model minority myth disavows the reality of current discrimination and the significance of past discrimination. The myth encourages us to conceptualize any discrimination that people of Asian descent may have endured or presently endure as negligible. Consider that during the early twentieth century, many states prohibited "persons ineligible for citizenship"—which, as discussed above, included all persons of Asian descent—from owning property, working in certain professions, and sending their children to school with white children; the result of this was that Asian people in the country were "denied quintessential American rights."[11] The model minority myth renders this embarrassing period in American history an inconsequence. Similarly, the myth makes Japanese internment during World War II an irrelevance—just water under the bridge. If it was meaningful, asks the model minority myth, how could Asian Americans be more affluent and better educated than most other racial groups?

Further, APACrit insists that the model minority myth elides that not all Asian Americans are doing well. Specifically, disturbingly large numbers of people of Hmong, Laotian, and Cambodian descent live in extreme poverty and have low levels of education.[12] The model minority myth might completely blind us to the destitution and distress of these Asian groups.

APACrit argues that the myth of the model minority also serves to "legitimize the oppression of other racial minorities and poor whites" because it declares the truth of the proposition that with hard work and determination, anyone living in the U.S. can pull herself up by the bootstraps and achieve the American Dream. The myth might assert that those individuals and groups that have not

---

[10] *Id.* at 1260.

[11] *Id.* at 1293.

[12] Rebecca Y. Kim, *Ethnic Differences in Academic Achievement Between Vietnamese and Cambodian Children: Cultural and Structural Explanations*, 43 SOCIOLOGICAL Q. 213, 216 (2002).

achieved the American Dream have only themselves to blame; they need to work harder, revise their ethical codes, and refuse corruption in the form of public assistance and the other "crutches" that the welfare state offers. In this way, APACrit proposes, the model minority myth is a justification for state inaction in the realm of social services provision.

Finally, APACrit contends that the model minority myth makes Asian Americans into tools with which other less successful racial groups can be chastised, thus setting the stage for antagonisms between Asian Americans and other nonwhite racial groups. The myth also reveals that racial groups are not simply defined vis-à-vis white people; they are also defined vis-à-vis other nonwhite people. Black people are defined not only in relationship to white people, but also in relationship to Asian, indigenous, and Latinx people. Latinx people are defined not in relationship to white people, but also in relationship to black, Asian, and indigenous people. And so on and so forth. Thus, any theory of race that solely considers a group's relationship to white people misses something important. Ignoring the fact that a multiplicity of differently racialized groups has always coexisted in the U.S. and around the world is a recipe for an impoverished theory or race, racism, and racial inequality.

II. QueerCrit

As mentioned above, CRT's earliest attentions were on black people's experiences with racial power in the United States. Although this focus is already quite problematically narrow—rendering invisible nonblack racial minority groups—early CRT's analytical privileging of black Americans becomes even more troublesome when one considers the erasure of those black Americans who are not heterosexual and cisgender. In other words, early CRT paid little to no attention to queer people of color. As Francisco Valdes describes it, "CRT [had] at times appeared to assume that 'people of color' are congenitally heterosexual."[13] As a result, "[q]ueers of color [had] been virtually invisible in the written record of CRT during its first decade."[14] Valdes writes that this lapse diminished the potential of early CRT to be as transformative as it might have been. In this diminished form, early CRT became a theory that strived "to make the world safe for 'our' race (or ethnicity) instead of unsafe for oppression."[15]

---

[13] Francisco Valdes, *Afterword: Theorizing "OutCrit": Coalitional Method and Comparative Jurisprudential Experience—RaceCrits, QueerCrits and LatCrits*, 53 U. MIAMI L. REV. 1265, 1280 (1999) [hereinafter Valdes, *Afterword*].

[14] *Id.*

[15] *Id.* at 1281.

Some might believe that analyzing the racial experiences of only those people of color who enjoy privileges of sexual orientation and gender identity is no oversight at all. The position would be that theorizing the lives of gay, lesbian, bisexual, transgender, and nonbinary persons of color would allow us to understand how *heteronormativity* and *cisnormativity* operate to privilege some lives while constraining others; however, theorizing these queer lives would not provide insight into how *racism* and *racial power* operate to privilege some lives while constraining others. This position would argue that ignoring queer people of color still allows theorists to produce a complete account of racism in the U.S. or anywhere else.

However, those utilizing a QueerCrit framework would disagree. They argue that just as a person's racial identity and ascription shape the form that homophobia and cisnormativity take in his/her/their life, a person's status as gay, transgender, or nonbinary shapes the form that racism takes in his/her/their life. This is to say that all people of color do not experience racial unprivilege in the same way. Just as a class-privileged person of color will live racial disadvantage quite differently from a poor person of color, a sexual minority of color will live racial disadvantage quite differently from a heterosexual, cisgender person of color. For example, while racial power operates to push heterosexual, cisgender persons of color into homes that are less valuable than the ones owned by white persons of the same income level,[16] racial power operates to push transgender persons of color into homelessness—thereby making them vulnerable to the violence that frequently follows that status.[17] QueerCrit argues that in order to develop a truly complete account of the myriad forms that racial disadvantage takes—and, as such, to develop a total theory of race, racism, and racial inequality—one has to account for and theorize the lives of queer people of color.

QueerCrit considers itself to be as much of a corrective to scholars of race as it has been to scholars of sexual orientation and gender identity. In the late 1970s and early 1980s, when legal academics were beginning to take up questions of sexual orientation,[18] these thinkers largely omitted queer people of color

---

16 John E. Farley, *Race, Not Class: Explaining Racial Housing Segregation in the St. Louis Metropolitan Area*, 38 SOCIOLOGICAL FOCUS 133, 147 (2000).

17 *Violence Against the Transgender Community in 2017,* HUMAN RIGHTS CAMPAIGN, http://www.hrc.org/resources/violence-against-the-transgender-community-in-2017 (last visited Sept. 21, 2018).

18 It would be inaccurate to say that legal academics began to take up questions of gender identity alongside questions of sexual orientation in the late 1990s. Transgender persons remained invisible within legal academic scholarship during this time—even while the legal status of gay, lesbian, and bisexual individuals was becoming legible within the pages of law reviews and at scholarly conferences.

from their inquiries. Writes Valdes, "[I]t was possible to read sexual orientation legal scholarship and walk away from that effort thinking that race, ethnicity, class, religion and other markers of identity and opportunity were marginal, if not irrelevant, to sexual minority lives. It was possible, for the most part, to assume that the heterogeneous sexual minority population was comprised substantially of male, affluent WASPs; it was possible to conclude mistakenly that all was well in the lives of this nation's nonheterosexual population but for the exception of majoritarian sexual orientation bias."[19] However, Valdes contends, many sexual minorities struggle beneath the weight of not only homophobia and transphobia, but also "racism, sexism, poverty, and other blights that have yet to be engaged in a sustained and critical way either by the legal academy or the nation's governing elites."[20] QueerCrit argues that this omission makes incomplete any analysis that scholars interested in questions of sexual orientation and gender identity could offer. In its view, the erasure of queer persons of color does not allow us to see how sexual orientation bias constrains the lives of sexual minorities; it only allows us to see how sexual orientation bias constrains the lives of Christian sexual minorities with class, race, gender, and citizenship privilege. The erasure of queer persons of color does not generate theories of how homophobia operates, but rather generates theories of how homophobia operates in the lives of affluent, gay, Christian, white, male citizens.

Thus, QueerCrit does not imagine itself to be against *discrimination* on the basis of sexual orientation or gender identity; it imagines itself to be against *subordination* on any basis. As such, to write within the QueerCrit framework means to center the lives of queer people of color—as varied as they are—in order to produce scholarship that challenges racism, classism, sexism, ableism, and xenophobia as vigorously as it challenges heteronormativity and cisnormativity.

III. TribalCrit

Tribal Critical Race Theory, or TribalCrit, is a theoretical framework that centers indigenous persons and communities in the analysis of racial power in the United States. TribalCrit builds on the CRT proposition that racism is a ubiquitous, unexceptional, and banal feature of American life by proposing that *colonialism* is a ubiquitous, unexceptional, and banal feature of American life.

We might ask whether transgender persons are visible within legal academic scholarship at present and, if not, why.

[19] Francisco Valdes, *Beyond Sexual Orientation in Queer Legal Theory: Majoritarianism, Multidimensionality and Responsibility in Social Justice Scholarship*, 75 DENV. U. L. REV. 1409, 1417 (1998).

[20] *Id.* at 1418.

TribalCrit defines colonialism as the practice of imposing outsider "thought, knowledge, and power structures" onto a dominated group.[21] Thus, TribalCrit investigates spectacular examples from history of white colonization of indigenous peoples, and it interrogates how those practices continue today in subtler, less conspicuous forms.

TribalCrit proposes that the education of indigenous children is a domain in which one can observe colonialism in its more modern iterations. It argues that when schools explicitly or implicitly transmit the "lesson" that western ways of thinking and living are morally and intellectually superior to their indigenous counterparts, we witness colonialism in an understated, but nevertheless devastating, form. Thus, TribalCrit condemns educational institutions in the United States for largely proceeding from the assumption that indigenous students ought to assimilate into the western society that exists outside of their tribal communities. The framework is committed to the idea that indigenous individuals ought to maintain an indigenous identity and, further, that this identity ought to be a source of strength and pride. Writes the architect of TribalCrit, Brian Brayboy, education "might also teach American Indian students how to combine Indigenous notions of culture, knowledge, and power with western/European conceptions in order to actively engage in survivance, self-determination, and tribal autonomy."[22] Thus, the goal of the TribalCrit paradigm is to imagine, and then implement, an educational system that protects the integrity of indigenous students' identities as indigenous while also exposing them to the most empowering aspects of western modes of thinking and doing.

As one might expect, race is significant in TribalCrit analyses. This is due to there being a tenacious relationship between racism and colonialism. TribalCrit observes that discourses about the racial inferiority of a colonized group have functioned to justify the group's colonization; indeed, colonialist governments have racialized populations *in order to* legitimate the practices that exploit and marginalize them.

However, TribalCrit reminds us that while racial discourses have played an important role in the colonization (and extermination) of indigenous peoples in the United States, indigenous peoples ought not to be conceptualized *solely* in racial terms. In truth, many tribes are also *political* entities.[23] Further,

---

[21] Bryan McKinley Jones Brayboy, *Toward a Tribal Critical Race Theory in Education*, 37 URB. REV. 425, 430 (2005).

[22] *Id.* at 437.

[23] Brayboy quotes an Executive Order issued by George W. Bush in 2004 that concisely describes indigenous people's political status:

critical thinkers warn that to ignore the political nature of these groups is dangerous in our current constitutional landscape, as this is a landscape wherein the judiciary presumes the unconstitutionality of all uses of race within law—even those uses that are designed to benefit historically disadvantaged racial groups. If indigenous people and communities are *only* racialized groups, then the federal programs that benefit them do not embody a special relationship between two sovereign governments, but rather are race-conscious efforts that likely run afoul of the Equal Protection Clause. Thus, TribalCrit emphasizes that indigenous peoples are as much political entities as they are racialized entities. Further, it endeavors to investigate how the political status of these individuals and groups impacts their racial status, and vice versa.

Finally, TribalCrit enthusiastically embraces the practice of storytelling, which many critical race theorists have employed in their scholarship. TribalCrit's particular affinity for storytelling is due to many indigenous communities having longstanding oral traditions. In these communities, stories are the repositories of the tribe's history, values, philosophies, practices, and worldviews, and storytelling is the means by which this knowledge is transmitted across generations. For this reason, TribalCrit rejects critiques of storytelling that denounce it as problematically unobjective, hopelessly unempirical, and altogether unrelated to reason and rationality.[24] Indeed, to dismiss storytelling as an illegitimate way of gathering information about the world or sharing knowledge with others is to declare a cultural practice embraced by many indigenous communities to be inferior to western ways of doing things. This is precisely what TribalCrit is reacting against in its critique of colonialism. As the framework rejects the idea that western approaches are necessarily superior to nonwestern approaches and, consequently, are appropriately imposed on dominated groups, it rejects the idea that western approaches to collecting and sharing knowledge are simply better than other means of doing the same. Brayboy writes, "TribalCrit recognizes that the statistical power of the 'n' is not necessarily the marker of a 'good, rigorous' study. Stories may also be informative of structural barriers or weaknesses. In this respect, 'proof' is thought of in different ways. Stories as 'data' are important, and one key to collecting these data is 'hearing' the

---

> The United States has a unique legal relationship with Indian tribes and a special relationship with Alaskan Native entities as provided in the Constitution of the United States, treaties, and federal statutes. This Administration is committed to continuing to work with these federally recognized tribal governments on a government-to-government basis, and supports tribal sovereignty and self-determination.

Quoted in id. at 433.

[24] See Chapter 3 for a discussion of critiques of storytelling in legal scholarship.

stories."[25] Thus, TribalCrit understands storytelling to be a valuable methodology for producing and disseminating knowledge, and it supports its use when theorizing the distinct experience of indigenous individuals and communities in the United States.

IV. ClassCrit

Like many of the other "crits" that this chapter describes, ClassCrit emerged in response to a perceived omission within CRT. As the name suggests, ClassCrit is a consequence of some self-identified critical race theorists' beliefs that the framework had largely failed to theorize class and the role that it plays in constituting and sustaining existing racial hierarchies. ClassCrit is a reaction to the reality that many critical race theorists conceptualize race as discourse: their work analyzes racial meanings that circulate in society and examines how law both reflects and perpetuates these ideas about race. Scholars writing from within the ClassCrit framework are much more interested in the material consequences of these racial ideas. They are attentive to how race subjects some to the most vicious of poverties while facilitating others' access to extravagant wealth—all while portraying the resulting economic and racial hierarchies as natural and inevitable.

ClassCrit theorists propose that the failure to investigate class is more than a harmless oversight. On the contrary, they propose that the failure to put class under the most rigorous of analyses makes it less likely that those who are interested in racial justice will be able to fully understand existing racial injustices; as a result, it makes it less likely that these scholars and activists will be able to produce the world about which they dream. According to ClassCrit, racial hierarchies will not be dismantled without also dismantling the structures that create and sustain class stratification. And the reverse is also true: the structures that create and sustain class stratification will not be dismantled without also dismantling race. As one of the primary architects of ClassCrit, Athena Mutua, writes, "it [is] not clear that the economic harms of lower class suffering would be eliminated without addressing both the material and psychological seductions embodied and structured by race."[26]

Class Crit proposes that class inequality and racial inequality are mutually constitutive. Thus, to conceptualize racial inequality apart from class inequality is to misapprehend the nature of racial inequality. Mutua has cogently explained the interdependency of

---

[25] Brayboy, *supra* note 21, at 439–40.

[26] Athena D. Mutua, *Introducing ClassCrits: From Class Blindness to a Critical Legal Analysis of Economic Inequality*, 56 BUFF. L. REV. 859, 891 (2008).

race hierarchies and class hierarchies. She writes that race is "central to discussions and practices of class."

> [A]lthough both slavery and Jim Crow, as well as today's oppressive racial spatial isolation, were racial systems that oppressed and offended human dignity, they also were economic systems meant to facilitate the exploitation of black labor, to deny black material well-being, and to assist the few in hoarding the resources created by the many. This racial system relationally also privileges whiteness both materially and psychologically through the full range of social systems and institutions including the economy, political system, educational system, etc., setting up a hierarchy of the "races" that renders black racial identity, among others, a racial status within a caste-like system where large numbers of blacks are part of the working poor but in which almost all blacks, even those of the black middle class, are both materially and expressively subordinate.[27]

Also central to ClassCrit is the conviction that one will not understand economic inequality without also understanding the law. With this tenet, ClassCrit is reacting against a school of thought that avows that economic inequality is the result of natural differences among people. This school of thought claims that the more affluent among us have managed to accumulate their wealth because they are simply more talented, more hardworking, more virtuous, or simply luckier than the poor. Alternately, the affluent might be wealthy because they have pursued careers that society values more highly than the careers chosen by the poor. This understanding of economic inequality disavows that the law plays any role in facilitating the accumulation of wealth by some sectors of society and the destitution of other sectors of society.

ClassCrit believes this to be an inaccurate rendering of economic life. It posits instead that the law has shaped the circumstances whereby some individuals (and not others) are empowered to develop talents, work hard, be "virtuous," get lucky, and choose careers that society values. The law also acts to protect the wealth that some accumulate. (One might imagine a legal system that does not protect property rights, or that disallows some from accumulating more than what they need when others have none of what they need.) Further, the law acts by playing a discursive role; it provides a narrative that justifies the economic lay of the land. Writes Harris, "[L]egal rules and institutions serve a distinct ideological function in stabilizing liberal societies: making class relations and market institutions seem

27 *Id.* at 908.

natural, normal, and necessary."[28] Thus, according to ClassCrit, the law is an important actor in the economy, and one must understand it in order to understand economic inequality.

In this vein, ClassCrit rejects understandings of the market that imagine it to be a domain that exists entirely outside of the law. Within some philosophies, the market is nothing more than a constellation of individuals' tastes and preferences interacting with the availability of goods and services. However, this conception of the market elides that individuals' tastes and preferences—as well as the availability of goods and services—are artifacts of material circumstances. Further, the law has helped to shape those material circumstances. ClassCrit encourages us to recognize that the market is "subject to human agency"—the product "not just of supply and demand in the abstract, but of concrete political choices by groups of people, communities, etc., about production, distribution, and consumption."[29]

ClassCrit scholars have a vexed relationship to Marxism. On the one hand, they tend to embrace Marxist conceptions of class as *relational*. That is, Karl Marx emphasized the interdependent nature of classes—observing that the wealth of the more affluent classes depends on the poverty of the lower classes. More precisely, Marx observed that the poverty of the indigent *generates* the affluent classes' wealth. This is an observation with which ClassCrits wholeheartedly agree. Consequently, they find incomplete Max Weber-inspired understandings of class wherein there are differences between the middle-class and the upper-middle class, for example, but there are no antagonisms between the two. If the comfort of one class is fundamentally unrelated to the discomfort of another, then there is no reason for the two classes to be in conflict. On the contrary, scholars writing within the ClassCrit framework are sympathetic to Marxist theories which propose that "structured impoverishment . . . relates to structured privilege."[30] Thus, they analyze class as a site of inherent tension. Further, they understand that *all* of the parties involved in the conflict ought to be investigated. As such, ClassCrit rejects the idea that only the poor should be subjected to sustained analysis. It proceeds from the assumption that we can learn a lot about how economic power and disempowerment operates by also studying the wealthy and their "structured privilege."

---

[28] Angela P. Harris, *From Precarity to Positive Freedom: ClassCrits at Seven: Introduction*, 44 SW. L. REV. 621, 626 (2015).

[29] Mutua, *supra* note 26, at 868.

[30] *Id.* at 881.

While ClassCrit scholars accept Marxist notions of the relational nature of class, they are more skeptical of other claims that Marx made. For one, those writing within the ClassCrit framework tend to reject the *primacy* that Marx and his intellectual acolytes place on class. Specifically, Marxists tend to conceptualize everything as a function of class. Thus, religion is a function of class within vulgar Marxisms; it exists because it is an "opiate of the masses"—placating the proletariat and diminishing its resolve to rebel against the unjust systems that subordinate it on earth. Similarly, the law is a function of class within vulgar Marxisms; it exists in order to sustain structures of economic subordination and protect the property that the bourgeoisie comes to possess. And perhaps most provocatively, race is a function of class within vulgar Marxisms; it exists because racial divisions pit members of the proletariat against one another. Race prevents individuals who belong to the exploited class from seeing that they are similarly situated vis-à-vis the capitalist class; it prevents their recognition that the real enemy is not the racial other beside them, but rather the economic other above them.

Marxists' commitments to the primacy of class oftentimes leads them to believe that because institutions like religion—and identities like race—are simply epiphenomena of class, then dismantling class will lead to the dissolution of these institutions and identities. If true, then we do not *really* need to focus on race, as race is merely a symptom of a larger pathology. We ought to focus our energies, always and in every case, on class, as class is the real problem. According to this species of Marxism, solving our class problem will solve our race problem (as well as all of our other problems). ClassCrit rejects this variety of Marxist thought. Writes Angela Harris, "ClassCrits scholars take the position that arguments about the primacy of class, race, or gender have been counterproductive; these dynamics are so enmeshed that they should be considered mutually constitutive."[31]

Additionally, many ClassCrit scholars are not interested in the wholesale overthrow of capitalism.[32] While Marx saw socialism as the end towards which the world's economic systems desirably moved, ClassCrit scholars are not uniformly committed to that proposition. Instead, many of them are committed to *more just*

[31] Harris, *supra* note 28, at 625.

[32] This is not to say that *some* ClassCrit are not interested in ridding the world of capitalism. Like critical thinkers about race more generally, ClassCrit theorists are heterogeneous. While some writing within the framework would like to see the defeat of capitalism—believing that justice cannot exist within capitalist economic systems—others simply want to eliminate the more exploitative and excessive aspects of capitalism. Thus, revolutionaries and reformists alike have found an intellectual home in ClassCrit.

capitalist formations—not the absence of these formations altogether.

V. DisCrit

Dis/ability Critical Race Studies, or DisCrit, might be understood as a race intervention into disability studies and a disability intervention into race studies. With respect to the first term, the architects of DisCrit observed that much of the scholarship around disability had failed to interrogate race and the role that it plays in 1) how we come to define disability and 2) the choices that we make about how to treat those we have defined as having a disability. With respect to the second term, the DisCrit architects observed that thinkers about race have ignored the intersection of race and disability. DisCrit scholars argue that this is an unfortunate lacuna in race scholarship, as race and disability have always been intricately intertwined.

While the historical and present interrelationship of race and disability will be explored more expansively in Chapter 15, we will simply note here the DisCrit observation that disabled persons of color are embodiments of intersectionality. Critical race theorist Kimberle Crenshaw offered the concept of intersectionality to refer to some individuals experiencing disadvantage on account of several axes of their identity.[33] The case that Crenshaw used to introduce the concept was the black woman. She argued that black women are unprivileged by virtue of both their sex and their race. Thus, they are marginalized more than black men (who are unprivileged by virtue of race, but privileged by virtue of sex) and white women (who are unprivileged by virtue of sex, but privileged by virtue of race). Intersectionality means that, as women, black women have different experiences of racism than black men; and as black people, they have different experiences of sexism than white women. DisCrit observes an analogue in the experiences of disabled persons of color. They are marginalized more than disabled white people (who are unprivileged by virtue of ability, but privileged by virtue of their race) and non-disabled people of color (who are unprivileged by virtue of race, but privileged by virtue of ability). Accordingly, disabled people of color have different experiences of ableism than disabled white people, and they have different experiences of racism than non-disabled people of color. If true, then in order to develop a *complete* understanding of ableism, one has to analyze the lives of disabled people of color. Likewise, in order to develop a *complete* understanding of racism, then the experiences that disabled people of color have with racial power ought to be considered.

---

[33] The concept of intersectionality will be explored more extensively in Chapter 12.

The architects of DisCrit originally applied the theory to the field of education, inviting scholars to interrogate "the ways in which race, racism, dis/ability, and ableism are built into the interactions, procedures, and institutions of education, which affect students of color with dis/abilities qualitatively differently than white students with dis/abilities."[34] However, there is nothing that prevents DisCrit from being used to investigate other arenas and institutions. One can easily imagine DisCrit explorations of prisons, hospitals, the economy, the family, and religion.

VI. Critical Race Feminism

Adrien Katherine Wing explains that the name *Critical Race Feminism* brings together the multiple intellectual formations that informed the framework: Critical Legal Studies, Critical Race Theory, and feminist jurisprudence.[35] As this might suggest, Critical Race Feminism, or CRF, uses a critical lens to examine the lives of women of color, specifically focusing on the law's role in mitigating, perpetuating, or exacerbating their marginalization. CRF is also pointedly global in scope—theorizing the experiences of women of color outside of the United States as thoroughly as it theorizes the experiences of women of color living within the nation's borders.

As mentioned above, Crenshaw offered the concept of intersectionality to describe how individuals are multiply disadvantaged (or multiply advantaged) on account of different axes of their identity. And while men are appropriately theorized within the intersectionality framework—that is, men have intersectional identities too, although one of their axes of identity (their sex) is a privileged one—it is also true that intersectionality has come to be identified as a theory that is "about" women of color.[36] As such, CRF might be understood as an anthology of intersectional scholarship—a body of work that deploys Crenshaw's theoretical intervention to analyze the lives of women of color in domestic and international contexts. As Wing describes it, "[E]xisting legal paradigms under US, foreign, and international law have permitted women of colour to fall between the cracks—becoming literally and figuratively voiceless and invisible. [CRF] attempts to not only identify and theorise about

---

[34] Subini Ancy Annamma, David J. Connor & Beth A. Ferri, *Dis/ability Critical Race Studies (DisCrit): Theorizing at the Intersections of Race and Dis/ability*, *in* DISCRIT: DISABILITY STUDIES AND CRITICAL RACE THEORY IN EDUCATION 9, 14 (David J. Connor, Beth A. Ferri & Subini A. Annamma eds., 2016).

[35] Adrien Katherine Wing, *Global Critical Race Feminism: Legal Reform for the Twenty-First Century*, 34 DE JURE 446 (2001) [hereinafter Wing, *Global Critical Race Feminism*].

[36] This is, in large part, because Crenshaw first offered the theory to critique black women's simultaneous erasure from feminist movements and movements against racism. Because intersectionality was introduced as a project to make women of color visible, it has come to be associated with women of color.

those cracks in the legal regime, but to formulate relevant solutions as well."[37]

It is worth emphasizing that it might be misguided to conceptualize CRF as a body of scholarship that is distinct from CRT. Crenshaw—who is one of several scholars who launched CRT as a scholarly movement—offered the concept of intersectionality for many reasons, one of which was to illuminate the sexism of antiracist movements that did not consider women of color and their experiences with racism. Crenshaw's intervention worked to ensure that CRT would be an antiracist movement that did not repeat this error. In this way, intersectionality was not offered as a corrective to CRT; instead, it *is* CRT.[38] As a critical race theorist, Crenshaw's introduction of the concept of intersectionality ensured that CRT's antiracist efforts would be antisexist, as well.[39] Thus, if CRF is an anthology of intersectional feminism—and if intersectional feminism *is* CRT—then CRF is CRT. Thinking of CRF and CRT as separate might do an injustice to intersectionality's location within CRT.

However, CRF's insistence upon centering the lives of women of color who live outside of the United States might represent an important contribution to critical race scholarship, which we might still accuse of problematically analyzing the domestic context to the exclusion of everything else.[40] CRF has observed that women of color in other nations often exist in a fraught position, subordinated by both the forces of globalization as well as the local society that globalization disrupts. As Wing describes it:

> Women of colour may be simultaneously dominated within the context of imperialism, neo-colonialism or occupation as well as local patriarchy, culture and customs. They have often had to choose between the nationalist struggle for independence or self-determination and the women's

---

[37] Wing, *Global Critical Race Feminism*, *supra* note 35, at 447.

[38] This is a claim that Wing would dispute, as she has written that CRF is "a feminist intervention within CRT." Adrien Katherine Wing, *Introduction: Global Critical Race Feminism for the Twenty-First Century*, *in* GLOBAL CRITICAL RACE FEMINISM: AN INTERNATIONAL READER 1, 12 (Adrien Katherine Wing ed., 2000) [hereinafter Wing, *Introduction*]. CRF can only be a feminist intervention into CRT if, at some point in its history, CRT had failed to consider sex and gender. This might inaccurately describe CRT.

[39] This account departs from the one that Wing and Christine Willis offer. They write that "critical race theory . . . often assumes that the experiences of women of color are the same as that of men of color." Adrien K. Wing & Christine A. Willis, *From Theory to Praxix: Black Women, Gangs, and Critical Race Feminism*, 4 AFR.-AM. L. & POL'Y REP. 1, 3 (1999).

[40] This statement is only true if LatCrit—which conceptualizes the theorization of non-domestic contexts as central to its approach—is analytically distinct from CRT. If LatCrit is CRT, then it is incorrect to describe CRT as provincially focused on the United States. For a discussion of the ambiguous relationship between LatCrit and CRT, please see chapter 4.

> struggle against patriarchy. The nationalist struggle usually has prevailed and the women who have just helped throw off the yoke of outsider oppression have then been forced back into the "women's work" of taking care of the house and the children. Open acceptance of feminism can be seen as an unpatriotic embrace of western values that may be regarded as inimical to local culture.[41]

Thus, CRF offers insightful analyses of the "complex interrelationships between feminist, antiracist, and nationalist struggles"[42] and women's careful negotiation of the loyalties that have been made to compete against one another.

VII. Questions and Discussion

1. Valdes has argued that homophobia plays some role in the erasure of queer people of color from early CRT. He writes that the failure of early CRT to consider the lives of LGBTQ individuals of color "no doubt is due at least in part[ ] to the culture of constant homophobia that envelops us all, inducing uncritical (even if unintentional) replication of straight privilege within CRT and other outgroup venues at different times and places."[43] Interestingly, queer people of color were involved in the creation of CRT. Is it fair to describe these individuals as infected with homophobia as well? What might explain these individuals' refusal (or inability) to foreground their experiences with racial power and their failure (or inability) to insist that those experiences are integral to understanding how racial power operates?

2. Many have argued that the prioritization of marriage equality by LGBTQ advocacy organizations is a direct consequence of the absence or erasure of queer people of color within these organizations. For example, Russell Robinson has noted critiques of the marriage equality movement that sound in this register. He observes the argument that "[w]ealthy white males dominate the gay rights agenda, which prioritizes rights that are most meaningful for people who are middle or upper class and neglects the discrimination faced by poorer LGBT people, such as in the contexts of immigration and mass incarceration."[44] Many activists agree, arguing that "marriage is not even a first step for addressing the needs of queer

---

[41] Wing, *Introduction*, *supra* note 38, at 12.

[42] *Id.*

[43] Valdes, *Afterword*, *supra* note 13, at 1281.

[44] Russell K. Robinson, *Marriage Equality and Postracialism*, 61 UCLA L. REV. 1010, 1038 (2014).

people."[45] This perspective argues that the energies of the LGBTQ community are better spent working to produce change that could make the lives of the most marginalized sexual minorities less precarious. Given the tragic vulnerability of many poor black and Latinx LGBT persons, and given the likelihood that marriage equality will do nothing to change their desperate circumstances, these voices argue that fighting for the right to marry is an exorbitant luxury—a disastrous waste of resources.

Do you agree? Do you believe that even the most marginalized LGBTQ persons benefit from the legalization of same-sex marriage? If so, how? If not, do you believe that marriage equality advocates ought not to have fought as hard as they did for the right to marry?

3. It is likely that early CRT's failure to interrogate the experiences of racial minorities who were not black Americans disallowed it from developing a complete understanding of the racial subordination of *black Americans*. For example, in taking no notice of indigenous persons, early CRT neglected to develop a critical understanding of colonialism. However, through its centering of indigenous subjects, TribalCrit has developed a rich comprehension of the practice. This deep knowledge of colonialist practices, and a cultivated awareness of the varied forms that colonialism has taken, may actually generate insights about black Americans' experiences in the United States. That is, TribalCrit encourages us to ask questions like: how have black Americans been colonized? How has their colonization been different from indigenous peoples? How has it been similar?

Do you think that colonization is a helpful framework for thinking about black Americans' experiences in the country? How might the framework be harmful?

4. What are your thoughts on the model minority myth? In what ways might the model minority myth be helpful to people of Asian descent living in the United States? In what ways might it be harmful *even to those Asian groups that are successful in terms of income and education*?

5. Iglesias has written that "[t]he plight of Japanese Americans interned during WWII is just one example of the way inter-state conflicts have, throughout this country's history, been articulated in the configuration of domestic repression, the activation of racialized public discourses and the ebb and flow of race hate crimes."[46] Do you find this framework helpful for thinking about

---

[45] Marlon M. Bailey, Priya Kandaswamy & Mattie Udora Richardson, *Is Gay Marriage Racist?*, *in* THAT'S REVOLTING!: QUEER STRATEGIES FOR RESISTING ASSIMILATION 113, 119 (Mattilda Bernstein Sycamore ed., 2008).

[46] Iglesias, *supra* note 3, at 363.

Donald Trump's campaign promises to ban Muslim immigrants from the United States and to require the registration of Muslim individuals already present within the country? Why or why not?

Part II
CORE CONCEPTS

Chapter 6

THE LEGAL CONSTRUCTION OF RACE

One of the cardinal tenets of Critical Race Theory is that race is a social construction and, further, the law plays a vital role in constructing race. But, what exactly does that mean? This chapter unpacks this truism of CRT.

I. Race as a Biological Entity

To say that race is socially constructed is to deny that the races that we speak about (i.e., black, white, Asian, etc.) are "natural," genetically-determined things that preexist human interaction. The latter is the idea of biological race, a concept with origins in the sixteenth century, when Europeans first arrived on the African continent.[1] By the mid-eighteenth century, various thinkers in Europe had formulated their own schematizations of race. While these theorists often disagreed about the names and number of the races, they agreed with one another insofar as they all assumed that biology distinguished the races that they identified.

The concept of biological race has been the logic behind many social tragedies. The eugenics movement in the U.S. is a case in point. This movement was informed by the idea that characteristics such as "intelligence, 'feeble-mindedness,' criminality, alcoholism, [and] pauperism" were genetically determined.[2] Eugenicists sought to prevent the dissemination of the genes that purportedly determined these traits and behaviors through efforts such as immigration restrictions, anti-miscegenation laws, and forced sterilizations. Moreover, nonwhite racial groups were on the receiving end of many eugenic policies, as the racial "scientists" of the day were confident that the genes that led to antisocial characteristics were disproportionately found in nonwhite races.

The idea that race is a socially constructed entity, and not a biological one, began to gain wide acceptance in the 1940s, when the Holocaust demonstrated one of the most ghastly, but logical, consequences of the concept of biological race.[3] By 1951, the United Nations Educational, Scientific, and Cultural Organization

---

1 *See, e.g.*, WINTHROP D. JORDAN, WHITE OVER BLACK: AMERICAN ATTITUDES TOWARD THE NEGRO 1550–1812 (1968) [hereinafter JORDAN, WHITE OVER BLACK].

2 Garland E. Allen, *Eugenics and Modern Biology: Critiques of Eugenics, 1910–1945*, 75 ANN. HUM. GENET. 314, 314 (2011).

3 *See* AM. ANTHROPOLOGICAL ASS'N, STATEMENT ON 'RACE' (May 17, 1998), http://www.aaanet.org/stmts/racepp.htm (last visited July 20, 2018).

(UNESCO) was so certain that biological race is a fiction that it issued a "Statement on Race" declaring that race "is not so much a biological phenomenon as it is a social myth."[4] The American Anthropological Association (AAA) issued yet another "Statement on Race" in 1998, reaffirming what, by then, was close to becoming an indisputable truism: race is a social construction.[5] The AAA spoke unambiguously for the discipline:

> In the United States both scholars and the general public have been conditioned to viewing human races as natural and separate divisions within the human species based on visible physical differences. With the vast expansion of scientific knowledge in this century, however, it has become clear that human populations are not unambiguous, clearly demarcated, biologically distinct groups.[6]

That biological race is a fiction appeared to receive its ultimate, and most unanswerable, verification with the Human Genome Project's revelation in 2003 that all persons, irrespective of racial ascription or identification, share 99.9% of the same genes.[7] Indeed, one of the Human Genome Project's definitive conclusions was that humans could not be divided into coherent, discrete biological races. The death of biological race was announced in optimistic statements, including then-president Bill Clinton's affirmation that "one of the great truths to emerge from this triumphant expedition inside the human genome is that in genetic terms, all human beings, regardless of race, are more than 99.9 percent the same."[8]

But, like a zombie, biological race rose from the dead as observers turned their attention to the 0.1% of genes that all humans do not share. Specifically, biological race devotees began asserting that the 0.1% of genetic difference was meaningful in explaining health outcomes among differently raced individuals. Paradigmatic of this phenomenon is psychiatrist Sally Satel's *New York Times* article, salaciously titled "I Am a Racially Profiling Doctor."[9] In it, she wrote, "In practicing medicine, I am not colorblind. I always take note of my patient's race. So do many of my colleagues. We do it because certain diseases and treatment responses cluster by

---

[4] ASHLEY MONTAGU, STATEMENT ON RACE: AN EXTENDED DISCUSSION IN PLAIN LANGUAGE OF THE UNESCO STATEMENT BY EXPERTS ON RACE PROBLEMS 15 (1951).

[5] *See* AM. ANTHROPOLOGICAL ASS'N, *supra* note 3.

[6] *Id.*

[7] DOROTHY ROBERTS, FATAL INVENTION: HOW SCIENCE, POLITICS, AND BUSINESS RE-CREATE RACE IN THE TWENTY-FIRST CENTURY 49 (2012).

[8] *Id.*

[9] Sally Satel, *I Am a Racially Profiling Doctor*, N.Y. TIMES (May 5, 2002), https://www.nytimes.com/2002/05/05/magazine/i-am-a-racially-profiling-doctor.html.

ethnicity. . . . It may seem counterintuitive, but the 0.1 percent of human genetic variation is a medically meaningful fact."[10]

Those who insist that race is a social construction—a group that includes social scientists and social theorists as well as those working in the "hard" sciences, like population geneticists, medical doctors, and health sciences researchers—respond to arguments like Satel's by disputing that the 0.1% of genetic difference proves the existence of biological race. They look to science that demonstrates that it is simply not true that two unrelated people of the same race share more of the same genes than two unrelated people of different races. They explain that the 0.1% of genetic difference among humans does not function to divide the inhabitants of the globe into four or five discrete races. Instead, they assert, the 0.1% difference is spread across the globe in a spectrum—making the demarcation of the human population into four or five (or more, or fewer) races an exercise in arbitrariness.[11]

The modern form of the argument that race is a biological entity usually does not appear as an assertion that there are "black genes," "white genes," "Asian genes," etc. that demarcate the races. Instead, it usually appears as a declaration that race is a useful indicator of a person's genetic composition. This assertion is grounded in the fact (which few challenge) that some genes are traceable to specific geographic locations. That is, there may be genes that are "from" a particular location on the Arab Peninsula; other genes might be "from" another site in present-day Turkey. The traceability of genes to particular geographic locations results when many members of an ancestral group that lived in a location possessed a gene. A gene would become frequent among group members when they tended to reproduce with other group members, a practice known as endogamy. The geographic locations in which these endogamous ancestral groups, called *populations*, lived are the sites where certain genes are "from." If an individual's ancestors hailed from those places, then there is an increased chance that the individual will possess the genes found in the population that once resided there. This is the concept of geographic ancestry. The declaration that race is a useful indicator of a person's genetic composition—the modern form of the biological race concept—presupposes that race is a proxy for an individual's geographic ancestry and, accordingly, indicates the populations from which an individual hails. It presupposes that black people are more likely to possess a gene because they are descendants

---

[10] *Id.*

[11] *See* Deborah A. Bolnick, *Individual Ancestry Inference and the Reification of Race as a Biological Phenomenon*, *in* REVISITING RACE IN A GENOMIC AGE 70, 72 (Barbara A. Koenig et al. eds., 2008) ("Allele frequencies change gradually across geographic space, with few sharp discontinuities.").

of populations that resided in Africa; white people are more likely to possess a gene because they are descendants of populations that resided in Europe; and so on and so forth.

Yet, the problem with extrapolating the truth of geographic ancestry into the notion of biological race, say those who believe that race is a social construction, is that it is inaccurate to assume that genes that can be traced to regions in Africa can only be found in black people, and that genes that can be traced to regions in Europe can only be found in white people, and so on. In other words, *races are not populations*. Dorothy Roberts explains:

> If you look at a map of the world, you will see that parts of Africa are very close to Europe and the Middle East and other parts are very far from these regions. Because they are closer to the Arab Peninsula, African Somalis are genetically more similar to people in Saudi Arabia than they are to people in western or southern Africa.[12]

Accordingly, a gene that traces to the Arab Peninsula may be found in the descendant of a Somali (who, according to popular racial logic, is usually identified as a black person) and in the descendant of a Saudi (who, according to popular racial logic, is usually *not* identified as a black person). Roberts goes on: "The same is true for Europe and Asia. . . . Europe occupies the same land mass as Asia. England is much closer to Turkey, the nation seen as bridging the two continents, than it is to the eastern edge of Russia. Most of Russia is much closer to China than it is to Germany."[13] Accordingly, a gene that traces to Turkey may be found in the descendant of a Russian person (who is likely to be identified as white) and in the descendant of a Chinese person (who is likely to be identified as Asian). In short, geographic ancestry, say adherents of the notion that race is a social construction, does not prove the biological or genetic coherence of the racial groups that exist in our racial schemas.

Moreover, it is important to note that it is not at all rare for a white person to possess genes that can be traced to regions in Africa and for a black person to possess genes that can be traced to regions in Europe. Indeed, this is a rather commonplace occurrence. "Studies have shown that . . . a person whose skin color is perceived as white can have eighty percent recent West African ancestry, while a person whose skin color is perceived as black can have a predominance of alleles that indicate European ancestry."[14]

---

[12] ROBERTS, *supra* note 7, at 74–75.

[13] *Id.* at 75.

[14] Kimani Paul-Emile, *The Regulation of Race in Science*, 80 GEO. WASH. L. REV. 1115, 1137 (2012).

Biological race devotees may respond by observing that there are variations in the rates by which racial groups possess certain genes. For example, black people may be twice as likely to possess a gene as, say, white or Asian people. The conclusion that may be drawn from this observation is that it makes sense to define biological race as these statistically significant variations in the rates by which racial groups possess certain genes. However, persons committed to the idea that race is a social construction respond by pointing out that

> [i]t is possible to make arbitrary groupings of populations (geographic, linguistic, self-identified by faith, identified by others by physiognomy, etc.) and still find statistically significant allelic variations between these groupings. For example, we could examine all the people in Chicago, and all those in Los Angeles, and find statistically significant differences in allele frequency at *some* loci. Of course, at many loci, even at most loci, we would not find statistically significant differences.[15]

It is stating the obvious, say social constructionists, that these genetic variations do not make genetic entities out of "Chicagoan" and "Angeleno." Building on this insight, Jonathan Kahn notes, "Given that researchers may find differences in allele frequencies between Chicagoans and Los Angelinos, it is hardly surprising that they may find differences between groups somehow marked as 'Black,' 'White,' or 'Asian.' "[16] Considering that there likely are variations in the rates by which Chicagoans and Angelenos possess certain genes, why make "Black," "White," and "Asian" the stuff of biological race, but not make "Chicagoan" and "Angeleno" racial categories? The answer, argues Kahn and others, has nothing to do with biology or genetics, but everything to do with our socially constructed ideas about race.

II. Race as a Social Construction

If a race is not a grouping of humans who are genetically or biologically similar, then what *is* race? How do we define race beyond the simple assertion that "race is a social construction"? Ian Haney López, who has done extensive work in this area, has provided a particularly insightful definition, offering that race is "historically contingent systems of meaning that attach to elements of morphology

---

[15] *See* Troy Duster, *Buried Alive: The Concept of Race in Science*, *in* GENETIC NATURE/CULTURE: ANTHROPOLOGY AND SCIENCE BEYOND THE TWO-CULTURE DIVIDE 258, 265 (Alan H. Goodman, Deborah Heath & M. Susan Lindee eds., 2003).

[16] Jonathan D. Kahn, *Race-ing Patents/Patenting Race: An Emerging Political Geography of Intellectual Property in Biotechnology*, 92 IOWA L. REV. 353, 361 (2007).

and ancestry."[17] This is a rich definition that deserves some unpacking.

López's reference to "morphology and ancestry" refers to race having always had a physical component. That is, race is corporeal—it pertains to the physical body—in the sense that inherited physical characteristics (i.e., the shapes and sizes of noses, lips, and eyes; the curl pattern of hair; the color of skin) have always been taken to denote the boundaries and content of racial categories. But, López warns, to say that inherited physical characteristics are the stuff of race should not be taken as an assertion that "features and lineage themselves are a function of racial variation."[18] Instead, inherited physical characteristics have racial significance "because society has invested these with racial meanings."[19] In other words, we take wide noses, thick lips, and dark skin as characteristics of the black race not because those features "naturally" correspond to this racial group. Instead, wide noses, thick lips, and dark skin are characteristics of the black race because we, as a society, have decided that we are going to categorize people in terms of those features. We could have decided that we were going to construct racial categories around eye color, the prominence of cheekbones, and whether ears lobes are attached or unattached. In this hypothetical alternative landscape, race would still be defined in terms of the physical body. Yet, social constructionists argue, if one thinks that it is arbitrary to bestow significance to eye color, cheekbones, and earlobe structure, one ought to recognize how arbitrary it is that we have endowed significance to the shapes of noses, the size of lips, and

---

[17] IAN HANEY LÓPEZ, WHITE BY LAW: THE LEGAL CONSTRUCTION OF RACE 10 (10th ed. 2006) [hereinafter HANEY LÓPEZ, WHITE BY LAW].

Rubén Rumbaut offers another particularly poetic definition of race:

> Race is a pigment of our imagination. . .[It] is a social status, not a zoological one; a product of history, not of nature; a contextual variable, not a given. It is a historically contingent, relational, intersubjective phenomenon—yet it is typically misbegotten as a natural, fixed marker of phenotypic difference inherent in human bodies, independent of human will or intention . . . Racial statuses and categories (and the putative differences that they connote) are imposed and infused with stereotypical moral meaning. . . What is called "race" is largely the sociopolitical accretion of past intergroup contacts and struggles, which establish the boundaries and thus the identities of victors and vanquished, of dominant and subordinate groups, of "us" and "them," with their attendant conceits of superiority and inferiority and invidious taxonomies of social worth or stigma. As such "race" is an ideological construct linking supposedly innate traits of individuals to their rank and fate in the social order.

Rubén G. Rumbaut, *Pigments of Our Imagination: The Racialization of the Hispanic-Latino Category*, *in* HOW THE U.S. RACIALIZES LATINOS: WHITE HEGEMONY AND ITS CONSEQUENCES 15, 15 (José A. Cobas, Jorge Duany & Joe R. Feagin eds., 2009).

[18] HANEY LÓPEZ, WHITE BY LAW, *supra* note 17, at 10.

[19] *Id.*

the color of skin—the characteristics that are privileged in our existing racial schemas.

When López defines race as "systems of meaning" that attach to inherited physical features, he is referring to the fact that although race always has been about physical bodies, it never has been *solely* about bodies. Rather, it always has been about what those bodies mean in terms of mental, emotional, and political capacities. For example, consider the racial schema that physician and botanist Carl Linnaeus offered during the mid-eighteenth century. He first proposed that the species of *Homo sapiens* could be divided into four distinct types: *H. sapiens africanus*, *H. sapiens europaeus*, *H. sapiens asiaticus*, and *H. sapiens americanus*.[20] He went on to offer descriptions of the physical appearance *and character traits* of these racial groups:

> American[:] red, choleric, erect. Hair black, straight and thick; Nostrils wide; Face freckled; Beard scanty. *Obstinate, content, free*. Paints himself with fine red lines. Regulated by habit; European[:] white, sanguine, brawny. Hair abundantly flowing. Eyes blue. *Gentle, acute, inventive*. Covered with close vestments. Governed by customs; Asiatic[:] yellow, melancholy, rigid. Hair black. Eyes dark. *Severe, haughty, covetous*. Covered with loose garments. Governed by opinions; and African[:] black, phlegmatic, relaxed. Hair black, frizzled. Skin silky. Nose, flat. Lips tumid. Women's bosom a matter of modesty. Breasts give milk abundantly. *Crafty, indolent, negligent*. Anoints himself with grease. Governed by caprice.[21]

Race has never been simply about describing Asian people as having yellow skin, black hair, and dark eyes; it has *also* always been about knowing that those particular physical features correspond to severity, haughtiness, and covetousness. Race has never been about describing black people as having black, frizzled hair, silky skin, flat noses, and tumid lips; it has *also* always been about knowing that those particular physical features correspond to craftiness, indolence, and negligence. This is to say that the physical traits of race always have been imagined to correlate with nonphysical traits. Social constructionists underscore that the psychological attributes and tendencies that society has imagined racial groups to possess have been taken to justify all manner of different treatment and to legitimate all manner of social inequalities.

---

[20] *See* JORDAN, WHITE OVER BLACK, *supra* note 1, at 220–21 (quoting Carl Linnaeus's description of the races that he identified).

[21] *Id.* (emphasis added).

López elaborates on this point by observing that notions about the psychological attributes and tendencies of racial groups—that is, ideas about what physical bodies *mean*—are made to appear true as they come to be reflected in the social environment. He writes that "these meaning-systems, while originally only ideas, gain force as they are reproduced in the material conditions of society. The distribution of wealth and poverty turns in part on the actions of social and legal actors who have accepted ideas of race, with the resulting material conditions becoming part of and reinforcement for the contingent meanings understood as race."[22] So, López would ask us to consider the idea that black people are, in Linnaeus's schematization, "crafty, indolent, and negligent." He would ask us to consider as well that, due to a variety of structural transformations and governmental decisions, disproportionate numbers of black people have come to live in hyper-segregated, extremely impoverished neighborhoods that are physically distant from jobs that pay livable wages. The idea that black people are "crafty" gains believability as many of them have to resort to exceedingly creative measures to make ends meet while impoverished—efforts that can be read as proof of their guile. The idea that black people are "indolent" gains believability as disproportionate numbers of them find themselves unemployed—a condition that can be read as evidence of their laziness. Finally, the idea that black people are "negligent" gains believability as the neighborhoods in which they are compelled to call home feature the physical markers of extreme poverty, i.e., buildings in various states of disrepair, uncollected garbage, gatherings of residents on street corners. These physical markers can be read as a substantiation of black people's carelessness. Thus, the material conditions of society confirm the truth of ideas about race. Yet, López asserts that, at the same time, ideas about race justify the material conditions of society. (If black people are crafty, indolent, and negligent, then there is nothing wrong with disproportionate numbers of them living in hyper-segregated, extremely impoverished neighborhoods that are physically distant from jobs that pay livable wages. Indeed, this might be *expected*, given their craftiness, indolence, and negligence.) Meanwhile, the material conditions of society confirm the truth of ideas about race. . . . . And the dialectic between ideas about race and the material environment turns and turns.

Lastly, when López states that race is "historically contingent" systems of meaning, he is referring to the notion that our current ideas about race are products of the needs that race has satisfied over the course of human history. Indeed, many social constructionists conceptualize race as a *pragmatic* entity: race has been constructed

[22] HANEY LÓPEZ, WHITE BY LAW, *supra* note 17, at 10.

because it serves purposes. At the dawn of the nation, the black race was constructed as crafty, indolent, and negligent in order to justify enslaving them in a country that was built on the promises of liberty, freedom, and equality for all. If, as a consequence of nature, black people possess problematic psychological characteristics, then it explains why the promises of liberty, freedom and equality could not apply to them. It explains why they were unfit for the freedom that the new nation purported to guarantee to everyone. Analogously, if "Americans" were "obstinate," it explains why it would be futile to try to get them to agree to be ruled by a government of white men. It explains why extermination and banishment was a more suitable course to pursue vis-à-vis the indigenous peoples who lived on the lands that would become the U.S. And so on and so forth.

III. The Role of the Law in Constructing Race

If we are satisfied that race is a social construction, the next question to ask is: how is the law implicated in constructing race?

CRT contends that the law has played many different roles in the task of constructing race. Sometimes the law has played an obvious and undeniable role—as when the courts determined which ethnic groups and nationalities were white and, as a consequence, were able to naturalize as U.S. citizens. (The racial prerequisite cases are discussed below.) At other times, the ways by which the law has functioned to construct race have been subtle and oblique—as when a myriad of policies and judicial decisions produce and protect residential segregation, allowing ideas about racial groups to be reflected in the material environment. Law, of course, is not the only institution doing the work of constructing race. But, CRT claims that it is an important one. As López writes, "Law is one of the most powerful mechanisms by which any society creates, defines, and regulates itself. . . . It follows, then, that to say race is socially constructed is to conclude that race is at least partially legally produced."[23]

A. The Legal Construction of Race in the Pre-Civil Rights Era

As noted above, CRT argues that the law has constructed race in ways that are both direct and indirect. It asserts that the law tended to take a more direct approach in the pre-civil rights era, when there was no widely-accepted norm against speaking about race in public. CRT identifies many areas in which the law explicitly constructed race during this period of time. Three are explored below.

---

[23] *Id.* at 17.

1. *Racial Identity Trials*

Trials in which individuals attempted to demonstrate their whiteness were once a ubiquity. In the days of chattel slavery, these trials typically arose when an enslaved person sought to prove that she was a white person and, therefore, had been wrongly held as a slave. In these cases, juries held the power to grant freedom with a determination that the plaintiff was, in fact, white. Ariela Gross tells the story of Alexina Morrison, who had been held as a slave in Louisiana.[24] She ran away from a man by the name of James White, who claimed to own her, and sought protection from William Dennison, an administrator at the local jail. Dennison believed Alexina when she told him that she was white—in part because she had "blue eyes and flaxen hair"—and he took her home with him, eventually introducing her "into white society."[25] After some time, Alexina decided to sue James White for her freedom, and the case hung on whether Alexina could prove that she was white; if she was white, after all, she could not be a slave. The trials that resulted were highly contentious: "Several doctors testified on her behalf that the shape of her hair follicles and the arches of her feet proved her whiteness. James White, by contrast, tried to prove her 'negro blood' by calling her sexual virtue into doubt, accusing her jailer of having fathered her child, and questioning her witnesses about her behavior at public balls."[26]

After the end of chattel slavery, racial identity trials tended to arise in the context of marriage. Because many states had passed anti-miscegenation laws that made interracial marriage a crime, couples who were prosecuted under these statutes sometimes attempted to avoid prosecution by proving that both husband and wife were white and that they were not actually an interracial couple. At other times, "family members tried to have heirs disinherited by alleging that they were of mixed race and therefore the product of an illegitimate marriage."[27] And finally, more than a few husbands attempted to "avoid the obligations of marriage"[28] by asserting that the women they had married had concealed their true racial identities and were not, in actuality, white. Such claims tended to produce exquisitely salacious trials, as white men attempted to prove that their marriages were interracial, and thus illegal and voidable.

---

[24] ARIELA J. GROSS, WHAT BLOOD WON'T TELL: A HISTORY OF RACE ON TRIAL IN AMERICA 1 (2008).

[25] *Id.*

[26] *Id.* at 2.

[27] *Id.* at 5.

[28] *Id.*

In all of these situations, the racial identity of an individual was put on trial.

What is important to observe here is the law's role in fixing the race of individuals. Racial identity trials always ended with an official determination that a litigant was or was not white. This observation—that the law could give and take away whiteness—serves to undermine the claim that race is a pre-social, pre-legal entity that is found in the blood. This is especially true in light of the reality that many of these trials did not involve attempts at measuring or quantifying how much "white blood" and "nonwhite blood" any individual litigant had. Instead, they involved determining whether an individual *behaved* as white people were imagined to behave. Gross writes that, in these trials, race was not something that a person was; "it was something they did."[29] She continues:

> Who was a white man? A civic being who voted, served on juries, and mustered in the militia. Degraded black men were not capable of such things, while honorable white men could not keep from doing them. Thus we can see that the law—the public sphere—was involved not merely in recognizing race but in creating it; the state itself—through its legal and military institutions—helped make people white.[30]

2. *Immigration*

The law has also explicitly constructed race through its regulation of immigration. López observes that immigration laws have functioned to bring some groups into the country while keeping out others. This, he argues, has constructed race inasmuch as it has impacted the frequency at which certain inherited physical features—which, as noted above, are the stuff upon which race is built—are present in the country. He writes that immigration laws "determined the types of faces and features present in the United States."[31] These laws interacted with the anti-miscegenation laws mentioned above, as well as other laws that stripped women who married nonwhite, noncitizen men of their citizenship, to skew reproductive choices. The consequence was that racial intermixtures that might have changed the appearance of the physical features that code for race were kept to a minimum.

This point deserves some elaboration. Imagine if persons from Asia always had been allowed to immigrate at the levels at which

---

29 *Id.* at 53.

30 *Id.* at 53–54.

31 HANEY LÓPEZ, WHITE BY LAW, *supra* note 17, at 11.

their counterparts from Europe had immigrated. Imagine further that laws did not prohibit intermarriage between white and Asian people. (Indeed, imagine if the law had actually encouraged such unions.) López's point is that, if the country had this alternate history, Asian and white people would not *look* the way that they do today. It is possible that the inherited physical features that code for "Asian"—i.e., almond eye shape, straight hair texture, olive skin tones—would not be as readily discernable in individuals in our contemporary present. López's fascinating point is that immigration laws, together with laws that regulated who could marry and procreate with whom, worked to perpetuate "the 'pure' physical types on which notions of race are based in the United States."[32]

The racial prerequisite cases are another example of the law functioning to construct race quite explicitly in the context of immigration. The Naturalization Act of 1790 restricted the ability to naturalize and become a citizen to "free white persons." The question that this explicit racial restriction raised was: well, then, who is a white person? Were Armenian people white? What about people from Iran? South Asia? What about the Japanese? Syrian folks? In a number of cases, the judiciary explicitly determined which groups were white and which were not, with the Supreme Court weighing in twice. (The Court decided that neither Japanese nor South Asian people were white.[33])

These racial prerequisite cases are significant beyond the impact that they had on the lives of the individual petitioners whose ability to naturalize hinged on a judge's determination that they were or were not white. The cases are also significant because they illustrate how the law subtly constructs racial meanings. In one sense, there is nothing at all subtle about the law explicitly and formally declaring that a nationality—Japanese, for example—is not white. But, there is some subtlety in the way that the declaration generates racial meanings. When the Court explicitly held that the Japanese were not white in *Ozawa v. U.S.*, it did not also explicitly say that the Japanese were unrefined, untrustworthy, disloyal, and dishonorable. But, that was the arguable effect of the decision. Writes López, "To be unfit for naturalization . . . implied a certain degeneracy of intellect, morals, self-restraint, and political values; to be suited for citizenship . . . suggested moral maturity, self-assurance, personal independence, and political sophistication."[34] In this way, with each determination that a group was white, the judiciary communicated the virtue of a group and the individuals

---

[32] *Id.* at 82.

[33] Ozawa v. United States, 260 U.S. 178 (1922); United States v. Bhagat Singh Thind, 261 U.S. 204 (1923).

[34] HANEY LÓPEZ, WHITE BY LAW, *supra* note 17, at 11–12.

who belong to it. And with each denial, the judiciary communicated that virtue was not to be expected from the people who comprised the group.

Further, CRT finds the cases significant because of the way that they worked to fabricate a social landscape wherein nonwhite people are disproportionately impoverished and vulnerable to further subordination. When the Court declared that a group was not white, CRT reminds us that members of the group became incapable of participating in the political process. They were unable to elect representatives into city halls, legislatures, and executive offices who would look after their interests. There arguably is a direct connection between the vulnerabilities produced by exclusion from the political process and economic and social marginalization. (At the very least, the denial of the capacity to naturalize did not *improve* the economic and social status of groups.) We might then consider how the marginalization that political exclusion produced became reflected in the material environment—in the Chinatowns to which the Chinese were largely confined and the "ethnic" enclaves into which other immigrant groups were sequestered. These environments, and the fact that impoverished people resided in them, served to confirm the truth of the idea that nonwhite people possessed a "degeneracy of intellect, morals, self-restraint, and political values," in López's words. And ideas about the character of those racialized as nonwhite led to discriminatory laws and policies, which then contributed to a material environment that confirmed those ideas. . . . And the dialectic between ideas about race and the material environment turns and turns.

Finally, the racial prerequisite cases are significant because they arguably altered the course of history. For example, we might imagine what our present would like had the Court decided in *U.S. v. Thind* that South Asian people were white. Had the Court taken this alternate path—a path that was suggested by the Court's precedents and the racial truths that the discipline of anthropology had generated—today, we might think of South Asian people as incontrovertibly white. The inherited physical features that code for South Asian—dark skin, straight, dark hair—might be taken as "white" physical features today. While many may react to this claim with the sense that it is simply wrong to think that South Asian people are white, we should be aware of the possibility that one of the reasons we believe that South Asian people *clearly* are not white today is the Court's declaration of the same almost a century ago. The law has shaped our commonsense notions of race.

3. *The Curious Case of Mexicans' Whiteness*

In 1897, the Court declared in the case of *In re Rodriguez* that as a matter of law, people of Mexican descent were white.[35] The declaration did not come because the Court had consulted the science of the day and this science confirmed Mexicans' whiteness. (In fact, the Court acknowledged that the science of the day disputed the claim that people of Mexican descent were white.[36]) Instead, the declaration was the result of an interesting logical deduction. In 1846, the U.S. signed the Treaty of Guadalupe Hidalgo, which ended the Mexican-American War. The treaty provided that hundreds of thousands of square miles of land that belonged to Mexico would become property of the U.S.; it also gave to the Mexican nationals who were living on that land the right to become U.S. citizens. Meanwhile, as discussed above, the immigration laws at the time provided that only "free white persons" could naturalize as U.S. citizens. The Court in *In re Rodriguez* reasoned that because Mexicans could become citizens by virtue of the treaty of Guadalupe Hidalgo, and because only white people could become citizens by virtue of the nation's immigration laws, then it followed that Mexicans were white people. As such, *In re Rodriguez* is another example of the law explicitly constructing race.

However, the experience of people of Mexican descent in the U.S. may complicate the argument above that a formal declaration of nonwhiteness by a court of law worked to produce and/or exacerbate the political, economic, and social marginalization of groups declared nonwhite. The argument might presuppose that a formal declaration of *whiteness* by a court of law would protect groups from political, economic, and social marginalization. Curiously, this was not the experience that people of Mexican descent had with whiteness. Instead, by all accounts, they were treated like second-class citizens. As George Martinez describes, "Mexican-Americans were excluded from public facilities and neighborhoods, and were the targets of racial slurs. Mexican-Americans typically lived in one section of town because they were not permitted to rent or to own property anywhere except in the 'Mexican Colony,' regardless of their social, educational or economic status."[37] Although white by law, Mexican-American were the victims of unjustified police violence. They were discriminated against in the labor market. Their children were forced to attend inferior, segregated schools. Indeed, being "white" did not afford people of Mexican descent much in the way of privilege.

---

[35] *In re* Rodriguez, 81 F. 337 (W.D. Tex. 1897).

[36] *See id.*

[37] George A. Martínez, *African-Americans, Latinos and the Construction of Race: Toward an Epistemic Coalition*, 19 CHICANO-LATINO L. REV. 213, 219 (1998).

Ironically, being "white" might have *intensified* the subordination of people of Mexican descent. Because they were legally white, they had a difficult time availing themselves of antidiscrimination provisions barring discrimination on the basis of race. How could white people discriminate against other white people? This was the logic of the lower court in the case of *Hernandez v. Texas*.[38] The litigation began when a Mexican-American defendant, who was being prosecuted for murder, was tried and convicted by a jury that contained no Mexican-American jurors. He claimed that his equal protection rights had been violated by the absence of persons of Mexican descent on the jury that convicted him. The Texas appeals court affirmed the conviction. The court's reasoning was that as long as there were white people serving on juries in Texas, then defendants of Mexican descent were being tried by juries of their peers, as Mexicans were, technically speaking, white. The Texas court concluded, "The grand jury that indicted appellant and the petit jury that tried him being composed of members of his race, it cannot be said, in the absence of proof of actual discrimination, that appellant has been discriminated against in the organization of such juries and thereby denied equal protection of the law."[39] In this way, Mexicans' "whiteness" was deployed to frustrate their ability to achieve equality with their white counterparts. Their "whiteness" was deployed to maintain their marginalization.

The Supreme Court ultimately overturned the Texas court's opinion, finding that "the attitude of the community" in which the defendant was tried showed that people of Mexican descent were treated as a class apart from white people.[40] Thus, in subsequent cases, people of Mexican descent challenging discriminatory conditions had to prove that their lived conditions belied the whiteness that the law had bestowed.

B. The Legal Construction of Race in Modern Times

In the present day, the law clearly does not construct race as explicitly as it has done in previous historical eras. The judiciary is not adjudicating the racial status of nationalities anymore. Neither are individuals petitioning courts for an official declaration of their whiteness.[41] Although the law is not constructing race as

---

38 Hernandez v. Texas, 347 U.S. 475 (1954).

39 Hernandez v. State, 251 S.W.2d. 531, 536 (1952).

40 Hernandez, 347 U.S. at 479.

41 Gross writes that the last racial identity case occurred in Louisiana in 1983, "when Susie Phipps disputed the racial designation on her birth certificate as 'black' because she had always 'lived white'; the Louisiana courts found her black according to a '1/32 degree of African blood' statute, and the legislature promptly repealed the statute." GROSS, *supra* note 24, at 294.

spectacularly as it did in the days of yore, CRT insists that the law continues to construct race. The difference is that the mechanisms of the legal construction of race in modern times are much more understated than the mechanisms of yesteryear. Explains López, "[T]oday race is legally constructed principally indirectly by legal institutions that produce and bolster deleterious racial ideologies without forthrightly engaging the categorical debates that so preoccupied race law through the early twentieth century."[42]

López contends that law no longer constructs race through coercion—compelling individuals to occupy racial categories. Instead, he argues, law constructs race through ideology—creating a world where the racial ideas that we have "make sense." So, for example, we have ideas about black criminality. And then, CRT argues, the criminal justice system comes along and legitimizes those ideas by vigorously policing black men and incarcerating them at historically high levels. We have ideas about Muslim terrorists. And then, CRT argues, the state comes along and legitimates those ideas by targeting Muslim communities for extensive counterterrorism surveillance—all the while refusing to call the violence perpetrated by non-Muslim individuals "terrorism." We have ideas about Latinx illegality. And then, CRT argues, the state comes along and legitimates those ideas by erecting massive bureaucracies to identify undocumented Latinx immigrants while largely overlooking undocumented immigration from countries other than those in Latin America. Writes López, "Legal rules and decisions construct race through legitimation, affirming the categories and images of popular racial beliefs and making it nearly impossible to imagine nonracialized ways of thinking about identity, belonging, and difference.[43]

CRT has identified several areas in which the law *ideologically* constructs race, facilitating the attachment of particular racial meanings to racial categories. While not at all an exhaustive list, these areas include: residential segregation and laws and policies that contribute to the manufacture of racialized spaces; the War on Terror and the production and perpetuation of discourses that describe Muslim individuals and communities as dangers to the nation; mass incarceration and the way that it produces and legitimates discourses that describe men of color, particularly black and Latinx men, as social problems; and our system of public benefits and the work that it does to pathologize poverty, especially when it intersects with pregnancy and motherhood. Subsequent chapters will explore these areas in more depth. The balance of the chapter

[42] HANEY LÓPEZ, WHITE BY LAW, *supra* note 17, at xv.

[43] *Id.* at 87.

turns its attention back to immigration law as a site of racial construction.

1. *The Construction of Race in Modern Immigration Law*

Much scholarship in the CRT genre has observed that the nation's immigration policies function to construct Latinx individuals as "illegal." An uncritical lens might lead an observer to conclude that this construction is unproblematic. A person with this lens might assert that Latinx individuals are constructed as "illegal" because many of them *are* "illegal." To bolster her claim, she might look to statistics illustrating that that individuals from Mexico represent the largest population of undocumented immigrants in the U.S. today.[44]

While a person with a critical lens on immigration would not dispute that individuals from Mexico are well-represented among those who are undocumented, she would observe that this group's undocumented status is as much a function of the behaviors in which its members have engaged (i.e., entering or remaining in the country without authorization) as it is a function of the *law*. That is, the border between the U.S. and Mexico, delineating the boundaries of the two nation states, is a product of law. Further, the various visas that bestow the visa holder with an authorized status are all products of law. Finally, the U.S.'s choice to limit the avenues by which an immigrant can come to obtain a visa or permanent resident card that would authorize her presence within the legally-constructed borders of the country is reflected in law. Thus, although the U.S.—or any nation-state, for that matter—may have very good (or very bad) reasons for attempting to restrict immigration, it remains true that the *law* creates undocumented, or "illegal," immigrants.

Moreover, despite the large numbers of undocumented immigrants from Mexico living in the U.S., the state has elected not to create pathways by which those persons could become authorized to live and work in the country. Again, the question of whether the state *should* authorize immigration to the country is another matter. The point here simply is that if large numbers of Mexican immigrants are undocumented, that fact is, in very important respects, the work of the law. In this way, the law is responsible for "Mexican 'illegality.'"[45] The law is responsible for Mexican persons

---

[44] Vivian Yee, Kenan Davis & Jugal K. Patel, *Here's the Reality About Illegal Immigrants in the United States*, N.Y. TIMES (Mar. 6, 2017), https://www.nytimes.com/interactive/2017/03/06/us/politics/undocumented-illegal-immigrants.html.

[45] Nicholas De Genova, *The Legal Production of Mexican/Migrant "Illegality," in* LATINOS AND CITIZENSHIP: THE DILEMMA OF BELONGING 61 (Suzanne Oboler ed., 2006).

being the face and figure of undocumented immigration in the present day.

Some progressive race scholars have pushed this observation further, claiming that the law has made "illegality" attach to the Latinx racial category. This claim suggests that just as blackness arguably has come to represent criminality and/or procreative irresponsibility and state dependence, Latinidad has come to represent immigrant "illegality." Pursuant to this claim, all Latinx individuals (or all individuals who may be thought to be Latinx) are constructed as presumptively undocumented, without regard to their actual immigration and citizenship status. As evidence, these thinkers look to Arizona's Senate Bill 1070, which allows police officers to question an individual she has stopped or arrested about her immigration status when she has reasonable suspicion that the individual might be undocumented.[46] Because the physical markers that distinguish an unauthorized immigrant from a citizen or authorized immigrant are elusive, critics of SB 1070 assert that the law allows police officers to racially profile anyone who appears to be "Mexican"—that is, any Latinx person. If this assertion is correct, then all Latinx persons—whether U.S. citizen or fresh from an unauthorized border crossing—are constructed as presumptively undocumented. As Martinez writes, Latinx persons become "always subject to the violence of heightened scrutiny that occurs at the border."[47]

In sum, there is no court decision, statute, or executive order that says "Latinx people are presumptively undocumented and should be treated as such." However, according to these critical thinkers, the effect of our immigration laws and policies is to attach "illegality" to the Latinx racial category.

IV. Questions and Discussion

1. Khaled Beydoun's work on the construction of Arab-American identity might be taken as a study of the racialization of religion.[48] His examination shows that prior to 1952, when the country's laws restricted naturalization to "free white persons," immigrants hailing from Arab countries were presumed to be disqualified from citizenship because they were assumed to be Muslim, and Muslims were considered nonwhite. However, if an immigrant from an Arab country could show that he was not Muslim, but was instead Christian, he could establish his whiteness and

---

[46] ARIZ. REV. STAT. ANN. § 11–1051(B) (2010).

[47] George A. Martinez, *The Legal Construction of Race: Mexican-Americans and Whiteness*, 2 HARV. LATINO L. REV. 321, 345 (1997).

[48] Khaled A. Beydoun, *Between Muslim and White: The Legal Construction of Arab American Identity*, 69 N.Y.U. ANN. SURV. AM. L. 29 (2013).

would be allowed to naturalize. Beydoun's analysis demonstrates how "Islam was treated as an ethno-racial identity, as was Christianity."[49]

However, the construction of Muslims as nonwhite, at least as a matter of law, was not enduring. In 1944, a district court decided *Ex parte Mohriez*, in which an Arab Muslim was granted citizenship after the court found that he satisfied the whiteness prerequisite in the statute.[50] Beydoun argues that this shift in the racial construction of Muslims was a direct result of the U.S.'s changing economic and political needs. He writes that at the time of the decision in *Mohriez*, U.S. businesses were moving into the Arab Peninsula in search of oil. On top of this, the U.S. was jousting with Russia over which nation would become the most powerful in the world. "Extending citizenship to Muslim immigrants from the Arab World, particularly those hailing from nations with considerable value, made the United States a more attractive superpower with whom governments of these countries could align during the Cold War."[51] Thus, a combination of factors—none of which concerned discoveries in "science" or genetics—functioned to re-racialize Muslims and make them white (at least by law).

Do you believe that Muslims are considered white or nonwhite at present? What factors do you think have contributed to their current racialization? Can you imagine the group ever being re-racialized? Under what circumstances do you believe such re-racialization would occur? Chapter 14 does a deep dive into the thorny questions surrounding the racialization of Muslims.

2. As noted above, if the law constructs race in modern times, it does so in ways that are significantly more oblique than the ways that it employed in the pre-civil rights era. However, one arguable exception to this is the matter of the census. The census is sometimes described as an example of the law constructing race—instead of the law merely *measuring* race—because the census involves the law coercing individuals to self-identify with the racial categories that the government has delineated.

Recent research has suggested that we ought not to underestimate the ability of the census to construct race. Rubén Rumbaut has observed that although the census asks individuals to identify whether they are "Hispanic," the term is a relatively new invention whose significance might be limited to the United States. The term first appeared on the census in 1970 after activists demanded that the state cease constraining persons with Latin

---

[49] *Id.* at 33.

[50] *Ex parte* Mohriez, 54 F. Supp. 941, 942 (D. Mass. 1944).

[51] Beydoun, *supra* note 48, at 69–70.

American ancestry to identify as "white." However, the term might only be meaningful in the U.S., as "[t]he groups subsumed under the label 'Hispanic' or 'Latino'—the Mexicans, Puerto Ricans, Cubans, Dominicans, Salvadorans, Guatemalans, Colombians, Peruvians, Ecuadorians, and the other dozen nationalities from Latin America and even Spain itself—were not 'Hispanics' or 'Latinos' in their countries of origin; rather, they only became so in the United States."[52]

Although "Hispanic" is a term of fairly recent vintage with constrained geographic importance, Rumbaut notes that in a recent survey of youths with Latin American origins, 41 percent indicated that their race was "Hispanic" or "Latino."[53] Thus, this group identifies with a label that was externally imposed by law, and recently so. Writes Rumbaut, this is "a label developed and legitimized by the state, diffused in daily and institutional practice, and finally internalized—and racialized—as a prominent part of the American mosaic."[54]

3. Thomas Joo has argued that one of the meanings that has attached to the Asian racial category is "foreignness."[55] He contends that the origins of this racialization are in the exclusionary policies that the U.S. once had with respect to Asian immigrants. He notes that, as discussed above, Asian immigrants were unable to become citizens because the naturalization laws limited citizenship to white persons. Further, although individuals of Asian descent who are born in the U.S. have enjoyed birthright citizenship, laws functioned to keep this number to a minimum. This was accomplished by "restrictions on Asian immigration generally, restrictions on the immigration of Asian women, and laws against interracial marriage."[56] The consequence was that for most of our country's history, the overwhelming majority of persons of Asian descent in the country "were thus literally 'foreigners' in the legal sense."[57]

Joo argues that the conflation of Asian-ness and foreignness lives on in the present day. He claims that *Asian* still is racialized such that persons of Asian descent, regardless of nationality, continue to be considered irretrievably alien to the U.S. He writes, "The foreignness of the Oriental has not simply been an issue of national citizenship or place of birth. It has been treated as a

---

[52] Rumbaut, *supra* note 17, at 16.

[53] *Id.* at 30.

[54] *Id.* at 17.

[55] Thomas W. Joo, *Presumed Disloyal: Executive Power, Judicial Deference, and the Construction of Race Before and After September 11*, 34 COLUM. HUM. RTS. L. REV. 1 (2002).

[56] *Id.* at 15.

[57] *Id.*

permanent, inheritable characteristic. . . . American racial logic posits that an Oriental is not, and his or her descendants can never become, American. As a non-White racial category becomes identified with foreignness, that racial category, like foreignness, becomes incompatible with Americanness. And foreignness, like non-Whiteness, becomes a permanent impurity, impervious to alteration by immigration, naturalization, assimilation, or even American birth. Just as one cannot be both Black and White, one cannot be both racially 'foreign' and American."[58]

What do you make of Joo's argument? Do you believe that Asian-Americans are not considered American in the way that white people are? If so, how much of that is a product of law, i.e., legal restrictions on Asian immigration, naturalization, marriage, and procreation?

A related question: do you believe that indigenous persons are considered American in the way that white people are? If you answer this question in the negative, note that we cannot attribute the construction of indigenous persons as foreign or un-American to exclusionary immigration policies. To what might we attribute indigenous persons' un-American-ness?

Do you believe that *black* persons are considered American in the way that white people are? Why or why not?

4. A white racial identity that has received a lot of attention of recent is the one associated with white nationalists, neo-Nazis, and the Ku Klux Klan. Individuals with this particular variety of white identity caused a national controversy when they protested the removal of a statue memorializing a leader of the Confederacy in Charlottesville in 2017.[59] Arguably, their protest was less controversial than President Trump's willingness to defend them as well as those who protested alongside these groups.[60]

This chapter argues that we ought to pay attention to the laws, policies, and other processes that construct racial identities. What laws, policies, and processes, if any, have helped to construct the *white* racial identities that would identify as, or ally themselves with, white nationalists, neo-Nazis, and the Ku Klux Klan?

5. In *Racism on Trial: The Chicano Fight for Justice*, López writes about the racialization of people of Mexican descent as

---

[58] *Id.* at 17–18.

[59] Jason Wilson, *Charlottesville: Far-Right Crowd with Torches Encircles Counter-Protest Group*, GUARDIAN (Aug. 12, 2017), https://www.theguardian.com/world/2017/aug/12/charlottesville-far-right-crowd-with-torches-encircles-counter-protest-group.

[60] Maggie Astor, Christina Caron & Daniel Victor, *A Guide to the Charlottesville Aftermath*, N.Y. TIMES (Aug. 13, 2017), https://www.nytimes.com/2017/08/13/us/charlottesville-virginia-overview.html.

Chicanos in California in the late 1960s.[61] The primary force for this racialization, López argues, was police violence. López tells of how persons of Mexican descent in the community that he studied were the targets of incessant police harassment and brutality. Instead of defending themselves against this repression by claiming a white identity and contending that, as virtuous white persons, they did not deserve such treatment by the state, many embraced a decidedly nonwhite identity—that of the Chicano.

López looks to a study that showed that persons who identified as *Chicanos* were much more likely than those who identified as *Mexican American* to be aware of police misconduct, to believe that the police violated individuals' constitutional rights, and to think that the police used excessive force and violence when engaging with individuals. He notes that the traditional interpretation of this data is to suppose that those with politicized identities—that is, those who identified as Chicano—were more willing to see the conduct in which the police engaged as illegitimate. However, López argues that this interpretation misses an important element of the story. He argues, "More likely, the relationship ran in both directions: participation in the Chicano movement prompted negative views of the police, *while perceptions of police malpractice precipitated involvement in Chicano politics*."[62] López contends that "Mexicans did not possess a fixed racial identity that law enforcement officials and Chicano activists recognized and reacted to; rather, the actions of the police and the protesters also helped to fashion Mexican racial identity."[63]

Essentially, López's argument is that injustice practiced by law can construct race. What recent injustices do you perceive as having the capacity to create race?

The inverse of López's proposition might also be true: *justice* can construct race. What recent justices do you perceive as having the capacity to create race?

6. While most critical scholarship exploring immigration laws and policies focus on the question of how immigration restrictions construct their racialized targets in specific ways, some new scholarship has examined how these restrictions construct their racialized *proponents* in specific ways. In other words, instead of analyzing how immigration laws and policies racially construct nonwhite populations, this new scholarship analyzes how these laws and policies construct white populations.

---

[61] IAN F. HANEY LÓPEZ, RACISM ON TRIAL: THE CHICANO FIGHT FOR JUSTICE (2004).

[62] *Id.* at 152.

[63] *Id.* at 175.

Justin Steil and Jennifer Ridgley have examined the Illegal Immigration Relief Act (IIRA), which was passed by the city of Hazleton, Pennsylvania in 2006.[64] The act attempted to restrict or reduce the number of undocumented immigrants in the community by authorizing the city to fine individuals who rent apartments to undocumented individuals and to revoke the licenses of businesses who employ undocumented workers. Steil and Ridgley observe that in the decades preceding the passage of the law, the city had reversed economic positions with neighboring communities and no longer boasted the highest incomes and home values. The city "had gone from being a prosperous economic center to a forgotten city with shuttered storefronts. Instead of a regional retail destination, Hazleton had become a town where lower wage workers lived and trucks rumbled past on their way from warehouses out of town."[65] Steil and Ridgley argue that, in this context, the IIRA worked to rehabilitate the identity of the city and the persons who had called it home for their entire lives. They write that the IIRA represented

> the space of Hazleton as an "all-American town" [and] served to construct a social group consisting of "legal, hardworking citizens" of the town in opposition to "illegal aliens" flooding in from big cities. The positioning of the ordinance as a defense of small-town quality of life against the threats of foreigners and urban ills forged the descendants of diverse European immigrants with varied class backgrounds and interests into a singular identity as residents of this small town, intrinsically connected with all the other American small-town residents.[66]

In this way, the immigration restriction not only produced Latinx individuals in Hazleton as presumptively "illegal" threats to the community, but it also produced the city's white residents as a unified community with small-town, all-American values.

Steil and Ridgley's work might be taken as a reminder that racial categories tend to be relational. That is, white is defined in relation to black, which is defined in relation to Asian, which is defined in relation to indigenous, which is defined in relation to white, and so on and so forth. Thus, when immigration laws and policies construct nonwhite groups in a particular way, they oftentimes are simultaneously constructing white groups. Paying

---

[64] Justin Steil & Jennifer Ridgley, *'Small-Town Defenders': The Production of Citizenship and Belonging in Hazleton, Pennsylvania*, 30 ENV'T & PLAN. D: SOC'Y & SPACE 1028 (2012).

[65] *Id.* at 1035.

[66] *Id.* at 1041.

attention to only one side of the process is ill-advised if we also want to understand whiteness as a racial category.

In 2018, the Trump administration began a "zero tolerance" immigration policy at the U.S.-Mexican border, which resulted in thousands of children being separated from their parents.[67] How does this immigration policy construct whiteness? Blackness? Asian-ness? Indigeneity? Latinidad?

---

[67] Miriam Jordan, *How and Why 'Zero Tolerance' Is Splitting Up Immigrant Families*, N.Y. TIMES (May 12, 2018), https://www.nytimes.com/2018/05/12/us/immigrants-family-separation.html.

Chapter 7

STRUCTURAL/INSTITUTIONAL RACISM

Political activist Stokely Carmichael and sociologist Charles Hamilton usually are credited with coining the term "institutional racism." In their 1967 tome, *Black Power: The Politics of Liberation in America*, they distinguished individual acts of racism from a racism that was more covert and subtle. They wrote:

> When white terrorists bomb a black church and kill five black children, that is an act of individual racism, widely deplored by most segments of society. But when in that same city—Birmingham, Alabama—five hundred black babies die each year because of the lack of proper food, shelter and medical facilities . . . that is a function of institutional racism.[1]

The concept became popular over the course of the next several decades, as it supplied an explanation for the persistence of racial inequality in the post-civil rights era—an era that did not feature pervasive acts of overt racism perpetrated by individuals. Although widely used, even those on the political left criticized the concept as not being fully fleshed out and, therefore, deficient in explanatory power. Indeed, early in the concept's life, one social theorist "warned that the term 'institutional racism' would forever be a political slogan lacking in analytical rigour until it could be more precisely conceptualised, theorised, and subject to empirical investigation."[2]

Interestingly, commentators have made a similar assessment of the concept in more recent years—decades after it was first critiqued as being undertheorized. More than thirty years after Carmichael[3] and Hamilton coined the term, critical race theorist Ian Haney López observed that " '[i]nstitutional racism' seems to function more often as a label for a problem than as a theory of social behavior. A theory of 'institutional racism' has been elusive."[4]

---

1 STOKELY CARMICHAEL & CHARLES V. HAMILTON, BLACK POWER: THE POLITICS OF LIBERATION IN AMERICA 4 (1967).

2 Coretta Phillips, *Institutional Racism and Ethnic Inequalities: An Expanded Multilevel Framework*, 40 J. SOC. POL'Y 173, 173 (2011).

3 Carmichael later changed his name to Kwame Ture. Michael T. Kaufman, *Stokely Carmichael, Rights Leader who Coined 'Black Power,' Dies at 57*, N.Y. TIMES, Nov. 16, 1998, at B10.

4 Ian F. Haney López, *Institutional Racism: Judicial Conduct and a New Theory of Racial Discrimination*, 109 YALE L.J. 1717, 1727 (1999).

Scores of scholars have attempted to answer the call to define and theorize institutional, or structural, racism with precision. One can identify four elements that routinely recur in these definitions.

First, most definitions include a lack of intentionality. Most scholars posit that the laws, policies, procedures, and programs that function to produce racial inequality—specifically, a racial hierarchy in which white people, as a group, are doing much better than nonwhite groups—do not have racial subordination as their purpose or design. These scholars note that intentionality characterized the initial construction of the racial hierarchy. Certainly, actors *intended* to strip indigenous persons of their lands and sovereignty during the days of the pursuit of Manifest Destiny. Actors *intended* to subordinate black people during the centuries of chattel slavery and the decades of constitutionally protected formal inequality that followed the end of Reconstruction. Actors *intended* to exclude nonwhite persons from the polity during the time when the naturalization laws explicitly permitted only "free white persons" to become United States citizens.[5] However, most definitions of institutional/structural racism propose that sustaining the racial hierarchy that was intentionally constructed and maintained during the pre-civil rights era is now the unintended, if not unforeseeable, consequence of contemporary laws, policies, procedures, and programs.

Second, most definitions include an element of banality. That is, the practices that sustain racial inequality are not spectacular. Quite the contrary, they are daily, prosaic, mundane, ordinary. As Daria Roithmayr has written, racial gaps "are produced by the *everyday* decisions that structure our social, political, and economic interactions."[6]

Third, most definitions include an element of race neutrality—the absence of any explicit invocation of race. The idea is that the things that sustain racial inequality are myriad, and the most consequential of them reproduce racial hierarchies without mentioning race at all.

Fourth and finally, most definitions note the irrelevance of the "bad actor." That is, there is no evil "man behind the curtain" designing and operating the institutions that form the stuff of institutional racism. Undeniably, individuals animate these institutions. But, the fault lies not with the individual actors who

---

[5] Act of Mar. 26, 1790, ch. 3, 1 Stat. 103 (repealed 1795); Act of Jan. 29, 1795, ch. 20, 1 Stat. 414 (repealed 1802); Act of June 18, 1798, ch. 54, 1 Stat. 566 (repealed 1802); Act of Apr. 14, 1802, ch. 28, 2 Stat. 153 (repealed 1906).

[6] DARIA ROITHMAYR, REPRODUCING RACISM 4–5 (2014) (emphasis added).

bring institutions to life.[7] According to most definitions of institutional racism, actors—be they good, bad, or indifferent—are irrelevant in the grand scheme of things, as they play a minuscule role in something that is much bigger than themselves.

Although these four elements form the core of most definitions of institutional/structural racism, significant divergences in theorists' understandings of the concept remain. One interesting variance concerns the question of whether institutional racism is a synonym for structural racism, or whether the terms refer to two different phenomena. While most theorists conceptualize the two as synonymous, some differentiate *institutions* and *structures*, and thus differentiate *institutional racism* and *structural racism*. For example, john powell contends that the term *institutional racism* focuses on "intra-institutional dynamics," referring to the "practices and procedures within an institution" that may have the unintended consequence of disadvantaging racial minorities as a group.[8] He theorizes that the concept of *structural racism* is different, referring to the way that several institutions "interact to produce racialized outcomes."[9] Thus, within powell's schema, a theorist concerned with identifying and dismantling *institutional racism* will be looking within a single, isolated institution for those programs that act to reproduce racial hierarchies. Meanwhile, a theorist concerned with identifying and dismantling *structural racism* will be observing how the practices of multiple institutions, operating within multiple fields, combine to sustain racial minorities, as a group, within a subordinate social position. While the goal of powell's intervention is to encourage theorists to engage in more systemic, wide-ranging, sweeping analyses of racism, that work has been done under the banner of *institutional racism* as often as it has been done under the banner of *structural racism*. Consequently, today, most theorists thinking about race consider the two terms to be interchangeable.

Perhaps the most disagreement pertaining to the concept of institutional/structural racism relates not to its definition or its contours, but rather to its existence. That is, many persons—especially those on the political right—are skeptical that there is such a thing called institutional or structural racism; if they recognize its existence, they are doubtful that it explains as many social outcomes as those on the political left believe. For example, in his dissent in *Grutter v. Bollinger*,[10] in which the Court upheld the

---

7 Of course, some culpability may attach to those who participate in a scheme that they know has harmful consequences.

8 john a. powell, *Structural Racism: Building Upon the Insights of John Calmore*, 86 N.C. L. REV. 791, 795–96 (2008).

9 *Id.* at 793.

10 Grutter v. Bollinger, 539 U.S. 306 (2003).

constitutionality of race-based affirmative action, Justice Clarence Thomas expressed his disapproval of the concept of institutional/structural racism. Thomas theorized that the admissions plan at issue in the case "nearly guaranteed" black people with less than stellar LSAT scores admission to the University of Michigan Law School.[11] He conjectured that, as a result, black people were less incentivized to study vigorously for the LSAT. He suggested that maybe this was the real reason why black people, as a group, do not perform as well as white people on the LSAT and other standardized tests. He then acknowledged the speculative nature of his claim and, in the process, took a jab at the concept of institutional/structural racism:

> It is far from certain that the LSAT test-taker's behavior is responsive to the Law School's admissions policies. Nevertheless, the possibility remains that this racial discrimination [in the form of race-conscious admissions programs] will help fulfill the bigot's prophecy about black underperformance—just as it confirms the conspiracy theorist's belief that "institutional racism" is at fault for every racial disparity in our society.[12]

To Thomas and others of like mind, institutional racism is the stuff of conspiracy theory. Believing that it has much, or any, explanatory power when it comes to understanding the causes of present-day racial stratification is akin to believing that the moon landing was staged in a movie lot in Hollywood, or that Tupac is alive and living in Cuba with his mother.

Critics of Thomas would likely respond that while it may take an irrational level of skepticism to believe that Neil Armstrong actually was in Los Angeles instead of on the moon in July 1969, and that Tupac Shakur miraculously dodged the hail of bullets that reportedly killed him in September 1996, it does not take an irrational level of naiveté to believe that ostensibly race-neutral policies operate so as to make black people and other racial minorities poorer, sicker, more incarcerated, and less politically represented than their white counterparts. Indeed, progressive race thinkers have identified numerous mechanisms that they believe produce and reproduce existing racial hierarchies. The following have all been offered as examples of institutional/structural racism:

1. Public schools are typically funded with property taxes. This means that schools in poorer neighborhoods, where property values are low, tend to receive less funding than schools in more affluent neighborhoods, where property values are higher. These

---

[11] *Id.* at 377 (Thomas, J., dissenting).

[12] *Id.*

funding disparities typically translate into schools in poorer neighborhoods having more rundown physical plants, older books and equipment, limited access to adequate technology (i.e., computers, broadband internet), and fewer course offerings. Additionally, teachers in schools in poorer neighborhoods "are likely to have less experience, shorter tenure, and emergency credentials rather than official teaching certifications."[13]

Because people of color disproportionately bear the burdens of poverty in this country, poorer neighborhoods are often populated by people of color. Therefore, children of color are disproportionately those who are forced to attend under-resourced schools.

2. The Court has interpreted the Fourth Amendment to shield from the police only that which is shielded from private citizens. Thus, if individuals cannot erect a buffer between themselves and private actors, they enjoy no Fourth Amendment protection from the state as it goes about trying to prevent and punish crime. One effective buffer is space—simple distance from others. And people without money have a harder time accessing space. Many poor people in cities live in close proximity to their neighbors in buildings that are in various stages of disrepair—buildings through which sounds and smells travel easily. This makes the poor more vulnerable to the state's power to observe and punish.

Again, because people of color disproportionately bear the burdens of poverty in this country, those with a poverty-induced vulnerability to the state's power to observe and punish are disproportionately people of color.

3. Chester, Pennsylvania is the site of a number of commercial waste facilities. To be more precise, Chester has one of the largest collections of waste facilities in the nation. Not only do these facilities process all of the waste that the county in which Chester is located produces, but they also process waste from other states on the East Coast. Across the street from a housing complex in Chester sits one of the largest garbage-burning incinerators, which, in addition to burning local trash, also incinerates garbage that has been shipped to it from sites far outside of Pennsylvania. Thermal Pure Systems, which was the largest infectious medical waste treatment facility in the nation when it was in operation, was once located in Chester. The plant often left medical waste in adjacent lots, exposing residents to the risk of illness, injury, or worse. The pollution to which Chester's residents were exposed certainly took its toll. In the 1990s, the rate of infant mortality in the city was the highest in Pennsylvania. Sixty

---

[13] Devah Pager & Hana Shepherd, *The Sociology of Discrimination: Racial Discrimination in Employment, Housing, Credit, and Consumer Markets*, 34 ANN. REV. SOC. 181, 198 (2008).

percent of the city's children had blood-lead levels that exceeded recommended levels.

Notably, Chester is a predominately black city located in a county that is over 91% white. The rate of poverty in Chester is one of the highest in the state. Importantly, Chester is not that unusual. Studies have documented that persons in poor communities are more likely to be exposed to hazardous environmental conditions than those living in more affluent communities. Because people of color disproportionately bear the burdens of poverty, people of color are more likely to be subjected to environmental harms than are white people.[14]

4. As will be discussed in Chapter 17, critical thinkers about race have challenged traditional definitions of merit in the context of college admissions. Merit conventionally is defined as having a high GPA, a high standardized test score, and a résumé that features extracurricular activities, travel, AP classes, and honed skills and talents (i.e., the ability to play an instrument). However, affluent persons are much more likely than poor persons to be able to accumulate the stuff of merit. That is, there is a strong correlation between the wealth possessed by an individual's family and the score that she will receive on a standardized test; poor individuals are more likely to have to work after school and, consequently, are less likely to have the time to engage in extracurricular activities; it frequently takes money to travel and to develop a talent, which will preclude many poor individuals from doing so; and schools in poor neighborhoods are more likely to be under-resourced and, as a result, less likely to offer AP classes.

Because people of color have significantly less wealth than white people, and because they disproportionately bear the burdens of poverty, people of color have a more difficult time being "meritorious" according to established definitions of merit.

* * *

Now, there is little doubt that the practices in the four examples above have, in fact, disadvantaged racial minorities. However, there

[14] However, there is some evidence that nonwhite people's likelihood of being exposed to hazardous environmental conditions is due to their race, and is not simply an effect of class. As early as 1983, the U.S. General Accounting Office conducted a study that showed that three of the four most hazardous landfills in the South were located in poor black communities. The study went on to state that the siting pattern could not be attributed to the communities' poverty, as similar facilities in the South were not located in poor white communities. *See* U.S. GEN. ACCOUNTING OFF., GAO/RCED-83-168, SITING OF HAZARDOUS WASTE LANDFILLS AND THEIR CORRELATION WITH RACIAL AND ECONOMIC STATUS OF SURROUNDING COMMUNITIES (1983).

is a world of disagreement around the question of whether it is appropriate to identify them as institutional/structural *racism*.

Many progressive thinkers insist upon including the term "racism" in their description of the above phenomena. That is, they insist upon identifying them as examples of institutional/structural *racism*. Haney López has offered a particularly eloquent defense of this choice. He states that characterizing the phenomena above as a form of *racism* is "an analytic and political decision."[15] He continues:

> Referring to "racism" aims to evoke a sense of moral repugnance and social duty by vivifying the fundamental injustice of entrenched racial inequalities. . . . To call current racial patterns "racism" is to make a claim on that national moral obligation; in contrast, to relinquish the notion of racism, and even of race, is to cede one's claim on the nation's conscience.[16]

I. Questions and Discussion

1. Where do you come out on the question of calling race neutral practices that have the effect of harming people of color institutional/structural *racism*? What are the benefits of using the word *racism* to describe these practices? What are the dangers?

2. In *Washington v. Davis*, the Court embraced the discriminatory intent standard, which requires that persons challenging a law that has the effect of disadvantaging a racial group prove that the architects of the law *intended* to disadvantage the aggrieved racial group when they passed the law.[17] In accepting the discriminatory intent standard, the Court rejected the disparate impact standard, which would only necessitate a finding that the law has the effect of harming a racial group. Part of the reason for the Court's rejection of the disparate impact standard was the concern that it would have made a large number of laws and policies constitutionally suspect. The Court wrote:

> A rule that a statute designed to serve neutral ends is nevertheless invalid, absent compelling justification, if in practice it benefits or burdens one race more than another would be far reaching and would raise serious questions about, and perhaps invalidate, a whole range of tax, welfare, public service, regulatory, and licensing statutes

[15] Ian F. Haney López, *Post-Racial Racism: Racial Stratification and Mass Incarceration in the Age of Obama*, 98 CALIF. L. REV. 1023, 1071 (2010).

[16] *Id.* at 1071–72.

[17] Washington v. Davis, 426 U.S. 229 (1976).

> that may be more burdensome to the poor and to the average black than to the more affluent white.[18]

Now, there is a close relationship between the disparate impact standard and the concept of institutional/structural racism. Indeed, one would not be wrong to say that the disparate impact standard is designed to eliminate institutional/structural racism, as it is designed to bring the most rigorous judicial scrutiny to procedures and practices that, although race neutral, nevertheless have the effect of disparately impacting racial minorities, and negatively so.

The Court hesitated to embrace the disparate impact standard because it was too sweeping. Is that a good reason for rejecting the concept of institutional/structural racism—because it, similarly, is quite broad? Is it helpful or harmful to conceptualize "a whole range of tax, welfare, public service, regulatory, and licensing" regimes as *racist*? Does the identification of something as *racist* lose its moral punch if everything—or most things—are *racist*?

3. Social psychologists Michael Unzueta and Brian Lowery conducted a study that sought to shed some light on why some white people are willing to recognize institutional/structural racism as *racism* and others are not.[19] They began by noting that the concept of institutional/structural racism presupposes that people of color not only are unfairly disadvantaged by race neutral processes, policies, and procedures, but that white people are unfairly *advantaged* by the same. For example, while funding public schools through property taxes disadvantages children of color in poor neighborhoods, the practice actually benefits children in wealthier neighborhoods, who are disproportionately white. Therefore, if the way that we finance our public school is a species of institutional/structural racism, it is a racism that works to benefit white people as it harms people of color.

The idea that white people are unjustly enriched by institutional/structural racism may be a motivation for them to deny its existence, as it would suggest that the economic and social privileges that they enjoy are not the product of their hard work, talent, intelligence, and discipline, but rather are *unearned* in many important respects. Unzueta and Lowery hypothesized that those individuals who had strong perceptions of themselves as hardworking, talented, intelligent, and disciplined would be more inclined to acknowledge institutional/structural racism as *racism* than those individuals whose positive perceptions of themselves were more fragile.

---

[18] *Id.* at 248.

[19] Michael M. Unzueta & Brian S. Lowery, *Defining Racism Safely: The Role of Self-Image Maintenance on White Americans' Conceptions of Racism*, 44 J. EXPERIMENTAL SOC. PSYCHOL. 1491 (2008).

In order to test the hypothesis, Unzueta and Lowery subjected a group of study participants to a self-affirmation manipulation. (The researchers asked participants to identify values that were central to their self-concept, and then they affirmed those values by asking the participants to explain why those values were important to them.) Another group of study participants were not exposed to the self-affirmation manipulation. Unzueta and Lowery found that the group whose self-concepts had been affirmed was more likely to identify race neutral processes that disproportionately burden nonwhite people as *racism* than the group whose self-concepts had not been affirmed.

What are your reactions to Unzueta's and Lowery's study? What are the implications of the research?

4. You might have observed that all of the examples that this chapter provides of institutional/structural racism ended by noting that the practices disproportionately harmed nonwhite people because nonwhite people disproportionately bear the burdens of poverty in this country. Does that suggest that the race problem will be solved if the nation solves the class problem? That is, does it suggest that racial inequality will go away if society eliminates class inequality? Does it suggest that the *real* problem is not race, but rather class? Why or why not?

Some have argued that the reason the country has not eliminated class inequality—indeed, the reason many refuse to think of class inequality as a social problem—is because of race. The argument, explored in Chapter 11 and again in Chapter 19, is that if people of color did not disproportionately bear the burdens of poverty, the nation would do more to reduce poverty, establish a generous safety net, and diminish the size of the great chasm that exists between the haves and the have-nots. This argument insists that race is, in fact, the *real* problem. Is the argument convincing to you? If so, why? If not, what would it take to convince you that it is true? What sort of evidence would you require?

Chapter 8

IMPLICIT BIAS

Implicit bias might be most easily defined by contrasting it with explicit bias: where explicit biases are those feelings and attitudes of which a person is completely aware, implicit biases are those same feelings and attitudes of which she is not cognizant.

Implicit bias certainly has been much-discussed,[1] and critical thinkers about race have been open to the concept, finding it helpful for explaining existing racial stratification. Indeed, many progressive race scholars have devoted their scholarship to it. They have theorized the relationship between implicit racial biases and white dominance, documented the prevalence of implicit biases against racial minorities, and proposed reforms that might work to eliminate or reduce the impact of implicit racial biases. While this work around implicit bias has been well-received for the most part, some have been a bit more apprehensive about it. This chapter provides an overview of implicit bias research, describes proposals for its application in the law, and then discusses critiques that have been levied against it—both from those on the political right and political left.

I. What Are Implicit Biases?

We might begin with some terminology. In the field of social psychology, "attitudes" are defined as "evaluative dispositions"—the sense that one likes or dislikes something.[2] So, for example, many (but definitely not all) vegetarians have a favorable attitude towards tofu and an unfavorable attitude towards steak tartare. In other words, many vegetarians like tofu (which, if prepared properly, can be delicious) and dislike steak tartare (it is raw meat, after all).

Meanwhile, a "stereotype" is an "association between a social group or category and a trait."[3] A stereotype about vegetarians might be that they are very health-minded individuals; in this example, the social group of vegetarians is associated with the trait of health-mindedness. Now, if it were true that all vegetarians were, indeed, health-minded, then it would not be a stereotype to say as much:

---

[1] A search of the term in LexisNexis in July 2018 came up with close to 25,000 hits.

[2] Anthony Greenwald & Linda Hamilton Krieger, *Implicit Bias: Scientific Foundations*, 94 CALIF. L. REV. 945, 948 (2006).

[3] *Id.* at 949.

health-mindedness would be a "defining attribute" of the group.[4] However, in reality, many vegetarians do not possess this characteristic; they drink alcohol, smoke cigarettes, eat fried foods, and fail to exercise regularly or at all. Thus, it is accurate to say that any association between vegetarians and wholesome living is a stereotype—even if vegetarians are statistically more likely to be health-minded than are non-vegetarians.

People may or may not be aware of the attitudes that they possess or the stereotypes that they harbor. We define "explicit attitudes" and "explicit stereotypes" as the attitudes and stereotypes about which individuals are aware; implicit attitudes and implicit stereotypes are the ones about which individuals are unaware.

We arrive now at our definition of "implicit biases": they are "discriminatory biases based on implicit attitudes and implicit stereotypes."[5] Biases may be positive or negative. You might have an unconscious fondness of vegetarians—because you may unconsciously associate them with a healthy lifestyle. If so, then you have an implicit bias *in favor of* vegetarians. Or, conversely, you may have an unconscious animosity towards vegetarians—because you may unconsciously associate them with the trait of self-righteousness. If so, then you have an implicit bias *against* vegetarians.

The Implicit Association Test, or IAT, is the most widely used measure of implicit biases. As described by Dayna Bowen Matthew, the IAT is a "computer-based test that works on the straightforward premise that when people are asked to associate photographs with words that are consistent with their implicitly held beliefs about those pictures, they will make those associations quickly. But when people are asked to connect photographs with words they would not naturally or automatically associate with those photographs, their response times will be too slow to allow them to override their automatic instincts."[6] For example, if someone wanted to measure whether you are implicitly biased against vegetarians, she would generate an IAT that asks you to press a key on the right when you see prompts for vegetarian-related words (i.e., tofu, vegetables, PETA) as well as when you see prompts for pleasant words (i.e., good, nice, happy); you would be asked to press a key on the left when you see prompts for non-vegetarian-related words (i.e., steak, filet, hamburger) as well as when you see prompts for unpleasant words (i.e., bad, evil, sad). The test would then shift the pairings; you would

---

[4] Jerry Kang et al., *Implicit Bias in the Courtroom*, 59 UCLA L. REV. 1124, 1128 (2012).

[5] Greenwald & Krieger, *supra* note 2, at 951.

[6] DAYNA BOWEN MATTHEW, JUST MEDICINE: A CURE FOR RACIAL INEQUALITY IN AMERICAN HEALTH CARE 45 (2015).

then be asked to press a key on the right when you see prompts for vegetarian-related words and *negative* words and a key on the left when you see prompts for non-vegetarian-related words and *positive* words. If your response times are quicker for the second pairing—when you are asked to press the same key for vegetarian-related words and negative words—then we might reasonably conclude that you are implicitly biased against vegetarians.

The kicker is that implicit biases often contradict what people explicitly report. An individual may report that she is neutral towards a social category; but, the IAT may reveal that she is, in fact, averse towards that very category. Interestingly, social psychologists have concluded that implicit biases are a better predictor of behavior than explicit biases. Essentially, an individual's behavior is not dictated by her conscious associations and aversions, but rather by her *unconscious* associations and aversions.

People have become interested in implicit biases for two primary reasons. First, the science of implicit bias challenges traditional conceptions of our cognitive processes. In the past, most believed that attitudes and stereotypes of which we were conscious were all there was. Most were aware that people might *lie* about their explicit attitudes and stereotypes; the meat-eater might conceal the fact that he hates vegetarians, or the vegetarian might claim that she finds steak tartare disgusting when, in fact, she thinks that it is delightful. However, in bygone years, most assumed that there were no associations or likes and dislikes at the unconscious level that might contradict people's conscious thoughts and influence their behavior. The field of implicit social cognition blows this assumption out of the water.

Second, people have become interested in implicit biases not because social psychologists have documented a prevalence of deep-seated, albeit unconscious, distaste for *vegetarians* among the general population. Rather, implicit biases have become the subject of much conversation and research because social psychologists have documented a prevalence of unconscious *racial* biases among the general population. They have shown that many people harbor stereotypes that associate black people with problematic traits, like criminality and laziness. Further, they have shown that many people have deep-seated, albeit unconscious, negative attitudes towards black people. Indeed, IAT test takers of all racial identities and ascriptions tend to show implicit anti-black biases. This is true despite the fact that, in the post-civil rights era, few individuals report having any *explicit* anti-black biases.

Scholars working in the field have conducted numerous studies that purport to show the disturbing consequences that implicit racial biases may have. In one interesting study, a researcher developed a simulation designed to test how implicit racial biases might influence the likelihood that an individual will shoot a person who may or may not pose a threat.[7] Users were shown images of black and white persons in different cityscapes. Some of the people in the images held weapons; others held items that could be mistaken for weapons, like cellphones. Users were instructed to "shoot" those characters who had weapons. Disturbingly, users shot armed black men more quickly than they shot armed white men. Additionally, they were much more likely to shoot unarmed black people than they were to shoot unarmed white people.[8] Further, users were much more likely *not to shoot* armed white persons than were not to shoot armed black persons. Another study showed that users were quicker to shoot black persons with features that were more stereotypically "black" (i.e., wide nose, full lips, dark skin) than black persons without those features.[9] Importantly, there was no correlation between a user's reported *explicit* biases and the likelihood that she would shoot an unarmed black person, fail to shoot an armed white person, or quickly shoot a black person who looked more stereotypically black.

In another fascinating study, researchers attempted to demonstrate the implicit association between blackness and criminality.[10] Users were divided into three groups: one group was flashed an image of a black face, another was flashed an image of a white face, and the last was not flashed any image at all. Significantly, none of the users were aware that they had been shown an image; the image was shown so quickly that it only registered in the user's subconscious. The users were then shown fuzzy pictures of items that slowly became more distinct and identifiable. The users who had been subliminally primed with a black face more quickly

---

[7] Joshua Correll, *Across the Thin Blue Line: Police Officers and Racial Bias in the Decision to Shoot*, 92 J. PERSONALITY & SOC. PSYCHOL. 1006 (2007).

[8] Cynthia Lee observes that this has important, and disquieting, ramifications for self-defense cases. She notes that in order to claim self-defense successfully, a defendant has to prove that she believed that she faced an imminent threat and her belief that she needed to use force to defend herself was reasonable. However, "[i]f most individuals would be more likely to 'see' a weapon in the hands of an unarmed Black person and thus more likely to shoot an unarmed Black person when they would not shoot a similarly situated White person, then jurors in self-defense cases may also be more likely to find that an individual who says he shot an unarmed Black person in self-defense because he believed the victim was about to kill or seriously injure him acted reasonably, even if he was mistaken." Cynthia Lee, *Making Race Salient: Trayvon Martin and Implicit Bias in a Not Yet Post-Racial Society*, 91 N.C. L. REV. 101, 130 (2013). Thus, implicit anti-black biases may make it easier for people to kill black people, even when unarmed, and suffer no criminal consequences.

[9] Kimberly Barsamian Kahn & Jean M. McMahon, *Shooting Deaths of Unarmed Racial Minorities: Understanding the Role of Racial Stereotypes on Decisions to Shoot*, 1 TRANSLATIONAL ISSUES PSYCHOL. SCI. 310, 314 (2015).

[10] Jennifer Eberhardt et al., *Seeing Black: Race, Crime, and Visual Processing*, 87 J. PERSONALITY & SOC. PSYCHOL. 876 (2004).

identified pictures of weapons than the users who had been primed with a white face or no face at all. Further, the relationship between blackness and criminality—or, at least, weapons—worked the other way, as well: users who had been subliminally primed with images of weapons paid more attention to black male faces that appeared on the screen than white male faces.

In another noteworthy study, researchers tested the effect that race had on individuals' memories.[11] Researchers gave study participants a fact pattern that described an altercation that a man, the defendant, had outside of a bar. One group of participants was given a fact pattern in which the defendant had a "black-sounding" name, Tyronne. Another group was given the exact same fact pattern; however, the defendant's name had been changed so that it was "white-sounding": William. The participants who read the fact pattern in which the defendant was black remembered more aspects of the story in which the defendant acted in an aggressive manner as compared to participants who had read about a white defendant. "[P]articipants who read about Tyronne had a recall accuracy rate of 80.2 percent. That is, they failed to recall just 19.8 percent of facts accurately relating to the actor's aggressive actions. . . . [P]articipants who read about William failed to recall 32.2 percent of these aggressive facts."[12] As is de rigueur with these studies, the facility at remembering Tyronne's aggressive actions, and the relative inability to remember comparable actions taken by William, had no correlation with the participants' reported *explicit* biases.

The existence of implicit biases may have significant implications for racial justice. Implicit racial biases may play a key role in the persistence of racial inequality in the post-civil rights era. For example, the fact that an overwhelming majority of people associate black people with negative traits, like criminality, may explain why people of color are stopped, frisked, arrested, indicted, and convicted more often than their comparably situated white peers. Indeed, it may explain the nation's choice to use the criminal justice system as a principal means for addressing its social problems. It may explain the lack of real public outrage over the reality that this approach to addressing social problems has resulted in the mass incarceration of high numbers—both absolute and relative—of black and Latinx people.

Further, the likelihood that people oftentimes are not aware of their disaffection towards historically disadvantaged groups, like black people, may reveal why the law has arguably been an

---

[11] Justin D. Levinson, *Forgotten Racial Equality: Implicit Bias, Decisionmaking, and Misremembering*, 57 DUKE L.J. 345 (2007).

[12] *Id.* at 399.

incompetent tool for addressing racial inequality. Antidiscrimination law tends to reflect traditional conceptions of our cognitive processes, regulating public and private spaces with the assumption that discriminatory behaviors are invariably the result of conscious commitments. If this is not really how discrimination works anymore, then we ought not to be surprised that antidiscrimination law has failed to produce a racially just society. The law might be chasing an anachronism, allowing the mechanisms that perpetuate racial exclusion and subordination in the current era to go unpoliced. This next Part discusses this possibility.

II. Implicit Bias and the Law

What should the existence of implicit biases mean for the law? A contingent of legal scholars called themselves behavioral realists have argued that the law ought to reflect the insights that social psychology has yielded about how humans actually process information and act in the real world.

Linda Krieger and Susan Fiske have offered a particularly compelling defense of behavioral realism in the context of antidiscrimination law.[13] In an influential article, they respond to skeptics who caution against revising the law in light of discoveries about implicit biases. These skeptics have asserted that the law ought not to reflect new empirical research about human behavior—empirical research whose validity may be disproved in due course. Krieger and Fiske note that these disbelievers imagine that the options available to us are either to create a law that reflects the theory of human behavior suggested by implicit bias research, or to create a law that reflects no theory of human behavior at all. But, Krieger and Fiske argue that this misrepresents our choices. The observe that it is incorrect to believe that our antidiscrimination law in its current formulation is free of theory. Quite the opposite, they argue that antidiscrimination law currently reflects a theory of human behavior; moreover, this theory of human behavior is one that social psychologists believe they have disproved. They write that "those who criticize the use of insights from the empirical social sciences in constitutional lawmaking often fail to recognize that the alternative to empiricism is often bare judicial surmise, posing as common sense, and having a lesser claim to validity than the imperfect science such critics would exclude from the legal analytical process."[14]

---

[13] Linda Hamilton Krieger & Susan T. Fiske, *Behavioral Realism in Employment Discrimination Law: Implicit Bias and Disparate Treatment*, 94 CALIF. L. REV. 997 (2006).

[14] *Id.* at 1016.

How Do Implicit Biases Work?

Social psychologists offer a multi-step model to explain the operation of implicit biases.

1. The first step involves the individual's accumulation of knowledge about the social environment. During this stage, individuals are exposed to—and accept—the stereotypes and attitudes about groups that are present in society. We learn to associate black men with criminality, Latinx people with illegality, Asian people with intelligence, etc. These lessons—which do not have to be explicitly taught and which are essentially unavoidable—come from a variety of sources, "including music, television, books, family members, friends, teachers, childhood experiences, stories shared by others, news media, movies, and so forth."[15]

Importantly, these lessons are learned at extremely early ages: psychologists have found that children as young as three years-old demonstrate awareness of cultural and societal narratives about groups. The early introduction to racial (and gender-related, sexual, etc.) stereotypes and attitudes makes them especially durable. Thus, even when we become older and commit ourselves to the proposition that all persons, without respect to racial identification and ascription, are equal, we can never really *unlearn* the lessons that we learned during early childhood.

2. The second step in the operation of implicit biases takes place when we encounter another person. One of the many lessons that we learn at young ages is how to sort people into social categories. We learn what characteristics identify a person as a "man, "woman," "black," "white," "Asian," "fat," "skinny," etc. Thus, when we meet another person, we engage those lessons and immediately sort him/her/them into socially salient categories. We generally are unaware that we are engaging in this sorting. It tends to rise to consciousness only when a person is not easily categorized—when he/she/they is/are racially ambiguous, or defy norms about how the genders ought to present themselves. The most important point, however, is that within milliseconds of encountering another person, we know what "type" of person we are dealing with.

3. The third step occurs within moments of the initial sorting. While the first identification is value-neutral—i.e., when we (usually unconsciously) think to ourselves, "I am looking at a black male"—in less than a second, values flood in. Indeed, "within five hundred milliseconds from the moment of identification[,] we retrieve from our memory the most dominant associations we have stored with regard to that person's racial or ethnic group."[16] Thus, if we have been exposed to social narratives that describe black males as criminals, we will think, albeit unconsciously, about the possibility of criminality within less than a second after encountering a black male.

Further, our unconscious associations tend to override information that the individual we have encountered presents that might contradict those associations. So, if the black male in question is dressed in a suit and carrying a suitcase, we will still unconsciously think about criminality—even though business attire is not typically associated with crime (at least not the violent variety). Indeed, it is possible that we will not even *see* that he is dressed in a suit and carrying a suitcase, instead perceiving him as wearing a dark hoodie and matching jeans while toting a backpack. We will still unconsciously think about criminality even though, if asked, we might deride the construction of black males as criminals and profess our commitment to equality and racial justice.

4. The fourth step involves acting on the implicit biases. Again, without conscious reflection, we may engage in behavior that is consistent with our implicit biases (and inconsistent with our explicit biases). So, we may refuse to make eye contact with the black male in question, stand farther away from him that we would a white male, or cut the conversation short. We may decide to sit in the open seat on the subway car that is not next to him. If we are police officers, we may decide to stop and frisk him, or arrest him, or shoot him. If we are jurors, we may decide to convict him, or vote in favor of the death penalty as punishment for the crime for which he has already been convicted. If we are employers, we may decide not to hire him. The gamut of responses that we may have to our implicit biases is vast, ranging from minor improprieties to devastating outrages.

Neuroscientists have augmented this model by identifying different areas of the brain that play a role in the operation of implicit biases. Brain scans reveal that there exists some relationship between implicit biases and the amygdala, a small mass of grey matter on both the left and rights sides of the brain. Interestingly, the amygdala controls our reactions to stimuli and produces our emotions—including fear.

The dorsolateral prefrontal cortex (diPFC) and the anterior cingulate cortex (ACC) also appear to have a role in the operation of implicit biases. Neuroscientists believe that these two areas of the brain work to keep unconscious the implicit associations that we have, functioning to suppress them such that they never rise to the level of consciousness.[17]

As a case in point, they look to *Price Waterhouse v. Hopkins*, in which the Court endorsed a "mixed motive" analysis in proving disparate treatment under Title VII.[18] A violation of Title VII occurs

---

[15] MATTHEW, *supra* note 6, at 40.

[16] *Id.*

[17] *Id.* at 42.

[18] Price Waterhouse v. Hopkins, 490 U.S. 228 (1989).

whenever race, color, sex, national origin, or religion is a "motivating factor" in a decision to hire, fire, promote, or not promote. The "mixed motive" analysis provides that even if the employer has legitimate reasons for an employment decision—i.e., reasons that have nothing to do with an employee's race, color, sex, national origin, or religion—it is still actionable discrimination if the employer *also* allows any of those protected characteristics to inform the employment decision. In the latter situation, the protected characteristic nevertheless "motivates" the decision. Writing for the plurality, Justice Brennan explains this concept: "In saying that gender played a motivating part in an employment decision, we mean that, if we asked the employer at the moment of the decision what its reasons were and if we received a truthful response, one of those reasons would be that the applicant or employee was a woman."[19]

Krieger and Fiske observe that Brennan's approach is not *theory-free*. Instead, it reflects notions of humans' cognitive processes that behavioral realists believe they have debunked. They write:

> This description reflects two "common sense" theories about the nature of discriminatory motivation. In speaking of the decision maker providing a "truthful" (as opposed to an "accurate") response, this description reflects an unstated assumption that, when disparate treatment discrimination occurs, the discriminator is consciously aware, "at the moment of decision," that he or she is discriminating. . . . [T]hese two lay psychological theories—the belief in transparent mental processing, and the modeling of perception and decision making as two discrete processes—have not withstood empirical scrutiny. Decision makers are often *not* aware of the impact of a target's social group membership on their judgments, and those biased judgments are often formed quite early in the social perception process, long before the moment that a decision about the target person is made.[20]

Thus, Krieger and Fiske argue that judges tasked with developing and construing antidiscrimination law should take into consideration the insights that social psychology has yielded and, using them as "a jurisprudential corrective," rid the law of its erroneous "common sense" theories about how human cognitive processes work.[21] They contend that jurists should construct a law that is mindful that not only do individuals tend to be unaware of their problematic associations and negative evaluations of

---

[19] *Id.* at 288.

[20] Krieger & Fiske, *supra* note 13, at 1010.

[21] *Id.* at 1006.

historically marginalized groups, but also that these biases can pervert the decision making process by distorting perceptions of relevant information and influencing the ability of decision makers to retrieve this information from memory.

Behavioral realists believe that social psychology can make many other contributions to the law. Many scholars in this camp have proposed reforms in light of what the research around implicit bias has revealed. For example, studies have demonstrated that negative implicit biases about outgroups are weakened if individuals actually have quality interactions with members of the outgroup. Behavioral realists see in this research a justification for affirmative action and other measures that increase diversity within environments. According to these scholars, workplaces, educational institutions, juries, police departments, judges' chambers, and the offices of prosecutors and defense attorneys could all see a reduction in the implicit biases held by the people who operate in those spaces if some degree of heterogeneity was found in them.

In a similar vein, Song Richardson advocates the adoption of policies that encourage or facilitate interactions between police departments and the communities of color that they are supposed to protect and serve.[22] Noting the prevalence of the implicit association between blackness and criminality, and noting as well that implicit biases are reduced when individuals interact with members of groups against which they are biased, Richardson proposes that police officers would be less inclined to implicitly associate the people of color who they police with criminality if they simply had positive contact with them.

Other scholars observe that the law might simply mandate or encourage the implementation of policies that require decision makers—like admissions and hiring committees, jurors, legislators, prosecutors, and defense attorneys—to be informed about implicit bias and the probable effects such bias has on behavior. Evidence shows that people who believe themselves to be wholly objective tend to act on their implicit biases more than those who believe themselves to be partial in some way. Thus, informing decision makers about implicit bias—and the likelihood that they have more than a few—may make them doubtful of their objectivity and thus less likely to allow their implicit biases to influence their behavior. Indeed, some have suggested that decision makers should be required or encouraged to take the IAT so that proof that they have biases is put plainly in front of their faces.

---

22 *See* L. Song Richardson, *Police Racial Violence: Lessons from Social Psychology*, 83 FORDHAM L. REV. 2961 (2015).

Some reforms that behavioral realists have suggested are quite easy to implement. For example, in view of studies having demonstrated that individuals misremember (and fail to remember) facts in a way that is consistent with their implicit biases, some scholars have proposed that jurors simply be allowed to take notes during court proceedings, thus reducing their need to rely on their faulty memories.[23]

Other suggested reforms require more effort. For example, some scholars have proposed that institutions take a continuous accounting of the decisions made by decision makers. Why? Well, most people, save the exceptional few, embrace egalitarian principles and would be disturbed if they knew that they have acted in an unfair, prejudicial manner. The objective of keeping a detailed record of all of a decision makers' decisions "is to create a negative feedback loop in which individual[s] . . . are given the corrective information necessary to know how they are doing and to be motivated to make changes if they find evidence of biased performances."[24] In order to shock decision makers with evidence that they have been making biased decisions, the data about those decisions have to be accumulated and synthesized first.

Now, the field of implicit bias is not without its critics. A rough way to schematize these critics is to divide them into those who launch their critiques from the political right and those, including critical race theorists, who launch their critiques from the political left. The next section discusses the conservative critique of implicit bias.

III. Critiques from the Right

Gregory Mitchell and Philip Tetlock probably have written the most extensive critique of the field of implicit social cognition.[25] They have a number of different questions about the "science"[26] that has generated evidence of implicit biases, and they are skeptical about the advisability of incorporating this science into the law.

A. What Is the IAT Measuring?

Mitchell and Tetlock note that researchers describe the IAT as measuring the test taker's unconscious associations and evaluations. However, they are not entirely convinced that associations and

---

[23] *See* Levinson, *supra* note 11.

[24] Kang et al., *supra* note 4, at 1179.

[25] Gregory Mitchell & Philip E. Tetlock, *Antidiscrimination Law and the Perils of Mindreading*, 67 OHIO ST. L.J. 1023 (2006).

[26] I use quotation marks around "science" to reflect Mitchell's and Tetlock's wariness of the rhetorical move made when implicit bias researchers "claim the mantle of science" to describe their discoveries. *Id.* at 1029.

evaluations are, in fact, what the IAT measures. They observe that the IAT purports to determine the existence of biases by calculating differences in the speed at which test takers respond to two sets of pairings. As noted above, the IAT assumes that a user will respond more quickly to categories that are linked in the unconscious—like white person and businessman, or black person and criminal. However, Mitchell and Tetlock argue that there is no proof that differences in reaction time measure *bias*; they are open to the possibility that those differences could very well measure other emotions. They write that "[p]romoters of the IAT have presented no evidence that current reaction time measures can reliably distinguish qualitatively different cognitive-emotional states, such as frustration, sorrow and anger. . . . [I]t is not clear what emotions are implicated, and no reason is given to presume that the results are attributable to racial animus as opposed to guilt, shame, or another emotion."[27] Essentially, Mitchell and Tetlock propose that the reason many individuals take longer to link "black people" with "businessman" or "white people" with "criminal" may be that many individuals are sad that the number of black businesspersons is disproportionately low, or they feel guilty that white people are not overrepresented among the population of persons with criminal records, as are black people.

Perhaps a more convincing critique is the observation that implicit bias researchers have not demonstrated that a high IAT score demonstrates that the test taker actually subscribes to the association or evaluation that the test reveals. Mitchell and Tetlock write that test results indicating that a test taker associates "black people" with "criminal" do not prove that the test taker herself actually believes that black people are appropriately linked to "criminal." Instead, the results may simply indicate that the test taker is aware that there are societal discourses linking black people to criminality. In essence, they argue that an IAT score may simply reflect awareness about cultural narratives pertaining to social groups: "mere knowledge of cultural stereotypes about minorities should be sufficient to cause people to manifest 'prejudice' on the IAT."[28]

B. Does Implicit Biases Translate into Biased Behavior?

Mitchell and Tetlock argue that there is a paucity of evidence that connects the possession of implicit biases, as measured by the IAT, to biased behavior. They write that "IAT scores remain meaningless until empirical studies link specific ranges of scores to

---

[27] *Id.* at 1082–83.

[28] *Id.* at 1084.

specific acts that . . . represent discrimination.[29] To be most persuasive, a study would show that an implicit bias *causes* a discriminatory behavior. No study has been able to show such a causal relationship. The best that scholars in the field have been able to do is to show that there is a *correlation* between a high IAT score (showing that a test taker has implicit biases) and biased behavior. However, Mitchell and Tetlock are dissatisfied with these correlational studies, arguing that they "rarely control for a variety of confounding factors that could explain the pattern of results without assuming implicit prejudice or stereotypes at work."[30]

Further, Mitchell and Tetlock are skeptical of the studies that show that persons with anti-black implicit biases interact differently with black people as compared to white people. These investigations document that anti-black implicit biases are correlated with subtle behaviors, like decreases in eye contact or increases in speech errors, that make the individual appear to be less friendly when interacting with a person of color. Their critique is that these understated changes in body language and speech patterns are not the stuff of actionable discrimination. Indeed, a Title VII suit that alleged discrimination due to a potential employer having leaned forward when talking to white interviewees and leaned backward when talking to black interviewees would be promptly dismissed. Mitchell and Tetlock want proof that slight behaviors, like changes in the rate at which an individual blinks her eyes, are correlated to behaviors that constitute *legal* discrimination, like the failure to hire a qualified candidate due to his race. In the absence of such proof, they conceptualize these studies as much ado about nothing.

In response, implicit bias researchers counter that their critics hold them to impossibly high standards of proof—standards that they do not demand of current, unreformed laws and policies. Jerry Kang and Kristin Lane write that "science rarely provides perfect information, and demanding total understanding of every possible mechanism or boundary condition of a process will both guarantee inaction and stunt future research."[31] They underscore that it is doubly unfair for critics to demand that implicit bias research meet standards that most science cannot meet because "this stringent epistemological requirement is rarely required of the laws and policies embedded in the status quo."[32]

---

[29] *Id.* at 1032.

[30] *Id.* at 1032–33.

[31] Jerry Kang & Kristin Lane, *Seeing Through Colorblindness: Implicit Bias and the Law*, 58 UCLA L. REV. 465, 508 (2010).

[32] *Id.*

C. Do Implicit Biases Matter in Institutional Contexts That Have Proscribed Discriminatory Conduct?

Mitchell and Tetlock have expressed skepticism about whether implicit biases, if they exist, survive in real-world institutions, which are constrained by antidiscrimination laws and policies that prohibit discriminatory conduct. It is one thing, they say, to have implicit biases on which one is inclined to act. It is another thing, they say, to operate in institutions that strictly and unambiguously prohibit such behavior. Absent evidence proving otherwise, they conclude that "there is no reason to believe that these safeguards will not be effective against discrimination motivated by implicit biases."[33]

Defenders of implicit bias research respond to this claim by flipping the question and asking: why should we believe that the antidiscrimination safeguards that are already in place *will be* effective against discrimination motivated by implicit bias? Essentially, this question shifts the burden of proof. While Mitchell and Tetlock ask for evidence of the law's inefficacy, supporters of implicit bias research ask for evidence of the law's efficacy. Differently stated, Mitchell's and Tetlock's critique asks for justifications for changing our current approach to producing racially equitable outcomes; the response to this critique asks for justifications for the status quo.

D. Is It Not Rational to Have Biases—Either Implicit or Explicit—Against Historically Disadvantaged Groups?

The final critique that Mitchell and Tetlock lob at implicit bias research relates to the rationality of implicit, or even explicit, associations between social categories and problematic traits. For example, consider the association between black people and criminality once again. Mitchell and Tetlock would ask whether this association is a *bias* inasmuch as black people are, for a host of reasons, statistically more likely than other social groups to be criminals. This association is not a *bias*, they say. It is a "perfectly rational reaction[ ] to existing socioeconomic conditions."[34] Accordingly, persons who harbor such associations are not *biased*, they argue. They are merely "rational observers of the social scene."[35] Mitchell and Tetlock suggest that if it is rational to have these associations, then possessing them—and acting on them—is morally justified, and ought to be legal.

Proponents of implicit bias research find this argument unconvincing. First, they note that decades of research in the

---

[33] Mitchell & Tetlock, *supra* note 25, at 1034.

[34] *Id.* at 1085.

[35] *Id.*

behavioral law and economics field have proven that individuals are not very good at both calculating probabilities and engaging in behavior that is consistent with those calculations. This research suggests that we overestimate and underestimate risk, probabilities, and likelihoods all the time. They contend that it is overly optimistic to believe that, all of a sudden, we become perfectly rational when it is time to assess the appropriateness of linking blackness and criminality. Second, they observe that discriminating against an individual on the basis of a protected characteristic, like race, is illegal—even when it is rational. Indeed, we might formulate the claim more strongly and say that discriminating against an individual on the basis of race is illegal *especially* when it is rational. Writes Samuel Bagenstos, "The prohibition of rational discrimination is a central component of antidiscrimination doctrine—and it may be the most important aspect of antidiscrimination on the ground."[36]

* * *

On the whole, social scientists working in the implicit bias field are unpersuaded by the critiques made by conservative scholars like Mitchell and Tetlock, describing them and others like them as "islands of consensus within a sea of controversy."[37] Defenders of the field tend to observe the political motivations for these conservative critiques. Kang has noted that research findings that show that implicit biases permeate society challenge the conventional narrative that conservatism offers. The conservative narrative maintains that the U.S. used to have a problem with racism, but then the Civil Rights Movement happened and successfully purged racist ideologies from people's hearts and minds (save for the anomalous few who still retain anachronistic prejudices and hatreds). The narrative proposes that, after great effort, we fortunately now live "in a meritocratic, color-blind, gender-blind, social category-blind, market-based" world.[38] The narrative does not deny the existence of racial and other inequalities in the modern present. However, it understands these inequalities to be the just results of a fair competition. The narrative proclaims that if people of color, or women, or the indigent are losing the competition and are poorer, sicker, more incarcerated, etc. than their white, or male, or wealthy counterparts, then the former have

---

[36] Samuel R. Bagenstos, *Implicit Bias, "Science," and Antidiscrimination Law*, 1 HARV. L. & POL'Y REV. 476, 486 (2007).

[37] John T. Jost, *The Existence of Implicit Bias is Beyond Reasonable Doubt: A Refutation of Ideological and Methodological Objections and Executive Summary of Ten Studies No Manager Should Ignore*, 29 RES. ORGANIZATIONAL BEHAV. 39, 42 (2009).

[38] Jerry Kang, *Implicit Bias and the Pushback from the Left*, 54 ST. LOUIS U. L.J. 1139, 1140 (2010).

only themselves—and their shoddy work ethics, or their problematic lifestyles, or their unhealthy genes—to blame. Kang writes that implicit bias research challenges this narrative, demonstrating that individuals *without* prejudices or aversions in the post-civil rights era are actually the anomalous few. He posits that the research on implicit bias calls into question one of the foundational premises upon which conservatism is based. This, he suggests, explains the conservative impulse to challenge it and deny its relevance to the law.

IV. Critiques from the Left

If implicit bias research is, in fact, a challenge to one of the fundamental assumptions that undergirds political conservatism, then it is easy to understand the motivations behind critiques from the right. However, critiques from the left might be bit more complicated. This is because those on the left tend to find the results of implicit bias research—showing the ubiquity of prejudice against historically marginalized groups—quite convincing. (It might be more accurate to say that many of those on the left, especially critical race theorists, do not need any convincing about the ubiquity of prejudice against racial minorities. Implicit bias research offers to "prove" what critical race theorists already know.) Moreover, many of those on the left are sympathetic to the implications of implicit bias research inasmuch as it may lead to a reevaluation of our current antidiscrimination laws and the implementation of more mechanisms to guard against the reproduction of racial hierarchies. However, there are some aspects of implicit bias research that folks on the left find deeply troubling.

It may a bit incongruous for critical race theorists, in particular, to find fault with the field of implicit social cognition. This incongruity is owed to the fact that one of the most prominent and renowned critical race theorists, Charles Lawrence, wrote an article that paved the way for discoveries in implicit social cognition to be applied to the law. In 1987, Lawrence published "The Id, the Ego, and Equal Protection," in which he argued that the Court was wrong when it interpreted the Constitution to require plaintiffs to show that a defendant had an intent to discriminate in order to prove a violation of the Equal Protection Clause.[39] Lawrence wrote that in the post-civil rights era, individuals frequently do not possess a discriminatory intent when they take actions that harm racial minorities, arguing instead that harmful actions oftentimes are the products of unconscious processes. To buttress his claim, he looked to Freudian psychology and a field that was still in its embryonic stages

---

[39] Charles R. Lawrence III, *The Id, the Ego, and Equal Protection: Reckoning with Unconscious Racism*, 39 STAN. L. REV. 317 (1987) [hereinafter Lawrence, *The Id*].

at the time that Lawrence was writing the article: implicit social cognition.

"The Id, the Ego, and Equal Protection" has become one of the most cited articles in the CRT genre. (Indeed, Justice Brennan cited the article in his dissent in *McCleskey v. Kemp*, using Lawrence's arguments about implicit bias to contest the majority's decision to uphold the constitutionality of the death penalty.[40] The majority rejected the constitutional challenge to the death penalty because no one could show that a discriminatory intent was behind the penalty being administered in a racially discriminatory fashion. Brennan cited Lawrence for the claim that in the post-civil rights era, bias is frequently implicit and an intent to discriminate rarely will be found.) The article continues to be cited for a proposition that forms the crux of the voluminous research that has been generated about implicit biases: "Americans share a historical experience that has resulted in individuals within the culture ubiquitously attaching a significance to race that is irrational and often outside their awareness."[41]

However, Lawrence has expressed some regrets about writing this highly influential piece of CRT scholarship. His first regret relates to the individualist nature of implicit bias research, while the second regret relates to the possibility that social psychology may naturalize bias.

A. Individualizing Racism

Lawrence's first regret is at the heart of the progressive critique of implicit bias research. Lawrence has observed that his article, and the field of implicit social cognition more generally, is focused on the individual and the prejudices and aversions that he may or may not possess. Note how this focus is apiece with traditional understandings of racism, which posit that racism is what happens when racist individuals think racist thoughts and then do racist things. As discussed in Chapter 7, progressive theorists of race and racial inequality have fought tooth and nail to challenge this narrow formulation of racism, positing instead that in the post-civil rights era, racism is better defined as what happens when institutions and structures operate in a race neutral manner that nevertheless perpetuates historical racial disadvantage and produces new forms of racial disenfranchisement. However, implicit bias research remains squarely in an individual-centered paradigm—a framework

---

[40] McCleskey v. Kemp, 481 U.S. 279, 322 (1987) (Brennan, J., dissenting).

[41] Lawrence, *The Id*, *supra* note 39, at 327.

that causes "us to think of racism as a private concern,"[42] thus mitigating the responsibility that the state, and society more generally, has for the eradication of racism and racial inequality. Thus, many critical thinkers about race are skeptical of implicit bias research because they believe that it commits the error that noncritical thinkers of race make: it focuses on individualist racism and ignores institutional racism.

One might respond to this critique by observing that interrogating these two modalities of racism need not be mutually exclusive. Research that documents the prevalence of implicit racial bias does not contradict research that explores how institutions function to reproduce racial hierarchies through frequently race-neutral means. Kang writes that implicit bias research complements this other institution-focused research, adding "an explanatory layer to the deepest understanding of persistent inequalities among social groups."[43]

Progressive race scholars might reply that the problem is not that individuals have implicit biases; the problem is that we have constructed a society wherein people of color are at the bottom of most measures of social wellbeing. People of color are more indigent than white people, have a poorer quality of life than white people, are sicker than white people, and die earlier than white people. And it is doubtful that implicit biases alone can explain these disturbing inequalities. More likely, the reverse is true: we can likely explain implicit biases in terms of these inequalities. It is for this reason that Justin Levinson, who has done extensive work around implicit racial biases, writes that the best approach to dealing with implicit biases is "through a sustained process of cultural change" that results in the elimination of "the socially disfavored status of a subordinated group."[44] If people of color are not invariably located at the bottom of social hierarchies, individuals likely will not have implicit biases against them.

Most researchers doing work around implicit racial biases would agree that the problem lies less with the existence of implicit bias than it does with the existence of racial stratification. They would think that the whole point of their documenting the prevalence of implicit biases and the behavioral consequences that flow from them is to undo existing racial hierarchies. Rick Banks and Richard Ford have noted this and argued that, for these researchers, proving the existence of implicit biases actually may simply be a way to justify

---

[42] Charles R. Lawrence III, *Unconscious Racism Revisited: Reflections on the Impact and Origins of 'The Id, the Ego, and Equal Protection,"* 40 CONN. L. REV. 931, 942 (2008).

[43] Kang, *supra* note 38, at 1147.

[44] Levinson, *supra* note 11, at 419.

reforms.[45] For example, if we prove that contact with members of outgroups reduces implicit biases, then it validates affirmative action and the integration of most social spaces—from juries and judge's chambers to corporations and boardrooms. However, the problem, according to Banks and Ford, is that the focus on implicit bias may cause us to lose sight of our goals. As a result, we may come to believe that the "elimination of implicit biases," as opposed to the "alleviation of substantive inequalities," is what we have been fighting for the whole time. They write, "If people accept the eradication of unconscious bias as the goal of racial reform (and they will have to if the rhetoric is to be persuasive), they would be likely to push the theory in directions that siphon energy away from problems of substantive inequality and that may be undesirable in their own right."[46]

B. Naturalizing Bias

Lawrence also expresses concern that the research on implicit bias may normalize racial bias, presenting it as the result of natural, regular cognitive processes. He is certainly on to something. Consider the following description:

> Implicit racial biases refer to the unconscious associations we make about racial groups. The existence of these biases is consistent with the conclusion of more general research that we automatically and unconsciously use heuristics to cope with the enormous amount of information that bombards us. Implicit racial biases facilitate our ability to manage information overload and make decisions more efficiently and easily by filtering information, filling in missing data, and automatically categorizing people according to cultural stereotypes.[47]

In this description, implicit biases are depicted as effects of the way our brains operate. Implicit biases appear to be doing us a favor, actually—saving us from being overwhelmed by the innumerable stimuli that we encounter at any given moment, allowing us to make sense of it all. Note that if implicit biases are natural, normal, or inevitable—indeed, if they are *healthy*—it becomes difficult to criticize individuals for having them. It becomes akin to castigating someone for shivering when it is cold and sweating when it is hot.

Thus, many progressives are wary about implicit bias research when it emphasizes (or is taken to emphasize) the naturalness and

---

[45] Ralph Richard Banks & Richard Thompson Ford, *(How) Does Unconscious Bias Matter?: Law, Politics, and Racial Inequality*, 58 EMORY L.J. 1053 (2009).

[46] *Id.* at 1059.

[47] Song L. Richardson & Phillip Atiba Goff, *Implicit Racial Bias in Public Defender Triage*, 122 YALE L.J. 2626 (2013).

normalness of category creation. This emphasis may lead us to lose sight that something about our social world makes it such that people of color are on the losing end of this "natural and normal" process of categorization. In other words, implicit bias research may lead us to direct our attention to the inescapability of creating categories and away from the content of the categories that we create.

V. Questions and Discussion

1. Have you taken the IAT? If so, why did you take it? What was your reaction to your test results? Were you surprised by them? Did they cause you to behave differently? Would you feel comfortable sharing your results with friends? Classmates? Potential employers? Why or why not?

If you have not taken the IAT, why haven't you done so?

2. Some scholars have proposed that individuals with high IAT scores, indicating a high amount of implicit bias, should be prohibited from serving in certain roles. For example, a person who the IAT shows has a lot of anti-black biases might be disallowed from serving on a jury for a trial in which a black person is a defendant. How do you feel about such proposals? If you are uncomfortable with them, what *should* we do with persons with high scores on the IAT?

3. Almost a decade before the IAT was developed, psychologists John Dovidio and Samuel Gaertner developed the theory of "aversive racism."[48] The theory proposes that people, born into a social milieu that links racial minorities with negative traits and characteristics, absorb these stereotypes early on in their life courses. However, society also expresses commitment to egalitarian principles that propose the equality and humanity of all individuals and that declare that discrimination and prejudice are wrong. The negative associations that individuals harbor conflict with these egalitarian principles. Aversive racism is the consequence of this conflict. Dovidio and his co-authors explain,

> Because aversive racists consciously recognize and endorse egalitarian values—they truly want to be fair and just people—they will not discriminate in situations in which they recognize that discrimination would be obvious to others and themselves. Specifically, we propose that when people are presented with a situation in which the appropriate response is unambiguous—in which right and wrong are clearly defined—aversive racists will not discriminate against Blacks. However, because aversive racists still possess negative feelings, these negative

---

[48] Samuel L. Gaertner & John F. Dovidio, *The Aversive Form of Racism*, *in* PREJUDICE, DISCRIMINATION, AND RACISM 61–89 (1986).

> feelings may eventually be expressed, but they will be expressed in subtle, indirect, and rationalizable ways. Discrimination will occur when it is not obvious what constitutes appropriate or inappropriate behavior, or when an aversive racist can justify or rationalize a negative response on the basis of some factor other than race. Under these circumstances, aversive racists may discriminate, but usually in a way that insulates them from having to acknowledge the possibility that their behavior was racially motivated.[49]

While people who were already convinced of the prevalence of anti-black racism embraced the theory of aversive racism, it was not until more "technical" explanations of implicit bias were developed that the concept really gained traction in the literature. That is, it was not until we could refer to it as the *science* of implicit bias and point to areas of the brain that might be responsible for it that those were not already convinced of the persistence of anti-black bias, prejudice, and behaviors became more receptive to the possibility that such unegalitarian phenomena are widespread in the post-civil rights era. In their critique of implicit bias research, Mitchell and Tetlock pick up on this, contending that scholars working in the field have purposely "claim[ed] the mantle of science."[50] They note that some scholars in the field resist even identifying their work as *social* science—preferring to describe it as a *science*, without any qualification.[51] The goal of this rhetorical move, of course, is to claim legitimacy for implicit bias studies and experiments.

In some sense, Kang, a leader in the field of behavioral realism, admits to this. He writes about his awareness that "language and arguments based on 'science,' as regularly practiced by 21st century scientists tenured at research universities, pack a more persuasive punch."[52] He does not claim that it is *right* that people find "science" more convincing than other forms of argumentation. He states that he is "merely describing the brute fact that scientific evidence culled through standard hypothesis-testing procedures deploying modern statistics and published in peer-reviewed journals is considered to be the 'gold' standard to policymaking, including legal reform.

---

[49] John F. Dovidio, Samuel Gaertner & Kerry Kawakami, *Reducing Contemporary Prejudice: Combating Explicit and Implicit Bias at the Individual and Intergroup Level*, *in* THE CLAREMONT SYMPOSIUM APPLIED SOCIAL PSYCHOLOGY, REDUCING PREJUDICE AND DISCRIMINATION 137–63 (Stuart Oskamp ed., 2000).

[50] Mitchell & Tetlock, *supra* note 25, at 1029.

[51] *See id.* at 1029 n.21.

[52] Kang, *supra* note 38, at 1145.

Accordingly, if the Left wants to be pragmatic about its agenda, it seems sensible to pay attention to what science says."[53]

However, there is a counterargument. This is the position that science is not going to save us. This is the assertion that all of the science in the world cannot convince persons who do not want to be convinced. As an analogy, consider the debate around climate change. The weight of good research—the stuff that is "published in peer-reviewed journals" and "is considered to be the 'gold' standard to policymaking, including legal reform"—suggests that climate change is real and will have disastrous consequences for the planet and its inhabitants if we do nothing about it. Nevertheless, a significant cadre of people, including people in positions of great power, are unconvinced. They are not motivated to be convinced. Indeed, it is contrary to their interests to be persuaded. The same is true in the context of implicit bias. When confronted with the science demonstrating the existence of implicit bias, the person unmotivated to believe in its existence will dismiss it as "junk science," invalid, inconsequential, etc.

Moreover, even if science manages to persuade the skeptic that implicit biases against historically disadvantaged groups exist, science cannot tell us what we should do about them. That is, the descriptive claim that implicit biases are pervasive does not translate into the normative claim that they should be addressed in law and policy. Consider that Justice Scalia once argued that the existence of implicit bias should mean *nothing* for the law, even though he was convinced that such bias is real. Recall *McCleskey v. Kemp*, the case in which the Court declared the constitutionality of the death penalty despite good statistical evidence that racial bias made it more likely that black defendants would be sentenced to death. The evidence suggested that the biases that led juries to vote for the death penalty for black defendants—and the biases that led prosecutors to seek the death penalty in the first instance—were implicit: these actors likely were not aware of them. In response to this evidence, Justice Scalia wrote a memo to his colleagues in which he stated that while implicit biases likely made the criminal justice system a deadlier space for black people, this fact was insignificant to him.

> I do not share the view, implicit in [the draft opinion in *McCleskey v. Kemp*], that an effect of racial factors upon sentencing, if it could be shown by sufficiently strong statistical evidence, would require reversal. Since it is my view . . . that the unconscious operation of irrational sympathies and antipathies, including racial, upon jury decisions and (hence) prosecutorial [decisions], is real,

---

[53] *Id.*

> acknowledged [in the decisions] of this court and ineradicable, I cannot honestly say that all I need is more proof.[54]

Where do you come out in this debate? Should people interested in racial justice devote significant amounts of energy to buttressing their claims with "science"? What should be the role of science in the struggle for racial justice? What should be the relationship between science and law?

4. Banks and Ford have suggested that the reason implicit bias research is, for the most part, widely accepted is due to the "comforting narrative it offers about our nation's progress in overcoming its racist history."[55] They argue that claiming that most people have *unconscious* biases is much less disagreeable than claiming that most people have *conscious* biases that they are hiding. They continue:

> The invocation of unconscious bias levels neither accusation nor blame so much as it identifies a quasi-medical problem buried deep within us all, an ailment that distorts our thinking and behavior. People may be willing to accept that unconscious bias influences their behavior, even if they would vigorously deny harboring conscious bias. . . . The unconscious bias discourse promotes a (superficial) consensus that the race problem persists precisely by bypassing potential sources of disagreement.[56]

CRT has never been a theory that is interested in "comforting narratives" and "bypassing potential sources of disagreement." On the contrary, it has proudly proclaimed its desire to upset the status quo by telling unpleasant and unnerving truths about our racial past and present. It stands to reason that for some critical race theorists' shying away from implicit bias research is due to the arguably nonconfrontational and, in some senses, conciliatory nature of the concept.

Do you think that it is nonconfrontational or conciliatory to propose the existence of implicit racial biases and to declare that they lead to biased behavior? Do you believe that there may be something provocative and/or inflammatory about this claim? Why or why not?

---

[54] *See* Dennis D. Dorin, *Far Right of the Mainstream: Racism, Rights and Remedies from the Perspective of Justice Antonin Scalia's* McCleskey *Memorandum*, 45 MERCER L. REV. 1035, 1038 (1994).

[55] Banks & Ford, *supra* note 45, at 1058.

[56] *Id.*

5. In May 2018, Starbucks closed all of its 8,000 stores to give implicit bias training to its 175,000 employees.[57] The impetus for the training was a widely-reported incident in which a manager at one of the stores called the police on two black men who had been waiting in the store for a friend. The two were arrested although, by all accounts, they did nothing wrong.

Do you think that trainings of the sort that Starbucks provided are helpful? Why or why not? What sort of efforts, if any, do you think employers should make to address biases in their employees?

---

[57] Rachel Abrams, Tiffany Hsu & John Eligon, *Starbucks's Tall Order: Tackle Systemic Racism in 4 Hours*, N.Y. TIMES (May 29, 2018), https://www.nytimes.com/2018/05/29/business/starbucks-closing-racial-bias-training.html.

Chapter 9

RACIAL MICROAGGRESSIONS

A black male college student recounts an incident that occurred on the campus of his elite university:

> I was [in the department building] and I was walking down the hallway . . . [and] one of the teacher's doors was open. . . . She's like, "Oh, I should have locked the door. My purse is in there." I was just [thinking to myself], wow . . . maybe [she] should have kept that to [herself] or something, like, oh, I reminded you that you should lock your door![1]

This student describes what researchers have come to call a *racial microaggression*, a "brief and commonplace daily verbal, behavioral and environmental indignit[y], whether intentional or unintentional, that communicate[s] hostile, derogatory, or negative racial slights and insults to the target person or group[.]"[2] In this particular incident, the teacher's remark informs the student that, because of his race, people will associate him with criminality despite his privileged status as a student of one of the nation's most prestigious institutions of higher learning.

I. Understanding Racial Microaggressions

Chester Pierce, a black psychologist, is credited with birthing the concept of the racial microaggression. Pierce, who wrote more than 180 books and articles over the course of a career that spanned four decades, focused much of his scholarship on the study of racism in its modern iterations, endeavoring to strategize ways to preserve the mental and physical health of people of color in an age where overt and obvious acts of racism had become relatively uncommon. In a chapter titled "Offensive Mechanisms," published in 1970, Pierce introduced the term "microaggression," writing:

> Most offensive actions are not gross and crippling. They are subtle and stunning. The enormity of the complications they cause can be appreciated only when one considers that these subtle blows are delivered incessantly. Even though

---

[1] Daniel Solórzano, Miguel Ceja & Tara Yosso, *Critical Race Theory, Racial Microaggressions, and Campus Racial Climate: The Experiences of African American College Students*, 69 J. NEGRO EDU. 60, 68 (2000).

While this chapter focuses on microaggressions that are race-based, scholars have also identified and theorized sex-based and sexuality-based microaggressions that impact women and sexual minorities, respectively.

[2] Derald Wing Sue et al., *Racial Microaggressions Against Black Americans: Implications for Counseling*, 86 J. COUNSELING & DEV. 330, 330 (2008).

> any single negotiation of offense can in justice be considered of itself to be relatively innocuous, the cumulative effect to the victim and to the victimizer is of an unimaginable magnitude. Hence, the therapist is obliged to pose the idea that offensive mechanisms are usually a microaggression.[3]

Pierce asserted that in the post-civil rights era, people of color are much more likely to encounter racial microaggressions than they are to encounter the more spectacular, wholly unambiguous demonstrations of racism that characterized the days of formal racial inequality. He wrote that, in modern times, scholars of racism "must not look for the gross and obvious. The subtle, cumulative mini-assault is the substance of today's racism."[4]

Pierce, alongside other researchers who have come to develop the concept further, contend that microaggressions are meaningful and deserve study for many reasons. First, they propose that there is a close relationship between microaggressions and implicit bias, a topic that has received much attention in recent years (Implicit bias is explored in Chapter 8). Microaggressions oftentimes are described as "automatic"—as manifestations of implicit attitudes or associations.[5] Consider the white professor who sees a black student and remembers, quite suddenly, that she forgot to lock her office door. When asked, the professor would likely deny that she associates young black men with criminal behavior. She would likely profess her belief that all people ought to be judged by the content of their character and not the color of their skin. She might even take offense if anyone were to suggest that the race (and gender and age) of the black student that she encountered prompted her comment. However, a reasonable observer might conclude that race had *something* to do with her abruptly remembering her unlocked door. Researchers who study microaggressions would propose that the professor harbors an implicit bias that links young black men with criminality and that the racial microaggression that she perpetrated was an expression of that unconscious association. Thus, these researchers argue, if we are interested in implicit bias, then we ought to be interested in microaggressions, as the latter oftentimes are indicators of the former.

---

[3] Chester Pierce, *Offensive Mechanisms*, *in* THE BLACK SEVENTIES 265, 265–66 (Floyd B. Barbour ed., 1970).

[4] Chester Pierce, *Psychiatric Problems of the Black Minority*, *in* 2 AMERICAN HANDBOOK OF PSYCHIATRY 512, 516 (Silvano Arieti ed., 1974).

[5] Daniel Solórzano, Walter R. Allen & Grace Carroll, *Keeping Race in Place: Racial Microaggressions and Campus Racial Climate at the University of California, Berkeley*, 23 CHICANO-LATINO L. REV. 15, 17 (2002) (defining microaggressions as "subtle verbal and non-verbal insults directed toward non-Whites, often done automatically or unconsciously").

Second, scholars working in this field believe that racial microaggressions are significant because they understand them to be visible manifestations of the more indiscernible structures and systems of white dominance that people of color navigate throughout their lives. In this way, they argue, microaggressions serve as evidence of white supremacy. They propose that just as the statistics describing the high numbers of people of color who are presently incarcerated serve as evidence of the racial power that white people enjoy, the fact that many people of color can tell a story similar to the one recounted at the beginning of the chapter has an analogous evidentiary function. Scholars working in the field argue that racial microaggressions allow us to "see" the racist ideologies that are impacting, shortening, and reducing the quality of the lives of people of color. They allow us to look at the narratives and discourses that produce and justify the racial inequalities that we all live every day.

Third, theorists propose that racial microaggressions are important because these quotidian offenses have a powerful impact on the people of color who endure them. For example, recall once again the white professor who, after seeing a black student, remarks offhandedly that she should have locked her office door. In the grand scheme of things, the incident seems small. No one has died. No one is maimed. No one has been called a racial slur. No one has lost his job or his livelihood. However, theorists avow that the incident is extremely damaging. They note that the effects of racial microaggressions accumulate over time. This interaction is just one of many frequent—some researchers say *daily*—indignities that this student will have to endure over the course of his lifetime. Researchers insist that we diminish the significance of the affront when we view it in isolation from the rest of his life. These slights add up, they say, possibly contributing to the increased morbidity and mortality that hound communities of color in the United States.

Further, individuals may experience any given racial microaggression as profoundly disturbing. In the story that begins this chapter, the student essentially has been informed that even when he is walking on his college campus, others view him with suspicion. They perceive him to be an outsider, someone who threatens their safety and security. The incident communicates to the student that he does not quite *belong* at his college: despite his sitting through several hours of classes every day, living on campus in a dorm, and wearing clothes embossed with the school's name and mascot, it is not *his* college. That is a powerful message, researchers in this field say. And it is not unreasonable to believe that some people may be extremely distraught to hear it.

Thus, the term *microaggression* may be misleading inasmuch as it suggests that the events that it describes are minor, small, or insignificant. Scholars insist that they are not. Instead, they insist that they are "a form of everyday suffering that has become socially and systematically normalized and effectively minimized."[6] Explains Catharine Wells, "A microaggression is not 'micro' in the sense that it is less disturbing and less hurtful than [other kinds] of hate speech. It is only 'micro' in the sense that privileged members of the community will regard it as trivial, if they notice it at all."[7]

A. Types of Racial Microaggressions

Scholars have schematized microaggressions in various ways. However, most schematizations note that microaggression can be verbal or nonverbal, interpersonal or institutional, and can take the form of microassaults, microinsults, or microinvalidations.

1. *Verbal v. Nonverbal Microaggressions*

This division is fairly intuitive: while some microaggressions take the form of spoken comments, others are simply behaviors. Accordingly, the incident that begins this chapter is a verbal microaggression: the professor *said* something that demeaned or denigrated the black person in her presence. However, the professor might have communicated the same association of blackness and criminality without using any words at all. If she was carrying a purse, she might have clutched it tightly when the black student came into view. She might have walked to the other side of the hallway so as to avoid any contact with the student. She might have walked away from her open office door, only to circle back and securely lock it when she saw the black student walking down the hallway towards her. All of these alternatives to the actual encounter communicate the same message. However, because no words are used to express the message, they are understood as nonverbal microaggressions.

2. *Interpersonal v. Institutional Microaggressions*

This categorization derives from the identity of the perpetrator of the microaggression, with individuals carrying out interpersonal microaggressions and institutions carrying out institutional microaggressions. Interpersonal microaggressions might be the most familiar of this pair, as most people likely think of individuals as those who inflict microaggressions on others. Accordingly, the story that begins this chapter is an example of an interpersonal microaggression.

---

[6] Lindsay Pérez Huber & Daniel G. Solórzano, *Racial Microaggressions as a Tool for Critical Race Research*, 18 RACE ETHNICITY & EDUC. 297, 304 (2015).

[7] Catharine Wells, *Microaggressions in the Context of Academic Communities*, 12 SEATTLE J. SOC. JUST. 319, 329 (2014).

Institutional microaggressions might be a little less familiar. These microaggressions refer to organization-level arrangements that communicate negative or hostile messages to people of color.[8] Tara Yosso and her coauthors give the example of a college that has hired relatively few faculty of color, fails to offer classes or courses of study that allow students to explore issues of race, language, immigration, colonialism, or globalization, and refuses to offer programming that would be of particular interest to students of color. Yosso and her coauthors describe the state of affairs as an institutional microaggression: the university has engaged in "racially marginalizing actions and inertia" that have produced "structures, practices, and discourses that endorse a campus racial climate [that is] hostile to People of Color."[9]

Legal scholar Peggy Cooper Davis has argued that the law itself can be understood as an institutional microaggression.[10] As an example, she points to the Court's decision in *McCleskey v. Kemp*, in which the Court held that Georgia's death penalty was constitutional despite good statistical evidence suggesting that it was being administered in a racially discriminatory fashion.[11] The Court had been presented with a study, conducted by statistician David Baldus, that examined 2500 murder cases in Georgia. Controlling for a wide variety of variables, the Baldus study showed that "prosecutors sought the death penalty in 70% of the cases involving black defendants and white victims; 32% of the cases involving white defendants and white victims; 15% of the cases involving black defendants and black victims; and 19% of the cases involving white defendants and black victims."[12] It demonstrated that those who had killed white victims were 4.3 times more likely to be sentenced to death than those who had killed black victims. It proved that black persons who killed white individuals—as had the defendant in the *McCleskey* case—had the greatest chance of being sentenced to death. Despite this persuasive, and disturbing, evidence, the Court

---

[8] Derald Wing Sue and coauthors use the term "environmental microaggression" to describe the same phenomenon. *See* Derald Wing Sue, Christina M. Capodilupo & Aisha M. B. Holder, *Racial Microaggressions in the Life Experience of Black Americans*, 39 PROF. PSYCHOL.: RES. & PRAC. 329, 332 (2008). They observe that "physical surroundings" may convey a negative message about people of color. To illuminate this variety of microaggression, they quote a research participant who reflects on his office environment: "And you notice that, all right, yeah . . . there's a lot of minorities. But what positions are they in? Entry-level. Maybe middle management. And then they thin out, you know, if you're talking about execs and, you know, managing directors." *Id.* at 332.

[9] Tara J. Yosso et al., *Critical Race Theory, Racial Microaggressions, and Campus Racial Climate for Latina/o Undergraduates*, 79 HARV. EDUC. REV. 659, 673 (2009).

[10] *See* Peggy C. Davis, *Law as Microaggression*, 98 YALE L.J. 1559 (1989).

[11] McCleskey v. Kemp, 481 U.S. 279 (1987).

[12] *Id.* at 287.

held that the Georgia death penalty offended neither the Equal Protection Clause nor the Eighth Amendment prohibition against cruel and unusual punishment.

Davis argues that black people might reasonably experience *McCleskey* as an institutional microaggression. She writes:

> The *McCleskey* decisions exemplified and reinforced a pattern of hierarchical judgment predicated upon race. In pronouncing the Georgia capital sentencing system constitutional, the Court gave legitimacy, and a claim of inevitability, not only to the immediate wrong to the defendant and the secondary wrong to blacks as actual or potential crime victims, but, far more importantly, to the invidious racial heuristics that are as embedded in legal decisionmaking as they are in everyday life. . . . [T]he *McCleskey* decisions strike the black reader of law as microaggression—stunning, automatic acts of disregard that stem from unconscious attitudes of white superiority and constitute a verification of black inferiority.[13]

If Davis is right, then we might similarly understand as institutional microaggression the Court's finding in *City of Richmond v. J.A. Croson* that the state's desire to remedy the effects of past societal discrimination is not a compelling governmental interest that can sustain a race-based affirmative action program from constitutional challenge.[14] People of color might understand the Court's holding in that case as a declaration that the attempt to acknowledge and redress some of the racial wounds that the country has inflicted on them and their forebears is just not that important. In the same way, we might understand as institutional microaggression the Court's decision in *Wyman v. James* to uphold warrantless searches of the homes of parents who receive public benefits.[15] We might wonder about the discourses that link race, poverty, and deviance that possibly underlay the Court's decision to diminish indigent welfare recipients' Fourth Amendment rights against unreasonable searches. By the same token, we might understand as institutional microaggression the failure to indict police officers who have killed unarmed black men. People of color might experience these nonindictments as denigrating messages about the low value that has been placed on black lives.

---

[13] Davis, *supra* note 10, at 1576.

[14] City of Richmond v. J.A. Croson Co., 488 U.S. 469 (1989).

[15] Wyman v. James, 400 U.S. 309 (1971).

3. *Microassaults v. Microinsults v. Microinvalidations*

Derald Wing Sue, a clinical psychologist who has done extensive work on microaggressions, identifies three varieties of the phenomenon: microassaults, microinsults, and microinvalidations.[16]

Microassaults are defined as "intentionally and explicitly derogatory verbal or nonverbal attacks."[17] Moreover, they are committed with the intent "to hurt, oppress, or discriminate against a person of color."[18] Thus, if someone calls another individual a racial slur, spray paints a swastika on a building, or refuses to serve a person of color in a restaurant, these events would be understood as microassaults. Indeed, we might think of microassaults as anachronisms—holdovers from the pre-civil rights era, when explicit, deliberate and unambiguous displays of racial hostility were a normal, accepted, and expected feature of American life.

Microinsults are defined as actions that "convey insensitivity, are rude, or directly demean a person's racial identity or heritage."[19] The story that begins this chapter is an example of a microinsult. Inasmuch as an association between blackness and criminal behavior generated the teacher's comment, it demeaned the student's racial identity. Arguably, an example of a microinsult that got a lot of media coverage was President Trump's suggestion during his campaign that Mexican immigrants are distinctive inasmuch as they, unlike those who immigrate to the United States from other parts of the world, bring drugs, are rapists, and are criminals.[20] Proposing that immigrants from Mexico have a unique predisposition to drugs, sexual assault, and crime is demeaning.

Microinvalidations are defined as "actions that exclude, negate, or nullify the psychological thoughts, feelings, or experiences of people of color."[21] Sue writes that telling a black person that she is "articulate" is a microinvalidation, arguing that the "compliment" conveys the "hidden message" that "[p]eople of color as a group are unintelligent."[22] Another example of an microinvalidation is when individuals of Asian descent are asked (sometimes repeatedly) "where are you *really* from" or when they are complimented for speaking "good English" or speaking without an accent. These

---

[16] Sue et al., *supra* note 2, at 330.

[17] Yosso et al., *supra* note 9, at 662.

[18] Sue et al., *supra* note 2, at 331.

[19] *Id.*

[20] Suzanne Gamboa, *Donald Trump Announces Presidential Bid by Trashing Mexico, Mexicans*, NBC NEWS (June 16, 2015), https://www.nbcnews.com/news/latino/donald-trump-announces-presidential-bid-trashing-mexico-mexicans-n376521.

[21] Sue et al., *supra* note 2, at 331.

[22] *Id.*

varieties of comments evidence an assumption that people of Asian descent are invariably foreign-born. They demonstrate that the speaker does not intuitively associate "American" and "Asian," and they call forth discourses that declare that the only racial group that is properly linked with "American" is "white." For the Asian American individual who knows no other home but the U.S. and whose identity is closely wrapped up with his nationality, the suggestion that he is not *truly* American can be quite disturbing.

While microassaults are proverbial blasts from the past—archaisms from the dark ages of racial enlightenment—microinsults and microinvalidations are born from the soil of a land that professes commitment to racial equality. That which makes microassaults the old-timey, less fashionable cousins of microinsults and microinvalidations is that perpetrators of the former invariably act with the conscious purpose to harm the target of the action. Researchers propose that, quite distinctly, those who inflict microinsults and microinvalidations usually do not intend for their actions to be hurtful; indeed, these actors oftentimes are well-meaning and have the best of intentions. As such, researchers say that microinsults and microinvalidations, unlike microassaults, are the products of implicit biases, with the offending parties being largely or completely unaware of the problematic associations and evaluations that give rise to the offensive behavior.

B. Effect of Microaggressions

Researchers insist that although microaggressions may appear minor and inconsequential, they nevertheless have a profound effect on the individuals who are subjected to them. As noted above, scholars observe the cumulative nature of these offenses. They contend that it would be unfortunate, but relatively insignificant, if the only racially insulting incident a black student has to live through is an offhand comment indicating that he has reminded a professor that her office door is unlocked. However, theorists assert that such incidents are never individual. Instead, they occur in a context of constant microaggressive behavior. Thus, the student hears the casual observation about an unlocked office door after having to endure "compliments" about his articulate speech, deny suggestions that he attends his elite college on a sports scholarship, and correct assumptions that he grew up in the ghetto—all while attending a college that does not offer a major in African American Studies or the like. Theorists propose that the additive nature of these interpersonal and institutional microaggressions makes them tremendously burdensome.

Daniel Solórzano writes that the strain of negotiating regular microaggressions produces Mundane Extreme Environmental Stress, or MEES. He notes that MEES is

> *mundane,* because this stress is part of our day-to-day experience and is so common that we almost take it for granted; *extreme,* because it has an extreme impact on our psyche and world view, how we see ourselves, behave, and interact; *environmental,* because it is environmentally located, induced and fostered; *stress,* because the ultimate impact is indeed stressful, detracting and energy-consuming.[23]

Scholars assert that microaggressions are energy-consuming in part because the affected party has to spend time and effort processing the event. The student in the story that opens this chapter has to deal with the anger and sadness of being told that he, essentially, looks like a criminal. (Researchers insist that the emotions that microaggressions generate are often quite intense. Sue writes that victims of microaggressions "frequently report feelings of racial rage, frustration, low self-esteem, depression, and other strong emotional reactions."[24]) He might talk to his friends to get their perspective on the incident, asking how they would have reacted and deliberating over whether he ought to have confronted the professor. He may also have to deal with the anger and frustration of being told that he is being paranoid or that he is overreacting to an insignificant slight. Sue specifically observes that it is not unusual for people of color and white people to reach different conclusions about whether a microaggressive incident was, in fact, racially motivated. According to Sue, white people's relative lack of experience with racial hostility may make it difficult for them to agree with people of color when the latter assert that race motivated a particular event or interaction. Even more disempowering to people of color, observes Sue, is that white people's perceptions usually "win." He writes, "Microaggressions inevitably produce a clash of racial realities where the experiences of racism by Blacks are pitted against the views of Whites who hold the power to define the situation in nonracial terms. The power to define reality is not supported at the individual level alone but at the institutional and societal levels as well."[25]

If the victim of a microaggression is not already convinced that an incident was prompted by his race, he has to make some effort to answer that question for himself. As noted above, microinsults and microinvalidations tend to be much more ambiguous than

---

[23] Solórzano, Allen & Carroll, *supra* note 5, at 17.

[24] Sue et al., *supra* note 2, at 331.

[25] Sue, Capodilupo & Holder, *supra* note 8, at 335.

microassaults. This ambiguity can wreak havoc on the peace of mind of the individual affected by the behavior. Scholars underscore that the time and energy that victims of racial microaggressions spend processing the event *could be spent on something else*. Thus, we might understand the ability to devote one's psychic resources to matters unrelated to contemplating and dealing with the emotional fallout from a racially degrading incident as a racial privilege that many white people enjoy and many people of color do not have.

William Smith and co-authors have theorized that the MEES produced by racial microaggressions causes "racial battle fatigue." Racial battle fatigue involves the "psychological (e.g., frustration, shock, anger, disappointment, resentment, hopelessness), physiological (e.g., headache, backache, 'butterflies,' teeth grinding, high blood pressure, insomnia), and behavioral responses (e.g., stereotype threat, John Henryism, social withdrawal, self-doubt, and a dramatic change in diet) of fighting racial microaggressions."[26] Again, if racial microaggressions are something that people of color mostly endure, then we might understand the ability to avoid the psychological, physiological, and behavioral responses to these offenses as a racial privilege that many white people enjoy and many people of color do not have.

Scholars who study microaggressions also link them to the large-scale racial stratifications that we witness in the nation today, arguing that they play a role in the persistence of racial disparities in education, employment, and other arenas. For example, Solórzano and co-authors contend that microaggressions produce college campuses as hostile environments. They write that students of color react to these hostile spaces in many ways. Some of these reactions might be considered productive. For example, many students of color who Solórzano studied reported that, when confronted with a microaggression that evoked narratives about the inferiority of racial minorities, they endeavored to prove the narrative wrong; they reported working harder in an effort to avoid fulfilling the stereotype of nonwhite inadequacy. However, other students of color reacted to microaggressions in ways that were quite damaging and destructive. "The sense of discouragement, frustration, and exhaustion resulting from racial microaggressions left some African American students in our study despondent and made them feel that they could not perform well academically. . . .Several students commented that racial microaggressions had affected their academic performance in overt ways such as pushing them to drop a class, changing their

---

[26] William A. Smith, Man Hung & Jeremy D. Franklin, *Racial Battle Fatigue and the Miseducation of Black Men: Racial Microaggressions, Societal Problems, and Environmental Stress*, 80 J. NEGRO EDUC. 63, 68 (2011).

major and even leaving the university to attend school elsewhere."[27] Thus, researchers suggest that racial microaggressions, MEES, and racial battle fatigue can help explain racial disparities in academic achievement and the higher rates of attrition of racial minorities in colleges and universities.

Moreover, some scholars look to psychologists Joshua Aronson's and Claude Steele's research into *stereotype threat* to explain how racial microaggressions may contribute to the underperformance of people of color in educational institutions and elsewhere.[28] Stereotype threat refers to a phenomenon whereby negative stereotypes about the group to which an individual belongs adversely affect the individual's performance. However, the effect is situational: a negative stereotype about an individual's group will only impair the individual's performance when she is reminded that she is a member of that group. The converse is also true: if an individual belongs to a group about which positive stereotypes exist, she will do better on a task if she is reminded of her group membership. An oft-cited study revealed that when a group of Asian-American women were prompted to think about their Asian descent just prior to taking a math test, they achieved higher scores than a group of Asian-American women whose racial identities were not made salient. Notably, when the group was prompted to think about the fact that they were women, their scores decreased.[29] Theorists propose that stereotypes of Asian individuals being good at math led the research subjects to be confident about their abilities and worked to boost their scores; meanwhile stereotypes of women being bad at math undermined their confidence and worked to depress their scores.

Because of the existence of stereotypes that describe people of color—specifically black, Latinx, and indigenous people—as intellectually inferior, researchers propose that stereotype threat will diminish their performance when their race is made salient. Now, researchers assert that racial microaggressions are ubiquitous—they are constant and unavoidable. If so, then black, Latinx, and indigenous people are relentlessly made aware of their racial identities. Accordingly, they live in a perpetual state of stereotype threat—something that Yosso and her coauthors call an "environmental stereotype threat."[30] As a consequence, they are

---

[27] Solórzano, Ceja & Yosso, *supra* note 1, at 69.

[28] Claude M. Steele & Joshua Aronson, *Stereotype Threat and the Intellectual Test Performance of African Americans*, 69 J. PERSONALITY & SOC. PSYCHOL. 797 (1995).

[29] *See* Margaret Shih, Todd L. Pittinsky & Nalini Ambady, *Stereotype Susceptibility: Identity Salience and Shifts in Quantitative Performance*, 10 PSYCHOL. SCI. 80 (1999).

[30] Yosso et al., *supra* note 9, at 675.

always achieving at levels that are lower than what they would be in a world without racial microaggressions.

In this way, these scholars claim that racial microaggressions *cause* white dominance. They cause white people, who do not have to endure MEES, racial battle fatigue, or the negative effects of stereotype threat, to outperform nonwhite people. They also cause spaces that have excluded people of color historically—like college campuses, boardrooms, and resource-rich neighborhoods—to remain racially exclusive. As Catharine Wells has argued, microaggressions "operate in predictable ways to insure that the interests of insiders are protected from newcomers. . . . [T]hey have the overall effect of maintaining current patterns of exclusion. . . . [They] form a barrier against inclusion that has persisted long after more formal barriers have disappeared. Microaggressions impede integration."[31]

However, theorists invite us to understand microagressions as not only a cause of white dominance, but also an *effect* of the same. Individuals inflict racial microaggressions because discourses about the inadequacy, foreignness, and/or deviance of people of color exist. Institutions inflict racial microaggressions because people of color are not in positions of power where they can implement policies and programs that can make institutions less hostile places and can reduce the incidence and effects of interpersonal microaggressions.[32] In this view, white dominance creates the conditions under which racial microaggressions can occur.

Essentially, scholars in the field argue that any theory of racial inequality in the present is incomplete if it does not consider microaggressions. Writes Solórzano and coauthors, "Ultimately, theories about structural/institutional racism and racist ideology/attitudes provide at best only partial explanations for persistent social hierarchy and inequitable outcomes by race in contemporary America. Interpersonal relationships between human actors combine with structural patterns and ideological perspectives to reproduce racial hierarchy."[33]

---

[31] Wells, *supra* note 7, at 320, 327.

[32] In this vein, consider Ron Wheeler's experience of being called a racial and homophobic slur while walking across the campus of his law school. He writes, "There was no precedents of the university caring about, investigating, or punishing what we now call hate crimes. If there had been an organizational culture in existence at the university where a student would have been expelled for incidents such as these, would this incident have occurred?" Ronald Wheeler, *About Microaggressions*, 108 LAW LIBR. J. 321, 324 (2016). Essentially, Wheeler's law school had organized itself in such a way that interpersonal microaggressions could be inflicted without consequence.

[33] Solórzano, Allen & Carroll, *supra* note 5, at 18.

II. Questions and Discussion

1. The biggest criticism of the concept of microaggressions is probably the claim that they are no big deal. Everyone endures slights. You get cut off in traffic. You hold a door for someone and the person does not say "thank you." Your coworker sends you a passive aggressive email that ends with "please advise." You get tagged in an unflattering photo on social media. Essentially, the criticism is that *stuff happens*. Racial microaggressions are stuff like all the other stuff that happens to people.

How do you feel about this criticism? Are researchers in this area making a mountain out of a molehill? Or is there something about *racial* slights (or sex-based, or sexuality-based slights) that make them more significant than the petty indignities and inconveniences that everyone experiences on a daily basis?

2. Have you ever been on the receiving end of a microaggression, racial or otherwise? How did you react to it? If you have never been on the receiving end of a microaggression, what do you think has protected you from such an experience?

3. As noted above, scholars have argued that not only can racial microaggressions cause their targets to have intense emotional responses ranging from rage to depression, but can also explain large-scale racial inequalities, like the racial performance gap and racial disparities in health. Do you find such claims convincing? Why or why not?

4. As discussed above, racial microaggressions are defined in such a way that they include egregious acts (like calling someone a racial slur) and criminal acts (like punching someone because he is a racial minority). It seems intuitive that we lose something by calling these acts *microaggressions*, inasmuch as the "micro" in the term might diminish the significance of such heinous behavior. However, do we *gain* something by calling such contemptible acts microaggressions?

5. Smith and his coauthors have argued that people of color who have achieved some upward social and economic mobility face more racial microaggressions than those who reside at the bottom of social and economic hierarchies. They write that black men, specifically, encounter an increasing incidence of racial microaggressions as they achieve higher levels of education, acquire higher status jobs, and move into neighborhoods where white people reside. They observe that

> as education increases, Black men are being exposed to more historically and predominantly White communities and institutions where the bedrock of racial

> microaggressions and faulty racial ideologies are more imbedded and less subtle. . . . In predominantly White communities, African Americans have fewer opportunities to maintain the relative comfort of community social support found in predominantly Black communities and its social and religious organizations.[34]

Smith's argument might be interpreted to suggest that less affluent people of color have a privilege that their more affluent counterparts do not have: their poverty insulates them from racial microaggressions, to a certain degree. How do you feel about the suggestion that indigence might be a privileged status in this respect?

---

[34] Smith, Hung & Franklin, *supra* note 26, at 75.

Chapter 10

WHITE PRIVILEGE

One of the most frequently cited definitions of white privilege comes from feminist educator Peggy McIntosh, whose essay on the topic brought the term into common usage. In her essay, McIntosh describes white privilege as "an invisible package of unearned assets which I can count on cashing in each day, but about which I was 'meant' to remain oblivious. White privilege is like an invisible weightless backpack of special provisions, maps, passports, codebooks, visas, clothes, tools and blank checks."[1] McIntosh's description of white privilege suggests that simply being white is an advantage. It makes goals more accessible. It makes harms more avoidable. While it does not insure that every white person will win, it makes it harder for them to lose.

Critical thinkers about race have argued that the concept of white privilege does not index a new or unexpected phenomenon. If one believes that racial hierarchies exist, then it is fairly unremarkable to note that those hierarchies will benefit some to the detriment of others. As Devon Carbado and Mitu Gulati put it, the claim that white privilege exists "is nothing more than a claim about the existence of discrimination. . . . To the extent that race discrimination is a current social problem, there will be victims and beneficiaries of this discrimination. The former are disadvantaged; the latter are privileged."[2] Thus, white privilege is just a term for the spoils of racial hierarchy: white privilege is what white supremacy begets.[3]

In her essay, McIntosh identifies several examples of white privilege, ranging from the arguably minor and insignificant to the profound and consequential. She writes that, as a white person:

- When I am told about our national heritage or about "civilization," I am shown that people of my color made it what it is.
- I do not have to educate my children to be aware of systemic racism for their own daily physical protection.

---

1 Peggy McIntosh, *White Privilege: Unpacking the Invisible Knapsack*, PEACE & FREEDOM MAG., July/Aug. 1989, at 10.

2 Devon Carbado & Mitu Gulati, *The Law and Economics of Critical Race Theory*, 112 YALE L.J. 1757, 1777 (2003).

3 *See* john a. powell, *Whites Will Be Whites: The Failure to Interrogate Racial Privilege*, 34 U.S.F. L. REV. 419, 420 (2000) (noting that he prefers to call "White racial privilege" "White supremacy").

- I can worry about racism without being seen as self-interested or self-seeking.
- I can take a job with an affirmative action employer without having my co-workers on the job suspect that I got it because of my race.
- I can choose blemish cover or bandages in 'flesh' color and have them more or less match my skin.
- I can be late to a meeting without having the lateness reflect on my race.[4]

Those who believe that white privilege exists would propose that McIntosh's list is just the tip of the iceberg. They might add to it, observing that white people have an easier time securing loans than people of color; moreover, the terms of the loans that white people secure tend to be more favorable than those secured by people of color.[5] White people are much more likely than people of color to get from point A to point B, whether driving or walking, without police stopping them.[6] Black women die three to four times more often than white women during childbirth or shortly thereafter;[7] black babies die twice more often in their first year of life than white babies.[8] Homes in white neighborhoods are worth more than comparable homes in nonwhite neighborhoods[9]; white children get to attend better schools as a direct consequence.[10] A significant portion of people in the U.S. think that efforts to disestablish what progressives believe to be existing racial hierarchy, like affirmative action or race-consciousness in the fabrication of voting districts, are equivalent to efforts to erect and protect that same hierarchy; further, the Court has constructed a jurisprudence that reflects that belief.[11] Progressive race scholars would cite all of these social facts as evidence of white privilege.

---

[4] McIntosh, *supra* note 1, at 11.

[5] Drew Desilver & Kristen Bailik, *Black and Hispanics Face Extra Challenges in Getting Home Loans*, FACTTANK: NEWS IN THE NUMBERS (Jan. 10, 2017), http://www.pewresearch.org/fact-tank/2017/01/10/blacks-and-hispanics-face-extra-challenges-in-getting-home-loans/.

[6] Chapter 18 delves into race and policing.

[7] THERESA CHALHOUB & KELLY RIMAR, CTR. FOR AM. PROGRESS, THE HEALTH CARE SYSTEM AND RACIAL DISPARITIES IN MATERNAL MORTALITY (2018) https://cdn.americanprogress.org/content/uploads/2018/05/09121820/HealthSystemDisparitiesInMaternalMortality-Brief.pdf.

[8] T.J. Matthews, Marian F. MacDorman, & Marie E. Thoma, Dep't of Health & Human Servs., *Infant Mortality Statistics From the 2013 Period Linked Birth/Infant Death Data Set*, 64 NAT'L VITAL STATS. REPS., no. 9, 2015, at 1.

[9] Nancy A. Denton, *The Role of Residential Segregation in Promoting and Maintaining Inequality in Wealth and Property*, 34 IND. L. REV. 1199 (2001).

[10] Chapter 20 explores race and education.

[11] Adarand Constructors, Inc. v. Peña, 515 U.S. 200 (1995).

Some have proposed that the general tendency exhibited by white people not to think of themselves in racial terms is an example of white privilege. The idea is that nonwhite people are much more likely than white people to describe themselves by reference to their racial identities. Further, people of color are much more likely to *think* about their racial identities over the course of the day. While a woman of color may wonder whether her race informed a stranger's failure to hold open a door for her, it is unlikely that a white woman will ask herself the same question. Scholars describe this as a benefit that white people possess: they enjoy "a feeling of racelessness or invisibility."[12] Only rarely are they made to be aware of their race.

Critical scholars claim that while white privilege bestows a "psychological wage"[13] to white people—in the sense that there is an emotional or mental value involved in knowing that one is a member of the group that holds the most power and prestige in society—it is also valuable in terms of dollars and cents. As Marion Crain and Ken Matheny argue, white privilege "confer[s] material advantages[ ] in the form of higher wages and fringe benefits[ ] on members of the privileged groups . . .[,] giving them an economic advantage in the market."[14]

In essence, progressive theorists have identified what they believe to be many expressions of white privilege, proposing that it "can manifest itself in many currencies: education, employment, social networks, hobbies and even character traits like confidence."[15]

I. Formulations of White Privilege

Two different, but ultimately complementary, descriptions of white privilege recur in the literature. One focuses on the normativity of whiteness, the other on the statistical likelihood that a white person will do better than a similarly-situated person of color.

The description of white privilege that focuses on the normativity of whiteness contends that white people occupy a privileged position in society because whiteness has been constructed as the norm. In this view, whiteness is the site from which all things are measured and from which everything else deviates. An example of this might be found in the "flesh" colored bandage or the "nude" pantyhose. The color of "flesh" or "nude" in beauty products and apparel, at least historically, has approximated the skin tones of a

---

[12] Camille Gear Rich, *Marginal Whiteness*, 98 CALIF. L. REV. 1497, 1513 (2010).

[13] W.E.B. DU BOIS, BLACK RECONSTRUCTION 700–01 (1935).

[14] Marion Crain & Ken Matheny, *Labor's Divided Ranks: Privilege and the United Front Ideology*, 84 CORNELL L. REV. 1542, 1568 (1999).

[15] Jeremy Dunham & Holly Lawford-Smith, *Offsetting Race Privilege*, 11 J. ETHICS & SOC. PHIL. 1, 8 (2017).

white person.[16] As such, the skin tones of people of color are denied as "flesh" or "nude." They are something else—"brown" or "suntan," perhaps. In this way, the skin color of (some[17]) white people is constructed as the norm; the skin colors of nonwhite people are deviations from that norm.

Thinkers have expanded this insight into the proposition that white people's norms have come to constitute the norms of society, more generally. Thus, braids and dreadlocks—hairstyles that originated among black people and still are much more likely to be worn by this racial group—have been considered "unprofessional" and inappropriate for the workplace.[18] However, hairstyles that white people have worn—the crewcut, the bob, bangs, the ponytail (when worn by women)—are considered unremarkably proper ways to wear one's hair while at work. More abstractly, thinkers have proposed that the characteristics that white people have considered important have become the standards against which all people are judged. For example, elites in the legal academy—who, historically speaking, were mostly, if not all, white—have thought that the mark of a good law professor is an extensive publication record; significantly less important to this group was the quality of the instruction a professor gives in a classroom. Because this group prized publishing while thinking less highly of teaching, all law professors are judged in terms of where and how often they have published; the question of whether they are effective teachers is of secondary importance, if important at all. White privilege, say proponents of the concept, consists of everyone being measured against a yardstick composed of things that a select group of white people have thought to be valuable. Moreover, the particularity of this yardstick—that it reflects one group's values—is erased. Instead, it is simply called, without qualification, "standards."

Progressive scholars of race have proposed that what is true of notions of "professional" hairstyles and "standards" within the legal academy is true more broadly. They have argued that because most institutions in society today were built by white people with white people in mind, they reflect white norms.[19] As a result, they say that

---

[16] In 1962, Crayola renamed the "flesh" colored crayon, which had been introduced in 1949. *Frequently Asked Questions*, CRAYOLA.COM, http://www.crayola.com/faq/another-topic/why-does-the-color-quotfleshquot-not-appear-in-the-1958-limited-edition-box-of-64/ (last visited Sept. 22, 2018). The formerly "flesh" hue now goes by the name of "peach."

[17] It may be stating the obvious to observe that white people have a variety of skin tones.

[18] *See* Paulette M. Caldwell, *A Hair Piece: Perspectives on the Intersection of Race and Gender*, 1991 DUKE L.J. 365 (1991); Angela Onwuachi-Willig, *Another Hair Piece: Exploring New Strands of Analysis under Title VII*, 98 GEO. L.J. 1079 (2010).

[19] *See, e.g.*, Meera E. Deo, *Two Sides of a Coin: Safe Space & Segregation in Race/Ethnic Specific Law Student Organizations*, 42 WASH. U. J. L. & POL'Y 83, 116

white norms have been *structured* into society—placing all white people, who are better situated than nonwhite people to behave consistently with these norms, in a favorable position. According to this line of thought, white privilege describes the *structural advantages* that white people enjoy.[20] In this way, white privilege is not an individualistic concept of racial hierarchy. When properly understood, it does not "personalize racism."[21] It does not propose that racial advantages and disadvantages originate in individual white people. Quite the contrary, it suggests that these benefits and harms are institutional in origin. What this means, say critical thinkers of race, is that the way to dismantle the unearned and undeserved advantages that white people enjoy by virtue of their race is not to fix interpersonal relationships between individual white and nonwhite people, but rather to expose and challenge the fact that whiteness has become a hidden, uninterrogated, "universal norm" in all of our major institutions.[22] White privilege will only be eradicated, say these theorists, when we have reformed "the system that allows [white persons] to have race privilege in the first place."[23]

The idea that white privilege is the structurally advantageous position into which white people are placed by virtue of their race explains the second conception of white privilege that one frequently encounters in the literature: the statistical likelihood that a white person will do better than a person of color. Philosophers Jeremy Dunham and Holly Lawford-Smith have explained this formulation quite clearly. They argue that simply because structural advantages have been built into institutions does not mean that any individual white person will benefit from them. What it does mean is that he is *more likely* to benefit. They argue that the concept of white privilege "is premised on probabilistic advantage, rather than actual advantage."[24] It is a "statistical probability of advantage."[25] As such, white privilege refers to the *likelihood* that white people will have better outcomes than people of color. Dunham and Lawford-Smith observe that "African-Americans, Hispanics and Latinx people are

---

(2013) ("[T]he major institutions and social relationship of U.S. society—law, political organization, economic relationships, religion, cultural life, residential patterns, etc.—have been structured from the beginning by the racial order and continue to reflect racial privilege today.").

[20] *See* Denise A. Donnelly et al., *White Privilege, Color Blindness, and Services to Battered Women*, 11 VIOLENCE AGAINST WOMEN 6, 8 (2005).

[21] Zeus Leonardo, *The Color of Supremacy: Beyond the Discourse of 'White Privilege,'* 36 EDUC. PHILOSOPHY & THEORY 137, 140 (2004).

[22] powell, *supra* note 3, at 433. https://www.westlaw.com/Document/I89075ae14b0211db99a18fc28eb0d9ae/View/FullText.html?transitionType=Default&contextData=(sc.Default)&VR=3.0&RS=da3.0&fragmentIdentifier=co_pp_sp_3108_433.

[23] Dunham & Lawford-Smith, *supra* note 15, at 20.

[24] *Id.* at 9.

[25] *Id.*

more likely than white Americans to be killed by police while unarmed; more likely to be stopped, searched, arrested, and incarcerated; less likely to be hired by employers; less likely to be educated by prestigious institutions; and less likely to be protected by adequate healthcare."[26] Dunham and Lawford-Smith, and others who accept this formulation, refer to these probabilistic outcomes as white privilege.

To illustrate their point, Dunham and Lawford-Smith give the example of a disadvantaged white woman—a woman "whose parents were too involved with drugs to take care in raising her, who did not have the opportunity to receive a good education (or the necessary tools to take advantage of one, such as a quiet place to study and the relevant resources), [and who] now cannot find a job and relies on food banks and the kindness of her friends and neighbors."[27] They argue that although this woman is incredibly disadvantaged, her racial privilege means that she is more likely to be able to achieve economic and physical security than a similarly-situated black, indigenous, or Latinx woman.

This example raises an important aspect of racial privilege: it interacts with other axes of identity such that an individual who is privileged (or unprivileged) along the axis of race may or may not be privileged along axes of class, gender, sexuality, gender identity, nationality, etc. While the white woman in Dunham's and Lawford-Smith's example is privileged along racial lines, she is unprivileged in terms of class and gender—which increases the likelihood that she will encounter hardship in her life. Moreover, while the African-American, indigenous, or Latinx woman to whom Dunham and Lawford-Smith compare their hypothetical white woman does not enjoy the racial privilege that she enjoys—and, consequently, is more likely to be more disadvantaged than her—she might be straight. Or she might be a documented U.S. citizen. Or she might be cisgender. Thus, even though the African-American, indigenous, or Latinx woman in the example is *disadvantaged* vis-à-vis her white counterpart, she is *advantaged* vis-à-vis her lesbian, or undocumented, or transgender counterpart. In essence, it is important to recognize that there are interlocking webs of privilege and unprivilege. The failure to recognize this truth may result in overestimating the quality of the life that any racially privileged (i.e., white) person has.[28] Differently stated, it may guide one to the

---

[26] *Id.* at 2.

[27] *Id.*

[28] It may also result in *underestimating* the quality of the life that a racially unprivileged (i.e., nonwhite) person has.

mistaken conclusion that the possession of white privilege equals the possession of a charmed life.

II. White Privilege and Meritocracy

The concept of white privilege unsettles the notion that the nation is, or has ever been, a meritocracy. If some people are given advantages that they have not earned—indeed, if some people are *born* into a more advantageous position than others—then we cannot conclude that individuals occupy the statuses that they occupy as a sole consequence of their own effort (or lack thereof). On the one hand, we cannot conclude that the poor person of color, lacking in racial privilege, is indigent, marginalized, and vulnerable because he has done things (or failed to do things) that have earned him his subordinate status. And on the other hand, we cannot conclude that the more affluent white person, enjoying racial privilege, possesses wealth, health, safety, and security solely because he has *earned* this more comfortable social position. The latter claim may be most unsettling to those accused of having white privilege and, thus, deserves some elaboration.

Dunham and Lawford-Smith contend that when an achievement is "earned" in a context wherein individuals have undeserved advantages and disadvantages, we misspeak when we describe the achievement as an "earned" one. They write that

> [i]f promotion practices are unjust or educational access is unequal, then even a promotion that is "earned," or an educational qualification that comes as a result of one's skills and talents, may yet count as a morally problematic advantage (i.e., privilege). . . . [I]f educational access is unequal, then even an educational qualification that comes as a result of one's skills and talents may be the product of *undeserved advantage;* similarly, if promotion practices are unjust, then even a promotion that is 'earned' may be the product of *underserved advantage.*[29]

In this view, if a white person is placed in an advantageous position by virtue of his race—a personal characteristic that he has not earned—then we ought to drop an asterisk next to any achievements he has managed to accrue. His successes, feats, and triumphs are not *entirely* the product of his own efforts. Instead, they may have been *gifted* to him in some important respects. The idea that our achievements have not been wholly *achieved* may be disturbing to those whom the concept of white privilege accuses of enjoying undeserved, unearned racial advantages. This might explain why studies have documented that white people demonstrate

[29] Dunham & Lawford-Smith, *supra* note 15, at 4.

signs of anxiety during discussions of white privilege. Camille Gear Rich observes that this anxiety may be a product of white people's "fear that by acknowledging the role of white privilege in their success, they must confront questions about their own deservingness. Inquiries of this kind put whites at risk of self-invalidation, making them question whether they have actually earned or are entitled to the accolades and benefits that they have secured."[30]

III. White Privilege and the Law

Progressive race thinkers have argued that white privilege is no accident of history. Quite the opposite, they argue, the law has actively created it. In the pre-civil rights era, it did so through denying citizenship to nonwhite people, expropriating the lands on which indigenous people lived and relied, protecting the institution of chattel slavery, and assigning a denigrated legal status to black and other nonwhite people in the postbellum period. These thinkers contend that in the post-civil rights era, the law continues to create white privilege, albeit by different means. They assert that the law has constructed the distribution of wealth and opportunities that was the byproduct of the egregious, spectacular racism of the pre-civil rights era as the baseline. The law creates white privilege in the present day, argue critical thinkers of race, by conceptualizing efforts to redistribute these ill-gotten gains as presumptively unfair, immoral, and illegal.

These thinkers have observed that although the law has actively created white privilege, it has not acknowledged it for the most part. In their assessment, neither has it acted to dismantle it. Quite the opposite, scholars have identified several cases in which they believe that the Court has actively protected it.

John powell looks to the Court's decision in *McCleskey v. Kemp*, in which it upheld the constitutionality of the death penalty despite disturbing evidence that black people were more likely than similarly-situated white people to be put to death.[31] Part of the justification that the Court offered for its holding was the concern that if the plaintiff's challenge to the death penalty was legitimate, other challenges to the criminal justice system, more broadly, would also be legitimate. It argued, "[I]f we accepted McCleskey's claim that racial bias has impermissibly tainted the capital sentencing decision, we could soon be faced with similar claims as to other types of penalty . . . . [T]he claim that his sentence rests on the irrelevant factor of race easily could be extended to apply to claims based on unexplained discrepancies that correlate to membership in other minority groups,

---

[30] Rich, *supra* note 12, at 1563.

[31] McCleskey v. Kemp, 481 U.S. 279 (1987).

and even to gender."[32] Powell observes that the Court made a similar "slippery slope" argument in *Washington v. Davis*, in which it held that a showing that a law has a disparate impact on racial minorities was insufficient to establish a presumption of a constitutional violation, requiring instead that there be a showing that lawmakers intended to discriminate when they passed the burdensome law.[33] There, the Court argued that if it embraced the disparate impact standard, the consequences "would be far reaching and would raise serious questions about, and perhaps invalidate, a whole range of tax, welfare, public service, regulatory, and licensing statutes that may be more burdensome to the poor and to the average black than to the more affluent white."[34]

Powell argues that these passages from *McCleskey* and *Davis* demonstrate the Court's recognition of the extensiveness of racial privilege (and class privilege). However, it uses the extensiveness of racial privilege as a reason to do nothing about it. He writes that "the Court makes seemingly contradictory 'slippery slope' arguments that, in fact, suggest how deeply and concretely embedded in society systems of privilege really are. This final rhetorical technique recognizes the complexity and pervasiveness of privilege, but uses that as an excuse to turn away, rendering it invisible again."[35]

Instead of embracing a jurisprudence that allows the Constitution to reach and remedy what critical thinkers believe to be systemic racial privilege, the Court instead has embraced doctrine that makes unearned racial advantages and disadvantages legally irrelevant. It accomplishes this, say critical thinkers, through its definition of "discrimination," which the Court understands as "explicitly articulated, intentional, conscious racism."[36] Racial privilege is none of those things. Accordingly, it is constitutionally insignificant that white people arguably benefit from the unearned advantages that constitute white privilege. It is for this reason that some have argued that "our current concepts of discrimination perpetuate, rather than remedy, white privilege."[37] Indeed, the Court's current definition of discrimination might itself be a form of white privilege.[38]

---

[32] *Id.* at 315.

[33] Washington v. Davis, 426 U.S. 229 (1976).

[34] *Id.* at 248.

[35] powell, *supra* note 3, at 449.

[36] Sylvia Law, *White Privilege and Affirmative Action*, 32 AKRON L. REV. 603, 618 (1999).

[37] *Id.* at 616.

[38] *See id.*

IV. Critiques of the Concept of White Privilege

A. White Privilege Erases Domination

Some scholars on the left have critiqued the concept of white privilege because they feel that it focuses too intently on the recipients of racial advantages while ignoring that there are corresponding losers. Their complaint is that the concept elides that any racial benefits that white people accrue *are made possible* by disadvantaging nonwhite people. Privilege connotes that white people just have it easier than others. It erases that this ease comes at the expense of nonwhite people.

Scholars who articulate this critique endeavor to insert *subordination* back into the discussion. That is, they wish to underscore that white privilege is the consequence of racial domination. As Zeus Leonardo has written, studies of white privilege ought to "revolve[ ] less around the issue of unearned advantages, or the *state* of being dominant, and more around direct processes that secure domination and the privileges associated with it."[39]

The critique here is that when white privilege is understood as something that white people just happen to have, it ignores the harms that were perpetrated against people of color that have enabled white people to have the advantages that they enjoy. Scholars articulating this critique have insisted that inasmuch as the concept of white privilege obscures that white people have *done* things, historically and presently, that have subordinated people of color, it is "safe" to white people. It is a concept with which they can feel relatively comfortable. It seems to propose that there are no bad actors. No one has done anything wrong. To adapt sociologist Eduardo Bonilla-Silva's turn of phrase: there may be racism, but there are no racists.[40]

This perspective proposes that the concept of white privilege pushes the agents and acts of domination out of the frame. These critics want to bring them back in. As Leonardo contends, it obfuscates things to do as McIntosh did in her germinal essay and cite as evidence of white privilege the fact that white people can assume that their neighbors will be nice to them, the "person in charge" at a business will look like them, the police will not harass them, and "flesh"-colored bandages will match their skin color. Instead, the practices that have made these social facts possible need to be made visible. He writes:

---

[39] Leonardo, *supra* note 21, at 137.

[40] *See* EDUARDO BONILLA-SILVA, RACISM WITHOUT RACISTS (4th ed. 2014).

Whites have 'neighbors . . . [who] are neutral or pleasant' to them because redlining and other real estate practices, with the help of the Federal Housing Agency, secure the ejection of the black and brown body from white spaces. Whites can enter a business establishment and expect the "person in charge" to be white because of a long history of job discrimination. Whites are relatively free from racial harassment from police officers because racial profiling strategies train U.S. police officers that people of color are potential criminals. Finally, whites can choose blemish cover or bandages in "flesh" color to match their skin because of centuries of denigration of darker peoples and images associated with them, fetishism of the color line, and the cultivation of the politics of pigmentation. We can condense the list under a general theme: whites enjoy privileges largely because they have created a system of domination under which they can thrive as a group.[41]

B. The Stuff of White Privilege Is Ultimately Insignificant

There is a claim that the social facts to which the term white privilege refers are insignificant in the grand scheme of things. As noted above, scholars have argued that white privilege is evidenced by white people tending not to think about their race, finding beauty products that match their skin tones, and seeing people of their same race in positions of power in society. Critics argue that these social facts neither advantage white people nor disadvantage people of color. That white people can walk up to any makeup counter in most department stores and find a foundation that matches the shade of their skin might be *convenient*, but it does not amount to white supremacy or a racial hierarchy. These critics state that, quite the contrary, it is minor. To complain about it is to cry over the proverbial spilled milk.

Proponents of the concept of white privilege have two responses to this critique. First, they say that the critique both underestimates the psychological value of seeing oneself reflected as the norm in society and underestimates the mental and emotional harm of understanding oneself as a deviation from some identified valued. This is not crying over spilled milk, they say. It is more like mourning spilled blood. It is *serious*.

Second, proponents say that this critique ignores scholars' efforts to define and understand white privilege as a systemic phenomenon. It ignores conceptualizations of white privilege as

[41] Leonardo, *supra* note 21, at 148.

structured advantages—embedded in our institutions. As a structured advantage, proponents say that white people's ability to buy a concealer that transforms their skin into a seemingly blemish-free expanse is merely symptomatic of a more profound phenomenon: institutions in society are responsive to white people's needs because white people constitute the norms around which these institutions have been built. That every significant institution in society reflects the values of the white people who created them is reasonably referred to as white supremacy or a racial hierarchy, or so the riposte goes.

C. White Privilege Does Not Exist

And then there is the critique that white privilege does not even exist. This critique tends to be launched by people who argue that many of the supposed beneficiaries of white privilege are hardly privileged in any normal sense of the word. Consider the example given above of the white woman who grew up with neglectful, drug addicted parents, who was never able to receive a quality education, and who is now indigent and dependent on third parties to help her meet her basic needs. Critics would deny that her whiteness has benefitted her in any significant way. They would deny that it makes any sense to speak of this woman as having *white privilege*.

Moreover, the critique that white privilege does not exist sometimes expands into the claim that nonwhite people are not burdened with disadvantages on account of their race. Consider the millions of people who constitute the black middle-class. These folks are not stuck in hypersegregated ghettoes. They are not incarcerated. They are not trying to get decent educations in underfunded school districts. Quite the opposite, they live lives that are quite comfortable. Their class privilege appears to have saved them from the harmful effects that their supposed lack of racial privilege is supposed to cause. Some might go so far as to say that their class privilege has changed the meaning of their race. This critique takes seriously the possibility that class may "morph or elide racial identity."[42] If class can actually change what race means, then "black" may not be an unprivileged racial status. That is, it may be wrong for theorists, scholars, commentators, and laypeople to speak of "black" as always and necessarily a marginalized racial category. The argument is that when wealthy, a black person may have racial privilege—as their class privilege might have changed the meaning of their race.

---

[42] Audrey G. McFarlane, *Operatively White?: Exploring the Significance of Race and Class Through the Paradox of Black Middle-Classness*, 72 LAW & CONTEMP. PROBS. 163, 185 (2009).

If there is some truth to this proposition, then "white" is not always and necessarily a superordinate category. This is especially true when whiteness intersects with marginalization, as is the case when white people are poor, transgender, or undocumented. Essentially, the claim is that it may be wrong to assert, without qualification, that a person who is white enjoys racial privilege. When poor, transgender, undocumented, etc. a white person may lack racial privilege—as their lack of privilege along other lines might have changed the meaning of their race.

As noted above, there are interlocking webs of privilege and unprivilege, such that an individual may be privileged along axes of race and class, but unprivileged along axes of gender and sexuality, for example. This undeniably complicates the experience, if not the concept, of white privilege. It may be difficult for a white middle-class lesbian, for example, to feel *privileged* inasmuch as she is a female who is a sexual minority.

It might be important to recognize that it may be difficult for white people to feel privileged inasmuch as the benefits that accompany whiteness in the present day are significantly fewer than the benefits that accompanied this identity in times past. That is, it may be difficult for any white person to feel privileged when they compare the value of the whiteness they inhabit today, in the post-civil rights era, to the value of whiteness in the pre-civil rights days, when whiteness gave white people an "aristocratic standing."[43] Because whiteness is indisputably less valuable than it once was, it may be experienced today as lacking value altogether.

We see this sentiment expressed in the debate over race-based affirmative action, with opponents arguing that the white people who are put at a competitive disadvantage by these programs enjoy no racial benefits from their racial identities. Opponents deny that white people should be "asked to bear the costs of social justice programs to improve the standing of minorities," as they deny that we can comfortably assume that white people today, as a general matter, enjoy "the benefits of white privilege that put minorities at a relative disadvantage."[44] This opposition becomes a little more analytically sophisticated when one considers that, as discussed above, white privilege may be understood as the *statistical probability of advantage*. As political theorist Joel Olson observes, "[B]ecause [white privilege consists of] probabilities, not guarantees, the aggregated advantages of [present-day] whiteness hardly seem

---

[43] Joel Olson, *Whiteness and the Participation-Inclusion Dilemma*, 30 POL. RES. Q. 384 (2002).

[44] Rich, *supra* note 12, at 1526.

like privileges."[45] To be told that one must bear the burden of racial remediation because one is *likely* to have better outcomes than one's nonwhite counterpart may spark resentment and denial when a white individual has no proof that she *actually* has had better outcomes.

Where does this leave us? Well, it seems true that we tend to conceptualize white privilege along the paradigm of the individual who is privileged along *all* axes of identity—that is, the wealthy, straight, cisgender, white male citizen. Those who are white, but who are not similarly privileged in all respects—who are women, poor, gay, or transgender, for instance—certainly have different experiences than those of the wealthy, straight, cisgender, white male citizen. The question is whether it makes sense to describe these latter persons as enjoying racial privilege. One answer is to say no: their lack of class, gender, or sexuality privilege functions to defeat any racial privilege that they otherwise might enjoy. Another answer is to say yes: their lack of privilege along axes of class, gender, or sexuality might *change* their experiences with racial privilege. However, this answer would insist that white people, regardless of any other unprivileged characteristics they may have, still enjoy white privilege. They still benefit from their whiteness—economically, socially, culturally, politically, and psychologically.

As a general matter, critical scholars of race have concluded that white privilege is something that all white people enjoy, although they recognize that individuals may have different access to it as a result of their other characteristics. It misrepresents reality to propose that the fact of white privilege means that all white people win equally. Instead, white people are a varied group, and the racial privilege that any one individual enjoys will depend on his social circumstance. To believe that the benefits of white privilege are available to all white people in equal measure is to deny the incredible heterogeneity that exists within this group. If one believes that white privilege exists and is meaningful, then one has to recognize the uneven distribution of white privilege and think through the social and political consequences of that reality.

V. Questions and Discussion

1. The Court has occasionally acknowledged what progressives call white privilege. As Stephanie Wildman observes, the Court's recognition of white privilege led it to its decision in *Sweatt v. Painter*,[46] a precursor to *Brown v. Board*. *Sweatt* concerned Texas's effort to maintain racial segregation by opening a separate

---

45 Olson, *supra* note 43, at 392.

46 Sweatt v. Painter, 339 U.S. 629 (1950).

law school for black students in lieu of admitting them to the law school at the University of Texas. The Court held that Texas's plan ran afoul of the Equal Protection Clause inasmuch as the law school that had been erected for black students was patently inferior to the law school at the University of Texas, which the state was trying in earnest to reserve for white students. The Court noted that even if the newly-instituted law school for black people had been equal to the University of Texas Law School in terms of faculty size, course variety, or library offerings, it would still lack other more intangible, but extremely valuable, attributes. The Court observed:

> [T]he University of Texas Law School possesses to a far greater degree those qualities which are incapable of objective measurement but which make for greatness in a law school. Such qualities, to name but a few, include reputation of the faculty, experience of the administration, position and influence of the alumni, standing in the community, traditions and prestige.[47]

Wildman observes that the tangible and intangible qualities that made the University of Texas Law School a superior institution to the one that the state had hastily erected for black people is rightfully understood as the stuff of white privilege inasmuch as these qualities had been made only accessible to white people.[48] In holding that the Constitution required that black people have access to the tangible and intangible benefits of a University of Texas Law School education, the Court dismantled them as the stuff of white privilege (while, perhaps, maintaining them as the stuff of class privilege).

2. Caroline Mala Corbin has argued that the general tendency to describe white perpetrators of mass shootings as mentally ill, as opposed to terrorists, is an example of white privilege. She writes that the concept of white privilege explains why she, as a white person, likely would not be called a terrorist if she committed an act of violence that satisfied textbook definitions of terrorism, i.e., she engaged in ideologically-motivated violence in order to intimidate civilians or influence the government.[49] She writes that, "Rather than immediately becoming a demonized 'other,' I would remain an individual, albeit a deeply troubled one. The dehumanization of the

---

[47] *Id.* at 634.

[48] *See* Stephanie M. Wildman, *The Persistence of White Privilege*, 18 WASH. U. J. L. & POL'Y 245, 258 (2005).

[49] *See* Caroline Mala Corbin, *Terrorists are Always Muslim but Never White: At the Intersection of Critical Race Theory and Propaganda*, 86 FORDHAM L. REV. 101, 103 (2017).

Muslim perpetrator happens in an instant. The white Christian perpetrator, on the other hand, always retains his humanity."[50]

One of the many examples that she discusses is the case of Dylann Roof, who shot nine black churchgoers in Charleston, South Carolina with the explicitly stated purpose of starting a race war.[51] She notes that "[o]ne terrorist expert wrote that there is no definition of terrorism that the Charleston shooting fails to satisfy: 'There is no criterion or definition [of terrorism] that this incident does not plainly and fully meet . . . . Were I teaching such a course next year, I would begin with this Charleston event as a textbook example of domestic terrorism.' And yet, the Charleston shooter, like other white Christian extremists, is not routinely referred to as a terrorist, and other white Christian men are not profiled or expected to denounce him. That is white privilege."[52]

Some may argue that white people, as a general matter, gain nothing from this phenomenon; it only appears to benefit the rare white person who would commit a terroristic act. However, Corbin notes that one of the consequences of the individualization of the white perpetrator of mass violence is that white men, as a group, are saved from being treated as a potentially dangerous population. "Because these attacks are categorized as one offs, other white Christian men are spared the profiling that brown Muslim men are subjected to."[53] If Corbin is right, the benefit of identifying white terrorists as lone wolves with mental health issues accrues to all white men, who are not racially profiled when traveling and whose communities are not subjected to surveillance designed to sniff out the next perpetrator of ideologically-motivated violence.

Do you believe that the consequences of the racialization of terrorism and terrorists that Corbin observes are significant? Do you believe that we should understand it to be an example of white privilege?

3. Some critical scholars have emphasized that white people do not have a monopoly on racial privilege. That is, nonwhite people may enjoy racial privilege vis-à-vis other nonwhite groups. Tanya Katerí Hernández has argued that nonwhite individuals may even enjoy *white privilege*. She notes that this occurs when a nonwhite person positions himself "as an agent of White supremacy."[54] She argues that in certain contexts, nonwhite persons and groups may be

---

[50] *Id.* at 113.

[51] *See id.* at 116.

[52] *Id.* at 119.

[53] *Id.* at 115.

[54] Tanya Katerí Hernández, *Latino Inter-Ethnic Employment Discrimination and the Diversity Defense*, 42 HARV. C.R.-C.L. L. REV. 259, 307 (2007).

"functionally privileged" to the detriment of other nonwhite people and to the continued benefit of white people.[55] As an example, she discusses the protests that occurred in Los Angeles in the early 1990s. She writes that "both Koreans and African Americans were in turn positioned as functionally White-privileged in nativist constructs of the racial conflict in the public discourse. Korean Americans were described as immigrant foreigners in opposition to African Americans with 'White' U.S. citizenship, a description that alternated with the description of Korean Americans as pursuing the American entrepreneurial dream as Whites in opposition to African Americans as a socially problematic Black underclass."[56]

Do you think that it is helpful to describe nonwhite groups as, at times, possessing *white privilege*? What are the benefits of describing the racial advantage that these groups enjoy as *white privilege*? What are the dangers?

4. To the extent that race-based affirmative action benefits black, Latinx, and indigenous persons to the exclusion of white and Asian people, do you think it is fair to say that black, Latinx, and indigenous persons enjoy a racial privilege in that context? If not, why not?

If you do think that black, Latinx, and indigenous persons are fairly described as having racial privilege in the context of race-based affirmative action programs, can you identify other scenarios where these groups have racial privilege?

5. Sylvia Law has argued that "[e]ven if we accept that white privilege is a pervasive yet invisible fact, it is not clear that it is a wrong for which there should be a legal remedy, or what form that remedy might take."[57] Do you think that there should be a legal remedy for white privilege? Why or why not? If you believe that the law ought to remedy white privilege, what form should that remedy take?

6. In one of the most generative articles in CRT scholarship, Cheryl Harris famously argues that the law has come to protect white privilege and, as a result, whiteness has become a species of property.[58] She writes that "whiteness as property is the reification, in law, of expectations of white privilege."[59]

She argues that, at the dawn of the nation, the concept of property was deployed in a way that enabled white people to

---

[55] *Id.* at 309.

[56] *Id.* at 308.

[57] Law, *supra* note 36, at 616.

[58] *See* Cheryl I. Harris, *Whiteness as Property*, 106 HARV. L. REV. 1707 (1993).

[59] *Id.* at 1784.

dominate nonwhite people: specifically, the institution of chattel slavery allowed black people to be transformed into a species of property that could be bought and sold, enabling white people to generate and accumulate vast quantities of wealth. Additionally, the lands that indigenous peoples inhabited were expropriated because courts embraced concepts of property that denied that indigenous people "owned" those lands; instead, the practices in which white people engaged were the only ones that were legally sufficient to establish ownership. In this way, Harris argues, notions of property were essential to the subordination of black and indigenous persons and the simultaneous establishment of white supremacy.

Harris argues that in modern times, whiteness is helpfully understood as property because the law protects the expectations that white people have come to have—expectations that are the product of centuries of white racial domination. She identifies the law's protection of whiteness as property in the Court's approach to affirmative action. White people have come to expect that they will be able to compete for every seat in a university's incoming class, and they expect that none of the seats will be reserved for individuals belonging to historically underrepresented groups. White people expect that, when applying for a job, they will be evaluated according to the definitions of "merit" and "qualifications" that the nation has always used. They expect that they will not be evaluated according to alternative understandings of merit and qualifications that may function to produce a less homogenously white institution and that may result in them being less "meritorious" and less "qualified" for the position that they covet. Harris argues that the Court's jurisprudence around the question of affirmative action reveals that it is interested in protecting these expectations. Writes Harris,

> The Supreme Court's rejection of affirmative action programs on the grounds that race-conscious remedial measures are unconstitutional under the Equal Protection Clause of the Fourteenth Amendment—the very constitutional measure designed to guarantee equality for Blacks—is based on the Court's chronic refusal to dismantle the institutional protection of benefits for whites that have been based on white supremacy and maintained at the expense of Blacks. As a result, the parameters of appropriate remedies are not dictated by the scope of the injury to the subjugated, but by the extent of the infringement on settled expectations of whites. These limits to remediation are grounded in the perception that the existing order based on white privilege is not only just

"there," but also is a property interest worthy of protection.[60]

What do you think framing white privilege as a species of property adds to our understanding of this racial privilege? What does it take away or obscure?

7. McIntosh's formulation of privilege has made it into a Supreme Court opinion, albeit as an example of an unsavory "racial theory." In *Parents Involved in Community Schools*, the Court struck down a school board's plan to achieve more racially integrated schools in the district by taking students' race into consideration when making school assignments.[61] In Justice Thomas's separate concurrence, he argued that courts ought not to defer to school boards implementing race-conscious policies, as these boards may be constituted by people who have problematic views about race. As an example, Thomas noted that the Seattle school board, whose race-conscious school assignment plan the Court struck down in the case, had sent a group of high school students to a conference on white privilege. Thomas reports that at the conference, the students were instructed that white privilege was "an invisible package of unearned assets which I can count on cashing in each day, but about which I was meant to remain oblivious"—a definition of white privilege clearly lifted verbatim from McIntosh's essay.[62] However, far from finding the concept of white privilege enlightening and McIntosh's description of it illuminating, Thomas thought that they illustrated precisely why courts ought to review school boards' uses of race with strict scrutiny: school boards may harbor dangerous ideas about race.

Why do you think some conservatives believe that the concept of white privilege is a dangerous idea about race? Is it good or bad for some conservatives to find the concept dangerous?

8. Scholars have proposed a variety of terms for describing white persons who possess unprivileged nonracial characteristics. Camille Gear Rich describes these white individuals as possessing a "marginal whiteness."[63] She writes that these individuals have "more limited access to white privilege, and relatedly have a more attenuated relationship to white identity."[64] Analogously, I have described white persons who are unprivileged along nonracial lines

---

[60] *Id.* at 1767–68.

[61] *See* Parents Involved in Cmty. Sch. v. Seattle Sch. Dist. No. 1, 551 U.S. 701 (2007).

[62] *Id.* at 781 n.30 (Thomas, J., concurring).

[63] Rich, *supra* note 30, at 1505.

[64] *Id.*

as having undergone a "racial sullying."[65] The concept of racial sullying attempts to communicate that the racial privilege of a white person has been diminished in some respects—by drug addiction, or welfare dependence, for example.

Do you believe that the concepts of *marginal whiteness* or *racial sullying* effectively capture the idea that some white people are unprivileged along lines other than race and, consequently, face challenges? What other terms can you think of that capture this idea?

Do you think it is helpful to speak of disadvantaged white people as having *white privilege*?

---

[65] *See* KHIARA M. BRIDGES, REPRODUCING RACE: AN ETHNOGRAPHY OF PREGNANCY AS A SITE OF RACIALIZATION 239 (2011).

Chapter 11

THE RELATIONSHIP BETWEEN RACE AND CLASS

I. Introduction

People of color disproportionately bear the burdens of poverty in the U.S. today. In 2016, the poverty rate among indigenous people was 26.2%.[1] This means that one in four indigenous persons are impoverished. The poverty rates among black and Latinx people were better, but not by much—at 22% and 19.4%, respectively.[2] Asian persons, overall, are doing well; the poverty rate among this group was 11.4% in 2015,[3] better than the national average of 13.5%.[4] However, some groups of Asians are desperately impoverished. The poverty rate among Hmong persons, for example, was 28.3% in 2015.[5] Significantly, white people have the lowest poverty rate among all racial groups—at 8.8% in 2016.[6]

Progressive thinkers about race cite the statistics above as evidence of the close relationship between race and class in the U.S. That is, if one has race privilege, one is more likely to have class privilege. And the reverse is also true: if one lacks race privilege, one is more likely to be unprivileged along class lines. These scholars propose that there is a tight, frequently symbiotic relationship between race and class. Athena Mutua describes it in the following way: "[R]ace itself is a system for allocating resources but one that is part and parcel of, or intertwined with the class system, even as it operates independently and relatedly as a belief system that provides a ready justification for the racialized results of various distributions."[7]

To illustrate Mutua's description, we might think of racial disparities in wealth, which will be discussed in greater depth later in the chapter. The short of it is that, on average, nonwhite people

---

1 U.S. CENSUS BUREAU, AMERICAN INDIAN AND ALASKA NATIVE HERITAGE MONTH: NOVEMBER 2017, at 5 (2017).

2 JESSICA L. SEMEGA, KAYLA R. FONTENOT & MELISSA A. KOLLAR, U.S. CENSUS BUREAU, INCOME AND POVERTY IN THE UNITED STATES: 2016, at 12 (2017).

3 *Id.* at 13.

4 *Id.*

5 ARIANA RODRIGUEZ-GITLER, PEW RESEARCH CENTER, U.S. HMONG POPULATION LIVING IN POVERTY, 2015 (2017).

6 SEMEGA, FONTENOT & KOLLAR, *supra* note 2, at 12.

7 Athena D. Mutua, *The Rise, Development and Future Directions of Critical Race Theory and Related Scholarship*, 84 DENV. U. L. REV. 329, 392 (2006) [hereinafter Mutua, *The Rise, Development and Future*].

have a fraction of the wealth that white people possess. This is due, in part, to nonwhite people being much less likely to inherit wealth than are white people. Nonwhite people are less likely to inherit wealth because their parents, grandparents, and great grandparents before them were, on account of their race, prevented from accumulating it. Instead, their forebears were consigned to the laboring class: they were placed in the group in the class system whose labor would generate wealth for others. In this way, race has been intertwined with the class system in such a way that resources have been allocated toward some racial groups and away from others.

Further, Mutua's description proposes that when nonwhite groups disproportionately find themselves on the bottom of the socioeconomic ladder today—because they have inherited disadvantage, not wealth—racial narratives explain this result: black people are lazy and do not like to work, Latinx people prioritize family over work outside of the home, indigenous people are alcoholics whose addiction makes them unproductive, Hmong people prefer welfare over hard work, white people are naturally industrious, etc. In this way, race "provides a ready justification for the racialized results of various distributions."[8]

Mutua's point about the intertwining of race with our class system might deserve some elaboration. Many progressive scholars have observed the intermeshing of our systems of racial ordering with our economic systems. They invite us to think of slavery. The institution of chattel slavery in the U.S. explicitly created a racial hierarchy. Black people were the class that could be enslaved, while white people were those who could never be slaves. However, the reality that slavery was a profoundly race-based system should not detract from the fact that it was also an economic system. One of its purposes—some may even say its *primary* purpose—was to generate profit from the labor of the enslaved.[9]

These scholars assert that there are plenty of other examples of the intermeshing of our systems of racial ordering with economic systems. Consider Operation Wetback of 1954. Under this program, some one million people of Mexican descent, many of them U.S. citizens, were deported.[10] However, the reality that Operation

---

[8] *Id.*

[9] Indeed, Mutua describes slavery and Jim Crow as "economic systems meant to facilitate the exploitation of black labor, to deny black material well-being, and to assist the few in hoarding the resources created by the many." Athena D. Mutua, *Introducing Classcrits: from Class Blindness to a Critical Legal Analysis of Economic Inequality*, 56 BUFF. L. REV. 859, 907 (2008) [hereinafter, Mutua, *Introducing Classcrits*].

[10] Kelly Lytle Hernández, *The Crimes and Consequences of Illegal Immigration: A Cross-Border Examination of Operation Wetback, 1943 to 1954*, 37 WESTERN HIST. Q. 421, 421–22 (2006).

Wetback was a racial program—on what other basis can one justify deporting U.S. *citizens* on account of their Mexican ancestry?—should not detract from the fact that it was also an economic program. It was implemented as tens of thousands of soldiers who had served in the Korean War encountered a recession when they returned home. In this way, Operation Wetback was an economic program inasmuch as it helped reduce the competition for jobs faced by American citizens who were not of Mexican descent.

According to critical thinkers, the interrelationship of race and class continues to the present. Mutua has suggested that due to this continued symbiosis of race and class, decisions that are made about the economy are *racial* decisions and ought to be appreciated as such. She gives the example of the 2008 recession, which hit people of color the hardest: while this recession, which was the worst economic downturn since the Great Depression, caused white people to lose some 16% of their net worth, black and Asian American people lost 50% of their net worth, and Latinx people lost 65%.[11] She argues that in light of this,

> talk about unregulated markets, individual preferences, reduced investment in people and social and physical infrastructure, tax cuts for big business, and other policy choices is not just economic talk or class talk but race talk. That is, these policies have the effect of preserving the racialized status quo of current arrangements and their primary beneficiaries, with all its inequities, while also increasing economic inequality and the concentration of wealth in these beneficiaries' hands. In other words, free market talk is often race talk.[12]

Those who oppose significant government regulation of the market would vigorously disagree with Mutua's contention. They argue that the outcomes that a free market produces are fair, just, and sometimes constitutionally demanded. Some contend that a free market is the best hope that we have for generating the wealth that could, one day, eliminate poverty entirely. This line of argument concludes that, if people of color are disproportionately poor in this country, then they are *most* helped by a free market—which could lift their boats as well as the boats of everyone else. It might suffice to say that critical scholars like Mutua are unconvinced by these claims. The proof, they say, is in the pudding. And all that the bitter, not-at-all delicious pudding has revealed is the poverty statistics that open this chapter.

---

[11] Athena D. Mutua, *Stuck: Fictions, Failures and Market Talk as Race Talk*, 43 SW. L. REV. 517, 540 (2014) [hereinafter Mutua, *Stuck*].

[12] *Id.*

II. The Dialectical Relationship Between Race and Class

Critical scholars invite us to think of race and class as having a dialectical relationship: race produces class at the same time that class produces race. The next sections consider the two terms of the dialectic individually.

A. Race Produces Class

Scholars writing in this area work to identify the ways in which race produces class—that is, stratifications along the lines of power and wealth. The most obvious way race has performed this function is through denying unprivileged racial groups access to resources and/or relegating them to poverty while directing capital towards privileged groups. Moreover, say these scholars, the economic effects of historical events that impoverished nonwhite persons reverberate to the present. "[W]hen marginalized racialized groups come to the market in the modern moment, a market biased in favor of money, they often do so with less wealth, fewer assets . . . [and] a history and continuing experience of limitation and segregation."[13]

One visible location in which we might observe race producing class is the housing market. Here, various actors, including the federal government, worked together to ensure that black people were unable to purchase homes—an asset that "represents the primary source of wealth in our society."[14] As John Calmore explains, before the government got in the business of offering mortgages, owning a home was the exclusive province of the more affluent. "Prior to World War II, banks and other lending institutions as a rule demanded a down payment of fifty percent and required repayment of the mortgage within ten years."[15] This made mortgages unaffordable and put purchasing a home out of the reach of most. However, through the Federal Housing Administration (FHA) and Veterans Affairs (VA) programs, the government began offering mortgages that required only a five or ten percent down payment and could be paid back over the course of thirty years. These mortgages made home ownership accessible to those who were, or who would become, the middle-class. Yet, the federal government did not offer these mortgages to everyone equally. Black people found themselves overwhelmingly excluded. "Between 1934 and 1959, only two percent

---

13 *Id.* at 539.

14 John O. Calmore, *Spatial Equality and the Kerner Commission Report: A Back-to-the-Future Essay*, 71 N.C. L. REV. 1487, 1510 (1993).

15 *Id.*

of the FHA units were made available to the nation's minorities who comprised approximately fifteen percent of the overall population."[16]

Moreover, a constellation of actors—including "state and local governments, real estate brokers, developers and financial institutions"[17]—collaborated to ensure that communities were racially segregated. Thus, if black people could acquire a mortgage or had cash on hand to buy a house outright, racially restrictive covenants and other exclusionary local practices ensured that homes in white neighborhoods remained inaccessible to them. Significantly, the federal government endorsed these efforts to keep white neighborhoods racially segregated. "[T]he FHA manuals that guided the agency underwriters issuing federal insurance . . . provided a blueprint to prevent blacks from entering neighborhoods where their mere presence would bring down property values."[18] The result was that the only housing available to black families was in black neighborhoods—locations where state, local, and federal governments directed most low-income housing to be built and where the federal government refused to offer mortgage assistance.

These laws, policies, and practices directed a valuable asset—home ownership—toward white people and away from black people. Scores of white families were able to acquire this asset decades before black families. They were able to enjoy increases in the asset's value over the years, and they were able to pass this wealth down to their children. Black people were unable to do the same. This, argues Calmore, helps to explain racial disparities in wealth. In Calmore's view, the housing market is a site where we can witness race producing class: race created a white middle-class with wealth and assets and a black working class and underclass with neither.

An additional way that thinkers propose that race produces class—poverty, specifically—is through the welfare state. The argument is that poverty has come to be associated with nonwhite people. Specifically, when people think of the poor, they think of black people. The argument proposes that because people in the U.S., as a general matter, do not hold poor black people in particularly high regard, the programs that the nation has erected to care for the impoverished, who are imagined to be black, are only reluctantly charitable. These programs do not lift their beneficiaries out of poverty. Instead, they merely shift them to the low-skill, low-wage employment market, where continued poverty is virtually guaranteed. If this is true, then race produces poverty because it has

---

16 *Id.*

17 *Id.* at 1509.

18 *Id.* at 1511.

informed the harsh approach that the nation has taken towards caring for its poor. Chapter 19 explores this argument in depth.

B. Class Produces Race

The idea that race might produce class, specifically class stratification, may be more intuitive than the idea that class stratification has produced race. But, the concept of poverty and wealth producing race becomes easier to grasp when one accepts the proposition that race is a social construction. As discussed in Chapter 6, the claim that race is a social construction is the idea that race is not natural in any sense of the word. Rather, race is *ideas* that societies create about differences among humans. Importantly, these ideas become material—tangible, visible, capable of being apprehended by the senses—as they are reflected, and are made to be reflected, in material conditions. So, the idea that black people are averse to work becomes material as they endure higher rates of unemployment than their white counterparts. The idea that Latinx people are hardworking becomes material as undocumented immigrants from Latin America are compelled to accept any job that they can find. And so on and so forth. According to critical scholars, this is how class produces race: the circumstances in which unprivileged racial groups are forced to live reaffirms the "truth" about their race. Further, the relative wealth that privileged groups enjoy reaffirms their racial "truths" as well.

Feminist philosopher Nancy Fraser has contended that societies will be unable to undo the hierarchies that exist within them until they equalize the distribution of resources. Mutua describes Fraser as proposing that "the valuation and respect of different groups is more likely in an egalitarian society, a society where significant material inequalities between groups do not exist."[19] Mutua argues that a " 'politics of redistribution' that seeks to change the processes and conditions that create and structure the devaluation of differently-positioned individuals and groups is a more effective strategy for accomplishing the edification of different groups in a pluralist society."[20] If Mutua is onto something, it means that the racial stratification that we witness in the U.S. today will not be undone until we reduce, or eliminate, economic inequality. In other words, if class produces race, then when we not achieve racial justice until we have achieved economic justice. At the same time, other scholars warn that the achievement of economic justice will not necessarily lead to the achievement of racial justice. In other words, they assert that when class oppression has been eliminated, racial oppression may still endure. Accordingly, they caution us against

---

[19] Mutua, *The Rise, Development and Future*, *supra* note 7, at 393.

[20] *Id.*

reducing our racial problems to our class system. Race and class are intermingled with one another, they say. But, they remain distinct.

III. The Inadequacy of Law

Critical scholars have observed that the law is partly responsible for the enduring racial stratification that we witness in the post-civil rights era. Of course, from the perspective of CRT, the law's role in protecting and perpetuating racial hierarchy is fundamental. (Indeed, this entire primer is about CRT's conviction that the law has protected and perpetuated racial hierarchy!) However, critical scholars of race *and class* explore how law has operated *in the economy* to create racial inequality. They note that "class" itself, as well as "the market," are "product[s] of legal rules and state action."[21] So, for example, if "the market" is such that there are few decent jobs available in the hypersegregated neighborhoods where poor people of color live, then the law bears some responsibility for that fact. And if the jobs available to low-skill workers, who are disproportionately people of color, do not pay enough to lift their families out of poverty, then the law, which has created "the market," is answerable for this state of affairs.

Scholars also observe that even though the Constitution has been interpreted to protect individuals from harms suffered on account of their race, it has not been interpreted to protect individuals from harms suffered on account of their class. *This is true even though there is a close relationship between racial inequality and class inequality.* Calmore argues that the courts have been careful not to interpret the Constitution to empower them to "tinker[ ] with social inequality or the existing distribution of wealth and privilege."[22] The consequence is that when laws or policies harm poor people, generally—or poor people of color, specifically—the Constitution has nothing to say if that harm can be understood as economic in origin.

From critical thinkers' perspective, there is a certain irony in the law having disempowered itself from protecting the black poor. The irony lies in their confidence that the extreme marginalization and vulnerability that the black poor currently endures are consequences of the law's effort to help black people. This statement requires some explanation.

Observers across the political spectrum agree that the Civil Rights Movement was a momentous phenomenon in American

---

[21] Angela P. Harris, *From Precarity to Positive Freedom: ClassCrits at Seven: Introduction*, 44 SW. L. REV. 621, 626 (2015).

[22] John O. Calmore, *Exploring the Significance of Race and Class in Representing the Black Poor*, 61 OR. L. REV. 201, 235 (1982) [hereinafter Calmore, *Exploring the Significance*].

history, as activists and revolutionaries demanded the end to legal apartheid and racial caste. And the nation, through the law, responded to their demands. The Civil Rights Act of 1964 and the Voting Rights Act of 1965 were key pieces of legislation that the federal government offered to end black people's second-class citizenship. President Lyndon B. Johnson supplemented these efforts with the Equal Opportunity Act, the legislative piece of his War on Poverty. The Equal Opportunity Act complemented the Civil Rights Act and the Voting Rights Act by implementing job training and social welfare programs that were designed to help the poor acquire skills that could help them participate in the labor market and, ideally, emerge from poverty. In many respects, these efforts were successful. They certainly did not end racial inequality; but, they did help create the black middle-class, moving many poor black people into the economic mainstream of American life.

And this is the irony. While the legislative responses to the Civil Rights Movement helped the black middle-class, they did very little for the black people who remained impoverished. As Calmore puts it, "[A]dvances made in the name of race have enhanced the opportunities of more privileged blacks but have failed to address the problems of the black poor."[23] In Calmore's view, it is wonderful that the Civil Rights Movement prompted the government to initiate affirmative action programs in hiring and education. It is fantastic that the agitation led the government to establish the Equal Employment Opportunity Commission, which would enforce laws prohibiting employment discrimination. It is marvelous that the revolutionaries who took to the streets compelled the government to pass laws that allowed black people to share in public accommodations alongside their white counterparts. But, claims Calmore, these efforts have not done much for the black poor. In his assessment, they have "done little to change conditions which keep blacks unemployed and underemployed, educated in poorly funded and administered segregated schools, badly housed in segregated neighborhoods, and franchised with very little political power."[24] Quite provocatively, Calmore has suggested that the black poor being left behind by the Civil Rights Movement is not some perverse consequence of the social upheaval. Instead, he suggests that we might have expected the result. He writes, "The civil rights movement was undeniably a glorious thing. Yet . . ., [w]hile the reforms sought were radical in their call for inclusion of blacks in the American dream, the movement was not protesting so much against the 'system' as being left out of it."[25] According to Calmore, the

[23] *Id.* at 215.

[24] *Id.* at 222.

[25] *Id.* at 215.

activists were not challenging the exploitation of laborers that left-leaning economic thinkers say is part and parcel of capitalism; instead, they were challenging their inability to be exploiters. They were not rebelling against an economic system that creates poverty; they were simply rebelling against a race-based system that confined black people to poverty. If Calmore is right, then the civil rights activists "won" when some black people were permitted to escape poverty. They "won" even though millions of black people remained in desperate indigence.

In the most pessimistic rendering, the gains made by the Civil Rights Movement might have made it even more difficult to address the issue of black poverty. The nation might feel that it has done all that can be done—all that *should* be done—to address racial inequality. The existence of the black middle-class and the fact that black people can now be seen in elite institutions and in the halls of power might serve as evidence that the "race problem" has been solved. That some black people have succeeded might be taken to suggest that those who have not succeeded have only themselves to blame.

IV. The Disadvantage of the Black Middle-Class

Many critical theorists are very much concerned about the black poor who, as discussed above, are terribly impoverished without an apparent remedy. These thinkers have proposed that we need to turn our collective attention towards this group. However, another set of thinkers caution that we ought not to forget about the black middle-class *entirely*. In many respects, they are "precariously positioned."[26] Thinkers of this ilk underscore that the reason for the black middle-class's precarious positioning is *race*. That is, race has made it difficult for the black middle-class to enjoy the comfort and security that the white middle-class has.

We might begin by asking the question: how privileged is the black middle class? The answer that one gives to that question may depend on to whom one is comparing the group. Generally, the black middle class is compared to their black counterparts without class privilege—those folks who are sometimes referred to as the "underclass" or the "urban poor." When one compares the black middle class to this "truly disadvantaged" group, the former seems to be doing better than fine.[27] They appear to be successful, living the American dream. As one scholar recently put it, "Unlike the urban underclass, the black middle class lives in a world filled with options.

---

[26] *Id.* at 212.

[27] *See* Derrick Bell, *Racism is Here to Stay: Now What?*, 35 HOW. L.J. 79, 87 (1991) (noting that the black middle class has achieved "a success that is both enviable and—many whites and some blacks think—attainable by all blacks").

They are not restricted in the ways their forbears were by segregation. They are members of not just a race, but also an affluent, economic class."[28]

However, when one compares the black middle class to their white counterparts—that is, the white middle class—the picture becomes less rosy. Indeed, critical thinkers encourage us to judge wealthier racial minorities against those who share their class privilege, as opposed to those who share their racial ascription. It is then, they say, that their subordination is thrown into sharp relief.

We can begin with their health. Studies have documented that racial minorities endure increased levels of morbidity and mortality even when one controls for class. Consider racial disparities in maternal mortality. Class-privileged black women die during pregnancy and childbirth at rates that are significantly higher than their white counterparts.[29] That is, racial disparities in maternal mortality rates persist across income levels. Now, many are aware that there are racial disparities in maternal mortality in the U.S.; many may even be aware of the specifics—that three to four times as many black women as white women die on the path to motherhood.[30] However, the tendency has been to attribute this tragic disparity to poverty—to assume that because black people in the U.S. disproportionately bear the burdens of poverty, this disproportionate indigence is reflected in the rates at which black women die during pregnancy, childbirth, or shortly thereafter. However, this assumption is not entirely correct. It is not only poor black women who are dying on the path to motherhood. Wealthier black women are dying, too; and they are dying more frequently than wealthier white women. This means that it is not solely poverty that is killing black women.

For critical scholars of race and class, the excess mortality among wealthier black women attempting motherhood suggests that race matters. Race can be the difference between health and sickness, life and death. It also suggests to these thinkers that class privilege does not entirely erase the effects of the absence of race privilege. For pregnant black women who find themselves at the higher levels of the socioeconomic ladder, disadvantage persists despite their class privilege.

---

[28] Leland Ware & Theodore Davis, *Ordinary People in an Extraordinary Time: The Black Middle-Class in the Age of Obama*, 55 HOW. L.J. 533, 539 (2012).

[29] AMNESTY INT'L, DEADLY DELIVERY: THE MATERNAL HEALTH CARE CRISIS IN THE USA: ONE YEAR UPDATE 7 (2011), https://www.amnestyusa.org/wp-content/uploads/2017/04/deadlydeliveryoneyear.pdf [https://perma.cc/29ZB-ZRZU].

[30] Andreea Creanga et al., *Maternal Mortality and Morbidity in the United States: Where Are We Now?*, 23 J. WOMEN'S HEALTH 3, 4–5 (2014).

Further, the infants born to class-privileged black women die at rates that are much higher than the babies born to their white counterparts. Indeed, racial disparities in infant mortality and morbidity *increase* as one moves up the income ladder. That is, the rates at which poor black babies and poor white babies die are closer than the rates at which wealthier black babies and wealthier white babies die.[31] As one commentator put it, "contrary to what one might predict, these studies provide evidence that racial differences are larger among women perceived to be at lower risk for poor outcomes."[32]

What is true with respect to racial disparities in infant mortality is true as a general matter: Racial disparities in health tend to increase as one moves up the socioeconomic ladder.[33] In other words, poor black people and poor white people sometimes have levels of health that are more comparable to one another than the levels of health of wealthier black people and wealthier white people. This might mean that our antipoverty programs have managed to make race have less of an impact on poor people's health. This is a triumph, undoubtedly. But, it reveals that something that cannot be fixed by antipoverty programs is threatening the health of people of color. To progressive scholars, that something is race.

We can look beyond health for evidence that race disadvantages wealthier racial minorities. Consider their experiences in the housing market. Wealthier black people live in less affluent homes and neighborhoods than their white peers.[34] The neighborhoods in which class-privileged black people live tend to be closer to poor black neighborhoods[35] and, as a consequence, tend to feature the social dislocations (crime, poorer quality schools, etc.) that poverty so often causes.[36] The consequences of residential segregation for people of color are many, and most of them are bad. As Bennett Capers summarizes it: "Entrenched segregation tends to deny racial minorities equal access to jobs, government resources, amenities, and . . . quality schools. Segregation also tends to disproportionately

---

31 *See* Marsha Lillie-Blanton et al., *Racial Differences in Health: Not Just Black and White, but Shades of Gray*, 17 ANN. REV. PUB. HEALTH 411, 429 (1996).

32 *Id.* at 417.

33 *See* James S. House & David R. Williams, *Understanding and Reducing Socioeconomic and Racial/Ethnic Disparities in Health*, *in* PROMOTING HEALTH: INTERVENTION STRATEGIES FROM SOCIAL & BEHAVIORAL RESEARCH, 81, 89, 105 (Brian D. Smedley & S. Leonard Syme eds., 2000).

34 Bart Landry & Kris Marsh, *The Evolution of the New Black Middle Class*, 37 ANN. REV. SOC. 373, 388 (2011) (citing Richard D. Alba, John R. Logan & Brian J. Stults, *How Segregated are Middle Class African Americans?*, 47 SOC. PROBS. 543, 554 (2000)).

35 SHERYLL CASHIN, THE FAILURES OF INTEGRATION: HOW RACE AND CLASS ARE UNDERMINING THE AMERICAN DREAM 135 (2004).

36 Landry & Marsh, *supra* note 34, at 388.

burden racial minorities with society's detritus: Power plants and hazardous waste facilities, group homes for the mentally disabled, halfway houses, shelters for the homeless, and public housing projects."[37]

We can also look to income and wealth for evidence that race disadvantages wealthier racial minorities. Studies have shown that black professionals earn 75% to 85% of the incomes that their white counterparts earn.[38] Racial disparities in wealth are even more striking, with college-educated black people holding about 13% of the wealth that their white counterparts hold.[39] The disparity here is extraordinary: while white families whose heads hold a college degree have on average $180,500 in wealth, black families with similarly credentialed heads have almost an eighth of that wealth—$23,400.[40] While black families with annual incomes between $54,000 and $93,000 have $36,430 in wealth, white families in that income bracket have almost four times that much—$136,390.[41] Indeed, "[t]he poorest white families—those in the bottom quintile of the income distribution—have slightly more wealth than black families in the middle quintiles of the income distribution."[42] It is important to observe that the reason class-privileged black people have less wealth than their white counterparts has nothing to do with spending habits. Rather, critical scholars insist that it has everything to do with the weight of accumulated racial subordination. As legal scholar Deborah Malamud puts it, "all of the multi-generational disadvantages the black middle class suffers in housing, occupational segregation, education, and income translate into lower lifetime earnings, diminished return on housing capital, diminished likelihood of inheritance of wealth from parents, and therefore into reduced wealth accumulation over the life course."[43]

Progressive scholars look to the above as evidence that the middle-class that the Civil Rights Movement created continues to be burdened by race-based disadvantages—despite its class-privilege.

---

[37] I. Bennett Capers, *Policing, Race, and Place*, 44 HARV. C.R.-C.L. L. REV. 43, 44–45 (2009).

[38] *See* EDUARDO BONILLA-SILVA, RACISM WITHOUT RACISTS: COLOR-BLIND RACISM AND THE PERSISTENCE OF RACIAL INEQUALITY IN AMERICA 55 (4th ed. 2013).

[39] DARRICK HAMILTON ET AL., UMBRELLAS DON'T MAKE IT RAIN: WHY STUDYING AND WORKING HARD ISN'T ENOUGH FOR BLACK AMERICANS 3 (2015).

[40] *Id.* at 5.

[41] *Id.* at 7.

[42] *Id.* at 3.

[43] Deborah C. Malamud, *Affirmative Action, Diversity, and the Black Middle Class*, 68 U. COLO. L. REV. 939, 983 (1997).

V. The Conceptual Collapse of Race and Class

As discussed above, the black middle-class is not doing as well as it ought to be—at least when we compare it to its white counterpart. However, there has been little discussion of this. There are many reasons for this. Some might think that any disadvantage that the black middle-class encounters pales in comparison to that encountered by the black poor; accordingly, they believe that the relative vulnerability of the black middle class is irrelevant or unimportant. Others might think that the suffering of the black poor is so dramatic and visible that it blinds us to any suffering (if we can call it that. . .) that the black middle-class endures.

Another, more theoretical explanation for the invisibility of the black middle-class's disadvantage is the conceptual collapse of race and class. Under this schema, the close relationship between race and class is misunderstood such that race and class are taken to be the same thing. That is, the statement that black people disproportionately bear the burdens of poverty is taken to suggest that black people are poor—that *all* black people are poor. The statement that white people are underrepresented among the poor is taken to suggest that no white people are poor—that *all* white people are middle-class or better. This schema makes invisible black people who are not poor—the black middle class. It simultaneously makes invisible white people who are not middle-class or better—the white poor.[44]

The conceptual collapse of race and class is problematic for several reasons. On a basic level, it is just not true. Millions of black people are *not* poor; millions of white people *are* poor. Beyond that, the conceptual collapse might explain some of the vicious fights that the nation has around poverty and economic regulation. As briefly touched upon above, when compared to the nations that the U.S. considers its peers, the country does care for its poor very well. In other words, the social safety net that the country has erected is quite flimsy. Some scholars explain this in terms of the conceptual collapse of race and class—the idea that all black people, and no white people, are poor. If all black people, and no white people, are poor, then the

---

[44] Martha Mahoney offers a helpful rendering of the conceptual collapse of race and class. She writes:

> In America today only two social "classes" . . . are usually discussed in the media and popular politics—a "middle class," and an "underclass." Each has a presumptive race. "Middle class" is presumptively white or non-African-American, a notion easily identified by distinguishing the frequency with which "black" qualifies "middle class" in ways that "white" or "Asian" do not. In contrast, the category "underclass" is presumptively non-white, and the term is particularly likely to be used to refer to African Americans.

Martha R. Mahoney, *Class and Status in American Law: Race, Interest, and the Anti-Transformation Cases*, 76 S. CAL. L. REV. 799, 829–30 (2003).

safety net *only* cares for black people. To some, this explains the meager nature of our social welfare programs. They also underscore that if we have erected a porous, insubstantial safety net because we feel that it is a system "for" black people, then the millions of poor white people who also rely on that system are harmed by an apathy or contempt that is directed towards black people.

According to some theorists, the conceptual collapse of race and class makes working- and middle-class white people more insistent in their demands to hold onto any class privilege that they have. The conceptual collapse increases the stakes of becoming poor. If only black people, and no white people, are poor, then becoming poor means becoming black/becoming not-white. This could be a terrifying possibility for someone who identifies closely with whiteness. The conceptual collapse makes working class white people's battles over their economic interests into fights about racial status.[45] If true, it is no wonder that these struggles become so rancorous.

According to other theorists, the conceptual collapse of race and class also makes it easy to attack race-based remedies. If race-based remedies, like affirmative action, are premised on the assumption that all black people, and no white people, are poor, then the inevitable exceptions to that rule become justifications for abandoning the remedy. As Maria Grahn-Farley asserts, "The attack on affirmative action is based on this logic: if black poverty and disadvantage [are] no longer universal, then white privilege is no longer universal. If white wealth and power is no longer universal, then it is under threat, it is threatened by affirmative action."[46]

VI. CRT's Inattention to Class?

On occasion, scholars have critiqued CRT for what they perceive to be its failure to interrogate the relationship between race and class. Richard Delgado, one of the founders of the theory, has offered a particularly trenchant articulation of this critique.

Delgado proposes that when CRT was in its earliest stages, the thinkers who would come to be critical race theorists concerned themselves with what was happening out there on the ground. Delgado states that these thinkers were "realists," convinced that "material factors such as profits and the labor market" relegated people of color to the lowest rungs of the nation's racial hierarchy.[47] Racial realists examined "the role of international relations and

---

[45] *See* Mutua, *Introducing Classcrits, supra* note 9, at 910 ("[T]he white working class' 'economic' interests are primarily concerns about race status.").

[46] Maria Grahn-Farley, *Race and Class: More than a Liberal Paradox*, 56 BUFF. L. REV. 935, 942 (2008).

[47] Richard Delgado, *Blind Alleys: Recent Writings About Race, Crossroads, Directions, and a New Critical Race Theory*, 82 TEX. L. REV. 121, 123 (2003).

competition, the interests of elite groups, and the changing demands of the labor market in hopes of understanding the twists and turn of racial fortunes, including the part the legal system plays in that history."[48] Delgado contrasts racial realists—who focused "on how race works in the real world, and the way it functions as an ordering principle in a world of power, resources, and privilege"[49]—with "idealists," whose foundational assumption is that "race and discrimination are largely functions of attitude and social formation."[50] He writes that for racial idealists,

> race is a social construction created out of words, symbols, stereotypes, and categories. As such, we may purge discrimination by ridding ourselves of the texts, narratives, ideas, and meanings that give rise to it and that convey the message that people of other racial groups are unworthy, lazy, and dangerous. These writers analyze hate speech, media images, census categories, and such issues as intersectionality and essentialism. They analyze unconscious or institutional racism and show how cognitive theory exposes a host of preconceptions, baselines, and mindsets that operate below the level of consciousness to render certain people consistently one-down.[51]

Delgado concludes that racial idealists have taken over CRT, and he laments it. He remains firm in his belief that the more persuasive explanations of why racial inequality persists in the country will be found by looking to material factors—the economy, the demands of capital, class relations—and not discourse and ideas.

In light of Delgado's criticism, the first question that we might ask is: is he right? Have critical race theorists paid insufficient attention to material causes for racial hierarchy? Have they excessively focused on discourse—"texts, narratives, ideas, and meanings"? Well, it is undeniable that many progressive thinkers about race analyze discourse. However, there is a significant number of materialist analyses of race out there as well—by self-identified critical race theorists as well as those who might not identify as such, but who produce scholarship that undoubtedly qualifies as CRT.[52] So, the answer to the question of whether CRT has *excessively* focused on

---

[48] *Id.*

[49] Mutua, *The Rise, Development and Future*, *supra* note 7, at 384.

[50] Delgado, *supra* note 47, at 123.

[51] *Id.*

[52] *See*, e.g., Bell, *supra* note 27; KHIARA M. BRIDGES, REPRODUCING RACE: AN ETHNOGRAPHY OF PREGNANCY AS A SITE OF RACIALIZATION (2011); Calmore, *Exploring the Significance*, *supra* note 22; CASHIN, *supra* note 35; Ware & Davis, *supra* note 28; Grahn-Farley, *supra* note 46; Mahoney, *supra* note 44; Landry & Marsh, *supra* note 34; Priscilla Ocen, *The New Racially Restrictive Covenant: Race, Welfare, and the Policing of Black Women in Subsidized Housing*, 59 UCLA L. REV. 1540 (2012).

discourse relates to how much work one believes discourse does in producing and reproducing racial hierarchy. If one disbelieves that discourse plays an important role in creating and sustaining racial stratification, then any work exploring discourse is *excessive*.

In truth, it is probably wrong to say that discourse is wholly insignificant where questions of racial inequality are concerned. It undeniably plays *some* role. In Kevin Johnson's view, the material world is intimately connected with ideas about race. As such, understanding race requires an understanding of that interrelationship. "Idealist discourse helps us understand how society rationalizes racial subordination that power disparities create."[53] As an example, he looks to the poor education that many racial minorities receive. These are educations that are a product of material factors: residential segregation as well as the nation's practice of funding public schools through property taxes. How does the nation, which professes commitment to justice and equality, become comfortable with this unjust and unequal result? Johnson answers: discourse. "Discourse scholarship helps us understand how the dominant justify the current state of unequal affairs and forestall calls for reform."[54] For Johnson, this demonstrates how "the material and the ideal are inextricably linked."[55]

The thing is that Delgado and like-minded critics would not disagree. Delgado does not deny the importance of the ideal in racial stratification. However, he feels strongly that the material is doing most of the work. He writes of his sense that material factors *cause* much of the racial inequality that we see. Idealist factors—discourse—are merely an *effect* of the material. They come along afterwards to justify what material factors have done.[56] If Delgado is right, then one does not undo racial hierarchy by changing discourse. If he is right, we will not achieve racial justice, however defined, by transforming meanings around race. According to Delgado, racial justice will be won by intervening in the material factors that disproportionately make white people winners and nonwhite people losers. When the material has been altered, we can expect that the ideal will convert in light of it.

---

[53] Kevin R. Johnson, *Roll Over Beethoven: A Critical Examination of Recent Writing about Race*, 82 TEX. L. REV. 717, 720 (2004)

[54] *Id.*

[55] *Id.*

[56] *See* Delgado, *supra* note 47, at 145 (arguing that "changes in material conditions and social needs will precede and usher in changes of consciousness, rather than the reverse").

VII. Questions and Discussion

1. Scholars who believe that race and class are inextricably interrelated propose that if we examine many of the events from American history that we tend to think of in racial terms, we will find an economic cause underlying them and/or an economic effect resulting from them. Can you identify an economic aspect of Japanese internment during World War II? The Chinese Exclusion Act? Naturalization laws that only allowed "free white persons" to become citizens? The removal of indigenous people from their native lands? Jim Crow?

2. Mutua writes that because economic outcomes are so closely connected to racial outcomes, "free market talk is often race talk."[57] What do you think of that idea? Do you think that the reverse is also true—that talk about regulating the market is also race talk?

3. What do you think of Calmore's critique that the Civil Rights Movement sought *inclusion* in the system as opposed to *transformation* of it? Do you think that is an accurate description of the aims of the activists involved in the movement? If so, do you think that it is fair to critique the movement for not "thinking big" enough? Consider contemporary social movements—especially the ones that appear radical. Do you think that they are thinking big enough?

4. As discussed above, the black middle class is not doing as well as its white counterpart with class privilege, although it is doing much better than its black counterpart without class privilege. Do you think that we should care about the black middle class? In other words, what is at stake in its inferiority relative to the white middle class? What does it show us about race in the contemporary U.S.? About class? About the relationship between the two?

5. What do you think of Delgado's argument about the relationship between the material and the ideal—specifically, the theory that changes in the material cause changes in the ideal?

Think of the stereotype of the black male criminal. Scholars have argued that this stereotype—this idea—has produced a host of material consequences, including excessive police stops of black men, aggressive policing of black neighborhoods, and police shooting deaths of unarmed black men. What material factors can you think of that may have created the idea of the black male criminal? In order to produce fairer outcomes in the criminal justice system, do you think that the best course of action is to challenge the idea of the black male criminal or to alter the material factors that have produced the stereotype?

---

[57] Mutua, *Stuck, supra* note 11, at 540.

6. Of course, Delgado is not the only person who believes that CRT has insufficiently analyzed the material—namely class. Mutua has also shared this critique. She identifies three reasons for what she believes to be CRT's inadequate attention to class.[58]

First, Mutua reminds us that many of the scholars who would come to be critical race theorists were inspired by Critical Legal Studies (CLS), even while they rejected many of its premises and conclusions. (See Chapter 1 for an exploration of the relationship between CLS and CRT.) CLS relied heavily on postmodernist and poststructuralist philosophy, which foregrounds discourse, in its analyses of law. Accordingly, CRT, inspired as it was by CLS, came to foreground discourse in its analyses of race and law.

Second, Mutua proposes that CRT's reluctance to critique class relations "may result from fear of analyzing or critiquing capitalism, the reigning economic order, given the political environment that champions unfettered capitalism as a panacea for all ills despite its apparent tendency to concentrate wealth in the hands of a few."[59]

Third, Mutua provocatively suggests that CRT's hesitance to delve into issues regarding class is a product of the class privilege that critical race theorists enjoy. They are law professors, after all—most of whom have well-paying jobs, job security, and some degree of cultural capital. Mutua writes that critiquing class may "require race crits to acknowledge their own class standing and interest as part of an educated elite. This interrogation might suggest, among other things, that their interest in being and remaining a part of this elite class is in tension with the empowerment of the racialized underclass .... Said differently, in order for the masses of racialized underclasses to live well, the current system which privileges the educated elite will need to be transformed."[60] Less controversially, Mutua proposes that if critical race theorists ignore class, it may simply because class issues—namely poverty—does not affect them. Again, they are law professors, after all.

What do you think of the reasons Mutua identifies for CRT's arguably insufficient attention to class?

---

[58] *See* Mutua, *The Rise, Development and Future*, *supra* note 7, at 381–88.

[59] *Id.* at 386.

[60] *Id.* at 387.

Chapter 12

INTERSECTIONALITY

In 1989, Kimberlé Crenshaw published "Demarginalizing the Intersection of Race and Sex: A Black Feminist Critique of Antidiscrimination Doctrine, Feminist Theory, and Antiracist Politics."[1] With the publication of this article, Crenshaw introduced the world to the concept of "intersectionality," a term that refers to "the interaction between gender, race, and other categories of difference in individual lives, social practices, institutional arrangements, and cultural ideologies and the outcomes of these interactions in terms of power."[2] The impact of this article cannot easily be overstated: together with a subsequent article published by Crenshaw two years later that further developed the idea of intersectionality, it changed the way that academics in a variety of disciplines, practitioners, government actors, and activists all over the world think and talk about the experiences of multiply subordinated individuals and groups.

The concept of intersectionality was born of Crenshaw's frustration that courts had refused to recognize that black women could be discriminated against as *black women*. That is, courts had failed to see that the discrimination that black women faced in the workplace oftentimes was distinct from the discrimination that black *men* and *white* women encountered. A case in point was *DeGraffenreid v. General Motors*, in which a group of black women sued General Motors for implementing a lay-off policy that they argued perpetuated the effects of past discriminatory hiring practices.[3] The court held that although General Motors had failed to hire *black* women for a number of years, it had hired *white* women during that period of time. This suggested to the court that General Motors had not engaged in sex discrimination. The court then stated that the black women plaintiffs' suit ought to be joined with a race discrimination suit that had been filed by a group that included black male plaintiffs. This revealed the court's assumption that the discrimination confronted by black men and black women was

---

1 Kimberlé Crenshaw, *Demarginalizing the Intersection of Race and Sex: A Black Feminist Critique of Antidiscrimination Doctrine, Feminist Theory, and Antiracist Politics*, 1989 U. CHI. LEGAL F. 139 (1989) [hereinafter Crenshaw, *Demarginalizing the Intersection*].

2 Kathy Davis, *Intersectionality as Buzzword: A Sociology of Science Perspective on what Makes a Feminist Theory Successful*, 9 FEMINIST THEORY 67, 68 (2008) [hereinafter Davis, *Intersectionality as Buzzword*].

3 DeGraffenreid v. General Motors, No. 75-487C(3), 1975 U.S. Dist. LEXIS 15938 (E.D. Mo. Sept. 30, 1975).

indistinguishable from one another. The *DeGraffenreid* court's logic suggested that if an employer hired black men and white women while refusing to hire a single black woman, black women would have no recourse. The structural impediments or individual bias that might uniquely restrict black women's access to institutional spaces would be unchallengeable.

However, at the same time that some courts were denying that black women were sufficiently *different* from black men and white women, other courts were denying that black women were sufficiently *like* black men and white women. Crenshaw looked to a number of cases in which courts refused to certify black women as class representatives in class action suits for race or sex discrimination. In essence, these courts were saying that while black women might have been discriminated against as *black women*, that discrimination was not cognizable as "simple" race discrimination or sex discrimination: it was something more than that. It was different.

Crenshaw recognized that this phenomenon of courts schizophrenically perceiving black women to be too distinct, yet not distinct enough, from their black male and white female counterparts mirrored the schizophrenia that was taking place among social justice organizations that were agitating for racial and gender justice. She writes that among these groups, "Black women are regarded either as too much like women or Blacks and the compounded nature of their experience is absorbed into the collective experiences of either group or as too different, in which case Black women's Blackness or femaleness sometimes has placed their needs and perspectives at the margin of the feminist and Black liberationist agendas."[4]

In her subsequent article, "Mapping the Margins: Intersectionality, Identity Politics, and Violence against Women of Color,"[5] Crenshaw provided additional contour to the concept of intersectionality. She reiterated the claim that the agendas of feminist and antiracist organizations frequently overlook the specific needs of black women. And she offered a thesis as to why this is so: white women figure as the subject of feminism, and black men figure as the subject of antiracism. She continues:

> [R]acism as experienced by people of color who are of a particular gender—male—tends to determine the parameters of antiracist strategies, just as sexism as experienced by women who are of a particular race—

[4] Crenshaw, *Demarginalizing the Intersection*, *supra* note 1, at 150.

[5] Kimberlé Crenshaw, *Mapping the Margins: Intersectionality, Identity Politics, and Violence against Women of Color*, 43 STAN. L. REV. 1241 (1991) [hereinafter Crenshaw, *Mapping the Margins*].

> white—tends to ground the women's movement. The problem is not simply that both discourses fail women of color by not acknowledging the "additional" issue of race or of patriarchy but that the discourses are often inadequate even to the discrete tasks of articulating the full dimensions of racism and sexism. Because women of color experience racism in ways not always the same as those experienced by men of color and sexism in ways not always parallel to experiences of white women, antiracism and feminism are limited, even on their own terms.[6]

Crenshaw offered intersectionality as a theoretical lens that could redress those limitations.

I. Intersectionality and Antiessentialism

It is important to acknowledge that Crenshaw was not the first person to observe that black women and the issues that uniquely affect them tend to fall through the cracks of feminist and antiracist theorizing and organizing. As Kathy Davis notes, while Crenshaw coined the term "intersectionality," the ideas that the term indexed were not at all new.[7] She observes that "[a]s early as 1977, the Combahee River Collective, a Black US feminist lesbian group, issued a stirring and highly influential manifesto in which they argued that gender, race, class, and sexuality should be integral to any feminist analysis of power and domination. Several years later, the first anthology of Black feminist thought appeared with a title that provocatively stated what was at stake with intersectionality: *All the Women Are White, All the Blacks Are Men, But Some of Us Are Brave: Black Women's Studies*."[8]

---

[6] *Id.* at 1252.

[7] Now, while we ought to appreciate that "intersectionality" provides "a name to a pre-existing theoretical and political commitment," we ought to appreciate as well that something about Crenshaw's articulation of this pre-existing commitment has resonated. Jennifer C. Nash, *Re-thinking Intersectionality*, 89 FEMINIST REV. 1, 3 (2008). Indeed, intersectionality has been described as "the most important theoretical contribution that women's studies, in conjunction with related fields, has made so far." Leslie McCall, *The Complexity of Intersectionality*, 30 SIGNS: J. WOMEN CULTURE & SOC'Y 1771, 1771 (2005).

[8] Davis, *Intersectionality as Buzzword*, *supra* note 2, at 73.

Other feminist writings that might be understood as genealogical antecedents of intersectionality include BELL HOOKS, AIN'T I A WOMAN: BLACK WOMEN AND FEMINISM (1981); ANGELA Y. DAVIS, WOMEN, RACE, AND CLASS (1981); Hazel Carby, *White Woman Listen! Black Feminism and the Boundaries of Sisterhood*, *in* THE EMPIRE STRIKES BACK: RACE AND RACISM IN 70S BRITAIN 212 (1982); BARBARA SMITH, HOME GIRLS: A BLACK FEMINIST ANTHOLOGY (1983); CHERRIE MORAGA & GLORIA E. ANZALDÚA, THIS BRIDGE CALLED MY BACK: WRITINGS BY RADICAL WOMEN OF COLOR (1983); Evelyn Nakano Glenn, *Racial Ethnic Women's Labor: The Intersection of Race, Gender, and Class Oppression*, 17 REV. RADICAL POL. ECON. 86 (1985); Deborah King, *Multiple Consciousness: The Context of a Black Feminist Ideology*, 14 SIGNS: J. WOMEN CULTURE & SOC'Y 42 (1988); ELIZABETH V. SPELMAN, INESSENTIAL WOMEN: PROBLEMS

Theorists wrestling with the problem of the erasure of black women from feminist and antiracist politics had proposed a number of solutions. Some theorists writing in the 1980s, having been inspired by poststructuralism, suggested that the crux of the problem was, simply, categories. They argued that categories, by their very nature, presuppose homogeneity. The category of "women" presupposes that the people who will be placed in that category are alike in some important sense; likewise, the category of "black" presupposes that the people who can be described by that category share some intrinsic similarity. According to this line of thought, we do not avoid the problems of essentialism—that is, the notion that there is an "essential" element that all women or all black people possess—by simply identifying another category that is erased by existing categories. In other words, we do not avoid essentialism by identifying "black women" as having been erased by the categories of "women" and "black people." This is because, like all categories, the new category, "black women" presupposes homogeneity. As such, it erases the fact that black women are heterogeneous. They are stratified along lines of class, sexuality, gender identity, immigration status, and physical and mental ability, to name just a few. Thus, we should expect essentialism to rear its ugly head in the new category of "black women." Further, as those with the most power and who are least marginalized come to represent the entire category in the context of "women" and "black people"—that is, white women and black men—those with the most power and who are least marginalized will come to represent the entire category of "black women." Thus, we should expect those black women who enjoy class privilege, who are straight, who are cisgender, who are citizens, and who have no disabilities will come to represent the entire group of black women. We should expect their needs to be addressed to the exclusion of the needs of those black women who are more marginalized.

The solution that these thinkers, who came to be called *anti-essentialists*, proposed to this quandary involved the dissolution of categories altogether, as life is "too irreducibly complex—overflowing with multiple and fluid determinations of both subjects and structures—to make fixed categories anything but simplifying social fictions that produce inequalities in the process of producing differences."[9] Now, many anti-essentialists recognized that there has to be *some* categorization if we are to avoid being isolated from others and alienated from social life. However, anti-essentialists argued

---

OF EXCLUSION IN FEMINIST THOUGHT (1988); PATRICIA HILL COLLINS, BLACK FEMINIST THOUGHT: KNOWLEDGE, CONSCIOUSNESS, AND THE POLITICS OF EMPOWERMENT (1990).

[9] McCall, *supra* note 7, at 1773.

that because categorization was inherently silencing and disempowering, we should constantly problematize and deconstruct the categories that we are compelled to use. Writes Angela Harris in this vein, "My suggestion is only that we make our categories explicitly tentative, relational, and unstable."[10]

Intersectionality should be understood as a challenge to anti-essentialism and its will to discard categorical thinking completely. Crenshaw explicitly articulated as much in her "Mapping the Margins" piece. She argued that the trouble was not so much the existence of categories, but rather the ideas that have come to be attached to those categories and the material consequences that are the effect of those ideas. In other words, the issue is not that the category of "women" exists, but rather that we tend to believe that white women are the true and proper representatives of that category. The issue is not that the category of "black women" exists, but rather that we tend to believe that the people who populate that category are masculine and emasculating, reproductively irresponsible, lazy, unattractive, etc. Crenshaw argued that our energies should not be spent on attempts to dissolve the categories of "women" or "black women," but rather on attempts to challenge the dangerous values that have come to be associated with them. She writes, "a strong case can be made that the most critical resistance strategy for disempowered groups is to occupy and defend a politics of social location rather than to vacate and destroy it."[11]

Other proponents of intersectionality have described more extensively the problems that they see with anti-essentialism. They have worries that anti-essentialism will make political organizing difficult, if not impossible. That is, if "Latinx" is a category, "low-income" is a category, and "LGBTQ" is a category, how do you organize around issues that affect Latinx, low-income, LGBTQ individuals if one cannot name those categories? Writes Sumi Cho and Robert Westley, "[W]e cannot figure out what political organizing structures anti-essentialists propose as the alternative to group based political formations. How are they to be built under the formulation of a contingent, temporary, and relational identity? Upon what foundation can difference and creativity will political formations? How will such a program be effective in challenging established structures of subordination that are powerful and organizationally structured. . .?"[12]

---

[10] Angela P. Harris, *Race and Essentialism in Feminist Legal Theory*, 42 STAN. L. REV. 581, 586 (1989).

[11] Crenshaw, *Mapping the Margins*, *supra* note 5, at 1297.

[12] Sumi Cho & Robert Westley, *Critical Race Coalitions: Key Movements that Performed the Theory*, 33 U.C. DAVIS L. REV. 1377, 1417 (2000).

Additionally, proponents of intersectionality have worries that the dissolution of categories will not necessarily be simultaneous with the dissolution of the racism and sexism that have erased black women from feminist and antiracist movements, respectively. That is, simply because anti-essentialist organizations are agitating around *issues* as opposed to *social locations*—for example, simply because anti-essentialist organizations might agitate around the issue of Medicaid funding for abortion as opposed to the category of low-income women of color (who are disproportionately burdened by the refusal to fund abortion services with Medicaid funds)—this does not mean that their agendas, political strategies, or leadership structure will not reflect racism (or heteronormativity, or islamophobia, or xenophobia, etc.). As Cho and Westley explain, "[T]he proposed alternative of 'getting beyond identity politics' and moving toward 'radical and plural democracies' based on 'interests,' as a step up in the evolution of political group formations, begs the question of an historic and ongoing dynamic of racism within progressive political movements. This movement form of racism often expresses itself in the inability of white activists to respect or accept the autonomy of people of color, even when organizing around issues of racism."[13]

It is important to appreciate that intersectionality is a response to anti-essentialism, as this appreciation allows us to grasp more fully intersectionality's interest in "a politics of social location." We should also appreciate that when Crenshaw articulated this interest in social location, she used the language of "identity politics."[14] Perhaps it is for this reason that intersectionality has been accused of being nothing more than gussied up identity politics. This critique of intersectionality, and others, will be explored in the balance of the chapter.

II. Critiques of Intersectionality

While intersectionality has been received with open arms in a variety of disciplines, it has not been immune from critique. As this Part reveals, these critiques have been quite varied.

A. Intersectionality Has No Method

Many researchers have observed that while the intervention that intersectionality makes in the literature is important—

---

[13] *Id.* at 1418.

[14] She wrote, "With particular regard to problems confronting women of color, when identity politics fail us, as they frequently do, it is not primarily because those politics take as natural certain categories that are socially constructed but rather because the descriptive content of those categories and the narratives on which they are based have privileged some experiences and excluded others." Crenshaw, *Mapping the Margins*, *supra* note 5, at 1298.

certainly, it is imperative to investigate how a practice/ideology of subordination, like racism, differently impacts individuals and groups who have to confront other practices/ideologies of subordination, like sexism—it is not clear how one is supposed to *do* intersectionality. That is, there is no intersectional method. Crenshaw did not propose one in the articles that introduced the framework. And, since then, no one has designed a specific methodology that allows investigators to describe, explain, and interpret the complex social realities that intersectionality is all about.

This is not to say that researchers have not *done* intersectionality in the absence of a methodology that everyone agrees ought to attach to the theory. For example, an ethnography of a particular group at a particular social location might be an intersectional study inasmuch as it could enable the researcher to investigate how individuals in the group navigate a variety of subordinating discourses and structures over the course of everyday life. And Leslie McCall has proposed "intercategorical" research—which allows scholars to "document relationships of inequality among social groups" by comparing different categories of social groups with one another (i.e., white upper-class men v. white middle-class men v. white working-class men v. black upper-class men v. black middle-class men v. black working class men)—as a methodology that can competently document the complexity that intersectionality foregrounds.[15]

Many defenders of intersectionality are not disturbed by the theory's apparent lack of a methodology. As Crenshaw and her co-authors assert, "[A]ssessing intersectionality's value against the expectations of a grand theory seems off the mark since we do not understand intersectionality's use or objectives to be realized only through a full-fledged grand theory or a standardized methodology."[16] Essentially, they encourage scholars to use whatever methodology they deem appropriate for conducting intersectional investigations. Time will reveal whether one methodology emerges as best-suited for "doing" intersectionality.

B. Intersectionality Suggests That Subordination Is Additive

Some commentators have critiqued intersectionality with the claim that the theory suggests that one can understand a multiply-subordinated individual's life by adding together the different "-isms"

---

[15] McCall, *supra* note 7, at 1773.

[16] Sumi Cho, Kimberlé Williams Crenshaw, & Leslie McCall, *Toward a Field of Intersectionality Studies: Theory, Applications, and Praxis*, 38 SIGNS: J. WOMEN CULTURE & SOC'Y 785, 789 (2013).

that she faces. So, for example, if a poor black woman confronts racism, sexism, and classism, these critics suggest that intersectionality describes this woman's life as the combination of those three ideologies/practices of subordination. Differently stated, the claim is that intersectionality proposes that in order to analyze the life of the poor black woman, one needs to understand what it is like to be oppressed "as a poor person," "as a black person," and "as a woman." When one combines these three varieties of oppression, one will understand the oppression that the poor black woman experiences.

If this is what intersectionality in fact proposes, then the critique would be a devastating one. This is because oppressions cannot be disarticulated from one another. That is, no one experiences poverty "as a poor person." Instead, a person's experiences of poverty are always mediated through their status as a woman, man, or nonbinary individual at the same time that these experiences are being mediated through their race, sexuality, immigration status, etc. As Nira Yuval-Davis explains, when we imagine that there is a way to understand poverty "as a poor person," racism "as a black person," or sexism "as a woman," the essentialism that this chapter discusses above usually rears its ugly head, and the most powerful of the named group gets to stand in for the whole.[17] She writes:

> Any attempt to essentialize 'Blackness' or 'womanhood' or 'working classness' as specific forms of concrete oppression in additive ways inevitably conflates narratives of identity politics with descriptions of positionality as well as constructing identities within the terms of specific political projects. Such narratives often reflect hegemonic discourses of identity politics that render invisible experiences of the more marginal members of that specific social category and construct an homogenized 'right way' to be its member.

Defenders of intersectionality deny that the theory suggests that subordination is additive. They deny that Crenshaw has ever described the experiences of the black women who she argued had been erased by feminist and antiracist organizing as the sum total of the white women who represented feminism and the black men who represented antiracism. They argue that the theory understands the various subordinations that an individual encounters to be constitutive of one another.[18] Racism constitutes the sexism and

---

[17] Nira Yuval-Davis, *Intersectionality and Feminist Politics*, 13 EUR. J. WOMEN'S STUD. 193, 195 (2006).

[18] In this vein, Crenshaw and her co-authors propose that intersectionality "conceiv[es] of categories not as distinct but as always permeated by other categories,

poverty that the poor black woman confronts at the same time that sexism constitutes the racism and poverty that she confronts at the same time that poverty constitutes the sexism and racism that she confronts. Within this alternative understanding, there is no way to theorize racism separate from sexism and poverty. As such, there is no way to add them together in order to analyze any multiply-subordinated individual's or group's experiences in society.

What this means in practical terms is that the subordination experienced by the black women that Crenshaw centered in her early theorizations of intersectionality is not white women's subordination plus black men's subordination. Rather, when sexism and racism combine, the result is an oppression that is wholly distinct from the sexism that white women encounter and the racism that black men encounter. To propose a (bad) analogy: it is less cooking and more chemistry. That is, the additive approach that defenders of intersectionality reject would imagine black women's subordination to be *vegetable soup*: the combination of the vegetables of racism and the broth of sexism. The constitutive approach that defenders embrace would understand black women's subordination to be *water*: the synergistic result of the interaction of the two hydrogen atoms of racism and the oxygen atom of sexism.[19]

C. Intersectionality Is Only About Identity

As noted above, in one of Crenshaw's early articles, she defended identity politics in the course of arguing in favor of intersectional analyses of social life and against anti-essentialist efforts to dissolve categories altogether. Perhaps it is because of this early link between intersectionality and identity politics that some scholars have critiqued the theory as being solely interested in identity. The charge is that concerns about identity myopically focus on the subject while ignoring the larger social structures in which subjects are embedded. (Indeed, these are social structures that, in important ways, *produce* subjects and identities). If intersectionality is solely or overly concerned about identity, then it would be interested in, say, black women while being wholly uninterested in structural processes that both bring this group into existence and subordinate them. Along those same lines, those social justice organizations that are agitating for social change and that are inspired by an intersectionality that is

---

fluid and changing, always in the process of creating and being created by dynamics of power." Cho, Crenshaw & McCall, *supra* note 16, at 795.

[19] Adrien Wing offers another, less chemical, description of a constitutive model of subordination. She writes, "We, as black women, can no longer afford to think of ourselves or let the law think of us as merely the sum of separate parts. The actuality of our layered experience is *multiplicative*. Multiply each of my parts together, one × one × one × one, and you have one indivisible being." Adrien Katherine Wing, *Brief Reflections Toward a Multiplicative Theory and Praxis of Being*, 6 BERKELEY WOMEN'S L.J. 181, 194 (1990).

solely concerned about identity would be fixated on the liberation of black women and unconcerned about dismantling the social structures that burden this category of persons. If these organizations are successful, then black women would be better off; but, their Latinx, Asian, gender fluid, etc. counterparts would still find themselves struggling under the institutional processes that subordinate them.

It is true that a lot of research that proclaims itself to be intersectional examines identity. But, defenders of intersectionality observe that this should not be taken to mean that intersectionality is *only* about identity. The theory is not, as a matter of course, limited in that way. As Crenshaw and her co-authors note, "Intersectional work has . . . reflected different orientations toward the relative importance and centrality of various layers of society, ranging from the individual to the institutional."[20] Indeed, Crenshaw expresses a hope that studies utilizing the theory would be less concerned about identities as such and more concerned about the macro, large-scale forces that generate those identities.[21] Identity might be an entrée into a wider investigation into the institutional and structural processes that make identities coalesce as such. Perhaps Catharine MacKinnon, who was once accused of essentialism in her feminism, best describes this understanding of intersectionality:

> No question about it, categories and stereotypes and classifications are authentic instruments of inequality. And they are static and hard to move. But they are the ossified outcomes of the dynamic intersection of multiple hierarchies, not the dynamic that creates them. They are there, but they are not the reason they are there. Intersectionality, in other words, is animated by a method in the sense of an operative approach to law, society, and their symbiotic relation, by a distinctive way into reality that captures not just the static outcomes of the problem it brings into view but its dynamics and lines of force as well.[22]

D. So. . . . Just How Many Axes Are Intersecting?

In Crenshaw's early theorizations of intersectionality, she clearly evidenced an interest in the intersection of race and sex. However, those two axes are clearly not the only axes that matter.

---

[20] Cho, Crenshaw & McCall, *supra* note 16, at 787.

[21] *See id.* at 797 (noting the desire to "emphasize an understanding of intersectionality that is not exclusively or even primarily preoccupied with categories, identities, and subjectivities" and stating that the intersectional analyses that they want to foreground "emphasizes political and structural inequalities").

[22] Catharine A. MacKinnon, *Intersectionality as Method: A Note,* 38 SIGNS: J. WOMEN CULTURE & SOC'Y 1018, 1023–24 (2013).

Class is important. So is sexuality. So is gender identity. As is immigration status. As is religion. As is age. As is language. And so on and so forth.

Judith Butler refers to this problem as the "illimitable process of signification itself."[23] That is, because there are many aspects of identity and many practices/ideologies of subordination (and privilege), it might be impossible to identify all that are relevant. Further, even if they all can be identified, listing them all might be unmanageable, and analyses that endeavor to investigate their synergistic interaction may slip into incoherence. (Indeed, consider the above description of the way that poverty is constituted by racism and sexism, and racism by poverty and sexism, and sexism by racism and poverty. Imagine if that description had attempted to describe the co-constitutive nature of not only racism, sexism, and poverty, but also sexuality, gender identity, immigration status, religion, age, and language. If that description had been attempted, this chapter would be much longer than it already is. . . .). The problem of the "illimitable process of signification itself" counsels Butler and like-minded theorists to reject attempts to identify all possible axes by which power may subordinate (and privilege) and to embrace anti-essentialism, thus freeing them from the need to identify all the pathways through which power moves.

Those who are committed to intersectionality respond by asserting that simply because there are multiple axes by which individuals are privileged and subordinated does not mean that we must reject categorization as a matter of course. Anti-essentialism may be a bridge too far. Instead, they say, what theorists ought to do is identify the axes that are *most relevant* to their investigation. If one is studying, say, the experiences of Medicaid-reliant women receiving prenatal care in a public hospital in the U.S., then race, sex, class, language, and immigration status may be relevant to the investigation. But, sexuality, gender identity, religion, and age, are not. Thus, the intersectional investigation may safely ignore those characteristics.

The danger with the effort to identify the *most relevant* axes in a particular investigation is that the axes that are deemed less relevant and safely ignored are undoubtedly very relevant to an individual's experience.[24] The transgender man attempting

---

[23] JUDITH BUTLER, GENDER TROUBLE: FEMINISM AND THE SUBVERSION OF IDENTITY 182 (1999).

[24] Yuval-Davis explains this predicament quite clearly:

> [T]there are some social divisions, such as gender, stage in the life cycle, ethnicity and class, that tend to shape most people's lives in most social locations, while other social divisions such as those relating to membership in particular castes or status as indigenous or refugee people tend to affect fewer people globally. At the same time, for those who are affected by these

Medicaid-subsidized prenatal care in a public hospital will certainly have different experiences with state power than the cisgender woman. The burqa-wearing Muslim woman will have different experiences than the Protestant Christian woman. The danger is that those who are most privileged along the axes that are ignored will come to stand for the whole. Thus, if the intersectional researcher does not explicitly identify sexuality, gender identity, religion, and age as elements that may influence an individual's encounter with state power, then the straight, cisgender, Christian, 21- to 39-year-old will represent the entire group of persons confronting the Medicaid apparatus in public hospitals dispensing prenatal healthcare.

This problem—which one commentator has called "the Achilles heel of intersectionality"[25]—has no easy solution. And the stakes are high. As Crenshaw explained in her first article on intersectionality, the failure of anti-racist activists and scholars to consider the sexist aspects of racism led them to offer an incomplete rendering of racism. Similarly, she explained that the failure of white feminists to consider the racist aspects of sexism led them to offer an incomplete rendering of sexism. Ignoring axes by which power subordinates and privileges individuals led anti-racist thinkers and feminists to present "distorted analysis of racism and sexism."[26] If Crenshaw was right on that account, then the failure to analyze an axis along which individuals are subordinated and privileged because it appears to be irrelevant to an investigation will lead to distortions. Thus, the investigator of Medicaid-reliant women receiving prenatal care in a public hospital in the U.S. will offer a distorted analysis of racism and sexism if she fails to consider how cisnormativity and the othering of non-Christian religions impact an individual's experience with racism and sexism. A similar analysis can be done for poverty and xenophobia: the failure to consider cisnormativity and the othering of non-Christian religions will distort analyses of poverty and xenophobia.

Thus, intersectionality, as a theory, might be improved in the future if scholars working with and within the framework could proffer a satisfactory resolution to this theoretical pickle.

> and other social divisions not mentioned here, such social divisions are crucial and necessitate struggle to render them visible. This is, therefore, a case where recognition—of social power axes, not of social identities—is of crucial political importance.

Yuval-Davis, *supra* note 17, at 202.

25 Alice Ludvig, *Differences Between Women?: Intersecting Voices in a Female Narrative*, 13 EUR. J. WOMEN'S STUD. 245, 247 (2006).

26 Crenshaw, *Demarginalizing the Intersection*, *supra* note 1, at 140.

E. Intersectionality Does Not Theorize Privileged Groups

Some have argued that intersectionality is only interested in multiply-subordinated individuals and groups. As a result, they say, the theory is not useful to the task of helping us understand the experiences of individuals and groups that are privileged along one or many (or all) axes—like straight white men and women. Similarly, it does not help us understand how structural processes produce and support these privileged groups.

This criticism clearly results from Crenshaw having examined a multiply-subordinated group—black women—in her early work on intersectionality. And the criticism finds continued support in most studies that self-identify as intersectional investigating individuals and groups that are burdened along many axes. As Nash summarizes it, "[T]he overwhelming majority of intersectional scholarship has centered on the particular positions of multiply marginalized subject," making it "unclear whether intersectionality is a theory of marginalized subjectivity."[27]

One might begin a response to this critique by noting that while Crenshaw purported to analyze "black women" as a multiply-subordinated group in her early articles on intersectionality, the group that she actually analyzed was, in fact, privileged along some axes. In "Mapping the Margins," Crenshaw acknowledged that she was going to omit some factors—specifically, class and sexuality—from her analysis.[28] And she did. However, while many of the black women that Crenshaw discusses in the ensuing investigation are unprivileged along class lines, most of them are straight and cisgender. Thus, intersectionality, in its initial presentations, *did* theorize a group that was privileged—with respect to sexuality and gender identity. This suggests that intersectionality is not limited, as a matter of course, to theorizing subordinated groups.

Scholars have expanded upon the notion that intersectionality can theorize those who exist at the intersection of privilege—like the straight, wealthy, cisgender, white male—as capably as it can theorize those who exist at the intersection of unprivilege. (As Devon Carbado writes, "[I]t is a mistake to conceptualize intersectionality as a 'race to the bottom.' The theory seeks to map the top of social hierarchies as well."[29]) Some have noted that when we acknowledge that intersectionality can theorize the privileged, it actually reveals the instability of categories of privilege and unprivilege. For example,

---

[27] Nash, *supra* note 7, at 9.

[28] *See* Crenshaw, *Mapping the Margins, supra* note 5, at 1244–45.

[29] Devon W. Carbado, *Colorblind Intersectionality*, 38 SIGNS: J. WOMEN CULTURE & SOC'Y 811, 814 (2013).

black men, because of their gender, are usually imagined to be privileged vis-à-vis black women. However, consider the criminal justice system and mass incarceration. While black women are overrepresented among those who are under the jurisdiction of the criminal justice system (i.e., in jail or prison, or on probation or parole),[30] black men nevertheless outstrip them in this respect. Moreover, many would argue that gender—specifically, ideas about black masculinity—informs the overrepresentation of black men within the criminal justice system. That is, black men's *maleness* makes them vulnerable to the excesses of the criminal justice system. In this way—and in this specific social context—*maleness*, when it intersects with race unprivilege, may be an unprivileged position vis-à-vis femaleness. With respect to the muscular criminal justice system, femaleness—black, white, and other—may constitute the privileged side of the binary.

Darren Hutchinson has done a similar analysis of heterosexuality, which we tend to imagine as existing on the privileged end of the sexuality spectrum.[31] He notes, though, that throughout history and continuing into the present, black males' heterosexuality has been understood as a threat to white women; as such, gay black males' homosexuality has rendered them "safer" than their straight counterparts, saving them from some of the violence, like lynching, committed against the latter. Hutchinson observes, "Thus, heterosexual status, typically a privileged category, has served as a source of racial subjugation. This history complicates the apparent stability of privileged and subordinate categories; the meanings of these identity categories are, instead, contextual and shifting."[32]

* * *

In an insightful article, Kathy Davis has contended that intersectionality is an incredibly nebulous theory that, quite possibly, raises more questions than it answers. However, she argues that this quality of intersectionality may be responsible for the theory's pervasiveness and longevity:

> It is precisely because intersectionality is so imperfect—ambiguous and open-ended—that it has been so productive for contemporary feminist scholarship. Its lack of clear-cut definition or even specific parameters has enabled it to be

---

[30] Phyllis Gray-Ray et al., *African Americans and the Criminal Justice System*, 21 HUMBOLDT J. SOC. RELATIONS 105, 113 (1995).

[31] Darren Lenard Hutchinson, *Identity Crisis: Intersectionality, Multidimensionality, and the Development of an Adequate Theory of Subordination*, 6 MICH. J. RACE & L. 285 (2001).

[32] *Id.* at 312.

> drawn upon in nearly any context of inquiry. The infinite regress built into the concept—which categories to use and when to stop—makes it vague, yet also allows endless constellations of intersecting lines of difference to be explored. With each new intersection, new connections emerge and previously hidden exclusions come to light. . . . Intersectionality initiates a process of discovery, alerting us to the fact that the world around us is always more complicated and contradictory than we ever could have anticipated. It compels us to grapple with this complexity in our scholarship.[33]

This suggests that while there may be "wrong" ways to do intersectionality, there are many right ways to do it. It counsels that the critics of intersectionality are absolutely correct when they criticize the theory for being too capacious. But, it also counsels that defenders of the theory are also absolutely correct when they claim that capaciousness as part of the theory's strengths. Indeed, crafting the theory in a way that limits its capacity may be ill-advised. As Carbado writes, the aim might be to "push the theoretical boundaries of intersectionality rather than disciplining and policing them."[34]

III. Questions and Discussion

1. What do you think of the conflict between proponents of intersectionality and proponents of anti-essentialism? What tools does intersectionality offer to analyses of social life and political organizing that anti-essentialism does not? What tools does anti-essentialism offer to analyses of social life and political organizing that intersectionality does not?

2. Berta Esperanza Hernández-Truyol has written about the intersectional realities of Latinx women, whose particular experiences with racism and sexism are sometimes erased. She writes that the "dominant culture's gendered borders render all women less than full citizens simply because of their sex. The cultural borders create a Latina underclass within her own comunidad."[35] She expands on this notion:

> We are taught to be *pulcra* (pure) and passive; we are discouraged from activity and aggressiveness. We also are taught early, and severely, the meaning of *respeto* (respect): we must be deferential to our elders and all the men in our lives—fathers, brothers, husband and ask permission for

---

[33] Davis, *Intersectionality as Buzzword, supra* note 2, at 77–79.

[34] Carbado, *supra* note 29, at 841.

[35] Berta Esperanza Hernández-Truyol, *Borders (En)Gendered Normativities, Latinas, and a LatCrit Paradigm*, 72 N.Y.U. L. REV. 882, 914 (1997).

> everything. In sum, the Latina is supposed to be a self-sacrificing, virgin mother, a saint, superhuman. She is deemed a failure, however, if in her humanness she fails by falling short of this super- and suprahuman religious ideal. This mythical ideal Latina sharply contrasts with its better known counterpart: machismo, which molds men as cold, intellectual, rational, profound, strong, authoritarian, independent and brave.[36]

She observes the felt need to defend a notion of a Latinx culture from forces that seek to assimilate it. But, she worries that the subordination of women would be imagined to be an intrinsic part of Latinx culture such that a defense of the culture becomes a defense of sexism and patriarchy.

How do you feel about Hernández-Truyol's claim? How would her analysis change if instead of just theorizing the intersection of race and sex, she also theorized the intersection of class? Religion? Nationality?

3. What do you think of the theoretical pickle noted above—that is, it is practically impossible to identify all of the social axes of power that privilege and subordinate individuals and groups? Do you see a way out of it that stops short of the rejection of categories altogether and the embrace of anti-essentialism?

4. Catharine MacKinnon has written, "Intersectional subordination is a one-way ratchet, even as the analysis of it informs understanding of the status locations at both the top and the bottom of the hierarchies involved."[37] Think about this statement in the context of the question of whether intersectionality is only capable of theorizing the multiply-subordinated. Do you think that analyses of the experiences of, say, poor, black, transgender women, can help us understand the experiences (or the production) of wealthy, white, cisgender men? What can an analysis of one social category reveal about other social categories? What *can't* it reveal?

5. As noted above, some scholars have argued that intersectionality is as poised to theorize multiply-privileged individuals and groups as it is to theorize multiply-subordinated individuals. In line with this position, some, including Carbado, have claimed that multiply-privileged individuals and groups, like their multiply-subordinated counterparts, have intersectional identities. Thus, the wealthy, straight, cisgender, white male has as much of an intersectional identity as the poor, transgender, black lesbian. To deny as much is to render whiteness, maleness, heterosexuality, and

---

36 *Id.* at 915–16.

37 MacKinnon, *supra* note 22, at 1024.

cisgender-ness the norm and, as a direct consequence thereof, make them invisible.

However, there may be a danger that attaches to the claim that privileged individuals have identities that are as intersectional as those possessed by subordinated individuals. The danger is that it may suggest that the experiences of the dominant are *like* the experiences of the dominated. As Frank Rudy Cooper writes, "Extending intersectional analysis to the [privileged] risks creating a false sense that [their] subordination is equivalent to that of the multiply subordinated."[38] If intersectionality, when applied to dominant groups, does create this false sense, then it may sap the revolutionary potential of the theory.

What do you think? Do you believe that the dangers of thinking about dominant groups in intersectional terms outweigh the dangers of the failure to do so? Why or why not?

6. The chapter discusses scholarship that has proposed that, in some social contexts, heterosexuality may be the unprivileged sexuality and male may be the unprivileged sex. Are you comfortable with that reversal? Would you be comfortable with the argument that, in some contexts, cisgender may be the unprivileged gender identity? Would you be comfortable with the argument that, in some contexts, white may be the unprivileged race? Why or why not?

---

[38] Frank Rudy Cooper, *Against Bipolar Black Masculinity: Intersectionality, Assimilation, Identity Performance, and Hierarchy*, 39 U.C. DAVIS L. REV. 853, 856 (2006).

Part III

THE INTERSECTION OF RACE AND. . .

Chapter 13

THE INTERSECTION OF RACE AND SEXUALITY

What does it mean to analyze the intersection of race and sexuality? The answer to this question might depend on who you ask. Some folks would say that analyses of the intersection of race and sexuality focus on the intersection of racial identities and sexual identities in *individuals*. Studies in this vein might interrogate how heterosexuality impacts the experience of whiteness in straight white men. Or they might interrogate how a person's identity as an Asian-American impacts her experience as a transwoman. Analyses in this genre explore the intersection of race and sexuality on a *micro* level.

Other folks might say that studies of the intersection of race and sexuality focus on the intersection of racial and sexual *discourses*. Investigations of this type might, for example, interrogate how race and racism have been sexualized—as when white lynch mobs castrated their black male victims in the course of killing them. Or they might explore how pundits in the nineteenth century once argued that immigration from Mexico ought to be restricted because Mexican "greasers" posed a sexual threat to U.S.-born white women. Analyses in this genre explore the intersection of race and sexuality on the *macro* level.

This chapter will move from the micro to the macro—first exploring the intersection of race and sexuality in individuals, and then at the level of discourse.

I. The Intersection of Race and Sexuality in Individuals

Scholars who have explored the intersection of race and sexuality at the micro level have underscored the importance of such inquiries. Most of the early studies that employed the intersectionality framework as put forward by Kimberlé Crenshaw neglected to interrogate matters of sexuality.[1] As Chapter 12

[1] However, if intersectionality is understood more broadly—if it is disconnected from Crenshaw's particular articulation of the concept and understood as generally referring to scholarship or politics that is interested in the myriad ways that multiple systems of oppression (e.g., racism, patriarchy, heteronormativity) impact differently-situated individuals differently—then it is wrong to say that intersectionality was at any time uninterested in matters of sexuality. Consider that the Combahee River Collective, a group of black feminists, issued a statement in 1977 in which they emphasized that thinking about matters of sexuality alongside matters of race and gender was paramount if social justice was ever to be achieved. They wrote:

discusses, the concern that prompted Crenshaw to articulate the theory was black women's experiences having been ignored both within feminist and antiracist organizing. This led Crenshaw to be most interested in the intersection of race and gender. She, as well as the scholars who followed her intersectional call to arms in the early years, were not attentive, at least not significantly so, to matters of sexuality. Because of the failure to interrogate sexuality explicitly—and because heterosexuality tends to be presumed when sexuality is not explicitly indicated—many of these studies concerned themselves with (implicitly) straight black women.

But, as Darren Hutchinson has argued, an explicit interrogation of sexuality in intersectional studies actually improves intersectionality as a theory. In addition to making visible another system of oppression that impacts individuals' lives—heteronormativity—it destabilizes concepts of privilege and subordination. He notes that intersectionality has assumed that women are unprivileged relative to men; consequently, it has assumed that all black women are unprivileged relative to black men. However, he argues that if we fold sexuality into the mix, it would call "into question the construction of men of color as privileged, relative to women of color."[2] Indeed, straight black women might be privileged relative to gay or bisexual black men in many important respects. In this way, analyzing sexuality in intersectional studies might add a necessary complexity to the theory.

A. The Erasure of LGBTQ People of Color

Investigations of intersectionality on the micro level have tended to focus on individuals who are marginalized along both the axes of race and sexuality. That is, they tend to center LGBTQ people of color.[3] And these studies have observed, time and again, this group's erasure.

> The most general statement of our politics at the present time would be that we are actively committed to struggling against racial, sexual, heterosexual, and class oppression, and see as our particular task the development of integrated analysis and practice based upon the fact that the major systems of oppression are interlocking. The synthesis of these oppressions creates the conditions of our lives. As Black women we see Black feminism as the logical political movement to combat the manifold and simultaneous oppressions that all women of color face.

Combahee River Collective, *Combahee River Collective: A Black Feminist Statement*, OFF OUR BACKS, June 1979, at 6, 6.

[2] Darren Lenard Hutchinson, *"Gay Rights" for "Gay Whites"?: Race, Sexual Identity, and Equal Protection Discourse*, 85 CORNELL L. REV. 1358, 1367 (2000).

[3] Note the discussion in Chapter 12 of the claim that intersectionality is not necessarily or inherently "about" multiply-subordinated individuals. The claim is that intersectionality is just as capable of describing the lives of singly-subordinated or multiply-privileged individuals as it is of describing the lives of the multiply-subordinated. In other words, this claim proposes that intersectionality is as much

Scholars have claimed that the most powerful organizations fighting for the rights of sexual minorities have, for the most part, ignored LGBTQ persons of color. They say that these organizations, which usually are directed and funded by gay white cisgender men with some degree of class privilege, frequently assume that there is a singular Gay and Lesbian Experience. This presumed universal experience, however, aligns only with the experience of the directors and funders of these organizations—that is, gay white cisgender men with some degree of class privilege. The consequence is that these organizations represent the interests of wealthier gay white cisgender men, ignoring the needs of those sexual minorities who are poor, are women, are transgender, and/or are people of color.

At the same time that gay rights advocacy has paid little to no attention to the particular experiences of LGBTQ persons of color, advocacy for the equality of *racial* minorities has committed the same sin. That is, antiracist organizations, for the most part, have not conceptualized issues that affect LGBTQ persons of color as issues of *racial justice*. Many of these organizations have failed to recognize that homophobia and cisnormativity must be challenged if racism and racial disenfranchisement are to be defeated. Hutchinson points to the AIDS crisis as a powerful example of the heteronormativity of most antiracist advocacy. He writes, "Despite the devastation of AIDS within communities of color, anti-racist political organizations have largely ignored this issue, due to . . . a false 'belief' that the issues presented by AIDS lie outside the scope of 'traditional' anti-racist politics. . . . [I]ssues [of] equal access to health care and to preventative health counseling for persons of color . . . are squarely within traditional anti-racist politics. Only a heteronormative construction of anti-racism could define AIDS and HIV-related health care issues as *non-racial*, given the harmful racial impact of the epidemic."[4]

Hutchinson argues that antiracist political organizations' refusal to challenge the sexual subordination that LGBTQ people of color endure is doubly unfortunate in light of the fact that antiracist advocacy has always challenged sexual subordination. As Part II of this chapter discusses, racial disenfranchisement historically has taken sexualized forms. For example, since the first contact between

"about" straight white men—who, just like everyone else, have an intersectional identity—as it is about black lesbians or Latinx transmen. If this is true, then it might be appropriate to observe that although investigations of the intersection of race and sexuality on the micro level have tended to center LGBTQ persons of color, nothing precludes intersectionality, as a theory, from analyzing the meaning of heterosexuality in the lives of straight white men or women, for example.

[4] Darren Lenard Hutchinson, *Ignoring the Sexualization of Race: Heteronormativity, Critical Race Theory and Anti-Racist Politics*, 47 BUFF. L. REV. 1, 57–58 (1999) [hereinafter Hutchinson, *Ignoring the Sexualization of Race*].

persons who would come to be "black" and those who would come to be "white," black men have been thought to be so ruled by their gluttonous sexual appetites that they posed a threat to white womanhood. This narrative about black male (hetero)sexuality worked to justify brutal repression and inhumane treatment. Similarly, narratives about the excessive (hetero)sexuality of black women functioned to deny the possibility that a black woman would ever withhold consent to sexual contact. Accordingly, the law historically has failed to recognize the sexual abuse of black women as a crime. Hutchinson observes that antiracist politics, throughout history, have challenged both the construction of black people as problematically (hetero)sexual as well as the material consequences of that construction. Thus, antiracist politics are well-versed in recognizing how ideas about sexuality have supported and legitimated racial subordination. However, this recognition has not occurred when it is ideas about *homosexuality*, rather than heterosexuality, that produce the racial disenfranchisement. Hutchinson observes the "disparate anti-racist responses to homophobic and heterosexual forms of racism" and concludes, "Heteronormativity in anti-racist discourse creates a discriminatory model of racial justice in which heterosexual status serves as a prerequisite for obtaining the advocacy and creative analysis of anti-racist theorists and activists."[5]

The result of the interaction between the racial myopia of the dominant gay rights community and the heteronormativity of the dominant antiracist community is that LGBTQ folks of color have been made invisible in political discourse.

1. *Erasure During the Marriage Equality Debate*

The erasure of LGBTQ persons of color by both gay rights advocates and antiracist organizations occurred quite tellingly during the fight for same-sex marriage. The most dominant gay rights organizations prioritized marriage equality. For them, it was the only issue that mattered. They took the denial of the right to marry as *the* sign of sexual minorities' second-class citizenship. Consequently, they understood winning the right to marry as the achievement of full citizenship. Hutchinson notes that a senior attorney at Lambda Legal Defense and Education Fund described *Baehr v. Lewin*,[6] in which Hawaii's Supreme Court held that the state's constitution required the recognition of same-sex marriage, as

---

[5] *Id.* at 97.

[6] Baehr v. Lewin, 852 P.2d 44 (Haw. 1993).

"*the most important* gay rights victory that we have ever had."[7] He notes that another commentator argued that marriage equality ought to be the " 'centerpiece' of a 'new gay politics' ", and that " 'denying [marriage] to homosexuals is *the most public affront possible* to their public dignity."[8] This commentator continued by arguing that " '[i]f nothing else were done at all, and gay marriage were legalized, ninety percent of the political work necessary to achieve gay and lesbian equality would have been achieved. *It is ultimately the only reform that truly matters.*' "[9]

Critical scholars have argued that an important explanation for the prioritization of the right to marry by dominant gay rights organizations is that the right to marry was important to wealthier white gay cisgender men. The privilege possessed by this group immunized its members to issues that affect other less-privileged LGBTQ persons—issues that the latter group might have prioritized over marriage equality if they had been helming the political advocacy ship. For example, wealthier white gay cisgender men are not affected by prison policies that deny medical treatment to transgender persons or that misgender them altogether, leaving them on the wrong side of sex-segregated facilities and, consequently, vulnerable to abuse and violence. Similarly, wealthier white gay cisgender men largely are not affected by homelessness, restrictive immigration policies, mass incarceration, the shrinking pool of public benefits, and a host of other issues that make the lives of those who are poor, are trans, and/or are of color quite difficult. In other words, the inability to marry signaled the second-class citizenship of *white gay cisgender men with class privilege*. It was the only thing that was keeping *them* from being equal to their straight counterparts.

Meanwhile, critical scholars claim, the second-class citizenship of LGBTQ persons of color was, and still is, signaled in a variety of brutal ways. The inability to marry simply was not the most powerful of these signals. As a result, the presumption has been that LGBTQ persons of color likely would not have prioritized fighting for the right to marry, as there are a host of other issues that keep them from being equal to others. As Hutchinson has argued, LGBTQ persons of color would think it "extremely unlikely that a marriage license will close much of the gulf between them and the center of a heterosexual society that is stratified by race, class, gender, and sexuality."[10] Indeed, "only those individuals buffered from racial, class, and

---

[7] Darren Lenard Hutchinson, *Out Yet Unseen: A Racial Critique of Gay and Lesbian Legal Theory and Political Discourse*, 29 CONN. L. REV. 561, 596 (1997) [hereinafter Hutchinson, *Out Yet Unseen*].

[8] *Id.* at 597.

[9] *Id.* at 597–98.

[10] *Id.* at 591.

gender oppression . . . could reasonably expect as narrow a reform as legal marriage to bring them almost complete . . . equality and liberation."[11] In essence, the great amount of attention that was given to marriage equality—by those who supported it, by those who opposed it, and by those who agnostically observed the nation convulse towards the Court's decision in *Obergefell v. Hodges*,[12] holding that the Constitution protects the right of individuals to marry a spouse of the same sex—might be understood as a measure of the erasure of LGBTQ persons of color.

2. Erasure Through Analogizing Gay Rights and Black Civil Rights

In both of the great battles for gay rights that we have witnessed in the contemporary age—the struggle over the ability of LGBTQ persons to serve in the military and the struggle over marriage equality, discussed above—advocates for gay rights could be heard drawing an analogy between the discrimination that lesbians and gay men have faced on account of their sexuality and the discrimination that black people have faced on account of their race. Russell Robinson describes an advertisement that gay rights advocates ran in North Carolina that pictured two water fountains: one fountain was marked "Gay" while the other was marked "Straight."[13] The image invites the viewer to liken the discrimination LGBTQ people confront with the racial apartheid that black people endured in the Jim Crow south. Robinson also discusses a more direct comparison between the two systems of inequality: a sign held by a protestor at a march that says "GAY is the NEW BLACK."[14]

It is important to note that the comparison between anti-black racism and discrimination against LGBTQ persons might be attractive if one has one's eye on the courts. That is, arguing that homophobic discrimination is *like* anti-black racism, and contending that LGBTQ people presently are in a situation that is similar to the one in which black people found themselves during the days of formal segregation, might make sense in terms of litigation strategy. The Court long ago decided that it will use strict scrutiny to review laws that discriminate on the basis of race, making it extremely unlikely that such laws will survive challenge. If discrimination against LGBTQ persons is, indeed, like racial discrimination, then it, too, should be reviewed with the most rigorous scrutiny; and it, too, should be illegal in most cases. Thus, if the goal is the achievement

[11] *Id.* at 598.

[12] Obergefell v. Hodges, 135 S. Ct. 2584 (2015).

[13] Russell K. Robinson, *Marriage Equality and Postracialism*, 61 UCLA L. REV. 1010, 1012 (2014) [hereinafter Robinson, *Postracialism*].

[14] *Id.* at 1024.

of formal equality for sexual minorities—prohibiting public and private actors from treating them differently from their heterosexual counterparts—then analogizing racial discrimination and discrimination on account of sexual orientation is logical.

However, critical scholars have been displeased with the analogy because of their sense that it renders LGBTQ persons of color invisible. They have argued that the analogy compares "gay people" with "black people." This comparison, they say, obscures the existence of *gay black people*. It implies that the "gay people" being referenced are not black; indeed, they are white. And it implies that the "black people" being referenced are not gay; indeed, they are straight. Thus, the analogy functions to equate the discrimination that that gay white people have faced with the discrimination that black straight people have endured. Progressive thinkers believe this to be problematic for several reasons. First, they say, while few would deny that gay white people have been burdened on account of their sexuality, these burdens are different in kind, and arguably in degree, from the burdens that straight black people have endured. Second, they say, while the analogy invites us to compare the oppressions of gay white people and straight black people, it distracts us from the fact that *LGBTQ people of color exist* and, further, that they experience oppressions that are unlike those suffered by both gay white people and straight black people.

Beyond the erasure of LGBTQ persons of color, many scholars have criticized the analogy between anti-black racism and discrimination against LGBTQ persons because they feel that it obscures the privileges that many of those who made the analogy enjoy. Class-privileged white gay cisgender men have most frequently offered the analogy. To claim that their suffering is "just like" the suffering of people of color, particularly black people, is to obfuscate the benefits that wealthier white gay cisgender men enjoy on account of their whiteness, gender identity, and socioeconomic status. Writes Hutchinson, the analogy "ignore[s] a legacy of racial and class hierarchy—of racial and economic privilege and subordination. Consequently, under the analogy the white gay child of a white slaveowner—or even a white gay slaveowner—occupies the same (or lower) social position as a black heterosexual slave: the former is stripped of his or her racial and class privileges; the suffering of the latter is distorted."[15]

Other critics of the analogy are disturbed by its invitation to compare subordinations—an exercise that they argue is rarely healthy and usually unproductive. As an example, Alycee Lane cites a champion for racial justice who rejected the analogy because he

[15] Hutchinson, *Out Yet Unseen*, *supra* note 7, at 631.

denied that (implicitly white) LGBTQ persons' misery has been as great as that of (implicitly straight) black people, noting that gay people "were never declared three-fifths human by the Constitution."[16] Lane argues that this Oppression Olympics—the perverse debate about which group's suffering is the worst—is terribly divisive, working to prevent the creation of alliances between advocates for racial justice and advocates for gay rights. Lane asserts that an alliance *ought* to exist between these two groups because they both are struggling against the same enemy. He writes that black people (of all sexualities and gender identities) and LGBTQ persons (of all races) have been subordinated by a "*particular kind of whiteness and white privilege*, both of which are defined against all black people and which have been used to victimize white gays and lesbians as well."[17] Moreover, say critical scholars, the Oppression Olympics distracts us from doing what we ought to be doing: inquiring into the specificity of heteronormativity, investigating the particular and unique harms that homophobia and cisnormativity have wrought, and fighting for the dismantling of heterosexual and cisgender privilege because they, on their own terms, are unjust and inconsistent with the values and ethics that the nation proclaims to hold.

Finally, scholars with a critical bent have been disquieted by the way that the analogy suggests that black people have arrived—as if the fight against racism and racial hierarchies has been won. The analogy suggests that sexual minorities should want to be "like" racial minorities, particularly black people, because they are no longer subordinated. However, those interested in racial justice deny that we have arrived at a racial utopia that is worthy of any group's envy. Despite all of the existing legal protections against racial discrimination, Robinson notes that black people continue to struggle against "mass incarceration, homelessness, unemployment, and health disparities, such as HIV/AIDS."[18] In light of these social realities, a more appropriate analogy might propose that the discrimination that LGBTQ people currently face is like a particular form of discrimination that racial minorities once faced—formal disenfranchisement from a set of rights. While that narrow slice of racial discrimination has been defeated, there is still an entire pie of inequality with which we, as a society, still need to reckon.

---

[16] Alycee J. Lane, *Black Bodies/Gay Bodies: The Politics of Race in the Gay/Military Battle*, 17 CALLALOO 1074, 1079 (1994).

[17] *Id.* at 1086 (emphasis added).

[18] Robinson, *Postracialism*, *supra* note 13, at 1055.

B. Race and the Meanings We Attach to Sexual Identities

Many theorists have claimed that it is wrong to presume that society attaches a singular meaning to sexual categories like gay, straight, bisexual, gender fluid, or transgender. Instead, race might make these sexual categories mean different things.

Robinson's exploration of "the DL" discourse is a powerful example of this idea. The DL, short for "down low," refers to black men who present themselves to the world—especially their girlfriends and wives—as straight. However, beneath their heterosexual veneer is a seedy second life filled with unsafe sex with men. Black men on the DL have been framed as a social problem, responsible for the rising rates of HIV infection among black women. They are portrayed as dangerous predators, vectors of disease, and threats to the black community as a whole. Robinson contrasts this narrative about black men on the DL with stories that are told about white men who engage in identical behavior. Robinson observes that when white men do what black men on the DL do—when they present themselves as straight and have sexual and romantic relationships with women, but also secretly engage in sex with men—they are portrayed as "victims of the closet."[19] He cites as an example the critically-acclaimed movie *Brokeback Mountain*, which told the tragic story of Ennis and Jack, two men who loved one another deeply and maintained a loving (and sexual) relationship over the course of several decades—all while leading their wives, children, friends, and communities to believe that they were straight. Indeed, our hearts are supposed to break for Ennis and Jack. (In the interest of full disclosure, this author's heart did, in fact, break for Ennis and Jack. Their love was so beautiful, yet doomed!) The last thing that the viewer of the movie is asked to feel for them is disgust, repulsion, or fear. Yet, this is precisely what the DL discourse invites us to feel for black men who live the lives that Ennis and Jack live. Essentially, Robinson reminds us that homosexuality and homosexual behavior might acquire different meanings when they are refracted through the lens of race. Victimhood and innocence might attach to white homosexuality, while predation, culpability, pathology, and excess might attach to black homosexuality.

In a study that most would likely consider disturbing, Sarah Calabrese and her coauthors provide empirical support for Robinson's reading of *Brokeback Mountain*.[20] Calabrese and her coauthors sought to determine whether black gay men faced

---

[19] Russell K. Robinson, *Racing the Closet*, 61 STAN. L. REV. 1463, 1465 (2009).

[20] Sarah K. Calabrese et al., *Sexual Stereotypes Ascribed to Black Men Who Have Sex with Men: An Intersectional Analysis*, 47 ARCHIVES SEXUAL BEHAV. 143 (2017).

stereotypes that were unique to them—stereotypes that were not shared by black straight men or white gay men. To this end, they asked several groups of research subjects to write down the words that they associated with the following categories: "Black men," "Black gay men," "Black heterosexual men," "gay men," "White gay men," and "White men." The responses showed that there are, indeed, stereotypes that are uniquely associated with "Black gay men." And, perhaps unsurprisingly, these stereotypes are not at all flattering or positive. Black gay men—and *not* black straight men or white gay men—are stereotyped as "Down Low, Diseased, Loud, and Dirty."[21] The researchers conclude that the results "suggest that Black [men who have sex with men, or MSM] face multiple, largely derogatory stereotypes related to their sexuality, some of which overlap with stereotypes of Black men and MSM broadly and others of which may be unique."[22] This study might stand for the broader claim that we ought to take the intersection of race and sexuality seriously, as society associates different meanings to the various identities that lie at the intersection of these axes. These different meanings may, in turn, produce different experiences. These different experiences may, in turn, demand different political goals.

In a related vein, Shinsuke Eguchi and Myra Washington have explored the "racial types" that exist for gay men—a typology that constrains the racialized individuals who are forced to contend with it in their daily lives. They write:

> Black men continued to be framed as hypersexual beings with large penises. The hyper-macho hip-hop aesthetic of a homo-thug distinctly sexualizes and racializes Black or African American queer men. Brown Latino bodies are also eroticized as hypersexual beings due to cultural conceptions of machismo. Extending the "tough guy" imagery related to working class masculinity, both Black and Latino men are repeatedly symbolized as sexual tops—intercourse penetrators. Similarly, the Orientalization of Asian men imagines them as feminine foreigners. Asian queer men are frequently sexualized as bottoms—intercourse receivers.[23]

What this typology demonstrates is that the race of the individual that embodies the status of "gay" changes the meaning that we attach to that sexual orientation. When "gay" intersects with Black and Latinx, it means sexual excess and dominance. When "gay" intersects with Asian, it means sexual passivity and

---

[21] *Id.* at 148.

[22] *Id.* at 150.

[23] Shinsuke Eguchi & Myra S. Washington, *Race-ing Queerness: Normative Intimacies in LOGO's* DTLA, 40 J. COMM. INQUIRY 408, 410 (2016) (citations omitted).

submissiveness. In essence, the social meaning of "gay" is not singular. Rather, its intersection with race (and, likely, class, immigration status, age, etc.) makes it acquire a multiplicity of meanings.

C. The Politics of the Closet

Some scholars have observed that because LGBTQ persons of color have to negotiate racism in addition to homophobia, their ideas about liberation from the oppressions they face may differ from individuals and groups that only have to face racism (because they are straight and a racial minority) or homophobia (because they are white and a sexual minority).

To be more precise, dominant gay rights groups—which, as noted above, tend to be helmed by gay white cisgender men with some degree of class-privilege—have described the closet as invariably constraining and humanity-denying. As a result, they have argued that all LGBTQ persons ought to come out of the closet and be public with their sexual identities, orientations, desires, and behaviors. Further, liberation from the closet has also been framed as fruitful beyond the psychological benefits that the individual will reap from no longer having to hide his own sexual truth. Coming out has also been understood as a political move inasmuch as the more LGBTQ people who are out, the less deviant being queer will seem. Straight people will cease to think of LGBTQ people as some aberrant, abnormal other that lives, parties, and has promiscuous sex in the seediest neighborhoods of San Francisco and New York City; instead, straight people will come to see LGBTQ people as their neighbors, coworkers, siblings, and children.

In a provocative article, Berta Esperanza Hernández-Truyol has challenged the notion that coming out is universally desirable.[24] She argues that the model of coming out as an individually liberating and politically expedient endeavor actually is based on the experiences of a particular group: class-privileged gay white cisgender men. She argues that what may be true for this group is not necessarily true for groups that are marginalized along lines of race, class, nationality, etc. She writes that "[c]ontrary to the presumptions and assumptions implicit in this sexual outsider master narrative, the cost of coming out differs for different groups with differing social burdens, bases, and spaces."[25]

---

[24] Berta Esperanza Hernández-Truyol, *The Gender Bend: Culture, Sex, and Sexuality—A LatCritical Human Rights Map of Latina/o Border Crossings*, 83 IND. L.J. 1283 (2008).

[25] *Id.* at 1322–23.

Hernández-Truyol specifically considers the experience of Latinx lesbians—women who are differently situated from white lesbians as well as straight Latinx people. She observes that many Latinx communities embrace traditional gender roles, which dictate that women aspire towards (heterosexual) marriage while suppressing any indication that they are sexual beings (outside of those discrete moments when they are having sex with their husbands). She writes that in this cultural context, coming out may be particularly disruptive. When a Latinx lesbian comes out, it may threaten her ability to maintain the relationship that she has with her family and community which she often prizes dearly and considers vital to her happiness and psychological health.

As such, Hernández-Truyol concludes that although coming out may be "affirming, appropriate, and adaptive within a particular majority culture[, it] might be dysfunctional and destructive within a minority culture because of its particularized plots. . . . Thus the 'coming out' model should not be normalized, universalized, or presumed to be either adequate for or of utility to particularized groups."[26] She recognizes that a robust project of liberation ought to work towards a "cultural reconstruction" within Latinx communities—a cultural reconstruction that would dismantle the gender norms that constrain women (and men) and that make coming out ill-advised for the LGBTQ people who are part of those communities. However, Hernández-Truyol contends that at present, with the existing constraints being what they are, remaining closeted may be the best course of action for Latinx lesbians who are embedded in communities that are beloved, but nevertheless embrace narrowly conservative ideas about gender and sexuality. Dominant gay rights organizations likely would find such a proposal disheartening and dangerous.

D. Race and Gender Identity

After centuries of erasure, transgender persons increasingly have become more socially and politically visible. It may be true, however, that society is most willing to accept those who are the least transgressive of a transgressive group. And, as we might expect, race informs our understandings of what is and is not transgressive. Thus, while homosexuality may be disruptive to traditional norms around sex and gender, it is less disruptive when it is embodied by a person with race privilege. Similarly, while transgender identity may be disruptive to traditional norms, it is less disruptive—and, therefore, more palatable—when it is embodied by a white person. This may

[26] *Id.* at 1324.

explain why white transgender people have become the face of "acceptable" transgender identity.

Consider Christine Jorgensen, a transwoman who became a celebrity of sorts in the 1950s after several news outlets, including *Time*, *Newsweek*, and the *Los Angeles Times*, covered her story of having been raised as a boy, but transitioning into the gender with which she identified as an adult. Emily Skidmore contrasts the abundant and largely sympathetic coverage that Jorgensen received with the sparse and often salacious coverage that Delisa Newton, a black transwoman, received during that same time.[27] While Jorgensen appeared in the mainstream media, Newton appeared in tabloids or publications that catered to black communities. Skidmore writes that the "disparity between the media reception of Jorgensen and Newton highlights the significance of race within media representations of transsexuality and suggests that such public narratives of transsexuality are not simply about gender but also about race, class, and sexuality."[28]

Skidmore notes that not only did Jorgensen's race make the transgression that her transgender identity represented more acceptable, but she aided her case for public acceptance by presenting her story in a way that was "safest" to the dominant norms. Jorgensen made sure to underscore that she aspired to marriage and domesticity, in keeping with the hegemonic gender norms of the day. Moreover, she often went to great lengths to underscore her heterosexuality. Skidmore writes that for Jorgensen, publicizing and amplifying her heterosexuality was key, as "sexual deviance was often articulated through racialized tropes of difference."[29] One might describe this as the racialization of homosexuality. Thus, in order for Jorgensen's whiteness to remained unsullied, her heterosexuality had to remain intact. In essence, while Jorgensen was incapable of becoming a "true" woman, her whiteness, alongside her embrace of "domesticity, respectability, and heterosexuality," allowed her to approximate true womanhood in a way that her counterparts of color simply could not.[30] Skidmore concludes that this is why the bodies of the transwomen of color who were Jorgensen's contemporaries "were less intelligible as 'authentic' (read: white) women" and, thus, why "they appeared in the mainstream press as subjects of ridicule, not as 'authentic' transsexuals."[31]

---

[27] Emily Skidmore, *Constructing the "Good Transsexual": Christine Jorgensen, Whiteness, and Heteronormativity in the Mid-Twentieth Century Press*, 37 FEMINIST STUD. 270, 270 (2011).

[28] *Id.* at 271.

[29] *Id.* at 287.

[30] *Id.* at 271.

[31] *Id.*

Kylan de Vries has done fascinating research with transpeople that reveals the co-constitutive nature of race and gender—that is, the reality that while race informs our understandings of gender, gender informs our understandings of race. Noting that class-privileged, white individuals have been the subjects of most research about transgender persons, de Vries asked transpeople of color to discuss their experiences with transitioning from one gender to another—an interrogation that he hoped would allow him to uncover and understand the ways in which race impacts the experience of gender. The responses revealed that, for the transpeople with whom de Vries spoke, there was no such thing as learning to live "as a woman" or learning to be "a man." Rather, they frequently stated that their race affected the type of woman or man they had to learn how to be.

For example, an Asian transwoman observed that, upon transitioning from male to female, she had to learn how to be an *Asian* woman—a process that involved learning how to navigate the exoticization of the Asian female body. She states that while being an Asian man had made her less threatening to the various publics that she encountered, as an Asian woman, she is a " 'sought after item.' "[32] She continues, " '[I]nstead of trying to get into groups, you're trying to get away from them, like standing on a street corner [waiting for a taxi] is actually a really dangerous thing.' "[33] However, due to the particular racial discourses that attach to blackness, black transmen spoke about experiencing being *male* as a more dangerous status than being female. One black transman stated, "When I transitioned from being an African American woman, you know that's a double minority, to being an African American man, you're probably the scariest person in the United States of America. When I walk down the street, people walk to the other side so they don't have to be near me. When I walk through the mall they follow me around and make sure I'm not stealing anything."[34] De Vries's research counsels that we miss something significant when we fail to pay attention to the intersection of race and gender identity. Specifically, we may miss how race and gender inform one other—with race impacting the meanings of a gender, and gender impacting the meanings of a race.

De Vries also exposes how race and gender may so deeply inflect upon one another that *a change in gender produces a change in race*. He discusses one indigenous respondent who, prior to his transition from female to male, was taken by most people he encountered to be

---

[32] Kylan Mattias de Vries, *Intersectional Identities and Conception of the Self: The Experience of Transgender People*, 35 SYMBOLIC INTERACTION 49, 61 (2012).

[33] *Id.*

[34] *Id.* at 63.

nonwhite: the shape of his eyes led many to believe that he was Asian. However, his facial structure changed after his transition to male, with his cheekbone becoming less prominent. As a result, fewer people racialized him as nonwhite. Thus, for this respondent, "learning to become a man is intimately connected to learning what it means to be white, middle class, and heterosexual, because these are the assumptions others place upon him."[35] De Vries also discusses Diego, a transman who, although of Puerto Rican descent, had been racialized as white prior to his transition. However, after taking testosterone, the change in his physical features, combined with his shorter height, caused people to racialize him as Latinx. De Vries concludes that Diego's, and others', experiences "illustrate the significant and influential combinations of race, social class, gender, and sexuality and how meanings associated with these combinations are interconnected and influence others' actions toward them. Thus, intersected identity frames others attribute in interaction are not just about race *or* social class *or* gender *or* sexuality."[36]

II. The Intersection of Race and Sexuality as Discourses

Scholars studying the intersection of race and sexuality on the macro level have observed at least two situations in which the two discourses can be said to intersect. In the first, sexuality is weaponized in order to demonize racial others. In the second, race is sexualized in a way that justifies and legitimates violence on racial outgroups.

A. The Weaponization of Sexuality

We can observe the weaponization of sexuality when there is talk about the ways that a racialized other discriminates against or oppresses a sexual minority. When this talk is used for political purposes—to justify a military intervention, or to perpetuate narratives that portray the racial other as backwards and, therefore, appropriately subordinated—we might say that sexuality has been weaponized.

As an example, Umut Erel and co-authors discuss the concern that some individuals have expressed about the treatment of gay persons within Muslim societies. While the concern that repressive governments and private actors treat sexual minorities inhumanely is a valid one, Erel and co-authors caution that we ought to be wary when this solicitude for gay Muslims occurs in a "context of war, Islamophobia and backlash against multiculturalism and migrant

[35] *Id.* at 59.

[36] *Id.* at 60.

rights."[37] The worry is that these ostensible advocates for the rights and dignity of sexual minorities around the world are not *really* troubled by the treatment of gay Muslims in some countries. Rather, the plight of gay Muslims is remarkable only because "it confirms the rule that 'Muslims' are the most oppressive 'group.' "[38]

B. The Sexualization of Race

Sexual characteristics likely have been attributed to racial groups since the first contact between populations that would come to see themselves as distinct races. Several centuries after this first contact, the sexualized narratives around different racial groups are plentiful. Hutchinson walks us through several. He notes that:

- Historically, blackness has been sexualized in a way that emphasizes its excessiveness. Thus, the sexual appetite of black males was imagined to be so robust that they posed a danger to the white women who were compelled to share their social space. Writes Hutchinson, "The horrible 'institution' of lynching in the post-bellum South . . . was justified by the construction of black male heterosexuality as a violent threat to white women."[39] Of course, discourses that declared the excess sexuality of blackness were not confined to men; they also were thought to describe women. The figure of the Jezebel, a promiscuous black woman who was *always* sexually available, results from the intersection of discourses of black sexual extravagance with the female body.

- Latinx people have also been racialized as sexually immoderate. Hutchinson points to the "greaser" stereotype, which purported to "describe a treacherous Mexican male who was sexually threatening to and desirous of white women."[40] Meanwhile, Latinx women have been racialized as "hot-blooded," exotic, highly sexual, and promiscuous—a racialization that has justified disbelieving any claims that they make about rape or sexual abuse.

---

[37] Umut Erel et al., *On the Depoliticisation of Intersectionality Talk: Conceptualising Multiple Oppressions in Critical Sexuality Studies*, *in* THEORIZING INTERSECTIONALITY AND SEXUALITY 56, 62 (Yvette Taylor, Sally Hines & Mark E. Casey eds., 2010).

[38] *Id.*

[39] Hutchinson, *Ignoring the Sexualization of Race*, *supra* note 4, at 83.

[40] *Id.* at 87.

- Men of Asian descent have been racialized as, "effeminate, asexual, passive, and weak."[41] While Latinx and black people faced discourses that described their sexual drives as "too much," people of Asian descent faced discourses that declared that their sexual drives were "not enough."

However, the story of Asian sexuality is more complicated than one that simply suggests that it has always been constructed as nonexistent or insubstantial. Martin Joseph Ponce reminds us of the period during U.S. history when immigration from Asian nations was heavily restricted or banned altogether. During this time, the only Asian people who were permitted to immigrate to the U.S. were male laborers. The result was a stark gender imbalance, which contributed to the production of racialized narratives about Asian sexual deviance. Writes Ponce, "San Francisco's Chinatown . . . was perceived as a 'bachelor society' brimming with dissolute, sexually perverse, opium-smoking men who cohabited in 'queer domestic arrangements' and posed a health hazard as syphilitics and lepers."[42]

Ponce's observation cautions critical thinkers against being led into believing that sexualized discourses just randomly fall from the trees or haphazardly spring forth out of thin air. Rather, *law* functions either to produce them or to make the ones already in existence make sense. In this view, law produced the circumstances under which Asian men could be said to "prefer" the company of other men. With this in mind, we might consider the Progressive era laws that "pushed 'vice' to black, Filipino, and Chinese neighborhoods such as Harlem and Chicago's south side."[43] These laws worked to create associations between nonwhiteness and sexual deviance, as prostitution and homosexuality could be found in nonwhite neighborhoods. Writes Anne Enke, "As Progressive reform increasingly associated deviant sex with increasingly racialized neighborhoods, it reinforced the ideology that racialized space and the people within it create deviant sexualities."[44] In this way, concrete laws encouraged and supported the sexualization of race. For progressive thinkers, this invites a consideration of the ways that current laws lead to the creation of sexualized narratives about racial groups.

---

[41] *Id.* at 90.

[42] Martin Joseph Ponce, *Sexuality*, *in* KEYWORDS FOR ASIAN AMERICAN STUDIES 224, 225–26 (Cathy J. Schlund-Vials, Linda Trinh Võ & Scott Wong eds., 2015).

[43] Anne Enke, *Smuggling Sex Through the Gates: Race, Sexuality, and the Politics of Space in Second Wave Feminism*, 55 AM. Q. 635, 649 (2003).

[44] *Id.*

III. Questions and Discussion

1. Some scholars have argued that it is strange, if not inappropriate, to apply the concept of intersectionality to matters of sexuality. Their argument is that intersectionality is the investigation of multidimensional, yet fixed, social identities, i.e., straight white men, Latinx lesbians, black bisexual men. Scholars with this view argue that sexuality is fluid and, as such, is not stable enough to be described in the categorical terms that intersectionality theory uses. That is, the "straight" white man may be straight in terms of sexual identity, "bisexual" in terms of sexual behavior, and "gay" in terms of sexual desires. The Latinx "lesbian" might be lesbian in the U.S., but not so in other sociopolitical settings. If sexuality ought not to be understood in terms of fixed categories—and if intersectionality requires conceptualizing phenomena in terms of fixed categories—then it might be misguided to approach sexuality through a lens of intersectionality. For a discussion of this tension, see Leah R. Warner and Stephanie A. Shields, *The Intersections of Sexuality, Gender, and Race: Identity Research at the Crossroads*, 68 SEX ROLES 803, 807 (2013).

2. Hutchinson has noted that the failure to analyze the intersection of race and sexuality is problematic because it makes analyses of our social world incomplete. As an example, he discusses the case of Loc Minh Truong, a 55 year-old Vietnamese man who was attacked and left disfigured by a group of white teenagers. Truong had been walking down a street in Laguna Beach, California that had a reputation for being a place where LGBTQ people congregated. Truong's assailants said that they attacked him because he was "gay." As a result of this statement and the location of the attack, most commentators on the crime understood it as a homophobic assault. However, Hutchinson argues that understanding the attack as one that is solely about sexuality elides its racialized dimensions. He writes that

> the assailants' very conclusion that their victim was "gay" could have resulted from interlocking race, sexuality and gender constructs. Under the landscape of white supremacist and patriarchal stereotypes, Asian American males are constructed as effeminate, asexual and weak. These stereotypes, apart from asexuality, correlate strikingly with popular characterizations of gay men. Hence, race, gender and sexual stereotypes of Asian American males may have influenced the assailants' selection of their "gay" victim; they might have believed Truong was gay because he was Asian American and male. Under this interpretation of the crime, Truong's racial

> status was *sexualized*—the sexual (and gendered) stereotyping of Truong was inextricably intertwined with his status as an Asian American male.[45]

Hutchinson's reading of the attack on Truong might serve as a reminder that we ought to be attuned to the racialized dimensions of violence that is ostensibly "about" sexuality. Likewise, we ought to be attuned to the sexualized dimensions of violence that is ostensibly "about" race.

With this is mind, consider the 2016 mass shooting at Pulse nightclub in Orlando, Florida. In June of that year, Omar Mateen—a man who had sworn allegiance to the Islamic State of Iraq and the Levant (ISIL) and who had told police that his acts had been prompted by U.S. bombings throughout the Muslim world—walked into the nightclub one night and killed 49 people and wounded 58 others. Because of Mateen's last name, religion, and statements made to the police, the violence largely was taken to be an act of terrorism perpetrated by an Islamic extremist. This reading of the crime, however, might diminish the significance of the fact that 1) the Pulse nightclub was widely-known to be a place that catered to Orlando's LGBTQ community, 2) Mateen chose to engage in his mass shooting during Gay Pride Month, 3) Mateen elected to commit his violence during "Latin Night" at Pulse, and 4) over 90% of the 49 persons who were killed were Latinx.[46]

Analyze the Pulse nightclub mass shooting in a way that is attuned to all aspects of the tragedy, paying attention to the ways that race, sexuality, and anti-American sentiment intersected to produce the violence in the specific, spectacularly tragic form that it took.

3. As discussed above, Robinson has been critical of the analogy that many advocates for marriage equality have drawn between anti-black discrimination and discrimination against LGBTQ persons. He argues that the analogy is particularly problematic because it evidences a selective awareness of people of color. He writes, "The parties tend to pay attention to race when they think that the comparison advances the claim for marriage equality, but elsewhere they ignore race, seemingly because they imagine their clients as exclusively white and privileged."[47]

Robinson goes on to contend that the failure to pay close attention to race is demonstrated by marriage equality advocates' argument that discrimination against LGBTQ persons should be

---

[45] Hutchinson, *Ignoring the Sexualization of Race*, *supra* note 4, at 24.

[46] Judith E. Koons, *Pulse: Finding Meaning in a Massacre Through Gay Latinx Intersectional Justice*, 19 SCHOLAR 1, 23, 43 (2016).

[47] Robinson, *Postracialism*, *supra* note 13, at 1058.

reviewed with strict scrutiny—the level of review that courts use for racial classifications. Robinson claims that if marriage equality advocates really attended to race, they might retreat from this position. He argues that since the late 1970s,

> the designation of race as a suspect classification has facilitated civil rights retrenchment, not reform. The principal effect of the Court applying strict scrutiny to racial classifications in recent years has not been the protection of *blacks*, but rather the protection of *whites* claiming reverse discrimination. From contexts such as schooling to government contracting to voting rights, the Court has invoked strict scrutiny in order to scrutinize closely and often invalidate race-based policies meant to address racial subordination. Even though whites are not politically powerless and lack a history of being discriminated against on the basis of race, the Court has consistently deployed strict scrutiny to protect white claimants. Moreover, landmark cases that dismantled segregation could have been achieved without employing strict scrutiny. Indeed, *Brown v. Board of Education* (which marriage equality lawyers often cite) never mentioned strict scrutiny in denouncing "separate but equal."[48]

Robinson concludes that "[t]he pursuit of strict scrutiny represents another selective approach to race—marriage equality advocates invoke race to install gays as the paradigmatic victims of oppression, but they ignore what strict scrutiny has done to African American progress."[49]

What do you think of Robinson's argument? Do you think that the pursuit of strict scrutiny in the context of gay rights represents a failure to really engage with black people's experience with the law and civil rights? What should advocates for gay rights seek from the courts if not the use of strict scrutiny of laws that discriminate against LGBTQ persons?

4. What do you think of Hernández-Truyol's contention that there is no universal truth to the proposition that coming out of the closet is affirming and ought to done for the health of the individual and the liberation of the LGBTQ community? Specifically, what do you think of her proposal that, for some Latinx LGBTQ persons, remaining closeted may be the healthiest thing that they can do?

5. Umut Erel and co-authors have observed that the language that activists, advocates, and scholars have come to use to describe

---

[48] *Id.* at 1062–63.

[49] *Id.* at 1063.

trans people's lives and experiences frequently is borrowed from contexts that describe racial minorities' lives and experiences. They write that this appropriation of racialized language is, at best, ironic in light of the fact that trans activism "is notoriously white."[50] They continue, "[C]oncepts such as 'disapora,' 'migration,' 'segregation,' and, even, 'apartheid' that were developed with regard to ethnic and racialised differences are now applied to denote the experiences of white trans people. Trans people . . . are described as being 'exiled' from their birth gender, or they are seen as 'migrating' between genders, or suffering from the 'segregation of male and female'. This clearly invalidates the realities of migrants, Jewish people and people of colour, especially those who face racism as well as transphobia."[51]

Do you find this borrowing of racialized language problematic? Try to come up with a list of terms or concepts that can describe trans people's lives and experiences that is less racialized. Do you believe that the terms on your list are as powerful—politically, emotionally, and/or intellectually—as racialized concepts such as "segregation" and "apartheid"? Why or why not?

6. What do you make of the contradictory sexualization of Asian men? As noted above, in one historical moment, Asian men were sexualized as deviant, sharing "unnatural" homosocial spaces with other men. Yet, in another historical moment, they were constructed as asexual. How can those conflicting constructions coexist? To the extent that they do coexist, what does that tell us about the nature of sexualized racial narratives?

7. In the debate over marriage equality, some commentators cast black people as particularly opposed to the expansion of civil rights in this arena. The sense that black people, as a group, opposed same-sex marriages was strengthened by an exit poll purporting to show that black people's votes ensured the passage of Proposition 8 in California, which made same-sex marriage illegal in the state. Several commentators have challenged the contention that black people, as a whole, are opposed to gay rights. Adele Morrison has pointed out that it is not *black people* who oppose gay rights, but rather *religious people*. Further, because "Blacks have long been cast as very religious and because Black social movements have long been run by religious institutions, blackness and the Black community, as well as the Civil Rights Movement, are identified with religiosity."[52] Robinson builds on this critique by looking to scholarship that shows

---

[50] Erel et al., *supra* note 37, at 61.

[51] *Id.*

[52] Adele M. Morrison, *It's [Not] a Black Thing: The Black/Gay Split over Same-Sex Marriage—A Critical [Race] Perspective*, 22 TUL. J.L. & SEXUALITY 1, 12 (2013).

that, when it comes to casting votes, even *religious black people* might be supportive of gay rights. He notes that "[p]olls have frequently shown a gap between black attitudes toward homosexuality and their votes."[53] This leads him to conclude that "because of black religious traditions, black attitudes tend to be strongly judgmental, yet this does not inevitably translate into a stronger vote against gay rights."[54]

Consider the portrayal of black people as particularly opposed to gay rights in light of the discussion above of the weaponization of sexuality—when the claim that a group mistreats sexual minorities justifies understanding them as backwards, barbaric, and legitimately suppressed. Do you think the claim that black people are homophobic is an example of the weaponization of sexuality? What if greater percentages of black people than any other racial group *are* opposed to gay rights? Would that unsettle the claim that sexuality has been weaponized in this context?

---

[53] Robinson, *Postracialism*, *supra* note 13, at 1032.

[54] *Id.*

Chapter 14

THE INTERSECTION OF RACE AND RELIGION

I. Introduction

Erik Love begins his book, titled *Islamophobia and Racism*, with the story of an incident involving a young man named Cameron Mohammed:

> Mohammed and his girlfriend were walking to their car in a Wal-Mart parking lot near Tampa, Florida. A man suddenly approached, shouting, "Are you Middle Eastern?" Mohammed, who was raised in Florida and born in Trinidad, simply said no. "Are you Muslim?" Mohammed is Catholic, so again, he said no. The stranger scowled, "Nigger with a white girl." Suddenly, he pulled out a gas-powered pellet gun and fired at Mohammed's head, at point-blank range. A hailstorm of pellets lacerated Mohammed's face and neck. The shooter, a White man named Daniel Quinnell, fled the scene before police arrived. Fortunately, Mohammed recovered, but he needed surgery to remove some of the pellets. A few days after the shooting, Quinnell was captured by police. When an officer informed him that Mohammed was not Muslim, he did not seem to care. "They're all the same," he reportedly said.[1]

Was Mohammed a victim of racism? Religious animus? Both? Neither?

Along similar lines, what do we make of the fact that during his campaign for the presidency, Donald Trump stated "I think Islam hates us" and went on to declare that what the country needed was a "total and complete shutdown of Muslims entering the United States"?[2] After winning the election, he took steps to fulfill his campaign promise by issuing an executive order that banned nationals from seven Muslim-majority countries from entering the country for ninety days.[3] Tellingly, the order made an exception that allowed persons to immigrate from the identified Muslim-majority

---

[1] ERIK LOVE, ISLAMOPHOBIA AND RACISM IN AMERICA 1 (2017).

[2] Abed Ayoub & Khaled Beydoun, *Executive Disorder: The Muslim Ban, Emergency Advocacy, and the Fires Next Time*, 22 MICH. J. RACE & L. 215, 220 (2017).

[3] Michael D. Shear & Helene Cooper, *Trump Bars Refugees and Citizens of 7 Muslim Countries*, N.Y. TIMES (Jan. 27, 2017), https://www.nytimes.com/2017/01/27/us/politics/trump-syrian-refugees.html.

countries if they were "religious minorities," i.e., not Muslim.[4] As Abed Ayoub and Khaled Beydoun explain, "While the plain language of the Executive Order did not expressly identify Islam or Muslims as the specific targets of the immigration restriction, the religious composition of the seven states combined with the exception for refugees that are 'religious minorities' (within their respective states) made it tantamount to a Muslim Ban."[5] Is Trump's portrayal of Islam and his attempt to prevent Muslims from entering the country an example of racism? Religious animus? Both? Neither?

Many might be tempted to deny that the examples above are species of racism. The intuition might be that the term "Muslim" refers to those who follow Islam—a religion. Accordingly, "Muslim" would be a religious designation—not a racial category. In this view, any violence or inequitable treatment that Muslims (or people thought to be Muslim) experience would be properly understood as religious discrimination—not racial discrimination.

A similar analysis might apply to anti-Semitism. Jews are the targets of anti-Semitism, and like the term "Muslim," "Jew" might be a religious designation. If so, then anti-Semitism might be properly understood as religious discrimination—not a form of racism.

This is how most scholars have approached the question of discrimination against Muslims and Jews. They largely have refused to consider the experiences of these groups through the lens of race and racism, opting instead to view any subjugation that Muslims and Jews endure as a species of religious persecution. But, there are signs of change in the literature.

A recent batch of thinkers has acknowledged that "[c]ombining the notion of racialization with a religious faith category presents a significant difficulty for analysis"[6]; however, they are insisting upon doing so. Beydoun has culled this insistence into the claim that "although Islam is a religion—and its followers diverse along racial, ethnic, and cultural lines—legal and political machinations have constructed Muslims into a de facto racial group. Islam was treated as an 'ethnoracial identity' for centuries, and continues to be viewed in these terms today. Discursively, Muslim identity is imagined along racial lines as frequently—if not more—as it is along religious lines."[7]

---

[4] Ayoub & Beydoun, *supra* note 2, at 225.

[5] *Id.*

[6] Neil Gotanda, *The Racialization of Islam in American Law*, *in* RACE, RELIGION, AND LATE DEMOCRACY 184, 186 (John L. Jackson & David K. Kim eds., 2011).

[7] Khaled A. Beydoun, *Between Indigence, Islamophobia, and Erasure: Poor and Muslim in "War on Terror" America*, 104 CALIF. L. REV. 1463, 1466 (2016) [hereinafter Beydoun, *Between Indigence*].

This chapter explores the intersection of race and religion by discussing scholarship that proposes the *racialization of Islam and Judaism*. Scholars contributing to this literature have argued that if the discrimination that Muslims and Jews confront involves prohibitions on their ability to practice their religion or live their lives in accordance with their religious beliefs, we might be dealing with religious discrimination. However, these scholars suggest that when "discrimination against Jewish and Muslim minorities picks out individuals on the basis of supposedly discernible characteristics,"[8] we are dealing with something else. These thinkers have offered that anti-Semitism and Islamophobia, at least in their modern iterations, have frequently drawn "upon signs of race, culture and belonging [and we might add sect, nationality, and more] in a way that is by no means reducible to hostility to a religion alone."[9]

If these scholars are onto something, and if Islam and Judaism have been racialized, then "race" becomes a useful concept to use when theorizing, and politicizing, the experiences of Muslims and Jews. This chapter explores this possibility.

Before beginning, it is important to note that some critical scholars resist understanding Islamophobia as simply, or mostly, anti-Muslim racism. These thinkers insist that while Islamophobia may implicate race, it can also implicate sect, nationality, and culture. For example, the Obama Administration sought to gain the support, and collaboration, of Shia Muslims when it rolled out its Countering Violent Extremism (CVE) policing program, which attempted to prevent terrorism by forestalling the radicalization of individuals.[10] It endeavored to win Shia Muslims' support for CVE by framing the radicalization against which the administration was fighting as a Sunni Muslim phenomenon.[11] This tactic—misdescribing Sunni Muslims in order to pit Shia Muslims against them—is pointedly *sectarian* in nature, as Sunni and Shia Islam are *sects* of the religion. It does not implicate *race* inasmuch as Sunni and Shia Muslims are not thought of, and do not think of themselves, in racial terms. If Islamophobia *always* requires the deployment of racial categories, then we cannot understand the Obama Administration's claim that radicalization is a Sunni Muslim thing as a species of Islamophobia. In essence, these scholars push back

---

[8] Nasar Meer, *Semantics, Scales and Solidarities in the Study of Antisemitism and Islamophobia*, 36 ETHNIC & RACIAL STUD. 500, 511 (2013) [hereinafter Meer, *Semantics*].

[9] *Id.*

[10] *See* Khaled A. Beydoun, *Bisecting American Islam?: Divide, Conquer, and Counter-Radicalization*, 69 HASTINGS L.J. 429, 468–85 (2018).

[11] *See id.*

against definitions of Islamophobia as exclusively and only anti-Muslim racism by proposing that Muslims and Islam can be vilified in a number of ways. While race may be a tool of vilification, it is not the only one.

II. What Is Race?

In order to comprehend why some scholars believe that Islamophobia and anti-Semitism are forms of *racism*, we might need first to define *race*. What exactly is race?

As chapter 6 discusses, traditional conceptions posit that races are groupings of humans who are biologically or genetically similar to one another. According to this definition, black people are a race because the individuals who constitute this group are more biologically like one another than they are to individuals of any other race. However, as chapter 6 explains, the weight of good science does not support biological definitions of race; indeed, most science in this area suggests that, genetically speaking, it is impossible to divide up the human population into four or five distinct categories of people.

But, if race is not a biological reality, then what is it? Progressive scholars propose that race is a social construction. By this, they mean that races are "real," but only because society has made them so. In the words of Michael Omi and Howard Winant, races are "created, inhabited, transformed, and destroyed."[12] Omi and Winant also specify that, frequently—and, perhaps, invariably—power and the need/desire to dominate explain why races are constructed in the first instance.

Anthropologist Kamala Visweswaran has offered a particularly generative definition of race as a social construction. She writes:

> The middle passage, slavery, and the experience of racial terror produce a race of African Americans out of subjects drawn from different cultures. Genocide, forced removal to reservations, and the experience of racial terror make Native Americans subjects drawn from different linguistic and tribal affiliations: a race. War relocation camps, legal exclusion, and the experience of discrimination make Asian American subjects drawn from different cultural and linguistic backgrounds: a race. The process of forming the southwestern states of the United States through conquest and subjugation and the continued subordination of Puerto Rico constitute Chicanos and Puerto Ricans as races.[13]

---

[12] MICHAEL OMI & HOWARD WINANT, RACIAL FORMATION IN THE UNITED STATES: FROM THE 1960S TO THE 1990S, at 55–56 (2d ed. 1994).

[13] Kamala Visweswaran, *Race and the Culture of Anthropology*, 100 AM. ANTHROPOLOGIST 70, 78 (1998).

What Visweswaran suggests in this passage is that, far from being pre-social, biologically coherent entities, races are the products of social conflict. They are the residue of oftentimes violent struggles over resources, land, money, and power.

If there is some truth to the claims made by Visweswaran, Omi, and Winant, we do not need to argue that there is a biological essence that unites Muslims or Jews in order to establish that these groups are races. Instead, we would simply need to ask whether social conflicts have produced Muslims and Jews as races. Are they treated like races? Do we see some resemblance between their experiences and the experiences of other groups that we have no trouble identifying as races? Many scholars studying the intersection of race and religion in the context of Islam and Judaism have looked at the way that public and private actors have treated Muslims and Jews throughout history—in the U.S. and in countries around the world—and they have concluded that these groups are, indeed, races.

Further, thinkers increasingly are observing that the conclusion that Muslims and Jews are races is not as great a departure from historical understandings of race as it may initially seem. These scholars have claimed that we misunderstand history when we believe that when the concept of race first arose, it entirely ignored religious distinctions and, instead, solely was organized around the idea of biological difference. This is the common understanding of the origins of the race concept: historians have proposed that the idea of race was born when Europeans first arrived on the African continent in the fifteenth century and European thinkers of the day sought to explain the differences in physical appearance (and, supposedly, temperament and personality) between the European explorers and the various African peoples they encountered. As the story goes, these thinkers were unconcerned that the diverse African peoples who lived on the continent practiced religions that were wholly different from the Christianity that the Europeans embraced; the story claims that these incipient philosophers of race were only concerned with physical dissimilarities. According to this common understanding, religion had nothing to do with notions of racial distinctiveness when the race concept first emerged.

However, scholars examining the racialization of Muslims and Jews have disputed this rendering of the origins of race, arguing that religious difference has always figured prominently in conceptions of race. They contend that if we to look to a time period that predates the arrival of Europeans in Africa—specifically, if we look at conflicts between Muslims, Christians, and Jews in seventh- and eighth-century Europe—we will see that, during this time, the fact of religious difference generated ideas about racial otherness. Nasar Meer, for one, argues that "there is ample evidence that religious culture and biology [were] deemed co-constitutive of a racial category prior to its articulation in Atlantic slavery and Enlightenment-informed colonial encounters."[14] He contends that religious subjects were racialized during these struggles in Europe, suggesting that religion is implicated in the formation of race. Examining these conflicts and the discourses that surrounded them has led Meer to conclude that "modern biological racism has some roots in pre-modern religious antipathy."[15]

Nadine Naber agrees. Like Meer, she has argued that religion has always played a role in the formation of racial categories. Specifically, she argues that the "idea that religious and cultural differences were based upon biological differences" was once dominant.[16] Accordingly, religious otherness was taken to indicate biological otherness—the building block of traditional understandings of racial difference. She notes that when Spain began colonizing the New World in the fifteenth century, Spanish colonizers justified the conquest of indigenous peoples by looking to their religious otherness. She writes that the Spanish "transferred the concept of 'religious infidel' "—which had been developed in the context of their struggle against Muslims in the Iberian Peninsula—"onto what they defined as 'heathen Indians' in their conquest on the other side of the Atlantic."[17] As Muslims were taken to be a race apart due to their religious difference, the religious difference of indigenous people suggested to the Spanish colonizers that they, too, were racially distinct. Naber notes that it was not until much later, in the eighteenth century, that thinking shifted such that religious otherness was no longer considered the stuff of racial otherness. She writes that "biological, zoological, and botanical scientific theories

---

[14] Nasar Meer, *Racialization and Religion: Race, Culture and Difference in the Study of Antisemitism and Islamophobia*, 36 ETHNIC & RACIAL STUD. 385, 387 (2013).

[15] Meer, *Semantics, supra* note 8, at 505.

Etienne Balibar would agree with Meer's assessment, at least with respect to Jews. He has written:

> A racism which does not have the pseudo-biological concept of race as its main driving force has always existed . . . . Its prototype is anti-Semitism. Modern anti-Semitism—the form which began to crystallize in the Europe of the Enlightenment, if not indeed from the period in which the Spain of the Reconquista and the Inquisition gave a statist, nationalistic inflexion to theological anti-Judaism—is already a "culturalist" racism. Admittedly, bodily stigmata play a great role in its phantasmatics, but they do so more as signs of a deep psychology, as signs of a spiritual inheritance rather than a biological heredity.

Etienne Balibar, *Is There a 'Neo-Racism'?*, *in* RACE, NATION, CLASS: AMBIGUOUS IDENTITIES 17, 23–24 (Etienne Balibar & Immanuel Wallerstein eds., 2011).

[16] Nadine Naber, *Introduction: Arab Americans and U.S. Racial Formations*, *in* RACE AND ARAB AMERICANS BEFORE AND AFTER 9/11: FROM INVISIBLE CITIZENS TO VISIBLE SUBJECTS 1, 11 (Amaney Jamal & Nadine Naber eds., 2008).

[17] *Id.*

became essential to the formation of racial thinking" only *after* the "legitimacy of religion as a justification for racism" had diminished.[18]

If Meer and Naber are right, then the supposition that "Muslim" and "Jew" can be appropriately understood as racial designations does not represent a perversion of the concept of race. Instead, this supposition might simply represent a throwback—a reversion to early formulations of racial difference. One might even say that describing Muslims and Jews as races simply unearths and amplifies within the concept of race an element of religious otherness that, because present at the dawn of the idea of race, has always been embedded in the concept.

III. What Is Racism?

Once we are satisfied that we know what race is, we have to ask about the content of racism. Indeed, what is racism?

French philosopher Etienne Balibar's description of "differentialist racism" has influenced many scholars who contend that Islamophobia and anti-Semitism are fittingly understood as racism. Balibar has written that in our contemporary world, wherein ideas about biological race do not have as much believability as they did in previous eras, the certainty that some groups ought to be eliminated from the nation—or, if their presence there is inevitable, subjugated within the nation—can no longer be based on the conviction that the *biology* of the groups is that which renders them problematic.[19] Instead, Balibar contends that *culture* now does this work. He maintains that racism presently takes the form of "differentialist racism," wherein culture "function[s] like a nature."[20] Suad Joseph, Benjamin D'Harlingue, and Alvin Ka Hin Wong elaborate that the "work of differentialist racism is to construct essential cultural difference; to mark cultural distinctions as homogeneous, static, and embedded; to install boundaries between cultures; and to reproduce and represent a hierarchy of cultures based on the essentialization of cultural difference."[21]

Within differentialist racism, ideas about the "insurmountability" of cultural dissimilarities suggest the "harmfulness of abolishing frontiers" and the "incompatibility of life-styles and traditions."[22] People who are imagined to be from cultures that do not value the individualism that many believe to be part and

---

[18] *Id.*

[19] *See* Balibar, *supra* note 15.

[20] *Id.* at 22.

[21] Suad Joseph, Benjamin D'Harlingue, & Alvin Ka Hin Wong, *Arab Americans and Muslim Americans in the* New York Times, *Before and After 9/11, in* RACE AND ARAB AMERICANS BEFORE AND AFTER 9/11, *supra* note 16, at 229, 233.

[22] Balibar, *supra* note 15, at 21.

parcel of the American ethos, cultures that are not committed to the formal equality of all persons, or cultures that are thought to expect persons to dogmatically obey authority figures all emerge as threats to the nation inasmuch as they have fundamentally un-American norms, principles, and ethics. Within differentialist racism, some groups are inferior to "us" not because of the genes they possess, but rather because of the beliefs that their cultures lead them to possess. Differentialist racism proposes that we do not need ideas about natural, pre-social biological differences between groups to construct some groups as inevitably and fundamentally dissimilar from "us" and appropriately excluded from the nation—or "the West," more generally—as a consequence thereof.

IV. Muslims, Islam, Race, and Racism

If Balibar is on to something and culture can be racialized, how does this apply to Islam and its adherents? Scholars writing in this genre answer by noting that Islam oftentimes is represented as a religion that is composed of beliefs that are diametrically opposed to the values that the U.S. and other Western nations embrace. Edward Said laid the groundwork for this thinking in his canonical tome, *Orientalism*.[23] He argued that since the first European forays into the lands that would come to be "the Orient," the latter has been portrayed, thought of, and treated as the polar opposite of "the Occident"—that is, the West. He contends that the Orient has supplied the West with "one of its deepest and most recurring images of the Other,"[24] helping "to define Europe (or the West) as its contrasting image, idea, personality, experience."[25] This particular discourse about the Orient, called Orientalism, allows Islam—a religion that was birthed in the Orient—to be positioned as "the civilizational foil of the West."[26] Building on Said's insight, Naber notes that Islam is commonly portrayed "as homogeneous, uncivilized, culturally backward, and violently misogynistic toward women."[27] Similarly, Lisa Suhair Majaj states that Islam has been "represented as a 'menace' to the west and to Christianity, it has more recently been caricatured as the epitome of barbarism, repression and irrational political violence."[28] Andrew Shryock concurs, observing that Islam and its adherents have been thought

---

[23] EDWARD SAID, ORIENTALISM (Vintage Books ed. 1979).

[24] *Id.* at 1.

[25] *Id.* at 1–2.

[26] Khaled A. Beydoun, *Islamophobia: Toward a Legal Definition and Framework*, 116 COLUM. L. REV. ONLINE 108, 115 (2016).

[27] Naber, *supra* note 16, at 32.

[28] Lisa Suhair Majaj, *Arab-Americans and the Meanings of Race*, *in* POSTCOLONIAL THEORY AND THE UNITED STATES: RACE, ETHNICITY, AND LITERATURE 320, 324–25 (Amritjit Singh & Peter Schmidt eds., 2000).

to "reject the liberation of women, oppose religious freedom, hate democracy, deny Israel's right to exist, [and refuse] the separation of church and state."[29] Indeed, if this is actually what Islam required, we should note how incompatible the religion would be with the U.S.—a nation that purports to be dedicated to the full citizenship of women, organized around commitments to religious freedom, identified as the quintessential site of democracy, committed to the support and defense of Israel, and pledged to the separation of church and state. In this rendering of Islam, the religion would be everything that the U.S. is not—indeed, everything against which the U.S. stands.

If the beliefs that Islam required its adherents to hold were, in fact, irreconcilably inconsistent with "American values," that might be enough to get many people on board with conceptualizing Islam as a threat to the nation. However, Islam frequently is portrayed as understanding itself to be in an ongoing, violent war with nonbelievers. It is described as demanding a fanaticism from its adherents, obligating them to "do their part" to help Islam win this epic, just war. In this way, Islam is rendered as possessing a violence that exists at its very core. It is for this reason, the story goes, that Muslim terrorists and acts of Muslim terrorism are as ubiquitous as they are. Writes Amaney Jamal, "Terrorism, according to this logic, is not the modus operandi of a few radical individuals, but a by-product of a larger cultural and civilizational heritage."[30] In its strongest formulation, this representation of Islam suggests that the phrase "Muslim terrorist" is a redundancy.

The figure of the "Muslim terrorist" is an essential component of the racialization of Islam and Muslims. As Caroline Mala Corbin explains, "the idea that 'all terrorists are Muslim,' which sometimes even morphs into 'all Muslims are terrorists,' "[31] is quite popular in the U.S. Of course, this is not true. It should not take much to establish the falsity of the claim that "all Muslims are terrorists." It smacks of exaggeration. If the 1.6 billion Muslims on the planet were all terrorists, all non-Muslims would likely be dead by now. Moreover, the claim that "all terrorists are Muslim" is equally false. Many acts of terrorism are committed by people who are not Muslim. To take just two examples, Robert Dear's deadly attack on a Planned Parenthood clinic in Colorado in 2015, as well as Dylann Roof's

---

[29] Andrew Shryock, *The Moral Analogies of Race*, *in* RACE AND ARAB AMERICANS BEFORE AND AFTER 9/11, *supra* note 16, at 81, 107.

[30] Amaney Jamal, *Civil Liberties and Otherization of Arab and Muslim Americans*, *in* RACE AND ARAB AMERICANS BEFORE AND AFTER 9/11, *supra* note 16, at 114, 121.

[31] Caroline Mala Corbin, *Terrorists Are Always Muslim but Never White: At the Intersection of Critical Race Theory and Propaganda*, 86 FORDHAM L. REV. 455, 457 (2017).

murder of nine black churchgoers in South Carolina that same year for the express political purpose of starting a race war, were acts of terrorism under most definitions of the term.[32] Neither Dear nor Roof is Muslim. Critical thinkers propose that the reason many people believe that the statement that "all terrorists are Muslim" is true is the general refusal of law enforcement, the media, politicians, and other speakers with large platforms to identify acts of violence committed by individuals who are not Muslim as terrorism. That is, even though some acts of violence are textbook examples of terrorism—like Roof's horrific crime—many powerful actors refuse to understand them as terrorism because the perpetrators are not Muslim. In progressive thinkers' assessment, a requirement that the individual who commits the violence be Muslim has been folded into the definition of terrorism. This prerequisite ensures that the statement that "all terrorists are Muslim" becomes true.

Although many terrorists are not Muslims, critical scholars argue that the racialization of Muslims as prone to terrorism explains why Muslims (and people who are thought to be Muslim) have been targeted by antiterrorism efforts. Love describes how in 2002, the government implemented the National Security Entry-Exit Registration System (NSEERS), which required only those visitors who were traveling to the U.S. from Muslim-majority nations and North Korea to submit to photographs, fingerprinting, and other "special registration" protocols.[33] If Muslims are prone to terrorism, it would explain why suspicion was cast *only* over individuals hailing from countries where Islam is the dominant religion (as well as individuals hailing from North Korea, a country with which the U.S. has had relations ranging from strained to actively hostile for the past several decades.) In a similar vein, "the NYPD ran a clandestine program systematically targeting Muslim Americans for surveillance. Known as the 'Demographics Unit,' a secret counterterrorism task force sent teams of undercover police officers into neighborhoods with large numbers of Muslim inhabitants. These undercover 'rakers' kept records of mundane daily life at those cafes, restaurants, and bookstores where Muslims congregated. The

---

[32] The Uniting and Strengthening America by Providing Appropriate Tools Required to Intercept and Obstruct Terrorism Act defines "domestic terrorism" as deeds that

(A) Involve acts dangerous to human life that are a violation of the criminal laws of the United States or of any State;

(B) Appear to be intended—(i) to intimidate or coerce a civilian population; (ii) to influence the policy of a government by destruction, assassination or coercion; or (iii) to affect the conduct of a government by mass destruction, assassination, or kidnapping; and

(C) Occur primarily within the territorial jurisdiction of the United States.

18 U.S.C. § 2331(5) (2012).

[33] LOVE, *supra* note 1, at 102.

dragnet conducted background checks on people who had legally changed their names to (or from) Muslim or Arabic-sounding ones."[34] Again, if Muslims are prone to terrorism, it would explain why the government chose to focus its energies on surveilling Muslim communities.

Note that NSEERS and the NYPD's secret program were not acts perpetrated by private individuals or private institutions. Instead, they were fully state-sponsored programs, and they were executed, funded, and defended by the government. To critical thinkers, this is an important point. It demonstrates that Islamophobia is not simply anti-Muslim animus held by individuals. It is that, but it also takes institutional or structural forms. Beydoun argues that Islamophobia is based on the Orientalist "presumption that Islam is inherently violent, alien, and unassimilable," and it is "driven by the belief that expressions of Muslim identity correlate with a propensity for terrorism."[35] Individuals may act on this presumption, as did the man who attacked Cameron Mohammed in the story that begins this chapter. When they do, Beydoun understands it to be an act of *private Islamophobia*. However, the government can also act on this presumption. According to Beydoun, when the government institutionalizes the idea that Muslims inherently pose a danger to the nation and that Islam is fundamentally incompatible with the U.S., this is *structural Islamophobia*. NSEERS and the NYPD's surveillance program—as well as Trump's Muslim Ban and the Court's sanctioning of it in *Trump v. Hawaii*[36]—are just a few examples of this.

If Islam is a constellation of violence and un-American commitments, then we know what we are dealing with when we see a Muslim. Even if the particular Muslim in front of us has not perpetrated a terroristic act, we know that, as an adherent of Islam, he or she is willing to execute violence against nonbelievers as a religious duty. Additionally, we know that when we see a Muslim, we have before us a person whose values are at odds with those that the U.S. embraces and has enshrined in its founding documents and laws. We know that when we see a Muslim, as a follower of Islam, this person is likely to demonstrate "fanaticism, sexism, anti-Semitism, antidemocratic attitudes, disloyalty, terrorism, and an inability to identify sincerely with America and its values."[37] Indeed, progressive scholars write that counter-radicalization policing—by which the government seeks to prevent terrorism by preventing the

---

[34] *Id.* at 104.

[35] KHALED A. BEYDOUN, AMERICAN ISLAMOPHOBIA: UNDERSTANDING THE ROOTS AND RISE OF FEAR 28 (2018).

[36] Trump v. Hawaii, 138 S. Ct. 239 (2018).

[37] Shryock, *supra* note 29, at 94.

development of terrorists—is premised on the idea that the "more Muslim" a person is, the more likely he is to embrace the "un-American" values that frequently lead individuals to commit terroristic acts. Beydoun argues that these counter-radicalization policies and programs link "radicalization—or propensity for radicalization—with Islamic piety."[38] Thus, an individual becomes more suspicious—and, consequently, more closely surveilled—the more that he displays and/or embraces a Muslim identity, i.e., by attending Friday prayers, praying in public, taking an Arabic name, or growing a beard. The idea is that because Islam is a fundamentally violent religion that is profoundly incompatible with the U.S., the more that a person identifies with Islam, the more likely he will embrace values and ideologies that are dangerous to the U.S.

According to critical thinkers, there are two foundational problems with the foregoing description of Islam and its adherents. First, most Muslims and scholars of Islam deny, vehemently and vigorously, that Islam embraces the commitments that purportedly render it irreconcilable with the U.S. and the values the country proclaims to hold dear. They reject the claim that Islam requires women to be subjugated, religious freedom to be denied, democracy to be discarded, and the other parade of horribles that detractors of Islam avow are essential components of the religion. Further, they refute the claim that violence resides at Islam's heart—that "true believers" must maim, torture, and kill in the name of *jihad*. Quite the opposite of this rendering, they affirm that Islam is a religion of peace.

The second foundational problem that critical thinkers have with this perspective is that even if we knew that we were dealing with a violent person with un-American beliefs when we see a Muslim, it would be exceedingly difficult in most cases to know when we actually are seeing a Muslim. This is because Muslims do not have a single "look," as they are a supremely diverse group—both domestically and globally. As such, they can look like anybody. Because Islam is first and foremost a religion, anyone can follow it and, consequently, anyone can be a Muslim. Thus, Muslims can be white, Asian, Latinx, indigenous, and black. In fact, in the U.S., black people are 24% of the Muslim population.[39] Thus, if you are looking for a Muslim in the U.S., you might be well-advised to look for a black person.

Some contend that there are visual cues that can help us know a Muslim when we see one. An Arab "look" is thought to be one of

---

[38] Beydoun, *Between Indigence, supra* note 7, at 1487.

[39] Khaled A. Beydoun, *Between Muslim and White: The Legal Construction of Arab American Identity*, 69 N.Y.U. ANN. SURV. AM. L. 29, 42 (2013) [hereinafter Beydoun, *Between Muslim and White*].

those visual cues. However, while many Muslims are from Arab nations,[40] most, in fact, are not. Most Muslims live in Asia. As Naber notes, "The top six countries with the largest Muslim population are Indonesia (170.3 million), Pakistan (136 million), Bangladesh (106 million), India (103 million), Turkey (62.4 million), and Iran (60.7 million)."[41] All of these countries—with the exception, perhaps, of Turkey—are in Asia. (Most of Turkey is in Asia; however, a small portion of the country falls in Europe.)

Moreover, even if most Muslims were Arab, it would *still* be difficult to identify them. This is because Arabs, like Muslims, do not have a single "look." Arabs—who, as it turns out, are white, according to official racial schemas—resemble a whole range of people, and a whole range of people resemble Arabs. As Shryock describes, "Arabs are not uniformly light or dark in their complexions. Indeed, Arabs 'look like' a wide variety of people. Greek, Mexican, Pakistani, Italian, Cuban, Iranian, Bulgarian, Somali, Turk, Venezuelan, Israeli, French, or Portuguese: an Arab in the United States might be taken (or mistaken) for a person from any of these backgrounds on first sight."[42] Further, many people assume that even if most Muslims are not Arab, then most Arabs are Muslims; but, this is also untrue. The vast majority of Arabs (63%) are Christian; only 24% of Arabs are Muslim.[43] Nevertheless, there has been an " 'Arabification' of Muslims"[44]—with large numbers of people believing that most or all Muslims are Arab. Simultaneously, there has been a " 'Muslimification' of Arabs,"[45] with large numbers of people believing that most or all Arabs are Muslim. Both of these beliefs are false.

Scholars writing in this literature have proposed that, even while there are no set of physical traits that uniformly mark actual Muslims as Muslim, certain physical markers have come to attach to the racialized category of Muslim. Thus, people think that they are looking at a Muslim when they see someone with brown skin and black hair—especially if the person has a beard and/or is wearing clothing that looks like it might be a religious garb of some kind, i.e., a *hijab* or a *taqiyah*. The idea that Muslims look a certain way explains why Cameron Mohammed, whose story begins the chapter, was attacked despite his not being Muslim (or Arab). Indeed, the proposition that there are visual cues associated with being a Muslim

---

40 The nations that are considered Arab are those that have joined the Arab League: Algeria, Bahrain, Djibouti, Egypt, Iraq, Jordan, Kuwait, Lebanon, Libya, Morocco, Oman, Palestine, Qatar, Saudi Arabia, Somalia, Sudan, Syria, Tunisia, the United Arab Emirates, and Yemen. *See* Naber, *supra* note 16, at 5.

41 *Id.* at 5–6.

42 Shryock, *supra* note 29, at 92.

43 Beydoun, *Between Muslim and White*, *supra* note 39, at 38, 40.

44 *Id.* at 37.

45 *Id.*

that enable anyone to identify a Muslim on sight, in much the same way that one can identify a black or white person by looking at him/her, explains why many non-Muslims have been targeted by Islamophobic speech and acts. As Love puts it, anyone who "looks Muslim" is made "vulnerable to Islamophobia. Many South Asian Americans are Muslim, but many others are Hindu, Sikh, Christian, Buddhist, or have no religion at all. Whatever their ethnic, religious, or cultural heritage, South Asian Americans often get caught up in Islamophobia because of race. Similarly, many Arab Americans are Christian, Jewish, or agnostic, but race exposes them to Islamophobia all the same."[46] On this point, it is interesting to observe that black Muslims, for the most part, have found themselves excluded from the national conversation about Islamophobia. This is true although, as stated above, a quarter of Muslims in the U.S. are black. Perpetrators of violence against Muslims, like the man who attacked Cameron Mohammed, are unlikely to select a black person as a target for Islamophobic violence. Similarly, it may be unlikely that government agencies will elect to surveil black communities in their efforts to prevent acts of Muslim-perpetrated terrorism. Scholars contributing to this literature propose that the reason for the erasure of black Muslims is that the category of Muslim has been racialized in a way that excludes black people. *Light brown* skin is the physical marker that is associated with the racial category of Muslim. Black people fall into a different racial category—one that is thought to be mutually exclusive to the Muslim racial category.

Love underscores that it is *race* that makes it possible for people to believe that they know a Muslim when they see one. It is a *racial* logic that makes a whole range of people who are not adherents of Islam vulnerable to Islamophobic violence. It is race that exposes not only Muslims, but also non-Muslim Arab, Sikh, and South Asian people and communities to government surveillance and other efforts designed to address the threat that radicalized adherents of Islam are said to pose to the country. He notes the "obvious truth that it is basically impossible to accurately determine someone's religion based solely on their physical appearance. That racial lens is why it is possible to 'look Muslim' in America. In other words, there are a set of physical traits and characteristics that can mark someone as 'Muslim,' regardless of their actual religion, ethnicity, or nationality. Race is the only way to explain how this is so."[47] He posits that the racial logics that make Cameron Mohammed, a Catholic Floridian originally from Trinidad, a racial *Muslim* are

[46] LOVE, *supra* note 1, at 3.

[47] *Id.* at 2.

> the very same racial understandings that promulgated the "one-drop rule"—that any African ancestry demanded Black as the primary identity—which denied the vast ethnic and cultural diversity among Black Americans. The same racial processes reduced countless cultures and nations down to "Indian," which helped to justify the brutal ethnic cleansing of Native Americans. The very same racist logic underpinned the Asian Exclusion Acts that affected Chinese, Korean, Japanese, and dozens of other communities—it was because of race that these endlessly diverse communities were viewed by most Americans as one and the same. On precisely the same line, the racial formation of the Middle Eastern racial identity collapses the myriad ethnic and religious groups among Arab, Muslim, Sikh, and South Asian Americans. Afghan, Armenian, Berber, Chaldean, Druze, Egyptian, Lebanese, Moroccan, Persian, Palestinian, Punjabi, Sikh, Turk, Turkmen, Yemeni—all these groups and many more are denied their self-identity and reduced to a single racial category in contemporary American discourse.[48]

If Islam has been racialized and *Muslim* has become a racial category in the U.S., we ought to pay attention to the work that our existing racial schemas play in this process. That is, the U.S. is a nation wherein the concept of race is not a foreign idea with very little social salience. Quite the opposite, there are strong arguments to be made—and critical race theorists make them all the time!—that the country is organized (politically, economically, socially, culturally) around race. If this is true, then we ought not to be surprised that religious differences have been assimilated into our existing racial understandings. In other words, it ought to be expected that we may come to understand any difference—in the immediate case, religious difference—in racial terms. As Jamal explains, "[I]n a society that is already constructed along racial lines, any perceived . . . 'Other' tends to conform to racism's framework. This 'othering' process lends itself to the *already existing* paradigm of defining oneself vis-à-vis other groups along the lines of racial categories."[49] In a country without strong racial understandings, perhaps Muslims would not become a racial group. But, in the U.S., wherein racial discourses constantly swirl, we might expect the racialization of Muslims.

---

[48] *Id.* at 42.

[49] Jamal, *supra* note 30, at 119.

V. Jews, Judaism, Race, and Racism

We might think of anti-Semitism as analogous to Islamophobia inasmuch as the former, like the latter, describes discriminatory beliefs, acts, and institutions that oppress a group of people (i.e., Jews) because of their religion (i.e., Judaism). Differently stated, Jews might be analogous to Muslims inasmuch as the religions of both groups might have been racialized, making it appropriate to refer to the adherents of both religions as races. However, referring to Jews as a *race* poses a unique set of issues—raising questions that are not raised when we speak about Muslims. Specifically, the racialization of Jews led to one of the most heinous events in modern history: the Holocaust. Thus, the stakes of the argument that Jews have been racialized may be higher, or simply different, from those involved in the argument that Muslims have been racialized.

In contemporary times, it is hardly disputed that Jews are not a race in any biological or genetic sense of the term. As Shelly Tenenbaum and Lynn Davidman concisely put it, "There is no such thing as a Jewish gene, and since Judaism is a religion that accepts converts, Jewishness is not a biological construct."[50] Further, due to the horrible ends to which the racialization of Jews was put in Nazi Germany, many people might even recoil at references to Jewish people as a race. The idea is that if we look throughout the annals of history, we cannot identify a moment when thinking of Jews as a race accomplished something good. In the past, arguments that Jews are a race were deployed to explain their supposed physical deficiencies: as black people's "race" explained why they had dark skin, thick lips, wide noses, and kinky hair, Jews' "race" explained why "[t]hey were ugly and malformed, with long and beak-shaped noses, hunched backs, concave chests, and flat feet."[51] Further, arguments that Jews

---

[50] Shelly Tenenbaum & Lynn Davidman, *It's In My Genes: Biological Discourse and Essentialist Views of Identity Among Contemporary American Jews*, 48 SOC. Q. 435, 443 (2007).

It is true that Ashkenazi Jews are predisposed to certain genetic disorders, most notably Gaucher Disease, cystic fibrosis, and Tay Sachs Disease. *Jewish Genetic Diseases*, JEWISH GENETIC DISEASE CONSORTIUM, http://www.jewishgeneticdiseases.org/jewish-genetic-diseases/ (last visited July 29, 2018). However, the reality that Ashkenazi Jews carry the genes that cause these disorders at higher frequencies than the general population does not make the broader category of *Jewish people* into a race. Ashkenazi Jews can trace their ancestry to a small number of forebears who tended to marry within their own social group. This explains the high frequencies of some genes within the present-day Ashkenazi Jewish population: they have descended from a small genetic pool that featured high rates of the genes that cause these disorders. This is not true of Jewish people, more generally. The ancestors of present-day Jews are too numerous to count. Because there is no gene that *all* Jewish people have, nor a gene that *only* Jewish people have, it is wrong to contend that there is some genetic basis to "Jewishness."

[51] Mitchell B. Hart, *Jews and Race: An Introductory Essay*, *in* JEWS & RACE: WRITINGS ON IDENTITY AND DIFFERENCE 1880–1940, at xiii, xxii (Mitchell B. Hart ed., 2011).

are a race were deployed to explain the imagined mental, moral, or ethical deficiencies that went along with their claimed physical deficiencies. As black people's "race" explained why they were lazy, sexually aggressive and/or promiscuous, and prone to violence, Jews' "race" explained why they were "predisposed to capitalism, and thus to certain forms of making a living that revolved around the lending of money at interest, or buying and selling for profit."[52] And, of course, arguments that Jews are a race were deployed to justify the murder of several million Jews as the "Final Solution" to the problem that they were dreamed to pose to Germany and Europe, more broadly.

The negative, and ultimately genocidal, ends to which the racialization of Jews has been put makes plain why some Jewish people have rejected thinking of the community to which they belong as a race. This is true across various national contexts: Jews have resisted the racialization of their religion not only in Europe, but also in the U.S. Although the threat of genocide did not loom in the U.S. as it did in Europe, the stakes of the racialization of Judaism were still quite high there. This is due, in part, to the bipolarity of notions of race in the U.S. Eric Goldstein writes about the country's commitment to a black-white schema of race relations. In this schema, if an individual or group was not white, they were black. Thus, it became dangerous for Jews to be racialized as anything but white, as such a racialization threatened their ability to enjoy the privileges of whiteness. Goldstein discusses the anxiety that many members of the Jewish community felt when, at the turn of the twentieth century, government agencies insisted upon classifying Jewish people as "Hebrews," racially speaking. Goldstein notes that many Jews interpreted this racial classification for official purposes as "the first step toward their eventual exclusion from the rights of white American citizenship."[53]

While there have been powerful voices that have denied that any good can come from conceptualizing Jewish people as a race, this conviction has not been unanimous. Indeed, throughout history, some Jews have *insisted* upon thinking of themselves as a race of people. Goldstein notes that in the U.S., many Jewish people felt that denying themselves a unique Jewish racial identity meant that they had to be raced as white; moreover, being raced as white disallowed them from being identified (and identifying themselves) as part of a distinctive historical and cultural community to which they felt a special attachment. Writes Goldstein of the pre-World War II period, "As acculturation began to efface the social and cultural boundaries

---

[52] *Id.* at xxiv.

[53] Eric L. Goldstein, *Contesting the Categories: Jews and Government Racial Classification in the United States*, 19 JEWISH HIST. 79, 85 (2005).

that separated Jews from their non-Jewish neighbors, 'race' allowed them to express the emotional attachment to Jewishness that remained."[54]

Further, there were some very practical advantages to racializing Jewishness in the U.S. Namely, some U.S. antidiscrimination laws only protect individuals from discrimination on the basis of race—not discrimination on the basis of religion. Thus, in order for Jews to enjoy protections under these laws, they had to argue that they were, or were perceived as, a race. And this is precisely what they did in *Shaare Tefila Congregation v. Cobb*.[55] A synagogue sought the protections of the antidiscrimination laws after it had been defaced with anti-Semitic graffiti. Although the lower courts reasoned that Jewish people were not a race and denied the synagogue relief, the Supreme Court ultimately reversed. It reasoned that although most people reject the notion that the Jews are a race in contemporary times, at the time of the passage of the relevant antidiscrimination statute, Jews "were among the peoples then considered to be distinct races."[56] As a result, the Court granted the synagogue relief, essentially holding that anti-Semitism was cognizable as racism.[57]

Finally, it deserves mention that many Jewish people continue to think of themselves as belonging to a race. Some even consider themselves to be members of a *biological* race. Tenenbaum and Davidman conducted research among Jews who do not belong to synagogues, and a surprising number of them articulated beliefs in the biological or genetic nature of their Jewishness. They write that "[a]lthough race science lost its validity and 'race' disappeared as a term for self-definition among American Jews, the idea that Jewish identity is primordial persists in contemporary America. Jews continue to believe that Jewishness is both hereditary and permanently fixed."[58] Essentially, many Jews continue to believe that Jewishness is "in the blood."

* * *

After observing that many Jews writing before the Second World War embraced conceptions of Jewish people as a race, Mitchell Hart asks a series of questions: "What did Jews stand to gain by engaging with racial thought? Why was the idea of a Jewish race attractive to many Jews? What purposes did Jews serve by making 'the Jews' into

---

[54] *Id.* at 81.

[55] Shaare Tefila Congregation v. Cobb, 481 U.S. 615 (1987).

[56] *Id.* at 617–18.

[57] *Id.*

[58] Tenenbaum & Davidman, *supra* note 50, at 438.

a race?"[59] Hart's questions prompt us to consider why we might conceptualize any group—be it Jews, Muslims, Mexicans, black Americans, native Hawaiians, or any other—as a race. When we are engaged in the work of determining which groups have been constructed as races, we might ask *why* we might identify a group as such. Do the members of the group think of themselves as a race? Why or why not? What ends would be served by conceptualizing a group as a race? Would it be advantageous or disadvantageous to think of a group in racial terms?

Because groups are differently situated, it may make sense to conceptualize one group as a race while declining to do the same for another. When speaking about the intersection of race and religion specifically, it may be logical to racialize the adherents of one religion while declining to racialize the adherents of another religion. Thus, that Muslims might be a race in the contemporary U.S. does not mean that Jews are also a race. The reverse is also a possibility. What all of this means is that the intersection of race and religion is a complicated place. It may be just as wrong to say that *all* religions are racialized as it is to say that *no* religion is racialized. We may have to engage in a nuanced, detailed interrogation of the unique facts describing a specific religious group before arriving at an answer to the question of its racial status.

VI. Questions and Discussion

1. As noted above, many in the U.S. who advocate on behalf of Muslims and Jews have conceptualized the discrimination these groups endure as a type of religious persecution, and not as a species of racism. Love has argued that the reason many advocates have made this conceptual choice is that in the U.S., it is much less provocative to fight "religious discrimination" than it is to fight "racism." He writes, "Religious communities enjoy a great deal of respect and legitimacy in the United States, and standing up for religious freedom is almost never controversial (unlike standing up for racial justice)."[60] What Love suggests is that, when duking it out in the court of public opinion, claiming that the unfair treatment to which Muslims have been subjected in the U.S. in recent years is a variety of *religious* oppression is an argument that is more likely to win than claiming that this treatment is a variety of *racial* oppression.

Does Love's assessment strike you as true? Can you think of any circumstance in which arguing in the language of race might be more persuasive, or more likely to "win," than arguing in the language of

[59] Hart, *supra* note 51, at xvii.

[60] LOVE, *supra* note 1, at 24.

religion? Further, what if Love is right? What does that mean for those who are engaged in struggles against Islamophobia and anti-Semitism? *Should* they make claims in the language of religion—even if Islamophobia and anti-Semitism can be understood as racism?

Note that, as discussed above, some critical scholars disagree with the claim that Islamophobia is *always* understandable as racism. Their point is that while some acts of Islamophobia can implicate race, others can implicate nationality, culture, or sect—as when the Obama Administration endeavored to pit Sunni and Shia Muslims against one another in its advancement of its Countering Violent Extremism (CVE) programming. This certainly complicates the question posed above about whether Islamophobia should be resisted in the language of religion or race. Persons challenging the Obama Administration's policy around CVE could not say that it was a species of *racism* inasmuch as it did not involve race, but rather sect. Should advocates for Muslims be mindful of the particular form that an Islamophobic practice takes and tailor their language accordingly? Thus, should they challenge a "Muslim Ban" as *racist* to the extent that it is based on racialized and racist understandings of Muslim people, but challenge a policy like the one that the Obama Administration implemented as a type of *religious discrimination* to the extent that is based on problematic understandings of a religious sect? Or should advocates be consistent in the language they use when resisting Islamophobia—without regard to the form that the Islamophobic practice or policy takes?

2. Why do some scholars insist that we use the lens of race to theorize and think about the experiences of Muslims and people who could be mistaken for Muslim? Why not use the lens of *ethnicity*? Shryock, who believes that the concept of race adds something valuable to the study of Islamophobia, explains that "racialization," unlike the processes by which ethnicities are formed, is "a negative process that is imposed by an external agent, usually the U.S. government, the mainstream, the larger society, or 'white people.' "[61] Because "Muslim"—the racial category designates brown people who are thought to be fanatical followers of a violent Islam—is something over which Muslim people (and the various non-Muslim peoples who are nevertheless placed in the racial category) have had very little control, *racialization* might more accurately describe the power dynamics at play. That is, the racial category of *Muslim* has been imposed on the various brown people who it is thought to describe. Ethnicity does not suggest the same imposition of identity.

---

[61] Shryock, *supra* note 29, at 99.

Do you find Shryock's explanation compelling? In the context of Muslims and people thought to be Muslim, can you think of other things that the language of race appropriately suggests that ethnicity does not? Can you think of things that the language of *ethnicity* appropriately suggests that race does not?

3. As the chapter observes, there may be a racial category of *Muslim* that purports to refer to Muslims and people who might be mistaken for Muslim. As Love writes, "[W]hen most Americans today use the term 'Muslim' in conversation, they are probably not really talking about Muslims. Instead, they are calling up this longstanding racial category, one that haphazardly includes hundreds of ethnic groups containing both Muslims and non-Muslims."[62] Moreover, as the chapter observes, the racial category of *Muslim* does not refer to *all* Muslims, as black Muslims tend not to be indicated by this term. Accordingly, the racial category of *Muslim* might refer only to non-black Muslims and others who look like they might have Arab or South Asian ancestry.

Thinkers have attempted to come up with a term that more accurately describes what the racial category inaccurately designated by the term *Muslim* is getting at. They have not reached a consensus. Writes Love, "[T]here is no name for the socially constructed racial category that has been used to collectively ascribe Arab, Muslim, Sikh, and South Asian Americans."[63] Some have proposed that what people really mean when they use the term "Muslim" to refer to non-black Muslims and others who look like they might have Arab or South Asian ancestry is *Middle Eastern*. However, this term is problematic because it omits people from Muslim-majority countries in North Africa. To correct this omission, some have proposed the category of *Middle Eastern and North African*, or MENA for short. While this term is more inclusive, it excludes five of the six countries that are homes to the largest Muslim populations—Indonesia, Pakistan, Bangladesh, India, and Turkey. These countries (with the exception of a small portion of Turkey that falls within Europe) are in Asia—not the Middle East.

Do you believe that thinkers should continue to try to craft a racial designation for the group of people that the racialized category of *Muslim* indexes? Why or why not? What are the dangers involved in failing to craft this racial designation? What are the dangers involved in succeeding?

4. Are Muslims white? If we are using *Muslim* as a term that references adherents of Islam, the answer to this question is: some of them. Some Muslims are white, while others are black, Asian,

---

[62] LOVE, *supra* note 1, at 6.

[63] *Id.* at 5.

indigenous, etc. However, if we are using *Muslim* as a term that references a racialized group that includes both brown Muslims and people who might be thought to be Muslim, then the answer to this question is more complicated.

Some scholarship in this area has offered that Islam, as a religion, has been racialized as nonwhite, with the consequence being that Muslims, as adherents of the religion, are not white. Hisham Aidi's work is instructive on this question. He writes about the racial transformation that some white converts to Islam feel. He observes that John Walker Lindh, a white U.S. citizen who fought alongside the Taliban and was captured in Afghanistan when the U.S. toppled the Taliban regime, felt that his conversion to Islam engaged him in a process of racialization that diminished, or negated entirely, his whiteness.[64] Reportedly, Lindh was happy to become "nonwhite" as a Muslim because, to him, whiteness represented the West, and the West stood for "racism and white supremacy on a global scale."[65] Less controversial figures have also shared the sense that becoming Muslim entails becoming nonwhite. Writes Aidi, "For many white hip-hoppers in the U.S., the sought after 'ghetto pass'—acceptance in the hip-hop community—comes only with conversion to Islam, which is seen as a rejection of being white. The white rapper Everlast, formerly Eric Schrody of [the rap group] House of Pain, claims that conversion to Islam and mosque attendance allow him to visit ghetto neighborhoods he could never enter as a non-Muslim white."[66]

It is interesting to consider how the law has answered the question of Muslims' whiteness. Prior to 1952, U.S. naturalization laws required that an individual be a "free white person" in order to naturalize as a citizen. As a result, courts were faced with the task of determining the racial statuses of petitioners who hailed from many different parts of the world. Notably, the whiteness of Syrians—who, technically speaking, are Arab—was disputed. Some courts held that they were white people and, consequently, could become U.S. citizens; others denied the same. Fascinatingly, the religion of the individual Syrian petitioner before the court often determined his racial status. Like many people continue to do in the present day, most judges during this time assumed that all Arabs were Muslims and, thus, that all Syrians were Muslims. However, if the petitioner could demonstrate that he was Christian, courts were inclined to decide that he was white. If, on the other hand, the petitioner was Muslim, courts tended to decide that he was nonwhite. In other words, the law answered the question of Muslims' whiteness

---

[64] Hisham Aidi, *Let Us Be Moors: Islam, Race, and "Connected Histories,"* MIDDLE EAST REP., Winter 2003, at 42, 44.

[65] *Id.*

[66] *Id.* at 50–51.

in the negative. Explains Beydoun, "Islam was treated as an ethno-racial identity, as was Christianity, which functioned as a hallmark of whiteness and a prospective gateway toward citizenship for immigrants from the Arab World. Judges who performed these religiously determined racial associations were not doing so within a vacuum. They relied upon other discourses, including those from eugenicists who classified Christian immigrants from the Arab World as a racial group distinct from 'Arabs' solely on account of their Christianity."[67] Consequently, Syrian petitioners seeking naturalization "tended to stress their Christian identity and their historical, geographical and religious relationship to the Holy Land, and to accentuate their distance from Islam."[68]

Because Islam had been racialized as nonwhite, courts consistently denied the petitions of Muslim seeking to naturalize. However, this course was reversed in *Ex Parte Mohriez*, when a district court held in 1944 that a Muslim Arab was a "free white person" within the meaning of the law and, consequently, able to become a U.S. citizen. The court reasoned:

> As every schoolboy knows, the Arabs have at various times inhabited parts of Europe, lived along the Mediterranean, been contiguous to European nations and been assimilated culturally and otherwise, by them. . . . The names of Avicenna and Averroes, the sciences of algebra and medicine, the population and the architecture of Spain and of Sicily, the very words of the English language, remind us as they would have reminded the Founding Fathers of the action and interaction of Arabic and non-Arabic elements of our culture. Indeed, to earlier centuries as to the twentieth century, the Arab people stand as one of the chief channels by which the traditions of white Europe, especially the ancient Greek traditions, have been carried into the present.[69]

Essentially, the court argued that Arabs of various religions had helped Europe be great. Consequently, the religious specificity of the Arab person before it—his Muslim-ness—was not to be held against him. Thus, the court concluded that Muslims were white.

Beydoun reminds us that we ought not to read this decision in a vacuum, but instead ought to pay attention to the sociopolitical conditions in which it was handed down. He observes that *Mohriez* was decided at a time when the U.S. began to develop economic and political interests in Saudi Arabia and the Arab world, more

---

[67] Beydoun, *Between Muslim and White*, *supra* note 39, at 33.

[68] Majaj, *supra* note 28, at 323.

[69] *Ex parte* Mohriez, 54 F. Supp. 941, 942 (D. Mass. 1944).

generally. He writes, "A key factor in the United States' sociopolitical engagement with the region was the increased demand for oil. Industrialization fueled the global search for the natural resource, which ultimately led U.S. speculators and oil companies into the Arabian Peninsula."[70] Thus, American economic and geopolitical interests stood to benefit if the U.S. presented itself as a friend of the Arab world, specifically Saudi Arabia—the native land of the petitioner, Mohamed Mohriez. Allowing Arab Muslims to naturalize represented a kind of friendship bracelet. Writes Beydoun, "Extending citizenship to Muslim immigrants from the Arab World, particularly those hailing from nations with considerable value, made the United States a more attractive superpower with whom governments of these countries could align during the Cold War."[71]

Essentially, Beydoun reminds us that politics and economics play an important role in the racial status of any entity—be it a nationality, a community within a nation, or a religion. The race of a thing is not "out there," pre-existing society and the power relations that course through it. Instead, power plays an important role in racializing people, places, and things—including religions.

With that in mind: what do you think? In contemporary times, are Muslims white? How does the conflation of Muslim with Arab identity, and the formal imposition of whiteness on Arab persons, prevent the acknowledgement of the racial diversity of Muslims and, more specifically, the *seeing* of black, Latinx, and non-Arab Muslims as bona fide Muslims? Does the racialization of Muslim identity supplant the racial identity of, for example, a Mexican Muslim?

5. When large numbers of people from Ireland began to immigrate to the United States in the early nineteenth century, their whiteness had not been established fully. While in later years, it would become an uncontroversial fact that the Irish are white, during this time period, there were disputes over whether Irish immigrants were "really" white. Importantly, their religion—Catholicism—played an important role in popular understandings of their nonwhiteness. In other words, in a largely Protestant country, Irish Catholics' *religious* otherness suggested that there was some *racial* otherness going on. On this matter, Peter Guardino observes that when poor Catholic Irish immigrants arrived in the U.S. in the early- to mid-1800s, "[t]hese new immigrants were seen as racial Others, . . . and their Catholicism was crucial to this characterization."[72] Indeed, on Guardino's reading, Irish immigrants' "Catholicism was

---

[70] Beydoun, *Between Muslim and White*, *supra* note 39, at 68.

[71] *Id.* at 69–70.

[72] Peter Guardino, *"In the Name of Civilization and with a Bible in Their Hands": Religion and the 1846–48 Mexican-American War*, 30 MEXICAN STUD./ESTUDIOS MEXICANOS 342, 345 (2014).

the most important component of their non-white racial identity."[73] Joshua Paddison makes a similar observation, noting that during the post-civil war years, race and religion were "[u]nstable as categories of social difference" and, consequently, "collided and overlapped."[74] In California during this time, "Romanists," or Roman Catholics, were marked "as both racially and religiously inferior."[75] Guardino and Paddison might be read to suggest that Catholicism had been racialized as nonwhite, thereby putting in question the whiteness of adherents to the religion.

Do you believe that, in the present day, Catholicism continues to be racialized as nonwhite? Why or why not? If you answer this question in the negative, what do you think has changed between now and the early nineteenth century such that Catholicism carries different, or no, racial connotations?

---

[73] *Id.* at 346.

[74] Joshua Paddison, *Anti-Catholicism and Race in Post-Civil War San Francisco*, 78 PAC. HIST. REV. 505, 505 (2009).

[75] *Id.* at 507.

Chapter 15

THE INTERSECTION OF RACE AND DISABILITY

It has only been in recent years that scholars who concentrate on race have paid any sustained attention to disability. The reverse is also true: only recently have scholars that specialize in disability paid any serious attention to race. The historical siloing of "race studies" and "disability studies" has prevented theorists from recognizing that the processes that racialize people and subordinate some can work in tandem with the processes that disable people and marginalize those so disabled. On this point, Jennifer James and Cynthia Wu observe that "the categories of race/ethnicity and disability are used to constitute one another" and that similar practices and discourses have kept racial minorities and persons with disabilities "in strikingly similar marginalized positions."[1] If James and Wu are right, then studies of race *ought* to investigate disability, as it is only through investigating disability that we will come to truly and completely understand race, racialization, and racial inequality. And, of course, if James and Wu are right, the reverse is also true: studies of disability *ought* to investigate race, as it is only through investigating race that we will come to truly and completely understand disability, the processes by which individuals are disabled, and the subordination of persons with disabilities.

This chapter explores scholarship that exists at the intersection of race and disability, beginning with a description of Disability Studies and an exposition of some of the insights that the field has generated, and then exploring the discipline's turn to investigating race.

I. What Exactly Is the Disability Studies Intervention?

Disability Studies arrived on the U.S.'s academic scene in the 1990s as an effect of the social agitation in which persons with disabilities had been engaging since the 1960s. One of the primary interventions that the discipline has made since its arrival is its challenging of what scholars have called the "medical model" of disability. This model understands disability to be a biological or physiological fact that is located in the individual. Pursuant to this understanding, disability is pre-social, existing prior to and

---

[1] Jennifer C. James & Cynthia Wu, *Editors' Introduction: Race, Ethnicity, Disability, and Literature: Intersections and Interventions*, MELUS, Fall 2006, at 3, 4.

independent of society. Because this model posits that social arrangements have absolutely nothing to do with disability, it proposes that disability is best managed by medical specialists—professionals who might be able to "fix" or "treat" the disabled person or, at the very least, make her more comfortable.

Disability Studies rejects this medical model and, instead, offers a "social model of disability." This model proposes that while people may have impairments, it is society that *disables* people. This paradigm asserts that, we, as a society, have made choices about how we will build our physical environments, and we have established norms around behaviors that mark some behaviors as good and expected and others as bad and censurable. Thus, while an individual may have an impairment that prevents her from being able to use her legs to walk, we *disable* her when we build stairs instead of ramps that persons in wheelchairs can negotiate. And while an individual may have a mental impairment that renders her clinically depressed, we *disable* her when we do not make allowances for incapacity—when we expect everyone to go to work every day to earn a wage and to care for their children when they return home at night.

The social model of disability proposes that the way we have arranged society is not at all neutral. It claims that it is not *impartial* to order society in a way that privileges those who can walk and those who are not battling depression. Quite the contrary, it argues that "biases are built into [society's] very structures, norms, and practices."[2] While these biases may not produce the impairments that individuals have, they do produce disability.[3] Those incapable of walking are only disabled because we have chosen to construct our physical spaces in a way that makes it impossible for them to traverse it. Those with clinical depression are only disabled because we have chosen to expect self-sufficiency, productivity, and capacity

---

[2] Kimani Paul-Emile, *Blackness as Disability?*, 106 GEO. L.J. 293, 298 (2018).

[3] It might be important to note that some Disability Studies scholars would challenge the distinction between impairments and disability. To say that impairments are the stuff from which disabilities are socially constructed is to suggest that while disability is a social construction, impairments are "pre-social," "real," or "objective." Subini Annamma and co-authors argue that there is nothing "objective" about impairments. They write, "all dis/ability categories, whether physical, cognitive, or sensory, are also subjective. In other words, societal interpretations of and responses to specific differences from the normed body are what signify a dis/ability." Subini Ancy Annamma, David J. Connor & Beth A. Ferri, *Dis/ability Critical Race Studies (DisCrit): Theorizing at the Intersections of Race and Dis/ability*, *in* DISCRIT: DISABILITY STUDIES AND CRITICAL RACE THEORY IN EDUCATION 9, 10 (David J. Connor, Beth A. Ferri & Subini A. Annamma eds., 2016). This is to say that in order to know what counts as an "impairment," we have to identify those bodies that are not impaired—that are "normal." The identification of the "normal"—like the identification of the "impaired"—is not a value-free exercise. Quite the contrary, this perspective argues, the "norming" of some bodies and the "impairing" of others are value-laden choices. In this view, impairments are just as subjective and socially constructed as are disabilities.

from everyone at all times. In this way, disability is *socially constructed*. As James and Wu summarize, " '[D]isability' [is] a discursively engineered social category. What disability studies does, then, is call attention to how built and social environments disenable those with physical, sensory, or cognitive impairments and privilege those who are normatively constituted."[4]

II. Critical Race Theory and Disability Studies: Twin Bedfellows

After many years of not directly speaking to one another, Critical Race Theory and Disability Studies are now in conversation. However, this conversation is a young one, beginning not too long ago. Critical thinkers wonder why the two theoretical perspectives have not always been in dialogue. They share many similar commitments, after all. As noted above, Disability Studies proceeds from the assumption that disabilities are social constructions, rejecting any framework that would "biologize" them. Further, Disability Studies affirms that if persons with disabilities are subordinated, marginalized, or unable to participate as equals in society, it is not because their "nature" predestines them to this fate. Instead, it is because social arrangements, stereotypes, implicit biases, and explicit aversions have consigned them to a second-class citizenship. This, of course, should sound awfully familiar to the critical student of race. CRT has similarly proposed that race is not a biological essence located in individuals' genes. Instead, CRT offers, race is the result of political, economic, and ideological contestations. Simply stated, CRT proposes that race is a social construction. And mirroring the argument that Disability Studies makes regarding persons with disabilities, CRT argues that if racial minorities exist at the bottom of social hierarchies, it is not because of their biology. Instead, it is because we have ordered society in such a way—materially and discursively—that their second-class citizenship is somewhat inevitable.

Moreover, both Disability Studies and CRT conceptualize difference as relational. With respect to race, CRT has argued that whiteness has been constructed in opposition to nonwhiteness. For example, it says, the supposed dirtiness, laziness, and ugliness of black people have rendered white people clean, productive, and beautiful. The construction of indigenous people as savage, irrational, and backward has ensured that white people would be understood (and would understand themselves) as civilized, rational, and modern. The more that Asian and Latinx people could figure as irreducibly foreign, the more that white people could figure as inexorably "American." Interestingly, Disability Studies has made a

---

4 James & Wu, *supra* note 1, at 3.

similar observation with respect to the "disabled" and the "non-disabled." Ivan Watts and Nirmala Erevelles observe that "the monstrous body" "demarcate[s] the borders of the generic," and the "pathological" "give[s] form to the normal."[5] In light of this, they conclude that "our construction of the normal world is based on a radical repression of disability."[6] In essence, the disabled are rendered abominable and inadequate so that the nondisabled can be desirous and sufficient.

Another characteristic that CRT and Disability Studies share is an ambivalent stance towards the law—a stance that, at one moment, is convinced that the law has produced and protected hierarchies between groups and, at another moment, is convinced that the law has managed to move society away from its blatantly and unapologetically unequal past. Writes Erevelles, both CRT and Disability Studies "have critically confronted the dialectical complicity of liberal democratic law in upholding both white supremacy and ableism, while, at the same time, acknowledging that it is these same laws that have, at least, opened opportunities for participation in civil society that had formerly been denied."[7]

That CRT and Disability Studies have some important commitments in common should not be taken to suggest that the two theoretical perspectives have never been in tension with one another. One point of conflict has arisen in CRT's wholesale rejection of discourses and narratives that portray people of color as physically and mentally deficient—that is, disabled—and, thus, justifiably subordinated. As Part III.A. of this chapter explores, those interested in affirming the superiority of white people, in the past and at present, have described people of color as physically and mentally inferior to their white counterparts. In these narratives, white people represent the norm from which people of color deviate. Advocates for racial justice have tended to respond to these narratives by denying that racial minorities are deviants in this way. These advocates have argued that people of color are worthy of citizenship—they are deserving of participation in the body politic—because they are, in fact, "normal." Disability Studies scholars have observed how this response functions to justify the subordination of person with disabilities—those who *do*, in fact, deviate from the norm that society has established.[8] The response does not problematize the assumption

---

5 Ivan Eugene Watts & Nirmala Erevelles, *These Deadly Times: Reconceptualizing School Violence by Using Critical Race Theory and Disability Studies*, 41 AM. EDUC. RES. J. 271, 274 (2004) (citation omitted).

6 *Id.*

7 Nirmala Erevelles, *(Im)Material Citizens: Cognitive Disability, Race, and the Politics of Citizenship*, 1 DISABILITY, CULTURE, & EDUC. 5, 9 (2002).

8 *See* Watts & Erevelles, *supra* note 5, at 276.

that the physically and/or mentally impaired, due to their impairments, are not capable of fulfilling the obligations of citizenship or are not worthy participants in society. Writes Douglas Baynton, "Rarely have oppressed groups denied that disability is an adequate justification for social and political inequality," a fact that leads him to conclude that "disability has functioned for all such groups as a sign of and justification for inferiority."[9] Baynton and others would contend that a better response from advocates for racial justice might have been to refute the supposition that all people of color possess disabilities, but then to problematize the assumption that those who have disabilities are rightfully denied meaningful citizenship.

Another point of tension that has existed between Disability Studies and CRT concerns the analogy that some theorists of disability have drawn between disability and race. Some Disability Studies scholars have argued that disability is *like* race inasmuch as persons with disabilities have been relegated to a subordinate position in society because stereotypes about their capacities counsel that they lack the ability to be productive, valuable members of society. In a similar manner, narratives about the inferiority of people of color have counseled that they are properly relegated to a subordinate position in society. Some theorists of disability have made the analogy between disability and race explicit, as when one prominent scholar of disability argues that disability is a "form of ethnicity" and another compares "the disabled figure" to "the body marked as differently pigmented."[10]

Although the analogy between race and disability might be helpful when making arguments that persons with disabilities ought to enjoy legal protection from discrimination within law—if disability is like race, then discrimination of the basis of disability should be as illegal as discrimination on the basis of race—a number of scholars are wary of it. For one, those who propose the analogy oftentimes do not wish simply to make a comparison between persons with disabilities and people of color; rather, they wish to compare the persecutions that the two groups have endured in order to conclude that persons with disabilities "win" this Oppression Olympics. For example, two theorists of disability observe that "while literary and cultural studies have resurrected social identities such as gender, sexuality, class and race from . . . obscurity and neglect[,] disability

[9] Douglas C. Baynton, *Disability and the Justification of Inequality in American History*, *in* THE NEW DISABILITY HISTORY: AMERICAN PERSPECTIVES 33, 34 (Paul K. Longmore & Lauri Umansky eds., 2001).

[10] Anna Mollow, *"When Black Women Start Going on Prozac": Race, Gender, and Mental Illness in Meri Nana-Ama Danquah's* Willow Weep for Me, MELUS, Fall 2006, at 67, 69.

has suffered a distinctly different disciplinary fate."[11] These theorists suggest that the acceptance within the academy of analyses of gender, sexuality, class and race has been matched by the rejection of analyses of disability—a suggestion that two other scholars make more explicit when they observe a " 'sharp contrast' between the reception of disability studies . . . and that of 'radical analyses of racism and sexism that quickly won favor.' "[12] This is the Oppression Olympics; it is an argument that disabled people, ignored as they are within the academy, are more subjugated than people of color. We also bear witness to the Oppression Olympics when another advocate for persons with disabilities asserts that the "neglect and institutionalized exclusion of disabled people is 'more profound' than that of black people."[13] However, many progressive scholars warn that the Oppression Olympics is a dangerous game inasmuch as, whenever it is held, it tends to pit groups that could be allies against each other—allowing for the large-scale forces and institutional processes that marginalize them both to escape investigation, censure, and challenge. In essence, there are no winners in the Oppression Olympics. Many critical thinkers would propose that instead of analogizing histories of subordination, a more useful tack would be to analyze the specificity of any one group's oppression and to make a case that it deserves remedy on its own merits—not because it is worse than another marginalized group's suffering.

Additionally, many scholars reject the analogy between race and disability because, like the analogy between race and sexuality discussed in Chapter 13, it renders invisible those who live at the intersection of those two axes of identity: disabled persons of color. If disability is *like* race, then we assume that the people of color who we are comparing to the disabled are *not* disabled; moreover, we assume that the disabled persons who we are comparing to people of color are not, in fact, people of color. Thus, the analogy between disability and race assumes able-bodiedness of people of color and whiteness of persons with disabilities. Wholly erased are people of color with disabilities.

Scholars who theorize the intersection of race and disability conclude that analogizing race and disability assumes a separateness between the forces that subordinate racial minorities and the forces that subordinate persons with disabilities. This impoverishes our analyses, they say, because it disallows us from "understanding how disability has always been racialized, gendered, and classed and how racial, gender, and class difference have been conceived of as

---

[11] *Id.* at 89 n.5.

[12] *Id.*

[13] *Id.*

'disability.' "[14] In other words, the oppression that people with disabilities have endured is not simply *like* the marginalization that people of color have experienced. As Jess Waggoner puts it, the discourses that render both groups "unfit" for equality and citizenship have a "fundamental intertwining."[15]

III. What Can Studying the Intersection of Race and Disability Reveal?

As noted above, Disability Studies' attention to race has been a recent phenomenon. Perhaps unsurprisingly, the failure of scholars of disability to pay attention to race resulted in their focusing only on the experience of those disabled people who were white.[16] The oversight was so pronounced that Chris Bell, an early and enthusiastic proponent of studying the intersection of race and disability, argued that calling the discipline "Disability Studies" was a misnomer: he argued that the discipline was properly called "White Disability Studies." He contended that the field's failure to "engage issues of race and ethnicity in a substantive capacity" had the effect of "entrenching whiteness as its constitutive underpinning."[17] Bell claimed that the refusal to pay attention to race allows scholars to assume that there is a homogeneity of experience among those with disabilities. However, race (and class, and nationality, and sexuality, etc.) intersects with disability to produce qualitatively different experiences. In essence, Bell affirms that the blind white person has a different experience with his impairment than the blind person of color; the white bipolar person has a different experience with her impairment than the bipolar person of color.

As it turns out, race has a complicated relationship to disability. At times, race has had the effect of facilitating the recognition of a disability. As this chapter discusses below in Part III.B., children of color are disproportionately represented among students with an intellectual disability (ID, formerly called mental retardation, or MR), a learning disability (LD), or an emotional disturbance (ED). In this context, racial minority status *increases* the chances that an evaluator will conclude that a person is disabled.

---

[14] James & Wu, *supra* note 1, at 8.

[15] Jess Waggoner, *"Oh Say Can You ___": Race and Mental Disability in Performances of Citizenship*, 10 J. LIT. & CULT. DISABILITY STUD. 87, 89 (2016).

[16] This is "unsurprising" only if one accepts the proposition, offered by progressive race scholars, that whiteness is the norm within our society. This claim asserts that whiteness is the position from which nonwhite races deviate. As such, whiteness is unmarked. If true, then if one purports to study "the disabled person," one is actually studying the *white* disabled person. One only studies the disabled person of color if one intentionally and explicitly identifies one's project as such.

[17] Chris Bell, *Introducing White Disability Studies: A Modest Proposal*, *in* THE DISABILITY STUDIES READER 275, 275 (Lennard J. Davis ed., 2d ed. 2006).

However, at other times, race has the effect of *preventing* the recognition of a disability. Anna Mollow observes that although there is no reason to expect that racial groups should or would suffer from depression at different rates, white people are diagnosed with depression much more often than black people.[18] "People of color, especially African Americans, are less likely to be diagnosed with depression or prescribed medication when they report their symptoms to a doctor; even in studies controlling for income level and health insurance status, the disparities are great."[19] In this context, racial minority status *decreases* the chances that an evaluator will conclude that a person is disabled.

Why is this so? How do we explain the inconsistent effects that race has on the recognition of disability? Scholars of race and disability offer that the stories that we tell about race may have something to do with it.

On the one hand, in the context of ID, LD, and ED, progressive thinkers encourage us to consider that, as noted above, people of color historically have been described as mentally inferior. Perhaps this explains why evaluators have no trouble seeing ID, LD, and ED in children of color: narratives about race that have existed in our discursive repertoire since the dawn of the nation might lead some to *expect* these types of mental deficiencies in children of color. On this point, Annamma and her coauthors observe that science once proposed that intellectual inadequacy was part and parcel of blackness. They contend that these ideas, while no longer validated by science, nevertheless persist in our discursive milieu. Thus, according to Annamma and her coauthors, we ought not to be surprised when "seemingly 'objective' clinical assessment practices" purport to "prove" the truth of black intellectual inferiority.[20]

On the other hand, in the context of depression, we have narratives that describe black people as lazy, unmotivated, and unproductive. A lack of motivation and a decrease in productivity are also signs of depression.[21] This, suggest scholars of race and disability, may explain why evaluators are less likely to recognize depression in black people: existing racial narratives may counsel that there is nothing "abnormal" when black people exhibit depressive behavior.

Studying the intersection of race and disability also allows recognition of the reality that race may impact an individual's ability to access treatment, medication, or other tools that can help them

---

[18] *See* Mollow, *supra* note 10, at 74.

[19] *Id.* at 73.

[20] Annamma, Connor & Ferri, *supra* note 3, at 23.

[21] *See* Mollow, *supra* note 10, at 73.

manage their impairment. Mollow observes that poverty and racism often create "insurmountable barriers" to the ability of poor people of color to access the medical care that more affluent white people have at their disposal. She notes that while disability activists have railed against the coercive treatments to which people with mental impairments have been subjected in the past, forced medication may actually be indicative of a privileged position. Mollow writes, "[F]or many African American women with depression, lack of access to health care, rather than involuntary administration of it, is the most oppressive aspect of the contemporary politics of mental illness."[22]

However, things are more complicated than the simple claim that people of color cannot access the healthcare that will help them manage their impairments. While in some contexts, people of color are not able to access the medical treatment that is available to white people—Mollow notes that a study of the treatment of persons diagnosed with depression revealed that "44% of white patients and 27.8% of Black patients were given antidepressant medication"[23]—in other contexts, people of color are overmedicated relative to their white counterparts. "African Americans are diagnosed with schizophrenia at much higher rates and are also given antipsychotic medications more frequently and in higher doses. They are also institutionalized involuntarily more often."[24] Thus, we have to pay attention to race when we study disability, as race may mean that people with impairments are *dis*abled differently.

A. The Racialization of Disability

Theorists argue that paying attention to disability while studying race, and race while studying disability, reveals that, throughout history, the two have informed one another. To put it differently, society has taken the fact of racial otherness to be a sign of mental or physical deficiency; at the same time, it has taken mental or physical deficiency to be a sign of racial otherness.

Baynton has documented the attribution of disability to nonwhite racial groups at various moments in history. He notes that chattel slavery in the U.S. was justified by the assertion that black people had physical and mental incapacities that rendered them unable to care for themselves and, consequently, unfit for freedom. As an example, he looks to Dr. Samuel Cartwright's infamous research with black people—research that led him to conclude that a mental impairment, drapetomania, caused enslaved people to develop a desire to seek freedom and to run away from those who

---

[22] *Id.* at 68.

[23] *Id.* at 91 n.15.

[24] *Id.* at 74.

claimed to own them. Quoting Cartwright, Baynton notes that drapetomania was imagined to be " 'as much a disease of the mind as any other species of mental alienation' [and] was common among slaves whose masters had 'made themselves too familiar with them, treating them as equals.' The need to submit to a master was built into the very bodies of African Americans, in whom 'we see "*genu flexit*" written in the physical structure of his knees, being more flexed or bent, than any other kind of man.' "[25] Thus, Cartwright attributed a disability to black people that, as it were, made them marvelously suitable for slavery but woefully unsuitable for freedom.

Black people were not the only group that was imagined to bear physical and mental impairments that rendered them inappropriate participants in the body politic. Baynton observes that immigration restrictions were often justified by arguments that nonwhite (or not-yet-white) people from foreign lands had physical and mental incapacities that made their admission to the U.S. unwise. Explains Bayton, "[W]hile people with disabilities constituted a distinct category of persons unwelcome in the United States, the charge that certain ethnic groups were mentally and physically deficient was instrumental in arguing for *their* exclusion. The belief that discriminating on the basis of disability was justifiable in turn helped justify the creation of immigration quotas based on ethnic origin."[26] As such, physical and mental disabilities were attributed to nonwhite and marginally-white groups of immigrants. On the physical disability front, thinkers of the day contended that " 'South Europeans run to low stature. A gang of Italian navvies filing along the street present, by their dwarfishness, a curious contrast to other people. The Portuguese, the Greeks, and the Syrians are, from our point of view, undersized. The Hebrew immigrants are very poor in physique . . . the polar opposite of our pioneer breed.' "[27] And on the mental disability front, thinkers of the day posited the " 'slow-witted Slav,' the 'neurotic condition of our Jewish immigrants,' and, in general, the 'degenerate and psychopathic types, which are so conspicuous and numerous among the immigrants.' "[28]

In contemporary times, arguments that we can presume that some racial groups, on account of their racial difference, are disabled do not really appear in public discourse. Disability is no longer racialized in the manner. Instead, in present times, disability might be racialized in the sense that the burdens associated with racial minority status might generate impairments that are the stuff of disability. For example, Mollow writes that "the production of some

[25] Baynton, *supra* note 9, at 38.

[26] *Id.* at 47.

[27] *Id.* at 48.

[28] *Id.* at 47.

impairments itself is a political process."[29] This framing encourages us to consider how the phenomena that critical thinkers of race identify as instances of modern-day racism—i.e., mass incarceration, police violence, an inadequate safety net, residential segregation, the placement of environmental hazards in poor communities of color, and punitive immigration policies, to name a few—might manufacture impairments that become disabilities. This framing encourages us to think through how depression, schizophrenia, and a host of other mental illnesses might be products of the processes that progressive thinkers call institutional racism.

Indeed, this line of thinking incites us to contemplate how the *poverty* that people of color disproportionately bear produces physical and mental disabilities. Consider Watts and Erevelles's observation that

> [a]t a physiological level, there is an interesting correlation between race, disability, and class when one takes into account the ways in which poverty hurts children emotionally, socially, and physically. Kozol's text *Amazing Grace* describes how the predominance of asthma and lead poisoning among poor children contributes to neurological damage that manifests itself as mild disabilities and behavioral disorders in schools. . . . In terms of race, 36.7% of African American children, as opposed to 17% of Latino children and 6.1% White children, have been identified as experiencing lead poisoning. Such statistics point to environmentally induced damage . . . resulting directly from the lack of adequate housing, health care, clean air, and other basic necessities.[30]

These numbers might represent the racialization of disability in modern times. Unlike the days of yore, during which racial minorities were *imagined* to be impaired, the racialization of disability in the contemporary era occurs when racial minorities actually *become* impaired—physically, emotionally, cognitively—due to living in unhealthy environments and bearing inhumane stresses.

B. The Overrepresentation of Children of Color in Special Education Classes

Scholars working at the intersection of race and disability have written extensively about the overrepresentation of nonwhite students in special education classes. As Annamma and coauthors note, "African American students continue to be three times as likely to be labeled mentally retarded [or intellectually disabled], two times

[29] Mollow, *supra* note 10, at 78.

[30] Watts & Erevelles, *supra* note 5, at 290.

as likely to be labeled emotionally disturbed, and one and a half times as likely to be labeled learning disabled, compared to their White peers."[31] Further, Latinx and indigenous students tend to be overrepresented in special education classes when there are large numbers of Latinx and indigenous people in the state. While these figures would be disturbing if ID, LD, or ED could be objectively measured, they arguably are made more disturbing by the reality that the determination that an individual has any of these disabilities is a subjective one. A student is not diagnosed as having ID, LD, or ED after some blood test or brain scan reveals an incapacity. Instead, students are diagnosed with these disabilities after an evaluator concludes that, in his or her professional opinion, the student significantly deviates from the norm.[32] The worry, of course, is that ideas about the mental inferiority and behavioral deviance of people of color inform evaluators' subjective determinations of disability, leading them to find disability in children of color at rates that are much higher than their white peers. That there may be some validity to this worry is suggested by the fact that physical disabilities that are objectively measured—like blindness, deafness, or mobility impairments—tend to be evenly distributed across racial categories.

The overrepresentation of students of color in special education classes is not a new phenomenon. Scholars have noted that there was a stark rise in the number of students of color in special education classes after *Brown v. Board* held that formal segregation on the basis of race was unconstitutional.[33] As the numbers of black children attending formerly white schools increased, so did the number of black children assigned to separate special education classes—always in different classrooms, sometimes in different buildings, and occasionally in different schools. David Connor and Beth Ferri report that "school officials in Washington, D.C. placed over 24 percent of their newly admitted African American students in separate special education classrooms. . . . [B]etween 1955 and 1956, special education classes doubled in enrollment; over 77 percent of students

---

[31] Annamma, Connor & Ferri, *supra* note 3, at 11.

[32] It is important to underscore that ID, LD, and ED are measured by a departure from an average. Thus, disability is "bound to the parameters of normalcy defined by a given cultural group." Beth Harry & Mary G. Anderson, *The Disproportionate Placement of African American Males in Special Education Programs: A Critique of the Process*, 63 J. NEGRO EDUC. 602, 607 (1994). Accordingly, progressive scholars observe that even though evaluators use objective-sounding, biologically-suggestive language like "etiology, symptom, syndrome, diagnosis, and prognosis" when discussing and describing disabilities that affect educational performance, the determination that a student departs from the norm, as well as the norm against which students are measured, are not objective or biological in nature. *Id.* Both are culturally informed and socially embedded.

[33] Brown v. Bd. of Educ., 347 U.S. 483 (1954).

in these classes were African American."[34] In essence, the mandate to integrate was met by the impulse to achieve segregation through alternative means.

For critical scholars who are concerned about the disproportionate diagnosing of students of color with "invisible" disabilities that involve "the capacity to 'think' or learn and/or those of a social nature,"[35] red flags are raised by the underrepresentation of students of Asian descent among those in special education classes. "Stereotyped as the 'model minority,' and often academically outperforming middle class white students, [students of Asian descent] are far less likely to be labeled in subjective categories of [ID, LD, or ED] than any other minority group."[36] The relative absence of Asian and Asian American students in special education classes suggests to these thinkers that racial narratives—the stories that we tell about race—are playing an important role in the discovery of (or failure to discover) disabilities in students. Because the stories that we tell about people of Asian descent portray them as educationally superior, evaluators do not find disabilities that can affect educational performance in them. Because the stories that we tell about people of African descent portray them as educationally suspect, evaluators spot these disabilities in them all the time.

For progressive theorists, red flags are also raised by the reality that when white students are diagnosed with a disability that can affect educational performance, it tends to be a learning disability.[37] Students have a learning disability when they have low school achievement despite having the potential for high scholastic performance.[38] In contrast, students have an intellectual disability when they do not have the potential to achieve in school. Again, these scholars wonder whether the stories that we tell about race lead

---

[34] David J. Connor & Beth A. Ferri, *Integration and Inclusion: A Troubling Nexus: Race, Disability, and Special Education*, 90 J. AFR. AM. HIST. 107, 108 (2005).

[35] *Id.* at 111.

[36] *Id.* at 115.

[37] This is not a new pattern. Connor and Ferri explain:

> Emerging as a label during the 1960s, students with a learning disability were characterized as having average or above average intelligence, specific rather than generalized deficits, and a white, middle-class cultural/familial background. The category of LD originally became associated with white students to such a degree that students with similar levels of academic achievement were given different labels based on their racial, ethnic, and class backgrounds. . . . While white students were overrepresented in the categories of LD and Gifted, African American students were overrepresented in the categories of MR and ED, and underrepresented in Gifted—even if they achieved comparable test scores to whites.

Id.

[38] *See* Linda M. Blum, *"Not This Big, Huge, Racial-Type Thing, but . . .": Mothering Children of Color with Invisible Disabilities in the Age of Neuroscience*, 36 SIGNS: J. WOMEN CULTURE & SOC'Y 941, 962 (2011).

evaluators to conclude that when a white student is not performing well in school, he has the potential to do so and, thus, has a learning disability; yet, when a black student is not performing well, he already is living up to his potential and, thus, has an intellectual disability.

The overrepresentation of students of color among the population of students with disabilities that impact educational performance is a thorny problem that is not likely to go away anytime soon. Critical scholars contend that the issue will not be resolved without theorizing race and disability simultaneously. As Annamma and her coauthors assert, "Neither institutional racism alone nor institutional ableism on its own can explain why students of color are more likely to be labeled with dis/abilities and segregated than their White peers with and without dis/abilities; instead, it is the two working together."[39] Thus, they argue, we have to think about the two—together—in order to bring equity to this space.

IV. Questions and Discussion

1. Kimani Paul-Emile has contended that it might be productive to think of blackness itself as a disability. She begins her provocative argument by observing, consistent with the social model of disability, that disabilities are socially constructed: many impairments only become disabling when they combine "with an inhospitable social or physical environment."[40] Similarly, she argues, being black is not inherently limiting. However, when blackness combines with an inhospitable social or physical environment, it severely limits the black individual. She then argues that the U.S., as currently constituted, is such an inhospitable environment. "[B]eing black, as a basic fact of daily life, now poses barriers to equality in employment, education, housing, medicine, and many other contexts."[41] As deafness impedes social participation when society is built for the hearing, blackness impedes social participation when society is built for those who are white. "In the same way that . . . social structures were built with the able-bodied in mind, so too is society structured to benefit Whites."[42]

What do you think of Paul-Emile's argument? What aspects of race or racial inequality does thinking of blackness as a disability illuminate? What aspects of race or racial inequality does thinking of blackness as a disability obscure? What are the benefits of this

---

[39] Annamma, Connor & Ferri, *supra* note 3, at 19.

[40] Paul-Emile, *supra* note 2, at 298.

[41] *Id.* at 299.

[42] *Id.* at 364.

framing of race and racism? What are the costs? Do you believe the costs outweigh the benefits?

2. Paul Longmore and Lauri Umansky have discussed the friction that has existed between Disability Studies scholars and scholars of race. Race scholars (as well as scholars of class and gender), they state, have at times been opposed to the establishment of Disability Studies departments or the inclusion of investigations of disability in already-established fields. According to Longmore and Umansky, these otherwise progressive thinkers have thought that "incorporating disability would 'water down' diversity requirements"—a position that has worked to "limit examination of disability in intellectual discourse."[43]

If what Longmore and Umanksy argue is true, why do you think that scholars of race have felt they were engaged in a zero-sum game with scholars of disability? That is, why have they felt that if Disability Studies "wins" any visibility, resources, or validation as a legitimate field of inquiry, thinkers of race would lose the same? Were they right?

3. With respect to the overrepresentation of children of color in special education classes, some have proposed that it is not race, but rather poverty, that is to blame. This position suggests either that poverty causes the development of disabilities that impact educational performance, or that evaluators are simply more prone to "see" these disabilities in poor children. Because people of color disproportionately bear the burdens of poverty in the country, they are disproportionately found among those with these kinds of disability.

A number of studies have challenged this position. For example, Russell Skiba and his coauthors observe that the position is unsettled by poor children not being overrepresented among students in "more biologically based 'hard' disability categories (e.g., visual or hearing impairment)."[44] Why, they ask, would poverty cause soft, invisible, judgment-based disabilities, but not the hard, objectively verifiable kind? They also observe that Latinx people also disproportionately bear the burdens of poverty. But, in some states, Latinx children are overrepresented among special education students; in others, they are not. If poverty is causing the development of these types of disabilities, why does poverty not always cause the development of these disabilities in Latinx children?

---

[43] Paul K. Longmore & Lauri Umansky, *Introduction* to THE NEW DISABILITY HISTORY: AMERICAN PERSPECTIVES, *supra* note 9, at 1, 9.

[44] Russell J. Skiba et al., *Unproven Links: Can Poverty Explain Ethnic Disproportionality in Special Education?*, 39 J. SPECIAL EDUC. 130, 132 (2005).

The smoking gun that suggests to Skiba and his coauthors that poverty cannot explain racial disproportionality in special education is found in research that suggests that the relationship between poverty and special education placement is not at all direct. While some studies have concluded that poverty is correlated to higher rates of placement in special education classes, other studies "have reported an opposite direction of effect, finding that as levels of poverty *decrease*, minority students are at greater risk for referral as [having a learning disability, intellectual disability, or emotional disturbance]."[45] Why, ask Skiba and his coauthors, would poverty cause the development of disability in some sites, but not cause the development of disability in other sites?

They conclude that many factors in addition to poverty—including race, but also "district resources and perhaps even disciplinary philosophy"[46]—explain racial disproportionality in special education placement.

---

[45] *Id.*

[46] *Id.* at 142.

Part IV
CONTEMPORARY ISSUES

Chapter 16

HEALTH

I. Introduction

When it comes to health care, the U.S. is a big spender. Indeed, the U.S. spends the most money on health care relative to other high-income countries.[1] However, the large sums of money spent on health care in the U.S. have not translated into a healthier population. In fact, the U.S. appears to be *unhealthier* than the nations that it considers its peers. When compared to countries like France, Japan, the United Kingdom, and New Zealand, the U.S. has the lowest life expectancies, the highest rate of infant mortality, and among adults aged 65 and older, the highest rate of chronic illnesses like diabetes and heart disease.

These facts raise many questions, and there are many avenues of inquiry one might pursue in light of them. For example, we might observe that the high spending on health care in the U.S. is, in part, a function of the higher costs of health care in the country. We might then question why health care costs are so high in the U.S, relatively speaking. Why are MRIs and CT scans more expensive in the U.S. than they are in other countries? Why is the price tag on a bypass surgery in Australia a little under $29K while that same surgery costs an average of $78K in the U.S.?[2]

Or we might observe that there have been changes in health care spending over time, note that the U.S.'s spending has appeared to plateau, and ask whether this steadying has had any consequences on population health. Have there been any significant changes in the rates of morbidity (i.e., the rate at which a disease appears in a population) and mortality (i.e., the rate of deaths in a population) since 2009, when spending began to level off?[3]

While critical thinkers about race may believe these avenues of inquiry to be worthwhile, their intellectual commitments convince them that the most compelling questions about the contradiction

---

[1] The U.S. spends the most on health care when measured in terms of per capita spending ($9,086) as well as percentage of the gross domestic product (17.1%). DAVID SQUIRES & CHLOE ANDERSON, COMMONWEALTH FUND, U.S. HEALTH CARE FROM A GLOBAL PERSPECTIVE: SPENDING, USE OF SERVICES, AND HEALTH IN 13 COUNTRIES, at 2 (2015).

[2] *See* INT'L FED'N OF HEALTH PLANS, 2015 COMPARATIVE PRICE VARIATION IN MEDICAL AND HOSPITAL PRICES BY COUNTRY (2015).

[3] *See* Anne B. Martin et al., *Growth in US Health Spending Remained Slow in 2010; Health Share of Gross Domestic Product was Unchanged from 2009*, 31 HEALTH AFF. 208 (2012).

between the U.S.'s high spending on health care and the low levels of health of its population involve race and racism. Indeed, many progressive thinkers are interested in how race and racism may explain the U.S.'s status as the sickest among the wealthiest nations.

"Health disparities" refers to differences in health states among groups within a population. We might interrogate health disparities in terms of sex (i.e., what are the differences in the rates at which men and women are diagnosed with hypertension?), geographic location (i.e., what are the differences in the rates at which people living in rural areas and people living in urban areas are diagnosed with hypertension?), or income (i.e., what are the differences in the rates at which people with incomes <$25,000/year and people with incomes >$25,000/year are diagnosed with hypertension?). Progressive race scholars are most curious about health disparities in terms of race (i.e., what are the differences in the rates at which white people and black people are diagnosed with hypertension?). Further, they focus their scholarly attentions on how racial disparities in health contribute to the relative sickliness of the U.S. when compared to other wealthy countries. They observe that if the country eliminated racial disparities in health, then the overall health of the U.S. would improve, moving the country closer to the health outcomes achieved in other industrialized nations.

As a general matter, people of color are sicker and die younger than their white counterparts.[4] For example, although the overall infant mortality rate has declined over the years, racial disparities persist. The infant mortality rate for black babies is 12.7%—a number that is more than twice the infant mortality rate for white babies (5.5%). The infant mortality rates for white babies is also lower than American Indian/Alaska Native babies (8.42%) and some categories of Latinx babies, namely those from Puerto Rico (7.3%).[5]

Another example: For the last forty years, black women have been dying during pregnancy, childbirth, or shortly thereafter at three to four times the rate of their white counterparts. Between 2011 and 2013, the maternal mortality rate for black women was 40 deaths per 100,000 live births, while the same rate for white women

4 For a comprehensive itemization of racial disparities in health, *see* Ctrs. for Disease Control & Prevention, *CDC Health Disparities and Inequalities Report—United States 2013,* MORBIDITY & MORTALITY WKLY. REP., Nov. 22, 2013, at 1, 184, https://www.cdc.gov/mmwr/pdf/other/su6203.pdf; *see also* INST. OF MED., UNEQUAL TREATMENT: CONFRONTING RACIAL AND ETHNIC DISPARITIES IN HEALTH CARE (Brian D. Smedley, Adrienne Y. Stith & Alan R. Nelson eds., 2002) [hereinafter INST. OF MED., UNEQUAL TREATMENT].

5 Ctrs. for Disease Control & Prevention, *supra* note 4, at 172–73.

was 12.4 deaths per 100,000 live births.[6] The Center for Reproductive Rights reports that in some areas of Mississippi, the maternal mortality rate for women of color is greater than the rate found in sub-Saharan Africa; meanwhile the maternal mortality rate for white women in these areas "is too insignificant to report."[7]

And yet another example: Hypertension can lead to heart disease and stroke, the first and fourth leading causes of death in the U.S. The rate of hypertension is highest among black adults—at 41.3%; the rates for white people and Latinx people are 28.6% and 27.7%, respectively.

Some may read the statistics above and ask, "What does race have to do with it?" Their instinct may be that racial disparities in health are much more about *class* than race. It is well-known that people of color are overrepresented among those living below the poverty line.[8] Because of this, some may be led to believe that *poverty*, not race, explains why people of color are sicker and die earlier than white people. The claim is that class, not race, explains racial disparities in health.

This claim is not at all outlandish. Social determinants of health refer to "the conditions in which people are born, live, work, and age."[9] They include the ability to access a good education and secure a nonhazardous job, healthy food, quality health services, safe and clean housing, a decent wage, and social support.[10] Social determinants of health certainly play a significant role in explaining racial disparities in health. The conditions under which poor people of color live undeniably lead to their poor health.

Now, if poverty is responsible for the poorer health outcomes that people of color have, then *class*—again, not race—is the real

---

[6] *Pregnancy Mortality Surveillance System*, CTRS. FOR DISEASE CONTROL & PREVENTION (July 25, 2018), https://www.cdc.gov/reproductivehealth/maternalinfanthealth/pregnancy-mortality-surveillance-system.htm.

[7] CTR. FOR REPROD. RIGHTS ET AL., REPRODUCTIVE INJUSTICE: RACIAL AND GENDER DISCRIMINATION IN U.S. HEALTH CARE 6 (2014), https://tbinternet.ohchr.org/Treaties/CERD/Shared%20Documents/USA/INT_CERD_NGO_USA_17560_E.pdf.

[8] In 2015, white persons constituted 41% of those in poverty, although they make up close to 65% of the total population. Black persons constituted 22% of those in poverty, although they represent only 13% of the total population. And Latinx persons constituted 28% of those in poverty, although they represent only 16% of the total population. BERNADETTE D. PROCTOR, JESSICA K. SEMEGA & MELISSA A. KOLLAR, U.S. CENSUS BUREAU, CURRENT POPULATION REPORTS, INCOME AND POVERTY IN THE UNITED STATES, at 12–14 (2016), https://www.census.gov/content/dam/Census/library/publications/2016/demo/p60-256.pdf.

[9] *About Social Determinants of Health*, WORLD HEALTH ORG., http://www.who.int/social_determinants/sdh_definition/en/ (last visited Aug. 1, 2018).

[10] *See NCHHSTP Social Determinants of Health: Frequently Asked Questions*, CTRS. FOR DISEASE CONTROL & PREVENTION (Mar. 21, 2014), https://www.cdc.gov/nchhstp/socialdeterminants/faq.html.

problem. And if class is actually the mechanism that leads to racial disparities in health, then progressive race scholars may be barking up the wrong tree when they seek to investigate the ostensible effects that race and racism have on nonwhite people's health statuses.

However, it seems that there is something up in that tree. More plainly, several studies show that people of color have poorer health outcomes *even when one controls for class*. Consider racial disparities in maternal mortality. Class-privileged black women die during pregnancy and motherhood at rates that are significantly higher than their class privileged white counterparts. That is, *racial disparities in maternal mortality rates persist across income levels*.[11] Thus, it is not only poor black women who are dying on the path to motherhood. Wealthier black women are dying, too; and they are dying more frequently than wealthier white women. This means that it is not solely *poverty* that is killing black women.

A similar phenomenon is in effect with respect to infant mortality. The infants born to class-privileged black women die at rates that are much higher than the babies born to class-privileged white women.[12] Indeed, racial disparities in infant mortality and morbidity *increase* as one moves up the income ladder. The rates at which poor black babies and poor white babies die are *closer* than the rates at which wealthier black babies and wealthier white babies die.[13]

What is true with respect to racial disparities in infant mortality is true in other health contexts, as well: At times, racial disparities in health do not only persist as one moves up the socioeconomic ladder, but these disparities actually *increase*.[14] In other words, poor black people and poor white people sometimes have health outcomes that are more comparable to one another than the health outcomes of wealthier black people and wealthier white people. This suggests that while we, as a society, ought to continue to try to ameliorate the effects that poverty has on health, we also need to try to ameliorate the effects that *race* has on health.

II. Explaining Racial Disparities in Health

Researchers utilizing a critical lens have identified a variety of mechanisms that might explain the existence and persistence of

---

[11] *See, e.g.*, Christopher T. Lang & Jeffrey C. King, *Maternal Mortality in the United States*, 22 BEST PRAC. & RES. CLINICAL OBSTETRICS & GYNAECOLOGY 517, 522–23 (2008); Elliott K. Main, *Maternal Mortality: New Strategies for Measurement and Prevention*, 22 CURRENT OPINION OBSTETRICS & GYNECOLOGY 511 (2010).

[12] *See* Marsha Lillie-Blanton et al., *Racial Differences in Health: Not Just Black and White, But Shades of Gray*, 17 ANN. REV. PUB. HEALTH 411, 416 (1996).

[13] *See id.* at 429.

[14] *See id.*

racial disparities in health. We can divide these explanations into structural causes of health disparities (which look to the structures within which people of color exist) and individualist causes of health disparities (which focus their attention on either the individual or the individual healthcare provider who cares for the patient).

Before exploring the explanations for racial disparities in health that critical scholars have embraced, it might be helpful to discuss explanations for health disparities that critical scholars have rejected. The first is the idea that genetic differences between the races explain the poor health outcomes of people of color. The second is the idea that the behaviors in which people of color engage—their culture—wholly explain their compromised health.

A. Rejected Theories

1. *Biological Race*

As discussed in Chapter 6, the view that a race is a genetically homogenous group of persons has a long history. After the Holocaust—when Nazi Germany relied on ideas of biological race to justify the murder of millions of Jews—the concept of biological race began to fall out of favor. The idea was further discredited decades later, when the Human Genome Project's mapping of the entire catalogue of human genes in 2003 revealed that all human beings, regardless of race, share 99.9 percent of the same genes.

If the concept of biological race persists into the present, it is because of uncertainty around the significance of that 0.1 percent of genes that humans do not share. While most scientists believe that the residuum of genetic difference is not distributed among the racial groups that we recognize (i.e., black, white, Asian, etc.) in a way that makes it possible to think about race in genetic terms, many people disagree. For example, in 2012, a group of researchers at Boston University probed the "role of genetics" in black women's experiences with cancer.[15] They concluded that "cancers can behave differently in different populations, so the medical establishment needs to stop treating them as if they were the same." A news story covering their research explained that

> [t]he phrase cancer disparities refers to more than racial or socioeconomic gaps in access to cancer diagnosis and treatment. As it turns out, all other things being equal, race and ethnicity account for significant differences in the incidence and survivability of certain cancers and in how well people respond to standard treatments. . . .

[15] Susan Seligson, *BU Takes on Cancer: Racial Disparities*, B.U. TODAY (April 9, 2012), http://www.bu.edu/today/2012/bu-takes-on-cancer-racial-disparities/.

> [C]umulative findings from several studies indicate that, regardless of their incomes and how early they are diagnosed, African American women are more likely to die from breast cancer than their white counterparts. "At all ages mortality from breast cancer is higher for black women, and it's clear now that it's not due to differences in access, care or treatments," [one researcher] says.[16]

The commitment in the scientists' research is that genetic variation between racial groups explains elevated breast cancer mortality rates among black women.

Indeed, peer-reviewed science journals are replete with articles purporting to demonstrate genetic distinctiveness among racial groups. For example, a group of researchers recently published a study in the peer-reviewed journal, *Cancer Control*, in which they explored differences in cancer-related mortality rates among U.S.-born black persons, Haitians, and Jamaicans.[17] Their study included a nod towards biological race: "While most intra-racial cancer mortality differences in our study seem to be determined by environmental factors, some of which are inherently related to place of birth, *it is important to note that some patterns are seemingly more related to race and possibly genetics, regardless of geography*."[18]

Critics of these studies respond by noting that proponents of the idea that genetic differences explain health differences between the races have never been able to identify a genetic variation that is specific to a racial group. These proponents have failed to identify race-specific genetic variations, critics argue, because such variations do not exist. Critics observe that proponents of biological race invariably conclude that genes cause racial disparities in health after they have controlled for other potential causes of the disparity—like income, socioeconomic status, or access to health insurance and health services. Although these researchers may eliminate many non-genetic causes of any given racial disparity in health outcomes, *they never identify the genetic cause of the disparity*. Their belief in biological race, critics argue, leads them to presume that such a genetic cause exists. Consider the BU researchers discussed above. Although they conclude that differences in access, care, or treatments do not explain racial disparities in breast cancer mortality, they never identify the genetic variation that is the culprit behind why breast cancer is deadlier for black women. They cannot do this,

---

[16] *Id.*

[17] Paulo S. Pinheiro et al., *Black Heterogeneity in Cancer Mortality: US-Blacks, Haitians, and Jamaicans*, 23 CANCER CONTROL 347 (2016).

[18] *Id.* at 353 (emphasis added).

progressive race scholars implore, as such a variation is a figment of our collective imagination.

Another example that progressive scholars cite as evidence of our imaginations leading us to conclude that genes explain racial disparities in health is the supposed "thrifty gene" that causes the individuals that bear it to retain salt.[19] Several researchers have proposed that this gene may explain elevated rates of hypertension among black persons. This theory of racial disparities in hypertension hypothesizes that this salt-retaining gene is more prevalent among African Americans because of the Middle Passage, through which newly-enslaved Africans were transported to the Americans in the most brutal and inhumane of fashions. The conditions that Africans endured during the Middle Passage, and later during chattel slavery, caused the salt-retaining gene to be selected for: those Africans who were genetically predisposed to retaining salt were able to survive dehydration, which the dire conditions during the Middle Passage and slavery inevitably produced. While this salt-retaining gene facilitated survival in the extreme environments found during the Middle Passage and slavery, it leads to morbidity in black people's present environment inasmuch as salt is now plentiful in their diets.

The thrifty gene theory, which is also known as the "slavery hypothesis," appears plausible at first blush. However, there are two problems with it. First, the thrifty gene theory is inconsistent with what scientists know about gene selection. In order for a thrifty gene to be as prevalent among African Americans as it must be if it is to explain their elevated rates of hypertension, the gene would also have to be quite prevalent among the African populations whose members were enslaved and brought to the U.S. However, West Africans, the group from which African Americans' ancestors came, have quite low rates of hypertension. In fact, the prevalence of hypertension among persons from Nigeria, a country in the region from which many enslaved Africans were captured, is lower than that among white Americans. This is good evidence that genes cannot explain racial disparities in hypertension. Second, and quite significantly, researchers have not been able to identify the thrifty gene in persons suffering from hypertension. As one commentator explains, "[T]he search for variant gene structures that contribute to blood pressure has not been particularly successful; those candidate genes that do appear to be associated with blood pressure are not differentially distributed across conventional racial groups, nor do

[19] For an accessible discussion of the "thrifty gene" and why it is an implausible explanation of higher rates of hypertension in black people, *see* Osagie K. Obasogie, *Oprah's Unhealthy Mistake*, L.A. TIMES (May 17, 2007), http://articles.latimes.com/2007/may/17/opinion/oe-obasogie17.

they differ between African Americans and first-generation African immigrants."[20]

Critical thinkers oppose explanations of racial disparities in health that rely on ideas of biological race not simply because they are convinced that empirical research cannot support them. (As critical race theorist Dorothy Roberts puts it: "It is implausible that one race of people evolved to have a genetic predisposition to heart failure, hypertension, infant mortality, diabetes, and asthma. There is no evolutionary theory that can explain why African ancestry would be genetically prone to practically every major common illness."[21]) They also oppose these explanations because they find them to be a dangerous distraction from the mechanisms that they believe actually explain why people of color are sicker and die earlier than their white counterparts.

When one is convinced that the poorer health of people of color is caused by structural factors—residential segregation and the inferior and unhealthy housing stock found in the neighborhoods that people of color call home, the clustering of environmental hazards in segregated neighborhoods of color, high unemployment rates, the unavailability of health insurance and quality health services—then any suggestion that their poorer health is caused by their *genes* sounds like an excuse not to address these large-scale contributors to morbidity and mortality. To critical scholars, genetic explanations of racial health disparities are no more than a cover for a distinctly *political* unwillingness to engage and change the social policies that make the country an unhealthy place for people of color. Roberts has made this argument quite forcefully in her scholarship. She writes, "Researchers still do not know why blacks get and die from heart failure at a much earlier age than whites. But if I were a scientist, I would start looking at the effects of young black men's seventy-five per cent chance of being incarcerated in some cities. Heart disease researchers should be more interested in the fact that black men are seven times more likely than whites to be imprisoned in this country than the less significant genetic differences many are so fixated on."[22]

In fact, if genetic differences between the races bear even a scintilla of responsibility for the racial disparities in health that are so well-documented, progressive scholars worry that these

[20] William W. Dressler, Kathryn S. Oths & Clarence C. Gravlee, *Race and Ethnicity in Public Health Research: Models to Explain Health Disparities*, 34 ANN. REV. ANTHROPOLOGY 231, 235–36 (2005).

[21] Dorothy E. Roberts, *What's Wrong with Race-Based Medicine? Genes, Drugs, and Health Disparities*, 12 MINN. J.L. SCI. & TECH. 1, 15 (2011) [hereinafter Roberts, *Race-Based Medicine*].

[22] *Id.* at 18–19.

differences may be taken to absolve society of responsibility for nonwhite people's poorer health. They worry that our energies will be drawn away from redistributing space, wealth, and opportunities such that people of color are not relegated to the bottom of social hierarchies; instead, our energies will be focused on developing medical treatments that can counteract the effects of racial minorities' unhealthy genes. They fear that society will be led to believe that the cure for racial minorities' elevated rates of morbidity and mortality involves these genetically-compromised folks simply taking care of themselves—taking their pills. The social arrangements that critical scholars believe actually bear the most responsibility for racial minorities' poorer health are not implicated in this technical cure.

Finally, for those who disapprove of the idea of post-racialism and its suggestion that the nation has entered a period wherein race is an insignificant fact of life, genetic explanations for racial disparities in health appear to be a convenient explanation for enduring racial inequality.[23] That is, few would deny that racial inequality endures in the present day; racial disparities in health are an instance of this enduring inequality. However, if we have entered a historical moment wherein race really does not matter—a post-racial time when race no longer plays the role that it did in previous eras in our nation's history, when it cruelly determined the content and trajectory of an individual's life—then *something* has to explain why racial groups are still socially, politically, and economically unequal to one another. Biological differences between the races supply that explanation. In identifying a cause for enduring racial inequality that is neither social nor political nor economic, biological race supports the post-racial sense that the nation, finally, has gotten beyond race.

Now, there is one species of the idea of biological race that progressive thinkers find intriguing: this is the possibility that social conditions have caused changes in gene expression. Socio-biological explanations for racial disparities in health will be explored later in the chapter.

2. *Culture*

It is undeniable that one's behavior affects one's health. There is a greater likelihood that a person who eats healthy foods and has high levels of physical activity in her daily life will have better health outcomes than a person who engages in different behaviors. Indeed, if a person eats fatty, high-sodium foods, drinks sugary beverages,

---

[23] For a cogent articulation of this argument, *see* DOROTHY ROBERTS, FATAL INVENTION: HOW SCIENCE, POLITICS, AND BIG BUSINESS RE-CREATE RACE IN THE TWENTY-FIRST CENTURY (2012) [hereinafter ROBERTS, FATAL INVENTION].

smokes cigarettes, and does not exercise, it is likely that she will have poor health. However, the undeniable truth that unhealthy behaviors lead to unhealthy outcomes might become more problematic when unhealthy behaviors are imagined to constitute a "culture" that explains racial disparities in health. Differently stated, critical thinkers are wary of arguments that racial minorities' "culture-bound lifestyle choices" lead them to engage in behaviors that compromise their health.[24]

One can hear cultural explanations of racial disparities in health ever so often. For example, there is an argument that the Tuskegee experiment[25] has led to a culture of distrust of physicians and other health care providers among black Americans; this culture is thought to have deleterious health consequences, as it leads black Americans to refuse to seek medical care when they ought to do so. Another example is the argument that "indigenous culture" leads the people steeped in it to consume excessive amounts of alcohol, which causes hypertension, stroke, liver disease, and an assortment of cancers. Another example is the argument that the foods that comprise the cultural repertoire of "soul food"—foods that black Americans are believed to eat because it is part of their "culture"—are the sugary or high-fat, high-sodium foods that lead to obesity, hypertension, and diabetes. One can hear this particular argument in a report on racial disparities in health authored by the Institute of Medicine [IOM]—a not-for-profit, non-governmental organization that is a division of the National Academy of Sciences.[26] (The IOM has since been renamed the Health and Medicine Division (HMD)). The report quotes an "African American patient" who recounts an experience that he had with his former primary care physician, who had diagnosed him with diabetes. "He said, 'I need to write this prescription for these pills, but you'll never take them and you'll come back and tell me you're still eating pig's feet and everything. . . . Then why do I still need to

---

[24] *See* Stephen B. Thomas et al., *Toward a Fourth Generation of Disparities Research to Achieve Health Equity*, 32 ANN. REV. PUB. HEALTH 399, 412 (2011).

[25] Beginning in the 1930s, the U.S. Public Health Service (USPHS) endeavored to study differences in how syphilis affected black and white persons. The hypothesis, which was based on ideas of biological race, was that syphilis would ravage the neurological systems of white persons while ravaging the cardiovascular systems of black persons. In an experiment that the USPHS conducted in conjunction with Tuskegee University, titled the "Study of Syphilis in the Untreated Negro Male," 600 poor, rural black men, two-thirds of whom had syphilis, were enrolled for analysis. The men were never told that they had syphilis. When it was discovered that penicillin could treat the disease, they were never told that there was a cure for their ailment, which ended up killing or maiming many of the study participants as well as their wives and children. Instead, the men were told that they had "bad blood." The experiment continued until the 1970s and ended only after a whistleblower exposed the operation. *See generally*, JAMES H. JONES, BAD BLOOD; THE TUSKEGEE SYPHILIS EXPERIMENT (2d ed. 1993).

[26] INST. OF MED., UNEQUAL TREATMENT, *supra* note 4.

write this prescription.' And I'm like, 'I don't eat pig's feet.' "[27] To this physician, his black American patient was so bound by his culture that he would continue culturally-dictated unhealthy behaviors despite hard evidence that they were compromising his health.

Critical thinkers dispute cultural explanations of racial health disparities on multiple fronts. First, they deny that culture is as fixed, unalterable, static, and constraining as these explanations imagine them to be. They note that when culture is imagined to be as deterministic as it must be if it is to explain the poorer states of health that people of color inhabit, the concept of culture functions to condemn groups of persons as effectively as did the race concept of yesteryear. As anthropologist Kamala Visweswaran explains,

> [B]ecause everyone 'talks culture' (that is to say, has access to the concept of culture), its relativist outlines have been increasingly filled by racist content. But does that not illustrate how culture has come to stand in for race? . . . [C]ulture is asked to do the work of race. This is perhaps what Walter Benn Michaels means by the title of his essay "Race as Culture." He writes, "Our sense of culture is characteristically meant to displace race, but . . . culture has turned out to be a way of continuing rather than repudiating racial thought."[28]

Second, progressive thinkers argue that it is distracting to conclude that when people of color engage in unhealthy behaviors, it is because their "culture made them do it." They say that this argument distracts from the reality that, oftentimes, the lives of people of color have been constrained in ways that make unhealthy behaviors the only option. In other words, these thinkers argue that the health behaviors of people of color may not be "chosen" in the usual sense of the term. If people of color do not go to the doctor as often as they should, it may be because they are uninsured or there are no health providers accessible to them. If people of color drink alcohol to excess, it may be because they are coping with poverty and racism. If people of color eat foods that are high in fat, salt, and sugar, it may be due to those foods being the only affordable options in their neighborhoods.

Third, progressive thinkers look to the droves of studies that show that behavioral differences cannot explain racial disparities in health. For example, one study shows that while more black people report being physically inactive when compared to their white counterparts, the risk of hypertension remained higher for black

---

[27] *Id.* at 90–91.

[28] Kamala Visweswaran, *Race and the Culture of Anthropology*, 100 AM. ANTHROPOLOGIST 70, 76 (1998).

people even after one controls for levels of physical inactivity.[29] While smoking increases the risk of a woman giving birth to an infant with a low birth weight, another study documents that there is no disparity in the rates at which black and white women smoke.[30] Similarly, another study shows that black people remain at increased risk of hypertension even when one controls for salt intake.[31] A group of scholars summarizes the literature succinctly: "As observed ten years ago,. . . health behaviors can be potent contributors to disease risk; there is little evidence, however, that alone or in combination health behaviors can explain racial and ethnic health disparities."[32]

* * *

There are several explanations for racial disparities in health that critical thinkers find convincing. The balance of the chapter details these favored accounts.

B. Accepted Theories

1. *Structural Explanations of Racial Disparities in Health*

As discussed above, social determinants of health are the conditions under which people live that affect their health. Critical scholars are committed to the idea that these structural factors—which include the availability of health care, quality schools and education, nonhazardous jobs, safe and secure housing, and nonviolent, unpolluted cities and communities—go a long way towards explaining the poorer health that people of color inhabit. There is a wealth of literature documenting that the environments in which racial minorities live, work, play, and age, and the relative lack of resources that are available in these environments, are all likely to compromise their health.

For example, residential segregation is quite high in the U.S., and it has resulted in poor people of color—especially poor black people—living in communities that are racially isolated from other communities. Further, the hypersegregated neighborhoods in which poor people of color live score poorly with respect to virtually all of the social determinants of health. The education that residents can access in the schools in these neighborhoods is deficient; secure,

---

[29] A. Colin Bell, Linda S. Adair & Barry M. Popkin, *Understanding the Role of Mediating Risk Factors and Proxy Effects in the Association Between Socio-economic Status and Untreated Hypertension*, 59 SOC. SCI. & MED. 275, 282 (2004).

[30] Charlotte A. Schoenborn et al., Dep't of Health & Human Servs., *Health Behaviors of Adults: United States, 1999–2001*, VITAL HEALTH STAT., Feb. 2004, at 1, 21.

[31] Steven G. Chrysant et al., *There are No Racial, Age, Sex, or Weight Differences in the Effect of Salt on Blood Pressure in Salt-Sensitive Hypertensive Patients*, 157 ARCHIVES INTERNAL MED. 2489 (1997).

[32] Dressler, Oths & Gravlee, *supra* note 20, at 238.

nonhazardous jobs that pay a livable wage are scarce; healthy foods are largely unavailable; quality health services are difficult to find; safe and clean housing is rare; the environment is riddled with pollutants and allergens; and social support is nonexistent or rapidly diminishing. Indeed, one study identifies residential racial segregation as the foundation of all racial disparities in health, proposing that a program to eliminate or reduce racial disparities would have to center integrating the communities that people of color call home.[33]

Consider as well that health insurance remains elusive for many. This is disproportionately true for people of color. Census data from 2010 showed that while "non-Hispanic White" persons made up 64.5% of the total population, they were only 47% of the uninsured population.[34] However, while black persons made up 12.7% of the total population, they constituted 16% of those who were uninsured. And most dramatically, while persons who were "Hispanic (any race)" comprised 16% of the total population, they were 30.7% of those who were uninsured. Contributing to racial disparities in health insurance coverage are laws that limit immigrants—even those who are lawfully present in the country—from accessing public health insurance. For example, the Affordable Care Act (ACA) includes restrictions that prevent lawfully present, documented immigrants from enrolling in Medicaid for five years after their arrival in the country.[35] (Texas, which has a significant immigrant population, does not allow lawful immigrants to enroll in the state's Medicaid program even after they have lived in the country for five years.[36]) And, as one might expect, undocumented immigrants oftentimes are completely prohibited from enrolling in states' Medicaid programs.[37] Further, the ACA prohibits undocumented immigrants from using health insurance exchanges to purchase private health insurance.[38] Because, persons from Central and South

---

[33] David R. Williams & Chiquita Collins, *Racial Residential Segregation: A Fundamental Cause of Racial Disparities in Health*, 116 PUB. HEALTH REP. 404 (2001).

[34] CARMEN DENAVAS-WALT, BERNADETTE D. PROCTOR & JESSICA C. SMITH, U.S. DEP'T OF COMMERCE, INCOME, POVERTY, AND HEALTH INSURANCE COVERAGE IN THE UNITED STATES: 2010 (2011), http://www.census.gov/prod/2011pubs/p60-239.pdf.

[35] *Immigrant Eligibility for Health Care Programs in the United States*, NAT'L CONFERENCE OF STATE LEGISLATURES (Oct. 19, 2017), http://www.ncsl.org/research/immigration/immigrant-eligibility-for-health-care-programs-in-the-united-states.aspx.

[36] ANNE DUNKELBERG, CTR. FOR PUB. POLICY PRIORITIES, IMMIGRANTS' ACCESS TO HEALTH CARE IN TEXAS: AN UPDATED LANDSCAPE (2016), https://forabettertexas.org/images/HW_2016_ImmigrantsAccess_FullReport.pdf.

[37] Elizabeth R. Chesler, Note, *Denying Undocumented Immigrants Access to Medicaid: A Denial of Their Equal Protection Rights?*, 17 B.U. PUB. INT. L.J. 255, 256 (2008).

[38] *Health Coverage for Immigrants*, HEALTHCARE.GOV, https://www.healthcare.gov/immigrants/coverage/ (last visited Aug. 2, 2018).

American make up a large portion of documented and undocumented immigrants in the country, Latinx persons are well-represented among those who find health insurance inaccessible by virtue of these rules. The disproportionate inability of people of color to access health insurance is a structural explanation of racial disparities in health.

Critical scholars underscore that there is nothing inevitable about resources having been distributed in a way that leaves people of color to inhabit the most polluted environments while also lacking the means, like health insurance, to protect their health. They find compelling the World Health Organization's position that the "unequal distribution of health-damaging experiences is not in any sense a 'natural' phenomenon but is the result of a toxic combination of poor social policies and [programs], unfair economic arrangements, and bad politics."[39]

2. *Individualist Explanations for Racial Disparities in Health*

a. Stress

Many researchers explain racial disparities in health by looking to the negative health effects produced by stress (which we might understand as an individualist cause of poor health outcomes inasmuch as it concerns an individual's physiological response to external stimuli). There has been some research supporting the proposition that stress contributes to disease and ill health. While some studies have concluded that stress does not have any long term effects on blood pressure, others have reached the opposite conclusion—affirming that stress can contribute to the development of hypertension.[40] Other studies show that women with high stress jobs give birth to lower birth weight babies than both those women whose jobs are not stressful and those women who can control certain aspects of their stressful jobs, like when and whether they can take a break.[41] Undisputed, though, is that individuals experiencing stress often cope by engaging in behaviors that can have negative effects on health—like drinking alcohol, smoking cigarettes, and using illicit drugs.[42]

If stress does, indeed, compromise health, then there is a possibility that it may contribute to racial disparities in health. This

---

[39] COMM'N ON SOC. DETERMINANTS OF HEALTH, WORLD HEALTH ORG., CLOSING THE GAP IN A GENERATION: HEALTH EQUITY THROUGH ACTION ON THE SOCIAL DETERMINANTS OF HEALTH, at 1 (2008).

[40] Chandra L. Ford et al., *Perceived Everyday Racism, Residential Segregation, and HIV Testing Among Patients at a Sexually Transmitted Disease Clinic*, 99 AM. J. PUB. HEALTH S137 (2009).

[41] *See* Dressler, Oths & Gravlee, *supra* note 20, at 240.

[42] *See* Williams & Collins, *supra* note 33, at 411.

would be true if racial minorities endure more stress in their daily lives, or over the course of their lives, than their white counterparts. Many scholars have been willing to make that argument, and they have identified several sources of stress that disproportionately, or uniquely, impact racial minorities.

The easiest and least contested source of stress is poverty. Poverty in most countries, including the U.S., invariably introduces the impoverished to a number of stressors—including financial uncertainty, state regulation by virtue of dependence on social welfare programs, violent neighborhoods, family separation due to the criminal justice system or the child welfare system, struggles with drug abuse and addiction, and chronic illness. Because racial minorities disproportionately bear the burdens of poverty, they disproportionately are exposed to these poverty-related stressors.

A source of stress around which there is more disagreement is racism—something with which racial minorities of all socioeconomic statuses have to contend, according to progressive race scholars. They argue that even wealthier people of color have to experience the physiological, emotional, and psychological responses to individual acts of racism, i.e., being racially profiled by the police, followed around stores while shopping, passed over for employment opportunities, promotions, and raises, and assumed to be the undeserving beneficiaries of affirmative action programs in the educational institutions that they attend and at the jobs that they secure. They also have to experience the physiological, emotional, and psychological responses to institutional/structural racism, which Chapter 7 defines and explores. Researchers in this vein argue that racism is a race-specific stress—something that white people, as a general matter, do not have to encounter regularly or at all. Moreover, it is something against which class privilege does not immunize wealthier people of color. Accordingly, these researchers advance the claim that stress might explain racial disparities in health, and it might explain the persistence of those disparities across income levels.

Another contested source of stress may be that associated with the phenomenon of "John Henryism." John Henry is the name of an American folk hero, a black "steel driving man" who hammered steel drills into rocks to assist in the construction of railroad tunnels. Legend has it that he was challenged to race a steam-powered hammer. John Henry won the race, besting the machine. However, he died soon after his victory from the stress that the effort placed on his heart.[43] "John Henryism" refers to a theory that people of color,

[43] The legend of John Henry has been the subject of many songs. The lyrics to the jazz standard vary, but all variations are quite poignant:

especially those who do not have class privilege, endure stresses attendant to attempts to overcome the various socioeconomic barriers that they face. Like the folk hero, these people of color die prematurely as a result of the effort involved in beating forces that are bigger and more powerful than them.[44]

b. Provider Bias

In 2005, the IOM (which is now the HMD) released a report documenting that the poverty in which black people disproportionately live cannot account for black people being sicker and dying younger than their white complements. The IOM found that people of color receive lower-quality health care than white people—even when one controls for insurance status, income, age, and severity of condition.[45] By "lower quality health care," the IOM

Now the captain he said to John Henry,
"I'm gonna bring that steam drill around,
I'm gonna bring that steam drill out on these tracks,
I'm gonna knock that steel on down, God, God,
I'm gonna knock that steel down."

John Henry told his captain
"Lord a man ain't nothin' but a man,
But before I let that steam drill beat me down,
I'm gonna die with a hammer in my hand, Lord, Lord,
I'll die with a hammer in my hand."

John Henry driving on the right side,
That steam drill driving on the left,
Says, "Fore I let your steam drill beat me down,
I'm gonna hammer myself to death, Lord, Lord,
I'll hammer my fool self to death."

. . .

John Henry he hammered in the mountains,
His hammer was striking fire,
But he worked so hard;
It broke his heart,
John Henry laid down his hammer and died, Lord Lord,
John Henry laid down his hammer and died.

See, e.g., NORM COHEN, LONG STEEL RAIL: THE RAILROAD IN AMERICAN FOLKSONG 61–63 (2000).

[44] Some studies dispute whether "John Henryism" can explain elevated morbidity and mortality among people of color. One study shows that when individuals perceived racism on their jobs and directly challenged it, they had lower systolic blood pressure measurements than those who either had no reactions to perceived racism or who suppressed those reactions. Ford et al., *supra* note 40, at S137. "John Henryism" would suggest the opposite result; it would predict that those who attempted to overcome racism by challenging it would have higher blood pressures.

[45] INST. OF MED., ADDRESSING RACIAL AND ETHNIC HEALTH CARE DISPARITIES: WHERE DO WE GO FROM HERE?, at 3 (2005).

meant the concrete, inferior care that physicians give their black patients. The IOM reported that minority persons are less like than white persons to be given appropriate cardiac care, to receive kidney dialysis or transplants, and to receive the best treatments for stroke, cancer, or AIDS. It concluded by describing an "uncomfortable reality": "some people in the United States were more likely to die from cancer, heart disease, and diabetes simply because of their race or ethnicity, not just because they lack access to health care."[46]

Many studies have buttressed the IOM's findings by documenting that providers are less likely to prescribe and deliver effective treatments to people of color when compared to their white counterparts—even after controlling for characteristics like class, health behaviors, comorbidities, and access to health insurance and health care services. One study of four hundred hospitals in the U.S. showed that black patients suffering from heart disease received older, cheaper, and more conservative treatments while their white counterparts received newer, more expensive, and more invasive therapies.[47] For example, black patients were less likely to receive coronary bypass operations and angiography.[48] And after surgery, they tend to be discharged from the hospital earlier than white patients—at a stage in their recovery when discharge is inappropriate.[49] What is true with respect to heart disease is true with regard to other illnesses. Consider breast cancer. Studies have shown that black women are less likely than white women to receive radiation therapy in conjunction with a mastectomy.[50] In fact, they are less likely to receive mastectomies.[51] Consider end-stage renal disease. Writes one scholar, "Researchers have found that blacks are less likely than whites to be informed about [kidney] transplant treatment, referred for transplant evaluation, or placed on transplant waiting lists."[52] Perhaps even more disturbing is that black patients are *more likely* to receive *less desirable* treatments. For example, the rates at which black patients have their limbs amputated and are castrated are higher than those for white

---

[46] *Id.*

[47] *See* DAYNA BOWEN MATTHEW, JUST MEDICINE: A CURE FOR RACIAL INEQUALITY IN AMERICAN HEALTH CARE 58 (2015).

[48] *See* Edward L. Hannan et al., *Access to Coronary Artery Bypass Surgery by Race/Ethnicity and Gender among Patients Who are Appropriate for Surgery*, 37 MED. CARE 68, 75 (1999).

[49] *See* Katherine L. Kahn, *Health Care for Black and Poor Hospitalized Medicare Patients*, 271 J. AM. MED. ASS'N. 1169, 1171 (1994).

[50] *See* Nina A. Bickell et al., *Missed Opportunities: Racial Disparities in Adjuvant Breast Cancer Treatment*, 24 J. CLINICAL ONCOLOGY 1357, 1358 (2006).

[51] *See* Vickie L. Shavers & Martin K. Brown, *Racial and Ethnic Disparities in the Receipt of Cancer Treatment*, 94 J. NAT'L CANCER INST. 334 (2002).

[52] MATTHEW, *supra* note 47, at 59.

patients.[53] Additionally, black patients suffering from bipolar disorder are more likely to be treated with antipsychotics despite evidence that these medications have long-term negative effects and are not a particularly effective method for treating bipolar disorder.[54]

In light of these studies, some scholars have concluded that racial disparities in health can be explained by looking to the individuals who are choosing not to prescribe the most effective health- and life-conserving treatments to racial minorities. The argument is that if people of color are sicker and are dying at younger ages than white people, this may be because physicians have racial biases. Their biases cause them to give their patients of color inferior health care and, in so doing, contribute to higher rates of morbidity and mortality among people of color.

If physicians harbor racial biases, these biases can either be consciously-held or unconsciously-held. Dayna Bowen Matthew—who has done the most work of late around the idea that unconscious biases held by health care providers might explain racial disparities in health[55]—notes that physicians are like the general public inasmuch as precious few admit to harboring negative attitudes about any particular racial group. (And we probably do not gain much from disbelieving their accounts.) For this reason, Matthew concludes that physicians' *explicit* racial biases likely cannot account for racial disparities in health. If physicians' choices around which treatments to prescribe are harming their patients of color, it is unlikely that physicians are intentionally doing so.

However, Matthew notes that there is little reason to believe that physicians have not been exposed to the negative discourses and narratives about racial minorities that circulate in society—discourses and narratives that become the stuff of unconscious negative attitudes about racial groups. That is, Matthew proposes that physicians, like the rest of the American public, have *implicit* biases. They have views about racial minorities of which they are not consciously aware—views that lead them to make unintentional, and ultimately harmful, judgments about the care that they give people of color. Matthew observes that when physicians were given the Implicit Association Test ("IAT")—a test, discussed in Chapter 8, that purports to measure test takers' implicit biases by asking them to link images of black and white faces with pleasant and unpleasant words under intense time constraints—they tend to associate white faces and pleasant words more easily than black faces and pleasant

---

[53] *See id.* at 61.

[54] *See, e.g.*, David E. Fleck et al., *Differential Prescription of Maintenance Antipsychotics to African American and White Patients with New-Onset Bipolar Disorder*, 63 J. CLINICAL PSYCHIATRY 658 (2002).

[55] MATTHEW, *supra* note 47, at 49.

words. Indeed, research appears to show that these anti-black/pro-white implicit biases are as prevalent among providers as they are among the general population. This leads Matthew to conclude that physicians' implicit racial biases can account for the inferior health care that the studies discussed above document. As such, physicians' implicit racial biases can help explain racial disparities in health.

A number of experiments support her claim. For example, one study showed that physicians whose IAT tests revealed them to harbor pro-white implicit biases were more likely to prescribe pain medications to white patients than to black patients.[56] Another study administered the IAT to physicians and then asked them whether they would prescribe thrombolysis—an aggressive, yet effective treatment for coronary artery disease—to patients presenting with a range of symptoms for the disease. The experiment revealed that physicians that the IAT tests revealed to harbor anti-black implicit biases were *less likely* to prescribe thrombolysis to black patients and *more likely* to prescribe these same treatments to white patients.[57]

It is worth noting that some progressive race scholars are circumspect about the claim that implicit biases are responsible for racial disparities in health. This is due to their fear that people will disbelieve that individualist and structural mechanisms can operate simultaneously. They worry that if we, as a society, turn our attention to the possibility that providers' implicit racial biases are contributing to excess morbidity and mortality among people of color, it may lead us to ignore the structures, discussed above, that progressive scholars are convinced also compromise the health of people of color.

c. Socio-Biological Explanations

Epigenetics involves changes in the expression of genes that do not involve a transformation of the gene sequence itself.[58] Thus, epigenetics concerns changes in *phenotype* without a corresponding change in *genotype*. The idea behind epigenetics is that several factors, including the environment, can cause genes to be expressed differently without the genes having undergone a mutation. Further, and fascinatingly, individuals who have been exposed to environments that have caused changes in their gene expression—that is, their *epigenome*—may pass these epigenetic changes along to the children. As a result, it only slightly overstates the case to say that children can be exposed to the environments that their parents

---

[56] *See id.* at 69.

[57] *Id.* at 66.

[58] Cathérine Dupont, D. Randall Armant & Carol A. Brenner, *Epigenetics: Definition, Mechanisms and Clinical Perspective*, 27 SEMINARS IN REPROD. MED. 351, 351 (2009).

and grandparents lived. Epigenetics is the medium for that environmental exposure.

One study showed that the children born to women who survived the Dutch famine of 1944–1945 were more likely to develop coronary heart disease and obesity later in life.[59] The epigenetic explanation for this phenomenon is that the famine caused changes in the epigenome of the survivors; that is, the famine caused survivors' genes to be expressed differently. Although female survivors may not have been pregnant during the famine, their phenotype nevertheless had been altered. The women would eventually pass down this environmentally-transformed phenotype to their children. The phenotype ultimately contributed to the elevated rates of morbidity found in their children. Another study showed that the sons born to men who started smoking before the age of eleven had a greater body mass index.[60] Another study showed that women who were exposed to diethylstilbestrol (DES), a synthetic form of the estrogen hormone once used to prevent miscarriage, gave birth to daughters with elevated rates of reproductive disorders. Moreover, these daughters ultimately gave birth to *another generation of daughters* with elevated rates of reproductive disorders. Essentially, women's environments impacted their grandchildren. Again, epigenetics is the means for transmitting these trans-generational impacts.

The field of epigenetics is important to scholars interested in racial disparities in health because it may explain why poor health has persisted across generations in people of color. Epigenetics suggests that racial minorities living today may have inherited epigenomes that reflect the overtly hostile environments that people of color had to inhabit in times past—when they were the subjects of chattel slavery, internment, lynch mobs, forced removals and relocations to reservations, and the banal brutality of Jim Crow.

For example, consider that racial disparities in infant mortality rates persist across income levels above. (Indeed, as discussed above, racial disparities in infant mortality increase as one moves up the socioeconomic ladder.) Epigenetics might explain this phenomenon. Could it be that the unyieldingly antagonistic environments in which black people lived in the decades that preceded the civil rights era caused changes in their epigenomes? Could it be that these epigenetic changes—which might cause morbidity and mortality in the infants born with these genetic expressions—have been passed down over the generations, elevating the rates at which black infants die in the

---

[59] *See* Rebecca C. Painter, Tessa J. Roseboom & Otto P. Bleker, *Prenatal Exposure to the Dutch Famine and Disease in Later Life: An Overview*, 20 REPROD. TOXICOLOGY 345, 348 (2005).

[60] *See* Marcus E. Pembrey et al., *Sex-Specific, Male Line Transgenerational Responses in Humans*, 14 EUR. J. HUM. GENETICS 159 (2006).

present? Could epigenetics explain why wealthier black women's class privilege cannot protect the health of the infants that they birth?

While epigenetics is a burgeoning field that may help us understand the persistent nature of racial disparities in health, some critical scholars sound a warning about the endeavor. Roberts is one such scholar. She cautions that epigenetic understandings of racial minorities' compromised health may slip into arguments about racial minorities' genetic inferiority. She counsels that

> the line between the genome and the epigenome can seem blurred. When scientists write that epigenetic effects of racial discrimination are durable across generations, it sounds perilously close to biological theories of race. The point of this research should not be to consign another generation to the biological fallout of past discrimination. To the contrary, its hopeful message is that epigenetic changes are caused by the environment and therefore can be environmentally interrupted so that future generations can enjoy better health.[61]

III. Questions and Discussion

1. Why do you think other industrialized nations—like France, Japan, the United Kingdom, and New Zealand—have health care systems that are superior, when measured in terms of health care spending and outcomes, to the one found in the U.S.? Why do you think the U.S. has not committed itself to beating its peer nations in this regard? What is stopping it from doing better?

2. The "thrifty gene" explanation for higher rates of hypertension among African-Americans is quite popular. Indeed, Oprah Winfrey once touted it on a segment of her widely-watched talk show in which a physician, Dr. Mehmet Oz, answered audience members' burning health questions.[62] However, as discussed above, scientists who specialize in theories of gene selection have rejected the "thrifty gene" hypothesis. Nevertheless, it endures in popular thought. As Dressler and his coauthors describe it, "What is striking, however, is its wide acceptance based on virtually no empirical evidence."[63] What do you think explains the popularity of the "thrifty gene" explanation of racial disparities among rates of hypertension? Is its popularity a cause for concern? If so, what can be done to defeat it?

---

61 ROBERTS, FATAL INVENTION, *supra* note 23, at 144.

62 Obasogie, *supra* note 19.

63 Dressler, Oths & Gravlee, *supra* note 20, at 236.

3. In 2005, BiDil become the first drug that the FDA approved for use by a specific racial group. The manufacturers and marketers of BiDil, a combination of two generic drugs (hydralazine and isosorbide dinitrate) that widens blood vessels in the heart and could reduce mortality in people suffering from congestive heart failure, argued that the medicine worked better with African Americans than with any other racial group. The FDA accepted the claim, paving the way for the first race-specific medicine to hit the market. However, notably, the clinical trials that purported to prove the race-specific efficacy of BiDil could not say anything about "whether BiDil works differently or better with African Americans than with other groups because the trial enrolled *only* African Americans. . . . Without a comparison population there can be no scientific basis for a claim of differential efficacy based on race."[64] Indeed, no physician, biologist, or geneticist could explain just *why* BiDil purportedly worked better with African Americans than with other racial groups. In the absence of an empirically proven explanation, people hypothesized that African Americans possessed a gene with which BiDil acted differently and more effectively. Thus, the FDA hearings are filled with testimony like that of Steve Nissen, the chair of the Cardiovascular and Renal Drugs Advisory Committee, who claimed, in line with the "thrifty gene" hypothesis, that African Americans have inherited genes from their African ancestors that increase the amount of salt that they retain relative to white people.[65] BiDil, he argued, worked better with the race-specific biology produced by these race-specific genes. The company holding the patent to BiDil, NitroMed, made similar arguments elsewhere. In a press release, NitroMed argued that racial disparities in rates of death due to congestive heart failure "may be due in part to ethnic differences in the underlying pathophysiology of heart failure."[66] And in 2007, in an article published in the *Annals of Internal Medicine*, the FDA defended its approval of BiDil, writing, "We hope that further research elucidates the genetic or other factors that predict the usefulness of hydralazine hydrochloride-isosorbide dinitrate."[67]

But, BiDil *did* prevent deaths in black persons suffering from congestive heart failure. While there was no evidence that it was *more* effective in black persons, no one disputed its simple efficacy in black persons. Although the science did not support the claim that

---

[64] *See* Jonathan Kahn, *Exploiting Race in Drug Development: BiDil's Interim Model of Pharmacogenomics*, 38 SOC. STUD. SCI. 737, 739 (2008).

[65] *See* Susan M. Reverby, *"Special Treatment": BiDil, Tuskegee, and the Logic of Race*, 36 J.L. MED. & ETHICS 478, 481 (2008).

[66] Roberts, *Race-Based Medicine*, *supra* note 21, at 4.

[67] Dorothy Roberts, *The Social Immorality of Health in the Gene Age: Race, Disability, and Inequality*, *in* AGAINST HEALTH: HOW HEALTH BECAME THE NEW MORALITY 63 (Jonathan Metzl & Anna Kirkland eds., 2010).

BiDil worked *better* in black people, should the FDA have approved it because it could, and did, save black people's lives? Or should the FDA have rejected it because the science did not support its manufacturer's claims about the drug's race-specificity? Note that if the FDA refused to approve BiDil, the drug would have been inaccessible to everyone—including black people, who suffer elevated rates of congestive health failure.

4. The opioid epidemic has become a severe public health problem. In 2016, over 17,000 people died after overdosing on prescription pain relievers, and close to 16,000 people died after overdosing on heroin.[68] These numbers mean that 90 people died from an overdose related to opioids *every day* in 2016.

Progressive race scholars direct their attention to the racial aspects of the crisis. They note that it has disproportionately affected white people and white communities because, as noted above, physicians are more likely to prescribe them strong pain medications relative to people of color—even when the latter have the same access to health insurance, present with the same symptoms, and report the same level of pain.[69] Scholars have offered that the reason for this phenomenon is doctors' beliefs that black patients "are abusing prescription medication, diverting medication to the black-market, overstating symptoms, or failing to comply with protocols for taking medications or recuperating."[70]

Moreover, progressive thinkers are interested in how the opioid crisis's effect on middle-class, white communities has influenced the approach that cities, states, and the nation, more generally, have taken to address it. As the New York Times reports,

> When the nation's long-running war against drugs was defined by the crack epidemic and based in poor, predominantly black urban areas, the public response was defined by zero tolerance and stiff prison sentences. But today's heroin crisis is different. While heroin use has climbed among all demographic groups, it has skyrocketed among whites; nearly 90 percent of those who tried heroin for the first time in the last decade were white. And the growing army of families of those lost to heroin—many of them in the suburbs and small towns—are now using their influence, anger and grief to cushion the country's approach

---

[68] *See* Puja Seth et al., *Overdose Deaths Involving Opioids, Cocaine, and Psychostimulants—United States 2015–2016*, 67 MORBIDITY & MORTALITY WKLY. REP. 349, 352, 354, https://www.cdc.gov/mmwr/volumes/67/wr/pdfs/mm6712a1-H.pdf.

[69] Lior Jacob Strahilevitz, *Reputation Nation: Law in an Era of Ubiquitous Personal Information*, 102 NW. U. L. REV. 1667, 1696 (2008).

[70] *Id.* at 1697.

> to drugs, from altering the language around addiction to prodding government to treat it not as a crime, but as a disease.[71]

Can you think of a legitimate justification for addressing crack cocaine addiction through the criminal justice system and opioid addiction through alternative, non-punitive systems? What does racial justice look like in the context of the opioid epidemic? Does it look like more punishment of white people who are addicted to opioids? Does it look like less punishment of people of color who are addicted to other controlled substances?

5. As discussed above, lack of access to health insurance and health care is an important contributor to racial disparities in health. Should universal health care—whether it is provided through the ACA or through alternative legislation—be understood as an issue of racial justice? What are the benefits of framing it in those terms? What are the dangers?

---

[71] Katharine Q. Seelye, *In Heroin Crisis, White Families Seek Gentler War on Drugs*, N.Y. TIMES (Oct. 30, 2015), https://www.nytimes.com/2015/10/31/us/heroin-war-on-drugs-parents.html.

Chapter 17

AFFIRMATIVE ACTION

It understates the case to describe race-based affirmative action as a controversial issue in the U.S. today. Some passionately champion race-conscious admissions and hiring programs, believing them to be an essential part of the fight to undo the effects of the country's lamentable racial past. Folks in this camp conceptualize such efforts as necessary elements of a multifaceted program to bring historically disadvantaged racial groups into the body politic as equals. Others passionately oppose race-based affirmative action, believing it to be an immoral, divisive technique that is rife with irony: in order to cure the problem of racial discrimination against black, Latinx, and indigenous people, institutions propose to practice racial discrimination against white and Asian people.

On the whole, progressive race scholars tend to defend race-based affirmative action programs and policies, understanding them as the *least* that public and private actors could do to help produce a racially just society. Unsurprisingly, however, progressive thinkers are not *uncritical* of race-based affirmative action: they remain aware of the possibility that it might help to legitimate the exclusionary pathways that the powerful and privileged in society have used to keep power and privilege inaccessible to all but the precious few.

I. Historical Origins of Race-Based Affirmative Action

The Civil Rights Movement of the 1950s and 1960s is rightfully understood as the birthplace of race-based affirmative action. While those who participated in this social movement recognized that intentional racial discrimination was a key mechanism in the relegation of black people to the bottom of social, cultural, political, and economic hierarchies, they appreciated that other processes functioned to produce the same results. Indeed, Dr. Martin Luther King, Jr. argued that even if intentional racial discrimination was never again practiced in the country, "Black poverty, the 'historic and institutionalized consequences of color,' would continue."[1] Hence, thinkers of the day understood that *formal* legal equality for black

---

[1] Tomiko Brown-Nagin, *Rethinking Proxies for Disadvantage in Higher Education: A First Generation Students' Project*, 2014 U. CHI. LEGAL F. 433, 438 (2014).

people would not result in *substantive* equality for this historically disadvantaged group.

Accordingly, activists certainly celebrated the passage of the Civil Rights Act of 1964 ["CRA"], which outlawed race-based discrimination (as well as discrimination on the basis of color, religion, sex, and national origin) in significant areas of American life. However, they conceptualized the CRA as a necessary, but not sufficient, step in the fight for racial justice. They believed that the nation also needed to take steps to dismantle the race-neutral processes that destroyed black people's ability to enter, and succeed in, the labor market. They were convinced that exclusion from job opportunities were "as much a function of the way in which an employer traditionally did business as of an intent to discriminate. The networks ordinarily tapped, the tests ordinarily used might generate exclusion as effectively as intentional discrimination. Nondiscrimination was not enough. Nondiscrimination by an employer or by a college might still leave many blacks and minorities marginalized, outside the mainstream, and embittered candidates collectively for riots, or individually, for criminal acts."[2]

The Equal Opportunity Act ["EOA"], which was the legislative piece of President Lyndon B. Johnson's "War on Poverty," complemented the CRA inasmuch as the EOA implemented job training and social welfare programs that were designed to help the poor acquire skills that could help them participate in the labor market and, ideally, emerge from poverty.[3] But, still, many felt that the programs that the EOA implemented were incapable of accomplishing what civil rights activists demanded: full-throated racial justice. They proposed that race-based affirmative action programs were the means for fulfilling that demand. It was these programs to which President Johnson averted in a speech on Howard University's campus in June 1965, in which he argued that it was time for the country to enter the "next and the more profound stage in the battle for civil rights."[4]

Critical thinkers emphasize affirmative action's origins in the Civil Rights Movement because they reject depictions of these programs as handouts from kind-hearted, benevolent white people to agency-deprived, powerless black people. For example, in his vigorous dissent from the Court's approval of the University of

---

[2] John R. Howard, *Affirmative Action in Historical Perspective, in* AFFIRMATIVE ACTION'S TESTAMENT OF HOPE 19, 30 (Mildred Garcia ed., 1997).

[3] Some of the programs that the EOA made possible were Head Start for preschool children, Upward Bound for high school students entering college, and work study programs for those already enrolled in college.

[4] Lyndon B. Johnson, Commencement Address at Howard University (June 4, 1965).

Michigan Law School's affirmative action program in *Grutter v. Bollinger*, Justice Clarence Thomas describes the program at issue as one that has been dreamed up by a "cognoscenti"; he claims that it amounts to nothing more than a "social experiment[ ] on other people's children."[5] Critical scholars dispute this characterization of affirmative action. Inasmuch as civil rights activists involved in one of the country's most powerful social movements *demanded* affirmative action, progressive theorists argue that these programs ought not to be understood as something that generous and altruistic white people have gifted to the historically disadvantaged. Rather, they say, it is something that the historically disadvantaged *exacted* from the powerful in this country. These thinkers propose that affirmative action is rightfully conceptualized as something that the marginalized has forced power to concede. As prominent critical race theorist Charles Lawrence has written:

> The original vision of affirmative action proceeded from the perspective of the subordinated. [When t]he students and community activists who fought for affirmative action in the 1960s and '70s . . . demanded affirmative action—when they sat-in and sued and took over buildings and went on hunger strikes and closed down universities—they sought redress for their communities."[6]

II. The (Tenuous) Constitutionality of Race-Based Affirmative Action

A. *Regents of the University of California v. Bakke*[7] (1978)

Bakke was the first case in which the Court ruled on the legality of a voluntarily-initiated race-based affirmative action program. The case involved the Medical School of the University of California at Davis ["the Medical School"]. The Medical School implemented a race-conscious admissions program after it became apparent that racial minorities would be underrepresented at the school if it evaluated all applicants according to traditional standards of merit. The program required the school to reserve sixteen out of the 100 seats in the incoming class for individuals belonging to one of four designated groups: "Blacks," "Chicanos," "Asians," and "American Indians." After Alan Bakke, a white applicant, was denied admission to the school, he challenged the program on statutory grounds (i.e.,

---

5 Grutter v. Bollinger, 539 U.S. 306, 350, 372 (2003) (Thomas, J., dissenting).

6 Charles R. Lawrence III, *Two Views of the River: A Critique of the Liberal Defense of Affirmative Action*, 101 COLUM. L. REV. 928, 951–52 (2001).

7 Regents of Univ. of Cal. v. Bakke, 438 U.S. 265 (1978).

Title VI of the CRA) and constitutional grounds (i.e., the Equal Protection Clause of the Fourteenth Amendment).

In a fractured opinion, the Court struck down the program. Four justices voted to uphold it, finding it to be consistent with the demands of the Constitution and Title VI.[8] Five justices, however, voted to strike it down: four justices found it to be inconsistent with the demands of Title VI, and one justice, Justice Powell, found it to be inconsistent with the demands of the Constitution. Justice Powell's opinion in the case—an opinion onto which no other Justice signed—has come to shape the discourse around race-based affirmative action.

Justice Powell began by noting that the Equal Protection Clause "cannot mean one thing when applied to one individual and something else when applied to a person of another color."[9] This statement was a rejection of the dissenters' view that laws that burden historically advantaged racial groups (i.e., white people) are more constitutionally permissible than laws that burden historically disadvantaged groups (i.e., black, Latinx, indigenous people). The dissenters argued that "benign" uses of race—those uses that are designed to *include* racial minorities in institutions from which they have been excluded historically—should be reviewed with an intermediate scrutiny. This test would designate as constitutional those laws that bear a "substantial" relationship to an "important" governmental interest. The intermediate scrutiny test would be easier to satisfy than the test that the dissenters proposed for "invidious" uses of race—those uses that are designed to *exclude* racial minorities from institutions that they have been unable to access historically. The dissenters proposed using strict scrutiny on "invidious" uses of race, which would find constitutional only those laws that are "narrowly tailored" to achieve a "compelling" governmental interest.

The dissenters argued that while strict scrutiny was appropriate for laws that burdened racial minorities, it was inappropriate for laws that burdened white people, as the courts had been using strict scrutiny to protect groups that were unable to protect themselves. The dissenters asserted that the case law established that strict scrutiny was to be used to protect groups that had "traditional indicia of suspectness," i.e., groups that had been "saddled with such disabilities, or subjected to such a history of purposeful unequal

---

[8] Title VI prohibits discrimination "on the ground of race, color, or national origin" in institutions receiving federal financial assistance. Title VI of the Civil Rights Act of 1964, 42 U.S.C. § 2000d (1964). Accordingly, both Title VI and the Constitution constrain state-run schools that receive significant federal funds, like the schools in the University of California system.

[9] *Bakke*, 438 U.S. at 289–90.

treatment, or relegated to such a position of political powerlessness as to command extraordinary protection from the majoritarian political process."[10] Because white people had no such disabilities, had no history of purposeful unequal treatment, and were perfectly capable of defending themselves in the majoritarian political process, they did not need courts to rigorously review laws that burdened them.

Justice Powell rejected the dissenters' approach, arguing that both "benign" and "invidious" uses of race ought to be reviewed with strict scrutiny. He admitted that the drafters of the Equal Protection Clause had the intention of making one specific racial minority group—African Americans, who had recently been held as slaves—equal to the white majority. However, he claimed that the racial geography of the country had changed since the ratification of the Fourteenth Amendment. The shift in racial demographics made it inappropriate to speak of a "white majority." In Powell's view, the white majority was, in fact, a grouping that consisted of various minority groups: the Irish, the German, the Italian, the Russian, etc. According to Powell, all of the various minority groups, both white and nonwhite, were similarly situated to one another; they were as likely to be the perpetrators of racial discrimination as they were to be the victims of racial discrimination. Powell surmised that because every minority group could be oppressed on the basis of race, the Equal Protection Clause must be applied rigorously to all racial classifications, without respect to which racial groups are benefitted and which are burdened.

Having rejected the "benign" versus "invidious" schema that the dissent proposed, and having determined that strict scrutiny was the appropriate level of review for *all* laws containing a racial classification, Powell then assessed which, if any, of the interests that the Medical School's affirmative action program pursued was "compelling" enough to satisfy strict scrutiny. The Medical School had claimed that its program furthered four interests: it increased the number of racial minorities in medical schools and the medical profession; it addressed past societal discrimination; it increased the number of doctors willing to serve underserved communities, and it "obtain[ed] the educational benefits that flow from an ethnically diverse student body."[11]

Powell quickly dismissed the asserted interest in increasing the number of racial minorities in medical schools and in the medical profession, declaring that "[p]referring members of any one group for

---

[10] *Id.* at 357.

[11] *Id.* at 306.

no reason other than race or ethnic origin is discrimination for its own sake. This the Constitution forbids."[12]

Powell also denied that a governmental interest in remedying the effects of past societal discrimination was a compelling one. He observed that the notion of past societal discrimination was an "amorphous concept of past injury that may be ageless in its reach into the past."[13] He was concerned that in attempting to remedy this nebulous harm, numerous white persons who had not engaged in any discriminatory behavior would be injured. In order to avoid harming this class, Powell interpreted the Constitution to forbid states from attempting to make whole another class: racial minorities who had been wrongfully excluded from the avenues to upward social and economic mobility.

Powell went on to deny that the interest in increasing the number of physicians who will work in underserved communities was compelling. He thought it improper to assume that simply because a student is a racial minority, she will go on to serve racial minorities. He disbelieved that medical schools "must prefer members of particular ethnic groups over all other individuals in order to promote better health-care delivery to deprived citizens."[14]

However, it was the interest in obtaining the educational benefits produced by a racially diverse student body that most aligned with Powell's sense of what was compelling. Powell concluded that the "robust exchange of ideas" present in racially diverse classes of students was "of paramount importance."[15]

Yet, while Powell believed that the Medical School's affirmative action plan could be constitutionally defended on the grounds of diversity, he disbelieved that it pursued the benefits of diversity in a constitutionally permissible manner. That is, he believed that a quota—reserving a set number of seats in an incoming class for students from historically disadvantaged groups—was not a narrowly-tailored means of accomplishing the compelling end of diversity. On the question of what form an affirmative action program must take to satisfy his vision of narrow tailoring, he looked to Harvard University's admissions plan. Under this plan, racial minority status was just one of many elements to which an admissions office could give favorable consideration when reviewing an applicant's file. Powell approvingly quoted a description of the Harvard Plan, noting that "the race of an applicant may tip the balance in his favor just as geographic origin or a life spent on a farm

[12] *Id.* at 307.

[13] *Id.*

[14] *Id.* at 311.

[15] *Id.* at 313.

may tip the balance in other candidates' cases. A farm boy from Idaho can bring something to Harvard College that a Bostonian cannot offer. Similarly, a black student can usually bring something that a white person cannot offer."[16] The Harvard Plan considered racial minority status—and other characteristics, like having lived in a rural part of the country—to be a "plus" in an applicant's file. This "plus" system was attractive to Powell because it did not "insulate the individual from comparison with all other candidates for the available seats," as would a quota system.[17] Unlike the quota system, the Harvard Plan, in Powell's view, treated "each applicant as an individual in the admissions process."[18]

Because there was no majority opinion in *Bakke*, the question of the appropriate level of review for "benign" uses of race remained open after the case. Further, because no other Justice signed on to Justice Powell's opinion, there were disputes about whether it was binding precedent in the years following *Bakke*. In 1996, the Fifth Circuit declared in *Hopwood v. Texas*[19] that Powell's opinion in *Bakke* was not binding, and it went on to strike down the University of Texas's affirmative action program. It was not until 2003, in the Court's decision in *Grutter v. Bollinger*, that Justice Powell's views on diversity in higher education would come to receive the blessing of a majority of the Court.

B. *Adarand Constructors v. Peña*[20] (1995)

In *Adarand*, the Court struck down a federal affirmative action program that offered additional compensation to prime contractors who subcontracted with minority-owned businesses. The case marked the beginning of the modern era of race jurisprudence, wherein the Court interprets the Equal Protection Clause as presupposing an equivalence between historically advantaged racial groups and their historically disadvantaged counterparts. Justice Thomas made this principle clear in a separate concurrence, in which he asserted that there was a "moral and constitutional equivalence between laws designed to subjugate a race and those that distribute benefits on the basis of race in order to foster some current notion of equality."[21] Justice Stevens disputed this principle in his dissent, writing:

> There is no moral or constitutional equivalence between a policy that is designed to perpetuate a caste system and one

---

16 *Id.* at 316.

17 *Id.* at 317.

18 *Id.* at 318.

19 Hopwood v. Texas, 78 F.3d 932 (5th Cir. 1996).

20 Adarand Constructors, Inc. v. Peña, 515 U.S. 200 (1995).

21 *Id.* at 240 (Thomas, J., concurring).

> that seeks to eradicate racial subordination. Invidious discrimination is an engine of oppression, subjugating a disfavored group to enhance or maintain the power of the majority. Remedial race-based preferences reflect the opposite impulse: a desire to foster equality in society. . . . The consistency that the Court espouses would disregard the difference between a 'No Trespassing' sign and a welcome mat. It would treat a Dixiecrat Senator's decision to vote against Thurgood Marshall's confirmation in order to keep African Americans off the Supreme Court as on a par with President Johnson's evaluation of his nominee's race as a positive factor. It would equate a law that made black citizens ineligible for military service with a program aimed at recruiting black soldiers. An attempt by the majority to exclude members of a minority race from a regulated market is fundamentally different from a subsidy that enables a relatively small group of newcomers to enter that market.[22]

While the *Adarand* decision answered the question of what level of scrutiny was appropriate for laws containing a benign racial classification—"Strict!," said the Court—it did not answer the question of whether the pursuit of racial diversity was a compelling enough interest to satisfy the demands of the prescribed scrutiny. Specifically, it remained unclear whether a majority of the Court would agree with Justice Powell's position in *Bakke* that the educational benefits that come from student body diversity was a compelling governmental interest such that the government's narrow-tailored pursuit of it could satisfy the demands of the Equal Protection Clause. A majority of the Court would answer that question in the affirmative eight years later.

C. *Grutter v. Bollinger/Gratz v. Bollinger*[23] (2003)

Grutter and *Gratz* both concerned affirmative action in university admissions. *Grutter* involved the race conscious admissions program that the University of Michigan Law School ["the Law School"] had implemented—a program that closely mirrored the Harvard Plan approvingly referenced in Justice Powell's lone opinion in *Bakke*. The Law School defended its program under the banner of diversity, asserting that its race consciousness during the admissions process was in active pursuit of the educational benefits that flow from a racially diverse student body. Like the Harvard Plan, racial minority status in the Law School's

---

22 *Id.* at 245 (Stevens, J., dissenting).

23 Grutter v. Bollinger, 539 U.S. 306 (2003); Gratz v. Bollinger, 539 U.S. 244 (2003).

program was considered a "plus" as part of a holistic, individualized review of a candidate's file. And like the Harvard Plan, other nonracial characteristics of the applicant—like her geographic origin—could also be considered "plus" factors during the holistic review. Further, the Law School had not reserved any seats in the incoming class for racial minorities. Rather, the Law School simply sought to enroll a "critical mass" of students hailing from historically disadvantaged racial groups.

Gratz involved the race conscious admission program that the undergraduate college at the University of Michigan ["the College"] had implemented. While the College also defended its program under the banner of diversity, it pursued diversity by adding a set number of points to the applications of students of color. The result of the automatic conferral of points was that "minimally qualified" candidates from historically underrepresented racial groups were virtually guaranteed admission.

In *Grutter*, the Court upheld the Law School's affirmative action program after subjecting it to strict scrutiny. The Court affirmed the compelling nature of student body diversity, noting that it helps to cultivate "a set of leaders with legitimacy in the eyes of the citizenry."[24] Further, the Court held that the holistic, individualized application review process that the Law School employed was narrowly-tailored to its goal. Quite notably, the Court also said that a crucial part of narrow tailoring in the affirmative action context is that the deviation from a norm of colorblindness must be temporary. Thus, the Court articulated an expectation that race conscious admission programs would be unconstitutional in twenty-five years. Said the Court, "It has been 25 years since Justice Powell first approved the use of race to further an interest in student body diversity in the context of public higher education. Since that time, the number of minority applicants with high grades and test scores has indeed increased. We expect that 25 years from now, the use of racial preferences will no longer be necessary to further the interest approved today."[25]

Justice Thomas filed a dissent in which he reiterated many of the criticisms that opponents of affirmative action have levied against race conscious programs—criticisms that the following Part outlines. Interestingly, Justice Thomas also launched an attack against the elitism involved in the Law School's choice to look to traditional indicia of merit despite those indicia invariably functioning to rank applicants of color as less "qualified" than white applicants. Specifically, Justice Thomas critiqued the Law School's

---

[24] *Grutter*, 539 U.S. at 332.

[25] *Id.* at 343.

privileging of the Law School Admissions Test (LSAT) in its admissions process even though it, and every other law school in the U.S., has full knowledge that students of color do not score as highly on the test as do white students. He noted that the Law School continues to privilege the LSAT even though the test is only an imperfect predictor of future success in law school—a fact of which Justice Thomas claims the Law School must be aware inasmuch as it "regularly admits students who score below 150 (the national median) on the test."[26] He observed that the Law School could admit significant numbers of students of color if it stopped using traditional criteria of merit. The Law School chooses not to do this, Justice Thomas argues, because of its desire to retain its elite status. He concludes:

> Having decided to use the LSAT, the Law School must accept the constitutional burdens that come with this decision. The Law School may freely continue to employ the LSAT and other allegedly merit-based standards in whatever fashion it likes. What the Equal Protection Clause forbids, but the Court today allows, is the use of these standards hand-in-hand with racial discrimination. An infinite variety of admissions methods are available to the Law School. Considering all of the radical thinking that has historically occurred at this country's universities, the Law School's intractable approach toward admissions is striking.[27]

Parts of Justice Thomas's dissent in *Grutter* suggest that he opposes affirmative action because it is not radical enough. He writes that race conscious admissions programs like the one that the Law School implements do not "address the real problems facing underrepresented minorities."[28] He critiques the program because of his belief that it was not intended to "solv[e] real problems like the crisis of black male underperformance."[29] Remarkably, if these comments reflect a disquietude with race-based affirmative action that is born of a sense that racial inequality in this country will not be solved by the admission of a few racial minorities to a few elite institutions every year, then Justice Thomas—a staunch conservative—may find intellectual bedfellows with progressive race scholars. Their critique of affirmative action is described below.

While *Grutter* held that the Law School's affirmative action program passed constitutional muster, *Gratz* struck down the

---

26 *Id.* at 370 (Thomas, J., dissenting).

27 *Id.*

28 *Id.* at 372.

29 *Id.* at 373 n.11.

College's race conscious admissions program. Although the College similarly pursued the educational benefits that flow from a diverse student body, the Court concluded that the means by which the College pursued those ends were not sufficiently narrowly tailored. Specifically, the Court found that the point system, by which candidates of color were awarded a fixed number of points towards admission, was not "flexible enough to consider all pertinent elements of diversity in light of the particular qualifications of each applicant."[30] Unlike the Law School's system of holistic review, the Court found that the College's point system insufficiently allowed for "individualized consideration."[31] Justice Ginsburg filed a dissent in which she argued that the College's point system and the Law School's holistic review were one and the same; the only difference was that the College's approach was less opaque and more forthcoming about the goal being pursed. She contended that the Court's decision encourages colleges and universities to "resort to camouflage."[32] She concluded with the assertion that "[i]f honesty is the best policy, surely Michigan's accurately described, fully disclosed College affirmative action program is preferable to achieving similar numbers through winks, nods, and disguises."[33]

III. Critiques of Affirmative Action (and Critical Responses to Those Critiques)

Over the years, opponents of race-based affirmative action have levied a number of criticisms against it. This Part details these critiques and describes critical thinkers' assessment of them.

A. Affirmative Action Is Immoral

Some opponents of affirmative action argue that it is simply immoral to treat people differently on account of their race. As esteemed law professor Alexander Bickel once wrote, "The lesson of the great decisions of the Supreme Court and the lesson of contemporary history have been the same for at least a generation: discrimination on the basis of race is illegal, immoral, unconstitutional, inherently wrong, and destructive of democratic society."[34]

The critical thinker might observe that the assertion that race consciousness is immoral is nothing more than a conclusion: it does not reveal the premises of the argument or disclose the logic that leads to the conclusion. In this absence, people are free to reject the

---

[30] *Id.* at 334 (majority opinion).

[31] Gratz v. Bollinger, 539 U.S. 244, 271 (2003).

[32] *Id.* at 304 (Ginsburg, J., dissenting).

[33] *Id.* at 305.

[34] ALEXANDER M. BICKEL, THE MORALITY OF CONSENT 133 (1975).

conclusion. In fact, they are free to arrive at the opposite conclusion. Indeed, many critical theorists of race are convinced that it is immoral *not* to attempt to remedy the present-day effects of historic and current racial discrimination by treating people differently on account of their race. Many critical scholars argue that the real immoral practice is to ignore race in a world and in a society marred with such stunning racial inequality.

B. Affirmative Action Is Stigmatizing

A criticism that one frequently hears is that race-based affirmative action does more harm than good to the racial minorities that these programs are designed to benefit. The claim is that affirmative action programs stigmatize people of color as incapable of getting admitted to competitive colleges and universities or getting hired into competitive positions by their own lights. Justice Thomas has made this argument in a number of opinions. However, he may have argued this position most passionately in his dissenting opinion in *Grutter*. There, he wrote,

> It is uncontested that each year, the Law School admits a handful of blacks who would be admitted in the absence of racial discrimination. Who can differentiate between those who belong and those who do not? The majority of blacks are admitted to the Law School because of discrimination, and because of this policy all are tarred as undeserving. This problem of stigma does not depend on determinacy as to whether those stigmatized are actually the "beneficiaries" of racial discrimination. When blacks take positions in the highest places of government, industry, or academia, it is an open question today whether their skin color played a part in their advancement. The question itself is the stigma—because either racial discrimination did play a role, in which case the person may be deemed "otherwise unqualified," or it did not, in which case asking the question itself unfairly marks those blacks who would succeed without discrimination.[35]

It is difficult to deny the truth of Justice Thomas's claims: certainly, many believe that affirmative action perverts systems of meritocracy and, as a result, makes it safe to conclude that black, Latinx, and indigenous people are not qualified to study in the universities that they attend or to hold the jobs that they have. However, critical theorists observe that this narrative about the inferiority of racial minorities and their lack of qualifications is quite flexible. They assert that just as surely as black people's *presence* in

---

[35] *Grutter*, 539 U.S. at 373 (Thomas, J., dissenting).

certain institutions and job positions is taken to demonstrate their inferiority, their *absence* from these same institutions and jobs would be taken to demonstrate the same.

Those who challenge the legality or propriety of affirmative action programs by arguing that they stigmatize beneficiaries seem to assume that, if these programs did not exist, people would stop thinking that racial minorities were undeserving. But, critical thinkers see scant evidence to sustain that claim. Indeed, if one views the country's history through critical eyes, it appears to be one in which dominant society invariably explains racial minorities' existence at the bottom of social hierarchies in terms of their inferiority. This narrative about the inferiority of racial minorities is not at all dependent on the existence of affirmative action. Instead, progressive scholars argue, it appears to be an enduring, persistent feature of American life.

C. Affirmative Action Is Divisive

Opponents of race-conscious programs have argued that these efforts are illegal and ill-advised because they are divisive. As Justice O'Connor wrote in her dissent in *Metro Broadcasting v. FCC*, "the dangers of such classifications are clear. They endorse race-based reasoning and the conception of a Nation divided into racial blocs, thus contributing to an escalation of racial hostility and conflict."[36]

Like the stigma argument, the divisiveness argument against affirmative argument appears to assume that, without race-conscious programs, racial hostility and conflict will be *de minimis* or nonexistent; the argument seems to posit that racial blocs, if they currently exist, will wither away in the absence of affirmative action. But, critical scholars believe there may be good reason to believe that racial hostility and conflict will persist if we do not make race-conscious efforts to address racial stratification in the country. They observe the incredible racial segregation that characterizes the present—where people of different races live in different neighborhoods, learn in different schools, work in different jobs, pray in different houses of worship, etc. These conditions, they say, certainly do not foster racial understanding. Indeed, because the number of opportunities to interact as peers and colleagues—as equals—with people of different races is low, critical thinkers suggest that these conditions contribute to the "othering" of the racial outgroup. That is, they allow individuals to come to believe that members of races are fundamentally different from themselves. Critical thinkers conclude that we ought not to be surprised if racial

---

[36] Metro Broad., Inc. v. FCC, 497 U.S. 547, 603 (1990) (O'Connor, J., dissenting).

hostility and conflict—and the persistence of racial blocs—result from these conditions.

D. Affirmative Action Harms Innocent White Victims

Opponents of affirmative action have argued that race conscious programs harm white people by denying them jobs and seats in incoming classes that they would otherwise secure. The white persons who lose these employment and educational opportunities frequently are described as "innocent" because they have not engaged in any discriminatory acts that have harmed people of color. Nevertheless, affirmative action makes them pay the debt of the discriminators who have gone before them.

Critical thinkers find disquieting the attention shown, and the concern given, to persons belonging to historically advantaged racial groups. They think it odd for society to focus its attention on those who have been advantaged while allowing those who have been disadvantaged to receive only an ancillary concern. The analogy may be a car crash in which paramedics arriving on the scene first concern themselves with the bystanders—making sure that the emergency care that must be administered to those trapped inside of the burning car will not make these unwitting observers of the accident too queasy. Many theorists operating within a critical frame argue that centering white people's experiences—and judging the legality of efforts that address the harms endured by racial minorities in terms of the effects that those efforts will have on white people—is a glaring, and disturbing, example of white privilege.

A critical eye might also be skeptical of the notion that white persons denied job opportunities or refused seats in incoming classes are "innocent." As one progressive scholar observes, "[T]he rhetoric of innocence avoids the argument that white people generally have benefited from the oppression of people of color, that white people have been advantaged by this oppression in a myriad of obvious and less obvious ways. Thus, the rhetoric of innocence obscures this question: What white person is 'innocent,' if innocence is defined as the absence of advantage at the expense of others?"[37]

E. Affirmative Action Promotes/Depends on Racial Stereotypes

Opponents of affirmative action have argued that these programs foster stereotypical thinking about members of different races. Justice O'Connor articulated this argument in her dissent in *Metro Broadcasting*, which involved a federal law that gave

[37] Thomas Ross, *Innocence and Affirmative Action*, 43 VAND. L. REV. 297, 301 (1990).

preferences to minority-owned businesses in the distribution of broadcast licenses. Supporters justified the law on the grounds that it would help to produce a diversity of viewpoints on the airwaves. Justice O'Connor argued that policies like the one challenged in the case "presume that persons think in a manner associated with their race."[38] She claimed that they were unconstitutional because they "embody stereotypes that treat individuals as the product of their race."[39] Although O'Connor came to endorse the diversity rationale in her majority opinion in *Grutter*, the criticism that affirmative action programs rely on and promote stereotypical thinking when such programs are implemented to pursue a diversity of viewpoints in a context has endured.

Progressive race scholars do not dispute the proposition that a racial group is composed of individuals who hold a variety of different viewpoints and beliefs. Thus, these theorists would agree that if an affirmative action program assumes that a member of a racial group holds a particular viewpoint or belief, then that program is trading in stereotypes and, consequently, is unsupportable.

However, critical thinkers disbelieve that an individual's race has had no impact whatsoever on the viewpoints and beliefs that she has come to hold. They propose that we misrecognize the potency and omnipresence of race and racial discourses if we imagine that race and racial discourses have had no bearing or effect on the constellation of views that together comprise an individual's worldview. Now, critical scholars deny that race informs people's perception of the world in a uniform way. That is, they deny that the status of being a black person has impacted all black people's perception of the world in the exact same manner. However, critical thinkers insist that being black *has* impacted black people's worldviews in some respect. If this is true, then to admit students of varying racial backgrounds is to admit students with a variety of racially-informed views. To be conscious of race during admissions because one endeavors to admit a class with a multiplicity of racially-informed beliefs, they argue, is not to trade in stereotypes or to fall victim to stereotypical thinking; rather, it is to recognize that race matters, and powerfully so, in contemporary life.

F. Affirmative Action Is Problematic to Implement

Some have objected that implementing affirmative action requires institutions not only to identify the groups that will receive different race-based treatment under the law, but also to define the criteria by which an individual will be regarded as a member of a

---

38 *Metro Broadcasting*, 497 U.S. at 618 (O'Connor, J., dissenting).

39 *Id.* at 604.

racial group. Thus, if an employer decides that it wants to ensure that black apprentices comprise half of a training program, then the employer has to decide who qualifies as "black." Some have thought this to be a dangerous and repulsive pursuit. For example, Justice Stevens has argued that "the very attempt to define with precision a beneficiary's qualifying racial characteristics is repugnant to our constitutional ideals," and he noted that the institutions attempting to construct these definitions might look to Nazi Germany for guidance.[40] Similarly, Justice Kennedy has offered that institutions might turn to South Africa—specifically, the laws that implemented and administered the political and social system of apartheid—for precedent in crafting their definitions of race.[41]

A response to this critique is that race conscious programs need not define the criteria by which an individual will be regarded as a member of a racial group. Indeed, most affirmative action programs rely on individual self-identification: if an individual identifies as a member of a racial group, then he belongs to that racial group for the purposes of the program. Proponents of this approach posit that there is nothing particularly dangerous or repulsive—indeed, there might be something quite empowering—about allowing individuals' self-understanding with respect to racial membership to determine whether they "belong to" a racial group.

Perhaps a more compelling practical objection to the use of race in law is the observation noted above: there is an incredible amount of heterogeneity within one racial group. Indeed, a "racial group" may, in fact, be composed of various subgroups, and these subgroups may enjoy differing levels of social, political, and economic success. For example, in his dissent in *Fisher v. Texas II*, Justice Alito observed that the University of Texas's affirmative action program evaluated "Asian Americans" according to traditional indicia of merit (i.e., standardized test scores, GPAs, extracurricular activities) while refusing to privilege such indicia when evaluating black and Latinx people. The idea, of course, is that because the latter groups do not perform as well as Asian American and white persons when appraised according to traditional indicia of merit, they ought to be assessed by alternative criteria. But, as Justice Alito points out, "Asian Americans" is a group that includes a range of different subgroups, some of which also do not perform well when judged by traditional indicia of merit. He observes that "Asian Americans"

---

[40] *See* Fullilove v. Klutznick, 448 U.S. 448, 534 n.5 (1980) (Stevens, J., dissenting) (observing that "[i]f the National Government is to make a serious effort to define racial classes by criteria that can be administered objectively, it must study precedents such as the First Regulation to the Reich's Citizenship Law of November 14, 1935").

[41] *Metro Broadcasting*, 497 U.S. at 635 (Kennedy, J., dissenting).

include "individuals of Chinese, Japanese, Korean, Vietnamese, Cambodian, Hmong, Indian and other backgrounds comprising roughly 60% of the world's population."[42] Some of these subgroups are doing quite poorly, while others are succeeding quite magnificently in American life. For example, large percentages of persons with Japanese, South Asian, and Filipino backgrounds in the U.S. have decent educations and respectable incomes.[43] At the same time, the poverty rate among Hmong-, Cambodian-, and Laotian-Americans is staggering, and half of these persons have less than a high school education.[44] Thus, to treat "Asian Americans" as a homogeneous group, and to deny this group the benefit of being evaluated by alternative criteria, constructs all Asian Americans as socially, politically, and economically successfully. Yet, the experience of Hmong-, Cambodian-, and Laotian-Americans reveals that this practice is not empirically, and perhaps ethically, supportable.

Many progressives believe that this criticism is valid, and they take it to heart. Yet, they conclude that it does not counsel in favor of eliminating affirmative action programs entirely. Instead, they believe that it counsels in favor of crafting *better* affirmative action programs. That is, the broad racial categories that are supposed to represent humanity's racial divisions—white, black, Hispanic/Latinx, Native American, and Asian—may not be appropriate when the task involves identifying groups that have been advantaged and disadvantaged on account of race.[45] Indeed, persons of Hmong, Cambodian, and Laotian descent have certainly experienced race-based disadvantage[46]; yet subsuming them within the broad category of "Asian" obscures the particularity of their racial experience. Thus, critical thinkers propose that a more granular analysis is required. They argue that institutions implementing race-based affirmative action programs should identify, with a great degree of specificity, groups that are socially, politically, and/or economically disadvantaged and the cases in which that

---

[42] Fisher v. Univ. of Tex. at Austin (*Fisher II*), 136 S. Ct. 2198, 2229 (2016) (Alito, J., dissenting).

[43] *See* PEW RESEARCH CTR., THE RISE OF ASIAN AMERICANS 7 (rev. ed. 2013).

[44] *See* Bic Ngo & Stacey J. Lee, *Complicating the Image of Model Minority Success: A Review of Southeast Asian American Education*, 77 REV. EDUC. RES. 415, 418–20 (2007). From 2006 until 2010, twenty-seven percent of Hmong Americans were living in poverty; the poverty rates for Cambodian and Laotian Americans were 19% and 14%, respectively. *See* JOSH ISHIMATSU, NAT'L COAL. FOR ASIAN PAC. AM. CMTY. DEV., SPOTLIGHT ON ASIAN AMERICAN AND PACIFIC ISLANDER POVERTY 11 (2013), http://assetbuildingpolicynetwork.org/wp-content/uploads/2013/08/National-CAPACD-Asian-American-and-Pacific-Islander-Poverty.pdf.

[45] As Chapter 6 discusses, these racial categories are the products of questionable science.

[46] *See generally* AIHWA ONG, BUDDHA IS HIDING: REFUGEES, CITIZENSHIP, THE NEW AMERICA (2003).

disadvantage is traceable to race. Crafting and implementing an affirmative action program with this sophisticated understanding of race and race-based hardship is, of course, much more difficult than administering a program that imagines that there are five races and that there is a similarity of racial experience within those broad racial categories. Nevertheless, conclude many progressive thinkers, a level of sophistication with respect to what race is and how race operates is necessary if we are to put into practice policies and programs that move us closer to something that we can call racial justice.

G. Affirmative Action Postpones the End of Racial Thinking

Critics of affirmative action argue that the race-consciousness that is part and parcel of these programs delays the arrival of the day when we, as a society, can stop thinking about race. As Justice Scalia wrote in his opinion in *Adarand*, to administer race-conscious programs, "even for the most admirable and benign of purposes[,] is to reinforce and preserve for future mischief the way of thinking that produced race slavery, race privilege, and race hatred."[47] The corollary to this proposition appears to be that in the absence of race conscious programs, the way of thinking that produced race slavery, race privilege, and race hatred will go away.

Progressive race scholars challenge this claim by observing that while race slavery, race privilege, and race hatred are all undesirable things, they are not the product of thinking about race. Instead, they are the product of thinking about race *in a particular way*. They propose that there might not be anything inherently wrong or dangerous about race-thinking; race-thinking might only become problematic when it creates, sustains, and legitimates racial hierarchies. These thinkers theorize that a fear of race-thinking is justifiable if it *inevitably* leads to the species of thinking that led to Jim Crow and Japanese internment, for example. There is no evidence that this type of race-thinking necessarily flows from simply thinking about race.

The second challenge to the argument that affirmative action programs postpone the arrival of the day when we can stop thinking about race is to deny that race-thinking will disappear if race conscious programs disappear. Indeed, critical thinkers claim that there is a strong argument to be made that race-thinking will *persist* if race conscious programs disappear. Since the 1960s, race-based affirmative action in university admissions has been proposed as a method for making race matter less in future iterations of American

[47] Adarand Constructors, Inc. v. Peña, 515 U.S. 200, 239 (1995) (Scalia, J., concurring).

society. The idea is that affirmative action will lead to the inclusion of racial minorities into institutions from which they have been historically excluded. The hope is that, over time, people of all races will have access to the jobs, wealth, and power that these institutions provide. The plan is that, in future iterations of society, race will no longer determine fundamental aspects of a racial minority's life—such as whether she will live in poverty, be incarcerated, die during her first year of life, or die while giving birth. Proponents of affirmative action anticipate that these programs will produce this change—that they will make race matter less. Thus, supporters of affirmative action fear that without these programs, race will continue to be significant, and racial stratification will persist. A highly racially stratified society like ours leads people to think of black males as criminals; to think of black females as irresponsible procreators; to think of Puerto Ricans as welfare dependent and, therefore, lazy; to think of Mexican immigrants as criminals, rapists, and drug dealers; and to think of an incredibly heterogeneous group of Muslims as potential terrorists. People think in these ways not because of affirmative action, critical thinkers argue; they think in these ways because of our social failure to effectively address racial inequality—the primary goal of affirmative action programs.

The third challenge to the argument that race conscious programs delay the advent of an era wherein society has stopped thinking about race is to observe that this argument assumes that 1) such a society is desirable, and 2) such a society is possible. With respect to the desirability of such a society, there is no consensus among critical thinkers that a society in which no one thinks about race is the goal. That is, it is not clear that this society is what racial justice looks like—that this society is what we are fighting for. Some critical thinkers believe that a racial utopia is a society in which we think about race, but not in the problematic ways in which we think about it at present. The society for which we are fighting might be one in which we think about race because there are differences among the races, but those differences are not the stuff of hierarchy and stratification. Rather, they are the stuff of variety and celebration.

Finally, some critical thinkers are skeptical about the possibility of a society in which race-thinking has disappeared. Derrick Bell, a father of CRT, once declared that "racism is here to stay."[48] He argued that "Black people will never gain full equality in this country. Even those herculean efforts we hail as successful will produce no more than temporary 'peaks of progress,' short-lived victories that slide into irrelevance as racial patterns adapt in ways

[48] Derrick Bell, *Racism is Here to Stay: Now What?*, 35 HOW. L.J. 79, 79 (1992).

that maintain white dominance. This is a hard-to-accept fact that all history verifies."[49] If Bell is correct, then the argument that affirmative action delays the arrival of a society in which race-thinking has disappeared is specious: a society in which race-thinking has disappeared will never arrive, as "racism is here to stay."

H. Affirmative Action Benefits Those Who Are Not Disadvantaged

Some opponents of race-based affirmative action programs argue that they are illegitimate because they help people who are not truly disadvantaged. The argument is that the racial minorities who actually benefit from race conscious admissions programs enjoy a large degree of class privilege. Further, many beneficiaries are members of privileged subpopulations within the larger unprivileged racial group. For example, the children of African immigrants—a group that, on the whole, is economically and socially better off than U.S.-born people of African descent—tend to benefit from race-based affirmative action programs more often than the children of African Americans.

It is true that class-privileged people of color are more likely than poor people of color to benefit from affirmative action programs. However, some critical observers note that the class privilege that more affluent people of color enjoy does not allow them to escape disadvantage completely. For example, college-educated black people hold about 13% of the wealth that their white counterparts hold.[50] While white families whose heads hold a college degree have on average $180,500 in wealth, their black counterparts have almost an eighth of that wealth—$23,400.[51] Critical thinkers take these facts, and the others that are discussed in Chapter 11, as demonstrating that although wealthier people of color enjoy class privilege, they still experience race-based burdens and are subordinated relative to their white peers. Accordingly, if affirmative action programs benefit them, these thinkers conclude, then these programs are benefiting a group that is *disadvantaged*, relatively speaking.

I. Affirmative Action Results in Overmatch/Mismatch

A final criticism that is lobbed against affirmative action is that race-conscious admissions programs actually harm their beneficiaries by enabling students to attend colleges and universities that offer instruction that exceeds these students' capabilities. The

---

[49] *Id.*

[50] *See* DARRICK HAMILTON ET AL., UMBRELLAS DON'T MAKE IT RAIN: WHY STUDYING AND WORKING HARD ISN'T ENOUGH FOR BLACK AMERICANS 5 (2015).

[51] *See id.*

overmatch/mismatch theory—which finds its strongest endorsement in the empirical work of Richard Sander, a law professor and economist at UCLA Law School[52]—asserts that because affirmative action beneficiaries are academically "in over their heads," they do not thrive at institutions that look beyond traditional indicia of merit. The theory claims that the combination of the lower grades that affirmative action beneficiaries receive and the hits to their confidence that they must endure makes them more likely to drop out of school altogether. Overmatch/mismatch theory asserts that affirmative action beneficiaries would be better off if they did not "benefit" from race-conscious programs by gaining admission to institutions with student bodies that, on the whole, are academically stronger than them. The theory asserts that it is best for racial minority students to attend the schools that match their academic credentials.

The overmatch/mismatch theory has sprouted an added flourish in recent years with the claim that affirmative action has the effect of decreasing the number of students of color pursuing and entering into more technical careers.[53] The argument is that students of color with aspirations of careers in the sciences are less likely to pursue these professions when they are admitted to institutions in which they are "overmatched," as they find they cannot perform adequately in the majors that are prerequisites for the careers that they desire; consequently, they switch to less technical majors and pursue alternate career paths. The contention is that these students of color are more likely to achieve the careers in the sciences that they desire if they attend less selective colleges and universities; in these schools, the difficulty and pace of the workload in the more technical majors would match the students' capabilities, and they would be more likely to successfully complete the course of study and, ultimately, attain a job in the sciences.

Supporters of affirmative action look to the wealth of studies that discredit overmatch/mismatch theory.[54] While most of these

---

[52] *See, e.g.* RICHARD SANDER & STUART TAYLOR, JR., MISMATCH: HOW AFFIRMATIVE ACTION HURTS STUDENTS IT'S INTENDED TO HELP, AND WHY UNIVERSITIES WON'T ADMIT IT (2012).

[53] A recent empirical study that provides support for this claim is Peter Arcidiacono, Esteban M. Aucejo & V. Joseph Hotz, *University Differences in Graduation of Minorities in STEM Fields: Evidence from California*, 106 AM. ECON. REV. 525 (2016). This study offers evidence that students of color attending UCLA or Berkeley would be more likely to graduate with science majors had they attended UC Santa Cruz or UC Riverside—less selective schools in the University of California system.

[54] *See, e.g.*, Richard Lempert, *Mismatch and Science Desistance: Failed Arguments Against Affirmative Action*, 64 UCLA L. REV. DISC. 136 (2016) (citing and summarizing the findings of several studies that seem to disprove overmatch/mismatch theory).

studies do show that affirmative action beneficiaries earn lower grades at more selective institutions than they would have earned had they attended less selective ones, they also show that these students nevertheless do quite well in the more selective institutions that they attend. Moreover, these studies show that, when one considers the incomes that these students earn once they have graduated and the satisfaction that they report with their careers, the evidence suggests that being "overmatched" actually *benefits* students of color. Professor Richard Lempert, who has challenged mismatch/overmatch theory time and again in this scholarship, summarizes the available studies as showing that "[w]ith the exception of some controversial and deeply flawed research,. . . researchers are particularly likely to find that minorities who attend more selective schools tend to do better than similar students at less selective institutions."[55]

Now, empirical studies do appear to confirm that students admitted to more selective colleges and universities under race-conscious admissions programs are less likely to pursue more technical majors at these institutions than if they had attended less selective institutions. However, progressive thinkers do not believe that this is an argument for undoing affirmative action altogether. Instead, they say, it is merely a piece of information that a student who is interested in a career in the sciences ought to consider when choosing the college that she will attend. Lempert argues that the existence of "science mismatch" does not mean that a student will not graduate with a science major from a more competitive school; it may simply mean that she is more likely to graduate with a science major from a less competitive school. He notes, "But who should determine whether to prefer the higher payoff option or the option with the higher likelihood of success? To argue against affirmative action because the country needs more science-trained minorities is to say that society, rather than affected students, should determine the quality of the school the student attends. To foreclose a student's chance of admission to an elite school because the country needs more minorities with degrees in science is to argue that a minority student's educational preferences should be overridden for the good of the collective."[56]

Critical observers also respond to mismatch/overmatch theory by noting that it trains its focus on the *individuals* admitted to selective colleges and universities while paying no attention at all to the *institutions* within which these individuals study and learn. They propose that the environment that an institution creates—whether

[55] *Id.* at 145.

[56] *Id.* at 165–66.

an institution ensures that professors or teaching assistants are available to answer questions outside of class, provides tutoring services, facilitates and encourages the creation of study groups, introduces students to mentors or other individuals who are invested in a student's success, etc.—may impact whether an otherwise "overmatched" student will thrive. This response to overmatch/mismatch theory does not ask, "Why is the student failing?" Instead, it asks, "How are we failing students?" While overmatch/mismatch theory is an individualist explanation of student failure, this response is a structuralist explanation of student success.

Finally, critical observers are curious about overmatch/mismatch theory's sole concern with students of color who are "overmatched." They remind us that institutions admit students of all races whose academic credentials, in terms of GPA and standardized test scores, fall below the school's median. Studies show that *race* does not impact how well or how poorly an "overmatched" student will perform. That is, "overmatched" *black* students perform academically in ways that are comparable to "overmatched" *white* and *Asian* students.[57] However, proponents of overmatch/mismatch theory never articulate a concern with the latter students. Critical observers find it odd that proponents of overmatch/mismatch theory are troubled by the academic "underperformance" of black, Latinx, and indigenous students, but are unbothered by the comparable academic "underperformance" of white and Asian students. Now, say these observers, it could be that proponents of the theory are singularly devoted to ensuring the welfare of black, Latinx, and indigenous students. But, they say, it is more likely that the focused concern that overmatch/mismatch theorists have with the academic successes and failures of black, Latinx, and indigenous students does not evidence their interest in the prosperity and happiness of these students, but rather evidences their distaste for race-based affirmative action.

IV. Additional Critical Reflection on Affirmative Action

As noted at the beginning of the chapter, many progressive race scholars have been skeptical about affirmative action. Their sense is that race conscious admissions and hiring programs are not really a radical solution to systemic racial inequality. In their view, affirmative action leaves in place the problematic institutions and structures that make race conscious programs necessary. For example, consider that people of color are underrepresented among

[57] *See* Michal Kurlaender & Eric Grodsky, *Mismatch and the Paternalistic Justification for Selective College Admissions*, 86 SOC. EDUC. 294, 305 (2013).

legal academics. A race conscious hiring program would allow decision makers in a law school to consider the race of a candidate when deciding whether or not to hire her. However, that hiring program leaves in place all of the large scale forces that make the law professor of color a relatively rare phenomenon, i.e., residential segregation and the funding of public schools through property taxes; the phenomenon of "stereotype threat,"[58] which may explain why people of color underperform on standardized tests relative to white people; the reality that people of color disproportionately live below the poverty line, with poverty diminishing individuals' ability to achieve when measured by traditional indicia of merit. In leaving in place all of the systemic causes of black, Latinx, and indigenous people's failure to achieve at the same levels as white people, these progressive critics of affirmative action believe that the programs may be reinforcing, rather than challenging, the structures of power that lead to racial inequality. If that is what affirmative action is doing, they say, then it may be profoundly conservative.

Richard Delgado has been dubious about modern affirmative action programs because he believes that the national fight over them has worked to prevent us from conceptualizing as affirmative action the long history during which people of color were formally and informally excluded from jobs and educational institutions—an arrangement that benefitted white people greatly. He writes:

> For more than 200 years, white males benefited from their own program of affirmative action, through unjustified preferences in jobs and education resulting from old-boy networks and official laws that lessened the competition. Today's affirmative action critics never characterize that scheme as affirmative action, which of course it was. By labeling problematic, troublesome, and ethically agonizing a paltry system that helps a few of us get ahead, critics neatly take our eyes off the system of arrangements that brought and maintained them in power, and enabled them to develop the rules and standards of quality and merit that

---

[58] Stereotype threat refers to a psychological phenomenon where an individual unconsciously behaves in a way that aligns with stereotypes about the group to which she belongs. For example, due to stereotypes about black incompetence or low intelligence, black students will not perform as strongly on standardized tests when their race is made salient to them prior to test-taking. *See* Claude M. Steele & Joshua Aronson, *Stereotype Threat and the Intellectual Test Performance of African Americans*, 69 J. PERSONALITY & SOC. PSYCHOL. 797 (1995). Due to stereotypes about Asian people's superior ability at math, Asian students will perform more strongly on a math test when their race is made salient to them prior to test-taking. Margaret Shih, Todd L. Pittinsky & Nalini Ambady, *Stereotype Susceptibility: Identity Salience and Shifts in Quantitative Performance*, 10 PSYCHOL. SCI. 80 (1999).

> now exclude us, make us appear unworthy, dependent (naturally) on affirmative action.[59]

Thus, critical thinkers have been critical (unsurprisingly!) of affirmative action. Nevertheless, it is important to note that many other critical thinkers support affirmative action because they do not think it to be a conservative device, but rather a *radical* program for redistributing power, privilege, and opportunities in the country. Writes critical race theorist, Cheryl Harris, "CRT reflects an ideological position that takes up the fight for affirmative action as a means of addressing problems of institutionalized white privilege. Affirmative action, as articulated through a critical lens, is not an effort to repopulate hierarchy, but reflects the deployment of a tactic to attack white privilege as embedded within traditional definitions of merit and other exclusionary practices that were cast as neutral and fair."[60]

Harris's point deserves elaboration. Here she alludes to an insight that critical thinkers have made regarding traditional definitions of merit: the things that we have come to identify as the stuff of merit are not at all neutral or objective. Instead, they reflect the subject positions, experiences, and values of those who are in power and have been able to define what merit is. For example, consider what merit with respect to law professor hiring looks like: a JD from an elite law school, membership on that law school's law review, a Supreme Court clerkship, and articles that have been published in an elite law school's law review. Critical thinkers underscore that the decision to privilege these specific achievements is not *neutral* or *objective*. As Kimberlé Crenshaw notes, there is nothing "magical or intrinsically compelling" about these standards; they are "not the exclusive criteria for identifying candidates who [are] likely to make substantial contributions both to the educational mission of the school and to the broader goals of advancing legal knowledge."[61] The critical insight is that decision makers have made a value-laden *choice* to privilege these achievements and to identify them as the stuff of merit. Crenshaw argues that to call traditional criteria of merit "neutral" or "objective" is to "sanitize[ ] the racial power" at play."[62]

Further, critical observers charge that the reason decision makers have defined merit in the particular way that it has been

---

59 Richard Delgado, *Affirmative Action as Majoritarian Device: Or, Do You Really Want to Be a Role Model?*, 89 MICH. L. REV. 1222, 1225 (1991).

60 Cheryl I. Harris, *Mining in Hard Ground*, 116 HARV. L. REV. 2487, 2536 (2003) (book review).

61 Kimberlé Williams Crenshaw, *Twenty Years of Critical Race Theory: Looking Back to Move Forward*, 43 CONN. L. REV. 1253, 1269 (2011).

62 *Id.* at 1286.

defined is that it reflects the interests, preferences, and commitments of those who have enjoyed power in the country throughout most of history—class-privileged white men. Moreover, say observers, this group has no real incentive to change, or even challenge, traditional definitions of merit, as these criteria function to assure members of the group that they really are, objectively speaking, "the best." Writes Duncan Kennedy, who is fairly described as a class-privileged white man, "We are generally too dependent on, even addicted to, the continual reward of being told we are better, and that our law schools are better, according to an objective merit scale, than other people and law schools. . . . The hypertrophy of standards-talk . . . has a narcissistic payoff, since it endlessly reaffirms the merit of those who make judgments of merit."[63]

It bears noting that this is where those with liberal politics and those with critical politics part ways. Liberal defenders of affirmative action tend to conceptualize current definitions of merit as just and proper; they tend to be committed to the idea that those who have achieved the things that are the stuff of our traditional definitions of merit are "better", "smarter," "more deserving," and/or "more qualified" than those who cannot lay claim to similar achievements. Persons in this camp defend affirmative action, however, due to their conviction that, because of historical and contemporary discrimination, people of color have been unable to achieve the trappings of merit. Thus, they support affirmative action as a temporary deviation from a standard that they believe to be, ultimately, right.

However, critical defenders of affirmative action dispute that current definitions of merit are just and proper. Rather, they understand these definitions to be repositories of race-based and class-based privilege. Thus, their support of affirmative action is not a product of their sense that deviations from evaluating persons according to traditional indicia of merit are necessary in order to allow people of color to "catch up." Rather, their support is due to their sense that traditional indicia of merit are corrupt in the first instance. Further, they are committed to the idea that merit, as traditionally defined, has been a mechanism by which affluent white men have passed power and privilege to other affluent white men over the generations. Thus, to these thinkers, departures from traditional definitions of merit are not the equivalent of "lowered standards," a charge that opponents of affirmative action frequently make. To critical thinkers, departures from traditional definitions of merit are *different* standards that, crucially, disrupt the transgenerational transmission of power and privilege to wealthy

---

[63] Duncan Kennedy, *A Cultural-Pluralist Case for Affirmative Action in Legal Academia*, 1990 DUKE L.J. 705, 719–20 (1990).

white men. In this way, many critical thinkers believe that affirmative action threatens white supremacy.

Progressive race scholars observe that we might define merit entirely differently—in a way that reflects *other* interests, preferences and commitments. For example, Lawrence proposes that, instead of defining merit as the list of achievements that affluent white men have valued historically, we might "re-imagine merit in light of [our] commitment to the goal of fighting racism."[64] If merit was reimagined in this way, he says, we probably would not attach uncritical importance to high standardized test scores and GPAs. In many instances, those two achievements are purchased at the cost of other, more socially worthwhile endeavors: an applicant might have spent his time ensuring that his grades and SAT score are unimpeachable instead of devoting at least some of his time to providing services to society's most marginalized. If we defined merit in conversation with a commitment to undoing racial hierarchy, then our indicia of merit would attempt to identify those who would help the university achieve that goal. Those who are meritorious would not necessarily be applicants who have scored in the ninety-ninth percentile on a standardized test and who can boast a 4.0 GPA.

Critical thinkers realize that there is nothing *neutral* or *objective* about defining merit in relationship to a commitment to dismantling hierarchy. However, they remind us that there is nothing neutral or objective about defining merit in relationship to standardized test scores and GPAs. As the latter definition reflects the preferences of one group in society, the reimagined definition simply reflects the preferences of a different group.

The question of merit is not the only issue that distinguishes liberal and critical supporters of affirmative action. Also distinguishing the two groups is their understanding of how we ought to understand and defend affirmative action. Liberal defenders have described affirmative action as good for society generally. In this view, we ought to pursue race-conscious programs because when people of color are consigned to the margins of society, the conditions for social unrest, resistance, and revolt have been laid. Thus, an interest in social order counsels in favor of affirmative action.

Critical supporters of race conscious hiring and admissions programs reject the proposition that these programs ought to be pursued as a prophylactic technique that staves off social instability and conflict. Rather, they argue that such programs ought to be pursued in light of the country's history of racism and racial disenfranchisement. That is, critical supporters frame affirmative action as an effort to remedy the effects of past and present racial

[64] Lawrence, *supra* note 6, at, 972.

discrimination. They argue that in light of people of color having been formally and informally precluded from enjoying the incredible wealth that their bodies have generated, affirmative action is a moral imperative. In their assessment, society is morally obligated to address the wrong that has been done, and continues to be done, to people of color in this nation. Affirmative action is a means for doing just that.

However, liberal defenders reject this framing of race conscious programs—or, at least, they have come to reject it. When the Court first began considering the constitutionality of affirmative action, supporters argued that the state had an interest in remedying past societal discrimination and that race conscious admissions and hiring programs were a means to accomplish this interest. After the Court rejected the claim that an institution could constitutionally pursue this remedial interest, proponents of affirmative action began to defend such programs under the banner of "diversity"; they argued that employers and educational institutions should be allowed to be conscious of race in order to pursue the benefits that a racially diverse workforce or student body inevitably produces. Ultimately, in *Grutter*, the Court gave this rationale its blessing. Thus, liberal supporters of affirmative action now champion race conscious efforts with the claim that diversity is good for institutions.

However, progressive theorists are concerned that the diversity rationale seems to be just as worried about those who have benefited from the country's history of racial exclusion as it is about those who have been burdened by it. Indeed, the diversity rationale justifies affirmative action programs with the claim that racially diverse learning environments will improve the educational outcomes of everyone in them—including the white people who would be in those environments whether or not affirmative action programs are implemented. Consider the Court's discussion of this point in *Grutter*:

> [T]he Law School's admissions policy promotes cross-racial understanding, helps to break down racial stereotypes, and enables [students] to better understand persons of different races. These benefits are important and laudable, because classroom discussion is livelier, more spirited, and simply more enlightening and interesting when the students have the greatest possible variety of backgrounds.
>
> The Law School's claim of a compelling interest is further bolstered by its *amici*, who point to the educational benefits that flow from student body diversity. In addition to the expert studies and reports entered into evidence at trial, numerous studies show that student body diversity

> promotes learning outcomes, and better prepares students for an increasingly diverse workforce and society, and better prepares them as professionals.[65]

In critical thinkers' view, these passages seem to evince a solicitude for everyone but the racial minorities who have endured systemic oppression on account of race in this country. Instead, they appear to be most attentive to the white students in selective institutions who, in the absence of affirmative action, would not receive the benefit of learning with and from students of color. In this framing, affirmative action introduces students of color into white people's educational spaces—producing discussions that are "livelier, more spirited, and simply more enlightening and interesting." White students who have been able to access elite institutions like the University of Michigan Law School have fared quite well in this country—even when those institutions were formally and informally closed to students of color. But, the diversity rationale, argues progressive theorists, proposes that *those students will do even better* if they learned alongside racial minorities. In this way, critics argue, the diversity rationale constructs students of color in these institutions as tools with which white people can improve their educations, their careers, and their lives.

Critical thinkers do not deny that the learning outcomes of diverse student bodies may be superior to those of homogeneous student bodies. And they do not deny that students of color who gain admission to selective institutions benefit from the lively, spirited, enlightening, and interesting environments that their presence in these spaces helps to generate. But, many critical thinkers are disturbed that efforts to improve the wellbeing of dispossessed groups can only be made by centering the experience of those who have enjoyed power and privilege in this country. When these efforts centered the experience of the historically dispossessed—when affirmative action was conceptualized as a means to remedy past societal discrimination—the Court said that they were not constitutionally permissible.

Because many critical observers conceptualize affirmative action as both a threat to white dominance as well as something that society is morally obligated to implement in order to address the country's history and present of racial exclusion, they do not feel the need to apologize for it. Indeed, liberal defenders of affirmative action tend to conceptualize it as a temporary departure from a colorblind norm—a norm that we will finally be able to live up to as soon as we right the wrongs of our past. Because liberal defenders offer colorblindness as the proper center of our moral compasses,

---

[65] Grutter v. Bollinger, 539 U.S. 306, 330 (2003).

affirmative action gets conceptualized as an immoral pursuit that, nevertheless, must be pursued; it becomes a "necessary evil." Most critical observers agree that affirmative action is necessary; but they deny that it is evil. Instead, they conceptualize it as the good and just thing to do—indeed, the *right* thing to do—as it clears away some of the structural impediments that have made it difficult for unprivileged groups to succeed in the country.

V. Questions and Discussion

1. As discussed above, it is well-established that black, Latinx, and indigenous people do not perform as highly as white and Asian people on standardized tests—including the LSAT. It has also been established that LSAT scores are only an imperfect predictor of a student's success in law school—functioning to predict performance in the first year, but failing to predict how well a student will perform in subsequent years and in her career, more generally. Nevertheless, law schools continue to privilege LSAT scores when evaluating applicants. Part of the reason is pragmatic: many law schools receive thousands of applications in a given year, and applicants are wildly heterogeneous—hailing from different undergraduate institutions after pursuing different programs of study. A student's LSAT score is one way to compare her to another student when no other means of comparison exists. Another important reason that law schools privilege LSAT scores relates to the U.S. News and World Report, which publishes extremely influential rankings of law schools every year. One of the criteria that U.S. News and World Report uses when ranking law schools is the median LSAT score of the school's incoming class. Hence, if a law school wants to be competitive in this ranking, it needs to pay attention to its incoming class's median LSAT score.

Given the strength of the forces that encourage reliance on the LSAT score, how can law schools get out of the problem of depending on a test that does not accurately predict law school performance and functions to construct certain racial minority groups as "unqualified"? What solutions to this predicament can you propose?

2. As described above, Justice Powell argued in *Bakke* that the white majority was, in fact, an assemblage that consisted of various ethnicities, i.e., Italian, Irish, Greek. According to Powell, the U.S. does not have one majority white race and various nonwhite minority races. Instead, the U.S. is composed a plethora of nonwhite and white minority groups. Further, these groups have taken turns oppressing and being oppressed by one another.

Perhaps unsurprisingly, progressive race theorists have rejected Powell's version of U.S. history. These thinkers note that some racial groups have never had the social, economic, or political power to exert dominance over other racial groups. They observe that one cannot find any moment in history during which black people dominated any group belonging to the white majority. In other words, these thinkers find Powell's rendering of American history simply unsupported by the evidence.

Further, Ian Haney López has argued that Powell's description of American racial politics—whereby every minority group is equally capable of forming alliances with other minority groups and deploying those racial alliances so as to dominate out-groups—does not lead to the conclusion that strict scrutiny is the appropriate level of judicial review for laws containing a racial classification. Instead, it leads to the conclusion that the courts should be deferential to the results of a fair political process in which all of the players are equally situated. He writes:

> [I]f multitudinous ethnic groups stood in relations of shifting competition forming only temporary majorities, no special solicitude for racial groups seemed required. . . . Powell's ethnic theory not only failed to justify heightened review in the affirmative action context, it failed to justify it in every case. . ., thus drawing into question every modern case from *Korematsu* to *Loving*. Powell's ethnic analysis seemed to convert racial discrimination, both benign and invidious, into ordinary social legislation.[66]

What do you think of Powell's theory of race? Do you agree with López that it leads to the conclusion that racial classifications in law should be scrutinized with rational basis scrutiny?

3. Should proponents of race-based affirmative action be concerned that these programs may stigmatize their beneficiaries as undeserving? Is this an argument for the unconstitutionality of these programs? Does it make these programs bad policy? Is there anything that the law can do to reduce the likelihood that there will be those who believe that people of color are "unqualified" for the positions that they come to occupy in schools, jobs, and society?

4. Some have argued that institutions ought to replace race-based affirmative action with class-based affirmative action. They assert that race-talk is divisive, and to speak about racism and racial inequality is politically disadvantageous. These proponents of class-based affirmative action claim that class-conscious programs can get racial minorities admitted to institutions from which they have been historically excluded without having to use the "dirty" word of race. However, some critical observers are skeptical about class-based

---

[66] Ian F. Haney López, *"A Nation of Minorities": Race, Ethnicity, and Reactionary Colorblindness*, 59 STAN. L. REV. 985, 1038–39 (2007).

affirmative action because of its consistency with post-racialism's ideology of racial progress. They claim that class-based affirmative action denies that individuals—and groups—continue to be advantaged and disadvantaged on account of race. It denies that there is such a thing called race privilege that materially impacts people's worlds. Hence, these critical thinkers insist upon the race consciousness of race-based affirmative action, as it functions to assert that *race* matters in the contemporary U.S. and that we are far from a post-racial society.

Do you think that class-based affirmative action should be pursued because, pragmatically speaking, it may be superior to race-based affirmative action, as it is less likely to spark intense opposition? Or do you think that race-based affirmative action should be pursued, despite its political unpopularity, because it is important to remind society that we have not overcome our unfortunate racial past and that individuals continue to be disadvantaged *on the basis of race* in the contemporary U.S.?

5. Imagine that two schools, Alpha University and Omega College, have both implemented race-conscious admissions programs. Imagine that Alpha University issues a statement explaining that it has implemented the program because it wants to address the effects of past and present societal racial discrimination. Imagine that Omega College also issues a statement; however, its statement explains that the school has implemented its race-conscious admissions program in order to pursue the educational benefits that flow from student body diversity. Do you think that Alpha's and Omega's race-conscious admissions programs are substantively different? Is one school's program more legitimate than the other? Why?

6. Imagine that you are the dean of a law school, and you have been charged with constructing a definition of merit that the school's hiring committee will use when choosing professors to hire. What criteria would you include in your definition of merit? Why have you chosen those criteria?

7. As described above, critical thinkers have argued that traditional definitions of merit reflect the interests and experiences of affluent white men. However, even if one finds this claim untrue, one might still be convinced that these definitions of merit privilege the wealthier among us. For example, Abigail Fisher, whose challenge to the University of Texas's race-based affirmative action program was twice reviewed by the Supreme Court, was quoted as saying, "I took a ton of AP classes, I studied hard and did my homework—and I made the honor roll . . . I was in extracurricular activities. I played the cello and was in the math club, and I

volunteered. I put in the work I thought was necessary to get into UT."[67] However, as Osamudia James notes, "[Fisher] seemed unaware that the very things she identified as examples of her hard work also demonstrated privilege bestowed on her through no effort of her own. For instance, [she] was able to participate in extracurricular activities because her family's financial stability likely freed her from the necessity of an afterschool job; she could become a cellist because she had free time for instruction, possibly paid for by her parents; and she could enroll in AP classes because, even though many schools throughout the United States do not offer such courses, the one that she attended did."[68] Adapting Charles Lawrence's racial critique into a class critique, we might say that traditional indicial of merit "replicates and perpetuates a class-based distribution of educational opportunity and privilege by choosing to make the very opportunities denied to poor children the prerequisites for admission."[69]

What are your reactions to the claim that traditional indicia of merit are the stuff of class privilege? If they are, what should we do about it?

---

[67] *See, e.g.*, Mike Tolson, *Supreme Court to Take Up UT Admission Case*, CHRON (Oct. 8, 2012, 6:45 AM), http://www.chron.com/news/houston-texas/article/Supreme-Court-to-take-up-UT-admission-case-3927014.php.

[68] Osamudia R. James, *White Like Me: The Negative Impact of the Diversity Rationale on White Identity Formation*, 89 N.Y.U. L. REV. 425, 428 (2014).

[69] Lawrence, *supra* note 6, at 947.

Chapter 18

THE CRIMINAL JUSTICE SYSTEM

It is no overstatement to say that progressive race scholars have written *volumes* about crime and, particularly, the nation's responses to it. This chapter will not attempt to explore this voluminous literature in any great depth. Instead, it will describe the interventions that critical thinkers have made in public and scholarly conversations about just three issues concerning the criminal justice system: mass incarceration, policing generally, and police violence—specifically, police killings of unarmed people of color.

I. Mass Incarceration

There are currently 2.3 million people housed in the country's prisons and jails.[1] By most measures, this number is remarkable. It is remarkable because it means that the U.S. has the largest prison population in the entire world. China comes in second, imprisoning 1.7 million people—over half a million *fewer* people than the U.S.[2]

The 2.3 million people presently housed in the nation's prisons and jails is remarkable when one thinks of it in terms of incarceration rates. The number translates to the imprisonment of 698 people for every 100,000.[3] This rate dwarfs the incarceration rates of the countries that the U.S. usually thinks of as its peers. Indeed, the rate at which the U.S. incarcerates its population is seven times the highest rate of incarceration among western European nations.[4] Slightly more broadly, the U.S. has the highest incarceration rate among industrialized nations: Russia is a distant second, imprisoning 413 persons per every 100,000 in the country.

In fact, the 2.3 million people currently housed in the country's prisons and jails is remarkable when one compares the U.S. to *itself*. In 1980—just a couple of decades ago—the U.S. imprisoned only

---

[1] Peter Wagner & Wendy Sawyer, *Mass Incarceration: The Whole Pie*, PRISON POL'Y INITIATIVE (Mar. 14, 2018), https://www.prisonpolicy.org/reports/pie2018.html.

[2] ROY WALMSLEY, INT'L. CTR. FOR PRISON STUDIES, WORLD PRISON POPULATION LIST 1 (10th ed. 2013), https://www.apcca.org/uploads/10th_Edition_2013.pdf.

[3] Peter Wagner & Wendy Sawyer, *States of Incarceration: The Global Context 2018*, PRISON POL'Y INITIATIVE (June 2018), https://www.prisonpolicy.org/global/2018.html.

[4] Germany has the highest prison population among Western European countries, with 63,000 people. The highest imprisonment rate in Western Europe is in Luxembourg, with 112 per 100,000 people. ROY WALMSEY, INST. CRIM. POL'Y RES., WORLD PRISON POPULATION LIST 11 (11th ed. 2016), http://prisonstudies.org/sites/default/files/resources/downloads/world_prison_population_list_11th_edition_0.pdf.

500,000 people.[5] This means that in a relatively short period of time, the prison population increased nearly five-fold.[6]

While these numbers, in and of themselves, might be disconcerting to social justice-minded individuals, they become even more disturbing when the racial geography of the U.S.'s prison population is considered: people of color, particularly black people, are disproportionately represented among those who are presently incarcerated. While black people constitute 12% of the U.S. population, they constitute 33% of the prison population.[7] Thus, black people are dramatically overrepresented in the country's prisons and jails. Compare black people's *over*representation in the prison population to the *under*representation of white people: while white people comprise 64% of the U.S. population, they comprise solely 30% of the prison population.[8] Some scholars have noted that while there are black-white racial disparities across many areas of social life, the racial disparities in incarceration rates are the worst. Bennett Capers, for one, observes that black-white racial disparities in unemployment are two to one, wealth are one to four, and infant mortality are two to one; however, racial disparities in incarceration rates are eight to one.[9]

These figures have piqued the ire of progressive race scholars because they read the numbers as indicating that the U.S. is closer to its racial past—when racial hierarchy and the mechanisms that produced it were spectacular, obvious, and ordinary—than it is to the post-racial future that many claimed had arrived upon the election of Barack Obama to the presidency. Some scholars observe that the U.S. incarcerates more black people now than it did when *Brown v. Board* was handed down—during the heyday of Jim Crow and formal racial inequality.[10] On a similar note, Michelle Alexander, whose work on mass incarceration is explored more expansively in Part I.B.,

---

[5] *World Prison Brief Data: United States of America*, INST. CRIM. POL'Y RES., http://www.prisonstudies.org/country/united-states-america (last visited Aug. 3, 2018).

[6] *Id.*

[7] John Gramlich, *The Gap Between the Number of Blacks and Whites in Prison is Shrinking*, PEW RES. CTR. (Jan. 12, 2018), http://www.pewresearch.org/fact-tank/2018/01/12/shrinking-gap-between-number-of-blacks-and-whites-in-prison/.

[8] *Id.*

[9] I. Bennett Capers, *Critical Race Theory and Criminal Justice*, 12 OHIO ST. J. CRIM. L. 1, 1–2 (2014). We might add that racial disparities in maternal mortality are three to one. THERESA CHALHOUB & KELLY RIMAR, CTR. FOR AM. PROGRESS, THE HEALTH CARE SYSTEM AND RACIAL DISPARITIES IN MATERNAL MORTALITY 1 (2018), https://cdn.americanprogress.org/content/uploads/2018/05/09121820/HealthSystem DisparitiesInMaternalMortality-Brief.pdf.

[10] James Forman, Jr., *Racial Critiques of Mass Incarceration: Beyond the New Jim Crow*, 87 N.Y.U. L. Rev. 21, 22 (2012).

observes that the U.S. currently "imprisons a larger percentage of its black population than South Africa did at the height of apartheid."[11]

The extremely high rates of black incarceration mean that, in many communities, it is not unreasonable for black people—particularly black men—to *anticipate* going to jail at some point in their lives. Alexander observes that in Washington, D.C., "it is estimated that three out of four young black men (and nearly all those in the poorest neighborhoods) can expect to serve time in prison."[12] On a national scale, one out of three black men should expect to be incarcerated during their lifetimes.[13]

Critical observers might find racial disparities in incarceration rates less disquieting if they reflected the rates at which different racial groups committed crime. Thus, if black people committed 33% of all crime, then we might be less disturbed by their representing 33% of the prison population. However, there is good evidence that incarceration rates do not reflect crime rates—at least as it relates to drug crimes. Alexander's work here is particularly instructive. She writes, "Studies show that people of all colors use and sell illegal drugs at remarkably similar rates. . . . That is not what one would guess, however, when entering our nation's prisons and jails, which are overflowing with black and brown drug offenders. In some states, black men have been admitted to prison on drug charges at rates twenty to fifty times greater than those of white men."[14]

These facts suggest to many critical thinkers that there is something corrupt going on in the criminal justice system. Indeed, even if the large number of black people presently imprisoned simply reflected the fact that a large number of black people commit crime, many of these thinkers still would have a problem with mass incarceration. Writes Paul Butler,

> Imagine a country that has statistics like DC's in which more than one-third of the young male citizens are under the supervision of the criminal justice system: they either are in prison, on probation or parole, or have a trial coming up. Imagine a country in which two-thirds of the young men can anticipate being arrested before they reach age thirty. Imagine a country in which there are more young men in prison than in college. . . . Such a country sounds like a police state. When we criticize those kinds of regimes, we

---

[11] MICHELLE ALEXANDER, THE NEW JIM CROW 6 (2012).

[12] *Id.* at 6–7.

[13] *See id.* at 9.

[14] *Id.* at 7.

> think that the problem lies not with the citizens of the state, but rather with the government or law.[15]

Here, Butler suggests that mass incarceration says less about the problematic values held by those who would break the law and more about the problematic commitments of the nation that would incarcerate these lawbreakers with such impunity.

Now, progressive scholars might be less troubled by mass incarceration if the punishment of those convicted of crimes ceased when their prison term ended. However, this is not what happens. Instead, a series of disabilities, many of them permanent, come to attach to those with criminal convictions—especially if the conviction is for a drug crime. As James Forman summarizes, "[A] person convicted of a crime today might lose his right to vote as well as the right to serve on a jury. He might become ineligible for health and welfare benefits, food stamps, public housing, student loans, and certain types of employment."[16]

According to critical scholars, we ought not to discount the severity of these disabilities. The inability to obtain licenses to engage in certain occupations—coupled with the legality of discrimination against persons who have been convicted of crimes—means that persons with criminal convictions likely will have a hard time finding a (legal) job with which they can support themselves and their families. (At the same time, critical thinkers remind us that, in terms of employment prospects, people with criminal convictions likely were not doing that great before their convictions. Notes Rose Brewer and Nancy Heitzeg, "The overwhelming majority of those in prisons and jails were unemployed or employed in the minimum wage service sector at the time of their commitment offense."[17]) The inability to obtain federal student loans lowers ex-offenders' prospects of furthering their education so as to bring higher paying jobs within their reach. If unemployed, the inability to access food stamps and other welfare assistance usually means that it will be difficult for them to provide themselves with the basic necessities. The inability to access health benefits makes it more likely that they will be forced to inhabit states of ill health. The inability to receive public housing benefits makes them vulnerable to homelessness. As Alexander summarizes it, "[T]hese civil penalties . . . often make it virtually impossible for ex-offenders to integrate into the mainstream society and economy upon release."[18]

---

[15] PAUL BUTLER, LET'S GET FREE: A HIP-HOP THEORY OF JUSTICE 60 (2009).

[16] Forman, *supra* note 10, at 28–29.

[17] Rose M. Brewer & Nancy A. Heitzeg, *The Racialization of Crime and Punishment*, 51 AM. BEHAV. SCIENTIST 625, 628 (2008).

[18] ALEXANDER, *supra* note 11, at 143.

The legality of stripping convicted felons of the right to vote has deeply unsettled some progressive thinkers of race. In all but two states—Maine and Vermont—incarcerated persons are denied the ability to vote.[19] Most states continue to deny voting rights to convicted felons after they have been released from prison, when they are on probation or parole.[20] Some states permanently deny convicted felons voting rights.[21] Progressive thinkers have argued that these practices of felon disenfranchisement serve to decrease black voting power dramatically. Brewer and Heitzeg observe that "[o]f African American males, 13% are disenfranchised; in 7 states, 1 in 4 are permanently barred from voting. In Florida alone, nearly one third of all Black men are permanently disenfranchised."[22] We might wonder what our legal landscape would look like if those convicted of felonies were able to participate in selecting the persons who make the laws. We might wonder whether they, and the communities they call home, would vote to eliminate the laws that disenfranchise them. As the Sentencing Project's Marc Mauer argues, "[N]ot only are criminal justice policies resulting in the disproportionate incarceration of African Americans[,] imprisonment itself reduces black political ability to influence these policies."[23]

A. Women and Mass Incarceration

People tend to think of mass incarceration as an issue that solely involves men. However, the reality is that women have been swept into the criminal justice system at rates that are historically unprecedented. It is true that men constitute the overwhelming majority of inmates in the nation's prisons and jails. Nevertheless, women constitute a significant portion of the country's prison population. Moreover, their numbers are growing rapidly. As Brewer and Heitzeg report, "Whereas the adult male population has tripled in the past 20 years, the number of women incarcerated has increased tenfold during the same time span. Women represent the fastest growing sector of the prison population."[24] From 1970 to 2001, the number of women imprisoned increased 2,800%.[25] Further, women of color are overrepresented among the population of incarcerated women. "More than 90,000 prisoners are women, and

[19] THE SENTENCING PROJECT, FACT SHEET: FELONY DISENFRANCHISEMENT 1 (2014), https://www.sentencingproject.org/publications/felony-disenfranchisement-laws-in-the-united-states/.

[20] *Id.* at 4.

[21] *Id.*

[22] Brewer & Heitzeg, *supra* note 17, at 628–29.

[23] MARC MAUER, RACE TO INCARCERATE 206 (2d ed. 2006)

[24] Brewer & Heitzeg, *supra* note 17, at 628.

[25] Mary V. Alfred & Dominique T. Chlup, *Neoliberalism, Illiteracy, and Poverty: Framing the Rise in Black Women's Incarceration*, 33 WESTERN J. BLACK STUD. 240, 241 (2009).

they are overwhelmingly women of color. African American women are 3 times more likely than Latinas and 6 times more likely than White women to be in prison."[26] Although they make up only 13% of the total population of women in the country, black women represent 50% of the women who are incarcerated.[27]

Kimberlé Crenshaw has sought to ensure that women of color are included in any conversation that the nation has about mass incarceration. She has emphasized that mass incarceration poses a risk to women of color that is equal to the risk that it poses to men of color. She explains:

> [R]acial disparities in incarceration between men and women across all racial groups are in fact quite similar. This is partly because men in all these groups are more likely to be incarcerated than women. Thus, within their respective gender groups, men and women of color face racialized risks of incarceration that are similar to their white counterparts. In other words, the increased risk of incarceration relative to race is virtually the same for Black men and women as for whites.[28]

In the view of scholars like Crenshaw, it is important to include women of color, and women more generally, in discussions of mass incarceration because their experiences show how our penal policies are connected to other social institutions. Crenshaw and others writing in this vein highlight the relationship between the expansion of the nation's prison population, on the one hand, and the diminishment of support for the welfare state, on the other. They argue that the connection between incarceration and the contraction of the welfare state exists on two levels: on a material level, critical scholars propose that when funding for social problems designed to support indigent families is reduced, the heads of these families—who tend to be women—may feel compelled to engage in crime in order to sustain their families. On a more discursive level, critical scholars propose that social welfare programs have been racialized as nonwhite in the same way that crime has been racialized as nonwhite. Thus, if hostility or resentment towards nonwhite people exists, we ought not to be surprised if this racial displeasure is expressed in our penal policies (which punish implicitly nonwhite lawbreakers by giving them long sentences and saddling them with ruinous collateral consequences) as well as our public benefits policies (which punish implicitly nonwhite welfare mothers by

---

[26] Brewer & Heitzeg, *supra* note 17, at 628.

[27] *See* Alfred & Chlup, *supra* note 25, at 241.

[28] Kimberlé W. Crenshaw, *From Private Violence to Mass Incarceration: Thinking Intersectionally About Women, Race, and Social Control*, 59 UCLA L. REV. 1418, 1436–37 (2012).

denying them support and forcing them to rely on a labor market that does not contain jobs that pay a livable wage).

B. Mass Incarceration as *The New Jim Crow*

In 2010, Alexander published her widely-read account of the U.S.'s penal policies, *The New Jim Crow: Mass Incarceration in the Age of Colorblindness*. While Alexander certainly was not the first person to identify similarities between the nation's present criminal justice system and the formal system of racial control that the South administered for a century once Reconstruction came to an end in the 1870s, her account probably has been the most influential. She proposes that the country has always had a need and desire to subjugate people of color—black people, specifically. It initially accomplished this subjugation through chattel slavery. When that institution fell, the country secured the control and exploitation of black people through Jim Crow, a system of "laws, policies, customs, and institutions"[29] that reduced black people to second-class citizens. When the Civil Rights Movement forced the disestablishment of Jim Crow, the nation found itself without a formal mechanism by which it could dominate black people. Alexander proposes that the criminal justice system has come to serve that purpose. She writes:

> What has changed since the collapse of Jim Crow has less to do with the basic structure of our society than with the language we use to justify it. In the era of colorblindness, it is no longer socially permissible to use race, explicitly, as a justification for discrimination, exclusion, and social contempt. So we don't. Rather than rely on race, we use our criminal justice system to label people of color "criminals" and then engage in all the practices we supposedly left behind. Today it is perfectly legal to discriminate against criminals in nearly all the ways that it was once legal to discriminate against African Americans. Once you're labeled a felon, the old forms of discrimination—employment discrimination, housing discrimination, denial of the right to vote, denial of educational opportunity, denial of food stamps and other public benefits, and exclusion from jury service—are suddenly legal. As a criminal, you have scarcely more rights, and arguably less respect, than a black man living in Alabama at the height of Jim Crow. We have not ended racial caste in America; we have merely redesigned it.[30]

---

[29] ALEXANDER, *supra* note 11, at 13.

[30] *Id.* at 2.

Alexander contends that although the racial nature of the criminal justice system and mass incarceration is obvious, it nevertheless operates in an ostensibly race-blind fashion. Those who are its architects, as well as those who endorse it, have never needed to confess an aspiration to dominate or regulate black people. Instead, proposes Alexander, they have only needed to articulate a concern about "crime," declaring that they are worried about the decline of "law and order" and stating that the country needs to take back the streets from "criminals." Thus, Alexander proposes, defenders of mass incarceration never need to make the case that the present system of racial control is just and right—as segregationists and other defenders of the old Jim Crow had to do from time to time. Instead, defenders of mass incarceration only need to deny that it is a system of *racial* control in the first instance. As Brewer and Heitzeg put it, "[T]he reliance on the criminal system provides the color-blind racist regime the perfect set of codes to describe racialized patterns of alleged crime and actual punishment without ever referring to race. . . . There is no discussion of race and racism; there is only public discourse about crime, criminals, gangs, and drug-infested neighborhoods."[31]

Other critical scholars have argued that just as white people accrued benefits from the old Jim Crow, the "New Jim Crow" pays them dividends as well. For example, Butler identifies material and nonmaterial gains that white people reap from mass incarceration. On the material side of the ledger, Butler argues that the imprisonment of hundreds of thousands of people of color, together with the disabilities that formally incarcerated people are forced to bear, function to reduce the competition that white people have for jobs in the labor market. He proposes that, in this way, the criminal justice system operates as "an employment stimulus plan for working-class white people,"[32] who are significantly more likely to escape contact with the criminal justice system than their counterparts of color. Moreover, he observes that mass incarceration generates jobs for white people in the rural areas where many jails and prisons are located. Somebody needs to build these institutions and manage the people inside, after all. Thus, Butler argues, mass incarceration "delivers cash money to many working-class white people."[33]

The less quantifiable benefits that the mass incarceration of disproportionate numbers of people color gives to white people are equally significant, argues Butler. He writes about the psychological

---

[31] Brewer & Heitzeg, *supra* note 17, at 633.

[32] PAUL BUTLER, CHOKEHOLD: POLICING BLACK MEN 12 (2017) [hereinafter BUTLER, CHOKEHOLD].

[33] *Id.*

gains that white people experience as a direct consequence of the imprisonment of large numbers of nonwhite people. He contends that the "criminalizing of blackness . . . brings psychic rewards. American criminal justice enhances the property value of whiteness."[34] The more that nonwhite people are degraded, the more that white people's status is improved. Just as many poor white people supported slavery and Jim Crow because these systems forced people of color to occupy the lowest rung on the social ladder—thus freeing poor white people from being the dregs of society—mass incarceration in contemporary times does similar work. The argument is that although poor and working-class white people may not be "winning" at all within global capitalism, mass incarceration has so demeaned people of color that it makes white people feel better: it makes them feel that they are not "losing." Their whiteness may give them very little; but, at the very least, it gives them the invaluable knowledge that they are not black.

Alexander argues that the criminal justice system became the stuff of the "New Jim Crow" when former President Ronald Reagan decided to launch a War on Drugs. It was shortly after this "war" was initiated that the nation's incarceration rates began to skyrocket. Alexander contends, however, that a concern with drug use and abuse was not the impetus behind the war; neither was a concern with the violence that illegal drug markets tend to generate. Instead, Alexander proposes, the War on Drugs was a product of Reagan's desire to appeal to white voters who, consciously or unconsciously, wanted to reverse the gains that people of color had won through the reforms of the civil rights era.

It is true that Reagan's War on Drugs coincided to a great extent with the crack cocaine epidemic, which destroyed individuals, decimated families, and lay waste to communities of color across the nation. For this reason, many have concluded that Reagan's War on Drugs was his good faith effort to address a crisis that had ruined the lives of countless people of color. Alexander disagrees. She writes that although the havoc that crack cocaine brought certainly demanded a strong response, we, as a nation, had several choices about what that response would be. She observes that "some countries faced with rising drug crime or seemingly intractable rates of drug use and drug addiction chose the path of drug treatment, prevention, and education or economic investment in crime-ridden communities."[35] Faced with the crack cocaine crises, the U.S. chose to spend billions of dollars militarizing police forces and building prisons within which millions of people would be warehoused.

---

[34] *Id.*

[35] ALEXANDER, *supra* note 11, at 51.

Although the crack cocaine epidemic has come to an end, U.S. incarceration rates remain among the highest in the world. This is due, in part, to the nation's continued fixation with punishing drug use and sales though the criminal justice system—a fixation that both Democratic and Republican administrations have shared. (Alexander and others find it important to observe that although Reagan began the War on Drugs, Bill Clinton escalated it to previously unimagined heights during his administration—dramatically increasing the funding for anti-drug efforts, increasing the sentences for drug crimes, and making the collateral consequences of a drug conviction more incapacitating.)

Critical thinkers find this incredibly interesting, with some proposing that the reason for the nation's insistence upon criminalizing drug use is its association with people of color. In other words, some have argued that the reason for the nation's obsession with drug use is society's belief that black people are the folks who are using drugs. On this point, Capers writes that society has always "marked the crime engaged in by African Americans as particularly dangerous and in need of control. Thus, while Irish-Americans may have been associated with rum-running or Italian Americans with numbers rackets and organized crime, their criminal activity was deemed less threatening to the social order than crimes committed by blacks."[36] Capers goes on to suggest that part of the explanation of society's failure to criminalize or prosecute the harmful acts perpetrated by corporations and the individuals who animate them is that these behaviors are associated with white people. He implies that if white-collar crime had a black face, we would witness an obsession with rooting it out—quite possibly with the incredibly shocking tactics that the police currently use to root out drug crimes—and punishing those who would dare to commit it.

An important element of Alexander's rendering of mass incarceration as the "New Jim Crow" is that, in her telling of it, justice and fair outcomes are not to be found in the court system. Alexander observes that we tend to believe that persons who have been charged with a crime invariably will have the opportunity to prove their innocence in court. However, this is not the reality for the overwhelming majority of people facing criminal charges. Most individuals charged with a crime accept a plea bargain, where they agree to plead guilty "in exchange for some form of leniency by the prosecutor."[37] Plea bargains oftentimes are the most advisable course that criminal defendants can pursue. First, when a defendant is

---

[36] I. Bennett Capers, *Critical Race Theory*, *in* THE OXFORD HANDBOOK OF CRIMINAL LAW 25, 29 (Markus D. Dubber & Tatjana Hörnle eds., 2014) [hereinafter Capers, *Critical Race Theory*].

[37] ALEXANDER, *supra* note 11, at 87.

poor—indeed, some 80% of criminal defendants are living in poverty[38]—it is unlikely that he will be able to afford to hire a lawyer who can help him fight his case. This means that he likely will have to rely on a public defender. Alexander argues that this is far from ideal, as "our nation's public defender system is woefully inadequate. The most visible sign of the failed system is the astonishingly large caseloads public defenders routinely carry, making it impossible for them to provide meaningful representation to their clients."[39] Second, accepting a plea bargain tends to be advisable because many crimes—especially drug crimes—carry stiff statutory penalties. Many of these crimes have mandatory minimums, with the "typical mandatory sentence for a first-time drug offense in federal court" being five or ten years.[40] Thus, it is often prudent for an individual facing criminal charges to agree to plead guilty and accept the more lenient sentence that a prosecutor offers than to go to court and risk being sentenced to a decade, or more, in prison. As Alexander tells it, "Never before in our history . . . have such an extraordinary number of people felt compelled to plead guilty, even if they are innocent, simply because the punishment for the minor, nonviolent offense with which they have been charged is so unbelievably severe. When prosecutors offer 'only' three years in prison when the penalties defendants could receive if they took their case to trial would be five, ten, or twenty years—or life imprisonment—only extremely courageous (or foolish) defendants turn the offer down."[41]

1. *Critiques of* The New Jim Crow

While Alexander's account of mass incarceration has been influential, it is not without its critics. We might understand these critiques to fall into three camps: 1) those that believe that Alexander's account is accurate, but incomplete; 2) those that do not believe that the *old* Jim Crow is an appropriate frame through which to view mass incarceration, and 3) those that dispute that *race* is a valuable frame through which to understand mass incarceration.

a. *The New Jim Crow* as a Partial Account

Richard Delgado and Jean Stefancic have argued that while there is much to laud about Alexander's proposition that mass incarceration is a racial caste system that is appropriately analogized to the Jim Crow of the 1870s through 1960s, her account ultimately is deficient. They claim that the deficiency is a product of Alexander's almost exclusive focus on mass incarceration *as it affects black men.*

---

[38] *Id.* at 85.

[39] *Id.*

[40] *Id.* at 87.

[41] *Id.*

They contend that if Alexander had broadened her focus, she would have seen that other nonwhite racial groups confront societal institutions that function to subjugate them in a manner that is similar to the way in which the criminal justice system subjugates black people.

Delgado and Stefancic maintain that Alexander and others are correct when they propose that "[i]mprisonment removes African-Americans—particularly young men, often for drug offenses—from the street, the voting rolls, and the job market, thus reducing competition with whites over jobs [and] political power."[42] However, they note that while the criminal justice system is the institution that operates to exclude black people from the polity, other institutions operate to exclude Latinx, indigenous, Asian, and Muslim peoples. They write,

> Imprisonment, then, removes blacks from the American mainstream, whereas deportations and their specter accomplish the same for Latinos. . . . History reveals a similar pattern for Native Americans. The Discovery Doctrine and, a few years later, the Trail of Tears, the Dawes Act, and relocation to reservations removed them from land and opportunities that whites coveted. For Asians, Chinese Exclusion, alien land laws, and wartime removal of Japanese-Americans achieved much the same. For Muslims, and Middle Eastern people, close surveillance, profiling, and demands for immigration restriction send the message that they are unwelcome.[43]

Thus, Delgado and Stefancic contend that Alexander's narrow attention to the criminal justice system as a mechanism of racial control over black people causes her to miss the others systems that serve as mechanisms of racial control over other nonwhite groups.

b. The Old Jim Crow as an Inapt Lens

James Forman, Jr.—who, it might be important to note, is an avid critic of the criminal justice system and who has devoted much of his scholarship to advocating for its reform—has proposed that viewing mass incarceration through the lens of the old Jim Crow might obscure more than it illuminates. He argues that analogizing the current imprisonment of millions of people, a disproportionate number of whom are people of color, to the old Jim Crow misrepresents several aspects of the present problem.

---

42 Richard Delgado & Jean Stefancic, *Critical Perspectives on Police, Policing, and Mass Incarceration*, 104 GEO. L.J. 1531, 1537 (2016).

43 *Id.* at 1538–39.

i. Problematic Centering of Drug Crimes

Forman proposes that scholars who contend that mass incarceration is a "New Jim Crow" tend to blame the country's high imprisonment rates on the War on Drugs and the nation's aggressive approach to punishing drug crimes. However, Forman argues, this focus misses that while many people are incarcerated for drug offenses, many, many more people are serving time for violent crimes. Indeed, while a quarter of the prison population is serving time for drug crimes, half of the prison population is serving time for violent crimes. He concedes that the 550,000 people currently incarcerated for drug crimes is an "extraordinary and appalling number."[44] However, he notes that "even if every single one of these drug offenders were released tomorrow, the United States would still have the world's largest prison system."[45]

Forman observes that if one wants to make the argument that the criminal justice system is discriminating against black people, it makes sense to ignore violent crimes and to focus on drug crimes. As noted above, most studies have found that black people and white people use and sell drugs at similar rates; however, black people are much more likely to be arrested, prosecuted, and convicted of drug offenses. In the context of drug crimes, it appears that although black and white people are engaging in similar behaviors, they are being treated quite dissimilarly. Yet, Forman notes, when one considers violent crimes, any dissimilarity of treatment between the races disappears. While black people are overrepresented among those who are presently incarcerated for violent crimes, this makes sense, as black people are overrepresented among those who commit violent crimes. Thus, the argument that the criminal justice system discriminates against people of color by treating them differently from their white counterparts fails when we consider the fifty percent of the prison population that has committed violent offenses.

Forman also observes that ignoring violent crime allows for those who make the "New Jim Crow" analogy to argue that the nation's focus on drug crimes is appropriately understood as a racial backlash against the gains that black people made during the Civil Rights Movement. Forman argues that the backlash story obscures that "crime shot up dramatically just before the prison boom. Reported street crime quadrupled in the twelve years from 1959 to 1971. Homicide rates doubled between 1963 and 1974, and robbery rates tripled."[46] While we still might wonder why the nation did not choose a less punitive approach to address the increase in violent

---

44 Forman, *supra* note 10, at 48.

45 *Id.*

46 *Id.* at 35.

crime during this time—and we might wonder whether the nation felt comfortable locking up perpetrators of violent crime because those perpetrators were disproportionately people of color—Forman advises us to pay attention to the role that violent crime played in bringing the country on board with a plan that led the nation to have the largest prison population in the world.

ii. Black Support for Mass Incarceration

Forman contends that the "New Jim Crow" analogy obscures that people of color have been supporters and architects of mass incarceration. While the old Jim Crow was a system that white people imposed on black people, mass incarceration cannot be similarly described. In many cases, black people with an interest in protecting their families and communities from crime have imposed mass incarceration on other black people. He looks to Washington, D.C.—a jurisdiction that is controlled by black people, yet has incarceration rates that rival jurisdictions where white people are in control—as evidence of this. He concludes, "While racial animus or indifference might explain the sky-high African American incarceration rates in Baltimore and Detroit, they do not explain those in Washington, D.C."[47]

iii. Class Privilege and Mass Incarceration

Forman writes that an important element of the Jim Crow of the nineteenth and early twentieth centuries is its domination of *all* black people—men and women, young and old, rich and poor. Under that racial caste system, affluence did not allow a black person an exit from second-class citizenship. Forman argues that the same cannot be said of the "New Jim Crow." The vast majority of people who presently are incarcerated in the nation's prisons and jails were living in poverty prior to their incarceration. Forman underscores that the reach of mass incarceration "is largely confined to the poorest, least-educated segments of the African American community."[48] In most cases, class privilege works to safeguard an individual from becoming entangled in the criminal justice system.

On this point, Forman takes particular issue with Alexander's claim that mass incarceration has determined what blackness means in the contemporary U.S. Alexander proposes that just as slavery and the old Jim Crow defined what it meant to be a black person in the U.S.—i.e., it made blackness mean inferiority, subservience, marginality, and exploitability—mass incarceration as the "New Jim Crow" does similar work. She argues that the nation's imprisoning of disproportionate numbers of black people has made blackness mean

---

[47] *Id.* at 42.

[48] *Id.* at 54.

danger, criminality, violence, and deviance.[49] Forman disagrees. He might agree with the claim that mass incarceration has made blackness mean danger, criminality, violence, and deviance *when blackness intersects with poverty*. But, in light of the reality that "increased income and educational attainment can bring a measure of protection against some of the criminal justice system's historic anti-black tendencies,"[50] he rejects the suggestion that mass incarceration is as totalizing a system as slavery or the old Jim Crow such that it can "define[ ] the meaning of blackness in America."[51]

c. Nonracial Explanations of Mass Incarceration

Even though many people find racial disparities in mass incarceration disturbing, many observers have opined that, ultimately, race cannot explain why the U.S. currently has the largest prison population and the one of the highest incarceration rates in the world.

These explanations come in a variety of forms. Many of them tend to emphasize that large numbers of *white* people currently are imprisoned in the U.S. Indeed, close to one million white people are incarcerated today.[52] The argument is that the criminal justice system cannot be a system that is designed to, or simply functions to, subjugate nonwhite people when white people find themselves within its jurisdiction at significant rates. Essentially, this position proposes that if mass incarceration is the "New Jim Crow," it is one in which many white people also have to sit in the back of the bus, cannot eat at lunch counters, and must use "colored only" bathrooms.

Critics who insist that the criminal justice system is, either in purpose or effect, racist respond to the above observation by emphasizing that while there might be many white people who presently are imprisoned in the U.S., they are nevertheless *underrepresented* in the nation's prisons and jails. Several hundred thousand more white people would have to be incarcerated, and several hundred thousand nonwhite prisoners would have to be released, in order to eliminate racial disparities in incarceration rates.

Now, those who deny that race has any explanatory value when it comes to mass incarceration usually reply that, as noted above, racial disparities in imprisonment rates simply reflect racial

---

[49] *See* ALEXANDER, *supra* note 11, at 197.

[50] Forman, *supra* note 10, at 56–57.

[51] ALEXANDER, *supra* note 11, at 197.

[52] *See* E. ANN CARSON, U.S. DEP'T OF JUSTICE, PRISONERS IN 2016, at 3, 19–20 (2018), https://www.bjs.gov/content/pub/pdf/p16.pdf; ZEHN ZENG, U.S. DEP'T OF JUSTICE, JAIL INMATES IN 2016, at 9 (2018), https://www.bjs.gov/content/pub/pdf/ji16.pdf.

disparities in crime rates. Because nonwhite people commit more crime than white people, they are overrepresented among the prison population.

Racial critics of mass incarceration have at least two response to this position. First, they contend that society addresses crime with prisons and jails *because* people of color disproportionately commit crime. They propose that if white people disproportionately committed more crime than nonwhite people, society would find less punitive ways to deal with it. Instead of building more prisons and jails, society would try to address the root causes of crime. Alternately, racial critics of mass incarceration propose that if white people disproportionately committed crime, society simply might not identify their "criminal" behavior as crime. Writes Capers, "[M]uch conduct committed by white-collar individuals that causes extreme harm and could be criminalized is simply not made criminal at all, but is subject only to ethical or civil sanctions."[53]

The second response that progressive thinkers give to the suggestion that there is nothing racially problematic about racial disparities in incarceration rates, as these rates simply reflect crime rates, is to remind that this is not true across the board. As discussed above, when it comes to drug crimes, black and white offense rates are the same. Nevertheless, nonwhite people are much more likely to be arrested, prosecuted, convicted, and sentenced to jail or prison for drug offenses.

Interestingly, some have been willing to deny that racial disparities in punishment for *drug offenses* reflect racial discrimination. For example, William Stuntz has argued that punishing drug crimes is just a vehicle for governments to punish violent crimes. According to this argument, if black people are disproportionately punished for drug crimes, it is only because they disproportionately commit violent crimes, for which the drug conviction is simply a proxy. He writes:

> [T]he substitution of drug prosecutions for violent felony cases was natural. . . . [I]n 2006, the murder rate among whites stood at 3.1 per 100,000; among blacks, the analogous figure was 23.7. . . . [I]n the places where the most blacks live, clearance rates for violent crimes are lowest; in the whitest areas, clearance rates are highest. . . . Everything about the war on drugs and the politics associated with it make sense only on the assumption that drugs were not the war's primary target. Violence was. So, in the many cases in which direct punishment for violence

[53] Capers, *Critical Race Theory*, *supra* note 36, at 29.

was impossible, drug laws made indirect punishment easy.[54]

Finally, many of those who deny that race explains mass incarceration itself or, simply, racial disparities in mass incarceration, propose that class is actually the culprit. As Forman observes, the large majority of people under the jurisdiction of the criminal justice system are poor. If poverty, in some significant respects, causes crime, then we ought not to be surprised that people of color disproportionately commit crime, as they disproportionately bear the burdens of poverty in this country. Progressive thinkers of race respond by asking the question: if poverty causes crime, why not attempt to reduce poverty or, in the alternative, reduce its most harmful effects? Why spend money building prisons and jails when that money could just as easily be spent on creating a safety net that lifts people out of poverty?[55] They wonder: could the race of indigent lawbreakers have something to do with our societal choice to punish the poor instead of helping them?

II. Policing, Generally

It is probably not controversial to state that perceptions of the police vary widely among communities. Some communities celebrate the police, viewing them as heroes without capes—literal lifesavers who run towards danger when everyone else is running away. Other communities have far less laudatory opinions about the police, viewing them as the enemy—antagonists who occupy neighborhoods and cause more problems than they have ever solved. The latter communities tend to be communities of color.

Progressive race scholars have written extensively about some nonwhite communities' sense that the police do more harm than good. They have concluded that the communities that feel this way are on to something: their experience of the police as agents of the state who harass, bully, and terrorize people of color is not some bizarre misperception of reality, but rather is an accurate accounting of how the police operate in marginalized communities and treat marginalized individuals. Many progressive scholars underscore that the police's antagonistic relationship with nonwhite individuals and communities is not an accident or an unfortunate case of good intentions gone awry. Instead, in large part, these thinkers propose that the police's status as a dominating and dehumanizing force in

---

[54] William J. Stuntz, *Unequal Justice*, 121 HARV. L. REV. 1969, 2022–24 (2008).

[55] Sociologist Loïc Wacquant has argued that the neoliberal state purposefully uses its prisons and jails to manage those who are unable to survive and flourish within global capitalism. *See generally* LOÏC WACQUANT, PUNISHING THE POOR: THE NEOLIBERAL GOVERNMENT OF SOCIAL INSECURITY (2009). Chapter 19 will discuss Wacquant's scholarship in greater depth.

disadvantaged neighborhoods of color is by design. As Butler has written, "The work of the police is to preserve law and order, including the racial order."[56] According to Butler, the police are a mechanism by which white people's dominant status, and nonwhite people's subordinate status, can be maintained.

Many critical theorists have focused on the laws and policies that they believe enable the police to exist as a hostile force in disadvantaged communities of color. The Fourth Amendment, the part of the Constitution that most centrally regulates the government's relationship to the individual with respect to criminal matters on the street, has figured prominently in their analyses.[57] These scholars note that, as with all of the Amendments, the men who drafted the Constitution likely thought of the Fourth Amendment as a limitation on government power. However, in their critical assessment, the Court has not interpreted it in a way that imposes meaningful restrictions on the police. In Devon Carbado's telling, "By prohibiting the government from engaging in unreasonable searches and seizures, the Fourth Amendment is supposed to impose constraints on the police. However, the Supreme Court has interpreted the Amendment in ways that empower, rather than constrain, the police. . . . To put the point more provocatively, the Supreme Court has interpreted the Fourth Amendment to protect police officers, not black people."[58]

A. The Impotence of the Fourth Amendment

In progressive race scholars' view, several cases have created a jurisprudential landscape wherein the state is empowered to police individuals with few constitutional limitations. While the state has great powers vis-à-vis any individual—without regard to race, gender, class, etc.—these scholars emphasize that the state tends to use this power only vis-à-vis *some* individuals. And, more often than not, those individuals are poor and black or Latinx. Thus, in these scholars' assessment, formal equality exists; yet, there is vast inequality on the ground. Butler suggests that this is the only reason the status quo is allowed to exist. He writes, "If the police patrolled

---

[56] BUTLER, CHOKEHOLD, *supra* note 32, at 3.

[57] The Fourth Amendment provides: "The right of the people to be secure in their persons, houses, papers, and effects, against unreasonable searches and seizures, shall not be violated, and no Warrants shall issue, but upon probable cause, supported by Oath or affirmation, and particularly describing the place to be searched, and the persons or things to be seized." U.S. CONST. amend. IV.

[58] Devon W. Carbado, *Blue-on-Black Violence: A Provisional Model of Some of the Causes*, 104 GEO. L.J. 1479, 1505 (2016) [hereinafter Carbado, *Blue-on-Black Violence*].

white communities with the same violence that they patrol poor black neighborhoods, there would be a revolution."[59]

1. *Terry v. Ohio*[60]

In *Terry*, the Court was called upon to answer the question of whether police stops were cognizable as seizures under the Fourth Amendment. Prior precedent had provided that the police need "probable cause" in order to seize anyone and act consistently with the Fourth Amendment's prohibition of "unreasonable" seizures. In the world of criminal procedure, "probable cause" is a fairly high bar, requiring that a state actor possess some sort of evidence or know of some facts that would lead him to believe that a crime has been committed.

The *Terry* Court held that police stops *were* seizures under the Fourth Amendment. However, it concluded that the police do not need probable cause before conducting one. Instead, all they need is a "reasonable suspicion"[61] that crime is afoot—a lower bar than that represented by "probable cause." Further, the Court also licensed police officers to pat down individuals who they have stopped when they have a "reasonable suspicion," supported by "specific and articulable facts," that the person might be carrying a weapon.[62] While the police need probable cause to conduct a full "search" of an individual, police are permitted to "frisk" a person—involving a less invasive pat-down of the outer layers of a person's clothing—when a "reasonably prudent man [would be] warranted in the belief that his safety or that of others was in danger."[63]

Terry has been a disappointment to progressive thinkers because, as they see it, the case opened the door for the police to become a constant, regulatory presence in the lives of individuals of color. These critics have derided the opinion for failing to explore "the racial consequences of permitting police officers to search and seize people without having probable cause."[64] Indeed, Carbado decries the opinion for putting "in place a legal regime that effectively provides

---

[59] BUTLER, CHOKEHOLD, *supra* note 32, at 3.

[60] Terry v. Ohio, 392 U.S. 1 (1968).

[61] Carbado has described reasonable suspicion as "an evidentiary standard that is greater than a hunch but lower than probable cause." Devon W. Carbado, *From Stopping Black People to Killing Black People*, 105 CALIF. L. REV. 125, 157 (2017) [hereinafter Carbado, *From Stopping Black People*].

[62] *Terry*, 392 U.S. at 21.

[63] *Id.* at 27.

[64] Devon W. Carbado, *From Stop and Frisk to Shoot and Kill:* Terry v. Ohio's *Pathway to Police Violence*, 64 UCLA L. REV. 1508, 1533 (2017).

police officers with a constitutional mechanism to engage in [the wholesale harassment of African Americans]."[65]

Some have been skeptical that the decision in *Terry* could lead to the "wholesale harassment" of any group, as the police need to have a "reasonable suspicion" that an individual is about to commit a crime in order to stop her. Many progressive thinkers have responded by arguing that, despite what the Court in *Terry* may have intended, the reasonable suspicion standard does not operate as a bar that prevents police interactions with poor individuals of color. They identify two reasons for this.

First, there are many, many crimes on the books. Some of these crimes are serious—like the armed burglary that the defendants in *Terry* seemingly were preparing themselves to commit. However, many more are not serious—like the panhandling, loitering, littering, and "spitting in public places" that legislatures have made into criminal activity in some states.[66] While these "quality of life" crimes may make being in public spaces a more enjoyable experience for those with delicate sensibilities, they dramatically increase the number of crimes that an individual may commit—and, therefore, dramatically increase the number of occasions for police to become reasonably suspicious that "criminal activity is afoot." So, while *Terry* might not open the door to wholesale harassment if police had to be reasonably suspicious that an individual was about to commit a murder, rape, robbery, or theft, it is certainly more likely to open the door to wholesale harassment if police only have to be reasonably suspicious that an individual is about to panhandle, loiter, litter, or spit. As Carbado summarizes it, "[M]ass criminalization is not just a source of criminal sanction—it is a source of police empowerment. It provides police officers with a kind of . . . free-floating reasonable suspicion . . . that they can use to justify their repeated interactions with African-Americans."[67]

The second reason for the belief that the reasonable suspicion standard does not prevent harassment involves narratives about black criminality. Critical thinkers assert that these narratives propose that there is a close relationship between black people—specifically, black men—and crime. Because of these narratives, say thinkers, it is reasonable for anyone to believe that any given black

---

[65] *Id.*

[66] Carbado, *Blue-on-Black Violence*, *supra* note 58, at 1487–88. These laws are apiece with "broken windows" policing, which is premised on the idea that "if police officers do not vigorously focus their attention on low-level crimes and signs of disorder in a given community, that community will experience more serious and long-lasting problems of criminality and social upheaval. Broken windows policing, then, is expressly predicated on the view that police officers should enforce minor criminal infractions and surveil communities for signs of disorder." *Id.* at 1485–86.

[67] *Id.* at 1490.

man has committed, or will commit, a crime. If these discourses about black (male) criminality exist, then police officers will always have a reasonable suspicion that the black person who they encounter is engaging in crime. This paves the way for police to constantly engage black people in order to confirm their "reasonable" suspicions.

2. *Florida v. Bostick*[68]

The litigation that culminated in *Florida v. Bostick* began when police officers boarded a Greyhound bus in order to conduct a "drug sweep"—a procedure that Alexander tells us is a "common tactic in the War on Drugs."[69] She reports that these suspicion-less sweeps involve police entering buses and interviewing passengers in "dragnet operations [that] usually culminate in a request for 'consent' to search the passenger's luggage" for drugs.[70] This is precisely what the police did in *Bostick*: they boarded the bus on which Bostick was traveling and began looking for drug-carrying passengers. Eventually, they arrived where Bostick was seated. They asked him if they could search his bag. He said yes. And they found that he was, indeed, carrying drugs.

The question that the case raised was whether the police had "seized" Bostick when he sat in his seat and two armed, uniformed police officers stood in the aisle, effectively blocking any easy exit from the bus. If Bostick had been seized within the meaning of the Fourth Amendment, the police officers would have had to have, at the very least, a "reasonable suspicion" that he was carrying drugs—something they could not claim to have had. Of course, if Bostick had not been "seized," then the police could initiate an interaction with him and question him for a bad reason (i.e., because he is black) or for no reason at all.

The Court held that Bostick had not been seized. According to the Court, a "reasonable person" would have felt free to end the interaction with the police. The Court held that a person is only seized if a reasonable person would feel compelled to engage in a police encounter. The Court argued that a reasonable person in Bostick's shoes would have felt that she had the latitude to refuse to answer the police's questions and, if so inclined, pick up her things and exit the bus (although she would have to squeeze around the two police officers who were standing in the aisle).

Many progressive race scholars wonder who this reasonable person is. Would *any* person feel empowered to tell a group of police officers to leave her alone—especially when she is in the small space

---

[68] Florida v. Bostick, 501 U.S. 429 (1991).

[69] ALEXANDER, *supra* note 11, at 64.

[70] *Id.*

of a bus seat? These scholars criticize *Bostick* for articulating a legal standard that does not reflect how real people think and act in the real world. Further, they are suspicious that if such an empowered person does, in fact, exist, she likely is not poor and black. In their estimation, poor and black people experience the coercive power of the police much more frequently than people who are not poor and/or not black. Their experiences with the police—who patrol their neighborhoods much more aggressively than others—are likely to counsel them that they can never say no when a police officer approaches them. The argument is that poor black people's racialized knowledge about their relationship to and with the police would lead them, more than any other racial group, to believe things that are at odds with what the Court's hypothetical reasonable person would believe.

Tracey Maclin has suggested a way out of this predicament:

> My tentative proposal is that the Court should disregard the notion that there is an average, hypothetical, reasonable person out there by which to judge the constitutionality of police encounters. When assessing the coercive nature of an encounter, the Court should consider the race of the person confronted by the police, and how that person's race might have influenced his attitude toward the encounter. . . . Currently, the Court assesses the coercive nature of a police encounter by considering the totality of the circumstances surrounding the confrontation. All I want the Court to do is to consider the role race might play, along with the other factors it considers, when judging the constitutionality of the encounter.[71]

The Court's finding that Bostick, and any person in his situation, had not been seized within the meaning of the Fourth Amendment immunizes that particular police behavior from constitutional constraint. The Fourth Amendment dictates that *seizures* have to be reasonable. If something is not a seizure, all constitutional bets are off. In other words, while police have to defend the seizures they conduct, they are not required to justify non-seizures. Critical thinkers emphasize that police can engage in racial profiling and "non-seize" black people simply because they are black people. The Fourth Amendment does not prevent them from engaging in these practices.

But, returning to the facts of *Bostick*: what about the police officers' search of the bag? The discussion of *Terry* above counsels

---

[71] Tracey Maclin, *"Black and Blue Encounters"—Some Preliminary Thoughts About Fourth Amendment Seizures: Should Race Matter?*, 26 VAL. U. L. REV. 243, 250, 268–69 (1991).

that searches, at the very least, need to be supported by reasonable suspicion. If the police did not have reasonable suspicion that Bostick was carrying drugs, does not the search of Bostick's bag qualify as *unreasonable* and, therefore, violate the Fourth Amendment?

The Court thought not, concluding that while the police did not have authority to search Bostick's bag (inasmuch as they did not have reasonable suspicion), Bostick voluntarily consented to the search. Indeed, the Court concluded that Bostick voluntarily consented to the search even though he did not know that he had the right *not* to consent to the search. Unlike the right to remain silent, police do not have to inform individuals of their rights to refuse consent to police searches and seizures.

This is troubling to many critical scholars. They worry that poor people of color are less likely to know about their rights to refuse consent and, therefore, will be less likely to assert them.[72] Further, they are worried that even if poor people of color know about their rights, they will feel compelled to consent—even when their white counterparts will not feel similarly compelled.

3. *Whren v. United States*[73]

The litigation that culminated in *Whren v. United States* began when Michael Whren and a friend, James Brown, were driving in a part of town that the police had designated a "high drug area."[74] Vice detectives who were in the area had a feeling that Whren and Brown might have been carrying drugs or had been engaged in some drug-related activity. However, they lacked probable cause, or even a reasonable suspicion, that these drug crimes had been committed. So, they decided to follow Whren's car. After being tailed by the police officers (who, as vice detectives, were in plainclothes and in an unmarked car) for a while, Whren eventually made a sudden turn, without using his turn signal, and drove away at an "unreasonable" speed.[75] Thus, Whren broke the law—a traffic law. Having probable cause that Whren had committed a traffic violation—but, in actuality, more interested in investigating Whren for the drug crimes that they believed (without basis) that he and Brown were committing—the detectives pulled the car over. Upon approaching the car, they saw a bag of crack cocaine in Whren's lap and subsequently arrested the men for the drug crime. The question the

---

[72] Interestingly, studies have shown that when police officers tell people they have a right to refuse consent, it does not really change anything. People tend to give their consent anyway. *See* Marcy Strauss, *Reconstructing Consent*, 92 J. CRIM. L. & CRIMINOLOGY 211, 253–54 (2001–2002).

[73] Whren v. United States, 517 U.S. 806 (1996).

[74] *Id.* at 808.

[75] *Id.*

case presented for the Court was whether police officers can use traffic violations as an opportunity to investigate crimes that are unrelated to the traffic infraction—crimes for which they have no probable cause or reasonable suspicion to believe have been committed. A unanimous Court answered in the affirmative.

For critical thinkers, *Whren*—which established the legality of "pretext" stops—is a disaster. This believe this for several reasons. First, the Court's holding in *Whren* has the effect of authorizing police officers to stop any motorist at virtually any time. They say that this is because it typically is impossible to get from Point A to Point B in one's car without violating a traffic law. Laws prohibit motorists from driving too fast, driving too slow, rolling through a stop sign, stopping too long at a stop sign, etc. If a police officer is interested in pulling over a car and investigating the driver for a crime that he has no evidence to believe has been committed, all he has to do is follow the car for a bit. As soon as a traffic infraction is inevitably made, the police officer will have probable cause to stop the car and investigate the crime that he really is interested in investigating. Critical scholars emphasize that the police have the authority to question the driver about things that are unrelated to the traffic violation. Of course, drivers can refuse to consent to this additional line of questioning. But, even in the context of a traffic stop—that is, even in the context of a detention to which a person is not consenting—police officers have no obligation to inform an individual about her right not to consent to questioning that is tangential to the reason for the detention. This creates a confusing set of circumstances for a driver who has been stopped by a cop: she is obliged to answer some questions, but not obliged to answer others. Moreover, it is not always clear which questions must be answered and which ones can be ignored.

Second, critical thinkers about race are disturbed by their sense that *Whren* legitimizes racial profiling. Think about the facts of the case. They propose that the officers who stopped Whren and Brown had a feeling that they were engaging in a drug crime *because they were young black men*. According to these thinkers, *Whren* authorizes the police to follow up on their racialized hunches about criminal activity by waiting for the racially suspicious subjects to commit a traffic violation. They underscore that *everyone* commits traffic violations. However, they argue, the police will only be interested in the traffic violations committed by people of color because people of color are the folks who stereotypes and cultural narratives about criminality suggest are committing crime. Empirical evidence appears to confirm this intuition: although traffic violations are somewhat evenly distributed across the races, police officers disproportionately stop black and Latinx people for their traffic infractions.[76]

* * *

To progressive race scholars, perhaps the thing that is most disturbing about the Court's criminal procedure jurisprudence is that it effectively has closed the door to persons who want to challenge its racial consequences. In *Whren*, the Court ruled that if an individual believes that a police officer stopped him because of his race and wants to challenge the stop's legality on that basis, he cannot bring his claim of racial discrimination under the Fourth Amendment. In this way, the Court interpreted the Fourth Amendment to permit the police to engage in race-based policing. However, the Court did state that claims of racial discrimination could be heard under the Fourteenth Amendment and its Equal Protection Clause. But, as Alexander puts it, "This suggestion may have been reassuring to those unfamiliar with the Court's equal protection jurisprudence. But for those who have actually tried to prove race discrimination under the Fourteenth Amendment, the Court's remark amounted to a cruel irony."[77]

Alexander is referring to is the fact that, as discussed in Chapter 7, the Court has interpreted the Equal Protection Clause as only proscribing race-based actions that are conscious and intentional. Simple proof that a law or policy harms or subordinates people of color is not the stuff of an equal protection violation; one also needs to show the *intent* to harm or subordinate. Further, as Alexander notes "patterns of discrimination"—even those that showed that black people who killed white people were seven times more likely to get sentenced to death than white people who killed black people[78]—do not run afoul of the Equal Protection Clause. Alexander concludes that this leaves the police free to engage in patterns of discrimination, racially profiling and targeting people of color as much as they want. Provided that no one unwisely, or boldly, leaves concrete evidence of racial bias lying around—indeed, "[s]o long as officers refrain from uttering racial epithets and so long as they show the good sense not to say 'the only reason I stopped him was 'cause he's black' "—the Constitution imposes no constraint on these police behaviors and practices.[79]

---

[76] *See* Gregory M. Lipper, *Racial Profiling*, 38 HARV. J. ON LEGIS. 551, 551–52 (2001); Samuel R. Gross & Katherine Y. Barnes, *Road Work: Racial Profiling and Drug Interdiction on the Highway*, 101 MICH. L. REV. 651, 660 (2002).

[77] ALEXANDER, *supra* note 11, at 109.

[78] McCleskey v. Kemp, 481 U.S. 279, 327 (1987).

[79] ALEXANDER, *supra* note 11, at 133.

B. Consequences

What are the effects of a jurisprudence that has interpreted the Constitution to allow the police fairly unbridled powers when it comes to investigating crime and otherwise enforcing the laws? Some might say that the result is we live in communities that are safer than they otherwise would be. While this may (or may not) be true, critical thinkers about race are afraid about the excessively high costs of our arguably safer communities. Specifically, they are troubled by the servility that people of color are compelled to display to the individuals who are supposed to be protecting and serving them—servility that enables people of color to avoid violence, or death, at the hands of the police. Writes Alexander, "Like the days when black men were expected to step off the sidewalk and cast their eyes downward when a white woman passed, young black men know the drill when they see the police crossing the street toward them; it is a ritual of dominance and submission played out hundreds of thousands of times each year."[80]

Butler argues that these displays of "dominance and submission" have a pedagogical function: they are designed to teach the people of color who must be obsequious, as well as the people of color who bear witness to this obsequiousness, that the state is powerful and everywhere and that the individual is insignificant and easily destroyed. Drawing from French philosopher Michel Foucault, Butler argues that "[t]he police purpose then is served not so much by the investigation but by the stop itself, which is, in Foucault's words, a 'reassertion and public declaration of power by the sovereign.' . . . It . . . 'display[s] for all to see the power relation that gave . . . force to the law.' "[81]

III. Police Violence

Progressives have not taken lightly the police killings of unarmed black people—folks like Eric Garner, Michael Brown, Philando Castile, Alton Sterling, Freddie Gray, Rekia Boyd, Stephon Clark, and Tamir Rice. Progressive scholars argue time and again that the deaths of unarmed black people at the hands of the police should not be understood as the result of a racist cop going off the rails and doing bad things. Instead, they emphasize that police killings of unarmed black people are the expected consequence of police officers following the rules. That is, these deaths do not evidence a flaw in the system; instead, they evidence the system working as we should expect it to work. Differently stated: if one thinks that the deaths of the above-named individuals reflect a

---

[80] *Id.* at 136.

[81] BUTLER, CHOKEHOLD, *supra* note 32, at 108.

problem, critical thinkers insist that the problem is not bad apples, but rather bad *laws*. As Butler cogently explains:

> The ideas from critical race theory help us understand why the crisis in criminal justice stems more from legal police conduct than illegal police misconduct. . . . [M]any of the concerns about the police are about conduct that is legal. The problem is not as much "bad apple" cops as police work itself—what the law actually allows. That's why even when police officers are charged with brutality, they are often found "not guilty."[82]

Carbado has sought to foreground the role that the Fourth Amendment plays in producing police killings of unarmed people of color. According to him, the jurisprudence discussed in the previous part ought to figure prominently in any explanation of why we can count so many unarmed black people who have died at the hands of the police. He has argued that *Terry*, *Bostick*, *Whren*, and many other cases permit "[police] interactions with African Americans with little or no basis. This 'front-end' police contact—which the Fourth Amendment law enables—is often the predicate to 'back-end' police violence."[83] He stresses the "direct relationship between the scope of ordinary police authority, on the one hand, and African American vulnerability to extraordinary police violence, on the other."[84]

Again, the emphasis in these analyses is on structural explanations of police violence, and they are adamant about eschewing individualist explanations that focus on rogue cops. Moreover, the structures that these thinkers offer to explain police violence are incredibly complex: Mass incarceration reinforces (and reaffirms the truth of) stereotypes about black criminality. Broken windows policing enables the police to engage in frequent interactions with people of color. The failure of police departments to adequately train officers—and these departments' toleration of a policing culture within which police officers figure as "soldiers" fighting in a "war zone" of urban decrepitude—increases the likelihood that officers will be aggressive in their interactions with the individuals they encounter. People of color, who have to constantly demonstrate meekness to the police, occasionally get fed up. And they resist. . . . When violence does occur, the law works to legitimize it. Prosecutors decide not to bring charges. Grand juries refuse to indict. If cases are actually tried, juries conclude that a "reasonable person" would have believed that deadly force was necessary, and they vote to acquit. Because the killing offends no law,

---

[82] *Id.* at 187.

[83] Carbado, *From Stopping Black People*, *supra* note 61, at 127.

[84] *Id.* at 128.

nothing changes. And the complex process continues without interruption or significant challenge.

Because critical theorists believe that the cause of the problem is macro in scope, they believe that the solution is equally macro. They say that it involves the nation's retreat from mass incarceration, the development of alternative means to address violence in poor communities of color, racial and economic integration of neighborhoods, a rejection of broken windows policing, proactive efforts by police departments to address implicit and explicit biases in their officers, the generation of new Fourth Amendment precedent, the generation of new Fourteenth Amendment precedent, etc. Some have even proposed the abolition of the police.[85] The work, they say, must be truly transformative. If it is not, they are convinced that, as a nation, we will be doomed to continuously add names to the list of people of color who have been killed by the police.

IV. Questions and Discussion

1. Progressive race scholars have argued that one of many functions of mass incarceration is to hide social problems. Consider that those who are incarcerated are not counted in tallies of unemployment rates. Accordingly, mass incarceration makes it appear that fewer people are unemployed and that, in terms of economic health, the nation is doing better than it actually is. Further, racial disparities in incarceration rates mean that black and brown unemployment, in particular, is hidden. According to some critical thinkers, this makes it appear as though the nation's racial problems are closer to being solved than they really are. Explains Ian Haney López, "The invisibility of significant facets of continued nonwhite poverty and unemployment leads to false comfort about racial progress and undercuts calls for needed social reform. The seeming resolution of the extreme poverty and severe unemployment afflicting nonwhite communities has permitted a social consensus that racial inequality lies in the receding past."[86]

2. Some progressive thinkers have proposed that the only answer to the racial problems presented by mass incarceration is through prison abolition. As Butler puts it, "U.S. prisons are built for black men, and black men will be free, literally and figuratively, only when prisons are no more."[87] Butler is careful to emphasize that abolishing prisons does not mean that wrongdoers will escape

---

[85] Derecka Purnell, *What Does Police Abolition Mean?*, BOSTON REVIEW (Aug. 23, 2017), http://bostonreview.net/law-justice/derecka-purnell-what-does-police-abolition-mean.

[86] Ian F. Haney López, *Post-Racial Racism: Racial Stratification and Mass Incarceration in the Age of Obama*, 98 CALIF. L. REV. 1023, 1048 (2010).

[87] BUTLER, CHOKEHOLD, *supra* note 32, at 229.

punishment entirely. Instead, prison abolition means that we, as a society, will be forced to identify ways to punish those who violate the norms embodied in the criminal law that do not involve "lock[ing] them in a cage."[88]

Does the possibility of prison abolition sound appealing to you in an intuitive sense? Why or why not? Those who support abolishing prisons oftentimes emphasize that "[i]ncarceration, for people of all races and genders, is violent and dehumanizing."[89] Can you think of ways to punish that are not violent and dehumanizing? Can you imagine a prison system that is not violent and dehumanizing? If so, what are some of its features? Do you think that violence and dehumanization is, sometimes, an appropriate feature of punishment?

3. As discussed above, the Court has declined to fold race into the reasonable person standard when determining whether a police encounter is a "seizure" for the purposes of the Fourth Amendment. The question of whether someone is in custody for the purposes of *Miranda* warnings is a very closely related issue, and it also uses an objective reasonable person standard. In *J.D.B. v. North Carolina*, however, the Court recognized that children's reactions to police are different from those of adults.[90] Accordingly, the Court decided that it was appropriate to individualize the reasonable person standard in terms of the defendant's age and it is necessary to ask, for example, whether a reasonable 13-year-old would feel herself to be in police custody—as opposed to simply asking what a reasonable (presumably, adult) person would feel.

Do you think that the Court got it right in *J.D.B.* when it held that the reasonable person ought to reflect the defendant's age? Do you think that the reasonable person ought to reflect the defendant's race? Is there a difference between age and race that is so significant that one ought to be considered for the purposes of Fourth Amendment analysis while the other ought to be ignored? Why or why not?

4. Alexander's *The New Jim Crow* has sold over a million copies to date and remains at the top of bestseller lists some eight years after its initial publication. What do you think explains the appeal of Alexander's argument?

5. As discussed above, the defendant in *Bostick* agreed to let the police search his bags even though he knew that he had drugs in his suitcase. He could not have thought that the cops would miss the

---

[88] *Id.*

[89] *Id.*

[90] J.D.B. v. North Carolina, 564 U.S. 261 (2011).

large amount of cocaine that he was carrying. Why, then, do you think that Bostick gave his consent to the search?

6. As discussed above, Stuntz has argued that although there are significant racial disparities in incarceration rates, the problem is not, at bottom, a racial one. He proposes that the problem is that decisions about crime and criminal punishment have been moved from local political arenas to more general fora. Thus, people—who may not be directly affected by crime—are now making decisions about what to do about crime. Stuntz argues that this is a recipe for disaster. He explains:

> With respect to crime and criminal punishment, residents of *all* neighborhoods have two warring incentives. On the one hand, they want safe streets on which to walk and drive and go about their business; they want to travel to parks and sporting events and grocery stores without fearing for their lives and property. On the other hand, they are loath to incarcerate their sons and brothers, neighbors and friends. The desire for order and the longing for freedom, anger at crime and empathy for the young men whom police officers arrest and prosecutors charge—both forces are powerful, and they push in opposite directions. . . . Local political control over criminal justice harnesses both forces, without giving precedence to either.[91]

Thus, Stuntz proposes that if we want to see moderation in penal policies, we need to return control over these policies to local communities.

Does this proposal strike you as true? Why or why not? If there was a way to address racial disparities in the criminal justice system without engaging race directly, do you think that we should pursue that course? Why or why not?

---

[91] Stuntz, *supra* note 54, at 1981–82.

Chapter 19

THE WELFARE STATE

I. Introduction

In this chapter, we explore the U.S.'s welfare state—the constellation of government programs and services that aim to protect and foster the health and wellbeing of the nation's citizens and residents. This chapter pays particular attention to the programs that provide cash assistance to indigent families with children—namely the Temporary Assistance for Needy Families program (TANF), which replaced the Aid to Families with Dependent Children program (AFDC) in 1996.

Some may be a bit perplexed by the inclusion of a chapter on the welfare state in a primer that is about race. These folks may feel that the U.S.'s safety net is not a *racial* issue in the same way that the criminal justice system or education, for example, are racial issues. However, progressive scholarship seeks to challenge this belief. The work of Kimberlé Crenshaw—specifically, her theory of intersectionality, explored in Chapter 12—is instructive here. Crenshaw's work counsels that the intuition that the welfare state is not a racial issue, and that it fails to implicate questions of racial justice, is likely a product of the belief that the black *man* is the true racial subject.[1] Pursuant to this view, the issues that we understand as affecting black men, like mass incarceration, are easily understood as racial issues. Meanwhile, matters that disproportionately impact black women—like the approach that the welfare state has taken to supporting poor, female-headed households—are not thought to be racial issues. Guided by the lessons that intersectionality has taught, the inclusion of this chapter in this primer represents critical thinkers' commitment to bringing women, as well as non-binary people, squarely within our racial lenses. As such, it offers an invitation to readers to think of the welfare state and the public benefits that it offers (or refuses to offer) poor women, who are disproportionately women of color, as a matter of racial justice.

Additionally, many scholars have observed that the government's policies around public benefits mirror its criminal justice policies. They say that both sets of policies are born of the

[1] As noted in Chapter 12, Crenshaw argued that while the generic "black person" is male, the generic "woman" is white. Thus, antiracist efforts centered the experiences of black men, and feminism centered the experiences of white women. The result was that black women and their experiences were obscured in both of these social justice movements. Crenshaw offered the theory of intersectionality with the intention of making black women visible.

same impulses and concern the same population. Their argument, essentially, is that *if we understand the criminal justice system, policing, and mass incarceration as implicating racial justice, then we ought to similarly understand the welfare state.*

Sociologist Loïc Wacquant has offered a comprehensive articulation of this position.[2] He begins by observing that transformations in the economy have reduced the number of middle-skill, middle-wage jobs that used to support the middle-class. Many people who could once rely on these jobs have been pushed into the market for low-skill, low-wage labor and, consequently, into jobs that cannot support a family. They are forced into poverty as a result. Wacquant proposes that the contemporary welfare state and the criminal justice system are society's way of managing the population living in this precarious economic condition. Instead of protecting indigent people from the insecurity and deprivation that the market for low-skill, low-wage labor guarantees, the welfare state pushes them into it by making work a condition of assistance or by denying assistance altogether. Meanwhile, the criminal justice system incarcerates those who fail at making do with very little. Wacquant calls these dual systems a "*carceral-assistantial net*."[3]

Wacquant contends that both the modern welfare state and the criminal justice system are motivated by the same philosophy of the individual: both systems insist that the individual is wholly responsible for his/her social situation. If she is poor, it is because she does not possess the commitment to work that will allow her to achieve financial success within the market for wage labor; if he has committed a crime, it is because he is criminally-inclined and ethically-challenged. Wacquant claims that both the welfare state and the penal state accept the view that *moral deficiencies* explain why people are poor or why they break the law. While the welfare state attempts to "fix" the moral deficiencies of the individuals under its jurisdiction, the penal state simply aims to keep the morally deficient away from the general population. Importantly, says Wacquant, both systems reject the possibility that the transformations in the economy mentioned above—that is, *structural conditions*—explain the impoverishment of marginal populations and why some of those who are marginalized violate the criminal law.

Wacquant is not the only theorist who has championed the position that the welfare state and the penal state "are twinned state responses to the generalization of social insecurity"[4] and,

---

[2] *See generally* LOÏC WACQUANT, PUNISHING THE POOR: THE NEOLIBERAL GOVERNMENT OF SOCIAL INSECURITY (2009).

[3] *Id.* at 12.

[4] *Id.* at 69.

consequently, ought to be analyzed together. Political scientists Joe Soss, Richard Fording, and Sanford Schram note that the money that financed the expansion of the criminal justice system and the proliferation of jails and prisons in the 1980s had to come from somewhere.[5] They suggest that it came from public assistance budgets. They argue that " 'bloated correctional spending primarily siphoned funds from welfare expenditures' "—a fact, they say, that demonstrates that there had been a "substantive shift in the ways that states [are] 'dealing with poverty and the governance of marginalized populations.' "[6]

Indeed, Soss and his coauthors propose that there has been a general intermeshing of the welfare state and the penal state. They assert that jails and prisons used to bring in social services in order to help inmates. Now, they say, the welfare state has grown more punitive, and "the direction of influence has reversed: Penal logics have been imported into the welfare arena."[7] Critical scholars observe that, in fact, the penal state has infiltrated welfare offices quite literally. Kaaryn Gustafson has explored the use of the criminal law to punish welfare recipients who violate the rules of public assistance programs.[8] Beneficiaries who fail to report income, for example, are not just hit with civil penalties, like a fine or a loss of benefits. They are also charged with, and convicted of, felonies. Further, welfare offices have worked closely with law enforcement both to exclude individuals with criminal records from welfare rolls as well as to nab public aid recipients with outstanding warrants.[9] Soss and his coauthors observe that even similar *vocabularies* are used to describe indigent persons receiving cash assistance and persons who are under the control and supervision of the criminal justice system: people who return to welfare after a stint of working commonly are described as "recidivists."[10]

Wacquant insists that the welfare state and the criminal justice system are both issues of racial justice because they both manage the same population. He writes that the "social silhouette of [the persons who are beneficiaries of the programs that provide cash assistance to indigent families] turns out to be a *near-exact replica of the profile of jail inmates*."[11] He notes that in terms of class, race, education,

---

5 *See* JOE SOSS, RICHARD C. FORDING & SANFORD F. SCHRAM, DISCIPLINING THE POOR: NEOLIBERAL PATERNALISM AND THE PERSISTENT POWER OF RACE 103 (2011).

6 *Id.* at 103–04.

7 *Id.* at 47.

8 *See* KAARYN S. GUSTAFSON, CHEATING WELFARE: PUBLIC ASSISTANCE AND THE CRIMINALIZATION OF POVERTY (2011).

9 *See* SOSS, FORDING & SCHRAM, *supra* note 5, at 48.

10 *Id.* at 47–48.

11 WACQUANT, *supra* note 2, at 98.

marital status, and history with abuse and violence, the population that receives cash assistance for poor families is identical to the incarcerated population. The only difference that he observes between the two populations is gender: women disproportionately are the subjects of the welfare state, while men disproportionately are the subjects of the penal state. On this point, he writes, "[T]he primary clients of the assitantial and carceral wings of the neoliberal state are essentially the two gender sides of the same population coin drawn from the marginalized fractions of the postindustrial working class. The state regulates the troublesome behaviors of these women (and their children) through workfare and those of the men in their lives . . . through criminal justice supervision."[12] Here, Soss and his coauthors offer a friendly amendment—one that insists upon recognizing that women have been swept into jails and prisons at historically unprecedented rates. As the number of women receiving welfare benefits has decreased, the number of women incarcerated has increased, seemingly in lockstep.[13] In this way, Soss and coauthors propose that prison, and not the market for low-wage work, increasingly has become the place where welfare recipients go when they leave the welfare rolls.

Finally, and crucially, just as progressive race scholars insist that race is crucial to explaining why the U.S. has chosen to manage its social problems through the criminal justice system, they insist that race is crucial to explaining why the U.S. has erected a welfare state that, in their view, inadequately and only reluctantly cares for its poor. The balance of this chapter explores this position.

II. The Causes of the Porous Welfare State

When compared to the nations that the U.S. tends to consider its peers, the welfare state that the country has erected is quite meager. It is "more fragmented and less universal than the welfare states of most other developed democratic nations—prone to division between generous social insurance policies for workers and stingy and punitive public assistance benefits for the poor . . . and lacking policies that most other countries provide, such as universal health insurance, family allowances, [and] child-care."[14] Observers have attempted to explain this American anomaly.

---

12 *Id.* at 99.

13 SOSS, FORDING & SCHRAM, *supra* note 5, at 272 (observing that "[f]rom 1995 to 2005, as TANF caseloads fell by 60 percent, the number of women prisoners in the United States rose by 57 percent").

14 Robert C. Lieberman, *Race and the Limits of Solidarity: American Welfare State Development in Comparative Perspective*, *in* RACE AND THE POLITICS OF WELFARE REFORM 23, 26 (Sanford F. Schram, Joe Soss, & Richard C. Fording eds., 2003).

One popular explanation looks to the values that people in the U.S. are imagined to embrace. Under this view, Americans hold individualism and property rights in incredibly high esteem. The welfare state appears to be inconsistent with both of those things. The property rights of the haves must be infringed if the have nots are to be cared for. That is, some of the money to which those enjoying financial stability can lay claim has to be taken from them in order to finance the programs and services that will care for the financially unstable. Moreover, the welfare state refuses to permit the individual to be isolated. He is not isolated if some of his stuff can be taken from him in order to care for someone else; similarly, she is not isolated if she need not rely solely on herself, but can turn to other individuals for support. Because the welfare state runs afoul of both individualism and property rights, some observers have proposed that this explains the U.S.'s refusal to commit itself fully to it.

While this explanation for the anemic quality of the U.S.'s safety net may resonate, many observers identify problems with it. Namely, they say, it cannot explain why some safety net programs, like Medicare and Social Security, have enjoyed and continue to enjoy immense political popularity. Moreover, they say that it cannot explain why the public benefit programs that the U.S. now offers came into existence in the first place.

Another explanation for the insubstantiality of the U.S. welfare state is the absence of a labor-based political party in the country and the relative weakness of organized labor. If workers had been more powerful and had a louder political voice, this explanation proposes, then they would have demanded the creation of a robust welfare state. In the absence of labor's political clout, this explanation concludes, the welfare state that the nation developed was insubstantial.

While it is probably true that the existence of a labor-based political party might have led the U.S. to construct a safety net that is more expansive than the one that presently exists, some observers are dissatisfied with this explanation because it does not explain *why* such a party failed to develop or *why* industrial labor unions have remained weak when compared to their peers in industrialized nations around the world.

The answer that many critical thinkers have offered to these questions is *race*: race explains why labor unions in the country have been feeble, with white workers refusing to form alliances with black workers and, in the process, increasing the power that employers had over both groups. Race, they say, explains why a labor-based political party did not coalesce. And, more broadly, they say that race explains why the country has such a miserly welfare state. As Jill Quadagno has written, "Among the distinctive features of American state formation, none is more salient than the failure to extend full citizenship to African Americans. It is this characteristic, more than any other, that has influenced the development of the welfare state."[15]

Thus, progressive thinkers suggest that the welfare state in the U.S. grew patchily and unevenly because the desire to keep people of color at the bottom of the country's racial hierarchy prevented the welfare state from developing in any other way. Moreover, these scholars insist that the effect that race has had on the welfare system is ongoing. As Soss and his coauthors write, "The racial character of the contemporary system is more than just a legacy of our troubled racial past. It is a reflection of how race operates today as a *social structure* that organizes politics and markets and as a *mental structure* that organizes choice and action in governance."[16] In essence, scholars writing in this vein propose that if the welfare state remains inadequate and insufficient today, it is because it is associated with people of color. Society shows its contempt for people of color by being contemptuous towards the system that society imagines to care for them.

It is probably important to note before continuing that while people of color disproportionately bear the burdens of poverty in this country, there are still *more* white people in poverty than black in terms of absolute numbers. Further, while more nonwhite people than white people rely on the welfare programs that are designed to assist indigent families, *millions* of white people do so as well. Thus, if these programs have become paternalist and punitive because society imagines that black people primarily benefit from them, then the ire directed towards black people harms scores of white people as well.

III. Varying Levels of Support for Welfare State Programs

As a general matter, Americans profess support for the welfare state. Poll after poll has shown that when asked, a supermajority of Americans embrace the idea that the government has an obligation to care for the needy. Indeed, many polls show that Americans think that the government ought to be doing *more* than it currently does for the poor and vulnerable. Writes Martin Gilens, "Large majorities of Americans, for example, think that the government should be spending more money to fight poverty and homelessness, to improve

[15] JILL QUADAGNO, THE COLOR OF WELFARE: HOW RACISM UNDERMINED THE WAR ON POVERTY 191 (1994).

[16] SOSS, FORDING & SCHRAM, *supra* note 5, at 3–4.

our nation's education and health care, and to assist displaced workers and the elderly."[17]

While Americans might enthusiastically support the welfare state in the abstract, they do not wholly support the welfare state as the U.S. has implemented it. The country's welfare state is a patchwork of different programs that are designed to serve different parts of the population. Some of these programs, like Medicare and Social Security, are incredibly popular. Others, like TANF, are intensely reviled.

The American public tends to call the programs that fall in the latter, profoundly unloved category "welfare." Gilens proposes that the programs that people generally refer to as "welfare" have three things in common. First, they are "means-tested," which denotes that individuals can benefit from them only if their income falls below a certain level. Second, they provide assistance "in cash or in a near-cash form."[18] This contrasts with programs that provide assistance "in kind"—that is, through the direct delivery of a good or service. Third, "welfare" aids the "working-age, able-bodied poor."[19] Thus, disability benefits, which provide monetary assistance to individuals who cannot engage in wage labor, generally are not considered "welfare"—even though they are means-tested and provide cash assistance.

Relatively speaking, welfare—specifically, TANF—does not cost the government that much. In 2015, the federal government spent a little less than $20 billion on TANF.[20] It seems like a lot. However, the amount represented *less than one percent* (.54%) of total federal outlays that year.[21] As a point of comparison, Medicare, the popular and politically unassailable program that provides healthcare to the elderly, cost the federal government $675 billion and accounted for 15% of the federal budget in 2016.[22]

The next question becomes: why? Why do some safety net programs enjoy such immense popularity that any politician who dares to suggest that their funding ought to be cut risks burying himself in a watery political grave? Why are other programs, welfare, so passionately despised that any politician who proposes to expand

---

[17] MARTIN GILENS, WHY AMERICANS HATE WELFARE: RACE, MEDIA, AND THE POLITICS OF ANTIPOVERTY POLICY 12 (1999).

[18] *Id.*

[19] *Id.*

[20] Melissa S. Kearney, *Welfare and the Federal Budget*, ECONOFACT (July 25, 2017), https://econofact.org/welfare-and-the-federal-budget.

[21] *Id.*

[22] JULIETTE CUBANSKI & TRICIA NEUMAN, HENRY J. KAISER FAMILY FOUND., THE FACTS ON MEDICARE SPENDING AND FINANCING 1, 2 (2017), http://files.kff.org/attachment/Issue-Brief-The-Facts-on-Medicare-Spending-and-Financing.

them will likely find herself out of a job after the next election? Why do people hate welfare even though it represents a relatively miniscule portion of the federal budget? Scholars have proposed several possible answers.

Some scholars say that the distinction between contributory and non-contributory programs explains Americans' inconsistent support of safety net programs. Contributory programs are those into which individuals pay at some point in their lives. Social Security retirement benefits are a good example. Workers contribute a portion of their paychecks to Social Security throughout their working lives; when they retire, they get their money back in the form of Social Security benefits. Yeheskel Hasenfeld and Jane Rafferty argue that Americans tend to favor contributory programs because they are "well-anchored in the insurance metaphor and [they are] consonant with the principle of economic individualism."[23] In contrast, individuals do not pay into noncontributory programs, like TANF; they can collect from these programs without ever having funded them in any way. This, some scholars argue, explains their unpopularity. However, many observers find this explanation unsatisfying inasmuch as many exceptions to it can be found. As an example, blind persons can receive benefits through the Supplemental Security Income (SSI) program. Although blind people do not have to contribute to SSI, it is quite popular nonetheless.

Others say that the distinction between in-kind and cash assistance programs explains Americans' love-hate relationship with the welfare state.[24] The idea is that people dislike safety net programs that provide cash assistance, while favoring those that provide assistance in-kind. The difference in affinity is explained in terms of vulnerability to waste and abuse. Cash assistance is thought to be easily abused, while in-kind assistance is thought to be less so. For example, it is quite easy to fathom how an individual might misuse a $200 TANF check that is supposed to be spent on shelter and clothing. In contrast, it is difficult to see how a person might misuse the healthcare that the Medicare program provides directly. However, exceptions can be found here are well. For example, the benefits that SSI gives to the blind are in the easily abused form of cash. Nevertheless, SSI remains a popular safety net program.

A final explanation for the differing levels of support for the country's safety net programs is the distinction between the deserving and undeserving poor. The idea here is that some people are thought to be poor through no fault of their own. They are unable

[23] Yeheskel Hasenfeld & Jane A. Rafferty, *The Determinants of Public Attitudes Toward the Welfare State*, 67 SOC. FORCES 1027, 1032 (1989).

[24] *See, e.g.*, Greg M. Shaw, *Changes in Public Opinion and the American Welfare State*, 124 POL. SCI. Q. 627, 629 (2009).

to work because they are blind, or disabled, or old. Some tragedy has befallen this group, and they have been left impoverished as a consequence. These are the deserving poor. Unlike the deserving poor, however, the undeserving poor are thought to be those who can be blamed for their poverty. This group is poor because they are lazy, lack a respectable work ethic, and/or simply feel entitled to government handouts. Many thinkers have proposed that the safety net programs that Americans support are the ones that they imagine to benefit the deserving poor. The programs that Americans loathe—welfare—are the ones they imagine to benefit the undeserving poor.

And this is where race comes in. Critical thinkers in this area have proposed that when Americans think of poor *black* people, they think that they are undeserving. Thus, when confronted with black poverty, the collective intuition is to believe that black people are poor because they are indolent, do not want to work, and feel entitled to collect welfare checks to support their lifestyle. Of course, this presumption may be rebutted if evidence suggests that a poor black person is, in fact, hardworking or is a victim of circumstances beyond her control. But, the presumption of undeservingness exists in the first instance. Further, critical scholars have proposed that the reverse is also true: when Americans think of poor *white* people, they think that they are deserving. Thus, when confronted with white poverty, the collective intuition is to believe that white people are poor because of dynamics that they are powerless to affect.

According to critical thinkers, the result is that if a safety net program becomes associated with white people—or, at least, if it does not become associated with black people—then the beneficiaries of the program will not be thought to be responsible for their predicament. Society will think they are in need of public assistance because they have been affected by "larger forces or bad breaks."[25] That is, society will presume that they are deserving, and it will support the program that supports them. Conversely, if a safety net program becomes associated with black people, society will conclude that it benefits the undeserving poor and, consequently, will detest it. This is what has happened to welfare, say critical scholars. The American public believes that welfare programs primarily benefit undeserving black people. As a result, it generally wants to see these programs diminished or dismantled altogether.

Gilens has done extensive research in this area, and his statistical analyses of poll data lead him to conclude that the biggest predictor of attitudes about welfare is an individual's beliefs about black people. This is because welfare *has been racialized*; it has

---

[25] IAN HANEY LÓPEZ, DOG WHISTLE POLITICS: HOW CODED RACIAL APPEALS HAVE REINVENTED RACISM AND WRECKED THE MIDDLE CLASS 97 (2013).

become linked to black people, specifically. Thus, the way a person feels about black people determines how she feels about welfare. As such, if an individual believes that black people disproportionately bear the burdens of poverty in this nation because of, say, structural racism and/or inherited disadvantage, then she likely will throw her support behind the welfare programs that assist them, as she will believe that the beneficiaries of the programs are deserving. However, if an individual believes that black people are disproportionately impoverished because of "their own lack of effort"—that is, because they are lazy—she likely will oppose the welfare programs that assist them, as she will believe that the programs' beneficiaries are underserving.[26]

Critical scholars writing in this area underscore that the racialization of welfare has very real, material consequences. When lawmakers and the people they represent perceive black people as the actual or potential beneficiaries of a state's TANF program, that state's program will become much less charitable and much more penal and/or paternalistic. Gilens cites a study that shows that the states that have higher proportions of black people give smaller grants in their TANF programs compared to states with higher proportions of white people. Further, Soss and his coauthors observe that when states have higher proportions of black people in their welfare programs, the programs tend to be more disciplinary and punitive. They summarize this research: "Looking across the American states, one finds a tightly configured relationship consisting of higher black population rates, more stringent and locally controlled TANF regimes, and more aggressive applications of correctional control."[27]

IV. The Racialization of Welfare

Why did welfare come to be associated with black people? It cannot simply be due to the demographics of welfare recipients. That is, it might make sense for people to associate welfare with black people if all or most of the beneficiaries of these programs are black. However, black people presently constitute only 29% of TANF beneficiaries.[28] Certainly, black people are overrepresented among the population of folks receiving welfare, given that they represent only 13% of the general population.[29] Nevertheless, they still comprise less than a third of welfare recipients. Why, then, is *welfare*

---

[26] GILENS, supra note 17, at 3.

[27] SOSS, FORDING & SCHRAM, *supra* note 5, at 137.

[28] U.S. DEP'T OF HEALTH & HUMAN SERVS., CHARACTERISTICS AND FINANCIAL CIRCUMSTANCES OF TANF RECIPIENTS, FISCAL YEAR 2016, Table 10 (2017), https://www.acf.hhs.gov/sites/default/files/ofa/fy16_characteristics.pdf.

[29] *Quick Facts*, U.S. CENSUS BUREAU, https://www.census.gov/quickfacts/fact/table/US/RHI225217#viewtop (last updated June 21, 2018).

currently racialized as black? Why has it ever been racialized in this way?

Scholars writing in this area have observed that welfare—and poverty, more generally—has not always been associated with black people. They note that as late as the early 1960s, most Americans tended to think of *white* people when they thought of "the poor." As an example, Wacquant cites Michael Harrington's *The Other America*, which was published in 1962 and reportedly incited a national conversation about whether the government ought to do more about poverty. Significantly, this book featured "rural whites of the Appalachian hollows," not "urban blacks."[30] Gilens similarly observes that in the early 1960s, when the Kennedy administration was mulling over what could or should be done about the nation's impoverished, the "dominant image of poverty . . . was the white rural poor of the Appalachian coal fields."[31] Simply put, blackness and poverty had not been linked in the early 1960s.

Further, blackness and *welfare* also remained unlinked at this time. Now, while it would have been logical for blackness and *poverty* to be associated with one another during this period—as black people were disproportionately impoverished then, as they are now—it would have been quite strange for blackness and *welfare* to have come to be associated with one another in the early 1960s. This is true because black people were, on the whole, unable to avail themselves of the welfare programs that existed at that time. This point deserves some elaboration.

TANF's ancestors are the states' "mother's pension" or "widow's pension" programs, which began in the Progressive Era of the 1920s. These programs provided support to families headed by women whose husbands could no longer support them and their children. The idea was that the grants would save working age, able-bodied women with children from having to engage in wage labor outside of the home—thus allowing these mothers to stay at home and raise their sons and daughters. Motivated by the sense that "[f]amily life in the home is sapped in its foundations when the mothers of young children work for wages,"[32] mother's pension programs proceeded from the assumption that the best place for a mother was in the home and the most valuable labor in which she could engage was the care of her young.

Black women, in the main, were excluded from these state programs. The local administrators of the programs only allowed

---

[30] WACQUANT, *supra* note 2, at 82–83.

[31] GILENS, *supra* note 17, at 104.

[32] QUADAGNO, *supra* note 15, at 119 (quoting FLORENCE KELLEY, MODERN INDUSTRY IN RELATION TO THE FAMILY, HEALTH, EDUCATION, MORALITY 16 (1914)).

mothers who they thought could provide "suitable homes" for their children to receive assistance. In practice, this meant that the programs were limited to mothers who were single because their husbands had died—not mothers who were single because they were divorced, had been deserted, or had never married in the first instance. Black mothers, when unmarried, were more likely to be single for the latter reasons. Further, even when black mothers were widowed, racist narratives made it difficult for these women to convince local administrators that they qualified for assistance by meeting the high standards of female behavior that the programs had established. As Kenneth Neubeck and Noel Cazenave tell it, "Because African-American women were deemed incapable of meeting these criteria by virtue of their racial inferiority, they were customarily excluded from assistance at the local level of the racial state, no matter what their marital status, level of impoverishment, or family needs."[33] The result was that 96 percent of the beneficiaries of these programs were white, while only three percent were black.[34] Accordingly, if welfare was racialized during this era, it ought to have been racialized as white.

FDR's New Deal, which responded to the destitution that the Great Depression had brought to the country by rolling out an extensive safety net, did not appreciably change black women's relationship to welfare. The New Deal established a federal program called Aid for Dependent Children (ADC), which took the place of the states' mother's pension programs. (ADC later was renamed Aid to Families with Dependent Children (AFDC)). Although the federal government had now taken on the obligation of caring for poor mothers, much of the administration of the program—from defining the rules around eligibility to setting benefit levels—was left to the localities. And, as with mother's pensions, local administrators of ADC/AFDC tended to exclude black mothers from the programs.

The methods that they used were many. "Man in the house" rules denied benefits to women who might be receiving financial help from a boyfriend or male paramour. "To obtain evidence of such violations, caseworkers could enter and inspect recipients' homes at any time, sometimes during unannounced 'midnight raids.' "[35] Black women frequently found themselves the targets of these raids. Moreover, many states—especially the ones in the South—adopted "employable mother" rules, which denied benefits to women who might have been able to find wage labor outside of the home. Local

---

[33] KENNETH J. NEUBECK & NOEL A. CAZENAVE, WELFARE RACISM: PLAYING THE RACE CARD AGAINST AMERICA'S POOR 45 (2001).

[34] *See id.* at 44.

[35] Joe Soss, Sanford F. Schram & Richard C. Fording, *Introduction* to RACE AND THE POLITICS OF WELFARE REFORM, *supra* note 14, at 1, 17.

caseworkers in the South tended to find that mothers were "employable" when the harvesting and planting seasons came around. In this way, ADC/AFDC functioned to ensure that there would be low-wage laborers available for hire whenever employers needed them. Critical scholars observe an irony here: welfare during this time was premised on the idea that mothers should be protected from the necessity of working outside of the home, enabling them to spend their time raising their children. Nevertheless, ADC/AFDC was administered in a way that ensured that poor mothers, specifically poor black mothers in the South, would be forced to work for wages in order to satisfy the region's agricultural demands.

The upshot of all of the discretion that ADC/AFDC allowed localities was that black women largely found welfare rolls inaccessible. Thus, progressive observers conclude, if welfare was racialized during this time, it should have remained racialized as white.

But, clearly, something changed in welfare's racialization. Many scholars propose that the re-racialization began with the attention that the Civil Rights Movement increasingly paid to the poverty that black people disproportionately bore. While the movement's leaders initially focused on ridding the country of the laws that formally made second-class citizens out of black people, in the later days of the movement, they turned their attention to the economic privation that they believed would keep black people subordinated even if they enjoyed formal equality. Further, when violence erupted in the ghettoes of several cities across the nation in the mid-1960s, politicians and other observers concluded that poverty was the cause: the poor black residents of these communities were frustrated with having been cut off from the economic (and social and political) life of the nation. Observers offered that violence was black people's way of protesting their condition. Their protests, often called riots, became a spectacle—broadcast into millions of homes via the nightly news. These events, assert critical scholars, functioned to fashion a close relationship between blackness and poverty in the minds of the American populace.

Thus, when President Lyndon B. Johnson launched a "War on Poverty"—a series of programs that sought to "improve communities, train workers, and increase housing for the poor"[36]—in an effort to address the economic hardship that millions of Americans *of all races* endured, the link between poverty and blackness led Americans to believe that the safety net programs that he implemented were, at the end of the day, for black people. Now, in many respects, race *was* on LBJ's mind when he began the War on Poverty. As this chapter

---

[36] QUADAGNO, *supra* note 15, at 155.

describes, the New Deal had established a welfare state in the U.S. However, the New Deal welfare state, by design and/or as implemented, had not been made accessible to black people. Thus, in many respects, LBJ's War on Poverty was a conscious effort to extend the safety net that already existed for vulnerable white people to equally vulnerable black people. In seeking to bring black people into the fold of the welfare state, the War on Poverty—inevitably and, in many respects, intentionally—"promoted racial equality."[37]

Nevertheless, it is worth reiterating that black people are not the only folks living in poverty in this country; millions of white people (as well as Latinx, Asian, and indigenous people) are also impoverished. Thus, a welfare state that cares for "the poor" will, by necessity, care for people of all races. While indisputably true, progressive race scholars note that the close association between blackness and poverty that the urban protests in the 1960s had helped to forge increasingly led many Americans to believe that the War on Poverty and the expanded welfare state that it introduced was *only* for, and *only* about, black people. The racialization of welfare, they say, had begun.

Another crucial phenomenon that critical scholars claim helped to racialize welfare as black was the increasing success that black women had in accessing welfare. In the late 1960s, poor black women began challenging the many impediments that local governments and administrators had erected to block their access to public assistance. The National Welfare Rights Organization (NWRO) was a major player in this movement. The NWRO had 22,000 members and branches in all fifty states at its height in 1969.[38] Its members engaged in protests—including sit-ins and mass demonstrations—in order to force changes in the rules that had excluded poor black mothers, but not poor white mothers, from AFDC rolls. Further, litigation in the courts served as a complement to the agitation taking place in the streets. And the lawyers and the indigent black mothers that they represented won. In a series of cases, the Supreme Court struck down the "man in the house" and "employable mother" rules, constrained the discretion that local administrators and caseworkers had in determining eligibility, and established AFDC as a statutory right.[39]

As a direct consequence of these victories in court, the AFDC rolls grew, as poor black mothers accessed the benefits that had been available to their white counterparts. It is important to note that this

---

[37] *Id.*

[38] *See* NEUBECK & CAZENAVE, *supra* note 33, at 126.

[39] *See* Frances Fox Piven, *Why Welfare is Racist*, *in* RACE AND THE POLITICS OF WELFARE REFORM, *supra* note 14, at 323, 330.

growth was substantial. In 1965, there were 3.3 million people receiving AFDC.[40] By 1971, that number had more than tripled, with 11 million people on the AFDC rolls.[41] Quite significantly, black people had come to make up 45 percent of these recipients. The increasingly disproportionate number of black people receiving welfare certainly made it easier for welfare to be racialized as black in the late 1960s and 1970s.

Finally, several critical thinkers of race insist that there is another phenomenon that we ought not to forget when we are attempting to answer the question of how welfare became racialized as black. They point to several politicians *intentionally* seeking to link blackness and welfare in the U.S.'s political consciousness. As Neubeck and Cazenave write, "For decades, well known US politicians like Barry Goldwater, George Wallace, Robert Byrd, Richard Nixon, Ronald Reagan, David Duke, Newt Gingrich, and Bill Clinton forged and exploited the link between 'race' and 'welfare' to such a degree that the two terms are now politically and culturally inextricable."[42] Thus, if *black* and *welfare* are coupled in the minds of the American public today, these scholars argue that it is because powerful politicians insisted upon it.[43]

V. Attacking Welfare

Progressive scholars contend that now that race and welfare have become associated with one another, welfare has been the object

---

40 *See* NEUBECK & CAZENAVE, *supra* note 33, at 121.

41 Angela Onwuachi-Willig, *The Return of the Ring: Welfare Reform's Marriage Cure as the Revival of Post-Bellum Control*, 93 CALIF. L. REV. 1647, 1669 (2005).

42 NEUBECK & CAZENAVE, *supra* note 33, at 3.

43 Haney López argues that linking black people to ostensibly race-neutral things—like a powerful federal government, busing, and welfare—allowed politicians to attack black people (and to win the favor of disaffected white voters) by attacking these race-neutral things. The boon was that these politicians never had to mention race at all—at least, not explicitly. Consequently, they could easily deny any charge that they were race-baiting or appealing to the racist sentiments of the white voters that they courted. As support for his argument, Haney López points to a statement made by Lee Atwater, a Republican strategist and advisor to Presidents Ronald Reagan and George H.W. Bush:

> You start out in 1954 by saying, "Nigger, nigger, nigger." By 1968 you can't say "nigger"—that hurts you. Backfires. So you say stuff like forced busing, states' rights and all that stuff. You're getting so abstract now, you're talking about cutting taxes, and all these things you're talking about are totally economic things and a byproduct of them is, blacks get hurt worse than whites. And subconsciously maybe that is part of it. I'm not saying that. But I'm saying that if it is getting that abstract, and that coded, that we are doing away with the racial problem one way or the other. You follow me—because obviously sitting around saying, "We want to cut taxes and we want to cut this," is much more abstract than even the busing thing, and a hell of a lot more abstract than "Nigger, nigger." So any way you look at it, race is coming on the back burner.

HANEY LÓPEZ, *supra* note 25, at 57.

of fierce attacks across the political spectrum. The claim is that any disdain that individuals feel, consciously or unconsciously, for black people can be expressed by attacking or opposing welfare. Disapproval of black people can be manifested by disapproving welfare.

Now, there are many observers who propose that political and social displeasure with welfare is not really about race. They suggest that it is *really* about gender—about the feeling that welfare recipients violate norms about how women are supposed to behave. As discussed above, at its inception, mother's pensions and ADC/AFDC had been limited for the most part to mothers who were single because their husbands had died; mothers who were single because they were divorced, had been deserted, or were never married in the first instance made up a preciously small fraction of ADC/AFDC beneficiaries. In 1939, however, the federal government established the Old Age and Survivor's Insurance (OASI) program, which provided benefits to the widows of laborers who had worked in covered industries. Most of the widows who had been receiving benefits under ADC/AFDC switched to OASI when it was implemented. OASI came to be the province of widows, while ADC/AFDC came to be the province of women whose lives more flagrantly violated norms around sex and sexuality—that is, women who husbands had left them, or women who had never had husbands in the first instance. Today, say many scholars, people continue to associate welfare with women who violate norms around sex and sexuality, believing that most or all of welfare beneficiaries are unmarried women who have had sex and given birth to children out-of-wedlock. Under this reading, opposition to welfare is more about discontent with women who demonstrate sexual impropriety than it is about discontent with black people.

In reality, the unpopularity of welfare probably ought to be explained in terms of both race *and* gender. We find support for this conclusion in the fact that the negative stories that have been told—by politicians, pundits, members of think tanks, laypersons, and others—about welfare recipients represent an "explosive bonding of patriarchal thinking with racist stereotypes."[44] The reference here is to the "welfare queen," who came to stand for welfare beneficiaries as a whole and who represented everything that critics of welfare claimed was wrong with AFDC.

President Ronald Reagan often is credited with giving birth to the "welfare queen"—a figure who not only lived lavishly off the benefits that the government provided to her, but who also had children for the sole purpose of increasing the size of her welfare

---

[44] NEUBECK & CAZENAVE, *supra* note 33, at 30.

checks. Reagan often told the story of a Chicago woman who had " '80 names, 30 addresses, 12 Social Security cards' [and] 'tax-free income . . . over $150,000' "[45] And he asked the public to believe that this woman—who, in actuality, was "not a garden-variety cheat, but . . . rather a full-fledge psychopath and con artist . . . whose other possible crimes included murder and kidnapping"[46]—represented all AFDC recipients. Haney López—emphasizing that Reagan often "placed his mythical welfare queen behind the wheel of a Cadillac, tooling around in flashy splendor"[47]—explains the logic behind Reagan's deployment of this figure:

> Beyond propagating the stereotypical image of a lazy, larcenous black woman ripping off society's generosity without remorse, Reagan also implied another stereotype, this one about whites: they were the workers, the tax payers, the persons playing by the rules and struggling to make ends meet while brazen minorities partied with their hard-earned tax dollars.[48]

We should note that the welfare queen was as much about race as it was about gender. The figure—which, progressive thinkers emphasize, draws on timeworn stereotypes of black women that describe them as sexually licentious, reproductively excessive, and firmly lazy—is as race-specific as it is gender-specific. Differently stated, the welfare queen is a *black woman*, and these thinkers propose that her blackness is as crucial to her identity as is her womanhood. If she was white, or if she was a man, she might be an abuser of the system, a danger to the body politic, or an object of ridicule, they say. But, she could not be a *welfare queen*. They insist that the black femaleness, or female blackness, of the welfare queen makes her as detestable—and, consequently, as politically useful—as she is.

Critical thinkers about race propose that when chaste white widows were imagined to be the beneficiaries of welfare assistance, the public largely supported the idea that they should be given a grant that would relieve them from the obligation of working for a wage outside of the home, allowing them to devote themselves to their children on a full-time basis. However, when black welfare queens were imagined to be the beneficiaries of welfare assistance, the public developed the sense that these women ought to get a job—any job. Indeed, these mothers' failure to get a job—their indolence—

---

[45] THOMAS BYRNE EDSALL & MARY D. EDSALL, CHAIN REACTION: THE IMPACT OF RACE, RIGHTS, AND TAXES ON AMERICAN POLITICS 148 (1991).

[46] Ann Cammett, *Deadbeat Dads & Welfare Queens: How Metaphor Shapes Poverty Law*, 34 B.C. J.L. & SOC. JUST. 233, 244 n.66 (2014).

[47] HANEY LÓPEZ, *supra* note 25, at 58.

[48] *Id.* at 58–59.

was accepted as the reason for their being poor in the first place. Scholars propose that identifying laziness and personal irresponsibility as the cause of disproportionate rates of black poverty does well to distract from the other, more large-scale forces that might be to blame for black poverty. Calling black mothers lazy, explains Holloway Sparks, "constructs the woman as the problem, which draws attention away from structural reasons for poverty, and from the gender, race, and class discrimination that hinders the ability of black women to support and care for themselves and their families in the first place."[49]

Note that if laziness and personal irresponsibility are the causes of poverty, then the solution to poverty is to reform the behavior and morals of the impoverished person. And that is precisely what the welfare reform implemented in 1996 attempts to accomplish.

VI. Welfare Reform

Wacquant observes that "[a]lthough the cost of AFDC never reached 1 percent of the federal budget, every government since Jimmy Carter has promoted its reduction as a top priority."[50] Indeed, Democratic and Republican politicians have been united in their professed disdain for welfare. Thus, it was in keeping with the country's political past when Bill Clinton, a Democrat, promised to "end welfare as we know it" if voters put him in the presidency.[51] Voters did just that, and Clinton followed through on this campaign promise by helming the passage in 1996 of the Personal Responsibility and Work Opportunity Reconciliation Act (PRWORA), which replaced AFDC with TANF.

Most observers would agree that TANF represents a significant departure from AFDC. AFDC was a federal entitlement—meaning that individuals had a right to receive benefits from the program if they met the program's eligibility criteria. Accordingly, the federal government was obliged to increase funding to the states if the number of persons eligible for AFDC increased. TANF, however, abolished welfare as an entitlement. Instead, TANF is funded through a federal block grant. With this funding structure, the federal government gives the individual states a fixed amount of money with which they can administer their TANF programs and provide benefits to individual families. If a state runs low on its block

---

[49] Holloway Sparks, *Queens, Teens, and Model Mothers: Race, Gender, and the Discourse of Welfare Reform*, *in* RACE AND THE POLITICS OF WELFARE REFORM, *supra* note 14, at 171, 177.

[50] WACQUANT, *supra* note 2, at 49.

[51] Gwen Ifill, *Clinton: Promising a Changed Party*, N.Y. TIMES (Oct. 10, 1992), https://www.nytimes.com/1992/10/10/us/the-1992-campaign-the-ad-campaign-clinton-promising-a-changed-party.html.

grant monies, impoverished persons and families who meet the eligibility criteria that the state has established may not receive TANF benefits: they are no longer *entitled* to it. We should note as well that TANF specifically permits states to use their block grant funds on things that do not directly involve providing benefits to indigent families. States are allowed to spend federal monies on efforts to 1) promote "job preparation, work, and marriage," 2) "prevent and reduce the incidence of out-of-wedlock pregnancies," and 3) "encourage the formation and maintenance of two-parent families."[52] Providing "assistance to needy families so that children may be cared for in their own homes or in the homes of relatives"[53] is just one of four endeavors that states may pursue with their federal block grant funds. This, of course, increases the likelihood that states will run low on those monies and be unable to directly assist indigent families.

In addition to the change in the funding structure, TANF has increased the latitude that states have to design and implement their individual TANF programs. States can determine whether it wants to impose family caps (which attempt to discourage beneficiaries from having additional children by fixing the size of a family's grant), sanction beneficiaries whose children have poor school attendance records, penalize recipients for failing to identify the fathers of their children, and impose limits on the period of time that a family may receive benefits that are shorter than the five-year maximum that the federal program establishes.

In this way, TANF quite explicitly and consciously hands a great deal of discretion to the states. Many critical scholars observe that the dramatic increase in flexibility that states now have in administering their TANF programs represents a blast from the past—a return to the days when the federal government imposed few constraints on localities as they went about the task of distributing aid. These critics remind that these were the *bad old days* of "man in the house," "employable mother," and "suitable home" rules—the days when welfare assistance was even more directly and intentionally a weapon of racial denigration and control. Frances Fox Piven laments, "With the elimination of the AFDC program, many of the legal victories of the 1960s are now moot. The painfully established rule of law in the old welfare system was wiped out with a legislative stroke."[54]

Indeed, many critical scholars contend that while TANF proponents argued that the program amounts to something "new" in

[52] 42 U.S.C. § 601(a)(2)–(4) (1997).

[53] 42 U.S.C. § 601(a)(1).

[54] Piven, *supra* note 39, at 331.

welfare administration, it actually just recycles many old tools of poverty governance. Soss and his coauthors argue that the techniques that TANF employs to regulate the morals and behavior of its beneficiaries bear "a striking resemblance to . . . ideologies that attended nineteenth-century poorhouses, agencies for outdoor relief, and scientific charity movements. Indeed, even the major areas of behavior emphasized in poverty policy today—work, sex, substance abuse, marriage, child rearing, and so on—echo the main targets of earlier crusades to uplift and normalize the poor."[55]

Critical thinkers emphasize that TANF's focus on "fixing" welfare recipients is a byproduct of a philosophy that contends that the impoverished person's morals and behavior have caused their poverty. According to this philosophy, people are not poor because of residential segregation, the fact that we fund our public schools through property taxes, the destabilization of communities by mass incarceration, changes in the economy, etc. Instead, this philosophy asserts that people are poor because they are lazy, cannot delay gratification, like to have unprotected sex, etc. By reflecting this ideology of poverty's roots, these thinkers assert, TANF blames the poor for their poverty. It tries to "fix" them. In attempting to "fix" the poor, critical theorists claim that it convinces us that we do not need to "fix" "the highly organized social structures and processes that bring about and sustain [poverty], whose unraveling requires nothing short of radical change."[56]

A. The Obligation to Work

One of the most audible drumbeats in TANF is its insistence that beneficiaries of the program work outside of the home.[57] States are required to ensure that half of all unmarried recipients engage in statutorily defined "work activities"—which include subsidized and unsubsidized work in the public or private sector as well as job search and "job readiness assistance"—for at least 30 hours per week.[58]

---

[55] SOSS, FORDING & SCHRAM, *supra* note 5, at 4.

[56] NEUBECK & CAZENAVE, *supra* note 33, at 32.

[57] Soss and his coauthors propose that TANF's resolve to make its beneficiaries work is so strong that it insists upon viewing their life histories and present circumstances through this lens. Thus, all of the tragedies that may have befallen them—the personal catastrophes that may have impoverished them—are understood simply as events that have kept them out of the workforce. They write that beneficiaries'

> social responsibilities and needs are reframed as nothing more than aspects of their value as a worker on the market. Refracted through this prism, all facets of poor women's lives—mental illnesses, physical disabilities, educational deprivations, obligations to care for children or aged parents—are collapsed into the economic register, recast as "barriers" to work that must be overcome.

SOSS, FORDING & SCHRAM, *supra* note 5, at 49.

[58] 42 U.S.C. § 607(a)(1), (c)(1)(A), (d).

Meanwhile, 90 percent of married recipients must engage in these "work activities" for at least 35 hours per week.[59] Additionally, TANF imposes limits on the number of individuals who can "work" through pursuing an education: "only thirty percent of TANF families can meet the work requirement through vocational or educational training."[60]

Again, critical thinkers invite us to note the reversal that welfare has taken to work. At its inception, welfare was a program that sought to shield mothers from the labor market; now, it has become a program that thrusts them into it.

Of course, at the inception of welfare, in the 1920s, the gender norm was for women *not* to work outside of the home—especially after marriage. Times have changed, of course. Women's labor force participation rates now approximate those of men.[61] So, we might say that the reason for TANF's current insistence that mothers work for wages, when the mother's pensions of the Progressive Era were designed to relieve them of this same necessity, is that our existing gender norms insist that all women should work for wages.

Critical thinkers of race are not convinced by this, though. First, they note that women of color—specifically, black women—have always been expected to work for wages, even when gender norms insisted that women belonged in the house. In this way, they see TANF as just continuing the racialized expectations around work to which black women always have been held. Second, critical thinkers look to the distinction between a *right* to work and an *obligation* to work.[62] They contend that white feminists struggled for white women's right to work; they never claimed that women ought to be obliged to work. To the extent that TANF compels work out of its beneficiaries, they argue that it perverts feminism's demands and, in so doing, forces poor mothers, who are disproportionately women of color, into "involuntary servitude."[63]

B. TANF's Dubious Success

A crucial question: has TANF worked? Has it been a success? As it turns out, the answers to those questions depends on how one defines success.

---

[59] 42 U.S.C. § 607(a)(2), (c)(1)(B)(i).

[60] Michele Estrin Gilman, *Return of the Welfare Queen*, 22 AM. U. J. GENDER SOC. POL'Y, & L. 247, 255 (2014).

[61] *See Civilian Labor Force by Sex*, U.S. DEP'T OF LABOR, WOMEN'S BUREAU, https://www.dol.gov/wb/stats/NEWSTATS/facts/civilian_lf_sex_2016_txt.htm (last accessed July 30, 2018) (finding women make up 46.8% of the civilian labor force as of 2016).

[62] *See* GWENDOLYN MINK, WELFARE'S END 26–27 (1998).

[63] *Id.* at 27.

If one defines success by the size of the welfare rolls, then TANF is a roaring success. The number of beneficiaries of the program has positively shrunk since it was implemented over two decades ago. In 1994, approximately 14.2 million people in five million families received AFDC benefits.[64] In 2017, approximately 2.5 million people in 1.1 million families received TANF benefits.[65] By all accounts, that is a significant reduction.

However, if one defines success by the number of individuals and families moved out of poverty, then TANF has not worked very well at all. It appears that TANF has simply shifted many poor mothers from the welfare rolls to the low-wage labor market—a place where many people stay mired in poverty despite the fact that they are, indeed, working. Progressive thinkers ask us to bear in mind that the low-wage labor market is a challenging place for mothers to work: in addition to the jobs available in this sector paying below-poverty wages, they also typically fail to accommodate the needs of women with children. So, for example, when the child of a woman who works at a law firm gets sick, she might be able to bring the child to work with her, work from home, or take a personal day and focus on nursing her child back to health at home. Yet, when one works at McDonald's as a cashier, for example, this type of flexibility simply is not a part of the job. If a child gets sick, a mother who works at McDonald's certainly cannot bring the child to the store with her. Working from home is not a possibility. And if she calls out sick, she forfeits the day's wages and risks losing her job. As Wacquant expresses it, TANF "concentrates on making public aid beneficiaries 'work ready' while disregarding the fact that the jobs that single mothers find or need are themselves not 'mother ready.' "[66]

Critical thinkers also look to research that suggests that TANF has reduced the size of the welfare rolls in part because it is simply failing to reach poor families that need help. The Government Accountability Office estimated that, as of 2007, "87 percent of the caseload decline . . . was due to fewer poor, eligible families participating in the TANF program, as opposed to rising family incomes. If caseload decline had been restricted to people whose successes made them ineligible, 3.3 million additional families would

---

[64] *See* U.S. DEP'T OF HEALTH & HUMAN SERVS., INDICATORS OF WELFARE DEPENDENCE: ANNUAL REPORT TO CONGRESS, 1998, APPENDIX A: PROGRAM DATA, at A-5 (1998), https://aspe.hhs.gov/report/indicators-welfare-dependence-annual-report-congress-1998.

[65] *See* U.S. DEP'T OF HEALTH & HUMAN SERVS., TANF CASELOAD DATA 2017 (2018), https://www.acf.hhs.gov/ofa/resource/tanf-caseload-data-2017.

[66] WACQUANT, *supra* note 2, at 86.

have been receiving TANF support."[67] Essentially, TANF has withdrawn the safety net from individuals who could really use it.

Additionally, critical scholars note that TANF benefits are so low that even when an individual receives them, she will still remain below the poverty line. As Gilman reports, "The average monthly benefit is $427 for a family of three, while in fourteen states the benefit levels for a family of this size are less than $300. This means that in all states, benefits are below fifty percent of the poverty line, and in the majority of states they are below thirty percent of the poverty line."[68]

So, yes: TANF has reduced the welfare rolls significantly. But, the families that welfare once supported are as poor as they were before welfare reform, if not poorer. We should debate whether we ought to count that as a success.

* * *

For many critical thinkers, that the U.S. currently supports poor families reluctantly and in such a punitive and paternalistic way is an effect of race. Indeed, for these thinkers, race has never *not* played a role in the administration of welfare in this country. Certainly, the role that race has played has changed over the years. The argument is that at the dawn of the welfare state, race operated to exclude black mothers from the benefits that were available to white mothers. In the 1960s, as black people fought their way onto the safety net, race operated to make society feel aggrieved by the very existence of welfare. And, presently, race operates to make welfare paltry, corrective, and only begrudgingly charitable. Critical theorists assert that though the role of race has transformed throughout the decades, the constant is that race has played some role in the form that the welfare state has taken. In this way, critical thinkers of race propose that our welfare state is an *effect* of racism.

But, Piven reminds us that it may also be a *cause* of racism. Insofar as TANF functions to keep poor people, who are disproportionately people of color, in poverty, it "creates its own theater of racial degradation. Du Bois thought that if the freedmen had been allowed to live differently, then the racism of Philadelphians, and of Americans generally, would have faded. If the minority poor were allowed to live differently now, then contemporary racism might also fade."[69]

---

[67] SOSS, FORDING & SCHRAM, *supra* note 5, at 264.

[68] Gilman, *supra* note 60, at 267–68.

[69] Piven, *supra* note 39, at 334.

VII. Questions and Discussion

1. As discussed in this chapter, the welfare state in the U.S. consists of a wide variety of programs that are designed to support and protect citizens and residents. However, when most Americans think of *welfare*, they tend to think only of the most stigmatized and racialized programs that help poor people—ADC/AFDC and TANF.

At present, TANF, however, is far from the only safety net program that aims to assist the nation's poor. The Earned Income Tax Credit (EITC) is one of the largest government antipoverty programs. It provides assistance to poor families by allowing them to claim a credit on their federal income taxes, thus reducing the taxes that they owe to the government. It is not at all unusual for the credit to be larger than the amount of taxes that the family owes. In this case, the family receives a "refund," and the assistance provided by the EITC takes the form of cold, hard cash.

The EITC has been incredibly successful, bringing some 6.3 million people above the poverty line in 2010.[70] It is not cheap, though. In 2011, the program spent some 58.6 billion dollars on 26.2 million low-income families.[71] (Comparatively speaking, TANF spending can never exceed 16.5 billion dollars.[72]) Notably, most people do not think of the EITC when they think of welfare.[73] Why do you think this is?

The EITC raises the broader question of why we consider some benefits that the government gives to be welfare and not others. Consider that individuals who own homes can deduct the interest on their mortgages from their taxes. Essentially, the government provides a financial benefit to homeowners by demanding less taxes than it would otherwise. Why do we not consider this benefit to be a form of welfare?

Every year, the U.S. pays over 20 billion dollars in subsidies to farmers and other agricultural businesses. These subsidies are designed to stabilize the cost and supply of food, which arguably functions to stabilize the U.S. economy. Why do we largely refuse to consider farm subsidies to be a form of welfare?

2. As discussed above, welfare is thoroughly racialized, with most Americans associating it with people of color—black people, specifically. To a lesser extent, poverty itself is racialized, with many Americans believing that most poor people in the country are black. Gilens notes that many Americans are wrong: while black people

---

[70] *See* Gilman, *supra* note 60, at 267.

[71] *Id.*

[72] *Id.*

[73] See GILENS, *supra* note 17, at 17.

constitute anywhere from a fifth to a quarter of those living in poverty, Americans tend to believe that they constitute half of this population.[74]

Gilens blames the media for the racialization of welfare and poverty. He analyzed decades of stories about poverty in three major media outlets and discovered that black people were overrepresented in the pictures that accompanied these stories. As the chapter notes above, in the early 1960s, poverty had not yet been linked with black people. During this time, Gilens found that most of the pictures that ran with stories about poverty featured white people. However, beginning in 1965—after black people began violently protesting their condition in the ghettoes of cities across America—"the complexion of the poor turned decidedly darker. From only 27 percent in 1964, the proportion of African Americans in pictures of the poor increased to 49 percent and 53 percent in 1965 and 1966, and then to 72 percent in 1967."[75] Further, the overrepresentation of black people in stories about poverty continued even after the violent protests ended. Writes Gilens, "From 1967 through 1992, blacks averaged 57 percent of the poor people pictured in these three [outlets studied]—about twice the true proportion of blacks among the nation's poor."[76]

Further, Gilens notes that pictures of black people were more likely to be found in *negative* stories about poverty, while white people were more likely to be seen in more sympathetic stories. Magazines tended to use images of black people "to illustrate stories about waste, inefficiency, or abuse of welfare"[77]; meanwhile, "pictures of nonblacks dominate the more sympathetic coverage that accompanies periods of national economic hardship."[78]

Critical thinkers find Gilens's study instructive. But, many of them feel that he does not sufficiently interrogate the ease with which the public accepts the images of poverty that the media offers them. These thinkers propose that seeing a picture of a black person in a story about welfare fraud "makes sense" to most people. They propose that seeing a picture of a white person in this same story would be surprising—or, at least, unexpected. Similarly, they contend that seeing a picture of a white person in a story about the Great Recession and the blow that it dealt to homeowners would be unremarkable; yet, seeing a picture of a black person in this story would be more unanticipated.

---

[74] *See id.* at 102.

[75] *Id.* at 114.

[76] *Id.*

[77] *Id.* at 117.

[78] *Id.* at 6.

Why is this so? These scholars propose that racist narratives about black deviance explain this phenomenon. In this view, the overrepresentation of black people in negative media reports about poverty and welfare is an *effect* of the racialization of the poor, not its cause. Stated more bluntly, these thinkers assert that we already do not think highly of black people. As a result, an image of a black person in a negative story about poverty merely reinforces our beliefs. The image does not create them. As Schram has written, "[I]t takes more than numbers and images to create racism. It takes more than statistics and pictures of black women on welfare to reinforce that they are undeserving. The racist premises that inform such interpretations must already be available before these pictures can do their work."[79]

What do you think about Gilens's argument and Schram's response to it? Do you think that the media have some responsibility for the racialization of poverty and welfare? Or do you think that the media are simply a reflection of society's preexisting views? If you believe that, in some important respects, the media have created problematic views about welfare and poverty, what should we do about it?

3. As this chapter notes, many critical scholars assert that the reason the U.S.'s welfare state is patchy and meager is that it was built with the intention of keeping its nonwhite citizens in a subordinate position. If black people in the South could turn to public assistance, white employers could not exploit them as easily. The welfare state was constructed so as to protect white workers while keeping black workers vulnerable. The result, they say, was an uneven and decentralized welfare state.

Robert Lieberman proposes that part of the reason for the countries that the U.S. considers its peers having a more universal safety net is that their racial others existed outside of the national borders. In the U.S., black people were presumptive citizens and, therefore, entitled to make demands that were equal to those that white people could make. However, in other countries, like the United Kingdom, nonwhite people largely were outside the national borders—in the colonies, to be specific. In these nations, the creation of a universal welfare state could unite the citizens against the racial other who lived outside of the country. As Lieberman explains the effect that colonialism had on the creation of the safety net in Great Britain, "[T]he presumption of racial homogeneity at home allowed for the construction of welfare systems with more forceful and authoritative means of connecting individual citizens to the state. . . .

---

[79] Sanford F. Schram, *Putting a Black Face on Welfare: The Good and the Bad*, *in* RACE AND THE POLITICS OF WELFARE REFORM, *supra* note 14, at 196, 219.

[T]he challenge of imperial rule demanded an 'imperial race,' which placed a burden on the state to ensure the health and welfare of its own citizens."[80]

What do you think of Lieberman's argument? Does it ring true to you? Do you believe that had the U.S. established more colonies in various parts of the world, the safety net that it erected "at home" would have been more substantial?

4. Schram has observed that some supporters of an expanded welfare state have argued that we ought to emphasize that white people are also poor and also need a safety net that can help lift them out of poverty. These supporters argue that if welfare and poverty were not racialized as black, then the nation might get behind constructing a safety net that adequately cares for all Americans—of all races.

However, Schram is not convinced that erasing the racial demographics of welfare receipt is a program that we should pursue. This is because he believes that race matters. For him, race explains why black people are disproportionately poor in this country. Race explains why black people need to rely on the welfare state more frequently than their white counterparts. And race explains why poor white people find it easier than black people to climb out of poverty. He writes that we need to talk about

> why African Americans in particular, but other racial minorities as well, [are] more likely to be living in poverty and in need of public assistance at higher rates. Equity arguments need to be urgently made now that take race into account, indicating that there are good reasons why African Americans and Latinos need to rely on public assistance more frequently and that they *should* be seen, if only in this regard, as "different." They confront different circumstances, often facing greater need, and more often requiring the assistance of welfare. . . . As long as advocates cling to the myth of a white welfare population, we will neglect the problems of racism, the issue of racial barriers, and the extent to which race-related differences need to be addressed. Such neglect is dangerous; it can ignore the systemic sources of poverty for low-income families of color.[81]

What do you think? If you support an expanded welfare state, do you believe that we should make arguments for its expansion that take account of race? ("We need a generous welfare state in order to

---

[80] Lieberman, *supra* note 14, at 31.

[81] Schram, *supra* note 79, at 208.

remedy the effects of racism?") Or do you believe that it is better to make arguments that ignore both the reality that some races may need the welfare state more than others as well as the reasons for this being true?

5. Some observers have proposed that welfare is racialized as black because the programs that this label references are targeted—only benefitting some people, i.e., those who meet the eligibility criteria. These observers argue that universal programs—which do not have eligibility criteria and that benefit everyone—are not racialized and, consequently, enjoy much more public and political support than their targeted counterparts. The Social Security program is the paradigmatic universal, politically popular program. The way to gain support for welfare, they say, is to make these programs universal like Social Security. Construct welfare so that everyone benefits, they say.

Critical thinkers are skeptical that universalizing welfare would solve the problem. They argue that many of the services that the poor need *must be* targeted. Writes Quadagno, "Unlike income support in old age, not everyone needs job training . . . ."[82] Similarly, everyone needs food and clothing. But, not everyone will need the government's help in purchasing these goods.

Can you think of a way to make welfare universal? How would you structure the program such that everyone, including those who are quite comfortably middle-class, feels like they are benefiting?

6. As discussed above, the New Deal did not significantly change black women's relationship to welfare, as it left local administrators in charge of distributing welfare benefits; moreover, these administrators oftentimes were committed to keeping black women off of welfare rolls. Many scholars propose that the failure of the New Deal to upset black women's subordination through welfare was no accident. They argue that the entire New Deal was designed to ensure that black people would remain impoverished and exploitable and the country's racial hierarchy would remain intact. They assert that southern legislators would not vote to establish a welfare state that freed black people in the region from the necessity of working for whatever wage that those with power were willing to pay.[83] The only way that FDR could get the New Deal passed was to concede to the demands of these congressmen and construct the welfare state in such a way that black people would be left without a safety net. Thus, the act establishing Social Security only covered

---

[82] QUADAGNO, *supra* note 15, at 172.

[83] *See, e.g.*, LINDA GORDON, PITIED BUT NOT ENTITLED: SINGLE MOTHERS AND THE HISTORY OF WELFARE, 1890–1935, at 5 (1994).

employees in manufacturing and commerce.[84] It did not apply to agricultural or domestic workers—the two industries in which most black workers could be found.[85] In this way, the New Deal ensured that black workers would remain vulnerable to poverty and coerced to work for any wage that they could find.

Critical thinkers propose that ADC being administered on the local level, and the effect that this administration had of excluding black women from the benefits that were available to white women, should be understood in the context of a compromise that sought to establish the bare bones of a welfare state while also leaving black people destitute and, thus, exploitable. As Quadagno explains, "Southern congressmen . . . insisted that states retain the right to establish eligibility criteria and to decide who received benefits. Only if local welfare authorities retained control over the distribution of benefits would the southerners support the measure. As a result, most of the initial ADC beneficiaries were white, widowed women with young children."[86]

7. While progressive race scholars underscore the role of race when analyzing welfare, other thinkers have different emphases. As noted above, feminists tend to emphasize the role of sex and gender. They stress that "welfare state policies help to sustain and reproduce patriarchy," and they assume that the "drive to maintain male dominance and the patriarchal family is . . . the principal force shaping the formation, implementation, and outcomes of U.S. welfare policy."[87]

Other scholars emphasize the function that welfare policies have had in disciplining and regulating labor. This lens calls attention to the fact that

> the state expands its welfare rolls to reduce the possibility of serious uprisings, in effect by pacifying, co-opting, or buying off the poor. In times of economic and political stability, the state turns around and expunges recipients from the rolls, forcing poor people to seek ways to survive in the market economy, and providing only the most meager assistance to those who would not otherwise survive.[88]

Essentially, different aspects of the welfare state might be emphasized. How would you analyze the welfare state with an

---

[84] *See* William J. Nelson, Jr., *Employment Covered under the Social Security Program, 1935–84*, 48 SOC. SEC. BULL. 33, 33 (1985).

[85] *See* QUADAGNO, *supra* note 15, at 157.

[86] *Id.* at 119.

[87] NEUBECK & CAZENAVE, *supra* note 33, at 18.

[88] *Id.*

emphasis on sexuality and gender identity? Citizenship? Ability and disability?

Chapter 20

EDUCATION

For many, a book about racial justice in the U.S. is incomplete without a discussion of education. Education, many believe, is the key to racial equality. The idea is that if we achieve racial equity in education, then we can hope to achieve racial equity along other lines—like income, housing, wealth, and health. The converse might also be true: if there is no justice in education, then racial justice will never be realized. In this vein, Daniel Kiel describes the "[e]ducation of children [as] a crucial tool for a shaping society."[1] Education can engender inequality, and it can eliminate it. It can justify a group's marginalization, and it can empower that same group to dismantle the systems that marginalize it.[2]

Progressive scholars contend that in the U.S., denying education to people of color has been a means to ensure their inferiority. In their view, this was the reason for criminalizing the teaching of enslaved people how to read during the days of chattel slavery. And this was the reason that segregationists in the Jim Crow South compelled black children to receive whatever educations they could in ramshackle buildings with dated books, underpaid teachers, and few, if any, of the educational resources that were at white children's disposal.

Critical theorists of race have analyzed what they believe to be education's function in producing, maintaining, and naturalizing racial hierarchy in this country, examining "the role of education policy in the active structuring of racial inequity."[3] These theorists insist upon the centrality of *race and racism* in explanations of why our educational system looks the way that it does and why it is doing such a poor job of educating large numbers of children. They assert that without directly confronting race and racism, we cannot hope to fashion a system that provides a quality education to *all* students.

---

[1] Daniel Kiel, *No Caste Here? Toward a Structural Critique of American Education*, 119 PENN. ST. L. REV. 611, 614 (2015).

[2] This is the sentiment that Carter Woodson expresses in his tome *The Miseducation of the Negro*, writing, "The same educational process which inspires and stimulates the oppressor with the thought that he is everything and has accomplished everything worth while, depresses and crushes at the same time the spark of genius in the Negro by making him feel that his race does not amount to much and never will measure up to the standards of other peoples." CARTER G. WOODSON, THE MIS-EDUCATION OF THE NEGRO xiii (AMS Press 1977) (1933).

[3] David Gillborn, *Education Policy as an Act of White Supremacy: Whiteness, Critical Race Theory, and Education Reform*, 20 J. EDUC. POL'Y 485, 485 (2005).

Critical analyses of racial inequality in education are plentiful. This ample literature might be divided into two genres. The first consists of scholarship written by *lawyers and legal theorists*, who have primarily concerned themselves with the laws that permit education to be a good that is provided unequally along racial lines. The second genre consists of scholarship written by *educators*, who have interrogated policies and practices within districts, schools, and classrooms that they believe marginalize racial minorities and leave them without the means to succeed in society. This chapter explores each of these genres in turn.

I. Lawyers on Education

The two issues that seem to consume legal scholars writing about education the most are the persistence of racial segregation in schools and inequality in school funding.

A. Segregation, Desegregation, and Resegregation

1. *Brown v. Board of Education*[4]

The conviction that education is central to the organization of society likely explains why in the 1950s, the civil rights lawyers who fought against formal inequality decided to focus on schools. They could have focused on any area of social life. They might have attacked the institution of Jim Crow by seeking to integrate public accommodations like hotels and restaurants. They might have sought to overturn *Plessy v. Ferguson*, which had established the doctrine of "separate but equal," by challenging segregation in trains—the same arena that had prompted Homer Plessy to file his suit at the turn of the twentieth century.[5] They might have sought to rid the country of the "black" and "white" pools, beaches, and water fountains that comprised the iconography of the South. Yet, they pursued none of these routes. Instead, they trained their sights on integrating schools.

Brown v. Board is one of a handful of cases that most people in the U.S.—even those who have never set foot in a law school—can name and recite the gist of the holding.[6] In 1954, a unanimous Supreme Court declared that state sanctioned segregation of school children on the basis of race injured black children who were denied the ability to learn alongside their white peers. The Court said that forcing black children to attend separate schools—even when those black schools were equal to white schools in terms of physical facilities and other "tangible" factors—hurt black kids, generating "a

---

[4] Brown v. Bd. of Educ., 347 U.S. 483 (1954).

[5] Plessy v. Ferguson, 163 U.S. 537 (1896).

[6] *Roe v. Wade* likely is on that short list as well.

feeling of inferiority as to their status in the community that may affect their hearts and minds in a way unlikely ever to be undone."[7] For this reason, the Court concluded that "in the field of public education the doctrine of 'separate but equal' has no place."[8] In the Court's assessment, "[s]eparate educational facilities are inherently unequal"[9] and, as a consequence, states that operated segregated school systems violated the Equal Protection Clause of the Fourteenth Amendment.

On the day that the Court decided *Brown v. Board*, the decision must have felt like a complete and utter triumph to anyone with an interest in racial justice. More than sixty years after the decision was handed down, however, many progressive thinkers about race wonder whether the hullabaloo that surrounded *Brown* was much ado about nothing. Well over half a century after civil rights lawyers scored one of their most significant victories, racial segregation in schools appears to remain the order of the day. In a 2012 study, researchers describe the dramatic extent to which *Brown* has failed to produce racially integrated schools. They note that

> 80% of Latino students and 74% of black students attend majority nonwhite schools (50–100% minority), and 43% of Latinos and 38% of blacks attend intensely segregated schools (those with only 0–10% of white students) across the nation. Fully 15% of black students, and 14% of Latino students, attend "apartheid schools" across the nation where whites make up 0 to 1% of the enrollment. . . . The nation's largest metropolitan areas report severe school racial concentration. Half of the black students in Chicago metro, and one third of black students in New York, attend apartheid schools.[10]

This study also reports that while white children represent half of the population in public schools, most white students attend schools where 75% of the students are also white. In essence, just as black and Latinx children attend schools with high concentrations of black and Latinx students, white children attend schools with high concentrations of white students.

Racial segregation in schools appears to be as bad as it was before *Brown* was decided. Indeed, some wonder whether segregation today is *worse* today than it was during the heyday of Jim Crow. This

---

[7] *Brown*, 347 U.S. at 494.

[8] *Id.* at 495.

[9] *Id.*

[10] GARY ORFIELD, JOHN KUSCERA & GENEVIEVE SIEGEL-HAWLEY, THE CIVIL RIGHTS PROJECT OF UCLA, E PLURIBUS . . . SEPARATION: DEEPENING DOUBLE SEGREGATION FOR MORE STUDENTS 9 (2012).

situation led Derrick Bell—who, before going on to become one of the founding fathers of CRT, had fought in the proverbial trenches, litigating school integration suits in federal courts across the nation—to write that "the statistics on resegregation . . . painfully underscore[ ] the fact that many black and Hispanic children are enrolled in schools as separate and probably more unequal than those their parents and grandparents attended under the era of 'separate but equal.' "[11]

Importantly, racially segregated schools tend to mean class segregated schools, and schools where racial minorities predominate tend to be sites of concentrated poverty. "Nationwide, the typical black student is now in a school where almost two out of every three classmates (64%) are low-income, nearly double the level in schools of the typical white or Asian student (37% and 39%, respectively)."[12] This would not be so bad if schools attended by large proportions of poor kids still managed to provide decent educations to their students. Typically, they do not. "[T]he resources that are consistently linked to predominately white and/or wealthy schools help foster real and serious educational advantages over minority segregated settings."[13]

Simply put, *Brown* has not done what it was supposed to do. We should note, though, that at one time, *Brown* had borne remarkable fruit. Sheryll Cashin observes that "[c]ourt-ordered desegregation of black students in the late 1960s and 1970s resulted in the South becoming our nation's most integrated region. By 1988, the South reached a high point of 43.5% of black students attending majority-white schools, up from a mere 0.001% in 1954. But, by 2000, marking a twelve-year and continuing process of resegregation, only 31% of black students in the South attended majority white schools."[14]

So, what happened? What made *Brown* such an ineffective tool for achieving racial integration? In truth, a lot of things. Many observers point to *Brown II*, which declared that local school boards had to use "all deliberate speed" to remedy the constitutional violation that *Brown* found.[15] For many, this was a curious holding. In their eyes, if someone is violating your constitutional rights, they should be made to stop *immediately*; they should not be required to do so eventually, with deliberate speed. Not so with respect to

---

[11] DERRICK BELL, SILENT COVENANTS: *BROWN V. BOARD OF EDUCATION* AND THE UNFULFILLED HOPES FOR RACIAL REFORM 114 (2004) [hereinafter BELL, SILENT COVENANTS].

[12] ORFIELD, KUSCERA & SIEGEL-HAWLEY, *supra* note 10, at 7.

[13] *Id.* at 8.

[14] Sheryll D. Cashin, *American Public Schools Fifty Years After* Brown*: A Separate and Unequal Reality*, 47 HOW. L.J. 341, 352 (2004).

[15] Brown v. Bd. of Educ. (*Brown II*), 349 U.S. 294, 301 (1955).

segregated schools. Racial justice advocates became suspicious that the "deliberate speed" standard was the Court's attempt to avoid raising the hackles of segregationists even further. The standard essentially said, "You have to stop with this 'segregated schools' nonsense. The Constitution requires it. But, you can do it on your own terms—whenever you're ready." Bell writes, "Until *Brown II*, . . . constitutional rights had been defined as personal and present," but the Court decided to "sacrifice[ ] individual and immediate vindication of the newly discovered right of blacks to a desegregated education in favor of a remedy more palatable to whites."[16]

Arguably more damaging to *Brown*'s ability to integrate schools, however, was the government's apparent retreat from what had appeared to be an initial commitment to desegregation. In the first two decades following *Brown*, the Court seemed to want to ensure that the decision functioned to integrate schools. Although school boards attempted to avoid the requirements of the Constitution—sometimes openly and defiantly—the Court issued decision after decision that sought to make them comply. When the school board in Prince Edward County in Virginia tried to avoid desegregation by closing all of its schools and giving white families tuition grants that they could use to send their children to private, segregated schools, the Court struck down the scheme.[17] And in *Green v. County School Board of New Kent County*,[18] the Court acknowledged that integrating schools might necessitate massive restructuring. If it did, the Court said, the Constitution obligated school boards to do just that; the Court insisted that boards had "the affirmative duty to take whatever steps might be necessary to convert to a unitary system in which racial discrimination would be eliminated root and branch."[19] Further, in *Swann v. Charlotte-Mecklenburg Board of Education*, the Court held that lower courts could fashion expansive remedies when confronted with a school district that had operated racially segregated schools.[20] The Court declared that "the nature of the violation determines the scope of the remedy."[21] Thus, the more systemic the violation, the more systemic the remedy could be. Noting that lower courts had "breadth and flexibility" when endeavoring to produce a unitary school system, the Court gave its blessing to the use of busing to ensure that black and white children attended the same schools.[22]

---

16 BELL, SILENT COVENANTS, *supra* note 11, at 95.

17 Griffin v. Cty. Sch. Bd. of Prince Edward Cty., 377 U.S. 218 (1964).

18 Green v. Cty. Sch. Bd. of New Kent Cty., Va., 391 U.S. 430 (1968).

19 *Id.* at 437–38.

20 Swann v. Charlotte-Mecklenburg Bd. of Educ., 402 U.S. 1 (1971).

21 *Id.* at 16.

22 *Id.* at 15.

In essence, for several years after *Brown* was decided, the Court issued strong precedent with powerful language. Further, the executive branch was also on board, vigorously enforcing desegregation requirements. But, then the tide turned in 1968 when Richard Nixon was elected to the presidency. He stopped "administrative enforcement of desegregation requirements, shifted the position of the Justice Department from proactive enforcement to passive acceptance, appointed four conservative Justices to the Supreme Court and attacked desegregation rulings. Nixon's judicial appointments produced the first divided desegregation decisions since *Brown*."[23]

There is wide agreement that *Milliken v. Bradley*[24] was one of the most damaging decisions to the desegregation cause that the Nixon-configured Court issued. The case involved Detroit, which was predominately black, and the predominately white suburbs that surrounded it. After Detroit was ordered to desegregate its schools though the use of busing, the city became blacker and the suburbs whiter. That is, white families fled to the suburbs—to different school districts—in order to avoid the necessity of putting their children on buses so that black children in the city's school district could get a desegregated education. (We should note that the practice of white families moving out of cities and into suburbs when faced with the need to integrate schools was not at all unique to Detroit. The phenomenon was quite widespread.)

In *Milliken*, the lower court had observed that any desegregation order that involved Detroit's school district alone was doomed to fail; there simply were not enough white people left in Detroit to achieve racially integrated schools. If black and white children were going to attend schools together, then white children in the suburbs would have to be made to attend school with black children in the city; and black children in the city would have to made to attend school with white children in the suburbs. The lower court, observing that "[s]chool district lines are simply matters of political convenience and may not be used to deny constitutional rights,"[25] ordered the school board to construct an interdistrict, metropolitan-wide desegregation plan. The Supreme Court struck down this ruling. It reasoned that while Detroit might have operated segregated schools, there was no evidence that the surrounding suburbs had done the same. Absent evidence that the school districts in the outlying suburbs had committed any constitutional violation, they could not be forced to pay for the sins of another school district that had actually violated the law. The Court argued that local control of education was a

---

[23] ORFIELD, KUSCERA & SIEGEL-HAWLEY, *supra* note 10, at 4.

[24] Milliken v. Bradley, 418 U.S. 717 (1974).

[25] *Id.* at 733.

tradition with deep historic roots in this country, and it was not keen to see this tradition set aside so easily—even if was to be set aside in the interest of school integration.

Milliken horrified those who believe in the desegregation of schools. To these observers, it prioritized local control of schools over *Brown*'s command to integrate schools. Now, local control of schools has been valued because of the belief that school boards that are close to the students it serves will be better able to meet their needs than would boards that are distant. However, writes Cedric Merlin Powell, the idea that local control ought to take precedence over integration is "wholly foreign to *Brown* and its constitutional mandate to eradicate dual school systems."[26] He argues that the suggestion that "school district boundary lines are sacrosanct and cannot be breached"[27] is a "doctrinal fiction"[28]—one that the Court in *Milliken* made up in order not to burden the white families in the suburbs with *Brown*'s mandate.

According to critical thinkers, *Milliken* ignored the reality that housing discrimination and the country's history of racial disenfranchisement—which have caused black people to be poorer than their white counterparts—made it exceedingly difficult for many black families to move to the suburbs. Residential segregation, with people of color confined to urban centers and white people living in the outlying suburbs, is not the result of voluntary housing choices. Instead, they argued, it is the product of past and present racism. No matter, said *Milliken*. Suburban school boards are required to remedy neither historical racial disenfranchisement nor housing discrimination, and they are not required to get involved in the affairs of another school board that had engaged in *de jure* segregation in schools. In this way, *Milliken* "essentially insulated predominately white suburban school districts from the constitutional imperatives of *Brown*,"[29] making the suburbs safe havens for white families who either do not want to deal with busing or, more abhorrently, do not want to send their children to school with black kids.

To progressive race scholars, one of the most disturbing effects of *Milliken* is that it actually increased racial segregation in schools. It guarantees white families that they do not have to deal with desegregation orders if they move to the suburbs. As Powell explains, "[A] Detroit-only remedy all but guaranteed intensified segregation

---

[26] Cedric Merlin Powell, Milliken, *'Neutral Principles,' and Post Racial Determinism*, 31 HARV. J. ON RACIAL & ETHNIC JUST. ONLINE 1, 25 (2015).

[27] *Id.* at 10.

[28] *Id.* at 26.

[29] Cashin, *supra* note 14, at 347.

exacerbated by white flight. Forty years later, the demographics bear this out. There was an urban exodus out of the city to the suburbs; and, as the total population of school students in Detroit rapidly declined, the school population was recast as a predominately Black school district."[30] This phenomenon played out in school districts around the country.

Milliken stands for the proposition that while racial separation that results from intentional acts of lawmakers (that is, *de jure* segregation) is forbidden and must be remedied, racial separation that is not intentionally produced by lawmakers (that is, *de facto* segregation) is allowable and need not be addressed. Because *de facto* segregation is responsible for the statistics that open this Part, the Court's precedents cast the extensive racial isolation that those statistics describe as perfectly consistent with the Constitution. The *de jure/de facto* distinction—and the proposition that the Constitution does not tolerate the former, but completely countenances the latter—has been the target of critical thinkers' ire insofar as it, in their view, "obscures and diminishes the significance and complexity of race, racism (structural inequality), and the present day effects of past discrimination."[31]

The retreat from *Brown* continued after *Milliken*, with the Court creating precedent that released school boards that had committed constitutional violations from judicial oversight—relieving them of the obligation to continue attempts to achieve integrated schools *even when their schools remained incredibly segregated.* In *Board of Education of Oklahoma City Public Schools v. Dowell*, the Court said that as long as boards had taken all "practicable" steps to desegregate schools, then the demands of the Fourteenth Amendment had been satisfied, the "purposes of the desegregation litigation had been fully achieved," and lower courts were free to remove them from their dockets.[32] Instead of asking whether it was likely that the schools in a district would become segregated again absent judicial supervision, courts started asking easier questions—about "whether the district [had] made good-faith efforts toward desegregation, the number of remaining schools identifiable by race, and the feasibility of additional desegregation."[33] In essence, courts began ending judicial oversight of school boards on the finding that continuing efforts to desegregate schools would be tough—not on the

---

[30] Powell, *supra* note 26, at 22.

[31] *Id.* at 6.

[32] Bd. Of Educ. of Oklahoma City Pub. Sch. v. Dowell, 498 U.S. 237, 247, 250 (1991).

[33] BELL, SILENT COVENANTS, *supra* note 11, at 126.

finding that school boards actually had successfully desegregated their schools.

a. *Brown* and Buyer's Remorse

In the years that followed *Brown*, many who had been staunch believers in school integration began to reconsider their conviction. The road to meaningful integration had revealed itself to be a nightmare to travel. Civil rights lawyers had to spend copious amounts of time and resources battling defiant school districts in court, attempting to attain orders that would force compliance with the demands of *Brown*. It might have been easier for many of these lawyers to dedicate themselves to this work if the benefits of integration were apparent—if there was unimpeachable evidence that black children were profiting from attending the predominately white schools that had previously been unavailable to them. Unfortunately, the evidence that was coming back about black children's experiences in integrated schools was mixed. While attending integrated schools improved the educational outcomes of many black children, this was not a universal experience. For black children, desegregation meant being plucked out of all-black environments that, while underfunded relative to their white counterparts, were supportive and nurturing. Instead of learning in friendly and warm black schools, black children were being placed into unfriendly and unwelcoming white spaces. As Bell describes it, "In these white schools, black children all too often met naked race-hatred and a curriculum blind to their needs. Black parents, who often lived far from the schools where their children were sent, had no input into the school policies and little opportunity to involve themselves in school life."[34] The situation was so bleak that it led Bell, who had been fighting for desegregation in the courts, to wonder whether he was spending his time wisely. He reflected:

> Why was I trying to get these children admitted to schools where they were not wanted, where, unless they were exceptional, they would fare poorly, probably dropping out without a diploma, perhaps responding to their hostile treatment and getting into difficulties that would result in their expulsion? It did not seem that the unwillingness to treat blacks as full citizens, despite *Brown*, had really changed in the more than one hundred years since Chief Justice Shaw's prediction in the 1850 *Roberts v. City of Boston* case that the prejudice in segregated schools, "if it exists, is not created by law, and probably cannot be changed by law. Whether this distinction and prejudice, existing in the opinion and feelings of the community,

[34] *Id.* at 112.

would not be as effectually fostered by compelling colored and white children to associate together in the same schools, may well be doubted."[35]

Bell also regretted that when black students were sent to white schools, the predominately black schools that they previously had attended usually were closed. Black teachers, administrators, and principals—folks who had dedicated their lives to educating black children—lost their jobs and their livelihoods.

These facts led many who had been unyielding integrationists—people who once had fought tirelessly to end segregation in schools and who had celebrated *Brown* as the most important decision that the Court had ever handed down—to question whether they should have tried a different approach. They speculated whether, instead of fighting for school integration, they ought to have fought for the equalization of black and white schools. According to this line of thought, if the resources and facilities of black schools were equal to those of white schools, then the educational outcomes of black children would match those of their white counterparts. Folks in this camp were adamant that black children did not need to sit beside white children in order to learn. They just needed the resources that were available to white children.

The appeal of this position should be apparent. It obviated the need to plead to white schools to accept black children, saved black children from environments whose hostility was both overt and subtle, and would result in a self-sufficient, empowered black community. However, many found the position disquieting. For them, it sounded too much like a capitulation to *Plessy v. Ferguson*'s pronouncement of "separate but equal"—a doctrine that had been degrading and humiliating to black people, reducing them to second-class citizens. Moreover, many others doubted that equalizing black and white schools would result in black children achieving the same educational outcomes as their white counterparts. Although their segregated educations might be similar, black children would still be missing out on the networks that would allow them access to elite spaces. This debate is explored in greater depth in the discussion about inequality in school funding below.

b. *Brown* and Interest Convergence

Bell has proposed that part of the reason for *Brown*'s failure to desegregate schools was that the decision was not really about black children. According to Bell, the case was not a product of a concern for the "hearts and minds" of the black kids who were imagined to feel themselves inferior because of state-sanctioned segregation. To

[35] *Id.* at 105.

Bell, the case did not reflect a society realizing the error of its ways and vowing to do right by its racial minority citizens. In his view, *Brown* was not about racial justice. Instead, Bell claims that *Brown* came down the way that it did because the U.S. needed to save face on the world stage.

To support his claim, he observes that the Cold War between the U.S. and the Soviet Union began in the late 1940s. The two world powers were locked in a battle for influence over other nations, especially African states that had recently won independence from the countries that had colonized them a century prior. The U.S. wanted to portray itself to these states as a bastion of democracy, freedom, and liberty—in contrast to the deprivation and constraint that it said the Soviet Union represented. However, Jim Crow gave the lie to that portrayal. Indeed, there was a large population in the U.S. that had no idea what democracy, freedom, and liberty looked like—a fact that the Soviet Union had no problem publicizing to countries all around the world. Thus, Bell argues, if the U.S. wanted to achieve its foreign policy goals, it had to fix its Jim Crow problem. *Brown* was the fix.[36]

Bell cites this as an example of "interest convergence." This principle proposes that "[t]he interest of blacks in achieving racial equality will be accommodated only when that interest converges with the interests of whites in policy-making positions. This convergence is far more important for gaining relief than the degree of harm suffered by blacks or the character of proof offered to prove that harm."[37] For Bell, interest convergence explains why the Court held in *Brown* that separate schools violated the Equal Protection Clause. But, what explains why *Brown* failed to actually eradicate separate schools? According to Bell, "even when the interest convergence principle results in an effective racial remedy, that remedy will be abrogated at the point that policymakers fear the remedial policy is threatening the superior societal status of whites."[38] Thus, when white people's dominant position became threatened by their having to put their children on buses to attend schools with black kids, or by their schools in the suburbs having to share resources with predominately black schools in the cities, *Milliken*, *Dowell*, *Missouri v. Jenkins*,[39] and other cases were decided

---

[36] Historian Mary Dudziak's work confirms Bell's reading of *Brown* as a Cold War case. MARY L. DUDZIAK, COLD WAR CIVIL RIGHTS: RACE AND THE IMAGE OF AMERICAN DEMOCRACY (2011).

[37] BELL, SILENT COVENANTS, *supra* note 11, at 69.

[38] *Id.*

[39] *Missouri v. Jenkins*, 515 U.S. 70 (1995), concerned a district court's order that was aimed at producing racially integrated schools in the Kansas City, Missouri School District (KCMSD). The court recognized that many white students had moved to the suburbs and attended schools there, making it virtually impossible to realize

so as to protect white dominance. This is a decidedly cynical view of *Brown* and the fight for racial justice, more generally.

c. Other Critiques of *Brown*

Other progressive race scholars have asserted that *Brown* was a flawed decision not simply because subsequent iterations of the Court retreated from it, but rather because it reflected a limited vision of racial justice. The critique is that *Brown* did not endeavor to end white dominance and black subordination; it simply sought to dismantle racial hierarchy in the form that it took at the time of the decision. As a result, the case left open the door for racial inequality to be reconfigured in a different form. This, say these theorists, is precisely what happened with the *Milliken* Court's protection of white families' privilege to disconnect themselves from black families and children by fleeing to the suburbs.

Cheryl Harris has articulated this critique powerfully in her "Whiteness as Property" article, which most would agree enjoys a prominent place in the CRT canon.[40] She argues that in prohibiting the racial inequality that was the entire point of *de jure* segregation, while leaving untouched the racial inequality that was both a cause and an effect of *de facto* segregation, *Brown* did no more than usher in a newer, more contemporary form of white supremacy. According to Harris, we misread *Brown* when we take it to stand for the claim that the Constitution will no longer tolerate structures and institutions that subordinate nonwhite people. Instead, *Brown* merely stands for the claim that different mechanisms must generate the subordinate status of nonwhite people. She argues that *Brown* simply dismantled an old form of white privilege

> while simultaneously permitting its reemergence in a more subtle form. White privilege accorded as a legal right was rejected, but de facto white privilege not mandated by law remained unaddressed. In failing to clearly expose the real inequities produced by segregation, the status quo of

---

meaningful racial integration in the city center. To fix this problem, the court ordered the school district to transform all of its high schools and middle schools, as well as half of its elementary schools, into magnet schools. The goal was to make the schools so appealing that the white families who lived in the suburbs would voluntarily send their children to attend them. The intent of the order was to increase the "desegregative attractiveness" of KCMSD. *Id.* at 91–92. The Court struck it down. The Court argued that the lower court had attempted to circumvent the constraints that *Milliken* had established. It accused the lower court of "devis[ing] a remedy to accomplish indirectly what it admittedly lacks the remedial authority to mandate directly: the interdistrict transfer of students." *Id.* at 92. In Cashin's reading, "*Jenkins* suggested that eliminating the vestiges of *de jure* segregation was either too difficult, too expensive or both, and it was time to let school districts off the hook." Cashin, *supra* note 14, at 350.

[40] Cheryl I. Harris, *Whiteness as Property*, 106 HARV. L. REV. 1707 (1993).

> substantive disadvantage was ratified as an accepted and acceptable baseline—a neutral state operating to the disadvantage of Blacks long after *de jure* segregation had ceased to do so. In accepting substantial inequality as a neutral baseline, a new form of [white privilege] was condoned.[41]

Noting that *Brown* "did nothing to stop advantages attributable to race not mandated by law," Anita Hill similarly concludes that it "was not a bad decision, and it certainly was not a wrong decision. It was simply a limited decision, in part because of the limited perspective the Court had on race."[42]

2. *Contemporary Modes of Racial Segregation*

At present, the law is out of the business of explicitly assigning students to schools on the basis of race.[43] *De jure* segregation is dead. However, as described above, racial segregation in schools persists, and it approximates the segregation that reigned supreme in the days before *Brown* was decided. Large portions of black and Latinx students still attend schools where white students are few and far between; and white students still attend schools where the number of black and Latinx students is low. White flight, and the Court's precedents that make it impossible for remedies to reach the suburbs to which white families relocated, bears a lot of responsibility for the present state of affairs. However, scholars have observed other processes that have made it difficult for black and white students to learn beside one another.

a. Meritocratic Sorting

It is not unusual for black and white students to be taught in different classrooms even when they attend the same schools—a result that probably is not what the civil rights lawyers who litigated *Brown* had in mind. The racial segregation of students within schools occurs through what Kiel calls "meritocratic sorting," where students are placed in different classrooms according to their perceived ability. Forms of meritocratic sorting include "tracking,[44] the institution of

---

[41] *Id.* at 1753.

[42] Anita F. Hill, *A History of Hollow Promises: How Choice Jurisprudence Fails to Achieve Educational Equality*, 12 MICH. J. RACE & L. 107, 117–18 (2006).

[43] The only exception to this is when schools remain under a desegregation order. Interestingly, in *Parents Involved in Community Schools v. Seattle School District*, the Court prohibited school districts from considering the race of students when making school assignments when those districts were attempting to achieve integrated schools, but had not been ordered to do so pursuant to a desegregation order. Parents Involved in Cmty. Sch. v. Seattle Sch. Dist. No. 1, 551 U.S. 701 (2007).

[44] Tracking is the practice of grouping students according to ability—oftentimes as measured by standardized tests—and teaching them in different classrooms, sometimes with different curricula.

'gifted' programs, honors programs, and advanced placement classes."[45]

On first blush, meritocratic sorting appears to be a good idea. It seems to allow students to be challenged according to what they can handle, enabling students to receive educations that are tailored to their needs. Race, however, makes things messy on the ground, say progressive scholars. "African-American and Latino students are disproportionately placed into the lowest tracks and afforded fewer educational opportunities as a result."[46] Further, students of color tend to be underrepresented in programs of study for more advanced students—like gifted programs and advanced placement classes. The result is racially segregated classrooms, with white students being found in the classes for the "smart kids" and students of color being found in the classes for those who are "slow."

The practice of educating students with disabilities separately from those without identified disabilities is another form of meritocratic sorting. Again, the practice sounds good in theory. A student with a disability may need more time to learn, or may need to be taught with different methods. Placing those students in separate classrooms allows them to learn at the pace and with the tools that they require. However, as applied, sorting students on the basis of ability has generated some racial issues, which Chapter 15 examines in greater depth. "Segregated special classes have been populated with students from non-dominant racial and ethnic groups, from immigrant populations, and from 'lower' social classes and status since their inception. A disproportionate number of non-dominant racial, ethnic, and linguistic [students] continue to be referred, labeled, and placed in special education, particularly in the categories of Learning Disability, Intellectual Disability (formerly called Mental Retardation), and Emotional Disturbance or Behavior Disorder."[47] Thus, students of color are disproportionately consigned to the classrooms for kids with disabilities, leaving the classrooms for kids without disabilities to be white spaces.

Finally, Kiel notes that an additional type of sorting takes place when students of color are disciplined more harshly for the same infractions that their white counterparts commit. He writes:

---

[45] Gloria Ladson-Billings & William F. Tate IV, *Toward a Critical Race Theory of Education,* 97 TEACHERS COLL. REC. 47, 60 (1995).

[46] Adrienne D. Dixson & Celia K. Rousseau, *And We Are Still Not Saved: Critical Race Theory in Education Ten Years Later,* 8 RACE ETHNICITY & EDUC. 7, 8 (2005).

[47] Subini Ancy Annamma, David J. Connor & Beth A. Ferri, *Dis/ability Critical Race Studies (DisCrit): Theorizing at the Intersections of Race and Dis/ability, in* DISCRIT: DISABILITY STUDIES AND CRITICAL RACE THEORY IN EDUCATION 9, 10 (David J. Connor, Beth A. Ferri & Subini A. Annamma eds., 2016).

> Studies of student disciplinary practices have consistently shown that African American students are more likely to be suspended and expelled. Even in preschool, African American students, who make up only 18 percent of preschool enrollment, make up 42 percent of the students suspended. Overall suspension rates demonstrate similar disparities—24 percent of African American students have been suspended, compared to only 7 percent of white students. Such suspensions further steer those suspended students (disproportionately African American) toward academic disengagement, lower achievement, and increased risk of dropout, creating what many have described as the school-to-prison pipeline.[48]

Thus, *Brown* is not inevitably realized simply when black and white students manage to attend the same schools. Critical thinkers remind us that a variety of segregative practices function to foil the dream of providing children with desegregated educations.

b. School Choice

Historically, the school that any individual child attends has typically been the one that has been assigned to her—usually the school that is geographically close to her in her neighborhood. Of course, parents have always been able to opt out of the public school system, electing instead to send their children to private schools or to home school them. However, traditionally, if parents chose to educate their kids in the public school system, their children usually would attend the school to which the district assigns them. "School choice" has changed this.

School choice refers to the opportunity for parents to use the funds that the state would spend educating a child in an assigned school on other schooling options. These options include private schools (including religiously-affiliated ones), charter schools, home schools, and other public schools (including those that are outside of a family's school district). So, for example, if the state typically spends $1000/year on each pupil in a particular public school, school choice allows the parents of a child to put that $1000 towards educating their child elsewhere. The most popular forms of school choice have been charter schools (which are independently-operated primary and secondary schools that are funded with public monies, but are not controlled by the public school district in which they reside) and vouchers (which refer to programs that allow parents to use public education funds to pay their child's tuition at a private

---

[48] Kiel, *supra* note 1, at 625.

school). Both charter schools and voucher programs result in the diversion of public monies from a child's neighborhood school.

Proponents of school choice argue that it empowers parents by enabling them to select the school that will provide an education that is most suitable for their child. They also argue that school choice puts all schools, public and private, in competition with one another. As each school vies for public dollars by attempting to offer programs, facilities, and teachers that are better than those offered by other schools, educational options improve all around, "increasing the quality of education for all."[49] However, opponents condemn school choice because they claim that not only does it exacerbate existing racial segregation, but it also isolates the most marginalized and vulnerable families in troubled schools.

It does appear true that school choice has increased racial segregation in schools. For example, charter schools tend to be more segregated than their public school counterparts.[50] Analysts attribute this to the fact that charter schools are oftentimes rolled out in districts with low performing public schools—that is, districts that are predominately nonwhite.[51] If charter schools were established in districts with fantastic public schools, families would have little incentive to pull their children from these schools, as they would be receiving an effective education where they are. Consequently, the racial mix of the public school would be unthreatened. However, because charter schools tend to be located in districts with low performing public schools, families are more likely to move their children from these underperforming schools when given the option through a school choice program. Further, they tend to choose to place their children in the charter school that most appeals to them, i.e., the school that is identified with their race or ethnicity.[52] Black families send their kids to the "black school"; Latinx families send their kids to the "Latinx school"; and so on. The consequence is that charter schools end up being even more racially isolated than the neighborhood school. For persons who are strong believers in integrated schools, this result is disquieting.

Further, opponents of school choice are disturbed by the way that these programs operate to sequester the most disempowered families in the lowest performing schools. In order to exercise a real

---

[49] BELL, SILENT COVENANTS, *supra* note 11, at 175.

[50] *See* Erica Frankenberg, Genevieve Siegel-Hawley & Jia Wang, *Choice Without Equity: Charter School Segregation*, EDUC. POL'Y ANALYSIS ARCHIVES, Jan. 10, 2011, at 1, 46.

[51] *See* GARY ORFIELD & ERICA FRANKENBERG, EDUCATIONAL DELUSIONS?: WHY CHOICE CAN DEEPEN INEQUALITY AND HOW TO MAKE SCHOOLS FAIR 30 (2013).

[52] *See* Courtney A. Bell, *All Choices Created Equal? The Role of Choice Sets in the Selection of Schools*, 84 PEABODY J. EDUC. 191, 199–200 (2009).

choice about where to send a child for school, a parent needs to have information about her options; further, the information needs to be in a language that she can understand. If a preferred school is not within walking distance, a parent needs to have the means with which to transport her child to the school. If the school choice program involves vouchers, a family will need the money to cover the portion of the chosen school's tuition that exceeds the value of the voucher. And if a preferred school has admissions criteria, the child will need the ability to meet these criteria.[53] The least privileged families will have none of these things. Accordingly, as the more privileged families—with information and transportation and money for tuition and "merit"—remove their children from the neighborhood school, the children of the least privileged families will remain there. We should keep in mind as well that as more privileged families move their children out of the lowest performing neighborhood schools, public funding goes with them. Thus, these schools are left with fewer resources with which to educate the least privileged students. This is the last thing that we should be doing, say school choice opponents. Instead of "siphoning needed resources from schools already poorly funded,"[54] we ought to ensure that every school has the resources that it needs to educate its student population. School choice does not do that, they say.

Some scholars who are strong supporters of integration contend that school choice need not *inevitably* result in increased racial segregation and the isolation of vulnerable students and families. They insist that school choice simply needs to be done *right*. For example, James Ryan gives the example of a voucher program

> that is limited to low-income students, provides each student $6500 and covers full transportation costs, requires participating schools to accept students by lottery, aggressively disseminates information about schools to parents and assists them in choosing schools, ensures that public schools that lose students retain sufficient resources to provide an adequate education, and requires suburban schools to accept students if space allows will surely have a decent chance of improving the educational opportunities of students currently attending inner-city schools. By contrast, a plan that provides all students a $1000 voucher that can be used only at urban private schools, does not

[53] Opponents observe that because school choice places schools in competition with one another, schools benefit when they exclude students with challenges—that is, children who will not score high on standardized tests, with a record of disciplinary actions, with a disability, etc. *See, e.g.*, Frankenberg, Siegel-Hawley & Wang, *supra* note 50, at 4–5.

[54] BELL, SILENT COVENANTS, *supra* note 11, at 175.

> provide for transportation, provides little assistance and information to parents, and allows schools to use whatever criteria they choose to select students will probably not do much to help disadvantaged students and may cause some harm, insofar as the vouchers would mostly siphon off families that could afford to supplement them and that are savvy and motivated enough to select a good private school.[55]

We will have to stay tuned to see if a school board devises a plan like the one that Ryan proposes.

In the meantime, Hill concludes that claims that school choice will save our beleaguered educational system and the children struggling to acquire knowledge and skills within it represent a shift in the approach that society has taken to thinking about fairness in education. She contends that where we used to think about educational issues as involving questions of "equality and public responsibility," the movement for school choice has moved us to thinking about these issues as concerning "liberty and private choices."[56] In her view, which is shared by many other progressive scholars, this is a framework that promises to fail disadvantaged children.

B. Inequality in School Funding

The schools that children of color had been left to attend during the days of Jim Crow and *de jure* segregation were obviously and intentionally poorly-funded, lacking the educational resources that the white schools had. Black students' educational outcomes suffered as a result. The integrationist impulse was premised on the belief that if black children could attend the well-resourced, well-funded schools that had been reserved for white students, then their educational outcomes would come to match their white counterparts. However, when the judiciary began signaling its retreat from a commitment to actually integrating schools, civil rights lawyers and the communities they represented began wondering if there was another way that they could improve the quality of the education that children of color received.

Advocates began insisting that black students' underachievement was not caused by their inability to sit next to white students in a classroom. Rather, they said, black underachievement resulted from the underfunding of black schools. They argued that black children's educational outcomes were lower than white children's because black schools did not have the means

---

[55] James E. Ryan, *Schools, Race, and Money*, 109 YALE L.J 249, 312–13 (1999).

[56] Hill, *supra* note 42, at 158.

to provide them with anything but a subpar education. More and more people began to conclude that if the courts would not force school districts to produce racially integrated schools, then they should at least be forced to provide equal funds to racially segregated schools. Essentially, these advocates were comfortable with the predominately white schools in the suburbs remaining white as long as the predominately black schools in the cities were funded on the same level as their suburban counterparts. Thus, if the schools in the suburbs could afford to offer "science labs, computers and other state-of-the-art technologies, [and] appropriately certified and prepared teachers,"[57] the schools in the cities should be able to afford the same.

Because schools are largely funded through property taxes, there are gross disparities in the funds that schools in different school districts receive. Schools in areas with more valuable property (i.e., predominately white suburbs) have more money than schools in areas with less valuable property (i.e., disproportionately black and Latinx central cities)—even when the areas with more valuable property have *lower* tax rates.[58] Thus, in order to achieve funding equity between schools, advocates had to challenge the practice of funding schools through property taxes. These challengers essentially wanted to *bind* poor districts to wealthier districts. As Ryan explains, this strategy resembled the arrangement that proponents of integration sought. "Desegregation sought to tie the fate of black students to that of white students, and school finance equalization sought to tie the fate of poor districts to that of wealthier ones."[59] If the courts were unwilling to tie black and white students together in a race-conscious way, then advocates hoped that they would be willing to tie them together in a class-conscious way.

In *San Antonio School District v. Rodriguez*, the Court rejected the argument that, where education is concerned, the Constitution requires wealthier districts to be tied to poorer ones.[60] It held that disparities in funding between wealthier and poorer districts posed no equal protection problem. Further, it held that there was no

---

[57] Ladson-Billings & Tate, *supra* note 45, at 54.

[58] For example, let's say that poor district X has property that is valued at $10 million. If the government taxes property at a rate of 10%, it will have $1 million with which to fund its schools. Now, let's say that wealthy district Y has property that is valued at $100 million. Even if the government taxes property at 5%—half of X's rate—it will still have $5 million with which to fund its schools.

[59] Ryan, *supra* note 55, at 256.

[60] San Antonio Indep. Sch. Dist. v. Rodriguez, 411 U.S. 1, 54–55 (1973). The facts of the case demonstrate the extreme disparities in school funding that can be found across the nation. The plaintiffs attended schools in the Edgewood Independent School District, which served a large proportion of Latinx students. The state spent approximately $26 per pupil in that district. However, in the Alamo Heights district, in which 80% of the students were white, the state spent some $333 per pupil, "13 times the local funding in Edgewood." Kiel, *supra* note 1, at 628.

fundamental right to an education and that the Constitution is not offended if the students residing in poorer school districts receive subpar educations. Thus, the Court shut the door to federal challenges to school funding practices. Critical observers have noted that the holding in *Rodriguez* makes the Court's decision in *Milliken* even more pernicious: *Milliken* provides that white families who move their families across district lines into the suburbs need not be forced to attend schools with families who are compelled to remain in the central cities. And *Rodriguez* provides that the wealthier families in the suburbs need not share their collective wealth with the poor, underfunded schools that they left behind.

Nevertheless, advocates persisted in the face of *Rodriguez*, turning to state courts and looking for relief in state constitutions. Providing reason for optimism was that some state constitutions provide for an affirmative right to education—something that is wholly absent from the federal Constitution. Another reason for optimism was the race-blind nature of school finance litigation. While there is no way to deny that efforts to integrate schools is about race, school financing might be portrayed as simply being about class. Further, many have observed that class is typically much less controversial and provocative than race. Advocates hoped that more people would be willing to get behind—or, at least, not actively oppose—a movement that is about class inequality than one that is about racial inequality. Looking back on the decades of school funding litigation, Ryan has concluded that this hope did not bear out. "[F]ar from moving beyond race, school finance reform has been and will continue to be hamstrung by the obstacles created by poor race relations and the Court's desegregation jurisprudence."[61]

To be fair, litigators have had more success with challenging school financing disparities than they have had in integrating schools. In some cases, they have managed to close gaps in the funding of schools. But, they have not managed to do so across the board. Additionally, state constitutional provisions protecting a positive right to education have led litigators to seek educational *adequacy*, as opposed to educational *equality*. As Hill explains, adequacy asks questions about "whether the education provided was adequate to prepare children to be successful members of society"[62]—not whether the educations offered to all children, without regard to how rich or poor they are or where they live, are the same. Thus, as long as poorer children, who are disproportionately children of color, receive *adequate* educations, the Constitution is satisfied—even

[61] Ryan, *supra* note 55, at 255.

[62] Hill, *supra* note 42, at 126.

when the educations that wealthier children receive exceed poor kids' *adequate* educations by leaps and bounds.

Some critics observe that even if litigators could force the government to provide *equal* funds to rich and poor schools, problems would remain. Writes Bell, "[T]here is reason to doubt that equalizing funding . . . will always make a substantive difference. . . . Schools in poor, segregated neighborhoods that have been marginalized for decades will not suddenly achieve high-quality education and produce students competitive with those of the traditionally privileged schools just because they are now given equal funding."[63] Ryan expands on Bell's notion:

> Students from lower socioeconomic backgrounds come to school with greater needs than their more advantaged peers. Such students suffer more often from malnutrition and poor health care; lack of parental involvement and a nurturing, stimulating home environment; frequent changes of residence; and exposure to violence and drug use. . . . Greater needs require greater resources: Disadvantaged students simply cost more to educate, requiring additional educational programs and non-academic services such as health care and counseling. It follows that schools with large concentrations of impoverished students will face the greatest educational costs, even before factoring in such additional services as security or counseling. . . .[64]

Critical race theorists have taken inequities in school funding quite hard. Writes Gloria Ladson-Billings, "Perhaps no area of schooling underscores inequity and racism better than school funding. CRT argues that inequality in school funding is a function of institutional and structural racism. . . . Without suffering a single act of personal racism, most African Americans suffer the consequences of systemic and structural racism."[65]

It is important to note that many are uncomfortable with the idea of abandoning efforts to desegregate schools in favor of pursuing school funding equalization. Much of the discomfort comes from proponents of funding equalization being satisfied with children attending racially isolated schools. They are not disquieted by white children having few or no classmates of color, nor disturbed by children of color having no white classmates. Opponents of funding

---

[63] BELL, SILENT COVENANTS, *supra* note 11, at 163.

[64] Ryan, *supra* note 55, at 285.

[65] Gloria Ladson-Billings, *Just What is Critical Race Theory and What's It Doing in a Nice Field Like Education?*, 11 INT'L J. QUALITATIVE STUD. IN EDUC. 7, 20 (1998) [hereinafter Ladson-Billings, *What is Critical Race Theory?*].

equalization efforts are wary of any tactic that legitimizes racial segregation. According to this view, integration is a good in and of itself, and we should pursue it until it has been achieved.

Further, skeptics of efforts to equalize school funding argue that integrating schools is not just the morally right thing to do, but it also produces benefits that cannot be achieved simply by eliminating disparities in funding between schools. They point to studies that purport to show that poor students have lower levels of achievement in environments with high concentrations of other poor students, as compared to environments with more affluent students. There is also "empirical evidence that suggests that even substantial increases in school expenditures have little effect on student achievement when the student composition remains predominately poor."[66] If these studies are correct, then funding poor schools at the same level, or higher, as wealthier schools will not result in poor students having the same educational outcomes as more affluent students. In some cases, it may produce no change at all in outcomes. Ryan, a critic of school funding equalization efforts (especially when they take the place of integration efforts), has concluded:

> Advocates of desegregation have always been wary, justifiably, of implying that black students need to attend school with white students in order to improve their education, and critics of desegregation, particularly from the far left, often attempt to ascribe such a motivation to those promoting desegregation. While black students need not sit next to white ones in order to learn, the social science evidence strongly suggests that a poor student will benefit from sitting in a classroom of middle-class students.[67]

For this reason, he—and many others—believe that we ought to keep our eyes on the integration prize.

II. Educators on Education

Led by Gloria Ladson-Billings, a contingent of progressive educators have brought the insights and critiques generated by legal scholars operating within the CRT framework to the field of education. Proceeding from the premise that our contemporary system of education is failing children of color, they have sought to analyze why that is and what can be done to fix it.

Like the legal theorists and lawyers who employ a CRT framework in their work, educators who use CRT in their scholarship tend to believe that there is something fundamentally corrupt with the present order of things. As law-oriented critical race theorists

---

[66] Ryan, *supra* note 55, at 289.

[67] *Id.* at 300–01.

believe that our racial problems will not be solved by a different precedent here or an additional piece of legislation there, educators using CRT deny that there are easy solutions to the inequities present in our existing educational system. In their view, the entire apparatus needs to be reimagined. As William Tate explains, "[T]he question for the education scholar employing CRT is not so much whether or how racial discrimination can be eradicated while maintaining the vitality of other interests linked to the status quo such as federalism, traditional values, standards, established property interests, and choice. Rather, the new question would ask how these traditional interests and cultural artifacts serve as vehicles to limit and bind the educational opportunities of students of color."[68]

The development of CRT in the field of education is a response to what critical thinkers perceive to be a relative nonchalance and calm around the outcomes and experiences that children of color have in our schools. Critical thinkers believe the country to be in the middle of a racial *crisis* in education. Yet, they believe that the field of education does not recognize this. Edward Taylor laments, "We are hobbled by the paradox of a largely White teaching staff whose practices, consciously or not, contribute to the racial achievement gap yet who are unable to see what they are doing. Despite evidence of disproportionate expulsion rates, tracking into vocational or nonacademic programs, and limited access to Advanced Placement opportunities, we have yet to agree that these problems exist, much less craft co-racial approaches to fixing them."[69] In essence, CRT educators think that the building is on *fire*. Meanwhile, they believe that the field of education cannot even smell the smoke.

The development of CRT in the field of education is also a response to popular approaches that the field has taken to thinking about issues of race and racial inequality in education. A framework that has enjoyed a great deal of popularity in recent decades has been that of multicultural education. As Ladson-Billings and Tate describe it, "[m]ulticultural education has been conceptualized as a reform movement designed to effect change in the 'school and other educational institutions so that students from diverse racial, ethnic, and other social-class groups will experience educational equality.' In more recent years multicultural education has expanded to include issues of gender, ability, and sexual orientation."[70] The framework conceptualizes the question of justice in education as one of *inclusion*.

---

[68] William F. Tate IV, *Critical Race Theory and Education: History, Theory, and Implications*, 22 REV. RES. IN EDUC. 195, 234 (1997).

[69] Edward Taylor, *Introduction* to FOUNDATIONS OF CRITICAL RACE THEORY IN EDUCATION 1, 9 (Edward Taylor, David Gillborn, & Gloria Ladson-Billings eds., 2009).

[70] Ladson-Billings & Tate, *supra* note 45, at 61.

It declares that justice will be realized when marginalized groups have been *included* in educational institutions. But, these inclusive practices, from the perspective of critical race theorists, border on the trite, involving "eating ethnic or cultural foods, singing songs or dancing, [and] reading folktales."[71]

Further, CRT in education denies that racial justice in education will be achieved when historically subordinated individuals and groups simply have been included in the educational institutions that had excluded them in the past. Instead, it proposes that these educational institutions need to be *transformed*. They need to be undone and then reconstituted with the experiences, interests, and needs of the historically subordinated in mind. As Ladson-Billings and Tate explain, the multicultural framework does not propose "radically new paradigms that ensure justice"[72]—paradigms that CRT in education contend are desperately needed. The feel-good, non-confrontational, comfortable efforts that the multicultural framework offers propose "no radical change in the current order."[73] Critics say that they do nothing but give us a reason to congratulate ourselves for finally doing something about the "race problem."

* * *

CRT in education is very much concerned about school desegregation and funding—the issues that consume legal scholars. However, they also concerned about practices that take place in schools and classrooms that they believe are both the result and cause of racial inequality and white dominance. Of the many practices that are in the crosshairs of educators operating within a CRT framework, this chapter briefly describes critiques of the curriculum, instruction based on a model of deficit thinking, and the No Child Left Behind Act.

A. Curriculum

CRT in education has been critical of the content of the lessons that students typically learn in schools. They have been skeptical about what has been taught as well as what has not been taught. Students inevitably read Shakespeare at some point during their time in high school; but, many students will graduate without ever having analyzed the beauty and depth of a Toni Morrison novel. Students will study one (or more) of Mark Twain's classics; but, most will never encounter the works of Pablo Neruda or Gabriel Garciá Márquez. Will they be taught about the thousands of people who were lynched across the country? Will they learn that up until 1952,

---

71 *Id.*

72 *Id.* at 62.

73 *Id.*

the law explicitly provided that only "free white persons" could naturalize and become U.S. citizens? Will Japanese internment during World War II be a history lesson? Will they graduate knowing what happened during Operation Wetback?

CRT in education proposes that when we analyze the curriculum that commonly is taught in U.S. schools, we will see an erasure of the contributions that people of color have made throughout history, a prioritization of white people's achievements and works, and a general sanitization of the brutality that is embedded in the fabric of this nation. In the uncompromising words of Ladson-Billings, "Critical race theory sees the official school curriculum as a culturally specific artifact designed to maintain a White supremacist master script."[74]

B. Deficit Models of Black and Latinx Underperformance

There is an academic achievement gap between white and nonwhite students. Data show that black and Latinx children do not perform at the same levels as their white and Asian peers. Hill notes that according to the National Assessment of Educational Progress, up until the 1980s, there was a narrowing of the gap in the scores that black and white 17 year-olds earned on standardized tests that measured their reading ability. However, the gap stopped narrowing in the 1980s and has persisted with few changes since then. Moreover, while overall scores on the math and verbal portions of the SAT have risen over the past ten years, there is still a gap in scores earned by black and Latinx students and white and Asian students. "Even as the scores increased overall, the gap widened."[75]

Now, some have attributed these racial disparities in achievement to class. They say that *poor* children do not perform as well as more affluent children. They conclude that because black people disproportionately bear the burdens of poverty in this country, this disproportionate indigence explains why black children underachieve when compared to white children. However, this class-focused, race-blind explanation does not satisfy critical thinkers about race.[76] As Ladson-Billings and Tate assert, "the cause of their

---

[74] Ladson-Billings, *What is Critical Race Theory?*, *supra* note 65, at 18.

[75] Hill, *supra* note 42, at 108.

[76] In fact, it appears that even when one controls for class, black students do not perform as well as white students. As Ladson-Billings and Tate put it, class (and gender) cannot "explain all of the educational achievement differences apparent between whites and students of color. Indeed, there is some evidence to suggest that even when we hold constant for class, middle-class African-American students do not achieve at the same level as their white counterparts." Ladson-Billings & Tate, *supra* note 45, at 51.

poverty in conjunction with the condition of their schools and schooling is institutional and structural racism."[77]

There are many theories that attempt to explain the academic achievement gap. However, the theory that CRT in education has critiqued most thoroughly and denounced most vehemently is the cultural deficit model. This theory contends that black and Latinx children do not perform as highly as their white and Asian counterparts because there is something wrong with their families and communities. The deficit model says that the dominant values in black and Latinx communities—like "present versus future time orientation, immediate instead of deferred gratification, an emphasis on cooperation rather than competition, and placing less value on education and upward mobility"[78]—put the children from these communities at a distinct disadvantage in school. The model also proposes that unlike white and Asian families, black and Latinx parents do not prepare their children for school. Indeed, these parents are imagined not to value education very much. Instead, the parents of these children are thought to have a higher regard for other things, like family and community. The model posits that black and Latinx children come to learn that education has secondary importance to a host of other pursuits. Accordingly, they do not aim to perform well in school. And when they have a subpar academic performance, their families and communities do not penalize or stigmatize them for it.

A cousin of the deficit model is the theory of oppositional culture or identity. This framework, first proposed by anthropologists Signithia Fordham and John Ogbu, claims that poor black children in racially- and socioeconomically-isolated environments develop a counterculture that rejects dominant social norms and mores.[79] The children that Fordham and Ogbu studied came to scorn academic success as "white," and they criticized peers who sought academic success as "acting white." Like the deficit model, the theory of oppositional culture or identity explains the achievement gap in terms of black and Latinx shortcomings and problematic cultural values. To the extent that the oppositional culture framework indicts large-scale, structural forces, the indictment is for placing poor black and Latinx student in environments where they are stuck with one another.

CRT in education encourages us to notice how the deficit model and the theory of oppositional culture explain black and Latinx

---

[77] *Id.* at 55.

[78] Daniel G. Solórzano, *Images and Words that Wound: Critical Race Theory, Racial Stereotyping, and Teacher Education*, 24 TCHR. EDUC. Q. 5, 13 (1997).

[79] Signithia Fordham & John U. Ogbu, *Black Students' School Success: Coping with the "Burden of 'Acting White,'"* 18 URB. REV. 176 (1986).

underperformance in terms of the inadequacies of individuals and communities of color—completely releasing the educational system from any responsibility. Critics say that, as such, these frameworks free us from querying whether our continuing failure to desegregate schools may have something to do with the achievement gap. They liberate us from interrogating whether disparities in school funding and the financing of schools through property tax contribute to black and Latinx underperformance and, if so, how much. They exempt us from investigating whether teachers are doing things in classrooms that are failing certain students. Instead, critical scholars say, these frameworks allow us to point our fingers at communities of color and lament their embrace of values that promise to keep them consigned to an impoverished, subordinate position in society.

CRT in education invites us to notice as well that if the deficit model and/or theory of oppositional culture are correct, then we do not need to "fix" the educational system nor the techniques that teachers use to instruct children; instead, we need to "fix" individual students. We need to acculturate them to the values of dominant society—the values possessed by white and Asian students that cause them to perform so well in school. These approaches suggest that educators can comfortably assume that "schools work and that students, parents, and community need to change to conform to this already effective and equitable system."[80] Further, these explanations of the achievement gap assert that because students of color lack the knowledge and social skills that their more privileged counterparts have, schools serve them best by conceptualizing them as empty containers that need to be filled up with the things they lack. Indeed, critics worry that the deficit model might lead to more nihilistic approaches to educating children from marginalized communities: if something is "wrong" with black and Latinx students, then there might be nothing that education law and policy can do to address the problem. The existing achievement gap might be the best we can do. According to this nihilistic perspective, that we have narrowed the achievement gap as much as we have is a testament to our persistence and good will, not evidence that we can narrow it even further.

As one might expect, CRT in education rejects the deficit model and theory of oppositional culture for their failure to implicate the systems in which black and Latinx students struggle to obtain decent educations. Moreover, CRT in education criticizes these explanations for their refusal to identify the strengths that disadvantaged communities have—strengths that they transmit to their children. Tara Yosso identifies several types of capital that, even though not

[80] Tara J. Yosso, *Whose Culture Has Capital? A Critical Race Theory Discussion of Community Cultural Wealth*, 8 RACE ETHNICITY & EDUC. 69, 75 (2005).

appreciated by dominant society, are valuable and are the cultural patrimony of subordinated communities. These include: linguistic capital, which includes the intellectual and social skills that one acquires when one is able to communicate in more than one language or code; social capital, which includes the individuals who provide a person with both physical and mental support; navigational capital, which "refers to skills of maneuvering through social institutions," especially those institutions that were "not created with Communities of Color in mind"[81]; and resistant capital, which "refers [to] those knowledges and skills fostered through oppositional behavior that challenges inequality."[82] Yosso endeavors to remind us that marginalized people have managed to survive despite their marginalization. Instead of bemoaning all of the things that they lack, Yosso contends that we ought to identify what they actually possess. Once we have recognized the value of their possessions, we might figure out ways to empower them with it.

Other educators operating within a CRT framework also endeavor to shift the focus from what disadvantaged communities lack to other, arguably more productive sites of intervention. In this spirit, some theorists have proposed that instead of talking about an achievement gap, we need to be talking about an opportunity gap. That is, we might talk about differences in the performance of black and Latinx students as compared to their white and Asian peers in terms of differences in the groups' opportunities to learn. Because of inequities in school funding, school segregation resulting from residential segregation, biases in curricula, and instructional techniques that are effective only for some students, unprivileged students have had much fewer opportunities to learn than their more privileged counterparts. According to this theory, if we equalize opportunities to learn, we will eliminate the achievement gap.

Another alternative to the achievement gap is the concept of *education debt*, which Ladson-Billings first proposed.[83] The concept pays attention to the histories of subordination that have made it difficult for communities of color to access education. For Ladson-Billings, these histories are important to acknowledge because they go a long way towards explaining the achievement gap in the present day. She identifies three types of debt that have contributed to black and Latinx underperformance. The first is economic debt, which refers to inequalities in school funding, as well as the factors that have caused people of color to have lower incomes and to possess less wealth than their white counterparts. The second is sociopolitical

---

[81] *Id.* at 80.

[82] *Id.*

[83] Gloria Ladson-Billings, *From the Achievement Gap to the Education Debt: Understanding Achievement in U.S Schools*, 35 EDUC. RESEARCHER 3 (2006).

debt, which refers to the degree to which people of color have been unable to participate in the political process—the very same process that controls the educational system. The last is moral debt, which refers to what society owes to individuals and communities who "have been excluded from social benefits and opportunities."[84]

In essence, these alternative ways of theorizing the achievement gap assert that there is nothing *wrong* with students of color who are not doing well in school. Instead, there is something *wrong* with the society that has produced the current state of affairs.

C. No Child Left Behind

In 2002, then-President George W. Bush signed into law the No Child Left Behind Act ("NCLB"). Architects of NCLB professed a motivation to improve the academic outcomes of poor children, children of color, children with disabilities, and other vulnerable children. Indeed, the declared aim of the act is "[t]o close the achievement gap . . . so that no child is left behind."[85] However, progressive thinkers of race have been highly critical of the means that the act uses to accomplish its stated goal. They have concluded that, ironically, NCLB ends up leaving the most disadvantaged children behind.

NCLB establishes standards in reading and math that children in grades 3 through 8 must meet. In order to ascertain whether children are meeting those standards, they are given state-controlled standardized tests. Schools must make steady improvements on their students' proficiency levels on these exams, ultimately reaching 100% proficiency. If improvements are not made, the school—now designated as "failing"—must endure a series of consequences. Initially, students in failing schools are given the choice to transfer to another school in the district, even as the failing school receives additional funds and resources to help it meet the standards. If the school continues to fail, it must replace its administrators or close and reopen as a charter school or private school. As we might expect, failing schools tend to be those attended by poor children, who are disproportionately children of color. Hill notes that of the schools that had failed for two consecutive years or more, "80% of the students were from minority groups and 62% of students were from low-income families, compared to 46% minorities and 49% low-income students in schools not required to offer choice."[86]

One issue that critical thinkers have with NCLB is the emphasis that it puts on testing. Standardized testing, say these critics, is a far

---

[84] *Id.* at 8.

[85] No Child Left Behind Act of 2001, Pub. L. No. 107–110, 115 Stat. 1425 (2002).

[86] Hill, *supra* note 42, at 147.

from ideal method of measuring whether a student has acquired a skill. Writes Hill, "Standardized testing that treats all students alike may actually exacerbate the problems of equity in the public school system .... [H]igh-stakes testing [might] actually discriminate[ ] against some students because of differences in background and 'learning styles.' "[87] Further, while standardized testing may reveal what students do not know, they "fail to tell us what students actually know and are able to do."[88] Moreover, because of the severe penalties associated with students failing the test, teachers in poor schools, which are much more at risk of "failing" than their more affluent counterparts, have every incentive to do whatever it takes to ensure that students pass. This focus has consequences. "[R]ote skills and memorization have, in many instances, subsumed creative, engaging teaching. By contrast, students in middle-class schools normally have little trouble with high stakes exam, so the schools and teachers are free to broaden the curriculum."[89]

Additionally, critics take issue with NCLB's giving students the option to transfer from failing schools. Essentially, NCLB inserts all of the problems of school choice discussed above into the law. Moreover, students can only transfer to schools that are also in their district. The catch is that the problems that affect an individual school—the problems that may lead it to fail, like a lack of funds to meet the increased needs of indigent students—usually affect the other schools in the district. Thus, critics ask, what good is the choice to transfer from a failing school if the other options are also failing? Further, critics note that when there are decent alternatives available in a district, and when students do transfer to them, the students left behind in the failing school are usually the most vulnerable. These are the students without the ability to pay for transportation costs (which NCLB funds will cover . . . if they are available[90]), without information, without English language proficiency, etc.

Ultimately, NCLB's critics believe that the law takes a limited view of the problems plaguing the educational system—the problems that lead to the achievement gaps that NCLB was designed to address. To be precise, critics assert that the Act narrowly conceptualizes the underperformance of children: it views it as an issue of isolated, failing schools as opposed to systems of inequity. According to Hill, a better law would be one that views "the problem systematically" with an eye towards funding "disparities between

---

[87] *Id.* at 143.

[88] Ladson-Billings, *What is Critical Race Theory?*, *supra* note 65, at 20.

[89] ORFIELD, KUSCERA & SIEGEL-HAWLEY, *supra* note 10, at 7.

[90] The National Conference of State Legislatures predicted that NCLB would be underfunded by some $10 billion in 2005. *See* Hill, *supra* note 42, at 142.

schools"[91]—a view that she believes the architects of NCLB expressly rejected in favor of a market-based approach to educational equality.

* * *

In conclusion, we have left behind the days when the law mandated that children of color receive a separate and decidedly inferior education. Nevertheless, educational inequality endures. Because the law no longer explicitly commands racial inequity in schooling, many have become convinced that race has nothing to do with the fact that schools are letting down large numbers of children of color. As Kiel explains:

> When a racial effect does follow from a colorblind practice, the colorblind instinct is to argue that racial disparities are the result of some other type of non-racial inequity. For example, lower performance among African American students may be explained by disparities in teacher quality or parental involvement or self-motivation or peer effects or school safety or the all-encompassing effect of poverty. It is not that the system is racially biased, the argument goes. Rather, too much poverty exists in the black community or too many black students and families do not value education. These alternative explanations are more comfortable than a comprehensive indictment of the system as caste system .... In addition, these problems can be addressed within the system without disturbing the sorting that is so crucial to maintaining the nation's social hierarchy. If the problem is disparate access to teacher quality, then schools simply need more high quality teachers. If it is low parental involvement, then schools need programs to engage and educate parents. And so on.[92]

CRT in education interrupts this narrative by insisting that the system *is* racially biased. It is failing children of color. And it will not begin to serve them in the ways that it should until we directly, relentlessly, and tirelessly confront race.

III. Questions and Discussion

1. Why do you think that civil rights lawyers in the 1950s attacked Jim Crow by focusing on schools and not, say, swimming pools? What were the benefits of the approach that they chose? What were the costs of it?

2. Psychologist Claude Steele has offered an interesting explanation for the underperformance of people of color on high-

---

[91] *Id.* at 137.

[92] Kiel, *supra* note 1, at 637.

stakes, standardized tests. He argues that we cannot chalk up black underperformance to poverty because performance gaps persist across class. That is, "minority student achievement gaps persist even in the middle and upper socioeconomic classes."[93] So, how do we explain this? Steele proposes that individuals who are members of groups about which there are negative stereotypes about their intelligence or competency may not perform as well on tests when they fear that a subpar performance will serve to confirm those negative stereotypes. He calls this phenomenon "stereotype threat," which he defines as "a situational threat—a threat in the air—that, in general form, can affect the members of any group about whom a negative stereotype exists."[94] Because there are stereotypes that black people are bad readers, stereotype threat will result in black people underperforming on a test that measures reading comprehension. Because there are stereotypes that women are not good at math, stereotype threat will result in women underperforming on a test that measures math ability. Steele tested his hypothesis in experiments on different groups of students. Black students who were reminded that they were black before a reading test did not score as well as black students whose racial identity was not made salient before the test. The same held true in the experiments that he conducted with women. These experiments led Steele to conclude that "[s]tereotype threat may be a possible source of bias in standardized tests, a bias that arises not from item content but from group differences in the threat that societal stereotypes attach to test performance."[95]

What do you think? Do you find the theory convincing? What are the problems with psychological theories of racial stratification? Can psychological theories comfortably coexist with structural theories?

3. As discussed above, the Court's opinion in *Rodriguez* upheld the system of funding schools through property taxes, which results in schools in wealthier areas receiving more funds than schools in poorer areas. However, Amy Stuart Wells and her coauthors have argued that a different holding in that case—one declaring that all schools in a county must be funded on the same level—might not have improved the educations that poor students receive.[96] They examined the schools in Nassau County, a county

[93] Claude Steele, *A Threat in the Air: How Stereotypes Shape Intellectual Identity and Performance*, *in* FOUNDATIONS OF CRITICAL RACE THEORY IN EDUCATION, *supra* note 69, at 163, 166.

[94] *Id.* at 164.

[95] *Id.* at 168.

[96] Amy Stuart Wells, Lauren Fox & Alana Miles, *Still Separate, Still Unequal in a Post-*Milliken *Era: Why* Rodriguez *Would Have Been Good but Not Enough*, *in* THE ENDURING LEGACY OF *RODRIGUEZ*: CREATING NEW PATHWAYS TO EQUAL

with a variety of school districts. Some of these school districts have very poor neighborhoods, communities, and towns within them; others have extremely wealthy neighborhoods, communities, and towns within them. Nevertheless, the per-pupil funding levels across school districts were similar—with the wealthiest districts spending the same amount of funds per student as the poorest. This is a circumstance that a different holding in *Rodriguez* would have produced.

Nevertheless, one would be hard pressed to describe the educations received by the kids in the wealthier districts that Wells and her coauthors studied as equal to those received by the kids in the poor districts. This is due to the willingness and ability of wealthier families to donate their own, personal funds to the schools. The private donations that wealthier families made to their children's schools were quite substantial, leading Wells and her coauthors to conclude that "when private resources . . . are added to the equation, the mounting inequities between rich and poor school districts are startling and are major factors in *separate and unequal educational opportunities*."[97]

Further, even though the schools in the poor districts were funded on the same level as schools in the wealthier districts, the students attending the former schools, because of their indigence, had to turn to the school for help with the problems that they faced; meanwhile, students in wealthier schools could address these problems with private resources. Consequently, equal funding was not enough. They write, "When we factor in the social and emotional needs of the students served in low-income and predominately African American and Latino districts . . ., the resource gap seems even wider. As [a social worker who worked in one of the poorer schools] pointed out, it is not always the disparate problems facing students across these contexts but, rather, their parents' ability to help 'solve' such problems with private resources."[98]

Most disturbingly, perhaps, Wells and her coauthors observe that wealthier and poorer students come to expect different things from their schools based on what their schools can provide. They write, "[T]he curricular and educational distinctions across separate educational spaces shape not only what the students experience but also what they come to understand they *should* experience."[99] Poorer students come to expect that their schools will provide them with

---

EDUCATIONAL OPPORTUNITY 87 (Charles J. Ogletree, Jr. & Kimberly Jenkins Robinson eds., 2015).

[97] *Id.* at 97.

[98] *Id.* at 103.

[99] *Id.* at 111.

nothing more than an education that will help them pass state-mandated standardized tests; wealthier students come to expect that their schools will provide them an entrée to elite colleges and universities.

These findings have led Wells and her coauthors to conclude that a "pro-plaintiff ruling in *Milliken* would have made far more difference in the lives of disadvantaged students" than a pro-plaintiff ruling in *Rodriguez*.[100] Equal funding will not result in equal educations across class and race lines; instead, they argue, real integration is the only means to that end.

What are your reactions to Wells and her coauthors' research and their conclusions? Do you believe that a different holding in *Milliken* would have produced equity in educational outcomes? That is, would a different holding have made it impossible for white families to avoid desegregation orders?

---

[100] *Id.* at 89.

TABLE OF CASES

INDEX

References are to Pages